# THE
# EVANGELIZATION
## OF THE WORLD

# THE
# EVANGELIZATION
## OF THE WORLD

A HISTORY OF CHRISTIAN MISSION

WILLIAM CAREY
LIBRARY

JACQUES A. BLOCHER & JACQUES BLANDENIER

TRANSLATED BY MICHAEL PARKER

Scriptures taken from the Holy Bible, New International Version®, NIV®. Copyright © 1973, 1978, 1984 by Biblica, Inc.™ Used by permission of Zondervan. All rights reserved worldwide. www.zondervan.com

Published by William Carey Library
1605 E. Elizabeth Street
Pasadena, CA 91104 | www.missionbooks.org

Kelley K. Wolfe, editor
Brad Koenig, copyeditor
Crooks Design Inc., cover design
Josie Leung, interior design
Rose Lee-Norman, indexer

Cover image: Raphael Cartoon—*Paul Preaching at Athens: Acts Chapter 17: Verses 16-34*; by Raphael (1483-1520); Italian (Urbino); 1515-16. Bodycolour on paper, laid on to Canvas. Used by permission of Victoria and Albert Museum.

Book II image: Mary Slessor stained glass window, MacManus Art Gallery and Museum, Dundee Scotland. Photo courtesy of Deborah Talbert.

William Carey Library is a ministry of the
U.S. Center for World Mission
Pasadena, CA | www.uscwm.org

Printed in the United States of America

16 15 14 13 12    5 4 3 2 1 SFP

Library of Congress Cataloging-in-Publication Data

Blocher, Jacques A.

   [Evangilisation du monde. English]

   The evangelization of the world: A history of Christian mission / by Jacques A. Blocher and Jacques Blandenier ; translated by Michael Parker.

      p. cm.

   ISBN 978-0-87808-017-5

1. Missions--History. I. Blandenier, Jacques. II. Title.

   BV2100.B6613 2009

   266.009--dc22

                                                        2009027392

# Contents

PREFACE . . . . . . . . . . . . . . . . . . . . . . . . . . . . . . . . . . . . . . . . . . . . . .xi

PREFACE BY THE TRANSLATOR . . . . . . . . . . . . . . . . . . . . . . . . . . . . .xiii

INTRODUCTION . . . . . . . . . . . . . . . . . . . . . . . . . . . . . . . . . . . . . . . xv

## BOOK I: THE HISTORY OF MISSION THROUGH THE LATE EIGHTEENTH CENTURY

### SECTION I  THE CHURCH OF THE FIRST CENTURIES

1.  APOSTOLIC MISSION: FROM THE ASCENSION TO
    THE END OF THE FIRST CENTURY . . . . . . . . . . . . . . . . . . . . . . . . . 5

2.  THE MISSION OF THE PERSECUTED CHURCH:
    FROM THE APOSTLE JOHN TO CONSTANTINE (100–313) . . . . . . . . . . . . 17

3.  EVANGELIZATION IN THE FOURTH CENTURY: THE IMPERIAL CHURCH
    AND EXPANSION BEYOND THE ROMAN EMPIRE . . . . . . . . . . . . . . . . 41

### SECTION II  MISSION IN THE MIDDLE AGES

4.  THE WEST: FROM THE FIFTH TO THE EIGHTH CENTURY . . . . . . . . . . . . 53

5.  ISLAM AND THE DECLINE OF CHRISTIANITY IN THE EAST . . . . . . . . . . . 77

6.  THE LAST STEP IN THE EXPANSION OF THE CHURCH IN EUROPE:
    FROM THE NINTH TO THE TENTH CENTURY . . . . . . . . . . . . . . . . . . 81

7.  THE CHURCHES OF THE EAST AND WEST CONFRONTED BY ISLAM . . . . 103

8.  THE EXTENSION OF THE CHURCH BEYOND EUROPE (400–1450) . . . . . . . 119

**SECTION III** CATHOLIC MISSION: FROM THE RENAISSANCE THROUGH THE EIGHTEENTH CENTURY

9. NEW HORIZONS IN EUROPE . . . . . . . . . . . . . . . . . . . . . . 137
10. CATHOLIC MISSION IN THE AMERICAS. . . . . . . . . . . . . . . . 143
11. CATHOLIC MISSION IN AFRICA . . . . . . . . . . . . . . . . . . . .171
12. CATHOLIC MISSION IN ASIA AND OCEANIA . . . . . . . . . . . . . 177

**SECTION IV** THE EMERGENCE OF PROTESTANT MISSION

13. PROTESTANT MISSIONAL THOUGHT. . . . . . . . . . . . . . . . . . 197
14. THE BEGINNINGS OF PROTESTANT MISSION . . . . . . . . . . . . 213
15. THE FIRST MISSIONARY SOCIETIES (1670–1800) . . . . . . . . . . 245
16. THE MORAVIANS. . . . . . . . . . . . . . . . . . . . . . . . . . . . 263

# BOOK II: A CONCISE HISTORY OF MISSION FROM 1792 TO 1945

INTRODUCTION TO BOOK II. . . . . . . . . . . . . . . . . . . . . . . . . 283

**SECTION I** THE BIRTH OF THE PRINCIPAL PROTESTANT SOCIETIES IN THE AGE OF MODERN MISSION

1. PRECURSORS AND FOUNDERS . . . . . . . . . . . . . . . . . . . . 287
2. THE MISSIONARY SOCIETIES OF THE "SECOND WAVE" . . . . . . . . 291

**SECTION II** PROTESTANT MISSION IN ASIA

3. WILLIAM CAREY: "FATHER OF MODERN MISSIONS" . . . . . . . . . 307
4. PROTESTANT MISSION IN INDIA AND NEIGHBORING COUNTRIES . . . . 331
5. PROTESTANT PIONEERS IN CHINA:
   ROBERT MORRISON AND KARL GÜTZLAFF . . . . . . . . . . . . . 343
6. HUDSON TAYLOR AND THE CHINA INLAND MISSION . . . . . . . . . 353
7. PROTESTANT MISSION IN THE FAR EAST. . . . . . . . . . . . . . . 371

**SECTION III** THE EVANGELIZATION OF THE PACIFIC ISLANDS

8. TAHITI AND THE SOCIETY ISLANDS. . . . . . . . . . . . . . . . . . 409
9. TWO PIONEERS OF THE PACIFIC: JOHN WILLIAMS AND JOHN PATON . . 427
10. THE LOYALTY ISLANDS AND NEW CALEDONIA . . . . . . . . . . . . 447

# SECTION IV  THE EVANGELIZATION OF AFRICA

PART ONE: SOUTHERN AFRICA

11. THE FIRST MISSIONARIES IN SOUTH AFRICA . . . . . . . . . . . . . . . . 461

12. DAVID LIVINGSTONE: MISSIONARY AND EXPLORER . . . . . . . . . . . . 467

13. FRANÇOIS COILLARD: FOUNDER OF THE ZAMBEZI MISSION . . . . . . . 481

PART TWO: WEST AFRICA

14. DRAMATIC BEGINNINGS . . . . . . . . . . . . . . . . . . . . . . . . . . 497

15. A SELF-SUPPORTING CHURCH . . . . . . . . . . . . . . . . . . . . . . . 507

16. COASTAL REGIONS OF WEST AFRICA . . . . . . . . . . . . . . . . . . . 519

17. THE IVORY COAST . . . . . . . . . . . . . . . . . . . . . . . . . . . . . 529

18. PROTESTANT MISSION AND THE FOUNDATION OF THE CHURCH
    IN CAMEROON . . . . . . . . . . . . . . . . . . . . . . . . . . . . . . . 541

19. THE SUDANESE REGIONS . . . . . . . . . . . . . . . . . . . . . . . . . 553

PART THREE: CENTRAL AFRICA AND MADAGASCAR

20. THE BELGIAN CONGO: EXPLORATION, EVANGELIZATION,
    AND FOUNDATION OF A CHURCH . . . . . . . . . . . . . . . . . . . . . 561

21. AN AFRICAN PROPHET: SIMON KIMBANGU . . . . . . . . . . . . . . . . 575

22. THE PIONEERS IN THE REGION OF THE GREAT LAKES . . . . . . . . . . 581

23. THE HORN OF AFRICA . . . . . . . . . . . . . . . . . . . . . . . . . . . 597

24. FRENCH EQUATORIAL AFRICA . . . . . . . . . . . . . . . . . . . . . . . 601

25. ANGOLA . . . . . . . . . . . . . . . . . . . . . . . . . . . . . . . . . . . 613

26. MADAGASCAR . . . . . . . . . . . . . . . . . . . . . . . . . . . . . . . 623

PART FOUR: NORTH AFRICA AND THE NEAR EAST

27. EVANGELISTIC PRESENCE IN THE MAGHREB AND EGYPT . . . . . . . . . 639

28. THE GOSPEL IN THE NEAR EAST . . . . . . . . . . . . . . . . . . . . . 651

# SECTION V  PROTESTANT MISSION IN LATIN AMERICA

29. FROM PROTESTANT IMMIGRATION TO EVANGELIZATION . . . . . . . . . . 663

30. DEVELOPMENT OF PROTESTANT MISSION IN LATIN AMERICA . . . . . . . 673

## SECTION VI  CONCLUDING POINTS

31. PROTESTANT MISSION AND COLONIZATION . . . . . . . . . . . . . . . . . . . . 691

32. THE WORLD MISSIONARY CONFERENCES . . . . . . . . . . . . . . . . . . . . . 707


AFTERWORD . . . . . . . . . . . . . . . . . . . . . . . . . . . . . . . . . . . . . . . . . . 721

BIBLIOGRAPHY . . . . . . . . . . . . . . . . . . . . . . . . . . . . . . . . . . . . . . . 723

INDEX OF PEOPLE, INSTITUTIONS, AND ETHNIC GROUPS . . . . . . . . . . . . 731

INDEX OF PLACES . . . . . . . . . . . . . . . . . . . . . . . . . . . . . . . . . . . . . 743

# List of Maps

BOOK I

Map 1: *Witnesses to Pentecost* . . . . . . . . . . . . . . . . . . . . . . . . . . . . . . 8

Map 2: *Limits of Christianity in the West at the end of the Roman Empire*. . . . . 24

Map 3: *Christians in the East during the fourth century* . . . . . . . . . . . . . . 49

Map 4: *The barbarian invasions* . . . . . . . . . . . . . . . . . . . . . . . . . . . . 54

Map 5: *Irish monks and Benedictine missionaries* . . . . . . . . . . . . . . . . . . 69

Map 6: *The expansion of Islam* . . . . . . . . . . . . . . . . . . . . . . . . . . . . . 79

Map 7: *Christian mission in Central and Eastern Europe in
the ninth and tenth centuries* . . . . . . . . . . . . . . . . . . . . . . . . . . . 88

Map 8: *Christian expansion in the East from the fourth to
the fourteenth centuries* . . . . . . . . . . . . . . . . . . . . . . . . . . . . . 123

Map 9: *The great explorers (1492-1600)* . . . . . . . . . . . . . . . . . . . . . . . 138

Map 10: *North America and Mexico from 1500 to 1800* . . . . . . . . . . . . . 145

Map 11: *Missions from 1500 to 1800 in South America* . . . . . . . . . . . . . 158

Map 12: *Missions from 1500 to 1800 in Africa*. . . . . . . . . . . . . . . . . . . 174

Map 13: *Evangelism in the Far East, 1500 to 1800* . . . . . . . . . . . . . . . . 183

Map 14: *Missions of the Moravian Brethren, eighteenth century* . . . . . . . . 277

BOOK II

Map 1: *Bangladesh and Burma, mission fields of William Carey
and Adoniram Judson* . . . . . . . . . . . . . . . . . . . . . . . . . . . . . . . 313

Map 2: *India*. . . . . . . . . . . . . . . . . . . . . . . . . . . . . . . . . . . . . . . . 332

Map 3: *The penetration of the gospel into China in the nineteenth century* . . . 359

Map 4: *Indochina and Siam* . . . . . . . . . . . . . . . . . . . . . . . . . . . . . . 389

*Map 5: Malaysia, Indonesia, and the Philippines* . . . . . . . . . . . . . . . . . . . . . . . 400

*Map 6: The Pacific Islands.* . . . . . . . . . . . . . . . . . . . . . . . . . . . . . . . . . . . . . . . 409

*Map 7a: Tahiti and the Society Islands* . . . . . . . . . . . . . . . . . . . . . . . . . . . 413

*Map 7b: The islands of Tonga and Samoa* . . . . . . . . . . . . . . . . . . . . . . . . 423

*Map 7c: Rarotonga and the Cook Islands* . . . . . . . . . . . . . . . . . . . . . . . . 432

*Map 8: The islands of the West Pacific* . . . . . . . . . . . . . . . . . . . . . . . . . . . 446

*Map 9: David Livingstone's journeys of exploration in Africa* . . . . . . . . . . . . 470

*Map 10: West Africa in the colonial era.* . . . . . . . . . . . . . . . . . . . . . . . . . . 498

*Map 11: The Congo Basin and western equatorial Africa* . . . . . . . . . . . . . 563

*Map 12: East Africa.* . . . . . . . . . . . . . . . . . . . . . . . . . . . . . . . . . . . . . . . . . 585

*Map 13: Northwest Africa.* . . . . . . . . . . . . . . . . . . . . . . . . . . . . . . . . . . . . 640

*Map 14: Northeast Africa and the Near East.* . . . . . . . . . . . . . . . . . . . . . . 648

*Map 15: Latin America* . . . . . . . . . . . . . . . . . . . . . . . . . . . . . . . . . . . . . . . 672

# *Preface*

To write an accurate history of modern missions, whose activities span the entire globe over a period of a century and a half, is not an easy task. Many readers, on detecting errors and gaps in the record, will propose useful additions or corrections to the text. Let them not hesitate to send it to the publishers with the prospect of improving an eventual second edition.

I owe a debt of gratitude to numerous friends whose advice, contribution of documentation, and encouragement were a great help. Yannik Blocher, Jacques E. Blocher, Gauthier de Smidt, Gérald Delapierre, and Charles Abel Piguet read the text carefully and made many helpful suggestions for its improvement. Michel Wurtz prepared the maps, overcoming the difficulties caused by changes in borders and names that have occurred over the years. The Protestant Service of Mission in Paris and Stefan Schmid supplied many documents. Claudine Luthi scanned a large number of illustrations used in the text, and Silvain Dupertuis did the page layouts and prepared the index [of the French edition]. I must also thank the Union of the Assembled and Evangelical Churches of French-speaking Switzerland, which granted me the time necessary to write and edit this work while employed in its service. And, finally, I am grateful to my family for graciously acquiescing in my time being monopolized for so long by this work.

Jacques Blandenier

What may be the most important development in the Christianity of our time is the rise of what is often called the Global South, the phenomenon in which the majority of Christians now live in the southern regions of the world—principally in Latin America and Sub-Saharan Africa, but also increasingly in Asia. In the year 1900 two-thirds of all Christians lived in Europe while today only about twenty-five percent do so. Or to put it differently, of the one-third of the world's seven billion people who are now Christians, most now live outside the West. The rise of the non-Western church has come upon the world so quickly that academics and church leaders are still trying to comprehend it. What can be said with certainty is that to a very large extent this southern and eastern shift can be attributed to the mission movement, the church's greatest success story. Beginning with about seventy wary and unprepossessing people in an obscure upper room in Jerusalem, Christianity over the course of two thousand years has now spread out sufficiently over nations and continents that it can be called the world's first truly global religion. This remarkable story is told here from its origins in Palestine in the first century down to about the year 1945.

Originally written in French as a two-volume set, this history is being used in French-speaking Europe and Africa to great effect. I first encountered it while teaching a class in mission at a French-speaking seminary in Rwanda in the early 2000s. My students found the books enormously helpful. They appreciated the careful attention the authors gave to missiological issues and the obvious delight with which they attended to the fascinating and often dramatic stories of missionaries and the early responses to the gospel by indigenous peoples. Moreover, the style and layout of the books is inviting, and the information provided is easily accessible, reliable, and sufficiently comprehensive to make these volumes the first stop in whatever writing assignments I gave my classes. In fact, the success that I've had using the books is one of the main reasons I decided to undertake the task of translating them into English. A second reason is that there is a need for an up-to-date history of Christian mission that will appeal to a popular audience, and I can easily envision this book being read by church groups, clergy, and lay people interested in mission.

Jacques A. Blocher, co-author of the first volume, was a well-known professor of mission history at three French institutes: L'Institut Biblique de Nogent-sur-Marne, Faculté de théologie protestante d'Aix-en-Provence, and Faculté de théologie évanglique de Vaux-sur-Seine. Jacques Blandenier took Dr. Blocher's course in mission history at the latter college. When Blocher died in 1986, Blandenier took up the task of assembling and completing the professor's partially edited notes, filling in the missing gaps, adding commentary, attempting to create a seamless whole. As Henri Blocher, the author's son, put it in the French edition of this work, "The two voices of a duet were harmoniously joined into one."

Blandenier, who is the sole author of the second volume, is well qualified to have written a history of mission, having also been a professor of mission history at three institutions in France and Switzerland: Faculté de Vaux-sur-Seine, Institut biblique Emmaus, and L'Institut biblique de Nogent-sur-Marne. He has also been the editor of *Semailles et Moisson* (Sowing and Reaping), a monthly journal of the Evangelical Churches of French-speaking Switzerland. He has been the director of Formation au Service dans l'Eglise (Training for Service in the Church), and director of Editions des Groups Missionaries, a publisher of mission material.

It has been my pleasure to help make Jacques Blocher and Jacques Blandenier's work available to an English-speaking audience. This English edition has combined Volumes I and II into a single volume as Books I and II respectively. I have tried to remain faithful to the spirit of the original work, which attempted to present vast amounts of information in an easy-to-read format for a general audience. I have, however, eliminated many of the subtitles that appeared in the French edition, an idiosyncrasy that Anglophone readers might find distracting. I have kept the French footnotes in the text so that the reader will be aware of the many non-English sources on which this book is based, but I have often cited English sources and quoted from them directly when the original text acquired them from secondary French sources. In Book I, I quoted directly from an English translation of Eusebius's history as this was often used in the early sections of this work. In Book II, I translated quoted material directly from the text with the exception of quotations from Stephen Neill's *A History of Christian Missions* and Ruth A. Tucker's *From Jerusalem to Irian Jaya: A Biographical History of Christian Missions*. In both Book I and II, I also followed this procedure for quotations from David J. Bosch's *Transforming Mission*. All three books being frequently cited and readily available to English-speaking readers, I thought it best to quote from the original English texts. References to French sources in the footnotes and bibliography have been retained but put in a form standard in English usage. Because this book was based on the often incomplete notes of Jacques Blocher, both Jacques Blandenier and I took pains to find and cite the primary and secondary material that he used; however, we were not always successful. This will not inconvenience the casual reader for whom this book is intended, and for others, we can only commend a deeper study of the sources.

Michael Parker
Louisville, Kentucky

How exactly do we define the term *Christian mission*, whose history is to be presented in this text? Generally *mission*, in the singular, is taken to be the duty to proclaim the gospel to all people, according to the command of Christ to his disciples at the time of his ascension (Matt 28:19–20). This is distinguished from *missions*, in the plural, which are the organizations that permit the church to send out messengers of the good news.

The word *mission* is formed from the Latin root *mitto* ("I send"). It is synonymous with the word *apostolate*, which comes from the Greek work *apostello*, signifying in the same way, "I send." Hence the words *missionary* and *apostle* are close terms, even if they are not always used in the New Testament and even if, in current usage, they have taken on senses very different from one another. There is also a distinction in current usage between the terms *mission* and *evangelization*, which in their original meaning have practically the same sense: the proclamation of the gospel of Christ to all people. The word *evangelization* most often denotes this proclamation but only as it is addressed to people of the same culture and language; whereas the word *mission* is employed when it is intended for people faraway or of other cultures.[1] Until the sixteenth century, the term *mission* was used solely to speak of the sending of the Son by the Father, and the Holy Spirit by the Father and the Son. This was the *missio Dei* ("mission of God"). It was Ignatius Loyola and the Jesuits who first used this term to apply to the sending by the church of messengers to those not knowing the gospel—to those "heretical" Protestants.

---

1    Others mean by the term *mission* the global task that God conferred on the church in the world, including the social, cultural, and political responsibilities. They reserve the word *evangelization* for the verbal proclamation of the gospel. For this view see John R. W. Scott, *Christian Mission in the Modern World* (Downer's Grove, IL: InterVarsity Press, 1975), chapter 1. For the purposes of this book, we will envision mission as the proclamation of the gospel with the aim of planting the church where it does not exist, in the manner of which the Apostle Paul spoke of his ministry: "It has always been my ambition to preach the gospel where Christ was not known" (Rom 15:20). Hence, for example, although one can say at the threshold of the twenty-first century that Europe is a "mission field," we will not treat here the present evangelization of European countries, which would be the subject of another study.

This history of Christian mission, therefore, will seek to study how the church has proclaimed the gospel to the populations of the world since the time of Christ until our own era. Beginning with the Reformation in the sixteenth century, we will especially study the development of Protestant mission, which in the seventeenth and eighteenth centuries was very slow in getting started but blossomed remarkably in the nineteenth century and especially at the beginning of the twentieth century.[2] Our study will not go beyond the first four and a half decades of the twentieth century, the history of the contemporary period constituting a separate area of research. The current statistical data for it can be obtained elsewhere.[3]

As a subject of historical investigation, the field of mission is extremely vast in that it concerns nineteen centuries and six continents. In order to make this volume a manageable size, it was necessary not to include—as it would have been convenient to do—developments touching on the general history of people and civilizations, the area of study known as "the history of religion," and the history of the different currents, divisions, and revivals in the Christian churches. These divisions, however, have notably influenced the manner in which the church has either accomplished or neglected its missionary task. An examination of the discipline of missiology—the science of mission—will be occasionally but not extensively undertaken. Readers with an interest in this are advised to consult more specialized works.[4] Our modest purpose here concerns only the study of the geographic expansion of the church of Jesus Christ by the preaching of the gospel through the centuries. The history of mission, in sum, is the amassing of the basic materials from which a missiology can be elaborated that is based on the historical evidence.

There is much to say on this subject, things admirable and others humiliating. Everywhere the student of mission will find heroic sacrifices and shameful delinquencies, resounding successes and cruel failures. But despite our shortcomings, God's method has always been to use human beings, which is why this book includes a large number of missionary profiles. This is especially so in Book II,[5] which treats a

---

2　For a history of Catholic mission in modern times, readers should see Jean Comby, "Deux mille ans d'évangelisation," in *Bibliothèque d'histoire du christianisme*, no. 29 (Tournai/Paris: Desclée/Begédis, 1992), 172–73. This study has benefited much from the rich documentation of this excellent work, notably from the numerous citations.

3　Especially helpful is David Barrett, *World Christian Encyclopedia* (New York: Oxford University Press, 1982, 2001). Annual updates are published in the *International Bulletin of Missionary Research* by Overseas Ministries Study Center, 490 Prospect Street, New Haven, CT 06511. In French see the successive editions of Patrick Johnstone, ed., *Flashes sur le monde*, (Marne-la-vallée, France/La Bēgude de Mazenc, France: La Croisad du Livre Chretien [CLC], 1994).

4　The principal work consulted: David J. Bosch, *Transforming Mission* (New York: Orbis Book, 1991). The second part of the book is dedicated to a historical study of the paradigms in missiology that have appeared in the course of the centuries. The work of André Roux, *Missions des églises, mission de l'église* (Paris: Cerf, 1984), presents several aspects of the history of the mission starting with a missiological perspective. A classic, from the Protestant perspective: J. H. Bavinck, *An Introduction to the Science of Missions* (Philadelphia, 1960; originally ed. in Holland, 1954). Julien Ries, *Les chrétiens parmi les religions* (Paris: Desclée, 1987). Ries, who has a Catholic background, studied the manner in which Christian missions collided with or adapted to the various cultures and religions that it has encountered in the course of centuries.

5　Book II will be especially dedicated to the study of the explosion of Protestant mission that began at the end of the eighteenth century.

well-known period and one that is close to us in time. Both books take special care to give recognition to "pioneer missionaries," those believers in whom the grace of God appeared in striking fashion. This manifestation of grace is not to be sought in their perfection or in their exceptional capacities (one is always tempted to exalt failings), but in their human condition wherein we recognize ourselves. It is in their joys and their sorrows, their determination and their failures, that grace acts toward the sinner, which is why it is grace. Then as now, all glory be to God our Savior.

# BOOK I

# THE
# EVANGELIZATION
## OF THE WORLD

### THE HISTORY OF MISSION
### THROUGH THE LATE EIGHTEENTH CENTURY

JACQUES A. BLOCHER & JACQUES BLANDENIER

TRANSLATED BY MICHAEL PARKER

# SECTION I

## THE CHURCH OF
## THE FIRST CENTURIES

# *Apostolic Mission: From the Ascension to the End of the First Century*

## THE DATA OF THE NEW TESTAMENT

Everything began when Jesus rose from the dead and, upon leaving his disciples, gave them his final instructions: "Therefore go and make disciples of all nations, baptizing them in the name of the Father and of the Son and of the Holy Spirit, and teaching them to obey everything I have commanded you" (Matt 28:19–20). Jesus himself, sent among men to save them, was the first missionary. He declared, moreover, that the mission of the apostles would follow directly from his own: "As the Father has sent me, I am sending you" (John 20:21).

The book of The Acts of the Apostles is the first history of the church and, at the same time, the first history of the mission of the church in the world. Its plan visibly corresponds to the missionary program assigned by Jesus to the apostles before his ascension. According to Acts 1:8: "You will be my witnesses in Jerusalem, and in all Judea [Acts 1–7] and Samaria [chapters 8–12], and to the ends of the earth [chapters 13–28]." From the testimony of Acts, it is clear that the apostles did not readily understand that the command of the Master was to proclaim the gospel of salvation to all people. They thought that the Jewish people, long prepared by the law of Moses, the prophets of Israel, and the Holy Scriptures, were alone worthy to receive this message of liberation. The rest of humankind could not claim the privileges accrued from so long and painstaking a preparation. In order for the Jews who had become disciples of Christ to accept that pagans could be directly introduced into the church, God had to employ extraordinary measures. Hence we see how Peter needed a triple vision and a series of clear proofs in order to accept that the Roman centurion Cornelius had become a Christian without a Jewish initiation (Acts 10). The book of Acts and several of Paul's letters help us to understand that many Judeo-Christians of the first century could never accept this. The Holy Spirit had to interfere very often, directly or indirectly, so that the disciples of Christ would abandon a nominally Jewish conception of salvation.

Stephen, one of the Seven in Acts 6:1–6, was without doubt the first of the followers of Christ to see that Christ had not come to found a new Jewish sect, such as the one at Qumran. He understood that the gospel was supposed to move beyond the confines of Judaism. Philip, who no doubt shared the sentiments of his colleague Stephen, was the evangelist of Samaria and was sent to the Ethiopian eunuch (Acts 8:4–8,26–40).

Antioch of Syria, according to the book of Acts, was the first great city of the Greek world where the Christian community broke through the barriers of Judaism. (Alexandria, a capital of Hellenistic culture, was also evangelized very early, but precise information about it is lacking.)

## Paul's Missionary Journeys

The first attempt at the methodical evangelization of pagans reported in the book of Acts is the "first missionary trip" of Barnabas and Saul of Tarsus (Acts 13–14). Sent under the inspiration of the Holy Spirit by the church of Antioch, they went first to Cyprus where their success was considerable, and then to Asia Minor in the mountainous regions of the southern Roman province of Galatia. In the course of this expedition, some pagans became Christians without having fulfilled the conditions judged necessary to be integrated into Judaism. Naturally, this created a great scandal at Jerusalem. Paul and Barnabas were sent there to plead their cause, and it was necessary to assert all the authority of the apostles and elders, especially of Peter and James, to calm the opposition. In narrating this first trip, Luke, the author of the book of Acts, retained three distinctive samples of Pauline evangelism: a conversation with the political leader Sergius Paulus in Cyprus (Acts 13:7–12), a sermon in a synagogue in Pisidian Antioch (Acts 13:16–41), and a conflict with rural paganism in Lystra (Acts 14:8–20).

Following this voyage so rich in incidents, Paul undertook several others. We know of three of them from the book of Acts.

Paul chose Silas as his companion for the second expedition. This decision followed a dispute with Barnabas, who decided to depart on a different missionary journey in the company of his relative John-Mark. Paul and Silas, after passing through Cilicia, visited the young churches they had founded in Asia Minor during the preceding voyage. They wanted to extend their evangelistic efforts to the central region of Asia Minor, but being prevented in this "by the Holy Spirit," they continued on their journey until they reached the shores of the Aegean Sea, at Troas, in Mysia. There Paul had the vision of a Macedonian who was calling for his help. The missionaries and their team passed through the straights that separate Europe from Asia and disembarked at Macedonia. They sojourned in the city of Philippi and soon founded a church there that would remain particularly tied to the apostle.

They next evangelized other cities in Macedonia before arriving in Greece where Paul preached in Athens, without great success. They then moved on to Corinth where they stayed a long time and founded an important church. From there they traveled to Judea, before returning to Antioch of Syria (Acts 15:36–18:22).

The third trip took Paul, Silas, and their team from Antioch of Syria to Asia Minor, where they visited the communities previously founded. After this, Paul sojourned a long time at Ephesus, the capital and influential center of eastern Greece. He then traveled back through Greece, stopping particularly at Corinth, before returning to Jerusalem by a long sea voyage via Troas and Phoenicia (Acts 18:23–21:14).

The eventful trip from Caesarea to Rome, which Paul made as a state prisoner, was not, properly speaking, a missionary journey; however, it did permit the apostle to proclaim his faith to many Jews and pagans along the way (Acts 27:1–28:16). The book of Acts had previously reported in great detail the examination of Paul before the high magistrates of Israel (Acts 24:1–26:32). These narratives no doubt furnished a stimulating example for the numerous Christians of the first generations who were also called to appear at the bar of justice.

## THE EXTRA-BIBLICAL DATA

Outside of the information furnished by the book of Acts, what do we know of the missionary enterprises of the first-century church? In truth, not much.

Certainly their efforts would have included many events about which the book of Acts does not speak. Justin Martyr, who died in Rome about the year 105 and was therefore a relatively close witness of the apostolic generation, did not doubt that all the apostles obeyed the command of the Lord. "Twelve men," he wrote, "left from Jerusalem to travel through the world."

Admiration for the book of Acts and a conviction that Paul was the greatest missionary of history must not lead us to underestimate the ministry of the other servants of God, those not mentioned by Luke and who, for the most part, are anonymous. Even if formal evidence is lacking, it is reasonable to suppose that a considerable and highly fruitful work was set forth in all directions on the day of Pentecost, following Christ's ascension. This would have been due initially to the pilgrims who had come to Jerusalem "from every nation under heaven" (Acts 2:5), and who returned to their respective countries baptized and full of the Spirit. The names of the fifteen regions that Luke enumerated suggest an advance outward to the four points of the compass, and all of them are places where Christianity was planted very early in ancient times.

The activities of Paul himself were not all described in the book of Acts. In his epistle to the Romans, for instance, the apostle alluded to a voyage to Illyricum (15:19), of which the book of Acts does not speak. The New Testament mentions the names of about twenty of the colleagues who made up Paul's missionary team, but aside from Luke's narrative we have little knowledge of how their other missionary work might have unfolded, though one can suppose that it was widespread. It is only incidentally, for example, that 2 Timothy 4:10 indicates to us that Titus went to Dalmatia, a region north of Illyricum on the cost of the Adriatic Sea.

One scholar has counted that the New Testament alludes to the presence of churches in forty different localities. In most cases nothing is known of the circumstances of their foundation. This is true even of the two most important centers of the empire, Rome and Alexandria; and the same can be said for six of the seven churches of the Apocalypse (Rev 2–3), the groups of dispersed Christians in the remote regions of Asia Minor that Peter addressed in his first letter, the churches of Crete where Titus worked, and many others as well.

The fragmentary character of the history recorded in the book of Acts is due to the fact that Luke chose to follow one man at a time—first Peter, then briefly Philip, and finally and especially Paul—rather than to glean information scattered over the whole missionary endeavor of the first generation. His decision is admirable, for otherwise his work would have been too voluminous, a work the size of the whole of the New Testament. This would have been an insurmountable handicap to its dissemination, and the work would have consisted of little more than a fastidious and uninspiring enumeration of places and missionary names. Luke preferred, instead, a presentation more selective and personalized, and his choices were dictated by a solid theology of mission.

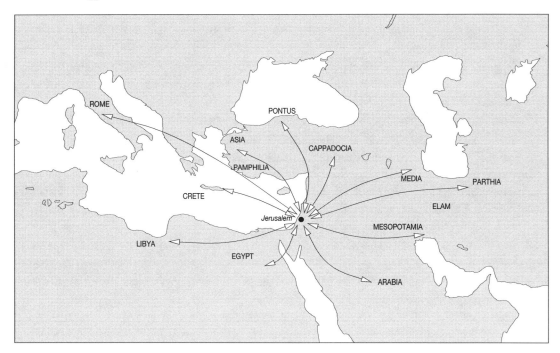

*Map 1: Witnesses to Pentecost*

If in most cases we know neither how nor by whom the gospel was preached in the first century, the better-known situation of the second century implies that the message spread very quickly in all directions. Some churches, it seems, were planted very early, not only on the Antioch-Ephesus-Rome axis, but also along the routes of Paul's journeys and, beginning in Jerusalem, toward the east and the south. It is necessary to insist on this point, for our Western ethnocentrism inclines us to think that the sole missionary enterprise worthy of interest in the apostolic era was that which led to Rome, the capital of the West. It is true, however, that this all-too-partial vision is also due to the unreliability of much of the extra-biblical information concerning the first century, information that contrasts sharply with the solidity of

Luke's account. Moreover, it is necessary to be conscious that the churches of the great metropolitan centers, solicitous of adding to their prestige, began very early and without serious evidence to claim a founder garbed in apostolic authority. This is why the task of laying out a first-century map of Christian communities is far from being an easy task. In many cases it is necessary to be content with hypotheses and imprecise testimony.

## The Testimony of Eusebius

In his *Ecclesiastical History*, Eusebius (the first great historian of the church and bishop of Caesarea in Palestine, 263–ca. 340) cites Origen, who himself was writing about 120 years after the end of the apostolic era. According to this citation, the apostles divided the task of evangelizing the diverse regions of the world, which is not at all implausible:

> But the holy apostles and disciples of our Savior, being scattered over the whole world, Thomas, according to tradition, received Parthia as his allotted region; Andrew received Scythia, and John, Asia, where, after continuing for some time, he died at Ephesus. Peter appears to have preached through Pontus, Galatia, Bithynia, Cappadocia, and Asia, to the Jews that were scattered abroad; who also, finally coming to Rome, was crucified with his head downward, having requested of himself to suffer in this way. Why should we speak of Paul, spreading the gospel of Christ from Jerusalem to Illyricum, and finally suffering martyrdom at Rome, under Nero? This account is given by Origen, in the third book of his exposition of Genesis.[6]

This text provides us with supplementary data to that of the New Testament. It is evident that, following Origen, Eusebius sought to respond to the question that many were posing: What did the apostles do after the ascension and after they had received the command to be witnesses to the ends of the earth? Would they have neglected the commandment of their Lord? Did they eventually return to their careers as fishers—of fish? Not only is this improbable, but the book of Acts implicitly witnesses in favor of their having set out as missionaries when it reports that elders slowly replaced the apostles as leaders of the church at Jerusalem.[7]

## The Apocryphal Acts of the Apostles[8]

The different versions of Acts contain narratives reporting that the apostles drew lots to determine which region of the world each would be given, and every story recounts how its hero was sent to his respective region by the resurrected one himself. Here is a sample of this literature from the *Acts of Thomas*:

> In this time, we the apostles were in Jerusalem—Simon, called Peter, and Andrew . . . [etc.] —and we divided the regions of the

---

6  Eusebius, *Ecclesiastical History* (Grand Rapids, MI: Baker Book House, 1989), 3:82.

7  For this implication compare Acts 15 and 21.

8  Condemned as heretical by theologians and bishops, this hagiographic and romantic literature appeared from the end of the second to the third centuries.

world, in order that each of us would go to the region for which he was responsible and to the people to whom the Lord was sending him.

According to the lots, India went to Judas Thomas, also called the Twin. But he did not want to leave, saying that he could not do it and that he was incapable because of the weakness of his flesh: "How can I, being a Hebrew, go to the Indians to proclaim the truth?" While he was reflecting and speaking in this way, the Savior appeared to him during the night and said to him, "Fear not, Thomas, leave for India and proclaim the Word there. For my grace is with you." [Thomas responded,] "Send me anywhere else you would like, but I will not go to the Indians." [The following summarizes the story:] But the Christ obliged him to leave in selling him as a slave to the Indian merchant Abbanes. He submitted and embarked on the boat of the merchant who, thanks to a favorable wind, soon arrived in Andrapolis. The apostle, a carpenter by trade, saw the need to construct the palace of King Gundaphore. Thomas decided that he would not construct for him a palace of stone and other perishable materials, but a spiritual and eternal house in the heavens, in distributing to the poor and afflicted the considerable funds that Gundaphore had put at his disposal for the construction. When the king asked him to see the palace, Thomas responded to him calmly: you cannot see now, but you will see it when you will have left this life. Furious, Gundaphore threw the apostle into prison. Miraculously delivered, Thomas finished by bringing the king to faith and baptism.[9]

Gathering all the data from the different versions of Acts would present a picture something like the following:

Mark founded the church at Alexandria; Bartholomew went on to the shores of the Black Sea[10]; Jude to Armenia; Matthew to Ethiopia; James the Lesser to Spain; Andrew to the north of Greece, in the Balkans and even in Dalmatia (Romania); and Simon the Zealot to Persia. As for Thomas, his prestige is astonishing; he became a quasi-myth. One finds traces of him just about everywhere—in Arabia, in Persia among the Parthians, in India (with a tomb at Malilapur, near Madras), and at Edessa (Mesopotamia, and also with a tomb). Could Thomas have been the "Saint Paul of the East," or at least the founder of a missionary school working especially in the medium of the Syriac language? No formal proof exists to confirm this, for the tendency of the Orthodox Church to claim him for itself resulted in the West marginalizing the witnesses concerning him. But why reject the account in its entirety? It would be difficult to claim that Thomas' omnipresence in the East is based on nothing substantive at all!

---

9   One part of this summary appears in *The actes apocryphes des apotres* (Geneva: Labor & Fides, 1981), 252–53.

10   Another tradition reported by Eusebius (*Ecclesiastical History*, 5:190) claims that Pantaenus, evangelist and theologian of Alexandria, visited India (though this could in fact have been Yemen) about the year 160. This is deduced from the churches founded there by Bartholomew who, according to the tradition, carried with him a Hebrew translation of *The Gospel According to Matthew*.

Nevertheless, even when it is admitted that several of the places mentioned in the apocryphal Acts were important Christian centers from the earliest times, on the whole the data of these works gives the thoughtful reader much cause for caution.

## Other Legendary Stories

One very ancient tradition asserts that the evangelist Mark was a native of Egypt, and that he returned there less than ten years after the day of Pentecost in order to found the church of Alexandria. He would have come again in the year 68, for it was here that he underwent martyrdom. There is no other historical evidence, however, to corroborate this story.

There is little time to linger over the "golden legend" according to which Martha, Mary, and their black servant fled persecution by sailing from the shores of Palestine and, pursued by a violent wind, landed at a location close to Marseille—Saintes-Maries-de-la-Mer—a very old place of pilgrimage. After disembarking, they lived for a time in a cave close to Aix-en-Provence, the grotto of Sainte-Baume, a pilgrimage site at least since the third century, if not before. The legend attributes a tomb at Saint-James-of-Compostelle (to the northwest of Spain) to James the Lesser, whom Joseph of Arimathea sent to evangelize England.

In conclusion, the extra-biblical information concerning this period is rare and lacks historical surety. Nevertheless, it does indicate the very early presence of the faith in the regions concerned. Still, it is hardly prudent from this evidence alone to affirm that by the end of the first century the entire Mediterranean basin had been visited by the bearers of the gospel.

# METHODS OF EVANGELIZATION

While possessing so little information, is it possible to discern the apostolic method of doing mission? Many have tried.[11]

It is necessary to recall that the gospel is good news, which, as such, must by all means be disseminated far and wide. In the first century the primary means was oral communication. The gospel of Jesus Christ was hence proclaimed everywhere where there were ears to hear; first in the Jewish synagogues, where the hearers were prepared to understand the Christian message because of their knowledge of the Holy Scriptures. Next the good news was announced everywhere where hearers were found: in the markets, public places, streets, schools, private houses. It is curious to observe that the construction of worship buildings troubled no one at this time.

The proclamation differed according to the listeners: Paul, for example, did not speak at Athens or at Lystra as he did in the synagogue of Pisidian Antioch or on the steps of the temple in Jerusalem. Throughout the Roman Empire the first missionaries had the advantage to have at their disposal a common means of communication: a commercial language, Koine Greek, that everyone understood.

The oral proclamation of the gospel is not disincarnated; it is accompanied by acts of charity, service, and the *diakonia* ("care" or "service") of Christians. Often the

---

11    The best-known study is that of Roland Allen, *Missionary Methods: St. Paul's or Ours?*, 8th ed. (1912; repr., London: World Dominion Press, 1976).

Word is also attested by miracles—"signs"—but this is not everywhere the case. In Athens, for example, they were not produced.

The agents of the mission seem to have been the apostles and those sent by the churches, as was the case with Barnabas and Saul of Tarsus (Acts 13:1–4). There were without doubt a large number of missionaries, who generally worked in sizable teams. However, the extraordinary progress of Christianity in the course of a generation can only be explained if most Christians—men and women—are seen to have been witnesses for Jesus Christ. The gospel was carried along Roman roads by Christian merchants or soldiers. The witnesses of Christ proclaimed the gospel message through the normal social channels of family members, neighbors, and work companions. Christians at this time were not disposed to meet in "sanctuaries," but assembled for their worship services in the homes of those among them who had houses best suited to the purpose. Often their meetings were held in the interior courtyards of houses where each was able to enter and leave freely. Paul very naturally envisioned that curious non-Christians would drop into a meeting of the church and there discover the gospel (1 Cor 14:23–25).

## A Prepared Ground

Since antiquity, historians and theologians have been struck by the convergence of various favorable factors that led to the rapid diffusion of the gospel in the first century. In the third century, Origen wrote:

> God was preparing the nations to receive his teaching, in subjecting everyone to the single emperor of Rome, and in preventing the isolation of the nations by a plurality of sovereigns that would have made it difficult for the apostles to execute the command of Christ: Go to all nations and makes disciples. It is clear that Jesus was born under the reign of Augustus who had, as it were, reduced to a uniform mass, thanks to his single sovereignty, most of the men of the earth. The existence of numerous [independent] realms would have been an obstacle to the dissemination of the teachings of Jesus through all the earth.[12]

There is more than a hint of ethnocentrism in Origen's reflection, for, in the first century, the Roman Empire only dominated a third of the population of the world.

## The Pax Romana

Though the preparation of the nations—the *praeparatio evangelica*, to use the sacred term—is a debatable concept, it remains instructive. The peace of Rome, the *Pax Romana*, was a notable advantage for the dissemination of the message. As noted above, the existence of a common language, Koine Greek, eased the task. Added to this were excellent routes of communication. The Romans had laid out and maintained a remarkable road network of eighty thousand kilometers that crisscrossed the length and breadth of the empire, reaching to the frontiers of Spain, Britain, the

---

12  Origen, *Contra Celsum*, 2:30.

Rhine, the Danube, and the entire south coast of the Mediterranean as far as modern-day Morocco. After the collapse of the empire, Europe would wait more than a millennium for the construction of a system of travel and communication as rapid and complete. In addition, in comparison to the other regions of the globe, the interior security of Rome was well-assured, and remarkable legislation fixed the limits of arbitrary action.

## The Role of the Jewish Diaspora and Synagogues

The Jewish Diaspora (dispersion through the nations) should be considered a factor of the first order in the preevangelization of the known world. Since the fall of the kingdom of Israel (721 BC) and of Judea (586 BC), Jewish colonies had been established throughout the Near East. The movement increased at the time of the Maccabees until all the great commercial and cultural centers of the Mediterranean basin and of Mesopotamia had a strong Jewish presence. In the time of Jesus, as today, the majority of the Jews were living outside of their ancestral land. The approximate numbers advanced are usually the following: 500,000–700,000 Jews in Palestine, and 3–4 million in the Diaspora. It is estimated that about 7 percent of the population of the Roman Empire was Jewish and that close to 1 million of the Jews were established outside the frontiers of the empire. This included Persia, the regions beyond the Tigris, Arabia, and Ethiopia.

As the place where the Scriptures were taught, the synagogues enjoyed an essential role in the maintenance of a common Jewish identity. The Greek translation of the Old Testament—a version called the Septuagint that was completed in the milieu of the Egyptian Diaspora—helped to create a bridge between the Jews and the surrounding Hellenistic culture. Many pagans crossed this bridge to become proselytes of Judaism. A sympathy for monotheism existed at this time in the ancient world, especially among the cultured people of the empire, and Judaism naturally exercised a strong attraction on these sympathizers.

As important to Jewish evangelism as the widespread existence of synagogues was the tendency to Hellenize the Jewish religion, which can be seen especially in the influence of Platonic philosophy. This Hellenization of Judaism to a large extent filled the gap separating the Jewish faith from Greek culture. Judaism, however, was divided on the subject of this extensive proselytism.[13] But certain renowned rabbis clearly pronounced in its favor, like Rabbi Eleazar, who said, "God dispersed Israel among the nations for the sole end of making numerous proselytes." The book of Acts attests that proselytes and "God fearers" (pagan sympathizers who abstained from conversion because of the rite of circumcision) were numerous converts to the gospel. It is reasonable to think that they were less rooted in Judaism than those who were Jews by race; moreover, they found Christian universalism attractive while Jewish particularism represented for them a permanent obstacle.

---

13   For reasons that have nothing to do with Jewish particularism, Jesus is scathing in the sole allusion that he made to Jewish proselytism: "Woe to you, teachers of the law and Pharisees, you hypocrites! You travel over land and sea to win a single convert, and when he becomes one, you make him twice as much a son of hell as you are" (Matt 23:15).

If Paul dared to leave behind freshly founded Christian communities, it is thanks to the presence of numerous Jews and proselytes in whose midst there were many responsible leaders who had a solid knowledge of the Scriptures. This was a very different historical context from other mission fields where an illiterate population might lack the least notion of either the biblical revelation or even monotheism.

### The Crisis of the Old Religions

The mythologies of Greek antiquity seemed to have had their time. The pantheon had become so cluttered that even the notion of divinity was devalued. In annexing new territories, Rome did not impose its religion on a people, except for the imperial cult; rather, the empire "naturalized" the local divinities. The denizens of the empire had arrived at what one has called, not without reason, a "coarse anthropomorphic polytheism." This discredited traditional religion in the eyes of many cultivated people or those who yearned for a higher level of morality. Besides, for several centuries some of the great philosophers, such as Xenophanes, Plato, and Aristotle, had been preparing the field for monotheism. The Christian apologists of the second century did not blench from drawing on the arguments of these philosophers in order to proclaim the one God more effectively. Had not Paul, in a certain manner, opened the way to this in his discourse to the philosophers of Athens (Acts 17:24–25)?

## NUMEROUS ADVERSARIES

However, in looking at the question from another angle, each of these advantages can also be seen as an obstacle to the mission of the early church. The Apostle Paul himself wrote: "A great door for effective work has opened to me, and there are many who oppose me" (1 Cor 16:9).

The remarkable organization of the Roman Empire gave authorities the means of effective coercion, which made it possible for them during times of persecution to ravage the ranks of the church. In order for this vast state to conserve its cohesion amidst great diversity, a political-religious cement was necessary: the imperial cult. To confess "Caesar is Lord (*Kurios*)" and to participate in ceremonies in which sacrificial offerings were made in his honor was required as proof of

*This graffiti, found on a wall in the quarters of the imperial pages at Mount Palatine in Rome and dating from the third century, represents a young boy with his arms raised in the direction of a crucified man with the head of a donkey. The inscription says: "Alexamenos adores his God." A short distance away, another engraved inscription (not reproduced here) responds: "Alexamenos is faithful." This document is taken from Michael Green, L'evangélisation dans l'eglise primitive, (Lavigny et Saint-Légier: Groupes Missionnaires et Emmaüs 1981), 209.*

civic loyalty. Proclaiming "Jesus Christ is Lord" and refusing all compromise with the imperial cult led innumerable Christians to the horror of state torture.

The emptiness of the old mythologies inspired, as an alternative, an interest in the mystery cults of the East, but this widespread interest also threatened "to contaminate" a large number of otherwise good Christians.

The extent to which Judaism had expanded throughout the empire had not only created a strategic bridge for the planting of new churches; it had also formed the venue in which Judaism would become Christianity's first adversary. Among the numerous early churches were ones that were begun by dissidents from the synagogues of the Diaspora. The animosity that the Jews had for Christians is easily imagined, and some naturally sought to enlist the population and authorities against the apostles and new Christian communities. The book of Acts furnishes several examples of this.

Moreover, it is well to be conscious of an intrinsic obstacle to the gospel: Jesus Christ crucified, a scandal for Jews and folly for Greeks (1 Cor 1:23). Dating from third-century Rome, a clumsily engraved caricature can be found on one of the walls of the buildings where the pages of the emperor lodged. It is a representation of a crucified man with the head of a donkey before whom is prostrated a young man, no doubt a Christian page who was being mocked by his comrades. It has this inscription: "Alexamenos adores his God." Pliny wrote that the Christian faith is a "contagious superstition," and the historian Tacitus said that Christians are a plague—"the enemies of the human species, meriting the most severe chastisements."

To attribute to favorable circumstances alone the extraordinarily rapid dissemination of the gospel in the first century would be to discount the zeal of the first missionaries and the consecration that often led to the sacrifice of their lives. Accustomed to sophisticated modern means of communication, we can only admire this handful of men and women who, deprived of power and exposed to a hostile political climate, spread the gospel like wildfire throughout the whole known world.

## MISSIONARY STRATEGY

Is it possible to speak of a missionary strategy in the first century? The answer is no if one imagines a major centralized state, drawing up plans and giving orders for others to execute. Jean Delorme, a professor of the Faculté de Théologie Catholique de Lyon, writes: "It is a fact that the church expanded because of the initiative of individuals, groups, and communities, without a preestablished plan, without more coordination than that accorded by the faith and agreement between the apostles."[14]

However, it is legitimate to speak of strategy if one considers how the Holy Spirit took possession of the first disciples, formed them, sent them, and guided them by the opening or closing of doors of opportunity before them. This divine strategy also relied on the reason and good sense of Christians. The good news was preached first in the great urban centers, which were also centers of commerce. Christianity very early established itself in Antioch of Syria, Ephesus, Corinth, Alexandria, and Rome.

---

14  Jean Delorme, "Diversité et unité des ministères d'après le Nouveau Testament," in *Le ministère et les ministères selon le Nouveau Testament* (Paris: Seuil, 1974), 296.

(Jerusalem, destroyed in AD 70, thereafter enjoyed no role in the diffusion of Christianity, hence depriving the movement of a mother church upon which the others could depend.) These centers, being dispersed throughout the empire, also served as good conduits of communication.

An aspect of the missionary strategy of the Apostle Paul was his desire to reach heads of state: the proconsul Sergius Paulus in Cyprus, the Asiarchans in Ephesus, the Roman governors Felix and Festus in Judea, and King Agrippa and Bernice of Caesarea (the dialogue reported by Acts is unforgettable; chiefly Acts 26:7–10). Without doubt Paul even had the hope of appearing before the emperor himself in Rome. In the eyes of God such personages did not have souls any more precious than that of a Corinthian slave, but as converts, the influence they could have exerted on the development of the Christian mission would have been considerable.

The evangelists, like the Jewish proselytizers, used the written word. The New Testament itself provides evidence that the Gospels and the apostolic Epistles circulated from one church to another. These texts were soon used as a means to propagate the Christian faith.

In the spread of the good news, every means at the disposal of the church was used.

## STATISTICAL EVALUATION

Though historians do not possess accurate statistics for this period, reasonable estimations can be made. From the slender archaeological evidence and various documents that have survived, historians venture that at the end of the first century the total number of Christians and sympathizers probably came to a half million, the majority still being of Jewish origin. It is important, however, to be aware of the tenuous nature of this evaluation and that many prudent scholars in the field prefer to avoid statistical estimations altogether.[15]

---

15    In the first century the population of the Roman Empire was around 60 million inhabitants, of which 4 million were Jews. As for the population of the world, it is estimated that there were about 180 million inhabitants in this period. The statistician Barrett (*World Christian Encyclopedia*) advances the figure of 1 million Christians at the end of the first century. Most other specialists, however, propose estimations distinctly more modest.

# The Mission of the Persecuted Church: From the Apostle John to Constantine (100–313)

From the beginning of the second century, Christianity appeared to be different from Judaism. Until then it had scarcely attracted the attention of the Roman authorities, with the exception of Rome in the year 64 during the reign of Nero and Asia Minor in the years 81–96 under the reign of Domitian. Now the churches multiplied, especially in the cities where many were becoming aware of the existence of Christians. The favorable circumstances for evangelization discussed in the preceding chapter continued. The empire, however, was becoming a theater of grave disorders, especially after the death of Emperor Marcus Aurelius in 180; the old beliefs that gave Rome its original power seemed exhausted. The new religions, in particular the mysterious oriental cults from the East, seduced many people. But in the eyes of others, the gospel of Christ came to fill a void and supply a hope that until then was unknown. Christianity appeared to be a young and dynamic force, a solution in opposition to and replacing the old beliefs and modes of life that now left their followers feeling disappointed and anxious.

There are few confirmed details on the progress of the church in the second century. The situation of the first century, when each Christian appeared to carry the message to others, no doubt continued. Clandestine communities existed more or less in all the great cities of the empire, and equally so beyond the frontiers toward the south and east. For the third century, extant documents and archaeological evidence indicate the wide distribution of churches through the time when persecutions ceased in 313 under the emperor Constantine. The following will review the different regions of the empire and beyond.

## GEOGRAPHIC SURVEY

It is appropriate to begin with Asia, for was not Asia the origin of the message of salvation? Yet, since the time when the book of Acts focused on the evangelization of regions to the west of Jerusalem and Antioch, Western Christians have had the tendency to forget all that was undertaken in the direction of the East.

## Palestine and Syria

From the beginning the Jews were the declared adversaries of Christianity, believing this offshoot of Judaism to be in fact a new religion that threatened the secure place that they occupied in Roman society. Though Jerusalem was in ruins since the year 70 and the revolt at the beginning of the second century, Syrian churches were numerous and prosperous. Therefore, Antioch, the great commercial city and door to the East, became the chief center of missionary activity.

It is estimated that, by about the year 300, churches could be found in all the cities and even the villages of Syria. The gospel had come to them from either Antioch or Galilee when numerous Christians fled one after another from the persecution and then the ravages inflicted by the imperial troops in the Judeo-Roman War. It is important to remember, too, that there were already Christians in Damascus even before the conversion of Saul of Tarsus! Syrian Christians were good missionaries and evangelists, as will be shown when the situation in Mesopotamia is presented.

## Asia Minor

Asia Minor was without doubt the region where the density of Christians was the most considerable during this period. At least half of the New Testament was either written in or intended for Asia Minor. The writings of Luke, Paul, Peter, and John attest to the presence of churches in nearly all of the great centers of this vast territory before the end of the first century.

In the second century, the movement continued, although certain remote regions where the Greek language was not understood remained pagan for a long time. It was only in the sixth century that the emperor Justinian would eliminate the vast numbers of pagans holding fast in their mountainous regions, which until then were impervious to outside influence.

The progress of Christianity in the second and third centuries took place largely in the provinces of the north that had almost never been reached before. The Christians "in Diaspora," who were addressed in the first epistle of Peter, were the first fruits of an abundant harvest, particularly in Bithynia. The letter of Pliny the Young to the emperor Trajan, in about the year 112, attests to the magnitude of the flood of conversions to Christianity in this region at the beginning of the second century.

> The affair appears to warrant that I consult you, especially due to the number of accused. There is a crowd of persons of all ages and of all conditions, the two sexes also, who are or will be called to justice. It is not only in the cities, but also throughout the villages and the countryside that the contagion of this superstition has spread: it seems to me, however, that it is possible to check and heal it.
>
> In fact, it can already be observed that the temples, which are about deserted, have started again to be visited; that some ritual ceremonies long interrupted have restarted; that everywhere is

sold the meat of animals sacrificed to idols, which until recently was no longer found because buyers were so rare.[16]

Whatever the success of the measures taken by Pliny, the picture he depicted shows that the gospel enjoyed a great success in the country, even more impressive than the one enjoyed in the time when Paul was at Ephesus (Acts 19).

Another example of fruitful evangelization in Asia Minor merits attention. It concerns the ministry of Gregory Thaumaturgus (ca. 215–ca. 270), the "wonder-worker," in the neighboring province of Pontus about a century and a half later. A spiritual son of Origen, he evangelized the region with astonishing power. Here is how one of his successors in the episcopate, whose relatives had been eyewitnesses to the event, described the ministry of Gregory:

> From daybreak, a crowd of people were pressing at the door of Gregory—the old, those demon possessed, those unhappy in all respects—to whom he was in turn preaching, questioning, exhorting, healing. It was his manner to bring the people the gospel: the people were seeing the power of God as long as they were hearing him speak.

Some years after the death of Gregory in 375, the bishop and theologian Basil of Caesarea wrote about his ministry, mixing history and legend:

> Gregory had by the assistance of the Spirit a redoubtable power over demons, but to bring the nations to the obedience of the faith he received a grace of eloquence. At the beginning of his ministry, having found only seventeen Christians, he brought the entire people, townsmen, and countrymen, to the knowledge of God. He moved a bed of flowers by commanding them in the powerful name of Christ, and dried the marsh that was an object of litigation between two greedy brothers. His predictions were such that he conceded nothing to the great prophets. In brief, it would take a long time to relate in detail the miracles of this man, who by reason of the superabundance of chrisms [gifts] that the Spirit was producing in him, such as works of power and signs and prodigies, was proclaimed a "second Moses" even by the enemies of the Church.[17]

Cappadocia, mentioned already in the address of the first epistle of Peter, was also gained in the second century and subsequently enjoyed a great role, as much theological as missionary. It is from there that Scythia was evangelized, as well as Armenia and even the nations of the Goths. Basil the Great created at Caesarea, in 370, the first Christian hospital, welcoming the poor and foreigners. Though of lesser importance than Egypt, Cappadocia was also distinguished as a place of Christian monasticism since the period of the fourth century.

---

16   Pliny the Younger, *Epistles*, 10:97.
17   Basil of Caesarea, *On the Holy Spirit*, 29.

## Edessa and the Realm of Osrhoene

Situated beyond the Euphrates, Osrhoene is a small buffer realm between the Roman Empire and Persia. Its capital, Edessa (present-day Urfa, to the south of Turkey; near Haran, the city of Abraham), is only 250 kilometers from Antioch. A legendary Syriac writing reports that following an exchange of messengers between Jesus and King Abgar V, known as Ucomo ("the Black"), a disciple by the name of Addai (Thaddeus?) was sent by the Lord to Edessa and baptized the king. Here are some extracts from Abgar's letter, included in *The Doctrine of Addai*, that was supposed to have been sent to Jesus by Hannon, the archivist of the palace of Edessa.

> I have heard the reports respecting thee and thy course, as performed by thee without medicines and without the use of herbs. For as it is said, thou causest the blind to see again, the lame to walk, and thou cleanest the lepers, and thou castest out impure spirits and demons, and thou healest those that are tormented by long disease, and thou raisest the dead. And hearing all these things of thee, I concluded in my mind one of two things; either that thou are God, and having descended from heaven, doest these things, or else doing them, thou art the Son of God. Therefore, now I have written and besought thee to visit me, and to heal the disease with which I am afflicted. I have, also, heard that the Jews murmur against thee, and are plotting to injure thee; I have, however, a very small but noble state, which is sufficient for us both.
>
> [According to the archivist, Jesus responded:] Blessed art thou, O Agbarus [latinized version of Agbar], who, without seeing, hast believed in me . . . But in regard to what thou hast written, that I should come to thee, it is necessary that I should fulfill all things there, for which I have been sent. And after this fulfillment, thus to be received again by Him that sent me. And after I have been received up, I will send to thee a certain one of my disciples, that he may heal thy affliction, and give life to thee and to those who are with thee. [The archivist, who was to paint the king, put in the painting the image of Jesus and brought it to King Abgar, who received it with joy and placed it with great honor among the pieces of his own palace.][18]

The first Christian writings circulating in Osrhoene were in the Syriac language, which is why the hypothesis has been ventured that the gospel was not carried there from Antioch where the language spoken is Greek, but from Adiabene, a realm allied to Osrhoene where a Christian community was very early established among the Jews of the Diaspora, who were numerous in these regions. It is certain that before the year 200 Edessa was an important Christian center, and that by the beginning of

---

18   This writing, *The Doctrine of Addai*, dated actually in the fourth century, is known to us because of its inclusion in the work of Eusebius (*Ecclesiastical History*, Book 1, 13: 44–45) who considered it authentic. The comments in the text are from Jean-Marc Prieur, *Apocryphes chrétiens* (Aubonne, Switzerland: Moulin, 1995), 73–74, according to the translation of Alain Desreumaux, *Histoire du roi Abgar et de Jésus* (Turnhout, Belgium: Brepols, 1993).

the third century it was linked to the seat of Antioch. In asking for baptism in the year 196, the king of Edessa, Abgar the Great (179–214), would have been, one could say, the first head of state in the world to become a Christian. According to tradition, he came to Rome to speak with Bishop Eleutherius, though historians now doubt the historicity of this conversion. The *Chronicle of Edessa*, dating from the fourth century, cites the municipal archives to show that the Christians' house of prayer had been destroyed at the time of an inundation that ravaged the city in the year 201. This is the first historical mention of the existence of a consecrated Christian sanctuary, but no traces of the building remain.

*Edessa in northern Mesopotamia was from the second century an important theological and missionary center of Syriac-speaking Christianity, whose reach throughout Asia was considerable during the first millennium. Edessa was the capital of Osrhoene, the first state in the world officially Christian, following the conversion of its king in the year 196. Today it is the city of Urfa, the entirely Islamic prefecture of a province in south Turkey. (Photo: J. Blandenier)*

Following this period, Prince Bardesanes (or Bardaisan) (154–222)—astrologer, musician, poet, Christian, and doctor—contributed handsomely to the very important Christian literature in the Syriac language. He composed 150 hymns as a Christian psalter. When he was later accused of Gnosticism, he defended himself with vigor.

From Edessa, missionaries went out to the entire East, from the Caspian Sea to the Persian Gulf.

## Persia and Mesopotamia

The realm of Persia, having inherited a vast empire from the sixth-century conqueror Cyrus the Great, still included a considerable territory at the beginning of the modern era. The people were not polytheists but, rather, professed a high religion, Zoroastrianism, which was founded by Zoroastra in the sixth century BC. The cultivated and learned Zoroastrian priests formed an influential and respected elite. They presented a lively opposition to Christianity, which was first carried to the region by Syrian merchants. There were soon churches dispersed throughout Mesopotamia, some using the Syriac language and others the Greek. At Dura Europus on the Euphrates exists the most ancient ruin to be identified as a Christian sanctuary, having been constructed about the year 230. By the third century, there were seventeen cities with a bishop in the region that lies on both sides of the Tigris valley and between the mountains and the Persian Gulf. Among these cities was Seleucia-Ctesiphon, which later became the capital of an immense Eastern church entirely detached from Rome. The Persian King Shapur I, a chief of state who favored Christians, was harried by his hereditary enemy, the Roman Empire. When Emperor Valerian temporarily occupied Persia, he expelled the bishops from it. But Shapur, who defeated and killed Valerien in 260, authorized them to return.

Opposition to Christianity, however, increased in the fourth century. When Christians, in effect, formed a state church within the Roman Empire during the reign of Constantine, the Persian church was suspected of being a fifth column of the enemy. An unfortunate letter from Constantine, in which the emperor recommended his Christian coreligionists to the benevolence of the king of Persia, evidently produced the opposite effect. The Persian Christians then experienced tragic persecutions, notably during the reign of Shapur II (334–345). Many had to flee their country, some going under the direction of Thomas Cana to the coast of Malabar in India, while others, such as Ephraim the Syrian and his school, took refuge at Edessa.

Under the reign of Emperor Theodosius I (379–395), relations between Rome and Persia improved. The Persian church was then able to reorganize itself and reestablish contact with the rest of Christianity. Nevertheless, the majority of the Persian churches used the Syriac language and preserved a spiritual heritage that differed from that of the Western church. Historian Jean Meyendorff writes, "Syrian Christianity represented a separate world, one culturally distinct from the civilization which, in the interior of the Roman *oikoumene* [inhabited world], was in the process of slowly elaborating a synthesis between Christianity and Hellenism. Their spiritual leaders, such as Aphraates (ca. 270–345) and Saint Ephraim (ca. 306–373), did not know Greek."[19] This church, even before becoming Nestorian, was characterized by a remarkable missionary enthusiasm, notably among its monks. John Chrysostrom acquired his missionary vocation from the Syrian monks, as is apparent from his correspondence with the monastic community of Zeugma on the Euphrates. Meyendorff continues, "Although the outset of the history of Christianity in India, Armenia, Georgia, and Ethiopia is replete with legendary figures, there is no doubt that through these four countries the Syrians decisively contributed to the establishment of the church . . . The Nestorian church of Persia would continue its missionary enterprise throughout Asia until the end of the Middle Ages."[20]

## The Realm of Adiabene

The small realm of Adiabene, a vassal state of the Persians that lay beyond the Tigris, included an ancient and important Jewish colony. It made numerous proselytes among the population, including some in the very bosom of the royal family. A monotheism inspired by Judaism was adopted as the state religion in AD 36. King Monobaze, who had a palace in Jerusalem, sent troops to fight at the side of the Jews against the Romans in the Judeo-Roman War of AD 66–70. The beginning of the second century saw the first conversions to Christianity from synagogue members, and the church thereafter grew rapidly. In the fourth century the greater part of the Adiabene population became Christian. But from this time forward the realm experienced Persian occupation, and the church suffered severe persecution from Shapur II. John of Arbeles, the first bishop attested by the surviving documents (Arbeles was the metropolitan seat of the region), underwent martyrdom in 343. His successor, Abraham, was also martyred.

By the end of the fifth century, the Nestorian Christians and Jacobites founded a number of monasteries.

## India

There are several differing hypotheses concerning the foundation of the first churches in India. The belief that the Apostle Thomas evangelized the Indies is a well-anchored belief among the Christians of south India, who have some intriguing arguments to make. According to the *Acts of Thomas*, between the years 52 and 72 the apostle founded seven communities on the coast of southwest India (present-day Kerala). The grotto that would have been his last place of abode, and where he would have been buried, can be seen today near Madras. According to the *Acts of Thomas*,[21] soldiers killed the apostle by spearing him. Though the texts that support this tradition have little credibility, they do mention a king named Gundaphorus (or Gundobar) as well as his brother Guda, who were converted thanks to the witness of Thomas. The existence of these two kings is today historically attested, notably by an effigy on surviving coins. The name of Gundaphorus has even been transcribed into Greek, which confirms that he had at least some interaction with the West. It seems,

---

19   Jean Meyendorff, *Unité de l'empire et divisions des chrétiens*, trans. François Lhoest (Paris: Cerf, 1993), 116.
20   Ibid., 118, and see especially 157–58.
21   The *Acts of Thomas* is an apocryphal writing drafted in the Syriac language in Mesopotamia in the third century.

however, that this Gundaphorus did not reign in India but in a realm within Persian territory that lay to the east of Iran (present-day Khorasan). Thomas is often called "the apostle of the Persians," but the veracity of the stories reporting his evangelization of India lack irrefutable proof. However, they stand on more solid ground than historians have believed until recently, for there were then frequent commercial and cultural exchanges between Persia and India.

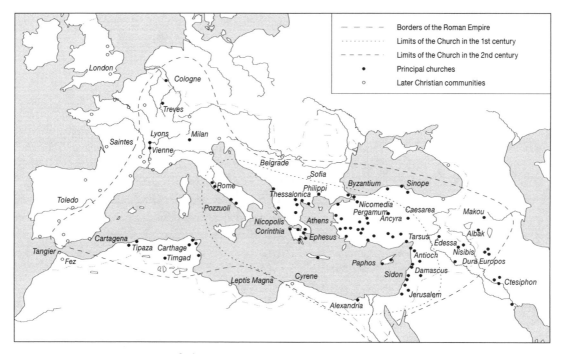

Map 2: Limits of Christianity in the West at the end of the Roman Empire

The first trace of written evidence for the evangelization of India is found in a chronicle dating from the year 295, affirming that Bishop David of Basra embarked on a journey from the Persian Gulf to India, where he "evangelized many people."[22] Thirty years later, in 325 at the Council of Nicaea, records show the presence of a bishop named "John of Persia and the great Indies."[23] Hence, there is little doubt that in the fourth century a church existed in India, though how it came to be there is not known with certitude.

## Armenia

At the end of the period studied in this chapter, the people of the independent realm of Armenia turned *en masse* toward the gospel. A considerable people, they were established in the region of the Caucasus that border on the Roman Empire. Setting aside the tiny realm of Osrhoene, Armenia was the first state to have officially adopted

---

22   See Chronicle of Seert.
23   The list of attendees is found in *Patrum Nicaenorum nomina Latin, Grace, Copice, Syriace, Arabice, Armeniace*, ed. Henricus Gelzer, Henricus Hilgenfeld, Otto Cantz, 2nd ed. (Stuttart: Teubner, 1995).

Christianity. The great missionary of Armenia, Gregory the Illuminator (240–326), first heard the gospel from the witness of his nurse, a Christian from the neighborhood of Cappadocia. Gregory was from a noble family of Parthian origin. During a time of conflict between rival noble clans, his father killed the Armenian king Chosroes I; and Gregory, then an adolescent, had to seek refuge in Cappadocia where he benefited from a Christian education and was baptized. When he received the call of God to proclaim the gospel to his own people, he returned to Armenia. Whereupon, King Tiridates (or Trdat), son of Chosroes, had him imprisoned.

Appearing before his persecutor in about the year 287, Gregory led him to the faith, and despite the opposition of the priests of the national goddess Anahid, from that time forward the king favored his ministry. The masses soon converted, and Christianity became the official religion in the year 301.

A very ancient chronicle describes these events:

> Having established the foundations of a church, Gregory built a house for the Lord. And in the villages of the neighboring nations, he founded churches, erected altars, and consecrated priests. All the inhabitants freely and with all their hearts converted and began practicing fasts, prayers, and the fear of God. At a fixed day . . . the holy man, having summoned the army, King Tiridates, Queen Aschken, Princess Khosrovitoukhd, and all the great people of the realm, went down to the shores of the Euphrates at sunrise and baptized them all at the same time in the name of the Father, Son, and Holy Spirit . . . Those who were baptized in the course of the seven days numbered four hundred thousand . . . Next he went to all the territories of greater Armenia and established churches in all the prefectures and all the provinces, cities, boroughs, villages, and countryside . . . Priests were installed everywhere, and the king ordered that only the one God, creator of heaven and earth, be worshiped and that provision be made for all the churches, altars of the Lord, servants, and pastors.[24]

Due to a powerful spiritual revival inspired by Bishop Mesrop Mashotz (361–440), Armenia was reevangelized in the following century to great effect.[25]

## Egypt

We move now to the African continent. As we have already seen, Eusebius reported a tradition that attributes to the evangelist Mark the founding of the church of Alexandria, one of the most important metropolitan centers of the empire. In fact, it is likely that this church was founded during the time of the first Christian generation. From Egypt have come several of the oldest fragments of New Testament texts ever found. One of these documents, which contains portions of *The Gospel According to John*, dates from the beginning of the second century.

---

24 For Gregory the Illuminator see Valerie Goekjian Zahirsky Agat 'angeghos, *The Conversion of Armenia: A retelling of Angathangelos' History,* (1985).

25 See pp. 119–20.

The list of the Alexandrian bishops that begins in the year 41 is no doubt fictive. The first bishop whose name is historically verifiable is Demetrius (189–232). But from a very early time, it is evident that, despite several severe persecutions, Alexandria was already a great theological center of Christianity. Its catechetical school, the first Christian university, was flourishing by the middle of the second century. It was founded in about the year 160 by Pantaenus, a converted Stoic philosopher. Here is the tradition reported by Eusebius:

> About the same time, the school of the faithful was governed by a man most distinguished for his learning, whose name was Pantaenus. As there had been a school of sacred learning established there from ancient times, which has continued down to our own times, and which we have understood was held by men able in eloquence and the study of divine things. For the tradition is, that this philosopher was then a great eminence, as he had been first disciplined in the philosophical principles of those called Stoics. But he is said to have displayed such ardor, and so zealous a disposition, respecting the divine word, that he was constituted a herald of the gospel of Christ to the nations of the East, and advanced even as far as India. There were even there yet many evangelists of the word, who were ardently striving to employ their inspired zeal after the apostolic example, to increase and build up the divine word. Of these Pantaenus is said to have been one, and to have come as far as the Indies. And the report is, that he there found his own arrival anticipated by some who there were acquainted with the gospel of Matthew, to whom Bartholomew, one of the apostles, had preached, and had left them the gospel of Matthew in the Hebrew, which was also preserved until this time. Pantaenus, after many praiseworthy deeds, was finally at the head of the Alexandrian school, commenting on the treasures of divine truth, both orally and in his writings.[26]

In this era geographical references were rather hazy, and often what was called the "Indies" referred to everything found to the east of the Arabian desert. Consequently, the region mentioned, as we noted above in regard to Bartholomew, could have been the southeast of Arabia or Yemen, and not India. On the other hand, what is interesting for our purposes is the expression used by Eusebius regarding the catechetical school: "The Holy Scriptures were taught there, *according to ancient custom*" (italics ours). Hence, in the year 160 Pantaenus was conforming to a custom that had already existed in Alexandria for a long time.

Clement of Alexandria (150–215) succeeded Pantaenus in the year 190. He was an illustrious professor and a zealous evangelist, as some of his writings, such as *The Address to the Greeks*, demonstrate. Clement pursued his ministry in an extremely troubled time: "Everyday we see with our own eyes streams of the blood of the faithful, burned alive, crucified, or decapitated," he wrote.

---

26  Eusebius, *Ecclesiastical History*, Book 5, 10:190.

Origen (ca. 185–ca. 254) also greatly contributed to the brilliance of the school of Alexandria. At the end of his life, and despite having seen intense persecution, he writes these triumphant lines: "All the cults will be annihilated, except the law of Christ, which alone will prevail . . . Its principles are implanted more and more in minds, and eventually it will triumph everywhere."

Among his copious writings, Origen left us *Contra Celsum*. It concerns the refutation of *True Discourse*, a polemical treatise against Christianity written about the years 177–180 by the Platonic philosopher Celsus. Though probably an Egyptian by birth, the author lived in Rome and sought to disparage Christians, whose activities he observed in the capital of the empire. The text of Celsus has been lost, but Origen cites it often in order to refute it, and through his citations we have a picture of the life and witness of Christians in the second century that one would suspect of being embellished had it not been written by one of their most inveterate adversaries.[27]

The school of Alexandria trained numerous missionaries that then traveled throughout Egypt. One Coptic translation of the New Testament asserts that not only the Hellenized centers but also the rural areas were reached with the gospel during the second century. The great persecution at the time of Emperor Septimius Severus in 202 produced numerous martyrs, from Alexandria to the region of Thebes, seven hundred kilometers from the Mediterranean coast. Bishop Heraclides consecrated twenty bishops between the years 231 and 247, the seat of Hermenopolis being four hundred kilometers to the south of Alexandria. In the third century, missionaries penetrated deeply into the African continent, sailing up the Nile as far as Sudan. About the year 300, the Bible was translated into Sahidic, a Coptic language of Upper Egypt. At the time of the synod of Alexandria in 320, there were a hundred Egyptian bishops.

Egypt was the cradle of Christian monasticism. The movement gained much notoriety through the monk Anthony (ca. 251–355), who lived as an ascetic first in a grotto near the Nile, then in the more distant desert, and finally in the vicinity of the Red Sea where he assembled a number of disciples in a monastery. It is there that he died, more than one hundred years old. The first great organizer of monasticism was Pachomius (292–ca. 347), who assembled at least three thousand monks into a very strict monastic discipline. Chenouda (or Shenoute), abbot in the period from 348–366 of the White Monastery near Atripe in Upper Egypt, directed 2,200 monks and 1,800 contemplatives and was the author of spiritual writings in the Coptic language.

Missionary efforts in Africa were vigorous, especially due to the monks. The regions of their principal activity were the upper Nile and, to the east, the horn of Africa.

## North Africa

The territories that are today Libya and Maghreb were reached with the gospel in the first century. The highly Romanized Carthaginian and Berber populations rapidly and in great numbers accepted the Christian faith at about the same time. This prosperous region, the breadbasket of Rome, became with Asia Minor a bastion of Christianity. At the end of the second century a veritable mass movement drew the

---

27  For a presentation of the treatise of Celsus, see Ries, *Les chrétiens*, 36–38.

people towards the church. In 197 Tertullian (160–ca. 230) wrote ostensibly to Roman provincial governors in *Apologetic*:

> We are of yesterday, and yet we already fill the earth and all that is yours: your cities, houses of commerce, the fortified posts, the camps themselves, your palaces, senate, forum . . . We leave you only your temples . . . In each city, more than half the inhabitants are Christians.

The same author explained, furthermore, that if the church grew, it was not in spite of persecution but because of it. Addressing high-ranking officials of the government, he wrote:

> You torture, martyr, condemn, and suppress us; your anxiety is the best proof of our innocence. It is why God tolerates that we endure all this . . . The greatest refinement of your cruelty serves you nothing. You succeed only in advertising our solidarity. We grow in number, but it is because you have started without ceasing to harry us: the blood of the Christians is a seed . . . When you condemn us, it is then that God acquits us.[28]

And he gave expression to this sense of triumph in a form so often cited that it has become part of the patrimony of the universal church:

> The more we are harried, the more numerous we are. The blood of the martyrs is the seed of the church. Your philosophers teach to confront suffering and death with courage, but they make fewer disciples than the Christians who do not lecture but preach by example.

Due at least in part to persecution, the church grew very rapidly. In the year 220, a regional council assembled seventy bishops; another thirty years later, eighty. It should be noted, however, that in North Africa the title of bishop was not reserved for the leaders of the church who lived in great cities; rather, the title corresponds to the current usage of the term pastor.

It is in North Africa that Christian literature in Latin first began to flourish, and it is here that the first Latin translations of the Scriptures appeared. Authors such as Tertullian and Cyprian gave these churches remarkable luster, and in the following century they would be succeeded by Saint Augustine.

The *Acts of the Scillitan Martyrs* is the first known Christian text in Latin. Written in North Africa about the year 180, it relates the trial and execution of a dozen recently baptized Berber peasants in Carthage. Appearing twenty years later, the *Passion of Perpetua* is a journal written in prison by a young mother of twenty-two who had recently come to the faith. With her newborn son in her arms, she was thrown to wild beasts in the Carthaginian arena in the year 203, giving until the end a radiant and triumphant witness. Such stories made a profound impression on Christians relentlessly threatened by persecution.

---

28  Tertullian, *Apologeticus*, 50:12–13.

*This cruciform baptistery amidst the ruins of the basilica of Bulla Regina, northwest of present-day Tunisia, witnesses to the importance of the Christian presence in fourth-century Maghreb before Islam arrived. (Photo: J. Blandenier)*

Cyprian, the great bishop of Carthage who died a martyr in 258, asked his tormentors why they used torture to obtain his "confessions" when he had for so long been evangelizing in the streets: "If I spontaneously confess and declare in a loud voice and several times over that I am a Christian, why do you employ torture to one who has confessed and dethroned your gods, not in some secret places, but publicly, in the market, in the presence of magistrates?"[29]

That the Christianity of North Africa extended rapidly to the western limits of the known world is evidenced by the existence of bishops in Tangier, Fez, and Rabat in the year 200.

## Greece

And now finally to the European continent, where we begin first with Greece, which for many years remained relatively impenetrable to the gospel. In the second century, Christians there were still a small minority. At the beginning of the third century, however, Clement of Alexandria wrote that Athens and all Greece was Christian. There is some rhetorical exaggeration in this remark, for it was not until 529 in the time of Emperor Justinian that the Athenian school of philosophy was closed, the last symbol of pagan antiquity. Moreover, certain regions of southern Peloponnesia remained recalcitrant to the efforts of evangelists until as late as the tenth century.

## Italy

Churches grew numerous quickly in Italy, at least in the south of the country in Latium (west-central Italy) and in Sicily. From the time of Nero, the capital could count about 800,000, and the number of Christians at that time is estimated to have been three thousand. In the year 94, Tacitus spoke of an "immense multitude of

---

29  Cyprian, *Ad Demetrianum*, 13.

Christians," perhaps to create fear and incite the authorities to react. In the year 166, Bishop Soter affirms that in Rome there were as many Christians as Jews.

Until the beginning of the third century, the names of the bishops suggest that there were many Greek-speaking Eastern immigrants among the members of the church of Rome. The first translation of the New Testament in Latin did not appear until the year 200, contemporaneous with the one in North Africa.

By about the year 250, there were close to thirty thousand Christians in the city of Rome, about 3 percent of the population. Eusebius cites a letter from Bishop Cornelius of Rome to his colleague in Antioch that dates from the year 251: the church, he said, includes forty-six presbyters and is subdivided into seven districts, each having in its service a deacon and a subdeacon to assist the fifteen hundred widows and other persons without resources.[30]

In contrast, before the accession of Constantine, Northern Italy was clearly less touched by the gospel. In the fourth century, however, Ambrose would give Milan a distinctively Christian glow, all the more important at a time when Rome was in decline and the Lombard capital threatened to supplant it as the seat of the western emperor.

## Gaul

Christian communities appeared very early on the Mediterranean coast, the Iles de Lérins, Fréjus, Marseille, and along the Rhone valley as far as Lyons, the capital of the Gauls. The gospel was carried there by merchants coming from Greece and Asia Minor. The language of the Christians was for a long time Greek, and it is in this language that the churches of Lyons and Vienna wrote to the churches of the East to recount the terrible persecution that ravaged them in 177, in the time of the emperor Marcus Aurelius. Among the fifty or so martyrs were Bishop Pothinus, who was more than ninety years old, and the young female slave Blandina. All the rest were recently baptized and gave a glorious witness. Perhaps, however, there were still only a few Gaullists among the converts. This changed with Pothinus' successor, Irenaeus (130–208), who, although he was from the East and had been trained in Smyrna by Polycarp, the disciple of the Apostle John, dedicated himself to the evangelization of the indigenous people.

A remarkable missionary, Irenaeus preached tirelessly in public places—in cities as well as towns—where he addressed the population in the Celtic language. In his correspondence, he spoke of Celtic and German converts. At the beginning of his treatise *Adversus haereses (Against Heresies)*, written about 180, he says that he had lost some of his mastery of Greek, for it was largely in the Celtic language that he practiced his ministry. In the same treatise, he affirms the uniqueness and the immense diffusion of the word of God. For Irenaeus, unity and universality are the authentic marks of the church, in contrast to heretical movements. And his treatise is also historically valuable in that it notes where the gospel had been planted by the end of the second century, according to what he knew of it:

---

30  Eusebius, *Ecclesiastical History*, Book 6, 43:265.

> The church, disseminated by everyone to the ends of the earth, received apostles in this faith in a single God . . . The message and the faith that the church received, although spread through the entire world, is kept with diligence as if it were living in a single house . . . The churches that are established in Germany do not have another faith and other traditions, nor do those in Spain, nor those that are Celtic, nor those that are in the East, nor Egypt, nor Libya, nor those that are in the middle of the world. The sun created by God is one and the same in the entire world, and like it the message of the truth shines everywhere and illumines all men who want to arrive at the knowledge of the truth.[31]

The witnesses of the gospel traveled from Lyons up the Saône River, penetrating farther north in Europe, following the string of garrisons and Roman government officials. There were some Christians in Metz in the second century, and by its tributary the Mosselle, the Rhine was reached by the time of Marcus Aurelius, before the year 180. This meant that Trèves, Mayence, and Cologne could be evangelized. Though the forests of Germany were to remain for a long time impenetrable to Christians, the Rhine is a navigable river permitting access to the Helvetian Plateau. Hence Basel and Zurich had probably already been reached by the beginning of the third century.

On the coastline of the Mediterranean, the evangelists divided their efforts equally between the west and center of Gaul. The witness of Gregory of Tours in these regions is confirmed by various sources:

> In the time of Decius [emperor from 249–251, but Gregory also refers to his consulate, sometimes years before], seven men ordained as bishops were sent to Gaul to preach there . . . These were the following: to Tours was sent Bishop Gatien; to Arles, Bishop Trophime; to Narbonne, Bishop Paul; to Toulouse, Bishop Saturninus; to Paris, Bishop Dionysius [Denys]; to Clermont, Bishop Austremoine; to Limoges, Bishop Martial. Among them, the blessed Dionysius, Bishop of the Parisians, having suffered from multiple torments for the name of Christ, finished his earthly life by being struck down by the sword . . . Saturninus, attached to a furious bull, was dropped high from a capitol. As for the others, after having lived in the greatest holiness, gained populations for the church, and everywhere spread the faith of Christ, they happily left this world confessing their faith.[32]

Other sources note the evangelists Martialis and Orientius at Bordeaux. Paris, as noted above, was evangelized by Dionysius (in about the year 270). With two of his companions, Eleuthèrius and Rusticus, Dionysius was martyred on a hill, ever afterwards called the Mount of the Martyrs (Montmartre). Quentinus, the converted son of a Roman senator, evangelized Picardie and was decapitated in 287. Bourges, Rouen,

---

31  Irenaeus, *Adversus haereses*, 1:9–10.
32  Grégoire de Tours, *Histoire des Francs*, 1:30–31.

and Rheims were also reached in the third century; and there were four martyrs at Rheims, also in 287.

In about the year 250, ten dioceses could be counted in Gaul. The persecution of Diocletien, so terrible in other regions, was relatively limited in Gaul. This was due, perhaps, to the tetrarch Constantius Chlorus, the father of Constantine whose spouse, Helene, was a Christian. At the Synod of Arles in 314, one year after the imperial edict granting toleration, sixteen bishops represented Gaul.

The regions of present-day Belgium were reached at a later period. The bishoprics of Tournai and Tongres were established in the fourth century. As for Flanders and Germany, with the exception of the Rhine valley, several more centuries would pass before their evangelization. Scandinavia and several of the Slavic countries would wait even longer, the gospel not being carried there until the end of the first millennium.

## Switzerland

We have noted that the gospel seems to have penetrated Helvetia (present-day Switzerland) at first from the north, coming from the valley of the Rhine. Close to Basel, the Roman city of Augustus was probably reached a little after the year 200, though conclusive archaeological remains attesting to a Christian presence have not been discovered there prior to the fourth century. The first known bishop to reside at Augustus was Justinian, who participated in the Council of Cologne in 346.

The oldest and most compelling archaeological witness to Christianity in Helvetia comes from the tomb of a young girl at Avenches in the canton of Vaud. Interred in the fourth century during the reign of the emperor Constantine, her tomb contained two glass goblets bearing Christian inscriptions.

At this time there were already some Christians in other regions of the country. In the fifth century, Bishop Eucherius of Lyons recorded the story of the martyrdoms of the Roman officer Mauricius and his legion at Agaune (present-day Saint-Maurice, in Valais) during the persecution of Diocletien between 303 and 305. The legion probably came from Egypt or, at the least, from an eastern province of the empire, for it was called Thebae (Thebes). Though the story was enlarged and embellished afterward, it is clear that Mauricius and his soldiers fell at the sword's edge for having refused to comply to the order of their general to search for and execute Christians living in the region. These elements of the story seem authentic and show that there were at least some Christians among the inhabitants of this country in the year 300. The gospel had no doubt been brought to them by travelers coming from Italy through the Alpine pass. At the end of the century, Theodorus, bishop of Octodurus (Martigny) from 381, was the founder of the cult of martyrs of Agaune.

The Rhone being difficult to navigate north of Lyons, a city like Geneva could scarcely have been reached before the year 350. The list of the bishops of Geneva begins about the year 400, and from this time the city became an important diocesan center, with extensive ecclesiastical buildings and two cathedrals separated by a baptistery.

## Great Britain

In the year 208, Tertullian affirms: "There are some regions in England where the Roman legions have not penetrated, but which have submitted to the law of Christ."[33] From the time of the persecution of the emperor Diocletien, there were some martyrs near London (at Saint Albans, previously Verulam) in 287 or 303. Three English bishops participated in the Synod of Arles in 314.

## Spain

Might Paul have traveled to Spain as he intended (Rom 15:28)? No evidence remains to confirm it. If he had not been able to do so, others soon realized his goal, for the gospel was undoubtedly proclaimed there from the first century and achieved rapid success. At the regional Council of Elvira in the year 300, there were nineteen Spanish bishops as well as twenty-four priests, representing altogether about thirty-five dioceses distributed throughout the country. Bishop Hosius, the first great name of the Spanish church, was subjected to torture at the time of Diocletien, but he survived it. He had some contacts with Constantius Chlorus, tetrarch of the Gauls, with whom his son, Constantine, had some influence. When Constantine became emperor, it appears that he had recourse to the old bishop on several occasions as a counselor. Hosius died in 357 at one hundred years of age.

# THE METHODS OF EVANGELIZATION
# IN THE SECOND AND THIRD CENTURIES

The methods of evangelization remained at this time the same as those of the first century, with the difference being that the synagogues were no longer accessible to Christian preachers. Some light is shed on this by the *Didache* (*The Teachings of the Twelve Apostles*), one of the most ancient noncanonical Christian documents, written about the beginning of the second century.

## Itinerant Preachers

The *Didache* mentions the ministry of the *apostoloi*, itinerant missionaries traveling from city to city to preach the gospel; and it gives some very practical counsel to the churches to aid them to discern, amidst the profusion of these itinerant preachers, which were authentic messengers of the gospel and which were heretics or parasites. Other texts from the second and third centuries also attest to the existence of these itinerant preachers, whom the monks would later succeed. The philosopher Celsus, according to a citation from Origen, turns these preachers to derision: "Here are those who, in public places, divulge their secrets . . . They would never have the audacity to approach an assembly of educated people to reveal their fine mysteries. Seeing some adolescents, a gathering of slaves or an assembly of imbeciles, they fall upon them and strut about."[34] "The Christians," Origen responded, "are not careless with regard to the mission of the sowers of the Word in the whole world. Some of them have even

---

33   Tertullian, *Adversus Judaeos*, 7. The authority for this citation is, however, in doubt.
34   Origen, *Contra Celsum*, 3:9.

chosen as their career to visit not only cities but also villages and cottages, in order to see the people and to turn them towards God. Let it not be said that they do this to enrich themselves since sometimes they do not even receive their subsistence."[35]

Eusebius did not disguise his admiration for these itinerant preachers:

> For most of the disciples at this time, animated with a more ar-
> dent love of the divine word, had first fulfilled the Savior's precept
> by distributing their substance to the needy. Afterwards leaving
> their country, they performed the office of evangelists to those
> who had not yet heard the faith, whilst with a noble ambition to
> proclaim Christ, they also delivered to them the books of the holy
> gospels. After laying the foundation of the faith in foreign parts as
> the particular object of their mission, and after appointing others
> as shepherds of the flocks, and committing to these the care of
> those that had been recently introduced, they went again to other
> regions and nations, with the grace and cooperation of God. The
> Holy Spirit also wrought many wonders as yet through them, so
> that as soon as the gospel was heard, crowds of eager men came
> voluntarily to embrace the true faith with their whole minds.[36]

## The Engagement of the Believers

The principal and most effective efforts were those made by spontaneous witnesses, the word spoken by Christians to their neighbors. Historians as divergent as Adolf von Harnack and Kenneth Scott Latourette are agreed on this point: "We cannot hesitate to believe," writes Harnack, "that the great mission of Christianity was in reality accomplished by means of informal missionaries." Latourette concurs: "The chief agents in the expansion of Christianity appear not to have been those who made it a profession or made it a major part of their occupation, but men and women who carried on their livelihood in some purely secular manner and spoke of their faith to those they met in this natural fashion."[37] Those who had professions that allowed them numerous contacts with their fellow citizens, in particular merchants and artisans, were the principal propagators of Christianity.

Celsus, the great enemy of the church, denounced a religion "that is preached by the workers and the ignorant." He pointed to the irony of "those sots who peddle the gospel in the wash-house." Far from contradicting this fact, a Christian author of the second century found it a source of pride: "Among us you can find the ignorant, manual workers, old women; if they are incapable of expressing the usefulness of their doctrine in words, they demonstrate the usefulness of their principles by their actions. They do not know the words by heart, but they exhibit them by good works."[38] The wise among the Christians shared the same zeal. In his *Panegyric* to

---

35 Ibid.

36 Eusebius, *Ecclesiastical History*, Book 3, 37:123.

37 The two citations of these renowned historians are found in Michael Green, *Evangelism in the Early Church* (Sury, France: Eagle, 1995), 208, 244–45.

38 Athénagore, *Suppliques*, 11.

Origen, Gregory Thaumaturgus gives this testimonial to the great theologian who was his spiritual father: "He was not trying simply to persuade by any intellectual argument; animated in his gentle spirit, affectionate and extremely generous, he had a single desire: to save us."

Conversions were most often of individuals or families. Sometimes, however, the conversion of the leader won over that of a group, even that of a people.

## Signs and Miracles

The signs, miracles, and exorcisms that were practiced in the first century continued into the second, as writers testified from diverse regions. Justin Martyr wrote:

> Jesus was made man for the salvation of believers and the ruin of demons. You can convince yourself of this by what happened under your own eyes. There are throughout the world and in your city [Rome] a number of demon-possessed that neither pleas, nor enchantments, nor filters have been able to heal. Our Christians,abjuring them in the name of Jesus crucified under Pontius Pilate, have healed them of it and continue to heal many today.[39]

Irenaeus wrote from Lyons: "The true disciples of Christ have received a grace, they perform miracles in his name . . . Some really expel demons and, frequently, those they have freed of these evil spirits believe in Christ and join the church."[40] Tertullian of North Africa also claimed to have witnessed numerous exorcisms and healings. And, as previously noted, there was the impressive ministry of Gregory Thaumaturgus in the province of Pont in Asia Minor.

Nonetheless, these miracles, exorcisms, and healings were becoming increasingly rare in the second century, except in certain marginal places. Moreover, as David Bosch remarks, "In the final analysis it was not the miracles of itinerant evangelists and wandering monks that impressed the populace—miracle workers were a familiar phenomenon in the ancient world—but the exemplary lives of ordinary Christians."[41]

## Living Testimonies

Christianity, in effect, presented through the behavior of its adherents an undeniable contrast to the ancient religions. The pagan divinities were often described as immoral, and religious practice had no effect on morality.[42] In contrast, conversion to the gospel brought about a transformation in lifestyle. Many Christian authors of antiquity insisted on this point, including among others Justin Martyr:

> Formerly, we took pleasure in debauchery; today chastity is our delight. We were given over to magic; today we are consecrated to the good and unbegotten God. We were searching only for money and domains; today we put in common what we have, we divide

---

39  Justin Martyr, *II Apology*, 6.
40  Irenaeus, *Adversus haereses*, 2:32.
41  Bosch, *Transforming Mission*, 191.
42  Cf. Green, *Evangelism*, 158.

it. Hatreds and murders divided us, different morals and institutions did not permit us to receive strangers into our homes; today, after the coming of Christ, we live together, we pray for our enemies, we seek to win over unjust persecutors.[43]

Already at the beginning of the second century Ignatius of Antioch was reminding the Christians of Ephesus of the importance of this living witness in the image of Jesus Christ.

> Give to your enemies at very least the lesson of your example: to their fits of anger, show forth sweetness; to their boastfulness, humility; to their blasphemies, prayer; to their errors, firmness in the faith; to their violent characters, humanity, without ever seeking to render to them the evil that they do to you. Let us show ourselves to be truly their brothers by our goodness. Let us strive to imitate the Lord.[44]

In his book *Contra Celsum*, Origen wrote: "Christianity detaches man from sin. It everywhere spreads new life and vigor . . . For the Word to come to and penetrate the heart, it must have a power only God can communicate."

### The Life of the Christian Community

The intensity of a communal life that was abolishing all social barriers, notably between freemen and slaves, was a characteristic of Christian communities that attracted numerous sympathizers—as did their solidarity with the more destitute. Women found in the church, at least in its beginning, a status that society refused to them. Justin Martyr, in describing the transformation affected by conversion to the gospel, underscored that the rivalries and hatreds inspired by the barriers of race and culture were replaced by a mutual acceptance and an authentic communion. Justin wrote elsewhere:

> Those who have plenty aid those who are in need, and we all lend mutual assistance. Those who are in abundance and who want to give, give liberally, each what he wants. What is collected is put into the hands of the president; he assists orphans, widows, the sick, the indigent, prisoners, and foreign guests; in a word, they help all who are impoverished.[45]

The church of Rome especially developed this dimension of the social gospel as is seen already in the spiritual gifts listed in Romans 12, which differ significantly from those given in 1 Corinthians 12. At the beginning of the second century, Dionysius of Corinth wrote to Rome to rejoice in the charitableness that from its origin characterized this community. He repeated with insistence:

---

43   Justin Martyr, *I Apology*, 14.
44   Ignatius of Antioch, *Epistle to the Ephesians*, 10.
45   Martyr, *I Apology*, 68.

> From the beginning, you have in various ways done well to all the brothers and have sent aid to the numerous churches in each city; hence, you relieve the destitution of the indigent, you support the brothers who are in the mines by the resources that you have sent from the beginning.[46]

This solidarity continued, if one believes the letter of Bishop Cornelius written in 251 and cited by Eusebius, as mentioned above (see p. 43, Italy). But Rome did not enjoy the privilege of the communal sharing modeled by the church of Jerusalem after the day of Pentecost (Acts 2:44–45; 4:32–27). At the beginning of the third century in the church of Carthage, according to Tertullian, Christians gave regular offerings, an expression of a communion encompassing all the aspects of daily existence.

> Everyone gives a modest contribution on a fixed day every month or when he wants to do so and it is possible. For no one is forced, one gives his offering freely . . . One can do it to feed and to bury the poor, to aid boys and girls without resources or relatives, and the servants who have become old, as also the shipwrecked; and the Christians who suffer in the mines, in the islands, in the prisons solely for the cause of our God . . . In the eyes of many this practice of charity imprints an infamous mark on us, "You see," they say, "how they love one another," but actually they detest one another; "You see," they say, "how they are ready to die for one another," but rather they are ready to kill one another . . . Hence therefore, closely united by spirit and soul, we do not hesitate to share our goods with others. All is employed for the common use among us, except our spouses . . . Our meals reveal the reason for their name: they are called by the word in Greek that signifies "love" [agape]. Whatever the expense may be, it is profitable to pay the cost for reasons of piety: in effect, it is a means by which we aid the poor . . . because, before God, the humble enjoy a greater consideration. One begins at the table only after having offered a prayer to God. One eats as long as hunger requires it; one drinks as long as sobriety permits it. One satisfies one's hunger as men who remember that, even in the night, they must adore God.[47]

At the end of the second century an epistle to Diognetus also evoked this quality of the communal life of the believers. The author Tertullian observed that the intensity of mutual relations aroused as much hostility in some people as it attracted others:

> They did not live in cities of their own . . . their type of life had nothing special about it . . . They dispersed themselves in both Greek and barbarian cities, they conformed to local customs, all the while manifesting the extraordinary laws and true paradoxes of the life in common . . . They obey all the established laws and their perfect manner of living shows them to be superior to the

---

46  Eusebius, *Ecclesiastical History*, 3:160.
47  Tertullian, *Apologetic*, 39.

laws . . . They are poor and enrich a great number. They lack all and have superabundance in all things. The Jews make war against them as if they were foreigners, they are persecuted by the Greeks, and those who detest them would not be able to explain the cause of their hate.[48]

The emperor Julian the Apostate, who tried to reintroduce the former religions in the Roman Empire that had been Christianized by Constantine a half-century before, was forced to encourage the pagan priests to rise to the challenge presented by the Christians' commitment to the needy. In the year 360 he wrote in a letter to Arsacio, a priest in Galatia:

> We have forgotten that the religion of the Christians has assumed principal responsibility for, namely, the philanthropy towards the foreigners, the tireless solicitude for a sepulture for the dead, and the seriousness of the moral life . . . [He announces that he will send important subsidies that Arsacio will have the responsibility to distribute:] The fifth must be remitted to the poor who serve the priests; you will divide the rest between the foreigners and the beggars. In effect, it is a shame that there are no beggars among the Jews, and that the impious Galileans [the Christians] feed not only their poor, but also ours.[49]

## The Witness of the Martyrs

Though martyrdom may not be considered a method of evangelization, it is undeniable that the confession and firmness of Christ before his judges and executioners made a strong impression. It is not by chance that the Greek word *martus*, which signifies *"witness,"* very early took on the sense of *"martyr."* Following the example of Paul before Festus and Agrippa (Acts 26:27–29), Christians at the bar of justice managed to entreat and warn their judges. Polycarp, the bishop of Smyrna, declared to the proconsul who sentenced him to the pyre: "You threaten me with a fire that burns an hour and is extinguished. For you know not the fire of the future judgment and the eternal chastisement that awaits the impious."[50] The quotation from Tertullian, given above, was confirmed many times over: "The blood of the martyrs is the seed of the Church."

## Literary Evangelism

This period is characterized by an abundant production of written works that convey the Christian faith and refute the caricatures of which it was the victim. Their authors are called the Apologists. Some of them were very combative against paganism, Judaism, and heretics. Others sought, rather, to demonstrate the points of convergence between philosophy and Christian faith and to present an interpretation of

---

48  Tertullian, *Epitre à Diognète*, 5:2–17.

49  Cited by Gottfried Hammann, *L'amour retrouvé: Le ministére de diacre, du christianisme primitif aux Réformateurs protestants du XVIe siècle* (Paris: Cerf, 1994), 77.

50  *Martyrdom of Polycarp*, 10:11.

Christian doctrine in the categories of thought accessible to their readers, a strategy not without the occasional risk of syncretism. The epistle *To Diognetus*, which was probably written by Pantaenus of Alexandria in about the year 180, is a treatise on evangelization particularly remarkable for its profoundly evangelistic tenor, devoid of both aggressiveness and doubtful compromises.[51]

But it is without doubt the Scriptures themselves that were the means *par excellence* of evangelization in the area of writing. Michael Green enumerates several Christian authors from the second and third centuries who profess to have been brought to the faith by the reading of the biblical text: Justin, Tatian, Athenagoras, Theophilus, and others still. He also reports the remarks of Jerome concerning Phamphilus of Caesarea in the third century, who "readily provided Bibles not only to read but to keep, not only for men but for any women whom he saw addicted to reading. He would prepare a large number of volumes, so that, when any demand was made upon him, he might be in a position to gratify those who applied to him."[52]

## STATISTICS OF CHURCH GROWTH

Unsupported by armed force, as with Islam, or by political power, as with Zoroastrianism and Buddhism, the growth of the Christian churches during these first three centuries is an extraordinary and unique phenomenon in the history of religions. In fact, not only did it lack military or political might, it was the victim of repeated persecutions throughout the Roman Empire.

Two authors of antiquity expressed an assessment of this period that needs no modern elaboration. Though he sometimes allowed himself to be carried away by enthusiasm, Eusebius' fourth-century evaluation merits attention:

> Thus, then, under a celestial influence and cooperation, the doctrine of the Savior, like the rays of the sun, quickly irradiated the whole world. Presently, in accordance with divine prophecy, the sound of his inspired evangelists and apostles had gone throughout all the earth, and their words to the ends of the world. Throughout every city and village, like a replenished barn floor, churches were rapidly found abounding, and filled with members from every people.[53]

Origen, writing in Egypt in about 220, was closer to these events than Eusebius and a direct actor in the expansion. He provides a moving witness to the glory of God:

> If we consider the immense progress of the gospel in several years despite persecution and torture, death and confiscation, despite the small number of preachers, the Word of Jesus Christ has been preached in all the creation under the heavens, to the Greeks and to the Barbarians, to the wise and to the ignorant . . .

---

51  Henri Irénée Marrou, trans., "Les ecrits des Pères apostoliques," in *Foi vivante*, no. 191 (Paris: Cerf, 1979), 3:57–74.

52  Jerome, *Adversus Rufin*, 1:9, cited in Green, *Early Church*, 283.

53  Eusebius, *Ecclesiastical History*, Book 2, 3:52.

> It is impossible to cite a single race that has refused to receive the teachings of Jesus . . . The goodness of our Lord and Savior is equally spread among the Bretons [in England], the Africans and the other nations . . . The preaching of the gospel throughout the entire inhabited earth shows that the church is powerfully aided by God. We cannot doubt that this surpasses the power of man, for Jesus taught with all the authority and the persuasion necessary for the Word to gain attention.[54]

Can the number of Christians be estimated for the beginning of the fourth century? Some venture the number 18 million, close to a tenth of the population of the world. By this time, too, the Scriptures had been translated into a dozen languages.

Concerning church growth in the first centuries, Henri Marrou offered a conclusion in the 1950s that is still valuable today:

> In the origin of the church, the missionary movement appears to have been, let us not say the most anarchic [in relation to later periods] but the most spontaneous, the most free and especially the most open—one should allow, especially in the first generation, a large place for spiritual gifts, for suggestions of the Spirit. The whole church considered itself to be involved in mission and to have a missionary duty, and every believer was a witness, felt called to the work of evangelization, even so far as the supreme witness of bloody martyrdom that was always on the horizon. This is perhaps the greatest lesson that Christians today can receive from their oldest brothers in the faith . . . The church of the first centuries was, thought of itself as, and wanted to be—as the conscience of each of the faithful held—an essentially missionary church.[55]

It is not necessary to search elsewhere for the secret of the extraordinary growth of the church during this period.

---

54  Origen, *De principiis*, 4:1.2.

55  Henri Irénée Marrou, "L'expansion missionnaire dans l'empire romain et hors de l'empire au cours des cinq premiers siècles," in *Histoire universelle des missions catholiques*, vol. 1 (Paris: Librairie Grund, 1956), 50, 62.

# Evangelization in the Fourth Century: The Imperial Church and Expansion Beyond the Roman Empire

## FROM PERSECUTION TO STATE RELIGION

In 313 a considerable event shook Rome and radically altered its history. After having attempted in vain to annihilate the church, the Roman Empire admitted its failure. The persecution of Diocletian began in the early fourth century and was the longest and most widespread, but it did not achieve its goal. It was then that political authorities rethought the situation and made their enemy an ally.

While the future emperor Constantine was devoted to the cult of the sun, his mother, Helene, was a fervent Christian. In the year 312, before the Battle of the Milvian Bridge against his rival for the imperial throne, Maxentius, he had a vision of the cross and had the Christian monogram inscribed on the shields of his soldiers. Maxentius was defeated, and, in the course of his flight, drowned in the Tiber. The sincerity of Constantine's conversion is not without question. Certainly his behavior following conversion was not that of a Christian. He was not baptized until 337 when he lay on his deathbed, and then the rite was performed by a bishop tending toward Arianism.[56] Whatever his true convictions, Constantine's conversion was an unexpected triumph for Christians who, until then, were despised and persecuted. In many respects, however, the prosperity brought about by Constantine for the church was a more redoubtable peril than the fire and sword of the persecutors. Pagan temples were hastily transformed into churches, and crowds rushed to the new sanctuaries. Church ministers were no longer destined for the pyre or torture, but for power and the favor of authorities. All was changed in the space of a generation. In 330 Constantine wrote of Constantinople: "So many people embrace Christianity in the city bearing my name that it is necessary to augment the number of the churches. Procure fifty copies of the Scriptures etched on parchment as fast as possible."

---

56   The doctrine taught by Arius, priest of Alexandria (ca. 280–336). In the name of a strict monotheism, Arius turned from the doctrine of the Trinity and affirmed that the Son has been created by the Father and that he is by nature divine but inferior in rank and glory. This heresy, which greatly reverberated in the ancient church and became a real threat to orthodox theology, gave impetus for the convocation of the Council of Nicaea in 325 where it was condemned. But the emperor Constance later took up the cause in support of Arianism.

Here are some extracts from the edict of Milan, issued in the year 313 by Constantine and Licinius—the latter was the emperor of the East, a pagan who had persecuted Christians and who would later be defeated by Constantine. The edict was addressed to the prefects of the provinces on the subject of the practice of religion. As such, this edict receives our approbation. Though it did not establish Christianity as the official religion of the empire, it offered liberty to all religions and constituted the first step, to be followed by many others taken by Constantine and his successors, that would lead to the mingling of the church and civil society.

> We, the Augusts Constantine and Licinius . . . have resolved to accord to Christians and to all others liberty to practice the religion that they prefer, so that the divinity that resides in heaven will be propitious and favorable to us as well as to all those who live under our domination. It appears to us that it is a very good and reasonable policy to refuse to none of our subjects, whether they be Christian or belong to another cult, [the right] to follow the religion that suits them best. In this manner the supreme divinity, whom each of us will honor henceforth freely, may accord to us his accustomed favor and bounty.

In the same year, the edict of Nicodemia declared that Christian places of worship that had been previously confiscated must be returned. Here is an extract:

> Here is what we have decided respecting the Christians: their local [places of worship], where they had the custom to assemble before, if the people appear to have bought them, either from our treasury or someone else's, they [the people] must restore them to the said Christians without payment and with no claim for compensation . . . and they [the Christians] must present themselves before the tribunal of the local magistrate, so that by our generosity a compensation can be accorded to them. All these goods must be rendered to the Christian people, without any delay and in full.

From the point of view of mission, the result of this new orientation was disastrous: the pagans to evangelize were no longer on the exterior but in the interior of the churches. In fact, it was not easy to distinguish between Christian and non-Christian. The church very rapidly blended with the surrounding world. Following the death of Constantine, his son Constance relied on a law of his father to prohibit pagan sacrifices. Moreover, he constantly meddled in theological controversies and exerted pressure on church councils to obtain the triumph of the Arian party. With his numerous banishments, Athanaeus personified the resistance of orthodoxy. After the brief reign of the pagan philosopher Julian the Apostate (361–363), who tried to return the empire to the worship of the traditional gods, the emperor Theodosius (379–395) brought to completion the movement begun by Constantine by prohibiting pagan cults. The state became officially Christian in 381. Rome imposed by diplomacy and force the new religion on the peoples who wanted to ally with it or who had been conquered by arms.

Now with official recognition, the church became an increasingly structured organization. Supported by the imperial power, the authority of the clergy grew considerably while the laity was increasingly turned away from posts of responsibility in the community. The spontaneous evangelistic activity of all the members of the church no longer made sense when all the inhabitants of the empire were supposed to be Christians. Christians were no longer a distinct group. Historian Henri Marrou writes: "Henceforth the notion of mission changed its sense: the problem that posed itself in the interior of the empire was no longer how to implant the church, but how to enlarge recruitment, how to convert the masses, the whole of the society, all the classes; the mission became a mission to the interior."[57]

Indeed, there remained a large number of true Christians, but they were hard put to make the fight against the corruption that was rapidly gaining in the church. Some among them preferred to quit the church community and live separately, either alone as hermits or in groups in monasteries.

Christianity, however, made great progress in the course of the fourth century. Several significant examples follow. With the exception of the first, they are located beyond the frontiers of the Roman Empire and, therefore, the Constantinian context.

## MARTIN OF TOURS, "THE APOSTLE OF GAUL"

Martin of Tours (316–397) was rightly called "the apostle of Gaul." Indeed, in the fourth century there were churches in all of the Gaullist cities, but the countryside was still pagan. Martin was born in 316 in Sabaria, in Pannonia (present-day Hungary), where his father, a pagan Roman officer, was garrisoned. While still a child, Martin, according to his own sayings, was attracted to monastic life. But, following his father's path, at the age of fifteen he became a soldier in the Roman army. At eighteen years, he was baptized in Amiens in the north of Gaul.

He was very early known for his charity. His biographer, Sulpicius Severus, recounts a well-known anecdote, one often dismissed as a legend. If true, the story occurred before Martin's baptism:

> One day Martin had with him only his arms and military cloak, made of a single piece of cloth. It was in the middle of a winter more rigorous than ordinary and so harsh that many people were dying of cold. At the city gate of Ambiens [Amiens], he encountered a poor, naked man. The unhappy man had prayed in vain that a passerby might take pity on him, but all walked past him. The man of God [Martin was at this time still engaged in his military career], seeing that the others were not touched by compassion, understood that this one was reserved for him. But what to do? He had nothing but the chlamydia [piece of rectangular wool serving as a cloak] in which he was dressed; he had already sacrificed his other goods in similar good works. Then he seized his sword, cut the cloak in the middle, gave part of it to the poor man, and draped himself again with the remainder. Among those around

57  Marrou, *L'expansion missionnaire*, 48–49.

him, some began to laugh, finding him unsightly in his truncated dress. But many others, with more wisdom, profoundly lamented that they had done nothing similar, for they would have been able to clothe the poor man without going naked.[58]

Following his baptism, Martin wished to abandon his military career, but he was not allowed to leave until 356. When he was forty years of age, he lived at Poitiers in order to follow the teaching of the theologian Hilary (ca. 300–367), "who was then celebrated for this unshakable faith in the things of God," according to Severus. Then Martin retreated for a dozen years to the neighboring country of Lugugé, where he settled into a modest hermitage in the ruins of a former Gallo-Roman villa. Disciples were not slow to surround him as his reputation for holiness became firmly established. The miracles that he was accomplishing were spoken of far and wide, even the resurrection of two who had died. In 371 the people of Tours came to ask him to be their bishop. At this time, however, he had not yet even been ordained a priest, having for humility's stake refused to be consecrated a deacon by Hilary, accepting only the position of exorcist. After having hesitated a long time, Martin accepted. Among the bishops who came to preside over his consecration were some opponents who "declared unworthy of the episcopate a man of so piteous a mien, poorly dressed and disheveled."

At heart he was not only concerned with the Christians of Tours but also with the evangelization of the multitude of the pagans in the countryside. He founded numerous parishes in the regions neighboring Tours and destroyed pagan sanctuaries with zeal. He organized a remarkable missionary effort, sending out carefully trained itinerant teams and founding several monasteries that became influential centers of the gospel. The one where he sojourned the most often was that of Marmoutier, located to the north of Tours in grottos on the shore of the Loire. His tours of evangelization and the work of his teams carried the gospel throughout the center of Gaul and into the Parisian region. Severus writes, "Although a bishop, Martin remained as he had been before: humble in soul, poor in clothing, but also full of authority and of good grace. He had all the dignity of a bishop, without abandoning the lifestyle and habit of a monk."[59]

Martin engaged in the life of the church of the Gauls, participating actively in several councils. He also went to the imperial court of Treves where he was readily heard and much respected. He died November 8, 397, at the age of eighty-one, being found in a rural parish that he had established. He was buried several days later at Tours, Severus writes, "escorted by an incredible multitude of persons. All in step before the body, they entered the city. All the inhabitants of the countryside and the villages were there, and many even came from the neighboring cities."[60] His memory remained alive not only in all of Gaul but also in all of Western Europe where many

---

58  Sulpice Sévère, *Saint Martin: Récits de Sulpice Sévère*, trans. Paul Monceaux (Paris: Payot, 1927), 101–3. Cited in Hammann, *L'amour retrouvé*, 90.

59  Sulpice Sévère, "Vita Martini," in *Sources chrétiennes*, no. 133 (Paris: Cerf, 1967), 8. See also Sulpice Sévère, "Vie de Saint Martin," in *Foi vivante*, no. 376 (Paris: Cerf, 1996).

60  Sulpice Sévère, *Lettres*, vol. 3.

churches and villages still bear his name. In France, seven hundred villages are called Saint Martin as opposed to 460 named for Saint Peter!

Beginning to write his *Vita Martini* while his subject was still living, Severus accentuated the holiness of his hero with miraculous and edifying anecdotes in order to encourage his readers. Born in Bordeaux about 360, Severus became a lawyer and, following his baptism, a monk. Often accused of confusing legend for historical fact, what follows is his description of Martin's struggle to evangelize some hostile pagans:

> Here is what happened in the country of Eduens. While Martin was in the process of knocking down a temple, a crowd of pagan peasants rushed upon him. One of them, more audacious than the others, having unsheathed a sword was going to strike him. Throwing away his cloak, [Martin] presented his neck to the assailant. The pagan did not hesitate to strike a blow, but in lifting his right arm too high, he fell over backwards. Struck immediately by a holy terror, he implored his forgiveness . . . But most of the time, since the peasants were opposing the destruction of their temples, he appeased the spirit of these pagans by the holiness of his preaching, enlightening them with the light of truth so that it was by their own hands that they demolished their temples.[61]

Severus completed his story with the vibrant lines that follow. But where enthusiasm replaces objectivity and admiration is without bounds, it is necessary to be reserved about this portrait of Martin as the image of an ideal Christian, as that was conceived by a theologian at the end of the fourth century:

> And then in his words, in his conversation, there is that of gravity, that of nobility! What ardor, what power! What promptitude, what facility to resolve the difficulties of the Scriptures! . . . I attest that never have I heard in the books of a person so knowledgeable, so talented, one so excellent and so pure of tongue . . . Never did anyone see him in anger, nor moved, nor afflicted, nor in the process of laughing. Always just the same, the appearance radiant of a heavenly joy as it were; he had an air foreign to human nature. Never was there anything but Christ on his lips, and goodness, peace, and mercy in his heart . . . As for me, I have a good conscience, having been spurred to write by the authenticity of the facts and by the love of Christ, to lay bare the evidence and say the truth.[62]

---

61   Sévère, "Vita Martini," 15.
62   Sévère, "Vie de Saint Martin," 36–38.

# THE CHRISTIAN PRESENCE BEYOND
# THE FRONTIERS OF THE ROMAN EMPIRE

In the second chapter the geographical overview showed that from the time of the first generations of Christians the gospel had been preached in regions outside of the limits of the Roman Empire—Armenia, Persia, and perhaps the Indies. This expansion is confirmed in the course of the fourth century, in a context obviously different from that of Constantinianism. Several examples follow.

## Ulfilas, the Evangelist of the Goths

The great Gothic people were evangelized in the course of the fourth century. Having come from Scandinavia, this bellicose nation was at first established in the basin of the Vistula. Later it infiltrated regions farther south, frequently attacking territories belonging to the empire, particularly in Asia Minor. With the approval of the Romans, the Goths came to settle on the lower Danube, where they at once protected and threatened the city of Constantinople. The gospel was transmitted to them by Ulfilas (ca. 311–383), a name in Gothic signifying "small wolf." Born among the Goths, he belonged to a Christian family of Cappadocia that was taken in slavery in 257. Consequently, he spoke the Greek and Gothic languages with equal felicity. Between 332 and 337, while he was still very young, his masters used him as an interpreter at their embassy in Constantinople.

*The "Codex Argenteus" is a translation of the Bible in the Gothic language carried out by Ulfilas in the sixth century. It is the oldest known document written in a Germanic language. Preserved at Uppsala, Sweden, the text reproduced here is Matthew 6:17–23. (© Uppsala University Library)*

Some years later, Ulfilas participated in the Council of Antioch and was conse-crated a bishop of the Goths in 341 by the patriarch Eusebius of Nicomedia, who had been consecrated a little before as bishop of Constantinople. As Eusebius was one of the leaders of Arianism, his disciple Ulfilas adopted this doctrine. When he returned to the land of the Goths, he evangelized them for forty years with an indefatigable zeal. One of his first undertakings was the translation of the Bible in the Gothic lan-guage. It is a masterpiece of linguistics and precious today for the light it sheds on the origin of the Germanic languages. Several important fragments of it have sur-vived and are now housed in the Museum of Uppsala, Sweden.

Ulfilas carried the gospel to different branches of the Gothic people from one part to another of the Danube and the mountains of the Balkans. It was in this way that some of the barbarian peoples who invaded the Roman Empire in the following century—Visigoths, Ostrogoths, Gepides, Vandals, and others less known—became Arian Christians. In 360 Ulfilas took part in the Council of Constantinople where he defended a moderate Arian position.

Because the Roman Empire was then Christian, some of the tribal chiefs suspect-ed the missionaries of being a fifth column. They severely persecuted the Christians, which forced Ulfilas to retire to the south of the Danube. Despite this, he reaped a remarkable harvest and is remembered as an intrepid missionary. According to his disciple and biographer Bishop Auxentius, "He blossomed gloriously and with a grace entirely apostolic, preaching without a break in Latin, Greek, and Gothic." In the Gothic community of Mesie, he became the uncontested chief, as much in the tem-poral as in the spiritual sense. According to Socrates of Constantinople, "his words had the force of law." He died and was buried in great pomp at Constantinople in 383, probably in the course of a synod dedicated to theological controversies.

We do not have many authentic details of his life. The church founded by Ulfilas, detached from orthodox doctrine and the contribution of the theological councils, was dogmatically poor. Moreover, the nomadic and rather rustic nature of the Gothic tribes in general hardly predisposed them to grasp theological subtleties. The Goths celebrated nocturnal cults in the forest that were accompanied by songs in a martial style that were very impressive. Their sermons exalted the moral principles of energy and courage, with a certain mystical dimension. Ulfilas declined to translate the bib-lical books of Kings and Chronicles, fearing that as people of so warrior-like a spirit they would be too inspired by the stories of bloody battles! On his deathbed, Ulfilas confessed his Arian faith in the following terms, which Eastern Orthodoxy would judge heretical:

> He is a unique God, eternal, not engendered, and invisible, who was alone before time existed. In time, he created his Son, the uniquely engendered God. He is the creator of all things, the Lord of the Holy Spirit that the Father created through the Son, having all things. The Spirit is subject to the Son in the same way that the Son is to the Father.[63]

---

63  Jacques Brosse, *Histoire de la chrétienté et d'Occident* (Paris: Albin Michel, 1995), 27.

## Nina and the Conversion of the Georgians of the Caucas
## (Beginning of the Fourth Century)

The historian Rufinus of Aquileia (340–410), translator of Eusebius' *Ecclesiastical History* that continued to the time of Thaddaeus, tells the story of Nina, who was also known by the name of Nino. Originating from Asia Minor, she became a prisoner of war and served as a slave in the court of the king of Georgia. Nevertheless, in about the year 330, she brought the Georgians of the Caucasus to conversion. Here is Rufinus' story:

> In this period, the nation that inhabits the region of the Caucasus committed itself to the Word of God and accepted a belief in the future life. There was a captive who was the origin of this great happiness. The people discovered that she was leading a life sober, pious, and full of self-control, that she was spending the days entirely in prayer, and that she was staying awake at night in order to pray to God. The novelty of these practices inspired the admiration of the barbarians, who asked her with much curiosity what they signified. Then this woman admitted simply what she was about: by these practices, she was adoring the Christ of God. Nothing was more astonishing to the barbarians than this new name. It was especially among the young that her perseverance provoked the greatest curiosity . . . One day a woman was carrying her sick infant from door to door, as was her custom. She could not find any medical treatment. After having visited all the houses, she came to show the infant to the captive and asked her if she knew how to heal him. She admitted that she knew of no human remedy but affirmed, instead, that the Christ, the God whom she adored, could accord to her the salvation of which men were despairing . . . Having put the infant down on its swaddling cloth, she addressed a long prayer to the Lord about this, and then returned a healthy infant to its mother.[64]

According to this account, in which history and legend are admittedly intermixed, Nina produced several miracles following the healing of the infant. Rufinus also reports the circumstances of the conversion of King Mirian of eastern Georgia, who was miraculously healed by the ministry of Nina. While hunting, he was very frightened by an eclipse of the sun. When the sun reappeared, he associated it with the figure of Christ, which delivers from darkness, saying: "At midnight, I saw a shining sun appear, our Lord Christ." At this moment, there were many Christians among his subjects, of which a good number had sprung from Judaism.[65] He caused a church to be built, the celebrated temple of Swtizchoweli. Rufinus continued: "After the church was completed, the people ardently desired to know the faith in God. Following Nina's counsel, they sent national ambassadors to the emperor Constantine,

---

64 Rufinas of Aquileia, *Historia Ecclesiastica*, 1:10.

65 According to an old legend, these Jewish converts offered King Mirian an extraordinary relic: the tunic of Christ, remitted to their keeping after the crucifixion. This relic was venerated throughout the Middle Ages in the great cathedral of Mtskheta.

who recounted to him their entire history and asked him to send priests who would distribute the gifts of God among them." Eprem Mzire, an evangelist who had come from Georgia at the call of Nina, compared the illumination of the king to that of the Apostle Paul on the road to Damascus. Since then, Mirian sensed a call to be the spiritual father of the country and ordered the construction of a number worship places.

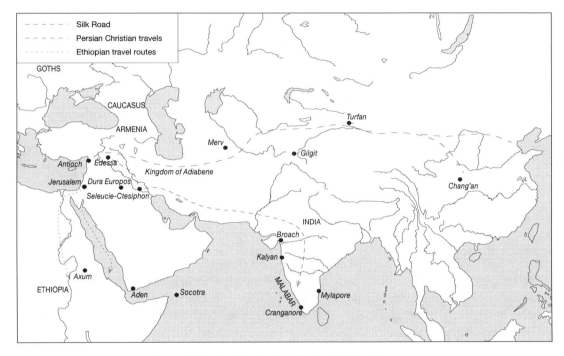

*Map 3: Christians in the East during the fourth century*

Since the fourth century, Mirian has been considered one of the most notable political figures in the history of the great realm that was Georgia. His role in the spiritual and cultural life of the nation permitted Christianity to supplant the Persian religion, which until then had been practiced by the Georgians.

## Aedesius and Frumentius in Ethiopia (Fourth Century)

The Ethiopian tradition attests the fact of a Jewish immigration having reached Ethiopia well before the Christian era. These Jews propagated the monotheistic faith among the people. The local religion was influenced by certain Jewish practices, and the Christian religion there would later, in its turn, be influenced by Judaism. The early existence of synagogues and proselytes in Ethiopia is suggested in the book of Acts, which speaks of an Ethiopian (or black) minister who had come to Jerusalem to worship and who on his return was reading a scroll of the book of Isaiah (Acts 8:26–40). Luke relates that the evangelist Philip was responsible for the conversion and baptism of this man, who may in fact have been from Cush (present-day North Sudan). Legend attributes to Matthew the evangelization of Ethiopia, but in fact, there is no historic evidence for an Ethiopian church before the fourth century.

The story is told that in this period two young brothers, Aedesius and Frumentius, from the Christian community of Tyre were sailing on the Red Sea when they were captured by pirates and sold as slaves to Axum. The king, impressed by their Savior and their conduct, freed them and charged them with the responsibility of educating his son Ezena. At the death of the king, they became the regents of the realm and used the opportunity to open the way to the Christian faith. Rufinus recounts:

> While Frumentius was holding the reins of power in his hands, God worked in his soul. When he was informed that among the merchants were some Christians, he counseled them and gave them the means to establish in their trading areas small chapels where they were able to assemble to pray. He did even more still, inviting them all to establish churches everywhere that there appeared to be an opportunity. He furnished all the things necessary so that Christianity could germinate in this land.[66]

Later, Aedesius returned to his own country and became a presbyter at Tyre, while Frumentius thoroughly dedicated himself to the evangelization of the Ethiopian population. He went to Egypt in 327 where he stayed for several years of training under Athanasius and to seek for missionary reinforcements. He was consecrated bishop and returned to Ethiopia. The date of the foundation of the Ethiopian church is fixed in the year 332. Upon becoming king, Ezena converted and in 341 made Christianity the official religion of his realm. Later, like the Egyptian church, the Ethiopian church adopted a Monophysite Christology under the influence of Jacobite preachers who had come from Syria. Remaining independent of the Roman Catholic Church, the Abouna (head of the Ethiopian Church) recognized the authority of the patriarch of Alexandria.[67]

Those who consider the story of Aedesius and Frumentius to be legendary attribute the initial evangelization of Ethiopia to the commercial relations of Mediterranean merchants with those of Aden, undertaken via the Red Sea. In fact a church could have been found in Aden at a very early date. The two traditions concern the same period and are not mutually exclusive. The legend of Frumentius, in effect, affirms the latter story insofar as it asserts that there were Christian traders from abroad in Ethiopia to propagate the gospel. Still another tradition attributes the founding of the Ethiopian Church to a Byzantine priest named John, who came from Arabia at the summons of the king of Axum.

The Ethiopian church afterwards maintained ties with the churches of Egypt. Between the fourth and sixth centuries, the Bible was translated into Ge'ez, the language of the people, at the instigation of Syrian missionaries. Though the Ethiopian church would later be cut off from the rest of Christianity by the Arab peoples encircling it, in large measure it would successfully resist Islamization (see p. 132).

---

66  Rufinus, *Histoira Ecclesiastica*, 1:9.

67  The Monophysites, disciples of Eutyches (first half of the fifth century), taught that Jesus Christ had only one nature, an idea that threatened the traditional doctrine of the Incarnation. The Coptic churches of Egypt and Abyssinia, the Jacobite Church of Syria, and the Armenian Apostolic Church have adopted this theology.

# SECTION II

## MISSION IN THE MIDDLE AGES

# CHAPTER 4

# The West: From the Fifth to the Eighth Century

## THE BARBARIAN CHALLENGE

We enter now a long millennium of uncertainty, of advances and setbacks, during which Christianity would perish in several places.

The fifth century was a major turning point in the history of the Western church. The Germanic peoples invaded *en masse* the frontier territories to the north of the Roman Empire, hunting down and often massacring the more or less Romanized inhabitants in these regions. They occupied the Danubian countries—modern-day Austria, southern Germany, and Switzerland. The Germanic peoples also moved farther north and farther south. This was particularly the case of the Goths. The Ostrogoths penetrated southward as far as the plains of Italy. Their king, Theodoric, became master of the peninsula and established his capital at Ravenna in 493. The Visigoths under King Alaric seized Rome in 410; but not content to remain in Italy, they settled in southwest Gaul and Spain. The Vandals, after laying waste to the west of Europe, crossed the straights of Gibraltar to invade and settle in North Africa. The Burgunds, Alamans, Lombards, and Franks, as well as other less important peoples founded Germanic kingdoms in different parts of the Roman Empire. These "Great Invasions," by people who had stayed relatively immobile through the centuries, are explained by the arrival in Central Europe of nomadic warriors from Asia, among whom the best known were the Huns—themselves pushed westward by the Mongol invasions. For the same reason, the Angles and Saxons in this era crossed the North Sea and occupied the eastern part of the British Isles, later known as England. Many of the inhabitants fled and took refuge in Armoric, present-day Brittany.

Most of these Germanic peoples were pagans. There were some exceptions to this, such as the Goths, who were evangelized by Ulfilas in the preceding century and became Arian Christians. Through them the Vandals and Lombards were also won over to Arianism. Their Christianity, however, was a thin veneer that did not prevent them in their travels from pillaging churches and monasteries and massacring priests and monks. This was an immense setback for the orthodox church and a grave threat to Greco-Latin culture.

Paulus Orosius, a Portuguese priest who had come to seek refuge with Augustine of Hippo in 414, had a less pessimistic interpretation of these events. In his *History Against the Pagans*, the oldest universal history written by a Christian, he sought to minimize the gravity of the fall of the Roman Empire by comparing it to the numerous other sad events that have afflicted humanity through the ages:

> Who knows? Perhaps if the barbarians had not penetrated the Roman Empire the churches would not be everywhere full, in the East and West, of Huns, Sueves, Vandals, Burgunds and other innumerable people who are now believers. Is it not then necessary to praise and celebrate the Divine mercy since, thanks to our ruin, so many nations have the knowledge of the truth with which, otherwise, they would not have been in contact?[68]

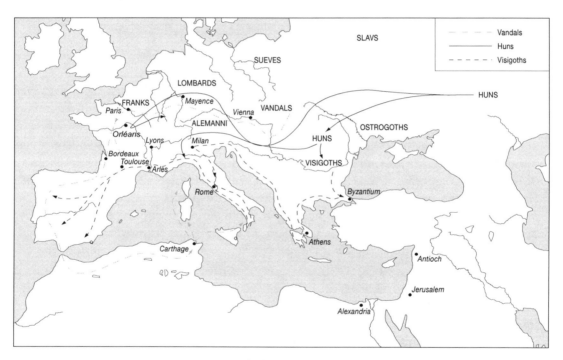

*Map 4: The barbarian invasions*

Faced with the repaganization of Europe, Christians took up the task of evangelizing it once again. Though the pagan and Arian tribes ended in effect by accepting orthodox Christianity, it took much time and many resisted. A little before the year 500, Avitus, the bishop of Vienna (ca. 450–518), expressed his anxiety in seeing orthodox Christianity shattered before Arianism: "We have no more than five or six [bishops] to resist. We must find a leader," he wrote. He was granted his wish by the conversion of Clovis to Christianity.

---

68 Paulus Orosius, *Historiarum adversus paganos*, 7:41.

# THE CONVERSION OF CLOVIS, KING OF THE FRANKS

The Franks, a Germanic pagan tribe, occupied the northern half of Gaul and eventually succeeded in imposing their name on the entire region. Clovis (c. 466–511), son of Childeric (d. 481), was a Salian Frank and a petty king of a tribe established in the environs of Tournai in 492 or 493. He married Clotilda, a Burgundian princess of Geneva. She was a fervent Christian, a Catholic rather than an Arian as were most of the Burgunds. Her influence on the pagan Clovis was decisive. It was said of her, "She did not cease to speak to her husband of the God of the Christians." With the aid of Remigius, bishop of Rheims, she eventually led Clovis to accept orthodox Christianity.

The story recorded by the chroniclers of the period, notably Gregory of Tours, openly compared the conversion of Clovis with that of the emperor Constantine. In a military campaign against the Alamans, Clovis found himself in great difficulty at Tolbiac, near Cologne. Historian Jacques Brosse writes, "It is then that he invoked the God of Clotilda so that he would come to his aid. All the Franks immediately took courage and crushed their enemies, who were soon discouraged by the death of their king. Being content with their submission, they then asked mercy of the king of the Franks, who accorded it to them. For this he was congratulated by Bishop Avitus, the most venerated of Burgundy's prelates. On his return, Clovis 'recounted to the queen how, in invoking the name of Christ, he had earned the victory.'"[69] As in the case of Constantine, it is difficult to evaluate how much of Clovis' decision was due to sincere conviction and how much to political opportunism. Remigius baptized the Frankish king on Christmas day in the year 496.[70] Learning of the news, Avitus wrote to Clovis:

> The choice that you have made is of value for all. Your faith is our victory . . . You walk in the path of your ancestors in the government here below; you open the way to your descendants in wanting to reign in heaven . . . By this act, you have consecrated your soul to God, your life to your contemporaries, your glory to your descendants . . . Thanks to you, this part of the world shines with a fine brilliance, and in our West sparkles the light of a new star!

In the time of his baptism, when it was said that three thousand of his Frankish warriors with drawn swords were also baptized, Clovis was exhorted by Remigius in these terms: "Incline your head meekly, Sicambrian, worship what you have burned, burn what you have worshiped," orders that Clovis and his groups applied to the letter, abandoning the various Franco-German religions and giving themselves over to "muscular" Christianity. The conversion of Clovis scarcely influenced his conduct since he went so far as to massacre half of the members of his family, notably the king of Cambrai and the king of Cologne, in order to seize their cities. His biographer, Gregory, was not overly anxious about this and did not seem to doubt his motivations: "He obviously killed many of those around him, but he went straight to God."

---

69  Brosse, *Histoire*, 85.
70  The date of 499 seems better attested today.

If from the missionary point of view Clovis' conversion is all but convincing, it nevertheless ensured that Christianity in those regions would assume an orthodox form.

Following the conversion of the Franks, and under the influence of Bishop Avitus, the Burgunds renounced Arianism in the year 500. Sigismond, king of Burgundy, allied himself with Clovis in order to conquer the Gothic tribes that remained Arian. In Limousin, Aquitaine, and the region of Toulouse, the churches were abandoned, for the Catholic clergy had been severely persecuted by the Visigoths. When the Burgunds invaded the Auvergne and Limousin in 507, the Franks of Clovis crossed the Loire and fought the Visigoths at Voulle, not far from Poitiers. Upon entering the campaign, Clovis declared: "It is with much pain that I endure these Arians to occupy a part of Gaul. Let us march with the aid of God, and when they have been vanquished, we will subject their territory to our rule." The Visigoth kingdom of Toulouse collapsed in its turn a little later, and Clovis' son Theodoric seized Bordeaux, Saintes, and Angouleme. Together with Clotilda, Clovis went to Paris to establish his throne. In discussing his military campaigns, Gregory of Tours employed the term "crusade."

Clovis' last initiative occurred in the year of his death, 511: he assembled the first great national council of the Frankish church at Orleans. Presided over by the Metropolitan Cyprian of Bordeaux, the bishop of Aquitaine, this council reorganized the church of the Frankish kingdom on the basis of the victory of Roman Catholic orthodoxy over against Arianism, but as an assembly of the national church it also showed that it was conscious of its autonomy. Jean Meyendorff concludes, "From now on, the Frankish church, although formally very respectful of the Bishop of Rome, was going to develop itself in total administrative independence and exercise a growing influence not only in the Germanic countries but also in Italy."[71]

Clovis' life quickly entered the realm of legend, which does not make it easy to determine what is historically accurate about the founder as he is presented in the later stories of his life. As Jacques Brosse writes, "The historian is well obliged to conclude that the conversion of the king of the Franks gave birth to the first Catholic barbarian state founded on the ruins of the Roman Empire. Also, if the commitment of Clovis to Catholicism assured the victory of the church over Arianism, it also permitted the Frankish kingdom to endure and later to revive the empire while the other barbarian kingdoms collapsed."[72]

As for Clotilda, she settled at Tours so that she could come regularly to pray at the tomb of Saint Martin. After the death of Clovis, she remained a widow for thirty-seven years and died at a little over seventy years of age. She was interred with Clovis at Paris in June 548 in the Basilica of the Holy Apostles that the couple had built on the left bank.

During this period of upheaval, there was little question as to the possibility of personal evangelization: mass conversions were the order of the day. War chiefs imposed on their soldiers and on the conquered their form of religion, if necessary by force. However, the evangelical faith of the apostles was not totally lost. It endured

71  Meyendorff, *Unité*, 150.
72  Brosse, *Histoire*, 93.

most notably in the monasteries. There are also many fine examples of lay believers, often great personages, who cared for the population during times of scarcity and made up for the incompetence of a weak and disorganized clergy. Gregory of Tours recounted the manner in which a zealous Christian senator fed the poor during a period of famine, demonstrating a truly evangelical spirit:

> In the time of Bishop Sidonius [between 450 and 480], a great famine ravaged Burgundy. As the people were dispersed in various regions and there was no chaplain to distribute goods to the poor, it is reported that Ecdicius, one of the senators and his relative, having put his confidence in God, then accomplished a great thing. Seeing in effect that the famine was growing, he sent his servants with horses and chariots to go through the neighboring cities to lead away those residents that the food shortage was torturing. They went therefore and gathered to his home all the poor that they could find and fed them there during all the time of barrenness, saving them from a murderous famine. As many said, there were more than four thousand of both sexes. Then when abundance returned, he once again organized transportation and returned each one to his home.[73]

## PATRICK: THE EVANGELIZATION OF IRELAND

A striking manifestation of the vitality of the faith, and one rich in consequences, is the evangelization of Ireland in the fifth century. This great island, peopled by Celts, lay outside the confines of the Roman Empire. Roman geographers knew of the island of Hibernia, though they sometimes confused it with Scotland. Greek and perhaps also Phoenician seaman had reached as far as the fogs of Ireland. However, in the fifth century of our era, the "Emerald Isle" was still under the authority of the Druids, strangers to Greco-Latin culture. The island was also a region of peace where German tribes had not brought the sword.

It is at this moment that the island was evangelized. Sadly, this beautiful history has been so embellished by those who have recounted it through the centuries that it is difficult for modern historians to see through the multiple and overlapping colors to the original fabric. In popular memory, "the apostle of Ireland" was Saint Patrick (ca. 385–ca. 460), who is still the island's patron saint.

Though it is certain that a man by the name of Patricius existed, it is possible that the lives of two or three contemporary missionaries were conflated into a single personage. Because of his *Confessions Before I Die*, historians have, however, a credible framework for his early spiritual development. This man, originally called Sikhat, was born between 385 and 390 in a British and Christianized family. Though the place of his childhood is the object of contradictory hypotheses, all agree that he lived on the west cost of present-day Great Britain. Some, however, prefer the village of *Bannauem Taburniae* (the term is uncertain, and some versions read *Bannaventa*) of

---

73   Gregoire de Tours, *Livre II*, 24. Cited in Hammann, *L'amour retrouvé*, 93.

which his *Confession* speaks. It was situated in the north of England, in a region close to Scotland and near the edge of the territory occupied by the Romans. Others favor the region neighboring the nation of Wales that lay near the mouth of the Severn, or perhaps at Somerset in the south of Bristol. The grandfather of Sikhat, Potitus, was a priest, and his father, Calpornius, a Roman *decurion* and a deacon in a small church. For some service rendered, he enjoyed the privilege of the title of *Patricius*, which his son inherited.

During his childhood, Sikhat (henceforth Patrick) knew troubled times. The Roman Empire was pressed from all sides by barbarian arms. The empire responded by recalling the Roman soldiers garrisoned in Britannica (England) to defend Italy, leaving the island at the mercy of the invaders. The Scots, Irish adventurers, and pirates began to cruise the north and west coasts of Britannica. When he was about sixteen years old, Patrick was captured with a number of other young people in a raid by Scottish pirates. He was carried to Ireland as a slave, put to hard labor, and mistreated by the peasant who had bought him. According to some sources, he was then placed in the service of a Druid named Milcho, which would explain his excellent knowledge of the practices of the Celtic religion that he put to good use in his later apostolate. In solitude and distress, he remembered the faith of his parents, who were zealous Christians. He wrote of his conversion experience in his *Confession*:

> The Lord opened the understanding of my unbelieving heart, so that I remembered, late as it was, my sins. I converted with all my heart to the Lord my God, who considered my baseness, took pity on my youth and ignorance, watched over me before I knew him and before I was sensible and able to distinguish between good and evil, strengthened me and consoled me as a father consoles his son.[74]

The sufferings affirmed and deepened his faith.

> I took the livestock to graze each day, and I prayed often in the day. The love of God and his fear invaded me more and more, my faith grew, my spirit followed its own desire, so that I was saying about one hundred prayers in a single day and about as many in the night, so that I was living in the forest and on the mountain, so that I rose before the day to pray in the snow, frost, and rain, so that I was feeling no evil, and so that there was no idleness in me—as I see it now—for then a spirit full of ardor was in me.[75]

After six years of captivity in the course of which he learned the Celtic language well, he had the conviction that God would aid him to escape. He was able to conceal himself in a quasi-miraculous manner on a pagan ship that was leaving Ireland for Gaul. He was captured, but he soon escaped again and finally managed to find his family. These events occurred about the year 407. He became a priest and perhaps a

---

74   St. Patrick, *Confession*, trans. Richard Hanson, in *Sources chrétiennes*, no. 249 (Paris: Editions du Cerf, 1978), 2.
75   Ibid., 16.

monk. It is then that the missionary call impressed itself upon him in the form of a vision. Here is the story that he gives in the *Confessions*:

> I was again in Britain [England] in the house of my parents, who welcomed me as a son and beseeched me not to leave to go elsewhere, henceforth all the more so after all the difficulties that I had endured. It was then that I saw in a nocturnal vision a man by the name of Victoricus, who appeared to come from Ireland with innumerable letters. He gave me one of them and I read the beginning where it was written: "Call of the Irish"; and while I was reading, I believed that I heard in the same instant the call of those who lived beside the forest of Voclute, which is close to the Western sea [the place it seems where Patrick had lived in captivity], and here is what they were crying as a single voice: "Holy boy, we pray to you to come again to walk among us." My heart was profoundly moved, and I could not continue my reading. At that point I arose. Thanks be given to God, for after numerous years, the Lord granted their plea.[76]

Patrick left for clerical training in Gaul where he sojourned for seventeen years (415–432), studying philosophy and theology. According to some sources, he first resided with the monks of Lerins, near Cannes, and then with the German monks at Auxerre.

He asked to be consecrated a bishop, a status that would permit him to found churches and consecrate priests, and then in 432 when he was about forty-seven years old, he returned to the island of his captivity with other missionary monks recruited in Gaul. They debarked at the far end of Strangford Lough, close to Downpatrick, about thirty-five kilometers south of Dublin, where Patrick's tomb is now located. Patrick was not the first Christian missionary in Ireland. The deacon Palladius, who was consecrated bishop for the purpose, had been sent several years before by Pope Celestinus I (422–432).[77] But Palladius died after three years, the same year of Patrick's arrival. His mission had enjoyed a limited success in that three small churches seem to have been founded in the region of Dublin. Some historians doubt the historicity of the mission of Palladius, who is ignored in the Irish sources.

Thanks to Patrick's knowledge of the Celtic language, he could immediately begin to preach the gospel to the population. He had to confront the implacable opposition of the local Druid priests. Remembering a particularly tragic moment, he wrote:

> They seized my companions and me. On that day they ardently desired to kill me, but my time had not yet come. They seized all that we had, and they bound me with iron chains. And on the fourteenth day, the Lord delivered me . . . Each day, I was supposed to wait to be slaughtered, or else for a treacherous attack . . . I feared to have lost the work begun . . . O God, may I never

---

76  Ibid., 23.
77  The dates given for the popes in the text are those of their pontificate.

be separated from this people that I am going to gain at the limits of the earth.[78]

Very quickly, and against great adversity, his prayer for divine aid was answered. He accomplished numerous miracles, which are not all necessarily to be classed in the category of legends. It seems, in effect, that God gave him these signs of power in order to confront the opposition of pagan religion and to succeed in planting a mission church as in the time of the first Christians. Loiguire, King of Tara, was not slow to convert and to give Patrick his full support.

Accompanied by a group of monks, Patrick traveled throughout Ireland during a period of thirty years. He built a church that, beginning in the north of Ireland, soon extended through the entire island. The monastic communities founded by Patrick and his companions were numerous, of high spirituality, and remarkably well-cultured. In the course of the fifth and sixth centuries, some count hundreds and sometimes thousands of monks. Their ascetic practices were very demanding, with prostrations or hands extended over many hours of daily prayer, as well as prolonged immersion in cold water, even in winter, to master the temptations of the flesh. In contrast to the cultural decline on the continent, Ireland became an island of civilization. Especially important centers of culture were the monasteries of Clonard, Clonmacnoise, Kilmacduagh, and Glendalough. Archaeology witnesses today to the importance of the early church in Ireland, with its agglomerations constructed around the principal monasteries.

Opposed by the Druids, Patrick knew how to conciliate the *filid*, the "onlookers," and at the same time those who maintained the ancient local culture: the poets, genealogists, jurists, and philosophers. Many converted and became in their turn missionaries. They stamped on the spirituality of the Celtic church their own unique traits, which clearly distinguished Irish religion from that of the Roman church.

Nonetheless, Patrick "Romanized" Ireland in some respects, for his monks had to learn Latin to be able to read and preach the Scriptures, and he introduced Latin characters to fix the written form of the Gaelic language. But because the church was established during a century when Europe was troubled by war and the British Isles were in effect "de-Romanized," Patrick and his successors were not in contact with Rome. Also, the distance that the Irish church stood from the Roman see was to some extent voluntary. At first organized according to the diocesan model that was current in the West, the Irish church slowly developed its own structure that followed the monastic form. Parishes were directed by communities of monks, with the abbey's authority soon supplanting that of the bishop's.

Jean Meyendorff writes, "The monastic communities monopolized the direction of the church so completely that the parish clergy and diocesan structures disappeared. The see of Armagh itself, created by Saint Patrick, was reorganized on a monastic basis."[79] One observes, furthermore, that the missionary dynamism of the Irish monks was remarkable and soon to be crucial for spiritual life on the

---

78 Ibid., 52–58 passim.
79 Meyendorff, *Unité*, 160.

European continent. But the Irish conception of church organization created conflicts with the local clergy, who continued to be organized according to the Roman canonical model. Meyendorff continues: "In the fifth to the sixth centuries, the Celtic church was leading a marginalized existence, one out of the mainstream of Christendom . . . There is no doubt that the Celtic church's 'indigenization'—its adaptation of the life of the church to local conditions—was made at the expense of its universalist consciousness. That the Celtic church really became indigenous posed certain ecclesiological and canonical problems. The question of the true nature of the episcopate was certainly one; another was the particular method of evangelization by the monks passing through, who were celebrating the Eucharist in private residences where the laity were assuming certain sacramental functions."[80]

*Ruins of the monastery constructed on the hill of Slane where, according to the legend, Patrick lit a great fire on the Easter of AD 433 to celebrate the complete Christianization of Ireland. (Photo: Michael Kooiman)*

According to Meyendorff again: "Rome had enjoyed practically no role in the origins of Irish Christendom, and the idea of an administrative disciplinary structure other than that of the abbots was entirely foreign to the Celtic church . . . The authority of the papacy had little weight in the eyes of the Celtic abbots, and in any event, it was not sufficient to convince them that their disciplinary and liturgical traditions should be abandoned in favor of Roman practice."[81]

One of the peculiarities of the movement of the Irish monks was the place that it accorded to women. Brigitte (ca. 450–520) assembled the first women's community and then founded a double monastery at Kildare, the monks and the religious

---

80 Ibid., 150.
81 Ibid., 162. Also note the remarks of Colomban writing to the pope (see p. 67).

directed by an abbess assisted by an abbot-bishop. Later, the disciples of Colomban founded several mixed abbeys in the countries of France. It is true that in Irish society women had a privileged position, and this was the case also in the church: they could assist the priest in his ceremonial roles and even distribute Communion—things rather shocking for Roman Catholics.

As for the theology of Patrick, it had an evangelical orientation, if one believes the most authentic documents, especially his *Confession*. His theology appears not only to have been centered on the person and work of Jesus Christ but to have excluded the traditions that the church had added onto the Scriptures. Moreover, it does not seem to have been influenced by the Pelagian tendencies then current among British theologians.[82] In any event, the fundamental experience of his life was his awareness of the sovereign grace of God. He testified that it was by pure mercifulness, rather than by virtue of his merits, that God had called him to evangelize Ireland:

> I who was at first a loutish fugitive and without education, I who do not know how to foresee the future, I know however one thing with certitude, it is that "before being humbled" I was as a stone lying in deep mud; but he came, the one who is powerful, and in his mercy he took me, he truly heaved me up very high and placed me on top of the wall; this is why I should lift up a loud voice to render something to the Lord for his goodness here below and in eternity, goodness so great that the spirit of men cannot appreciate it.[83]

The lines that conclude Patrick's *Confession* are equally revealing of his theology and of his experience of faith, founded on grace and oriented toward the glory of God:

> I address a prayer to the men who believe and fear God, who will deign to consider and welcome this writing, that Patrick, a truly ignorant preacher, has composed in Ireland: if I have done or revealed some small thing according to the good pleasure of God, may no one say that it is that ignorant one, even I, who did it, but think—and hold it as entirely certain—that this was a gift of God. This is my confession before I die.[84]

At his death in about the year 460, he left an Ireland that would soon be called "the isle of saints," a lasting home of cultural and spiritual influence, even if the Druids had not entirely disappeared and even if there continued to exist certain rites and practices of pagan origin among Christians. Patrick had also reformed the Irish judicial system and fought slavery, advocating an exchange of prisoners between victors and vanquished.

---

82   The English monk Pelagius (360–ca. 422), the adversary to Saint Augustine, affirmed the capacity of human beings to seek and practice the good, minimizing the role of divine grace. The monastery of the Isle de Lerins, where Patrick had perhaps sojourned, was known to have been influenced by Pelagianism. Certain Irish monks, such as Colomban, are sometimes considered "semi-pelagian."

83   Patrick, *Confession* 12.

84   Ibid., 62.

In the century following the death of Patrick, the Irish monks engaged in the missionary enterprise on a large scale. They were distinguished by the austerity of their discipline and their great intellectual knowledge. They were sometimes called Culdeens (*kelle dei* in Celtic: "servants of God") or Iro-Scots.

They did not all station themselves in Scotland and England. For example, the monk Brendan, called "the Navigator" (d. 577), reached the island of Greenland and perhaps even America. But there are no sure indications to attest that these explorations led to the evangelization of local populations or the foundation of monasteries. The Irish monks also went to the continent, which was still largely pagan or at best had come under a thin veneer of Christianity after the great Germanic invasions. A large number of European cities owe their names to such-and-such a missionary saint who devoted himself to their regions. To give some specific examples, these include in Brittany, France: Saint-Malo, Saint-Corenstin, and Saint-Brienuc. Often legendary exploits are attributed to the Irish monks. In the seventh century, Irish monasteries could be found from the west coast of Ireland all the way to Kiev in Russia.

These missionaries were not sent by anyone except the Holy Spirit and their abbots. Their home base was their monastery where they were being prayed for and where their marvelous adventures were being recounted, raising the enthusiasm of the novices who were impatient to leave on their own tour. They went out in teams full of joy and worked for the glory of God. Their task was both to evangelize and to civilize. Working themselves very hard, they labored, fenced, drained the marshes, cleared the forests, constructed bridges, and taught the population how better to cultivate the earth and to construct safer houses. Their monasteries were places of education and culture. The barbarian invasions had largely destroyed the cultural heritage of antiquity, which found refuge among the monks. They recruited many disciples among the local people, inculcating in them a work ethic and self-discipline, teaching them to read and write, and training them as evangelists. David Bosch writes, "In an age of insecurity, disorder, and barbarism, the monastery embodied the ideal of spiritual order and disciplined moral activity which in time permeated the entire church, indeed, the entire society. Each monastery was a vast complex of buildings, churches, workshops, stores, and almshouses—a hive of activity for the benefit of the entire surrounding community."[85]

In his book *Colomban and Gall*, Fritz Blanke writes: "In Ireland, a monk was considered to have reached the highest degree of perfection when, having in the first place left behind his entire family to dedicate himself to God in the bosom of a monastery, he next abandoned his monastery to found another in a foreign land . . . They were ready to make the sacrifice of leaving their own country, to exile themselves to an unknown soil, to devote themselves entirely to the heavenly country."

---

85  Bosch, *Transforming Mission*, 232.

# IRISH MONKS, EVANGELISTS OF EUROPE

## Colomba

One of the most famous of the Culdeens was Columcille (521–597), better known by the name of Colomba, "the apostle of Scotland." He was born in 521, close to a century and a half after Patrick, in the north of the island. He belonged to one of the royal families and was even a possible inheritor of the important kingdom of Tara. He became a monk and was the student of Finnian (d. 549), one of the principal successors of Patrick. But he remained a violent man, proud of his royal origins, his knowledge of science, and his virtues. He founded a monastery in 593, and others followed. He was accused of having incited the members of his clan against King Diamaid, who had reproached him for having behaved wrongly in a conflict with Finnian. Under the pretext that Diamaid had made a man die as a refugee in his monastery, Colomba launched a war in 562. The king was routed in a pitiless battle that resulted, it was reported, in three thousand deaths. Some supposed that it was remorse for having provoked this bloody confrontation that Colomba left Ireland to expiate his sins in a perilous mission.

In this era, the Highlands of Scotland and the Hebrides Islands were peopled by the Picts, fierce warriors from whom the Romans had protected themselves with Hadrian's Wall, an immense structure that stretched across the south of Scotland from the east to the west. Colomba decided to evangelize these Picts.

Hence in 563, he left Ireland with eleven companions in coracles, small wicker boats covered in animal skins. They journeyed to Iona, a small island that lay close to the Scottish coast and belonged to one of his relatives. It was part of the archipelago of the Hebrides, where "gray wind" blew three hundred days in the year, and where a warm sea current from the Caribbean generally protected the land from the frosts of winter.

Colomba established a monastery there, which consisted of several huts made of branches, as well as a chapel, library, study hall, and refectory. The monks lived very poorly, pulling the plow themselves in hard labor. Soon new companions came to enlarge the team. A veritable missionary fleet went to carry the gospel from isle to isle, reaching as far as the Shetlands and Faroe. On their fragile coracles, the monks plowed the sea, landing on the coast at the foot of the Highlands. From here they went up rivers, through wild countries, and everywhere established small churches. The missionaries of Colomba reaped an exceptional harvest. The most powerful king and the fiercest of the Picts, Brude MacMaelchon, who ruled in Inverness in the north of Scotland, converted in 565, and his subjects soon followed him.

At this point Colomba revealed himself to be a remarkable statesman. He organized the people who came to accept the gospel and unified them in a coherent kingdom, himself crowning their first king. The country of the Picts was henceforth called the country of the Scots: Scotland. The small island of Iona became for several centuries a missionary center, a nursery of imminent servants of God. Colomba died on June 9, 597, after thirty-four years of ministry in Iona. He was found dead that morning on his knees in prayer, like David Livingstone much later in the heart of Africa. Jacques Brosse concludes, "This violent, prideful man had become a man of peace, full of serenity and wisdom, having, said his biographer, 'an angelic visage,' leading at Iona a life of extreme austerity, fasting continually and lying on a prayer bench. Although for humility's sake Columcille had never received the episcopate, his authority was considerable, and his influence attracted to Iona a number of admirers who sometimes became his disciples."[86]

Aidan, his disciple and successor, traveled with a group of monks to the south where they evangelized the pagan Anglo-Saxon invaders established in Northumbria. In 635 Aidan founded a missionary center on the Isle of Lindisfarne, not far from Bamburgh, the capital of Northumbria. In time it was comparable to the one at Iona.

We have already noted the special place occupied by women in the Irish monastic tradition. Among the disciples of Aidan, Hilda founded a mixed abbey at Whitby on the east coast of England where monks and nuns lived under the direction of an abbess. Whitby rapidly became a spiritual and literary center.

## Colomban

An exemplary Culdeen missionary was Colomban (ca. 543–615). Having given a new impetus to monasticism, all the great founders of monasteries in the seventh century were either his disciples or his emulators. Colomban was born around 543 in Ireland and came from a noble family. At a young age he was both a lord and poet. Not knowing which way to follow, he went to consult a holy hermit known for his wisdom. The man convinced him to abandon all to follow Christ, which is what he did despite the pressure of friends and family. While still very young, Colomban became a monk in the famous abbey of Bangor where he studied under the direction of renowned masters. Benefiting from the rich culture of the Irish monasteries, he learned Latin and Greek perfectly and became an excellent student of the Scriptures. He wrote a commentary on the book of Psalms, composed poems, and already had a solid reputation as a man of letters and learning when he felt called by God to missionary work. He was then nearly fifty years old and had been teaching with honor for ten years at Bangor. However, an incessant, interior voice recalled for him the words of the Eternal to Abraham: "Leave your country, your people and your father's household and go to the land I will show you" (Gen 12:1).

He left with a team of eleven monks for Gaul where the church found itself in an unfortunate situation. Despite the conversion of Clovis, the Franks had retained numerous pagan practices. The clergy were corrupt and ignorant, not bothering to hide offerings made to Germanic divinities, sacrifices that included horses and even women and children. The Merovingiens had divided the Gallic territory between ephemeral kingdoms.

Colomban and his companions disembarked on the coast of Armoric between Saint-Malo and Mount Saint-Michel about 580, and then traveled slowly on foot as far as Burgoyne where they were welcomed, a dozen years later, by King Gontran

---

86  Brosse, *Histoire*, 158.

(545–592), the grandson of Clovis. They cleared a corner of a forest at the foot of Vosges at Annegray, in a region uninhabited since the invasions, and settled themselves in a ruined Roman fort. Soon dozens of young people rushed to Colomban for instruction, submitting themselves to his iron discipline. The missionary then founded another monastery at Luxeuil on the ruins of an ancient Roman spa town. This establishment rapidly became the principal missionary center of the movement and a school of civilization. Theology as well as classical, ancient letters and agriculture were taught there. The sick were also cared for. The monks followed the Irish liturgy and customs, which sometimes differed from those of the local clergy. Being censured for their immorality, the Gallica clergy complained of the missionary to the new king, Thierry II (587–613), a nephew of Gontran who had succeeded him. The debauched and cruel king, dissatisfied by the rigidity of Colomban and encouraged by his grandmother, the formidable Branehault, decided in 610 to expel Colomban and his companions. They were conducted *manu militari* (by force) as far as Nantes, where they were made to reembark for Ireland. From Nantes, Colomban wrote a farewell letter of great spiritual depth to the faithful at Luxeuil. Here is a portion:

> The gospels furnish us all that is necessary to encourage us; they have scarcely been written but for this: to teach the faithful to follow the crucified Jesus in carrying their cross; our perils are numerous . . . and the enemy frightening, but the recompense is glorious and liberty is our manifest choice. Without an adversary there is no struggle, without a struggle no crown . . . and without liberty no dignity.[87]

Loaded with sorrowing passengers, the ship left the port of Nantes, but soon a tempest broke out with such force that it ran aground on the nearby coast. Colomban's frightened escort allowed the missionaries to go where they wanted.

Colomban set out again for the east, sojourning sometimes in Soissons in the realm of Clothaire II, king of Neustria (584–629), who was well-disposed toward him. Then he went to Metz, the realm of Theodebert II, king of Austrasia (586–612), who asked him to evangelize the Suevi and the Alemanni who had settled in the valley of the Rhine after having eliminated Christianity in the process of conquering the region. Colomban agreed and went up the river to Basel. His disciple Ursinus left him to found a hermitage near the Doubs River. Colomban arrived at Bregenz, on Lake Constance, between Switzerland and south Germany. He took over all the ancient churches in the region that had been transformed into pagan temples, ejecting the idols from them. Confrontations with the pagan population were sometimes bitter, as will be observed later on. When in 612 he learned that his friend King Theodebert had been defeated at Tolbiac by his old enemy King Thierry II, Colomban crossed the Alps, leaving behind him Gall, one of his earliest companions. Gall, who sincerely wanted to remain behind to convert the Alemanni, founded a monastery in a valley of the Swiss Alps that eventually became a great center of intellectual and spiritual

---

87   Ibid., 194.

influence; and he gave his name to the city of Saint Gall.[88] Later called "the apostle of Switzerland," Gall died in his hermitage on October 16, 646.

As for Colomban, despite his seventy-two years, he pursued his travels in the direction of Italy. He sojourned at first in Milan in 614, where he published a treatise against the Arian heresy that was well entrenched in the region. Then he established himself at Bobbio, in the plane of the Po, and transformed an old, ruined basilica into a monastery. Over several centuries, this institution would be, like Luxeuil, Bregenz, and Saint Gall, a center of study and evangelization. At the request of the sovereigns of the region, he wrote to Pope Boniface IV (608–615), pleading with him to put the Arian heresy immediately to an end. This letter recognized the authority of the Apostle Peter but manifests a staunch independence in regards to Roman institutions.[89] Here is a brief passage from it:

> We Irish, who live at the extremity of the world, are the disciples of Saint Peter, Saint Paul, and the other apostles who have written under the dictation of the Holy Spirit. We have never accepted anything other than the apostolic and evangelical doctrine, and Ireland has never known neither heretics, nor Jews, nor schematics. The liberty of my race is the source of my daring. Among us, it is not the person but right that counts . . . We are submitted to the throne of Saint Peter: for, as glorious and powerful as Rome is, it owes, in our eyes, its grandeur and power to this throne alone.

In the darkness of the Merovingian times, Colomban shines with unequaled brightness. "The power of God was visibly shining in him," says his biographer. Not only was he a remarkable theologian, but this rude man was also a sensitive poet and very well-read: he knew and appreciated Virgil, Horace, and Seneca, and doubtless also Ovid and Juvenal, too. His works give testimony to a man of vast culture and great intelligence. His severity, which appeared in his monastic rule, can seem excessive to us, but this was necessary in a period when cruelty and barbarity reigned. He loved to repeat, "The one who affirms a belief in Christ must live as Christ lived, poor, humble, and always preaching the truth."

With a great beard and astonishing physical force, he was a tireless traveler until an advanced age—and this in a time when movement was a dangerous trial. He exercised a real fascination on those whom he encountered, and by his poverty and personal authority, he made a great impression on the young. He often said to them:

> Have always before your mind not what you are, but what you will be. The present endures only an instant, the future is eternal . . . You possess nothing on the earth, you will die as you were born and your body will return to the dust . . . Be alert not to lose heaven where your heritage is found, and for eternity. Sell yourself rather to buy life!

---

88 In the ninth and tenth centuries, the school of Saint Gall and its library, rich in sumptuous Irish manuscripts, enjoyed a role of the first rank in the diffusion of spirituality and culture in Western Europe (Brosse, *Histoire*, 195–96).

89 Concerning the relationship between the Celtic and Roman churches, see p. 61.

It is estimated that two hundred abbots were raised up through his influence. He died at Bobbio in 615.

In his *Life of Saint Gall*, Wahlafrid Strabon (d. 849) described the rather striking approach to evangelization practiced by Colomban:

> Colomban and his disciples, having received the king's permission to choose a place to settle and after having traveled through several countries, arrived in the land of the Alamans, on the shore of a river named the Limmat. In going upstream, they reached Lake Zurich . . . then a place called Tuggen. Seeing the beauty of the place and the easiness of habitation that it offered, they cried. Alas, the population that occupied it was cruel and impious. It was dedicated to the worship of false gods that it honored by sacrifices and had given itself up to the practice of augurs, oracles, and numerous other superstitions incompatible with the worship of the true God. The holy men began to live in the midst of this population and taught them the religion of the Father, Son, and Holy Spirit and the prescriptions of the true faith. But one day, Saint Gall, a disciple of the holy man, armed with a pious zeal, put fire to the temple where they were offering sacrifices to demons and threw all the idols that he could find into the lake.
>
> This vain gesture enflamed the pagans into anger and hatred: they rushed upon the holy monks, wanting to kill Gall and expel Colomban from their territory, but not before whipping him with the birch and subduing him with blows. The blessed father [Colomban], knowing their design and filled up with justice, cast an anathema on them with these words: "O God, you who by Providence preserve and govern the universe, order that the outrages that these people have inflicted on your servants fall on their heads. May their children die young; may on reaching old age they be struck with sudden folly; may they and their lands be overwhelmed by hard servitude; may their ignominy beat down on them all for eternity."[90]

Despite the unevangelical character of these proceedings and curses, the zeal and spiritual motivation of the Irish monks are incontestable. In their itinerant ministry of spreading the gospel, they were much more attentive to the needs of the population anxious for salvation than to affirmations of the power of the church. Their strategy was above all to found monasteries, and often the actual work of evangelizing the population would be accomplished subsequently by the disciples recruited on the spot and trained in a very strict disciple. These monasteries were nurseries of pious and well-instructed priests, remarkable for their zeal in the propagation of the gospel.

Daniel-Rops writes: "To be precise, the true Irish miracle, this second beginning of Christianity, was that a country only recently having received baptism was found

---

90   Cited in René P. Millot, *L'épopée missionnaire* (Paris: Fayard, 1956), 151–52.

immediately and marvelously faithful to the spirit of evangelization. In the Dark Ages of the West, Ireland was a second Palestine, a new cradle of the faith."[91]

# THE BENEDICTINE MISSIONARIES

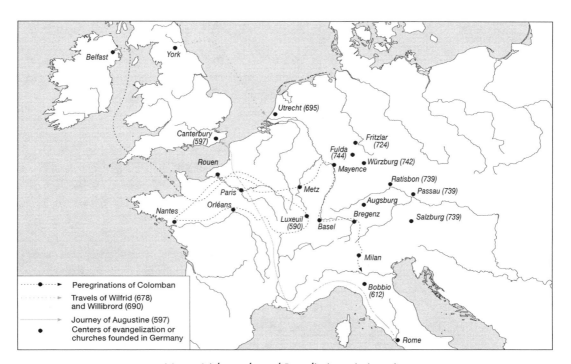

*Map 5: Irish monks and Benedictine missionaries*

For at least two centuries Iro-Scots missionaries evangelized Europe before being replaced, sometimes with a certain hostility, by the more "ecclesiastic" missionaries sent by the pope or in accord with him, belonging to the Benedictine order. This order was founded a little before the year 500 by a young Roman, Benedict of Nursia (ca. 490–547), who had retired from the world and from a church that he judged worldly in order to live out an ideal of purity and poverty. Benedict founded a monastery at Mont Cassin, 120 kilometers to the south of Rome. It was not only to be a home for monks but also a school for the training of disciples. Benedict expressed his intention in the introduction to the Benedictine rule, written in 529: "To found a school for the service of God in which, we hope, nothing too difficult or rigorous will be established." He described his ideal in this way: to help the monk to accede "to a love that, being perfect, chases away fear. Hence he would begin to observe, effortlessly and as if this was to him natural and habitual, all the precepts that he had until then observed by fear; and he would do it no longer for fear of hell, but for love of Christ and for a regular, joyous exercise in virtue."[92]

---

91 Henri Daniel-Rops, "La conversion des Barbares d'Occident," in *Histoire universelle des missions catholiques*, 1 (1956):92.

92 *The Rule of St. Benedict*, pp. 75 and 115.

For several centuries this order enjoyed a role of the highest importance in the missionary venture. This vocation was initiated in the end of the sixth century by Gregory, one of Benedict's successors. Born about 540, Gregory's father was the prefect of Rome. After having exercised high administrative functions in Rome, Gregory, while still young, turned in 574 to the monastic life. With the inheritance left by his father, he founded six monasteries in the domains of his family in Sicily. He then transformed his father's house in Rome into the monastery of Saint Andrew and became its abbot. The first and one of the most remarkable Benedictine missionaries was Augustine of Canterbury, who was dedicated to the evangelization of the pagan tribes of Great Britain.

## Augustine of Canterbury

During the Germanic invasions of Western Europe, the Jutes, Angles, and Saxons, who inhabited Germany near the North Sea, conquered the eastern section of Great Britain where they founded small kingdoms for themselves. As they were pagans, they destroyed every trace of Christianity in this region that belonged to the Roman period.

According to an oft-told legend, while Gregory was abbot of the monastery of Saint Andrew in Rome he saw one day in the slave market some tall, young, clear-skinned, blonde people who were to be sold. "Who are they?" he asked the merchant. "These are Angles," responded the latter. "These are not Angles, but Angels [*Non Angli, sed angeli*]!" replied the abbot. When he learned to his consternation that they were pagans, he added, "Alas! Must it be, therefore, that such handsome faces belong to the prince of darkness!" From that time on he burned with a desire to make known the true God to these foreign people, and a little later he set out as a missionary to accomplish the task. The people of Rome, who loved him for this goodness and piety, did not want to see him leave and sent a delegation in pursuit of him. He was found already three days' distance from Rome, but having been found, he consented with much personal anguish to return to the monastery.

A short time later, Pope Pelagius II (579–590) abruptly died of the plague, and by acclamation on the same day the people elected Gregory as bishop of Rome. He became Gregory the Great (590–604), one of the most eminent popes in history. But Gregory did not forget his missionary project, and in 595 he sent in his place Augustine (ca. 550–605), accompanied by eleven monks. Augustine was Gregory's successor as abbot of the monastery of Saint Andrew and, according to the pope, he was "filled with the science of the Holy Scriptures." The preceding year the pope had sent the priest Candidus to Marseille to buy young English slaves and to conduct them to the monastery of Lerins in order to train them to be missionaries to their own country.[93] These freed slaves scarcely had the time to acquire much knowledge, but some of them were nevertheless added to Augustine's expedition. On the way they recounted to Augustine horrible stories of the deaths in their country, the ferocity of the Angles, and the atrocities committed by the Saxons. At this Augustine took fright and retraced his steps. On returning to Rome, he beseeched Gregory to send someone else

---

93  With 3,700 monks, Lerins was then at the apogee of its influence.

in his place. The pope cast shame on him and sent him out again, this time with a reinforced troop of about forty monks.

As it turned out, those sent by the pope had nothing to fear when finally, in 597, they disembarked on the Isle of Thanet, separated from the mainland of Kent by the Wantsum Channel. Ethelbert (ca. 560–616), both the Saxon *bretwalda* (high king) and King of Kent, was a pagan who for political reasons had married a Christian princess, Bertha, daughter of the king of Paris, Charibert, himself the grandson of Clovis and Clotilda. On the advice of his wife, Ethelbert welcomed Augustine and his troop of monks. He only agreed, however, to receive them in the open air for fear that they might bewitch him.

The great English historian, Bede the Venerable (673–735), recounted these events a number of years later in *The Ecclesiastical History of England*:

> In this island landed the servant of our Lord, Augustine, and his companions, being, as is reported, nearly forty men. They had, by order of the blessed Pope Gregory, taken interpreters of the nation of the Franks, and sending to Ethelbert, signified that they were come from Rome, and brought a joyful message, which most undoubtedly assured to all that took advantage of it everlasting joys in heaven, and a kingdom that would never end, with the living and true God. The king having heard this, ordered them to stay in that island where they had landed, and that they should be furnished with all necessaries, till he should consider what to do with them. For he had before heard of the Christian religion, having a Christian wife of the royal family of the Franks, called Bertha; whom he had received from her parents, upon condition that she should be permitted to practice her religion with the Bishop Luidhard, who was sent with her to preserve her faith. Some days after, the king came into the island, and sitting in the open air, ordered Augustine and his companions to be brought into his presence. For he had taken precaution that they should not come to him in any house, lest, according to an ancient superstition, if they practiced any magical arts, they might impose upon him, and so get the better of him. But they came furnished with Divine, not with magic virtue, bearing a silver cross for their banner, and the image of our Lord and Savior painted on a board; and singing the litany, they offered up their prayers to the Lord for the eternal salvation both of themselves and of those to whom they were come. When he had sat down, pursuant to the king's commands, and preached to him and his attendants there present, the word of life, the king answered thus: "Your words and promises are very fair, but as they are new to us, and of uncertain import, I cannot approve of them so far as to forsake that which I have so long followed with the whole English nation. But because you are come from far into my kingdom, and, as I conceive, are desirous to import to us those things which you believe to be true, and most beneficial, we will not molest you, but give you favorable entertainment, and take

care to supply you with your necessary sustenance; nor do we forbid you to preach and gain as many as you can to your religion." Accordingly he permitted them to reside in the city of Canterbury, which was the metropolis of all his dominions . . .

There was on the east side of the city, a church dedicated to the honor of St. Martin, built whilst the Romans were still in the island, wherein the queen, who, as has been said before, was a Christian, used to pray. In this they first began to meet, to sing, to pray, to say mass, to preach, and to baptize, till the king, being converted to the faith, allowed them to preach openly, and build or repair churches in all places . . . Greater numbers began daily to flock together to hear the word, and, forsaking their heathen rites, to associate themselves, by believing, to the unity of the church of Christ. Their conversion the king so far encouraged, as that he compelled none to embrace Christianity, but only showed more affection to the believers, as to his fellow citizens in the heavenly kingdom.[94]

Ethelbert received baptism on the day of Pentecost in 597, bringing the majority of his subjects with him into the faith. The south of Great Britain was divided into seven kingdoms. The other Anglo-Saxon kings soon followed his example of conversion to Christianity. In a letter to the pope, Augustine cited works that innumerable missionaries have addressed to their mother churches down through the ages: "The harvest is plentiful but the workers are few" (Luke 10:2). In 601 Augustine received more reinforcements, a contingent of monks directed by Bishop Mellitus. The pope named Augustine archbishop for Britain, but the missionary had died a short time before, in 604 or in 605. He had just created two new bishoprics, one in the north at York and the other in the south at Canterbury—the latter would be the religious capital of England. After the death of Ethelbert in 616, a vigorous pagan reaction forced Mellitus and his colleagues to flee to Gaul.

The directives sent in 601 by Gregory the Great to his missionaries in England do not lack interest from a missiological perspective. They show that the line between a legitimate acculturation and a superficial syncretism is not always easy to draw.

I have reflected for a long time on the case of the Angles. Here is my response: let the smallest number possible of pagan temples be destroyed, but let only the idols they contain be destroyed. Let holy water be sprinkled on them, let altars be constructed and let relics be placed in the buildings, so that, if these temples are well constructed, only their object will be changed, which was the worship of demons, to consecration henceforth to the service of the true God. And from the moment that the people are used to it, when they assemble themselves for their sacrifices of cattle

---

94   J. A. Giles, ed., *Bede's Ecclesiastical History of England: Also the Anglo-Saxon Chronicle* (London: George Bell & Sons, 1903), chapters 25–26, pp. 37–39.

offered to the demons, it seems opportune to organize some cel-
ebrations for the people in compensation. The people will learn
to offer their livestock, not in honor of the idol, but in honor of
God and to feed themselves. When they have eaten and are filled,
they should render thanks to the author of all things. If we authorized these exterior joys for them, they will be better able to find
the way to the true interior joy. It is no doubt impossible to suppress completely all the abuses of these rude hearts. As when one
climbs a high mountain, one does not advance in great strides, but
slowly and surely by small steps.[95]

As for the Celtic churches founded by the Irish monks, they remained separated
for a long time from the Roman missionaries. The pope had given the mission to
Augustine, consecrated as bishop in this instance "to instruct" the abbots of the
great Celtic monasteries; that is to say, to work for their integration into the Roman
ecclesiastical system. But despite several meetings with the abbots, Augustine failed
in this task, and the Celtic church retained its independence.

### Wilfrid and Willibrord

Gregory the Great and his successors understood the importance for the church of
the conquest or the re-conquest of Europe and applied themselves to it. They were
able to use the qualities of the Culdeen monks. Wilfrid (ca. 633–ca. 709), the bishop
of York who was born into a noble family of Northumbria, had himself been influenced by the missionary vision of the Irish monks. The independent spirit of these
monks can be seen in their unique organization. Their church was clearly monastic
in that the bishop was placed under the authority of the abbot, the reverse of that
which prevailed on the continent. The Celtic monks who became missionaries were
itinerant and without ecclesiastical attachments. In fact, the Irish had no centralized
hierarchy. These characteristics were not lightly tolerated by the missionaries sent
by the pope. Wilfrid of York enjoyed an important role at the Council of Whitby in
664, which decided to impose Roman customs and organization on the Celtic monks.

Wilfrid traveled to several places on the continent. First he went to Gaul and then
in 678 to Frisia, which then covered a great part of the northwest of Germany, Holland, and present-day Belgium (at the mouths of the Rhine and the Meuse). Here he
converted several pagan chiefs, notably King Adelgisus I. As the abbot of the monastery
of Ripon at the end of his life, he asked his monks to go to the continent to evangelize
the peoples related to the Saxons of England, a bellicose and brutal people. The best
known among the missionaries who went was Willibrord of Ripon (658–739), who left
in 690 with eleven companions. Pepin of Heristal, the mayor of the palace of Austrasia,
wanted to convert his neighbors, the Frisians, to the gospel. He conferred this mission to Willibrord. With his companions, the missionary encountered great difficulties.
Persevering in the face of hostile pagans, he eventually founded several missionary
monasteries in Frisia. Pope Sergius I (687–702), wanting to grant him full authority

---

95 July 18, 601, in Gregoire, *Lettres*, 6:56.

in this region, ordained him archbishop of the Frisians in 695, with a seat at Utrecht. Willibrord also sought to evangelize Denmark, and King Ongendus received him favorably. He next went to other regions, notably Thuringia (eastern Germany) to which the French protectorate gave him access and where the prince, Heden, was already a Christian. Nevertheless, it does not seem that a true church was founded there in this period. Willibrord died in 739 at the abbey of Epternac in present-day Luxemburg.

In the same period, other missionaries evangelized more southern regions of Germany, Bavaria, and Alamannia—principally Swabia and present-day Alsace. Most of the population was Anglo-Saxon. Though attached to the Roman church, they had managed to inherit the missionary vision of the Irish monks. The missionaries had been preceded in these regions by Fridolin, a Scotsman sometimes called "the apostle of Germany." Coming in the time of Colomban, he founded the monastery of Sackingen and also evangelized several regions of south Germany. From the seventh century the monks of Luxeuil worked in Bavaria. Among them was the Irish Rupert, who died in 715. Another Irishman, the abbot Kilian, consecrated bishop by Pope Conon (686–687), preceded Willibrord to Thuringia and died a martyr there in 689. The most celebrated of these missionaries, if not the best known (for his biography was not fully recorded), is Pirmin, called "the apostle of Alsace." Probably coming from Aquitaine (or possibly from Visigothic Spain), he was also influenced by the Irish. With the support of Charles Martel in 724, he founded the monastery of Reichenau on an island in Lake Constance, which became a great and influential missionary and intellectual center. With the numerous monks that he trained, Pirmin evangelized Germany, establishing well-filled churches that he directed until his death in 753. Some of his disciples founded, sometimes amidst much adversity, monasteries in Bavaria. It was Boniface who reaped the fruit of this work, establishing four bishoprics there on the order of Pope Zachary (742–752).

## Boniface

The most illustrious of the successors of Willibrord was Winfrid of Crediton (ca. 675–754), whose name is sometimes written Wynfrith. He belonged to a noble family of west England. While still young, he entered the monastery of Exeter and later moved to the monastery of Nuthshalling, where he received a good education. He soon became a professor of rhetoric, history, and theology. But Winfrid was a man of action who was not content to live among books. Having a great passion for the adventures of Willibrord, he decided to leave England and travel to Frisia in order to lend his support to what appeared to be an uncertain but potentially fruitful missionary task. On his arrival in Frisia, he found a tense situation: the troops of Charles Martel had just undergone a bitter defeat in their struggle against the Frisians. It became impossible for Winfrid to remain where he was. But instead of returning to England, where it was proposed that he become the abbot of his monastery, he left for Rome to offer his services to the pope. Gregory II (715–731) welcomed him warmly and, after being assured of his unconditional obedience, on May 15, 719 made him a legate to the mission in Germany and gave him the Latin name Boniface. He charged him "to visit the savage peoples of Germany and to determine if their uncultivated hearts, worked by the evangelic plough, would receive the seed of preaching." Sent on his way by the pope, he went first to Thuringia, then learning that the situation had improved in Frisia, went to assist Willibrord. After three years, he journeyed next to Germany to found a monastery. Supported by the pope and aided by Pepin of Heristal, he also sought with the support of the regional councils to reform the corrupt French clergy.

In 734 Boniface began the evangelization of Thuringia, an enterprise that had been undertaken without great success by Amand (see p. 89) and by Willibrord. He dedicated himself to the Hessians, a people who lived in the great forest. He famously struck a great blow there by cutting down with his own hands, with the support of his missionary team, the gigantic oak of Thor at Geismar. This was an unheard-of provocation. But when the tree fell without the ones guilty of sacrilege being struck by lightning, the pagan crowd, overcome by such audacity, cheered the missionary. It was also said by some that the tree fell with the aid of a sudden gust of wind. Planks made from the sacred tree were used to construct a chapel dedicated to Saint Peter. Boniface recruited numerous disciples, establishing, in the fashion of the Culdeens, a network of monasteries in the German forest, notably at Ohrdruf and Fritzlar. This was a very effective means of disseminating the gospel, and soon Thuringia and Hesse were considered to be entirely Christian. It is important to note that Boniface also exerted much effort to suppress the desire for independence among the Irish missionaries who were also in Germany, and he succeeded in linking their churches and monasteries to Rome. A new pope, Gregory III (731–741), named him archbishop of all Germany with the right of oversight over Gaul. Boniface adopted the rule of Saint Benedict for his monasteries but maintained harmony by allowing it only to gradually replace the rule of Colomban. He was a remarkable organizer.

In addition to all the monasteries, in 747 he founded the abbey of Fulda where he decided to retire. He obtained from Pope Stephen II (752–757) an exemption for his abbey from all episcopal jurisdiction as well as permission to name his successor, the Englishman Lull. It was his intention to finish his days in prayer and meditation; however, when he learned that at this moment there were pagan Frisians who were continuing to persecute Christians, he left Fulda and went back up the valley of the Rhine, encouraging Christians along the way and going as far as Utrecht. On June 5, 755, when he had set up his tent on the shore of a river and was teaching young catechumens for confirmation, an armed crowd of pagans assailed them. Boniface refused the offer of anyone to come to his defense: "Do not render evil for evil," he repeated again and again. He placed his head on a large New Testament, and in this position his throat was cut. The bloodstained book of the martyr is preserved in the treasury of Fulda.

Boniface established in Germany a church well organized and closely tied to Rome. Lucien Musset writes of the saint, "It is difficult to form a judgment on a life as varied as that of Boniface. However, if a summary judgment must be given, we volunteer to say that he shone especially in his organizational capacities, neatness of thought, tenacity in execution, political sense, and elevated conception of the role of the Holy See and ecclesiastical discipline. It only remains, in this regard, to evoke the virtues of the apostle, which were also great . . . This opinion, without any doubt, would have discontented the saint: for him the mission was the essential thing; it marked his beginning, it occupied his end. However, during the most brilliant years of his active career, by the force of things it was sometimes relegated to the second rank."[96] One can say of Boniface, not without reason, that he had more influence on the course of continental history than any other Englishman.

A letter written to Boniface by his colleague Daniel of Winchester is revealing of the missionary apologetic of this period. Here are a few extracts in which he gives Boniface his advice on the manner of argument to be used against pagans:

> It is not necessary to directly combat the errors of the pagans or to contest the genealogy of their gods; you must proceed with discreet questions and make them explain their beliefs. First they should be brought to recognize that their gods and goddesses have not always existed, that they were born by generation in the manner of men. And the world, they should be asked, has it existed from all time? If it began, who created it? It was certainly not their gods, for they were not there before the world existed, when they would have had neither a place nor the means to live . . . For what reasons does one worship the gods? The good that one receives, or the eternal felicity? If it is for the goods, may they show us therefore how pagans are better off than Christians! For what reason would the gods take pleasure in sacrifices since they possess all? . . . If they need [the goods of the faithful pagans], why have they not taken them for themselves, and more still? If they do not need them, how can one hope to appease by offering them what they could make for themselves? All this must be shown with meekness and moderation, not in the tone of an impassioned and irritating controversy. From time to time, one can establish a comparison between their superstitions and the truth of our doctrine, but without insistence; the pagans will be more ashamed than irritated and will blush because of their ridiculous superstitions when they see that we know their myths and practices well . . . One must insist on this point that Christians constitute almost all of humanity: why then, in comparison to them, should this small herd of idolaters remain faithful to their ancient error? You should not leave the pagans in the grip of the false idea that the worship of their gods is legitimate because it has existed from all antiquity. Yes, the entire world was delivered to idols until Jesus Christ came to teach the truth.[97]

96 Lucien Musset, "La conversion des Germains," in *Histoire universelle des missions catholiques*, 1:124.

97 Godefroid Kurth, trans.,"Lettre de Daniel de Winchester," in *Saint Boniface* (Paris: Librairie Victor Lecoffre, 1902).

# CHAPTER 5

# *Islam and the Decline of Christianity in the East*

In the seventh century a major event occurred in the East that in several decades erased the missionary work that had been accomplished by the church over several centuries. This was due to the birth of Islam. This is not the place to examine its theology, but we will sketch its rapid and stunning expansion, which can be traced to the *Hijra* in 622 when Muhammad left Mecca to seek refuge with the faithful at Medina.

Born in Mecca about 570 and raised in Arab paganism, Muhammad was in contact with some Eastern Christians since his wife was the niece of a Nestorian priest. But the Christianity that he knew was rather debased and did not satisfy his thirst to know the absolute. He had also encountered Judaism and knew it well, but this too did not fulfill his expectations. It was not until he had a series of visions and revelations that he came to understand that God, the one God, had chosen him to be a prophet. This revelation was recorded in a book, the Qur'an, where elements of the Old Testament and the Gospels can also be found, Jesus being presented as a true prophet. When Muhammad had a conflict with the pagan citizens who wanted to kill him, he had recourse to holy war (*jihad*), which he imposed as a religious duty on his disciples. Muhammad's monotheistic doctrine hinged on the sovereign power and wisdom of God. All is written in advance and the believer must totally submit to the divine will—*Islam* means submission. Such a one is surrendered—*Muslim*—to God. Muhammad taught that Jews and Christians, having a part of the true revelation and adoring the sole God, should be tolerated by the Muslims. His successors, however, were generally less indulgent toward the "the people of the book."

Soon after the death of the prophet in 632, all of Arabia, where the churches had been numerous for centuries, embraced Islam. The Muslim conquest that followed was immense and moved rapidly in all directions.

In 638 Jerusalem was in the hands of the prophet's warriors. In 640 Syria and Palestine were Islamized, and the territories of the Byzantine Empire were reduced to the peninsula of Asia Minor. Jerusalem, Caesarea, and Antioch became Muslim cities. In 642 Alexandria and all of Egypt submitted themselves. Between 646 and 651 Mesopotamia and a considerable part of Persia succumbed.

Then the disciples of Muhammad turned toward the West. They founded Kairouan (in present-day Tunisia) in 670, and installed themselves at Carthage in 697. In 715 the kingdom of North Africa and the Iberian Peninsula were occupied. At the same time, Muslims reached southwest into Asia as far as the Punjab and India.

In less than a hundred years the most prosperous part of ancient Christendom had become Muslim. Christians were only rarely massacred. The conversions to Islam were made *en masse*, without violence. The churches that wanted to remain Christian were most often tolerated, which was the case notably in Egypt and Lebanon. Muslim authorities everywhere exerted over their conquered peoples a social, political, and economic pressure—the latter generally taking the form of heavy taxes. Resistance called for true heroism, but the times of the martyrs had long since past. And so Christianity slowly withered away in the conquered countries.

It is notable, however, that in certain cases Christianity was better able to resist the Islamic wave sweeping through than other religions, such as Zoroastrianism for example, which was held mostly by an elite. In the Near East until the twentieth century, numerous Christian minorities continued to reside, sometimes integrated into the broader community, sometimes grouped in compact blocks, as is the case with the Maronites in the mountains of Lebanon. In Egypt, the Arabs invaded the territory and seized power, without however seeking to eliminate the indigenous church.

As we will see later on (pp. 131–32), the kingdoms of Nubia established farther south, in the valley of the Nile, were Islamized with much greater difficulty. Ethiopia, protected by its mountains, moved its capital to more southern regions and came successfully to resist Islam, despite numerous attempts at penetration.

In North Africa (Maghreb), in contrast, the church receded rapidly. It had had a glorious past there, but it had also been undermined by numerous divisions. It never overcame the Donatist schism of the fourth century. Moreover, it underwent invasion in the fifth century by the Vandals, who drove out the Catholic clergy and replaced it with Arian priests who had no training. Then, in the sixth century, the emperor Justinian imposed the return of the Catholic clergy by force. In the beginning of the Muslim era, Christians preserved the liberty to practice their religion by paying a heavy tax. But being deprived of its priests, the population slowly abandoned this practice, and then Islam was rendered obligatory without risk of a popular uprising. To escape persecution, numerous Christians of Roman origin fled to Europe, while others went to the Atlas Mountains where they evangelized the Berbers. By the year 1053, there remained only five bishops in North Africa. Subsequently, even these were allowed to disappear.

In contrast, the Coptic church's resistance was eloquent of a deeper faith. In Egypt the Bible had been translated very early in the language of the people, which was not the case in Maghreb. Though translated in Latin by the year 200, the Bible had never been written in Berber and was reserved to an elite. The people depended therefore entirely on the teaching of the priests. In eliminating the clergy, the Arabs deprived the church of all the human resources that would have rendered it better able to resist. There is a fundamental missiological lesson here: a church in possession of a Bible translation in the popular language will have a capacity to resist persecution that is infinitely superior to one without. If the church's leaders are neutralized, which is relatively easy to do, believers can nevertheless find spiritual nourishment by themselves. It is not without reason that persecuting authorities, always and everywhere, try to make it impossible to publish and import Bibles!

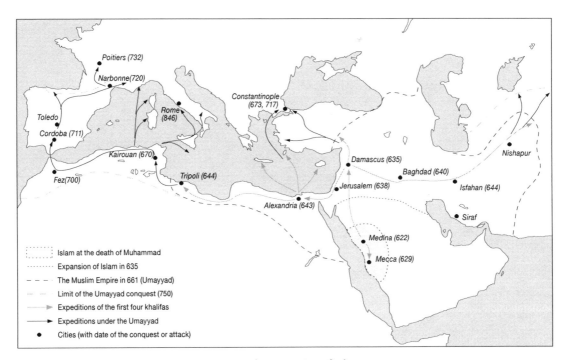

*Map 6: The expansion of Islam*

Although weak at the beginning of the eighth century, the armies of Muhammad seemed ready to conquer Western Europe when they were stopped in 732 between Poitiers and Tours by the army of the French king Charles Martel.

At the end of the eighth century, the church's situation in the world appeared more precarious than at any time since the emperor Diocletian. The Mediterranean, which had for so long been a "Christian sea," had become the domain of Muslim fleets—"Barbary pirates" as they were referred to in subsequent centuries.

The most important consequence of these events was that Christendom for a long time found itself limited to Europe, locked in as it were. Toward the south and east the border of Islam presented a nearly impenetrable barrier. Toward the north and northeast the way was barred by ice or sea.

# *The Last Step in the Expansion of the Church in Europe: From the Ninth to the Tenth Century*

Christendom as it was constituted after the conversion of the emperor Constantine in 312 was, following the Muslim invasion of the seventh and eighth centuries, nearly confined to Europe. However, even in the European continent there remained a vast field of non-Christians to evangelize. To the north and east lived a good part of the Germanic peoples, as well the Scandinavians and Slavs—all as yet untouched by the gospel.

## CHARLEMAGNE

The ninth century opens on the reign of an exceptional man who sought to revive the ruins of the Roman Empire. This was Charlemagne (768–814), a remarkable organizer and a great conqueror. Taking himself to be a new Constantine, he meddled in theological questions, named bishops, convoked synods and councils, was a great protector of popes, and believed it was his duty to convert pagans to the Christian faith. He conquered the countries of the rude Saxons hidden in the deep Germanic forest. He systematically organized conquered countries by establishing in them churches and monasteries, according to the customs and methods of the Culdeen monks. The vanquished, who would throw off the Carolingian yoke if they could, understood very well that for the emperor Christianity was a principal instrument of domination. At the first occasion of revolt, the church was the preferred target of the disaffected, who then always met with a rapid defense of the missionary establishment by the soldiers of Charlemagne. In some ways it is perhaps unjust to disparage the extensive evangelistic efforts of the emperor, but forced conversions such as that of Verden, a Saxon village on the Weser, cannot be forgotten. The victorious emperor assembled the Saxon prisoners on one of the banks of the river and offered them a choice: either they would move toward a group of priests who would baptize them, or toward a group of soldiers who would decapitate them. To convert or to die! The 4,500 Saxon warriors who in 782 preferred death to Christianity showed an admirable courage.

The *Capitulation of Charlemagne* in 785 shows unequivocally that baptism for conquered peoples was an act of political capitulation:

> Whoever shows contempt for Christianity by refusing to respect the holy fast of Lent by eating meat will be punished by death. Whoever delivers to the flames the body of a diseased person, following the pagan rite, will be put to death.
>
> Any nonbaptized Saxon who tries to dissimulate among his compatriots and refuses to have himself baptized will be put to death.

Army-enforced conversions raised numerous protests. The great theologian Alcuin, whose counsel was in general much respected, dared to write to Charlemagne: "You can oblige the pagans to receive baptism, but you cannot cause them by force to take a single step toward the true faith." He flayed those "who are not preachers but deprecators." In a letter dated 795, Alcuin returned to the charge and exhorted Charlemagne to practice more moderation and less superficiality in evangelization:

> May your very wise devotion, so pleasing to God, watch over this young people to provide them with preachers who will be at once honest in their morals, wise in theology, and well learned in the precepts of the gospel . . . It is also necessary to take into consideration, with greater attention, the fact that the work of preaching and baptism must be done methodically so that no one receives the water of holy baptism only on his body, but in his very soul and in a reasoned fashion: in no case must this precede the knowledge of the Catholic religion.[98]

Alcuin also denounced the heavy yoke of taxes that weighed upon the conquered peoples in the name of the Christian faith:

> Ah! If the easy yoke of Christ and his light burden had been preached to the people with as much warmth as the payment of tithes is required and the smallest fault is punished, perhaps the oath of baptism would not be so evaded . . . Did the apostles that Christ taught and sent to preach through the world impose tithes and ask for gifts? Without doubt the tithe is a good thing, but it is better to lose it than lose the faith.

Charlemagne, recognizing the disastrous effect of his coercive measures, convoked an assembly of bishops at Aix-la-Chapelle in 797. A number of new directions were taken there, including the abolition of the regime of terror instituted by the *Capitulation* a dozen years earlier. It was now thought necessary to appease the Saxon populations on most occasions.

When Charlemagne died in 814, the Saxons were pacified and submitted to Christianity. The emperor was then preparing to conquer the Scandinavian peoples, but fortunately the gospel was proclaimed to them by missionaries whose methods were rather different.

---

98  Alcuin, *Lettres*, 110.

# SCANDINAVIA

## Anskar

The first attempts to evangelize Scandinavia are due to Anskar of Corbie (801–864). Born near Amiens, at an early age he entered the celebrated monastery of Corbie in the north of Gaul, where he was an excellent student. He was known for his ability, piety, and goodness. When the abbot created an annex in Saxony, at Corvey, he was sent there as a professor. A short time afterwards, in 826, King Harald Klak, who was reigning over a part of Denmark, sought an alliance with the Franks. As a precondition, Louis the Pious imposed on him Christian baptism, which he accepted and which was administered to him at Mainz. He was asked to return to his country with a chaplain who would instruct him as well as his subjects in the religion that he had adopted. Harald consented to this. However, the Danish people had such a reputation for anti-Christian ferocity that no candidate presented himself to go with the newly converted king! Finally, Anskar accepted this perilous mission, finding to accompany him only a servant in the monastery. During the trip, he won the confidence of the king, and as soon as he arrived in Schleswig, he established a school at Hedeby to instruct adolescents and preach the gospel to them. But the resistance of the pagans was vigorous and obstinate, and in 827 the king had to send the missionary back, having been himself banished because of his faith. His rival, King Haarek, remained very suspicious of, if not hostile to, Christian missionaries.

A little later when Bjorn, a chief of a Swedish tribe, requested a missionary, the emperor sent Anskar to him. The journey, undertaken in 830, was very eventful—the ship being attacked by pirates. Anskar's life was spared, but he was robbed of almost all his baggage. When he finally disembarked in Sweden, he received a warm welcome from King Bjorn and was able to establish himself on the isle of Birka, situated in the great lake Mälar near the present-day city of Stockholm. He discovered in the vicinity several Christian slaves, whom he freed. He founded a school and a chapel, and soon several pagans converted and were baptized.

At that time, Emperor Louis the Pious decided to create a missionary institute at Hamburg for the countries of the north, the direction of which he conferred on Anskar. The latter left the developing work in Sweden to his companion Gautbert and settled himself in Hamburg in 832. Pope Gregory IV (827–844) named him "legate for the Swedes, Slavs, and other races of the north." At Hamburg Anskar constructed a church, library, and schools; and here he trained missionaries for all the countries of Northern Europe. The neighboring pagans were not tolerant of the incursion of evangelists coming from Hamburg, whom they considered—not perhaps without reason—as the agents of the emperor. In 845 a fleet of fast barks carried a troop of very excited Scandinavians who attacked Hamburg, thoroughly destroying Anskar's enterprise.

This was not the first time that missionary work had been obliterated. Anskar sought refuge in Bremen, enduring this period of trial and disaster with serenity.

In the meantime, all the missionaries had been driven out of Sweden. Undaunted, Anskar sent a new team there after a seven-year interruption. Under the direction of Gaubert, the team members again took up the work of evangelization. They found that some Christians had remained faithful and that, among those who had been the bitterest adversaries of the gospel, several had experienced a tragic death. Everything, therefore, was successfully restarted on the isle of Birka.

When the bishopric of Bremen became vacant, King Louis the German, son of Louis the Pious, sought Anskar for the position. The pope made him an archbishop and added to the bishopric the see of Hamburg. Archbishop Anskar was not slow to launch a new effort to evangelize Denmark. He obtained permission to rebuild a church at Hedeby, where the work soon began. He also visited Sweden in 852 and built the first stone church in the country. The results of this enterprise, however, were ephemeral.

The fruit of Anskar's ministry was not statistically impressive. Always hostile to the gospel, paganism had retained the loyalty of the great majority of the population. There were, however, some churches established in several of the northern countries. Anskar himself never renounced his mission and persevered until his death on February 3, 864, at Bremen, where he was buried.

In a world of violence and corruption, Anskar led a life of faith, love, and peace. Never in his missionary career did he have recourse to force. There were times when he had visions, and some said that he was a miracle worker, which he always denied. According to his successor and biographer, Rimbert, when someone once asked him if he had accomplished any miracles, he responded: "If I was worthy of it, I would ask God to accord to me this one miracle, to make me by his grace a good man."

Despite the efforts of Anskar and those who worked with him, the gospel would not be established in these regions for another century and a half. During this period the Scandinavian pirates, or Vikings, would devastate the churches and the monasteries throughout much of Europe. The Scandinavians of Normandy, despite a superficial conversion, remained for a long time attached to the paganism of their ancestors. In 931, at the time of the funeral of Duke Rollo, a Viking prince of Normandy who had been baptized at Rouen in 911, masses were celebrated for the repose of his soul while at the same time the throats of one hundred captives were being cut, according to custom, to appease the ancient divinities.

## Norway

By 933 Norway already had a Christian king, Hakon the Good. But his people refused to follow his religion and remained attached to their traditional gods. The most effective penetration of the gospel into Norway came in a surprising manner.

A Viking pirate, a cruel giant named Olaf Tryggvason, skirted the English coasts. On one of his forays ashore, he encountered a Christian hermit who impressed him by his peace and radiance to such an extent that he lived with the man, adopted his faith, and asked for baptism from the bishop of Winchester. In 995 Tryggvason returned to Norway to claim royal rule over all the country and to establish Christianity. Though he summoned numerous English missionaries, his conversion does not seem to have softened his morals. He soon sacked the pagan temples in his realm and committed other similar enormities. Conquered by the kings of Denmark and Sweden some years later, he threw himself into the sea and perished by drowning rather than surrender. But according to a popular legend, he was saved from drowning and traveled to the Holy Land to finish his life as a hermit.

By about the year 1000, Norway was nominally Christian. Another king continued the work of Christianizing the country but in a fashion less brutal and more profound. This was Olaf Haraldssön, called Olaf the Fat (1014–1030). He surrounded himself with English and German bishops and supported their missionary work. By the end of his life, paganism was in large measure eliminated, but the church was not yet organized. Olaf was killed in combat with pagan princes who had revolted against him. Considered a martyr, he became Saint Olaf. It was only at the end of the century that three stable bishoprics appeared. Some pagan slaves still continued to reside for a long time in some of the more remote regions of the country. Musset concludes, "Christ supplanted the gods of Valhalla; but it still took a long time for the Norwegians to truly accept the Christian idea, and see in him [Christ] a Redemptor more than a triumphant hero over his enemies. The reform of morals began only later, in the twelfth century."[99]

## Denmark

A century after the first attempts made by Anskar, another archbishop of Hamburg—Unni—entered into contact with the Danes and Swedes in 936. The king of Denmark, Harald Gormsson (Harald the Blue Tooth), born in 910, was a former Viking pirate. He had been captured by Emperor Otto I and freed after having taken a vow that he would become a Christian. He was baptized about 960. In the cemetery of what is today the most ancient church in Denmark can be found a great monolith dated 980. It was erected to the memory of his relatives and to the glory of "King Harald, who conquered all of Denmark and Norway and made the Danes Christians."

The adherence of Denmark to Christianity was especially due to King Knut (Canute) the Great. In 1016 his father, king of Denmark, gave him the crown of England, of which he had just taken possession. Knut went to England and converted when he came into contact with his new Christian subjects. He immediately manifested a great zeal for his faith. At the death of his brother in 1018, he also received the crown of Denmark, accompanied by several English missionaries. In 1027 he went to Rome for the crowning of Emperor Conrad II and had a conversation with Pope John XIX. A brilliant Latin culture developed in Denmark, and the country was filled with Benedictine and Cistercian churches and monasteries. When Knut died in 1035, he was reigning over a vast empire that included countries bordering on the North Sea—Denmark, England, and part of Norway. His nephew Sven Estridsen (d. 1074) completed the organization of the church. By 1060 the presence of overtly pagan people in the population could still be seen, but the king refused to convert them by force.

---

99  Musset, "La conversion," 138.

## Iceland

According to one tradition of doubtful historicity, the Irish monk Brendan (d. 577) reached Iceland in the sixth century. More reliable indications suggest that the gospel reached the island no later than the beginning of the eighth century when some Irish hermits came to retire in this savage and little-inhabited country. But the traces of this evangelization were swept away following the landing of Norwegian Vikings, who arrived in several waves beginning in 865.

In 999 the emissaries of the Norwegian Viking king Olaf Tryggvason also carried the Christian faith to this Nordic island. As the population was on the verge of civil war between partisans and adversaries of the new religion, a wise and respected old man was asked to study the entire question, and it was agreed that his decision would be followed. The wise man carefully studied the gospel and arrived at the conclusion that the message would be good for his people. A full assembly of Icelanders, the Althing, decided that henceforth Christianity would be the only authorized religion, and a curious decree was issued: "Everyone will receive baptism and believe in a single God; but one could sacrifice to the gods in secret if one wished it."

Most of the Icelanders accepted baptism without demur. It would still be another fifty years, however, before a church was organized around a bishopric. The Icelander Isleif Gissurarson was consecrated bishop at Bremen in 1056. In the following century, while some pagan customs such as infanticide continued to be more or less tolerated by the local clergy, an active monasticism developed. The first monastery was founded in 1133, and the monks undertook a deeper evangelization of the country than it had yet known. In the religious, social, and intellectual spheres, the monks enjoyed a role in the first rank of the island's population. It should be noted, however, that the Icelandic priests never accepted the rule of celibacy.

## Greenland

The monk Brendan may have reached this immense, icebound island with the gospel as early as the sixth century. It was rediscovered by a Norwegian Viking at the beginning of the tenth century and colonized on its western coast about 985 by the Icelander Erik the Red, who had to leave his country following a murder. Leif Eriksson, the son of Erik the Red, went to Norway and was baptized there a little before the year 1000. He received the mission to evangelize Greenland, but his father refused to convert. His mother, Tjorhilde, however, was baptized and constructed the first church in the country, whose foundations were discovered in 1961.

The Viking colonists quickly embraced Christianity, but it is not known to what extent the indigenous Inuits were reached with the faith. In 1261, there was an episcopal seat at Gardar, of which Bishop Arnal was the first titular.

Subsequently, contact with this not easily accessible country was nonexistent for several centuries, following a cooling of the climate. Nobody knows what became of its church. When Protestant missionaries returned there in the seventeenth and eighteenth centuries, they found no trace of an earlier Christian community.

## Sweden

Despite the efforts of Anskar in the ninth century, Sweden had remained pagan. Under the influence of Denmark, King Olaf Scotkonung converted in 1026 and summoned English missionaries. The population was far from sharing the interest of its king in the gospel, and several missionaries died as martyrs. Olaf failed in his attempt to destroy the temple of Uppsala, the high place of Scandinavian paganism. His successors, also Christians, made attempts in their turn but with little more success. King Inge was actually driven out in 1070 for having been too favorable to the Christian faith. It was only in about the year 1150 that the cause of Christianity was carried in Sweden. This was achieved under King Erik IX, the founder of a new dynasty. He was killed following a conspiracy of pagan rebels, and considered a martyr and saint. In 1287 his remains were transferred to the cathedral of Uppsala, where they were venerated by innumerable pilgrims until the era of the Reformation.

## Finland

Although Finland is not a Scandinavian country, with the exception of a region peopled by the Swedish, it figures here for reasons of geographic proximity.

Its first contacts with the gospel came in the ninth century from missionaries who had come from Hamburg and Bremen. The Christian penetration of the land, however, came belatedly, only really beginning in the twelfth century when the then-Christian Swedish kingdom became keenly interested in taking possession of Finland. In 1155 King Erik IX of Sweden occupied a major part of the country. Following "the crusade of Saint Erik," the inhabitants were asked to accept baptism. Erik allowed the bishop already in place, Henry of Uppsala, to organize the church with its center at Nousiainen. The pagan reaction was fierce, and Henry died a martyr. For a long time the Finnish were not receptive to the gospel, and Christians in the country were largely a minority of those of the Swedish language and race. The first indigenous bishop was Magnus of Abo, who was consecrated in 1291, marking the birth of the Finnish church.

# CENTRAL AND EASTERN EUROPE

The peoples of Central and Eastern Europe, often leading a nomadic life and meddling with each other, comprised a complex mosaic of different ethnic groups. For the most part these consisted of Slavs, but they also incorporated Germans from the west, Scandinavians from the north, and especially Asiatics—such as the Magyars or the Avars—from the east. Tribal groups were made and unmade according to the power of their enterprising chiefs. Their borders fluctuated from generation to generation, and now it is nearly impossible to imagine how they might have been distributed at any one time on a map of Europe. As for evangelization, or rather Christianization, it was done most often by force. A people vanquished by Christian conquerors received baptism as a mark of their submission. Consequently many of the subsequent revolts had an anti-Christian character. Christianization was achieved in successive waves, with the same people being converted many times and with many an ebb after the

Map 7: Christian mission in Central and Eastern Europe in the ninth and tenth centuries

flow. This is why ethnic groups are spoken of here rather than of territories, which were delimited much later. Moreover, many of the texts from this period have been destroyed, and the documents that have survived are rare, fragmentary, and often tendentious. It is only possible, therefore, to give a general view of these events and to locate the major historical landmarks through the centuries.

What further complicates the task is that the church of this period was divided in two, with the territories of Central and Eastern Europe coveted by the Germanic Roman emperors who were supporting the bishop of Rome, and by the emperors of Byzantium who touted the Ecumenical Patriarch of Constantinople. Bitter rivals, they held each other in mutual disdain, and their chroniclers often skewed their stories accordingly.

## The Slavs

The Irish monk Colomban had dreamed of evangelizing the Slavs but had not been able to realize his goal. A half century later, in the course of the seventh century, the first serious attempt was undertaken by the missionary Amand (ca. 590–679) who, by his lifestyle, evangelistic zeal, and intrepidity, distinguished himself in the great line of Irish monks. Born in Vendee, Amand became a monk on the isle of Yeu and then preached at Bourges. At first an itinerant bishop, he next received responsibility for the immense diocese of Tongres and Maastricht, which covered Holland and the German Rhineland. He founded churches in the region of Ghent, Antwerp, and Tournai. Redeeming slaves, he then instructed and ordained them to be priests, estimating their spiritual value to be superior to that of the local clergy. This practice and his personal austerity earned him the hostility of the clergy, and after three years he had to resign. He continued his work farther afield, traveling deeper into Europe in the hope of evangelizing the populations ignorant of the Christian message or recalcitrant to it. He preached the gospel to the Basques, and then went to Thuringia and in the countries of the Danube, and also evangelized the Slovenes and various Slavic tribes, dying in 679 an octogenarian. It is difficult to evaluate to what extent Amand planted the churches in the region of the Danube, for information concerning this area is imprecise and not always reliable. His biography, written a century later, often slipped into hagiography garnished with legends. Here is a brief sample:

> This holy man, having noticed that his sermons produced numerous conversions, was inflamed by a great desire to obtain still more. It is then that he learned of the existence of the Slavs, [a people] greatly given over to error and prisoners in the nets of the devil. His abiding dream was to earn the crown of martyrdom among them. He set out *en route* to find them beyond the Danube [no doubt he passed through Carinthia and Slovenia, on a route then in use among some French traders] and to fearlessly preach the gospel of Christ to them. Few however accepted baptism, and when he understood that he would not find among them the recompense of martyrdom, he returned to his flock.[100]

---

100 P. Duthileul, *L'évangélization des slavs: Cyrille et Méthode* (Tournai, Belgium: Desclée, 1963), 65.

In the following century, Boniface spoke of the Slavs in a letter of 745, but he seems to have thought of them with no more than a vague missionary desire, and perhaps he was even hostile to them. He considered them as entirely pagan and refractory to the gospel. The first movement toward their conversion occurred at the beginning of the ninth century with the conversion in 821 of Slavomir, the chief of the Abodrides tribe. Pope Gregory IV had named Anskar legate for the Swedes and the Slavs but, absorbed by his task in Scandinavia, had not been able to dedicate himself to Eastern Europe.

### The Slovenes

In the case of the Slovenians of Carinthia, with whom Amand seems to have failed, some attempts at evangelization were undertaken by the bishopric of Salzburg. Pepin, the son of Charlemagne, subjugated the Magyars in the region of the present-day southern frontier of Austria. Having come from Central Asia in the middle of the sixth century, this was a pagan tribe that deeply penetrated Europe, going as far as Bavaria and Italy. Charlemagne sent Bishop Arn of Salzburg, one of the great missionary bishops in this period and a friend of the theologian Alcuin. In the first years of the ninth century, Arn preached to the Slovenians, founded churches, and ordained and established Theodoric as their first bishop.

### The Croats

It was in the course of the ninth century that Croat chiefs on the coast of the Adriatic gradually adopted Christianity. But the rivalry between Rome and Byzantium disrupted the mission in these regions, compromising the enterprise and tainting it with violence. Zdeslav, the chief in this region, favored the work of the Greek priests, but he was driven from power by Branimir, who reigned over the country from 879–892. Branimir assured Pope John VIII (872–882) of his faithfulness to the see of Rome (879), and in turn the pope promised this brutal chief the blessing of Rome and victory over his adversaries. The first unified Croat state was founded in 925 by Tomislav, but it maintained its independence for only a century and a half. In 1097 the victory of the Catholic Hungarians put an end to this kingdom. From then on, the Croats were definitively integrated into the Roman Catholic system. The first written works in the Slavonic language undertaken by the population were translations of Latin books, and the Latin alphabet gradually replaced the Glagolitic introduced by the disciples of Methodius (see below).

### The Serbs

The Serbian princes were still pagan at the beginning of the ninth century. The pope of Rome was supposed to have renounced all claims to these regions, and Emperor Basil I of Constantinople (867–886) was threatened at this time by Arab invaders and was therefore occupied in raising an effective resistance to them. Consequently, it was the Bulgarian kings at the end of the ninth century who succeeded in imposing orthodox Christianity on the Serbs.

## Moravia: Cyril and Methodius

While most of the regions of Central and Eastern Europe were in the throes of discord between the pope and the Patriarch of Constantinople, Moravia was an exception. With many difficulties and delays, it was evangelized by two brothers from the East who were also well known in Rome.

These were Constantine (826–869) and Methodius (815–885). The various stories of their lives include some contradictions that are not easy to resolve. They belonged to a noble and senatorial family of Thessalonica in Macedonia. According to some traditions, Constantine was a librarian in Saint Sophia in Constantinople.[101] He refused a high ecclesiastical charge to the court of the patriarch, preferring to teach philosophy in the imperial university. His biography often refers to him as the Philosopher. Then he was made a monk and took the name of Cyril. Other sources claim that after having attempted to evangelize the Arabs, he joined his brother Methodius in a monastery at Mount Olympus. Doubtless, he had earned the reputation of an erudite, energetic, and independent man. His brother Methodius seems to have been marked out by the emperor of Constantinople for a high administrative charge in a Slavonic principality. Here he would have learned the Slavonic language. Later, he retired to the monastery with the simple ideal of living apart from the world and in solitude.

The two brothers were sent to Moravia at the call of Rastislav, prince of the Moravians, who desired the aid of Byzantium to resist an alliance between the Bulgarians and the Franks. At the same time, he asked the Byzantine emperor Michal III for a bishop capable of teaching the faith to the Moravians in their own language:

> Our countrymen have been baptized but we do not have an instructor to preach to us, to teach us, and to explain the holy books to us. We understand neither the Greek nor the Latin language: some instruct us in one fashion, others in another; consequently, we cannot make sense of the holy books or their power. Send us therefore some masters who are capable of explaining to us the holy books in our language and of teaching us the whole truth.

The emperor was anxious to evangelize Moravia and perhaps also to protect his land from the Western church and nations. On receiving this letter, he turned to his philosophers, who gave him this counsel: "There is at Thessalonica a man called Leo; he has some sons who know the Slavonic language well, two sons versed in the sciences and philosophy." The emperor summoned Constantine the Philosopher to say to him: "Have you heard, O philosopher, this word? None other but you can do it. Go with your brother Michal [Methodius] the higoumene.[102] For you are both Salonic and all the Salonicians speak Slavonic well."

---

101 The basilica of Saint Sophia, a Byzantine monument that was constructed in Constantinople by the Emperor Justinian between 532 and 536, was the most imposing religious building in Christendom until the construction of Saint Peter's in Rome. It became a mosque after the conquest of the Ottomans (1453), then a museum following the advent of the secular Republic of Turkey in 1924. In the ninth century, the library of Saint Sophia was one of the greatest in the world.

102 The title given to the superior of an orthodox monastery.

In this way Cyril and Methodius were called to go to Moravia. They arrived there in the spring of 863 and immediately began to translate the Gospels, Acts, and then the entire Bible, as well as some writings of the Fathers and some liturgical texts in Slavon, the language spoken in this period by the Moravians and by many other peoples as well. Even before leaving Constantinople, they had begun to perfect the alphabet that would allow them to translate the language, which until then was unwritten. The writing that they forged was called Glagolitic, and the modern Cyrillic alphabet is a direct descendant from it. Hence, as is true for innumerable languages throughout the world, the first texts written in the Slavonic language were the Gospels.

This translation was a great success. According to the *Life of Constantine*, "Rastislav assembled students for Constantine to instruct. He taught them the morning office . . . the short evening office, and the liturgy of the sacraments. According to the word of the prophet, the ears of the deaf were opened and the dumb began to speak clearly. God rejoiced in it and the Devil was filled with shame." But recourse to the Slavonic language raised the hostility of the German missionaries who claimed to represent Rome and the Latin language. They were opposed to the translation of the Scriptures and the liturgy of the Mass into the local language, for this was done nowhere else in the West. Cyril and Methodius, however, had prudently adopted the rite of the Roman Mass and not that of Eastern Orthodoxy, which they were accustomed to use. But their adversaries argued, "No people have the right to have their own language used for religious purposes. Rather, everyone must use Hebrew, Greek or Latin. The proof of this is Pilate's writing on the cross of the Lord."[103]

Due to these difficulties, after four years of ministry Cyril and Methodius went to Rome to ask for the support of the pope. There they encountered the "trilingual heresy," propounded by those who insisted that the word of God and the praise given in worship could only be worthy of God if they were said in Hebrew, Greek, or Latin. Pope Adrian II (867–872) received the two missionary brothers with all honors and ruled that they were right. He had the Mass celebrated in the Slavonic language in the principal basilicas of Rome and even agreed to consecrate to the priesthood the Slavonic disciples of Cyril and Methodius who had accompanied them. This concession was no doubt inspired by the desire above all to retain the Moravian church in the bosom of Rome. Better to pay the price of a "liturgical breach" than, by a strict adherence to principle, to throw the Moravians into the outstretched arms of the Patriarch of Constantinople.

Exhausted by his travels and struggles, Cyril died in Rome in February 869 and was interred in the church of Saint Clement. He was only forty-two years old and had served for years in Moravia.

According to the last desires of Cyril, Methodius departed alone for Moravia to complete his translation. Adrian II conferred on him the title of apostolic legate for all the Slavonic nations. When the pope died in 872, the German missionaries seized the opportunity to impose Latin. The new pope, John VIII (872–882), at first

---

103 The quotations are from the *Chronicle of Nestor* and date from the ninth century.

pursued the same policy as his predecessor, and he was irritated to learn that the Germans had actually dared to imprison Methodius despite his title of legate. The pope required that he be released and named him bishop of Sirmium, an area near Lake Balaton in Pannonia.

*In the church of Tyn at Prague a statue of Cyril and Methodius,*
*evangelists of the Slavonic peoples in the ninth century*
*and translators of the Bible in the Slavonic language.*

Being however subjected to various pressures, John VIII subsequently changed his mind and wrote to Methodius:

> It has been said to us that you sing the Mass in the barbarian language, that is to say in the Slavonic language, while we have already forbidden you in our letter, which was carried to you by Paul, Bishop of Ancone, to celebrate the solemnities of the holy Mass in this language. You can do it only in the Latin or Greek language, as do all the churches of God spread throughout the entire world and among all the nations. However, it is permitted to you to preach and to address the people in this language, since the apostle, with the psalmist, invites all people to praise God, in saying: "May all tongues proclaim that Jesus Christ is Lord, to the glory of God the father."[104]

Methodius then had to return to Rome to plead his case. The obvious spiritual ascendancy that Methodius had over his opponents and the art that he presented from the Moravian church so impressed this rather fickle pope that, accepting the arguments of Methodius, in 880 he declared himself convinced of his orthodoxy. Here is the letter that John VIII wrote to Duke Sventapluc to give his approval to the translation that Cyril had completed:

> We have questioned Methodius, our venerable archbishop whose case has been submitted to us by our brothers the bishops . . .
> We have judged that he was successfully defending the Catholic

doctrines and usages. We sent him out again, therefore, so that he can continue to govern our church, and you will receive him as your legitimate pastor with the honors and respect that are due to him. We entirely approve what the philosopher Constantine [Cyril] has written in Slavonic to the praise of God, and we order that the words and the works of our Lord Jesus Christ be proclaimed in this language; for it is not in three languages, but in all the languages that the holy authority directs us to praise the Lord, since it is written: "All nations praise the Lord, people, give all praise to him," since the apostles, filled with the Holy Spirit, spoke in languages by a prodigy of God and Saint Paul sounded the celestial trumpet "that all languages proclaim to the glory of God that Jesus Christ is Lord." There is nothing opposing you, therefore, in using the Slavonic language to sing the Mass, read the divine Scriptures in the Old and the New Testament, carefully translated, sing the hours and other offices.[105]

Methodius then traveled to Constantinople where he was received with the greatest honors by the emperor and the patriarch. Despite the still-brewing hostility to him in Moravia, he returned there to pursue his ministry. At the time of his death five year later, the new pope, Stephen V (885–891), under heavy German influence, reversed the authorization of his predecessor in these terms:

Methodius brought to his listeners not edification but superstition, not peace but polemics . . . The celebration of the divine offices . . . that Methodius was claiming to do in the Slavonic language has not been authorized by anyone . . . In the name of God and our apostolic authority, we forbid, consequently, under pain of anathema, except however for the simple souls who will not otherwise understand, that the gospel and the texts of the apostles be proclaimed in this Slavonic language by cultured people.

The German clergy had henceforth free hands: the two hundred priests and deacons who had been trained by Cyril and Methodius were imprisoned, while others who were younger were sold to the Jewish slave merchants. Fortunately a high Byzantine government official redeemed them, and they went to Bulgaria as refugees. It is there that the heritage of Cyril and Methodius was preserved, and from Bulgaria the Cyrillic alphabet passed to Serbia and Russia.

## Bohemia

Borivoj, the first Christian duke of Bohemia, was converted and baptized with his wife by Methodius in 874. At first he was driven out by his subjects because of his faith but later was reinstated. He died about the year 910. After the brief reign of his son, Vratislav I, Borivoj's grandson Wenceslaus (Vaclav) became king. Born in 907, he was too young to rule, and so the land was governed under the regency of the old king's widow, Ludmilla, who was very pious. Ludmilla was raised in the Christian faith, but

---

105 John VIII, *Letters*, no. 225, June 880.

her daughter-in-law Drahormira was very hostile to Christianity and brought about her assassination. She also sought to deprive Wenceslaus of the crown for the benefit of the second son, Boleslaus, who was a pagan. She ordered the expulsion of all the Christian priests and missionaries.

Wenceslaus, however, eventually acceded to the throne to which he had a right and organized the evangelization of his country. He summoned more priests into the country and built numerous churches, notably in his capital, Prague. Accused of selling his country to the German missionaries, he had to confront violent opposition directed by his brother Boleslaus, who organized a conspiracy. On September 28, 929, Boleslaus murdered his brother the king as he was leaving a church after Mass. Wenceslaus had thrown away his sword, saying: "A Christian should not commit fratricide," and he died while asking God to forgive his brother. He was only twenty-two years old. The population was indignant and began to organize pilgrimages to the tomb of the murdered king, whom they considered to be a martyr. Miracles were produced, and Wenceslaus was soon embraced as the patron saint of Bohemia. Although Boleslaus I was an anti-Christian and bloody king, his son, Boleslaus II, was called the Pious. He favored the foundation of bishoprics and monasteries while assuring the freedom of the country from Germany interference.

## Bulgaria

The Bulgarians, established in the Balkans, originated from Turco-Mongolian stock and were by the ninth century a mixture of Slavonic ethnic groups. For a long time they were the terror of Constantinople and remained impervious to the gospel until the day in 854 when their king, Boris I, was baptized. This baptism was a sign of capitulation following the nation's military defeat by the Byzantine emperor. Despite strong resistance, he urged his people to follow his example. Nevertheless, he dreaded having to depend on the Patriarch of Constantinople, who was himself a plaything in the hands of the Eastern emperor. He made several attempts to reattach himself to Rome, but without success. In 870 the Bulgarian church finally organized itself under the authority of Constantinople. A little later, the disciples of Methodius arrived, having been expelled from Moravia. They contributed to the strengthening of the Christian faith among the Bulgarians, as we have seen above.

When, in the last years of the ninth century, the Bulgarians inflicted a defeat on the Serbs, the emperor Basil I required that the vanquished receive baptism and submit to the patriarch of the East. Subsequently, the kings of Bulgaria also sent missionaries to Dacia of present-day Romania.

## Romania

The Dacians had been Romanized following the conquest of the emperor Trajan at the beginning of the second century of the Christian era. Christianity penetrated the country in the course of the third century, but the successive waves of barbarian invasions to which this region was particularly exposed swept all this away. Later Dacia was absorbed by the Bulgarian empire and integrated into and took on the appearance of Byzantine Christianity. By the end of the ninth century, Bulgarian missionaries had securely planted a church that celebrated the Mass according to the Slavonic liturgy. Transylvania, being occupied for a time in the tenth century by the Hungarians and then in the following century by the Saxons, was partially under the influence of Roman Catholicism. In the fifteenth century, the invasion and the occupation of the country by the Ottomans of the Muslim religion contributed to the unification of the church, the strengthening of a Romanian Christian identity, and the reattachment of the churches to Eastern Orthodoxy.

## Hungary

Christianity arrived in Pannonia in the era when the armies of the Roman Empire were stationed along the Danube, but this Christian presence crumbled to dust under the bludgeoning of successive barbarian invasions. The Magyars of Asiatic origin, who definitively settled themselves in this territory, were a mixture of Slavonic peoples and the survivors of the preceding invasions in this region of the middle Danube. Between 906 and 910, they destroyed a part of Moravia. Constantine VII, Byzantine emperor from 912–959, inflicted a severe defeat on the Magyar troops directed by Prince Gyula, who reigned over a part of southeast Hungary. Though baptized by force after his defeat in about the year 950, Gyula became a fervent Christian. He gave his daughter Adelaide in marriage to Duke Geza (972–997), another Magyar prince reigning in the west of the country.

Hence Geza, under at least some Christian influence, sought to impose his dominion on all the people living in the plains of the Danube and to unify them. As each ethnic group had its own hierarchical structure, there were regular confrontations, and the enterprise was fraught with difficulty. To achieve his goal, Geza needed to assure his security from external threats. To this end he decided to seek a rapprochement with Western Christianity, asking the emperor of Germany, Otto I, to send him evangelists. Bruno, a monk of the monastery of Saint Gall, was consecrated a bishop and arrived with a group of priests to establish a church in Hungary. Bishop Adalbert of Prague, a pious and zealous man, devoted himself to the evangelization of Hungary, as he had done for Poland. Geza received baptism and wished for the conversion of his people to Christianity.

After Geza's death, his son Vajk (or Waik) was baptized under the Christian name of Stephen (997–1038) and pursued the same end. He aided the work of the priests and abandoned the use of violence to unify his people. Because the church ignored social and racial differences, he believed that it alone was capable of supplanting bloodlines and tribal structures and of knitting together the diverse populations under his rule. He crushed several revolts and enlarged his kingdom. He obtained from Pope Sylvester II (999–1003) the ruling that the Hungarian church would come directly under the authority of Rome without the intermediary of an archbishop of the empire. In the year 1000, he also received from this pope the title of "Apostolic King." Stephen died in 1038 and became Saint Stephen, patron saint of Hungary.

## Poland

In the middle of the tenth century a vast grouping of Slavonic peoples in the east of Germany came under the direction of Mieszko, an energetic chief who had converted to Christianity after his marriage to the sister of the prince of Bohemia, Boleslaus the Pious. He was baptized in 966. For him, Christianity also acted as a cement between tribes difficult to unify. He established in 968 the first bishopric at Poznan, his capital. His successor secured a Polish church independent of the empire and placed under the direct jurisdiction of Rome, which avoided the ascendancy of a German mission that would have constituted a threat to the independence of the country.

More than a hundred years later in 1079, the bishop of Cracow, Stanislaus, was strangled during Mass by King Boleslaw II of Poland. The bishop had reproached the king for his life of violence and debauchery. Because of the general indignation against the murdering of a bishop, the king went into exile, dying two years later.

Poland endured a tortured history in the centuries that followed, but through it all the church was a major source of cohesion for the nation.

## Russia

In the east of Europe, in the great plains that are watered by the immense Dnieper, Don, and Volga rivers, Slavonic and Asiatic tribes had settled. Scandinavians, the Vikings, came from the north and created vast kingdoms and then merged into the mass of the population to form the Russian people. Their principal centers were Novgorod to the north, and Kiev to the south. The princess Olga, of Scandinavian origin, acceded to the throne of Kiev in 945 when her husband was assassinated. She governed with a mailed fist, but under the influence of a Greek priest at Kiev, she began to manifest an interest in Christianity. In 957 she went to Constantinople and was dazzled by Byzantine civilization. She converted and received baptism under the name of Helene. On returning to Russia, she attempted to send for Greek missionaries, but her son, Sviatoslav, who had since acceded to the throne, would not hear of it. Hostile to missionaries, especially Byzantine rather than German missionaries, he set in motion a violent anti-Christian reaction and came close to converting to Islam.

On the death of Sviatoslav in 978, his son Vladimir seized power at Kiev after having conquered and killed his elder brother. Some sources claim that under the influence of his grandmother, the princess Olga, he had been baptized at the age of thirteen, but this seems doubtful. Cruel and debauched, he lived in a manner resolutely pagan. According to the *Chronicle of Nestor* that was composed in the following century, he had more than five wives, "three hundred concubines at Vychegorod, three hundred at Bialogorod, two hundred at Bieriestovo . . . Insatiable of debauchery, he seduced married women and violated young girls."

Vladimir calculated, however, that paganism was a primitive and outdated religion, and that it would be better to opt for a more highly evolved religion. Hesitating between the available choices, he sent delegates to all the neighboring countries to investigate their religious practices. Neither Judaism nor Islam, whose worship services were judged too bare, gained their approval. Similarly, in Germany they found that the ceremonies of the Western church lacked luster. In contrast, Vladimir's ambassadors enthused about the worship services celebrated at the basilica of Saint Sophia in Constantinople: "We did not know if we were in heaven or on the earth. One cannot find greater splendor in all the earth, and it would be in vain to try to describe it . . . but we know that it is there that God lives with men. We could never forget such beauty!" According to this legend—written evidently by a Byzantine monk—Vladimir opted for the Byzantine form of worship. He was encouraged in this by his boyars who reminded him that his grandmother, renowned for her wisdom, had already accepted Byzantine Christianity.

He married Anna, the daughter of the emperor of Constantinople, who had followed him to Kiev against her will. To console her, the chronicler recounted that Vladimir sent away his five wives and his eight hundred concubines and showed thenceforth a great zeal for the Christian religion. Anna had come with icons and relics and was accompanied by a dozen ecclesiastical dignitaries who were to undertake the mission of converting the country. Vladimir was baptized at this time, though, as noted earlier, some claim that he had already been baptized as an adolescent at the instigation of the princess Olga, and others place his first baptism in the period of his youth when he was under the influence of his friend the king of Norway, Olaf Tryggvason. Vladimir's nobles followed him into the waters of Dnieper for baptism, the pagan idols in Kiev were destroyed, and baptism was imposed on the general population in 988—what is termed as "the Baptism of Russia." These facts are reported in the *Chronicle of Nestor* in a clearly embellished fashion:

> Vladimir saw that the following announcement was spread throughout the entire city: "Whoever is not found to be on the riverside tomorrow, rich or poor, wretched or artisan, will be my enemy." In hearing these words, the people came with jubilation . . . The next day, Vladimir went with the priests of the Empress Anna onto the shores of the Dnieper, and innumerable people assembled themselves. They descended into the water, some went as far as the neck, others as far as the chest . . . others were carrying their children, and the priests began saying the prayers. And there was joy in heaven and on earth to see so many souls saved. The prince ordered that churches be built in places where formerly there were idols. And he began to establish priests in all the cities and to bring the people to baptism in all the cities and the villages. Then he sought out all the children of the families with the aim of having them instructed in the [holy] books.

Christianity spread rapidly in its Byzantine form in the kingdom of Kiev and in the neighboring kingdoms. Vladimir piteously repressed a pagan revolt in the principality of Novgorod. The Russian church was soon independent but for centuries remained closely tied to Constantinople. The Christian influence remained superficial, and pagan beliefs and practices—founded on the worship of nature—mixed with it to form a decidedly debased Russian Christianity. The Christian identity, however, was reinforced in the thirteenth century by the reaction against the Mongol occupiers who were of the Muslim religion.

### Lithuania

The Baltic countries were first "evangelized" by the Danes, who led three military campaigns against them between 1197 and 1219 in an attempt to dislodge paganism. In the end, however, it was ecclesiastics from Germany who succeeded in planting the church in Estonia.

The last European country to adopt Christianity was Lithuania, the southernmost Baltic country. After various unfruitful attempts at evangelization, a church was planted there following the baptism of King Jagiello in 1386. Searching for an ally against Teutonic invaders, he had sought out the Polish, who promised him their aid under conditions that included his marriage to a Polish princess and his Christian baptism.

Hence the central and eastern parts of Northern Europe were Christianized. However, paganism continued to exist there even into the thirteenth century, though mostly in isolated places such as in the central mountains and along the shores of the Baltic Sea. Moreover, adherence to Christianity remained, on the whole, superficial.

## AN EVALUATION OF THE EVANGELIZATION OF EUROPE

After the barbarian invasions, the church had to begin by reconquering lost ground in a difficult *milieu*. There was instability due to tribal struggles, migration of populations, destruction of communications, brigandage, poverty, and cultural decline. The Catholic clergy, too small in numbers, often very ignorant, and weakened by their struggle against Arianism, was scarcely capable of carrying the gospel to the general population, still less of evangelizing the vast pagan groups in the less accessible regions of the continent. It was the missionary monks who undertook this task.

The evangelization of Northern and Eastern Europe took many centuries after that of Mediterranean Europe. A city like Cologne on the shores of the Rhine was reached for the first time before the year 200, thanks to the presence of Roman troops and administration. In contrast, the German forests or Frisia that lay some hundreds of kilometers from there had to wait another five centuries before the gospel could be proclaimed there for the first time.

In general Europe was a very arid, hostile field to the Christian faith. The missionaries were exposed to violent resistance by the pagan religions. Later, notably under Charlemagne, political and patriotic opposition often united together to reject the Christian religion, rendering the struggle for the gospel even more difficult. The confusion between the throne and the altar often led to annexations to the empire in the name of the gospel, which was consistent neither with the spirit of the missionaries nor the strategy of those who sent them. Naturally, the pagan tribes, fiercely jealous of their independence, often perceived the Christian religion as an enemy to be resisted.

Regarding the conversion of the German and Nordic peoples, Lucien Musset writes: "How can we not be struck by the diversity of the means of approach employed: by simple, commercial contact to military submission; by a variety of evangelistic methods, graduating from individual persuasion to collective baptism under pain of death; and finally by the many-colored character of the missionary personnel who included people from all over the West, the Irish, Spanish, Saxons, and Danish?"[106] Few of the established plans for evangelization, at least before Charlemagne, insisted on a uniform strategy; rather, the missionaries practiced a tenacious patience that was flexible enough to profit from all occasions, to adapt to all problems."[107]

In general the Christianization of the north and east of Europe was accomplished by force. Sometimes the religion was forced upon a people following the conversion of a king whose motivations were often foreign to the faith. At other times Christian baptism was imposed to gain allegiance to the conqueror. For the most part, people remained ignorant of the liberating message of Jesus Christ. The European church suffered from this unfortunate history of Christianization, and no doubt it continues to some degree to suffer from its consequences.

Some missionaries tolerated syncretism while others destroyed temples and sacred trees to manifest the victory of the Christian God over the ancient, local divinities. Intrepid and dedicated evangelists—monks like Martin and Patrick, Colomba and Colomban, Boniface, Amand, Anskar, Cyril, and Methodius—are the figures who give honor to the history of the church. Regrettably too many of their well-intentioned biographers have drowned the facts in a murky swamp of legends. These not only limit the value of their writings but unnecessarily complicate access to the simple, historical truth, which alone would have sufficed for our edification. Others among these missionary monks, whether known or anonymous, have accomplished their tasks with zeal, discipline, and a spirit of sacrifice. No doubt their example would better merit our attention if their stories could be retrieved from the omissions of history that have engulfed them.

In conclusion, here is a representative summary of the Christian teaching that was propagated by the evangelists of this period. Despite the presence of elements of fundamental doctrine, the message of salvation by the grace of God alone is, unfortunately, singularly absent. These lines are taken from a letter from the theologian Alcuin to Charlemagne:

> It is necessary first of all to instruct a man in the immortality of the soul, the future life, the judgment for good or evil actions, and the eternity of this judgment. Next he must be taught that he will suffer for his crimes and sins an eternal chastisement in company with the devil; but that by his good actions, he will enjoy eternal glory in the company of Christ. Then he must be carefully taught of the belief in the Holy Trinity and the coming for the salvation of every type of human of our Lord Jesus Christ, Son of God, shown in this manner: mystery of his passion; truth of his resurrection;

---

106 At the end of the eleventh century, even Monophysite Armenian bishops were evangelizing!
107 Lucien Musset, "La conversion," 111.

glory of his ascension into the heavens; his future coming to judge all the nations; resurrection of our hearts; eternity of chastisement for the evil and recompense for the good. Hence, as we have already said, the soul of the neophyte would be assured. In this fashion, a man who will have been fortified in this way will be ready to receive baptism.

# CHAPTER 7

# The Churches of the East and West Confronted by Islam

A s soon as the movement created by Muhammad weakened due to internal divisions, the churches of the East and West reacted energetically to force a Muslim retreat.

The Byzantine Empire, which was the most exposed, from the end of the tenth century and during the eleventh century had taken back Celica and even Syria from the Abbasids. Aleppo and Antioch also came back under Christian authority. In 975 the emperor John I retook Damascus, Nazareth, and Caesarea. These victories, however, were ephemeral, for at the end of the eleventh century the Seljuq Turks took the place of the Abbasids and pushed the Byzantines farther back from their former frontiers in Asia Minor.

As for the Christians of the West, in the eighth century they stopped the Muslim advance into France and pushed them back beyond the Pyrenees. In 801 Charlemagne retook Barcelona. The *Reconquista* ("Reconquest") of the Iberian Peninsula began in the ninth century. The caliphate of Cordoba was retaken in 1236, and all of northern Spain was soon reoccupied by Christian princes. The armies of the king of Catalan drove the Muslims out of the Balearic Islands between 1229 and 1232. The caliphate of Granada, the last Muslim bastion in Spain, capitulated only in 1492.

The Normans reconquered Sicily between 1061 and 1091, but the most important Western Christian enterprise against the Muslims was, no doubt, that of the Crusades.

## THE CRUSADES

Not to be confused in any way as missionary efforts, the goal of the Crusades (1095–1272) was to open the way to the Holy Land for Western pilgrims who in this period attached hitherto unheard-of merits to the work that they sought to accomplish. The Crusades were not a response to the Abbasid lords, who had never closed the pilgrim trail to Christians, but to the less tolerant Seljuq Turks when they forbade the free movement of pilgrims in their territories.

Historians generally count eight principal crusades, all of which differed from one another. The first was proclaimed by Pope Urban II (1088–1099) and preached by

Peter the Hermit, an enthusiastic monk. A wave of fanatic mysticism swept through the entire West, particularly through France and Italy. To the cry of "God wants it," disparate crowds assembled. Among the Crusaders were found noble lords, bold knights, skillful artisans, and humble peasants who were abandoning their women and children, castles, and fields "to liberate the tomb of Christ" from the hands of infidels. For most of those who departed on the first expedition of this Crusade, it was a horrible tragedy. Many perished *en route*, for few had foreseen how to feed and care for such large numbers of people.

The second expedition of the first Crusade that left in 1096 was more carefully prepared militarily. It was principally formed of Norman troops, and, after a famous siege, took possession of Jerusalem in 1099. A Christian kingdom was founded there that continued for a century. The old Christian cities of Antioch and Edessa were also retaken. But as with those that followed, this expedition scarcely led to more than the establishment of isolated fortresses, none of which had the ability to capture and hold extended territories.

The following Crusades, whose causes were not all religious, never managed to reconquer the Holy Land. The fourth was preached by Foulque of Neuilly (1202–1204), who saw his plans go completely away. Under pressure from the Venetians, the Crusade ended with the sack of Constantinople by Western Christians and the establishment of the Latin Empire there that endured from 1204–1261. This rendered seemingly irreversible the separation between Rome and the churches of the East, which had occurred a century and a half before in 1054.

The Crusades, which in their own time were a huge waste of human life, had considerable long-term consequences. They contributed greatly to the weakening of the Byzantine Empire, the rampart of Christendom against Islam; and Constantinople fell in 1453 under the bludgeoning of the Ottoman Turks and became a Muslim city. Moreover, for a long time the Crusades intensified the hostility of Islam *vis-à-vis* Christianity, and all subsequent missionary efforts among Muslims have been tainted by its memory.

## CHRISTIANS DISCOVER ISLAM: BIRTH OF A MISSIONARY CONSCIENCE

The Crusades nevertheless allowed Western intellectuals the opportunity to better understand Muslim civilization, which in many respects surpassed their own at that time. Moreover, the total sterility of these enterprises as missionary endeavors permitted some minds to grasp that violence could not produce true conversions. Hence the Franciscan Englishman Roger Bacon (ca. 1220–ca. 1294), the "Admirable Doctor," who lived in a time when the obvious failure of the Crusades called for a reassessment of their value, denounced the folly of a Christian movement that sought to massacre infidels rather than preach the gospel to them. According to Bacon, the failure of Christianity was in its abandonment of the apostolic objective of the primitive church and its desire to dominate people rather than to convert them to Christ. The sole means of enlarging the kingdom of God, he said, is the preaching of the word of

God. And the church has divested itself of this task, for no one is constrained to study the languages and beliefs of the people that need to be reached.

In the centuries that preceded the Crusades and certainly in response to the Crusades themselves, some theologians began to move toward a true definition of mission.

### John of Damascus

The first Christian author to seriously engage in controversy with Islam lived several centuries before the Crusades. This was the great Eastern theologian John of Damascus (ca. 650–ca. 749). Comparing the biblical stories in their versions as presented in the Qur'an, notably those that concerned the patriarchs, Jesus, and Mary, he was anxious to class Islam among the heresies, seeing it as close to Arianism. According to John, the doctrine of Muhammad was only a deviation from true Christian doctrine. He sought therefore to argue with Muslims on the basis of the Scriptures, placing the dogma of the Trinity at the center of the debate.

### Peter Alphonse

The Jewish convert Peter Alphonse (d. 1110) did pioneer work in putting at the disposal of Western theologians important information about Islam. Writing a little after the Fourth Crusade, between 1106 and 1110, he produced a *Dialogue* against his former coreligionists, the Jews. This work also included an important chapter dedicated to the beliefs of Muslims, and the text was disseminated throughout Europe.

### Peter the Venerable

At the time of the Crusades, Peter the Venerable (1092–1156) inquired into the weakness of the Christian response to Islam. As a member of the great abbey of Cluny since 1122, he translated the Qur'an in order to be able to refute it by reasonable arguments, and his translation would be in use until the seventeenth century. He attempted to show the things common to Islam and Christianity, notably the references in the Qur'an to the Jewish law, Gospel narratives, and the person of Jesus. He did not undertake, he said, a crusade by armies but, with reason and love, by the word. In a letter to Bernard of Clairvaux written in 1143, he ardently pleaded for the church to be fully engaged in better knowing Islam in order to be able to understand its errors.

> If a man can be found who has decided to write against this heresy, and who has the ability to do it, it is necessary that he know the enemy that he is going to combat . . . Until now, not only has no one responded to this heresy that, more than any other, has led to the eternal loss of the bodies and souls of a great part of the human race, but no one has been anxious to research or study that part of the world from whence this pestilent doctrine has come. This is the reason why I, Peter, humble abbot of the Holy Church of Cluny, when I was sojourning in Spain to visit the monasteries of our order that are found there, translated from Arabic

to Latin, at the price of much pain and expense, all the impious doctrines and the execrable life of its founder. I have laid it open to us in this way so that we will know in what points this heresy is suspect and ridiculous, and for the benefit of whatever servant of God, led by the Holy Spirit, undertakes to refute it in writing. As few are found, alas! in these times of tepidness, who will interest themselves in this type of study, I have promised to put myself to the task with the aid of God, but I would have preferred that this be done by one better than I.[108]

Peter the Venerable described Muslims here as heretics rather than as followers of another religion. Following the example of John of Damascus, he perceived the similarities between the doctrines of Islam and the heresies that arose in the first centuries of the church. But subsequently, faced with the refusal of Muslims to have any positive contact with the Christian community or to accept the sacraments instituted in the gospel, he would consider them as pagans: "May one give to the Mohammedan error the shameful name of heresy or, more infamously, the name of paganism. It is necessary to act against it; that is to say, to write."

He spoke later of a "mortal poison that has infested half of the globe." Whatever the good intentions of Peter the Venerable, the terms with which he explained his approach to Muslims reflect the aggressive contempt that characterized the attitude of the church toward Islam throughout the Middle Ages. However, Peter the Venerable was a pioneer figure in Muslim-Christian dialogue, for he managed to present Islam in a manner that demonstrates remarkable insight. Here is something like a confession of faith that he put in the mouth of a Muslim:

> We imagine nothing about God, and we conjecture nothing. What we think, what we profess, is not according to illusions coming from our body, but according to what was transmitted to us by Muhammad, our prophet, sent by God. He is the last of the prophets, the bearer of the divine law, not its author; he is not God, but the one he has sent. He received the heavenly precepts that were given to him by God through the intermediary Gabriel in their integrity, nothing more, nothing less; and what he received, he transmitted to us fathers to observe it. And it is this that we observe, that we conserve, this to which we have pledged our souls, our bodies, our lives, and our deaths.

## Raymond of Pennafort

A century later, the Dominican Raymond of Pennafort (1180–1275) wanted to train monks to be capable of engaging in discussion with Muslims. A contemporary of Francis of Assisi and professor at Bologna, he opened centers of study (language schools) in Tunis (1250), Barcelona, and Murcie (1265). As a missionary in Spain, he worked

---

108 Victor Segesvary, "L'Islam et la Réforme: L'age d'homme" (Doctoral dissertation in theology, University of Geneva, 1977), 169.

among Muslims and Jews. Repudiating recourse to the use of force, he pleaded for tolerance and the use "of reasonable arguments" alone to bring about conversions. "Enslavement to force does not please God," he wrote.

## Humbert of Romans

Other Dominicans in the thirteenth century also developed approaches to Islam. Humbert of Romans, master general of the Dominican order and fourth successor to Dominic, studied missionary methods and elaborated a program for Muslim evangelization. In his treatise *Charges of the Order* (1255), he made clear that the task of a master general is

> to show a special concern and ardor for the barbarian people, for pagans, Saracens,[109] Jews, heretics, schismatics and others who are out of the church . . . He should be ready to treat the various errors competently. He should desire that some of the brothers be capable of applying themselves to learn Arabic, Hebrew, Greek, and the barbarous languages . . . For this ministry, he must be there to encourage the brothers and designate . . . not just anyone among them, but only those who have a burning desire within them and, moreover, are adept at these various tasks.

## Thomas Aquinas

In composing the *Summa contra gentiles* and the *Arguments of Faith Against the Saracens, Greeks and Armenians*, Thomas Aquinas (1225–1274) attempted to respond to this need. As a believer in "just war" doctrine, he approved the Crusades against the Muslims. But he refused to see war as a means to convert them to Christianity. In effect, "the infidels, like the pagans and the Jews who have never received the faith, should not under any circumstances be constrained to accept the faith and to become members of the church, for belief must follow from the will."

## William of Tripoli

Having lived for a long time in the Holy Land, William of Tripoli (b. 1220) developed a syncretistic position regarding Muslim evangelism. In one chapter of his treatise titled "The State of the Saracens," he writes: "Here one witnesses that wise Muslims are very close to the Christian faith." He further explained:

> One can demonstrate that what the Saracens believe in their hearts is true: they declare as received from the mouth of God the words contained in the Qur'an and which concern the glory and praises owed to Jesus Christ, his doctrine and his holy gospel, the blessed Virgin Mary, his mother, and all those who imitate Jesus and believe in him. Although their faith contains many concealed falsehoods and numerous fictions, it appears in a fashion evincing

---

109 During the Middle Ages, Westerners commonly used the term "Saracens" to speak of the followers of Islam.

that they are close to the Christian faith and are verging on the way of salvation.[110]

William of Tripoli, therefore, strove to underscore the similarities between biblical and qur'anic teachings, hoping in this manner to facilitate a return to the bosom of the church by the followers of Muhammad. For he was convinced that before the arrival of Islam, Arabia was Christian. He counseled missionaries to learn the languages, avoid public controversies, refuse to seek to become martyrs by useless provocations, know Islam well, and cite the Qur'an.

He practiced this himself, preaching in Arabic, quoting the Qur'an and citing the Arabic commentaries on the Qur'an that he knew perfectly. He claimed to have administered baptism to one thousand Muslims—people he considered "truly spiritual, simple in heart, who were not allowed to take part in learned discussion, and who lived unharmed by any military pressure." Most of these converts were living in the Crusader states.

## Ricaldo da Monte de Croce

Ricaldo (Pennini) da Monte de Croce (1243–1320), a Dominican brother of Florence, dedicated himself to the study of the Qur'an in order to detect its contradictions. His book *Confutatio Alcorani* (*Refutation of the Qur'an*) was widely read throughout Europe over several centuries and available in Greek, Latin, and Spanish versions. In 1542 Martin Luther published a German translation in Wittenberg (see p. 200). Luther, however, held certain reservations about the objectivity of the text:

> One can clearly see that the author, with every good intention, wanted to show Christians the horrors of Muhammad so that they would live in the true faith in Christ. The fact that he has extracted from the Qur'an those things that are the most shameful and ghastly in order to make the Turks detestable and odious in the eyes of all the world, and that he has passed over in silence the several virtues that they posses (in appearance at least), engenders suspicion and casts discredit on the writing . . . For if someone only reproaches and attacks his enemy for his obvious faults and passes over the rest in silence, he makes himself suspect and seems to be prejudiced in his own cause. In effect, it is easy to refute what is obviously contrary to honor, virtue, and nature; such repugnant things denounce themselves. But the one who can fight and refute what in appearance seems of holiness and virtue . . . can demonstrate [that such things in fact] are scandalous, false, and contradict God and the truth, there is someone who is salutary and worthy of combat.[111]

For many years Ricaldo's *Refutation of the Qur'an* was the basis for much of the Christian polemic against Islam. Ricaldo also wrote a *Small Treatise for the Nations of*

---

110  Cited in Segesvary, "L'Islam," 54.
111  Ibid., 178.

*the East*, in which he described Buddhism, among other religions. Intended as a *vade mecum* ("handbook") for missionaries, he advised them not to allow themselves to become involved in polemics with the Jacobite Christians and the Nestorians of the East; and he encouraged them to master the Scriptures and to thoroughly learn the local language so as not to need an interpreter. In 1288 he left for the Holy Land and then sojourned for a long time in Baghdad among the Muslims.

In contrast to Raymond Lull (see below), he did not seek to explain rationally the Christian doctrines of the Trinity and the Incarnation but, rather, to expose the errors and contradictions of the Qur'an in order to show that it is unworthy to be held as the word of God. He also compared the violence of the Islamic law to the mildness of evangelical teaching. On the other hand, he conceded to his adversaries the seriousness with which Muslims practiced their strict morality, the probity of their public behavior, and especially their legendary hospitality that he cited as an example to Christians.

# TWO PRECURSORS

## *Raymond Lull*

In this troubled period, an exceptional man turned his efforts toward redefining mission in an evangelical sense: Raymond Lull (ca. 1233–1316). As the only son of a great Catalan lord, he hardly seemed destined to perform this task. He was born in Majorca, three or four years after the principal island of the Balearic Islands had been retaken from the Saracens. He served as a page to James I the Conqueror (1208–1276), king of Aragon. Then he became *seneschal* (servant) to James' son. Raised among the nobility of the period, he learned the knightly rules, trained for a career in arms, and mastered the life of a courtesan. But his more-than-common intelligence and universal interests protected him from the worst of the frivolities of court life. Poet and musician, he was at the center of every feast and festival, in which he took great pleasure.

One night when he was thirty-two years old and had a wife and children, he was composing a love song for a new lady that occupied his imagination. Then suddenly he had a vision of Christ on the cross. He attempted to forget this unfortunate incident, but when he took up his poem, a new vision, as incongruous as the first, came to trouble him. He refused to linger over it, but the vision kept coming back. No longer able to endure this trial, he prayed to God to reveal to him the meaning of the visions. After a period of agonized seeking, Lull understood that God was calling him to his service and that he must renounce his ambitions and his life as a man of the court. He immediately discerned that the nature of his service would be to work for the conversion of Muslims.

This objective became at once the *raison d'être* of his life. As he put it: "No one can render to Christ a greater or better service than to give his life and honor to him by going to convert the Saracens to the worship and service of the true God."

His vocation immediately took the form of a three-point program:

1. Agreeing to preach Christ even at the price of his life.

2. Composing a book in which clear arguments would be formed to persuade the infidels.
3. Securing the creation of monasteries and schools where Arabic would be taught so that the truth could be communicated to Muslims in their own language by those striving to lead them to conversion.

Lull decided to prepare in earnest for his mission by learning the Arabic language and by studying the Qur'an, as well as philosophy, logic, and theology. He sold most of his immense properties, reserving only what was necessary for his wife and children, whom he commended to the grace of God. To learn Arabic, he bought a Muslim slave and plunged himself into the study of the Qur'an and Islamic commentators and theologians. One day, nine years later, he was speaking of Christ to his slave when the unfortunate man allowed a blasphemy to escape from his lips. Lull was furious and slapped him. The Muslim then grasped a dagger and struck his master, giving him a serious wound. Lull had the man locked up, but the slave soon committed suicide. Humiliated by his recourse to violence, Lull asked forgiveness from God.

During these years Lull managed to master the Arabic language as well as Islamic philosophy and theology. At the same time he had also studied scholastic theology and philosophy, writing several works in which he presented a logical method to convince infidels of the truth of the Christian religion.

About the year 1275 King James of Majorca, accepting the advice of his childhood friend, Raymond Lull, founded the college of the Holy Trinity at Miramar. This was to be a school for language study and the training of missionary monks who were seeking to prepare themselves to present the gospel to Muslims. Lull taught Arabic there for a time, but he had difficulty recruiting students. Only the Franciscans showed interest in the project. In the same period, he wrote *Ars Major*, a book of apologetics that presented Christian doctrine in a rational, nearly mathematical, fashion that Lull considered "irrefutable."

With this work he rose to the challenge issued by Arab philosophers who claimed to have founded their religion on reason. They said to Christians, "If you claim that the law of the Christ is true and that of Muhammad is false, you must be able to prove it by compelling reasons." Lull placed the dogma of the Trinity at the center of his argument, expressing his conviction that the Christian doctrines of the Trinity and the Incarnation better safeguard the unity of God than qur'anic teaching. He also believed that Islamic doctrines placed the Muslims closer to Christ than the believers of any other religion, even Judaism. For this reason he believed that their conversions were possible, as long as God would "soften their hearts."

Lull went to the University of Paris, then shining with an unparalleled brilliance. He studied and taught there, as well as wrote new works on various subjects. Considered today as one of the great promoters of the knowledge of oriental languages in the West, in 1285 he succeeded in founding a school of oriental languages in Paris for which scholarships would be available to students. He sought to meet the pope to present his work to him and to ask him to encourage the training of missionaries for Muslim countries. Pope Honorius IV (1285–1287) appeared to be open to the project and agreed to meet with Lull, but just when he arrived in Rome, he learned that the pontiff had died. The cardinals at that time were no help, being immersed in the subtleties and intrigues of a papal election. Nicolas IV (1288–1292), the new pope, was not as interested in the project as his predecessor and only distractedly listened to the Catalan knight. This failure did not discourage Lull, who began to travel throughout Europe to sensitize the universities to the need to study oriental languages for the purposes of evangelization.

Among his writings of this period is the *Treatise on the Manner of Converting the Infidels* (1292), in which he advocated that centers for study of religions and sects be founded. Three centuries later this treatise inspired Ignatius Loyola, the founder of the Jesuit order, who read several of Lull's works during the time of retreat that followed his conversion. In this text, Lull wrote:

> First of all, a list of the different sects in the world that are opposed to the Catholic faith should be drawn up and those interested should apply themselves to numerous studies in order to learn the language of the infidels. Such work will be confided only to holy and pious men, ready to die for Christ, learned in philosophy and theology, of well-ruled morals.
>
> Next, they should be observed preaching and discussing among the infidels. May their polemic brandish necessary reasons, compelling arguments, and it will be the means to drive the infidels back and refute their objections—and also reinforce the doctrines and retorts of the faithful. These elements of argumentation are scattered in the pages of the Holy Scripture and among many wise authors; capable men must compose treatises based on these types of arguments and translate them into various languages, so that the infidels can study them and become aware of their errors.[112]

His pleas encountered little response from the king of France, Philip the Fair, who had other projects to consider besides that of a pacific mission to the Muslims. In the face of the indifference of churchmen and princes, Lull decided himself to depart for the Islamic world.

At sixty years of age in 1292, he was an old man in the eyes of his contemporaries. Nevertheless, he decided to go to Tunis, the capital of the Muslim West where Italian merchants had established trade relations. When he arrived at Genoa, he took passage on a ship due to leave and sent his bags aboard. According to what are probably autobiographical stories of his life, he suddenly became aware as he was preparing to depart of the folly of the enterprise, and panic seized him. As the sailors were weighing anchor, Lull ordered that his things be sent ashore, and then he disembarked as well, "overwhelmed with terror at the thought of what could happen to him in the country where he was supposed to go. The idea of suffering torture or life imprisonment presented itself to him with such force that he

---

112 Cited in Ramon Sugranyes de Franch, "Raymond Lulle: Docteur des missions," Supplementa 5, (Schoneck-Beckenrid, Suisse: Nouvelle Revue de science missionaire, 1954).

had difficulty controlling his emotions." What humiliation for so proud a man! But in his shame he mastered himself and overcame his weakness. No longer doubting the need for this mission, he took another Genoa ship and arrived in Tunis without incident.

He presented himself openly to the scholars of the city and proposed to them, as though he were in a Western university, a learned dispute. He added that he would convert to Islam if anyone could prove the truth of the Qur'an to him. The encounter took place, and never had Muslim intellectuals and teachers seen such a phenomenon: a *roumi* (foreigner) speaking Arabic perfectly, knowing the Qur'an and the great thinkers of Islam! Lull presented his famous "logical" argument to them: the attributes of Allah are unbalanced, for he lacks love in himself and the possibility to confer it to others.

The dispute ended badly. The scholars, who had only thought to make a fool of an uncultured old man, were astonished, and for the most part furious. Someone spoke of killing him, but others risked themselves in his defense. The sultan imprisoned him and eventually decided to expel him. Lull succeeded in escaping in a ship that had been forced to put in to shore and had remained clandestinely in Tunis for several weeks. He also made contact with several persons who wanted to convert. Finally, he set sail for Naples where he sojourned for a time and continued to write. Then he returned to the Eternal City. The new pope, Boniface VIII (1294–1303), had a reputation for being energetic, but he did not take the time to listen to Lull. Instead, Lull used the two years that he stayed in Rome to write numerous books and treatises.

The next period of his life, 1298–1305, was dedicated to many voyages. Lull went to Genoa; to Majorca; to Paris where he thought and continued to write; and to Montpellier, which at this period belonged to the king of Aragon, to study medicine, among other things. He also seems to have traveled in this time to Cyprus and Syria in order to better understand the Eastern church that lived in the midst of Islam.

In 1305 when he was seventy-three years old, the indefatigable Lull decided to return to North Africa. He chose Bugia, an important center in Algeria. Having barely landed, he went to a place swarming with people and wrote in Arabic: "The law of the Christians is holy, true, and pleasing to God. That of Muhammad is false and deceptive." The crowd fell on him to put him to death, but others snatched him away from the enraged people who wanted to tear him apart and brought him before the chief of the city. As a philosopher himself, the chief discussed many things with this prodigious scholar who knew Islamic thought so well. Lull was locked up in prison for six months, but he received numerous visits and used the time to write treatises in Arabic. Some attempted to convert him with many promises, but it was Lull who succeeded in converting several of his visitors. Finally, he was expelled. Suffering a shipwreck on his return, Lull succeeded in saving himself by swimming to shore on the coast near Pisa, but he lost all his manuscripts in the venture.

He then traveled to Avignon where the new French pope Clement V was to be found. But Clement turned a deaf hear to all his discourses. Then, in the period of 1309–1311, he sojourned in Paris, teaching at the university where he was recognized as one of the great teachers of the century. Learning of the convocation of a council at Vienna, not far from Avignon, he decided to go. Before the fathers of the council, he pleaded his cause, laying bare to them the need of the church for missionary training colleges. The council, which met in 1311 and 1312, was especially preoccupied with the condemnation of the Knights Templar. The church leaders, however, decided to respond to Lull's entreaties, creating chairs of Eastern languages in the great universities of Paris, Bologna, Oxford, and Salamanca. Lull also advocated, though without success, that a cardinal be put in charge of the missionary policy of the papacy. It was the Council of Trent (1545–1564) that finally took up this project, deciding to create the Congregation for the Propagation of the Faith that was to be directed by a cardinal. However these plans were not actually realized until 1622—three centuries after Lull had first advanced the idea.

A discouraged Lull returned to Majorca where he wrote several more works. In 1313 he drew up his last will and testament, being now eighty years old. When he learned that the king of Majorca had put his signature to a treaty with the sultan of Tunis, Lull determined to seize the opportunity. He left in 1314 for Bugia via Tunis. This time he hid himself among Italian merchants while he met secretly with sympathetic Muslim scholars. But this clandestine existence was not endurable. After several months in hiding, he went out in broad daylight to preach the gospel in the streets. The crowd immediately seized him, stoned him, and left him for dead. The merchants took up his body and carried it to a boat leaving for Spain. At the beginning of the year 1316, Raymond Lull died in view of his island home.

The missionary method advocated by Lull was remarkable. He was convinced that the conversion of infidels should be a work of love. "The preaching of the gospel," he often repeated, "is a work of love accomplished by understanding." He also said, "May all Christians who truly love Christ go before him . . . to love him, to adore him, and to contemplate him so that he will be honored in the entire world . . . Let us be the artisans of concord and love."

It follows that missionaries must first take seriously the people to whom they speak, respecting them and passionately seeking to understand them. To convince people, it is first necessary to understand their beliefs as precisely as possible. To the scientific study of religions, he would add the need to learn a people's morals, philosophy, and current intellectual fashions in order to evangelize them. Lull is incontestably the first to have understood that a knowledge of ethnology is an indispensable aspect of missionary training.

This vision guided him in developing a practical approach to Muslims. He saw in the Muslims to whom he spoke a religiosity that knew nothing of mystery. Believing that it was essential to fight them on their own ground, Lull adopted their methods of thought that consisted of supporting religious beliefs by rational arguments. In this respect, Sugranyes de Franch writes that Lull wanted "to rise to the challenge of Islamic scholars. Is Muslim theology seeking for demonstrable proofs? He would furnish them; he would support Christian dogma with proofs that its opponents could not reasonably reject. At the least, such was his intention."[113] Yet it is also important to note that for Lull God's love and transcendence were beyond human arguments. Consequently, his writings include an astonishing mixture of rational and mystical arguments.

Armed with these insights, Lull sought out Islamic scholars. He wanted to arrange public debates with them over doctrinal controversies, hoping that these would take place in an atmosphere of peace and mutual respect, for he was convinced of the sterility of acerbic polemics.

Some have incorrectly written that Lull preached in favor of the Crusades. Yet in one of his best-known books, *Blanquerna*, he attacked the Crusades on a spiritual level, comparing them to Muhammad's concept of holy war. Moreover, he deduced from the Crusaders' repeated failures to secure the Holy Land that God did not approve of these expeditions.

On the other hand, some of his works present the utopian vision of a City of God absorbing the city of men, and, in this universalist vein, he reasoned that the pope might rightly ask the secular princes to use force. This would not be to compel Muslims to receive baptism, but to open the door to allow Christian preaching and to impose tolerance on Islam. He dreamed of an armed international force that, having no territorial goal, would endeavor to establish religious liberty as a human right. Still, he never advocated anything but a "spiritual crusade." In this he was a follower of Francis of Assisi, whose disciple he was without becoming a Franciscan. According to Lull, conversion is a free act. There is no equivocation in his understanding of the missionary call: "Missionaries will convert the world by preaching, but also by shedding their tears and spilling their blood, by pain and effort, and even by a painful death."

Raymond Lull, not happy simply to teach others, lived the message that he proclaimed.

He left a considerable body of literary work. There are currently 247 of his authenticated works, and some are voluminous! He dealt with all subjects: from philosophy to grammar, from military art to chemistry. It was even said that he had discovered the secret of the philosopher's stone![114] He is considered to be the first and one of the greatest Catalan poets. The church, which is always suspicious of the ferment of original ideas and suspects heresy everywhere, has not canonized him. But all the same, it has recognized him as "Doctor Illuminatus." Circumstances did not permit him to create a body of work that would have an enduring impact on the church, nor was he able to accomplish a missionary work of much scope on Islamic soil. However, he can be seen as a visionary and a precursor of modern mission.

---

113 Ramon Sugranyes de Franch: "Raymond Lulle: Ses idées missionnaires," in *Histoire universelle des missions catholiques*, vol. 1 (Paris: Librairie Grund, 1956), 217.

114 Some works of Lull have been edited recently in French. We point out notably: Armand Llinarès, trans., "Principes et questions of théologie," in *Sagesses chrétiennes* (Paris: Cerf, 1989) and Armand Llinarès, trans., "L'art bref," in *Sagesses chrétiennes* (Paris: Cerf, 1991).

One of his biographers has written: "The idea of a return to early Christianity and to the evangelistic methods of the apostolic church is always present in the spirit of Raymond Lull."

De Franch concludes his story in these terms: "The call of Raymond to missionary activity was addressed to minds not yet ripe to receive it. But no good seed is lost in the storehouse of the church. What Raymond Lull planted and watered with his tears and blood would flourish splendidly several centuries later."[115]

## John Wycliffe

Before we close this section dedicated to the Middle Ages' diverse Christian perspectives on the world of Islam, it is apropos to mention the original perspective of a great English theologian, the eminent precursor of the Reformers, John Wycliffe (1320–1384). He read the Qur'an and, possessing a profound understanding of the teachings of the prophet Muhammad, developed an approach to Islam that was totally different from that of the medieval polemists. In comparing Christianity and Islam, he concluded that in practice the two religions are identical. They both give witness to humanity's insatiable pride, cupidity, and thirst for power. The dignitaries of the church have not behaved otherwise than Muhammad, seeking in the Bible only what justifies their desire for domination, pleasure, and glory. In contrast to a true evangelical church, Wycliffe saw that the prelates of the Catholic Church differed very little from their Muslim counterparts. The Crusades sprang from the same source from which Islam emerged: faith in the power of violence rather than in the way of the cross. Preaching and missionary work would accomplish nothing until the church reformed itself from the inside. The only way to conquer the religion of Muhammad, he believed, would be to change radically the conditions that originally brought it about. The church, which had turned away from Jesus Christ, must turn once again to him. The Reformers would adopt a view very similar to that of Wycliffe.

# THE MISSIONARY COMMITMENT
# OF NEW MONASTIC ORDERS

From the fourth century, monasticism constituted the most effective means of evangelization. This can be seen notably in the work of Martin of Tours and the Culdeen and Benedictine missionaries. Originally each community obeyed the rules of its founder, but then a uniform system slowly became fixed in the West. In general the monks obeyed the rule of Benedict of Nursia (ca. 490–547), who was seen by the church of the Middle Ages as an ideal Christian. As Europe became increasingly Christianized, the missionary role of the monks became less distinct, and they dedicated themselves to the internal problems of the church. Despite successive reforms, the monasteries had the tendency to modernize and enrich themselves, allowing the glowing lights of their founders to flicker and grow dim.

At the dawn of the thirteenth century, two new monastic orders were founded almost simultaneously: the Dominicans and the Franciscans. Their vocation was to

---

115 Sugranyes de Franch, "Ses idées missionnaires,'" 220.

work outside of the ecclesiastical institutions, and they had considerable importance in the history of evangelization and mission, as we will now see.

## The Dominicans

The Order of the Preaching Friars was founded at Toulouse in 1215 by a Spanish monk, Dominic Guzman (1170–1221). It was originally established to fight a crusade against the Albigensians by making the doctrine of the church better known to the people and by struggling against the heresy by combating ignorance. The Dominicans, often denigrated as the agents of coercion in matters of the faith, have nonetheless produced some great preachers. And they are frequently encountered in the history of Catholic missions.

Several among them have already been mentioned in regard to the controversy with Islam, in which they are more often distinguished by their scholarship and writings than by their actual activity in the field (see pp. 106ff). In later centuries, they can be found among the all-too-rare opponents of the plundering and massacre of the American Indians (see chapter 10).

In 1300 the Dominicans founded the "Society of friars living on foreign soil in the midst of pagans in the name and in the cause of Christ." It was, before the term was coined, the first "missionary society" in history.

## The Franciscans

Founded in 1209 by Francis of Assisi (1182–1226), the Order of Friars Minor was from the first the Catholic organization most directly oriented towards mission.

Francis was a part of the gilded youth of the city of Assisi, a center of commerce and prosperity in the heart of Italy. The son of a rich merchant, he was a carefree youth living in luxury; but then following a vision, he underwent a radical conversion. Having rediscovered the gospel, he sold all his possessions to distribute them to the poor and began to preach in the streets and public places. He had great success and immediately attracted numerous disciples to himself.

The clergy were at first concerned about his simple preaching. Who, after all, was this layman to address the people about the things of God? He was denounced as a heretic. Indeed, Francis was not a theologian, but his sole objective was to express his joy in knowing the love of Christ. When the pope summoned him to examine his doctrine, Francis showed so much humility and obedience that the pontiff approved his work, on condition that it remained submitted to the authority of the church. Francis organized his movement as a monastic order. He gave his disciples the name *Fratres Minores* ("Little Brothers"); and taking literally the words of Jesus reported in the Gospel of Luke (10:4) —"Do not take a purse or bag or sandals" —he launched an exceptional campaign of conquest. Without purse, sack, or sandals, and clothed in simple, gray robes with a cord for a belt, the Franciscans assumed the appearance of mendicants (beggars) and set out to preach the gospel to all Italy.

Francis quickly understood that the joy of the gospel was for all people, even Muslims and pagans. Hence he decided to join the fifth Crusade, that of John of Brienne, which left in 1217. He embarked June 24, 1219, at Ancone to join the Crusaders in Egypt.

According to one story, when he landed near Damiette on the Nile delta, Francis—without arms—advanced before the Muslim army, crying: "Soldan, Soldan!"[Francis' foreign pronunciation of "sultan."] The sentinels concluded that he wanted to see the sultan, Malek al-Kamil. He was conducted to his presence, and Francis preached the gospel to him with vigor. The Muslim was impressed by the courage of the radiant mendicant and by his energetic refusal of all the gifts that he offered to him "to try to weaken his soul with the riches of the world," as one of his biographers expressed it. He graciously returned the gifts, saying, "Pray God that he reveal to me the religion that is pleasing to him." The sultan gave him a safe-conduct to circulate freely in Muslim territory. This pacific mission, however, does not seem to have made any further advance.

Five of his friars had a tragic experience. In 1218 they were ready to evangelize the Muslims of southern Spain, who, at that time, were tolerating the presence of Christian minorities in their territory. Having scarcely arrived in Seville, the five Franciscans immediately began to preach the gospel by attacking Muhammad and Islam. They were arrested and brought before the local emir, who treated them with relative indulgence in releasing them and ordering them to remain calm and not to provoke anyone. Ignoring these orders, the brothers took up again the task of energetic street preaching. They were then arrested and expelled. The five missionaries next traveled to Morocco where they demonstrated a similar audacity. After several incidents, this time they were condemned to death by a horrible manner of execution. "When they refused to abjure," according to a Franciscan chronicle, "the king, mad with anger, took a sword and cut open the heads of the saints one after another, striking them in the forehead. He plunged the two-edged sword three times into each of their brains; hence by his own hand putting them to death with the cruelty of a wild beast."

In 1221 Francis added these words to his rule:

> If a brother, inspired by God, desires to go to the territory of the Muslims or other unbelievers, may he have permission for it . . . and may all the brothers, without exception, recall that they have given themselves and their persons as gifts to our Lord Jesus Christ, for which they must expose themselves to the blows of their enemies, visible and invisible.

The *Legenda antiqua* cites these same directives in greater detail:

> The brothers who, for the love of Christ, go in mission to the unbelievers can behave themselves in regard to them in two ways. The one consists of not discussing the faith in words with these unbelievers but of humbly showing them that they have submitted themselves to all creatures for the love of God, and by attesting as well that they are Christians. The other way is this: when the brothers perceive that this is pleasing to God, they may announce the divine word to the unbelievers, engage them to believe in the Holy Trinity, and baptize them so that they become Christians. But it is always necessary that the brothers remember that they have

abandoned their bodies to our Lord Jesus Christ and that, despite love for their bodies, they must keep themselves ready to give them up to adversaries, visible and invisible.

A desire for missionary activity was never absent from the Franciscan spirit. They were the only ones to encourage Raymond Lull and were among the first to travel through Central Asia. Still today, the Franciscans are present all over the world.

# CHAPTER 8

# The Extension of the Church beyond Europe (400–1450)

## CHRISTIANITY IN ASIA

### Armenia

We have already noted that Armenia adopted Christianity as its official religion in the year 301 (see pp. 24–25). After this event, Gregory the Illuminator returned to Caesarea in Cappadocia to be consecrated catholicos of Armenia.[116] He died in 326.

In the following century Mesrop Mashdotz, or Mashtots (361–440), a teacher and bishop in the Armenian church, was the instrument of a great revival in this otherwise superficially Christianized country. In his youth, Mesrop was at the same time a military chief and an impressively cultivated man of letters who knew the Greek, Persian, and Assyrian languages. He became the first minister, but as his interest in spiritual things grew, he asked to be ordained a priest. He became a hermit, and when a number of disciples joined him, he sent them to evangelize the population whose faith had been decided by a royal decree a century before and had since become mixed with paganism. He founded a school of theology where numerous students received training. Observing the great ignorance of his people, he translated the Bible into the Armenian language between 406 and 410. The language not yet being reduced to writing, he first had to create an alphabet for it. He next established schools to teach literacy. Mesrop's work, accomplished in collaboration with the catholicos Sahag, produced a great revival in the land. Hymns were sung and psalms read in every house and even in public places and in the streets. The faith produced an extraordinary joy and effervescence among a population profoundly moved by it.

Mesrop's translation of the Bible was a literary masterpiece and a decisive step forward in the creation of an Armenian cultural identity. Subsequently Armenia experienced a difficult history. Though attacked by neighboring powers, it remained faithful to its religion. The Armenian church, which had not accepted the Christological formulations of the Council of Chalcedon in 451, separated itself from Byzantium in 506 and

---

116 The term *catholicos* is used in certain Eastern churches to designate a leader whose functions correspond to those of bishop in the Western church.

thenceforth preserved its independence, becoming the Armenian Apostolic Church. Together with the Coptics and Ethiopians, it is ranked in the camp of the Monophysites.

*This statue in Erevan honors the memory of Bishop Mesrop Mashdotz (361–440), who created the Armenian alphabet and fixed the language in writing through his translation of the Bible. His ministry was also instrumental in bringing about a great spiritual revival in Armenia in the first half of the fifth century.*

Mesrop also participated in the translation of the Bible in Albania and Georgia. In the Caucasus region neighboring Armenia, Georgia had been evangelized in the preceding century by the Christian prisoner Saint Nina, and the churches of these two countries subsequently maintained close ties.

## Persia

Despite the opposition of the Zoroastrian clergy and the persecution that Christians endured beginning in the fourth century (see pp. 22ff), churches multiplied all over Persia. It is estimated that by the year 400 a quarter of the population of the Persian kingdom had adopted Christianity. The churches were geographically and politically distant from Rome and Constantinople, and this distance also became theological. Some churches leaned toward Monophysitism but most toward Nestorianism.[117]

The Nestorians, disciples of the fifth-century bishop Nestorius, reacted strongly against the cult of Mary and the orthodox belief that she is the "Mother of God" (*theotokos*). They believed, instead, that Jesus had two inseparable but distinct natures and that Mary was the mother of only his human nature.

Condemned by the Council of Ephesus in 431, Nestorius fled to Egypt and lived there secretly and in poverty. His disciples, pursued for heresy, also had in their turn to leave the Roman Empire. Many of them became refugees in Persia where they were active during the second half of the fifth century. In 495 they divided the country into seven metropolitan provinces. These were placed under the supervision of a catholicos whose seat would be established in Baghdad in 775.

---

117  For Monophysitism see p. 50, n. 67.

## Nestorian Missions in Asia

From Persia, the Nestorian missionaries traveled throughout all Asia.

In 345 a group of four hundred Nestorians, led by Bishop Thomas Cana, left Persia because of persecution and settled in India on the west coast of Malabar. They found Christian communities already established there. Also in this period, the Indian Ocean island of Socotra, which today is in the possession of Yemen, became Christian. It remained so for one thousand years.

About the year 450, numerous Nestorians evangelized Arabia and the countries of the Persian Gulf. There were at least six Nestorian bishoprics in Arabia, all under the authority of a metropolitan. Muhammad's wife Khadijah was the niece of a Nestorian priest, and there were numerous Christians in Arabia until the Muslim conquest.

In 520 the Nestorian Christians established several churches on the island of Ceylon (Sri Lanka), but it was especially to the north of Persia that they made progress. Beginning around the year 500, Turkish tribes began to turn to the gospel. The Huns, for example, became Christians in great numbers and even established an archbishop in 549.

It is known, from the rare documents that have survived, that in the seventh century a veritable missionary explosion occurred. The evangelization of the Turks of Central Asia was pursued with remarkable results. Great lords converted, and the churches multiplied. In the course of the same century, the Nestorians planted a church as far away as China, of which we will speak next.

## China

After an eclipse of four centuries, the Chinese empire experienced a renaissance with the advent of the T'ang dynasty (618–907). The empire then revived its relations with the West, notably by way of the Silk Road to the north of the Himalayas. Western explorers, merchants, and diplomats traveled along this long and perilous route through the high mountains and steps of Central Asia to Chang'An (present-day Xian), capital of the T'ang dynasty.

The Nestorian missionaries used the same route. The first to do so was a Syrian named Alopen, who reached Chang'An in 635. This is an established fact, thanks to an astonishing monolith erected in 781—the Nestorian monument at Hsianfu, sometimes called the "Nestorian Stele." It was found in 1625 by the Jesuits in the garden of a monastery. The monument, a granite paving stone of about three meters in height, is engraved with two thousand Chinese characters and topped with an effigy of a cross. Its title announces its purpose: "Monument commemorating the propagation of the illustrious empire of Ta Ts'in' [Syria]." It was erected to celebrate the generosity of the Christian Nestorian who came from Bactria, a region to the north of present-day Afghanistan, to reside at Chang'An. He gave considerable gifts to the poor, monasteries, and churches.

In speaking of this Christian, the monument recounts how his religion had arrived in China 150 years before, due to the missionary Alopen. Here are several extracts:

There was a bishop in Syria by the name of A-lo-pên. Directed by a brilliant cloud, he carried the holy book . . . he confronted the difficulties and the perils of the voyage. He rode to Chang'An where he arrived in the ninth year of Cheng-Kouan. The emperor sent a great minister at the head of an escort to the suburb of the west to welcome the visitor and introduce him. He gave him hospitality in the palace. The Scriptures were translated in the Imperial Library and the doctrine examined by the emperor personally. It is understood to be based on rectitude and truth and a special edict that expressly gave the ability to preach and propagate.

The monument begins with a summary of Christian doctrine as it seems to have been taught by the Nestorians. In the extract cited below, a Nestorian coloration in the statement concerning the incarnation can be detected, as well as recourse to Taoist and Buddhist terminology:

In truth, this one who is pure and pleasing, who, being without beginning, is the origin of origins, incomprehensible and invisible, always mysteriously existing until all ends, who, controlling the hidden axis of the universe, has created and developed all things, mysteriously giving existence to numerous wise men, being the first worthy of homage, is it not our God (Allaha), a Trinity, mysterious substance, not begotten and true Lord? [The narrative of the creation and the fall follows.]

However, the second person of our Trinity, the Messiah, who is the brilliant Lord of the universe in his veritable majesty, appeared on the earth as a man. The angels proclaimed the good news: a virgin gave birth to the Holy One in Syria. A brilliant star announced the blessed event: the Persian, seeing this brightness came to make homage to his presence . . . He fulfilled the Ancient Law; the Scriptures were transmitted in twenty-seven books . . . Founding the new religion of the Holy Spirit, the other person of the Trinity, he gave man the capacity to live out the true faith . . . He freed the world from sensuality and rendered it pure. Opening widely the door of the three virtues, he introduced life and abolished death . . .

He ordered baptism in water and the Spirit, which liberates from the vain pomp of the world and purifies as far as to restore to a perfect whiteness. His ministers carry the cross as a seal, which spreads his influence to the four regions of the world and unifies all without distinction . . . One time, each seven days, they have a nonbloody sacrifice.[118]

This monument also includes an edict of toleration promulgated by the emperor, authorizing a new monastery of twenty-one monks in the capital. It ends by proclaiming the benefits of Christianity: "If the empire is calm, if men act with righteousness,

---

118 These brief extracts from the text of the monument are found in a small work: John Foster, *A partir de Jérusalem* (Neuchatel, Switzerland: Delachaux & Niestlé, 1961), 47–48.

if the living prosper, if the dead possess joy, it is the merit of our illustrious religion." This suggests that there was a considerable Christian influence in China in the eighth century.

The authenticity of the monument has been questioned. However, the text of the edict of toleration engraved on the monument and attributed to the emperor T'ai Tsung was later found in the imperial archives. Today, specialists recognize the value of the monument. Also other imperial edicts concerning Christians—dated successively in 683, 745, and 845—provide official evidence for the existence of a Chinese church over a period of at least two centuries. These edicts mention the names of a dozen monasteries that were given authorization in good and due form. In another case, a document was found in the Gobi Desert that, dating from the eighth century, is contemporaneous with the monument. It contains a list of the translations of Christian books, including the books of the Old and New Testaments.

## THE CHURCHES OF CENTRAL ASIA

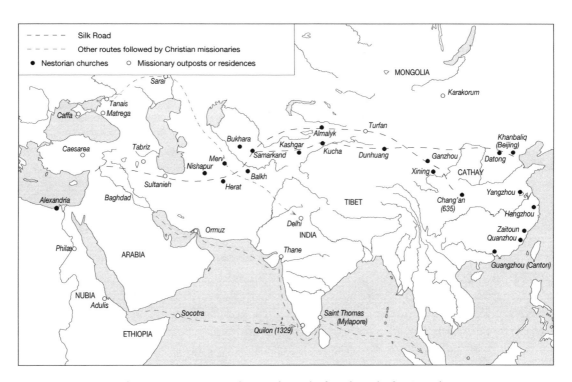

*Map 8: Christian expansion in the East from the fourth to the fourteenth centuries*

In Tibet the churches were so numerous at the end of the eighth century that a metropolitan was named there in 797.

About the year 800, Christianity was established in all of Central Asia from the Caspian Sea to western China. There are good reasons to think that it also reached Japan. But in the ninth century, a great ebbing of Christianity occurred, especially where Islam dislodged it, as in Arabia and India. In China it was the Taoist emperor

Wu Tsung in about the year 850 who destroyed Christianity as well as Zoroastrianism and Buddhism. Under his direction, forty thousand temples, churches, and monasteries belonging to one or another of these three foreign religions were destroyed. Persecution, however, did not stop the progress of the Nestorian churches in Central Asia. By about the year 1000, it is estimated that it could count at least 12 million members and 250 dioceses; it may in fact have even been larger than the Western church in this period.

## Mongolia

Occupying the high valleys and river tributaries of Lake Baikal, the Keraits are one of the more important Mongolian tribes. The tribe converted to Christianity in the year 1009 through the efforts of the catholicos of Merv (present-day Turkmenistan). The king of the Keraits became the ally of the emperor of China and received the semi-royal Chinese title of Unc-Khan. For a long time he was the most powerful prince of the Mongols. Two centuries later, one of his Christian successors was King Togrul. He was doubtless at the origin of the mythic dream that haunted the Western Christian imagination for centuries. Existing beyond the uncrossable frontiers of Islam at the very ends of the world, there was supposed to be a rich and marvelously powerful Christian kingdom whose king was Prester John. He was sometimes believed to live in Asia, at other times in Africa—specifically Ethiopia. Togrul was the suzerain of the young Genghis Khan, who fought and killed his overlord in 1203. This was the end of the ascendancy of the Christian Keraits in the area.

Islam had advanced far towards the east and south, and now it sought to conquer to the north. Nestorian Christianity, however, posed an obstacle to it. Some historians think that Muhammad and his successors respected the Nestorians and, therefore, consented to coexist with them. Nevertheless, after having conquered a part of Asia Minor and Armenia, the Muslims were for a long time simply interrupted in their march toward the north. But beginning in the thirteenth century, the Nestorian churches of Asia underwent a number of shocks that severely tested them.

The first shock was delivered by the great Mongol conqueror Genghis Khan (1160–1227). He was not animated by personal hatred of Christians, for his own mother was a Nestorian princess. An intrepid warrior, he employed the dreadful Mongol methods that worked so well for him. In 1211 he attacked immense China with a relatively small but extremely well-trained army of 130,000 men. In ten years he completed the conquest of the Chinese empire, massacring 35 million persons, including women and children. In 1220 he conquered Persia, annihilating a quarter of the inhabitants. In passing through Central Asia, he massacred entire populations. Among all these victims, from China to Persia, were numerous Christians. Many of the formerly flourishing cities of Central Asia were destroyed, never to be reconstructed. Several of them had been Christian.

Nevertheless, in the middle of the thirteenth century in Mongolia, Nestorian churches were still vital institutions. The four sons of Genghis Khan, who divided the immense empire of their father, were favorable to the Nestorian priests. A number of large populations followed the example of the Keraits and converted to Christianity.

These include the Ouigours (from which the word *ogre* is derived), the Onguts, and the Naimans. In 1266 Kublai Khan (1214–1294), a grandson of Genghis Khan, inherited an empire vaster and richer than was ever known by Greece or Rome. He reigned from Siberia to Indonesia, from Korea to the Caspian Sea. The khan favored the Christians and sought to establish relations with the Western church. He received a visit from the Venetian merchant Marco Polo who, with his father and uncle, sojourned in China from 1271–1295. Polo even became an employee of the emperor. When on his return to Europe he recounted his adventures in the *Book of Marvels*, most of his contemporaries took his stories to be fables and lies. They could not imagine a civilization that appeared to be more advanced than Europe! Historians continue to debate the authenticity of the travels of Marco Polo, but the information that he was able to glean from the various regions of China assuredly correspond to the reality. His book made mention of a number of important kings, princes, and Christian "barons," and of a great number of churches and monasteries scattered all over Asia, and particularly in China.

Polo's brothers, who had left Asia in 1269, carried a remarkable letter from Kublai Khan to Pope Gregory X (1271–1276):

> Our Christians [the Nestorians] are ignorant so that they are capable of very little and have even less influence . . . Go to your suzerain the Pope and tell him of our desire for wise men, enlightened in the Christian faith . . . I will receive baptism, and then my barons and high dignitaries will be baptized, and finally their subjects . . . In this way there will be more Christians here than in your regions.

Was he sincere or simply curious? He is known to have been very tolerant of other faiths but attached to the ancestral practices of the Mongols. None can know what would have happened if the pope and the kings of the West had understood the importance of this offer. After many hesitations, the pope sent only two Dominican monks, who left with Marco Polo in 1271. They retraced Polo's journey along the dangerous Silk Road. Regarding this lost opportunity, Polo wrote: "If the pope had sent people to him capable of instructing him in our faith, the great khan would have become a Christian, for, it is certain, he had a great desire for it." In response to the khan's request, five additional Franciscans were sent to China the following year, but no one knows what became of them. Some think that Kublai Khan eventually became a Buddhist before he died in 1294.

The Nestorians, for their part, were not hoping for the arrival of Roman Catholic missionaries. They had an archbishop at Khanbalik (Beijing), the new capital of the Mongol empire.[119] In contrast, the khan continued to seek out contact with the Western church. In 1274 at the Council of Lyons, envoys from the khan were received, and several of them were baptized. About the year 1280, Bar Sawma, a Nestorian monk of the Khanbalik region (a Mongol of the ethnic group Ongut, or Ouigour), wanted to go on pilgrimage to the Holy Land with a companion named Mark of Kawshang. When

---

119 Marco Polo wrote of it as "Cambaluc"; present-day Beijing.

the Turks barred access to them, they had to reside for a time at Baghdad. This occurred at the moment when the catholicos died, and the bishops assembled to elect Mark to succeed him. Hence in 1281 a Mongol monk, now under the name of Yahbh-Allaha II, was named catholicos of all the Nestorian churches, remarkable evidence of the importance of the Mongols in Asiatic Christianity. Yahbh-Allaha II continued to seek out contacts with the Western churches, and he also attempted to rectify certain theological errors of Nestorianism. He died in 1311. As for Bar Sawma, the Mongol khan of Persia made him his ambassador and set him again on his journey to the West.[120] He went to Constantinople and then to Rome, where Pope Nicolas IV (1288–1292) received him solemnly, and he continued his voyage as far as Paris and Bordeaux. Western dignitaries were astonished to hear him say: "Many Mongols are Christians, including princes and queens. The faith that we hold comes from the holy apostles and has been preserved until this day." Bar Sawma recounted how in 1287 at Bordeaux he was also presented before Edward I, king of "Alanguitar" (England), who asked him to celebrate Mass according to the Syriac liturgy. The king even received the Eucharist from the hand of this Mongol monk, a clear sign of the universality of the Christian faith at a time when Christianity is apt to be confused with the European nations! Beijing and England were literally at "the ends the earth," the extreme Orient and Occident of the then-known world. The mandate of Acts 1:8 seems to have been executed, and the prophecy of the Gospel accomplished: "People will come from east and west" (Luke 13:29).

## The Franciscan Missions in China and Southeast Asia

Though nothing is known of the ministry of the five Franciscans sent in 1270, much more is known about the Italian John of Montecorvino (1247–1328). Also a Franciscan, he was sent by Pope Nicolas IV to the Mongols some years later, following a reiterated call from Kublai Khan that had been sent by the khan of Persia.

Prior to this mission, Montecorvino had been a missionary to Armenia and Persia. In the course of his journey to China, he stopped in the Persian Gulf and south India: "For thirteen months I was in the country of India, and the Church of the Apostle Saint Thomas," he wrote. "I baptized one hundred persons there, and my companion, Brother Nicolas de Pistoia, died . . . Then I departed for Cathay [China] . . . I arrived at the kingdom of the Emperor of Tartars, the one called the Great Khan." He arrived at Khanbalik at the end of the year 1293, with the status of ambassador of the pope. It was more than twenty years since Kublai Khan had sent his message to Rome, and the khan died two months after Montecorvino's arrival. Temur, who succeeded him, allowed liberty to Christians but was not personally interested in the gospel. For eleven years Montecorvino remained the only Catholic missionary in the country until a German monk from Cologne arrived—Brother Arnold. Unfortunately, Montecorvino seems to have wasted much of his time and energy in a struggle against the Nestorians. He said regarding them:

---

120 The khan of Persia sought contact with Western Christendom; however, in 1295 the Mongols of Persia were adherents of Islam.

> The Nestorians, who claim the title of Christians, but who depart from much of the Christian religion, have gained such power in these regions that they permit no Christian of another profession to have the least opportunity to speak or preach any doctrine except their own . . . They have incited against me the gravest persecutions, claiming that I was a spy, a magician, and an impostor. This cabal continued for five years, years in which several times I have been brought before the courts and threatened with death. Finally, God helping me, the emperor recognized my innocence . . . Without these calumnies, and if I had had two or three companions to aid me, I would have baptized more than thirty thousand persons . . . maybe even the emperor Khan would have been baptized.

Montecorvino founded a school, a monastery, and two churches. In the course of his thirty-five-year ministry in China, he baptized thousands of people. He particularly sought to reach children, forming choirs of boys to help perform the liturgy of the Mass. He reasoned, in effect, that the beauty of the religious ceremonies was particularly apt to attract the population to the faith. He described his activities in rather surprising words, at least according to our criteria:

> I have bought one by one forty pagan children between the ages of seven and twelve. They do not yet know any law; I have baptized them and trained them in Latin literature and our worship service. I have transcribed for them the Psalter with thirty hymns, as well as two breviaries. Eleven among them already know our church services; they sing in the choir as in a monastery, whether I am present or not . . . From his chamber, the emperor can hear us when we sing. His majesty finds great pleasure in this . . . It is always a marvel to be able to celebrate the service in great pomp in our chapel. It is spoken of by all the pagans, which can have the happiest effects, with the aid of God.

In 1306 after sixteen years of ministry in China, Montecorvino sent a report to Pope Clement V (1305–1314) to ask for reinforcements. He spoke of four thousand baptized in the single year of 1305 and revealed his project "to translate for them the entire Latin liturgy, so that the Mass can be chanted and celebrated, not according to the Latin rite, but in their language and writing." He was also bringing a good number of Nestorians into the Roman church. Here is an extract from Montecorvino's report:

> At this moment (January 1305), I am in the process of building a new church to distribute the children in several places. I am getting old, I have turned gray, less by age (I am only fifty-eight years old) than by fatigue and anxiety. I have adequately learned the Tartar language and writing, that is to say the language common to the Mongols [that is usually called Ongut]. I have translated the entire New Testament and Psalter into this language and alphabet. I have seen that it has been transcribed in

superb calligraphy and I show it, I read it, I preach it and make it known publicly and witness to the law of Christ. I have commissioned six paintings of the Old and New Testament to teach the simple, with the captions in Persian, Turkish, and Latin characters so that all can read them.

This report aroused great enthusiasm in Rome, and the pope created the bishopric of Khanbalik in 1307, making Montecorvino its first titular. He sent six bishops, among whom three arrived in China and settled in the south of the country. An Armenian Christian had a church and monastery constructed for them in the city of Zayton (present-day Quanzhou), a three-month journey from Khanbalik.

John of Montecorvino certainly reached the Mongols, but it is not known to what extent the Chinese were ready to convert. He died in 1328 at the age of eighty-one, never having returned to the West. The news of his death took three years to reach Pope John XXII (1316–1334) at Avignon. It is not known if the archbishop he sent to succeed him reached his destination.

In any event, the Franciscan mission counted as many as sixteen mission posts in China and throughout Asia. The task was not easy as the following letter testifies, written in 1318 by the Franciscan Peregrinus de Castello, bishop of Zayton:

Concerning the infidels, we can freely preach, and we have preached several times in the mosques of the Saracens in order to convert them; the same for the idolaters in their great cities, by the intermediary of two interpreters . . . If we could speak their language, God would accomplish marvels. The harvest is great, but in truth there are few workers, and they lack sickles; for we are too few in number. In addition, we Brothers are too old and incapable of learning the languages . . . I have become the bishop of Zayton, for Brother Gerard, the bishop, is dead. And we remaining Brothers are not going to live a long time, and others have not yet come. The church will remain without baptism and without followers.

Peregrinus, in fact, died a few years later, but Pope Clement V sent a successor, Andrew of Perugia. Here is the news that he wrote to the pope in January 1326:

In this vast empire there exist men from all the nations that are under heaven, and from all the religious sects; and each is permitted to live according to his beliefs. For the opinion or rather the error that each can have salvation in his own religion is allowed here. We can therefore preach with all freedom and security. Among the Jews and Saracens, none are converted; the idolaters come to be baptized in great number, but several of the neophytes do not walk in the true ways of Christianity . . . I write neither to my spiritual brothers nor to individual friends because I do not know who is dead and who is living. Here, all the suffragan bishops created by Pope Clement have left in peace from Khanbalik to the Lord. I alone remain.

Other missionaries were sent to Asia. On the way to China a group of Franciscans, directed by Brother Thomas of Tolentino, stopped in India and lived there after having observed the urgency of the need. In 1320 four among them were put to death by the Muslims in Thana, near Mumbai (formerly Bombay). Their surviving companions saw little response to the gospel in these Islamic regions and went farther south where they had more success with the Nestorians. Cut off from their Baghdad base and becoming increasingly pagan, many Nestorians were easily won to Roman Catholicism by the Franciscans, who dedicated much of their time to this work.

In this period the Franciscans also had the opportunity to visit Southeast Asia and went as far as Java, Sumatra, and Borneo. It seems, sadly, that one of the tasks of these monks was to take the Nestorians into the bosom of the church. However, by being the first from the Western church of the Middle Ages to risk their lives without any human protection in distant countries, they pioneered a new dimension of evangelization.

A new archbishop of Khanbalik was named in 1370, but this date coincides with the beginning of a very rapid decline that nearly led to the complete disappearance of the church in China. A little before, in 1368, the Mongol khans, who had in general been favorable to Christians, were driven out by the Ming dynasty. The new rulers subsequently strove with much success to eliminate Christians from their land—especially Catholics rather than Nestorians.

### The Decline of the Nestorian Churches

It is at the beginning of the fourteenth century that the Nestorian churches of Asia reached their apogee. During the reign of the Mongol patriarch Yahbh-Allaha III (1281–1317), who originated from north China, they counted about thirty metropolitans. Each metropolitan had from six to a dozen suffragan bishops under his auspices, which doubtless represents at least 250 dioceses—from Cyprus to Manchuria, and from Turkestan to Malabar and Java. It is conservatively estimated that these Asiatic churches included more than 15 million members. Some current hypotheses even go well beyond this number, but due to a lack of documentation, these remain unverifiable.

It was the Nestorian churches of China that were the first to decline—suppressed, as were the Catholics—after the fall of the Mongols and the emergence of the Ming dynasty, which was hostile to all that came from abroad.

The severest blow to the Nestorian churches, after that of the persecution of the Mings, was the Black Death. This great plague seems to have originated in Mongolia, from whence it spread throughout Asia before infecting Europe. Its virulence was almost unimaginable; we know that in Europe, where it appeared in a less lethal form, the plague killed at least a third of the population. It seems that in Central Asia entire peoples were decimated.

The third blow to land squarely on the Nestorians of Asia was delivered by another conquering Mongol, Timur Leng ("Timur the Lame"), more generally known in the West by the name of Tamerlane (1336–1405). Born into a clan of the Turkish nobility and the king of Samarkand (in present-day Uzbekistan), this highly intelligent and cultivated prince practiced forms of cruelty that stagger the imagination. He took pleasure in erecting pyramids formed from the heads of his slaughtered adversaries. A Muslim fanatic, he wanted to expunge Christianity from Asia, and to a large extent he succeeded. Tamerlane could not conquer Ming China, but he undertook to destroy Chinese Christianity.

Most of the Christians who escaped from the Black Death were converted willingly or by force to Buddhism or Islam by Tamerlane and the Mings. This is doubtless what explains the considerable number of Muslims in China and the Christian-inspired paintings that are found in Buddhist monasteries of the Gobi Desert and elsewhere in Central Asia.

In several decades, Nestorianism disappeared or survived as a fossil in some small Mesopotamian islands and in the mountains of Kurdistan. It should also be added that Russian archaeologists have found, in places that are today deserts, immense Christian necropolises that witness to the faith of this population.

## India

Though the Mongols were not spared the Black Death, the epidemic passed India by because of its geographical isolation. We have seen that the gospel had been carried there from the first centuries. The Christians in India were numerous and widely dispersed in the country, as objects and documents found by archaeologists testify. It was between the seventh and tenth centuries that the churches were the most vigorous. Afterwards, Nestorian churches survived only in the south and southwest. In effect, the Muslim invasions caused Christianity to disappear throughout the north of the Indian subcontinent.

# CHRISTIANITY IN AFRICA

## North Africa

This region was for a long time one of the most beautiful jewels in the crown of the church. Augustine (345–430), bishop of Hippo (Annaba, in Algeria), was one of the greatest Christian theologians. In the fifth century the Arianism of the German invaders greatly weakened the churches. When Islam arrived between 680 and 720, Christians converted *en masse*, as noted above (see pp. 78-79). From Libya to the Atlantic, Christian churches almost completely disappeared while Jewish communities survived. Jewish and Christian groups, however, seem to have fled through the Sahara to settle farther south, notably in the regions of Lake Chad, Senegal, and Mali. It is one of the possible explanations for the ancient traces of a Christian presence found in these places.

## Egypt

The Egyptian church, becoming Monophysite in the fifth century, found itself in opposition to the orthodox doctrine of Chalcedon that Constantinople wanted to impose on it. Following the Islamic invasion, the church resisted the pressure of Islam. At first the Arabs permitted Christian buildings and guaranteed liberty of worship. In the eighth century, however, enforced Islamization began and reached its height in the form of overt persecution against Christianity in the fourteenth and fifteenth centuries. It is often difficult and always perilous to remain Christian in a Muslim country, but the Coptic church held its own throughout these assaults. Between the ninth and thirteenth centuries, the Coptics undertook the translation of the Old and New Testaments in Arabic. The Christian presence endured and, in the twentieth century, the church constituted about 7 percent of the population. The Coptics considered themselves, not without reason, as the legitimate descendants of the Egypt of the Pharaohs.

## Nubia

Three kingdoms were founded in Nubia in the fourth century: Nobatia, Alodia, and Makuria. Little is known of their origins except that they were pagan. The temple of Isis on the isle of Philae marked the frontier with Egypt. It was at the instigation of Emperor Justinian that they were evangelized in the fifth century by a presbyter of Alexandria—Julian, who was succeeded by another missionary by the name of Longinius. These kingdoms were then relatively prosperous and populous. Christianity developed there rapidly and became vigorous, as the numerous ruins of churches along the valley of the Nile attest. For a long time Philae continued to be a pagan center, but Theodore, its first bishop named in 526, converted the neighboring king of Nobatia. Arab Muslims arrived in about the year 650, penetrating as far south as Dongola, capital of the kingdom of Makuria. Christianity, however, continued as a tolerated religion, and the Islamization of the country was very slow. It would be another seven centuries, in 1316, before a Muslim king seized the throne of Dongola, and in this period the majority of the people were still Christians.

The bishops of the kingdom of Alodia, depending directly on the patriarch of Alexandria, were using a Greek rather than Coptic liturgy. A Muslim traveler in the tenth century described what he saw in this country, marveling at how the capital, Soba, was filled with churches and monasteries.

Beginning in the eleventh century, the Arab nomads of the Muslim religion settled down in many places throughout the three Nubian Christian kingdoms, thus reinforcing the process of Islamization. However, as late as the beginning of the thirteenth century an Armenian traveler claims to have seen as many as four hundred churches and numerous monasteries. At the beginning of the sixteenth century, Christianity continued to exist in Nubia, but the faith was hard pressed by Islam. Its leaders called on the king of Portugal for aid but without success.

It was the kingdom of Alodia, to the south of the Fifth Cataract, that resisted the Muslims most effectively. In 1504 it was the last to succumb, at which point, after a millennium of existence, the Nubian church disappeared.

Beginning in Nubia and continuing as far as Lake Chad, there is a long route that some Christian Nubian merchants used during numerous centuries. It may have been by this means that some African populations were evangelized. Church ruins have been found in Darfur (present-day west Sudan), around Lake Chad, among the Hausas of Nigeria, and even as far as Mali. Some, it is true—as was related above—attribute these traces of Christianity to the influence of Christian refugees driven from North Africa by the pressure of Islam. But whatever their origin, a pre-Islamic Christian presence is widely attested in the Saharan regions. Jean Meyendorff writes, "Following the example of the Nubian tribes, several other Christian centers were born among the nomadic populations of the Sahara. As far as the Atlantic Ocean, this is attested by archaeological vestiges, liturgical books in Greek and Nubian, and some residual Christian vocabulary in the language of the Touaregs. The total victory of Islam in all of the Sahara could well date only from the fifteenth century."[121]

## Ethiopia

As Ethiopia is situated farther south and protected by mountains, it could continue to resist the Arabs more easily than the inhabitants of the Nile plains. Little is known of its history between the seventh and thirteenth centuries, for it was then entirely cut off from the rest of Christendom and developed a unique church form. From the beginning of the fourteenth century, Arabs attempted over a period of two centuries to take possession of the high plateaus of Ethiopia, but without success. The situation, however, was becoming hopeless when the king asked, like the Nubians before him, for help from Portugal. In 1541 Cristóvão da Gama arrived with four hundred Portuguese troops to reinforce the Ethiopians in their struggle. Better equipped than the Arabs, they fought them in 1543, assuring the independence of a Christian Ethiopia.

# EVALUATION

From the human perspective, the future of Christendom at the threshold of the fifteenth century seemed somber. Even a century later, Martin Luther viewed the spectacle of the weakening of Western Christendom and arrived at the conclusion that the end times were close. With several exceptions, Europe remained the sole territory peopled by Christians. Europeans had been able to drive the Muslims from France, Italy, and Spain but were not able to prevent the Mediterranean Sea from becoming the domain of the Barbary States. To the east, pressure from Islam waxed ever stronger. The Mongols dominated the east and south of Russia. The finger in the dike was the city of Constantinople. When it fell in 1453, the bellicose Ottoman Turks swept through the Balkans. Their armies seemed invincible. Nothing now remained of the Eastern Empire, and the West appeared weak and vulnerable.

The first chapter of this work recalled that the missionary mandate conferred on the church by its Lord had a universal scope. On the basis of incontestable witnesses, we observed in the course of the first millennium of the Christian era, and even after, that the gospel was proclaimed not only around the Mediterranean basin and in Northern Europe but also in the immense regions of Asia and Africa. Before the advance of Islam in the seventh and eighth centuries, and again between the twelfth and fourteenth centuries, the church was widely established in the three known continents. Christianity was not perceived as a Western religion, and even the claim of universal hegemony by the Roman papacy could not discredit this idea. It was the Islamization of North Africa and the collapse of Asian Christianity that produced this concentration of the Christian church in Europe.

---

121 Meyendorff, *Unité*, 138.

Beginning in the fifteenth century, Europe would experience an extraordinary cultural renewal known as the Renaissance. Europe was then confined to narrow limits, restricted by the Atlantic Ocean on the west, the pole to the north, the Ural Mountains and the barrier of Islam to the east and south. The lid clamped down on the boiling pot of Europe produced an explosion, the Age of Discovery that will be discussed in the next section of this book. During this period, all the pieces would fall into place to produce the amazing expansion of European civilization throughout the rest of the world. Europe would come to dominate much of the world and enrich itself at the expense of the New World, Africa, and to a large extent Asia. It would impose on others its power and reckon it a duty to export to every corner of the globe its civilization—and its religion. A recent historian has written:

> From this time and through the twentieth century, Christian missions have been perceived as one of the principal manifestations of Western imperialism. When one speaks of "mission," it is often this image that the modern mind conjures up. This has left the church open to a massive critical broadside—criticism that at least at times is well founded. It is a handicap that can be surmounted only when the facts are seen in their proper historical context. A knowledge of the history of Christian missions from the seventh to the fifteenth centuries makes us aware of the decline of non-European Christianity that characterized this period. This permits us to better understand the period that followed, and its contingent aspects.

It is important to remember that Christian history has its own inner dynamics and hazards, which are not related to the essence of the gospel itself. It is in this uncertain and ambiguous medium that the missionary vocation of the church has had to be worked out. At the dawn of the twenty-first century, it is imperative that all the churches of the world—those of the Southern Hemisphere as those of the Northern, those of the Orient as those of the Occident—be conscious that from its beginnings in Jerusalem the gospel has spread to the four points of the compass. The universal expansion of the church that we know today is not simply a historical novelty that emerged from the age of European imperialism but the logical working out of the church's mission. Christianity certainly experienced a period of isolation on the European continent, but due to the internal logic of Christianity itself, it was inevitable that it would burst through these temporary confines. For, happily, Europeans did not believe that the Christian message was for them alone. Though the dissemination of the gospel beyond the seas is often badly understood, it is certain that the universality of the gospel and the expansion of the church throughout the entire world have neither been tied to the claims of the West to universal domination, nor to its power to impose its vision of the world on other civilizations.

# SECTION III

## CATHOLIC MISSION: FROM THE RENAISSANCE THROUGH THE EIGHTEENTH CENTURY

# CHAPTER 9

# New Horizons in Europe

Constantinople was conquered by the Ottoman Turks in 1453. From that point forward Western Christianity found itself under the direct threat of Islam. However, even while Europeans wondered if they were living in the end times of the world, a veritable resurrection was produced that has justly been called the Renaissance.

From a scientific viewpoint, it began modestly with technical improvements of minor importance. Naval construction was effectively improved: larger, stronger, and faster ships were leaving the dockyards. Progress in the use of the compass was achieved through the invention of a better-protected magnetic needle, making the instrument more reliable. There was the invention of the sternpost rudder, which remains firm in a storm. The old sea charts were retired, and new, more exact ones were designed. Navigation on the high seas became possible as the need for costal landmarks was overcome. It was then possible to risk exploration on the hitherto impassable sea.

For any change to occur it is necessary to have a person of vision to lead the way. Though largely forgotten today, this person was Henry the Navigator (1394–1460). Son of King John I of Portugal, he earned his spurs as a knight in 1415 at the battle of Ceuta in Morocco. It was here that he discovered the importance of Africa. He assembled a team of sailors and scholars to help him attain the goal that he had set for himself—the preaching of the gospel in Africa. In effect, this meant going around the Muslim world to the south of the Sahara. He dreamed, too, of discovering and joining forces with the famous Christian kingdom of Pester John, which he imagined to be in these regions.

Henry and his team moved from discovery to discovery. In 1418 he reached the island of Madeira, which was occupied in 1430 and became the base of later operations. Then farther west he discovered the archipelagos of the Azores in 1432, and in 1443 Rio de Oro on the west coast of the Sahara. He discovered the Cape Verde Islands in 1456, and eventually he reached as far south as Sierra Leone. The door of Black Africa was henceforth open. After Henry died in 1460, other expeditions became increasingly more frequent and more far-reaching. In 1470 the island of Fernando Po was reached at the base of the Gulf of Guinea, and the line of the equator was crossed the following year. Then in May 1488 Bartholomew Dias reached and then passed the Cape of Good Hope at the southern tip of the African continent. Soon after having entered a new ocean, the Portuguese Vasco de Gama in 1498 arrived in India, visiting Calcutta and Goa. Previously he had stopped at the Cape, then sailed on to Mozambique and the Arab ports of Kenya, Mombasa, and Malindi.

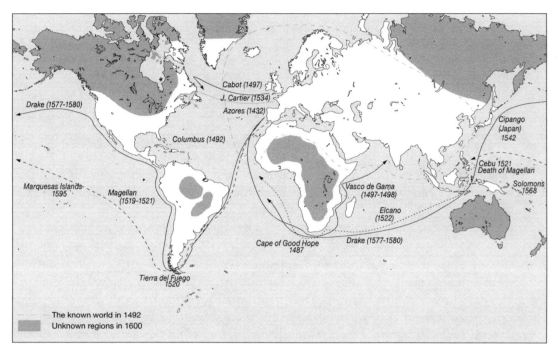

*Map 9: The great explorers (1492-1600)*

The Portuguese achieved their goal of overcoming the obstacle of the Arabs by circling around Africa to find the route to the Indies. Better navigators than the Arabs, the Portuguese destroyed an Egyptian fleet in 1509 and rapidly gained mastery of the ports of eastern Africa and Aden in Yemen. And they continued to push their advance toward the Far East. At the beginning of the sixteenth century, they arrived at the Strait of Malacca, and in 1517 reached China.

The French might have figured more prominently among the discoverers of the new world if the king of France had understood the importance of what was at stake. A Norman lord had, in fact, preceded even Henry the Navigator as an explorer. This was Jean de Bethancourt (1360–1425). Born in a family ruined by the Hundred Years War, he risked his life and what remained of his fortune in a maritime adventure to Africa. Accompanied by his friend Gadifer de la Salle, he embarked in 1402 for the Canary Islands. Forgotten over the centuries, they had been known by the Romans as "the Fortunate Islands." Bethancourt settled there in 1405 and converted the inhabitants, the mysterious Guanches, to Christianity. To protect against eventual enemies, he asked King Henry III of Castile to become his suzerain. Despite the opposition of the Portuguese, the archipelago was recognized as a Spanish possession in 1479. Subsequently the Guanches revolted against the Spanish and the church and were for the most part massacred.

## PORTUGUESE SETTLEMENTS IN AFRICA

The Portuguese established trading posts at several points along the western coast of Africa. In 1482 an expedition founded the first European establishment in Africa, the fort of Elima on the Ivory Coast. It was also at this time that the first Mass was celebrated in West Africa. In 1484 on the left shore of the immense mouth of the Zaire River, Diogo Cão (or Diogo Cam) discovered the extensive kingdom of the Congo. He established good relations with the king, who asked for priests for his land. The first missionaries, secular and religious priests of different orders, arrived in 1491. The king converted and, with his family, was baptized in 1492 and took the name of John. His capital, Mbanza or Monbassi, became São Salvador.[122]

## SPANISH SETTLEMENTS IN AMERICA

Queen Isabella of Castile, whose marriage in 1469 to Ferdinand II of Aragon singularly reinforced Spanish power, did not want her country to fall behind Portugal. She took the risk of engaging in her service the Genoese adventurer Christopher Columbus to discover a more direct route to India than had the Portuguese. The entire world knows how, in 1492, instead of arriving in Asia as he was counting on, the navigator disembarked on one of the islands of the Bahamas. Later he discovered Cuba and the magnificent island that he named Hispaniola (present-day Haiti and the Dominican Republic). By this voyage and the three following it, he opened to the Catholic kings the door of the New World, the country of gold—Eldorado. Thirty years later in 1522, Magellan reached the Indies and, instead of returning as he had come, sailed west, circled around South America, and hence became the first person to circumnavigate the globe.

Christopher Columbus wrote of the first indigenous people with whom he came into contact:

> I have given them much and have received nothing in return. My intention was to appease them and lead them to become Christians. Let us rejoice in Christ for the salvation of so many souls until now lost. Let us all rejoice in exaltation for our faith and for the addition to our goods.

This mixture of religious and economic motivations in the case of Columbus appears all too clearly in a letter to the Spanish sovereigns, written at Cuba in November 1492.

> I am certain that if zealous believers knew the language of the indigenous people, they would become Christians without delay. I wish that your Highnesses would be much concerned with this,

---

122 See p. 171.

so that the church may be given to numerous peoples and that they might be converted . . . Hence, they will learn our language and will adopt our customs and our faith, for I notice that these people are not idolaters and have no organized religion. They know only that there is a God in heaven and are convinced that we come from heaven. They make the sign of the cross and repeat each prayer that we say . . . These countries could become a place of commerce for all Christendom and principally for Spain, which must reign without division. Good Catholics alone, among Christians, must establish themselves here, for the initial goal of enterprise has always been the increase of the glory of the Christian religion.

Pope Alexander VI (1492–1503) had a lively interest in these events. He sensed their importance and considered himself to be the sole legitimate sovereign responsible for all the newly discovered countries. Since Christ is the king of the world, his vicar is, like him, the proprietor of the planet. According to the terms of the bull *Inter Caetera* (*Among Other* [*Works*]) of 1493, he recognized the existence of indigenous peoples "perfectly apt to receive the Catholic faith" and gave to the Spanish sovereigns the new territories with the responsibility to evangelize them:

In these countries, numerous people come pacifically, walking entirely nude and not eating meat . . . According to our envoys, these people believe that there is a single creator God in the heavens and seem apt to adopt good morals . . . Gold, herbs, and many other precious things have been found in this place . . .

We make it a duty for you, by virtue of the holy obedience that you have promised . . . to send to the mainland and the aforesaid islands virtuous and God-fearing men, scholars and men of experience, to instruct the indigenous people and the inhabitants in the Catholic faith and inculcate in them good morals.[123]

When the king of Portugal asserted his claims to the newly discovered territories, the pope divided the land into two hemispheres. The north-south line of separation passed to the west of the archipelago of the Cape Verde Islands. Spain had the western half of the world, and Portugal the eastern half. The following year on June 4, 1494, the Catholic kings of Spain and Portugal signed the Treaty of Tordesillas, which fixed the line of demarcation at 370 leagues to the west of the Cape Verde Islands. Hence Portugal received the eastern part of South America, which became Brazil, as well as Africa and India; and Spain had the rest of America, the Pacific, and the Philippines.

In conferring on the sovereigns of Spain and Portugal the responsibility to evangelize the populations among their new possessions, the pope established the *Padroado,* a system of royal "patronage." The Christian kings assumed "the duty to choose, prepare, send, and support the missionaries going to evangelize the countries discovered

---

123  Pope Alexander VI, *Inter Caetera*, May 4, 1493.

or to be discovered." The kings acquitted themselves in discharging these tasks by utilizing principally the Franciscans and Dominicans, and later the Jesuits too.

One can imagine the burden that fell on the shoulders of Phillip II of Spain when he annexed Portugal in 1580 and became its king the following year. The sun always shone somewhere on the countries in his possession. According to the customs of medieval Christendom, Christianity was imposed by force wherever this was possible.

The system of the *Padroado* remained the principal vehicle of Catholic missions for the better part of a century and a half, but it was not without grave disadvantages, for the dominating interests of the state did not always coincide with those of the church, let alone with those of the indigenous populations. Hence, when missionary work expanded, the popes preferred to direct it themselves. In 1622 the Catholic Church created *Sacra Congregation de Propaganda Fide*, the "Sacred Congregation for the Propaganda of the Faith." Based in Rome, the project had already been formulated sixty years earlier at the Council of Trent. This was a true ministry of mission, having its seat and its administration in the Vatican, under the supervision of a cardinal. The Catholic kings sought to neutralize the work of this institution that, they perceived, was designed to deprive them of a powerful tool for political action. From this moment forward, small missionary societies were established in all Catholic countries. Catholic missions, however, experienced a certain decline in the eighteenth century, but then they were rejuvenated in the nineteenth century, especially in France. In this latter period, four out of five Catholic missionaries in the world were French.

## THE SOCIETY OF JESUS

In the sixteenth century the Reformation, which so violently shook the Western church, did not slow down the expansion of the Catholic Church outside of the European continent. It even coincided with an explosion of the Christian religion. A religious order founded in this period contributed greatly to this effort: The Society of Jesus. The bishop of Rome knew how to gain great profit from this new instrument of evangelization, which was more effective in its work than all the others.

Ignatius Loyola (1491–1556) founded the Society of Jesus in 1534 at Montmartre, near Paris. Ignatius belonged to the Castilian nobility. Wounded in the siege of Pamplona in a war against France, he cared for his wounds at his home. During this time of forced inactivity, he plunged into the reading of pious books, particularly the lives of the saints. He was especially fascinated with the writings of the blessed Raymond Lull. Moved by these writings, he decided to dedicate the rest of his life to the service of God. He understood that he must prepare himself for this task and, as soon as he was fit, left for the University of Paris to undertake his studies there. He was doubtless shocked by the spirit of most of his fellow students and of several of his masters, for he assembled around himself friends who shared his desire to remain faithful to the piety and faith of the Catholic Church. Together they decided to form a new monastic order that would be different from the others. It was to have a semi-military organization, and its members would not only take the three classic monastic vows—poverty, chastity, and obedience—but also a fourth vow of total submission to superiors. The goals of the Society were to combat heresy, support the pope, and convert the Muslims and pagans.

Here are some lines from the fundamental Rule of the Society (1540):

> In order that the humility of our Society be greater still, and that the detachment of each of us and the abnegation of our wills be more perfect, we have concluded that it would be highly useful . . . for us to further commit ourselves by a particular vow, in such a way that, anything that the present Roman pontiff and his successors commands us to do concerning the good of souls and the propagation of the faith, we will be obliged to execute instantly without tergiversation or excuse, in whatever country that he may send us, either in the countries of the Turks or among any other infidels, or in the Indies, or among the heretics and schismatics [Protestants], or to any of the faithful.

Loyola gave his companions very strict principles and advice that is contained in his several works. The best known of these is *Spiritual Exercises*, a masterpiece of religious psychology and spirituality.

The Jesuits were the most effective agents of the Counter-Reformation in Europe, but the discussion of them here will be limited to their missionary activity, which by all accounts was remarkable.

# CHAPTER 10

# *Catholic Mission in the Americas*

## RAPID EXPANSION INTO THE AMERICAS

### The Antilles

The first religious mission that went to the New World sailed in 1493 on the second voyage of Christopher Columbus. However, though two Franciscan brothers remained behind, it had no lasting effect. The islands of the Antilles, the first American land discovered by Columbus, were also the first to receive the gospel, for in 1502 a Franciscan mission composed of seventeen religious disembarked on the island of Haiti. In 1510 King Ferdinand introduced the Dominicans onto the island, who were directed by Brother Pedro de Cordoba. The first American bishops were installed in 1511 at Santa Domingo (the present-day Dominican Republic), one being a Franciscan, the other a Dominican. The first bishop on the American continent proper was the Franciscan Juan de Quevedo. In 1513 he was put at the head of a diocese in Panama—Santa Maria de la Antigua, or Darien.

We will see later, in regard to Bartholoméw de Las Casas and Antonio de Montesinos, that the Dominican missionaries were the first rebels against the system of the *encomienda* ("commission" or "charge"). This was a form of slavery in which the land was given to the colonists in order to fully exploit it, and indigenous labor was allocated to them to this end. Of course it was necessary to hold the Indians as captives because they would otherwise have fled to the security of the mountains. To these arrangements was added the injunction that the proprietors were to be concerned with the conversion of their Indian subjects. Sadly, however, the Indians were for the most part treated as beasts of burden and forced, especially those in the mines, to a work beyond their physical ability, which produced considerable mortality.

By the seventeenth century all the inhabitants of the Caribbean Islands and of the isthmus between the two Americas were Christians; and all were Catholics except those who came under the control of Protestant masters: the English, Dutch, and Scandinavians.

The Caribbean Islands occupied by the French were Guadeloupe in 1619 and Martinique in 1624. The first missionaries were the Dominicans and Capuchins, and the

Jesuits arrived in 1635. Unfortunately later on there were rivalries between the religious orders. In the seventeenth century, these missionaries were often chaplains of the French colonists. It was in the eighteenth century that the population of African slaves began to expand.[124] In 1685 the Black Code defined the rights and duties of slaves. Among the most important of their rights was the opportunity to receive religious instruction, and it was the duty of the proprietors to procure this for them. Slave owners, however, were reluctant to allow missionaries among their laborers, at least in the beginning when some contested the system of slavery. According to a French traveler in 1652, the Capuchins affirmed "that the children of Christian Negroes were supposed to be freed from slavery after being baptized, and that it was a shameful thing to serve his Christian brother as a slave . . . Some Negresses killed their own children rather than allow them to be born into perpetual slavery." In fact, among the black population, there were freed slaves and some employed as house servants—a relatively easy position to obtain. By far the most miserable were those who worked on plantations, and there were hardly any missionaries among them. As for the numerous fugitive slaves (or "Marrons"), they were nearly impossible to recapture. A good number of Africans remained attached to their ancestral traditions and received the Catholic faith only as a thin veneer under which to continue to practice sorcery and other pagan activities. Hence African fetishism was kept alive and vigorous in the New World. There were no indigenous priests during the entire colonial period. The following text, which comes from the Jesuit Fathers, denotes the obvious paternalism that then reigned:

> Nothing can be added to the confidence and respect that these poor people have for the missionaries: they regard us as their fathers in Jesus Christ. It is to us that they come to in all their difficulties; it is we who direct them in their building projects and who reconcile them in their quarrels; it is by our intercession that they often obtain forgiveness from their masters for the faults that would have earned for them severe chastisements; they are convinced that we have their interests at heart.[125]

## Mexico

The evangelization of Mexico, also called New Spain, was inaugurated by Father Bartholoméw de Olmedo, chaplain to the conqueror Hernan Cortés. For Cortés evangelization was supposed to go hand in hand with the crushing of the Aztec civilization, and he insisted to Charles V that he send missionaries. The Franciscans began to arrive in 1523. The best known among them was Peter of Ghent, a lay religious who, despite the insistence of all, never accepted either the episcopate or even the priesthood. He founded a multitude of churches, convents, and schools, teaching the

---

124  E. Jarry, "Les missions d'Amérique du Nord, des Antilles et d'Amérique Centrale aux XVIIe et XVIIIe siècles," *Histoire universelle des missions catholiques* 2 (1957): 303, indicates the following numbers: 16,700 black slaves in Martinique in 1715, and 84,000 in 1789; 6,400 at Guadeloupe in 1715, and 90,000 in 1789; 100,000 in Santa Domingo and Haiti in 1726, and 400,000 in 1789.

125  Ibid., 304.

Indians mechanical arts, music, and the use of musical instruments. Encompassed all about by the veneration and gratitude of the Indians, he died in 1572. The Dominicans arrived in 1526, the Augustinians in 1533.

Despite some dissension, such as by Peter of Ghent, the evangelization of Mexico was characterized by its collusion with the military conquest. The circumstances, according to historian Robert Richard, "permitted [the missionaries] to proceed with conversions *en masse,* without true catechizing, due to the propitious fact that, under the shock of the conquest, three-quarters of the civilization and the indigenous society had collapsed."[126] In 1529 there were already 200,000 Christians. The Jesuit missionaries, who arrived in 1572, did not try to discover usable elements among the local beliefs; rather, they imposed on their neophytes a total rupture with their environment, a policy called *tabula rasa* ("blank slate"). Many years before the Jesuits in Paraguay, they organized Christian villages to protect the newly converted as much from the influence of the local religions as from the colonizers—in effect, the Spanish were entirely excluded from these villages.

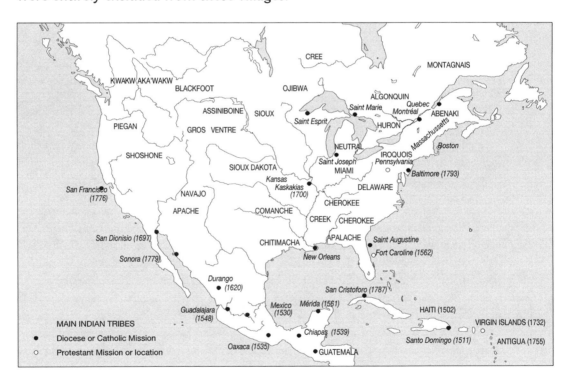

*Map 10: North America and Mexico from 1500 to 1800*

As in other regions of the world and in diverse periods, the missionaries often began by evangelizing children with the intention of making them unofficial missionaries to the adults. The children did this with some success and sometimes with as much zeal as someone prone to martyrdom. The missionaries were able to use the

---

126 Robert Richard, "L'expansion missionnaire du Portugal et de l'Espagne aux XVe and XVIe siècles," in *Histoire universelle des missions catholiques* 1 (1956): 244.

musical taste and gifts of the Indians to embellish their liturgy and church processions. The bishop of Mexico, the Franciscan Juan de Zumárraga, founded the College
of Tlatelolco in 1536, an institution reserved for the elite and intended to train a local
clergy. The college especially recruited the children of the former local aristocracy.
Though some attained a high level of literacy, it did not produce any priests of the Indian race. The undertaking, therefore, principally due to the hostility of the colonists
and the rivalry of the Dominicans, did not realize its own initial objective.

Since their earliest arrival, the Jesuits founded various colleges in the principal
cities. The first two priests, who were sent into an Indian territory in the province of
Sinaloa, were massacred in 1591. One of their successors, the Irish Father Wadding,
expressed himself in this way:

> During the long years, I was occupied in being obedient to the
> ministry of converting the Gentiles in a province that is called
> Sinaloa. On a burning earth, the missionaries walked along in all
> hours of the day and night, accompanied by naked barbarians,
> around big cats sleeping in the desert . . . Two religious, my com-
> panions, were wounded by being shot with arrows, and I was two
> times. I escaped through the mountains but not without having
> my house servant killed. These first fathers would go broken, torn,
> hungry, sad, exhausted, pursued, swimming the Rios in raw pain,
> crossing by foot the steep and high mountains and, despite the
> weight of all these difficulties, were serving God perfectly and
> converting many pagans . . . In no year did the number of bap-
> tisms drop below five thousand and in some years it rose to ten
> thousand. In the year 1624 there were more than eighty thousand
> baptized people residing in the province and since then it has risen
> to 120,000.[127]

As this witness describes, the first missionaries in the sixteenth century were
poor and they remained so voluntarily in order to be close to the Indians whose
cause they were also defending. Religious orders later benefited from very large gifts,
more often in gold and silver than land. Much of this came from the colonists. The
Franciscans in general refused to become landed proprietors, but this was not the
case with some of the other orders. As Jarry writes, the Jesuits notably "surpassed
the other orders in the art of enriching themselves and of investing their riches prof-
itably. Beginning with nothing, they soon had the largest flocks of sheep, the most
beautiful sugar shops, the best estates." This was an easy means for them to finance
their mission to the north.

Advancing from well-established bases in Mexico and Cuba, Catholic missionaries reached the Indians of California and Florida. Though this belongs to the history
of North America, it is included here because this work was linked to the mission in
Central America.

---

127 Jarry, "Les missions," 311.

## California and Florida

The first missionary ventures in California were made by the Franciscans who accompanied Cortés in 1535. These efforts were a failure, and the missionaries had to retreat to return another year. The Franciscans, Carmelites, and Jesuits made successive attempts in 1596, 1611, and 1672 respectively, but each was a failure. The Indian tribes believed in a spiritual world dominated by the great Manitou, whom it was necessary to conciliate by all sorts of ceremonies and rituals orchestrated by shamans. They practiced an eradicable polygamy, and were extremely bellicose, fiercely disputing among themselves the rights to hunting grounds. Their hostility in regards to all foreign incursion was seemingly implacable.

The Spanish government, renouncing any intention of occupying such difficult territories, finally signed a convention with the Society of Jesus in 1697, authorizing it to establish a mission in California. The Jesuits had to accept the condition that no part of the undertaking would be financed by the royal treasury and that possession of the territory would be made in the name of the king. In exchange, the Jesuits could raise troops and exercise enormous temporal power in the administration of justice. It was within these arrangements that the success of the Jesuits' financial interests in Mexico, spoken of earlier, came about.

In the same year as the convention, Fathers Salvatierra and Picolo set sail from Mexico with five bodyguards to disembark in the bay of San Dionisio. They were welcomed by a spray of arrows, and it was two years before they were able to subdue the indigenous people and master their language. The mission to California was one of the hardest that the Jesuits had ever undertaken. Nevertheless, they persevered tenaciously and, between 1697 and 1766, established a chain of seventeen missionary posts. In 1767 the Jesuits were expelled by a decree that preceded by several years the universal interdiction of the Society by the pope in 1773. The Franciscans took over from them in 1768, with the objective of going back up the Pacific coast toward the north as far as possible. Historians consider them the founders of Upper California (the present-day US state of California), while the Jesuits had essentially remained in Lower California. At the end of the century the Franciscans counted more than thirty thousand Christians in their parishes. In 1772 the Dominicans were in their turn authorized to establish themselves in California and, after working out an agreement with the Franciscans, concentrated themselves in the more southern regions, those that the Jesuits had previously evangelized in territory currently Mexican.

The first Franciscan missionaries arrived in New Mexico and Texas in 1598. A monastery was founded in 1622 in New Mexico. Some years later a revival suddenly occurred, and there were soon eighty thousand baptized in 1630. However the revolts of the Apaches in 1680 and 1696 almost entirely destroyed this work. Twenty-six priests were massacred and sixteen thousand Christians perished in the conflicts.

We will see later that the first Christians to encounter the Indians of Florida were French Calvinists who had come in 1562 to plant a colony where they could practice their faith in freedom. Sadly, this promising expedition terminated in a bloodbath when the Spanish dislodged the colonists in 1565 in the name of Spain and the Catholic faith.

After an unhappy attempt by the Jesuits, the first Franciscans arrived in Florida from Cuba in 1597. By 1634 there were thirty-five brothers serving forty-four missionary stations with thirty thousand Catholics. Here an Apache revolt in 1657 also swept away the work accomplished. Reestablishing it, even after the return of Florida to the Spanish following a period of English domination, was difficult due to the lack of available missionaries. The same shortage was felt in Louisiana where no Catholic enterprise was deployed before the arrival of French priest-explorers in 1672. Coming from the Great Lakes in Canada, they had followed the course of the Mississippi (see p. 168).

## South America

Brazil, the only territory in Latin America allowed to the Portuguese, was evangelized by the Jesuits beginning in 1551. The rest of the continent, under the domination of Spain, was conferred on the Franciscans and Dominicans, but later the Jesuits also came to work there.

Here as in other places, Christianization was made an integral part of the plan of colonization. In 1516 the Ordinances of [Cardinal] Ximenes stipulated that no ship could leave Spain for the New World without carrying missionaries. The local populations scorned colonization. In Peru, the Incas who resisted were annihilated. Other smaller and less developed Indian peoples, who were incapable of opposing the invaders, were subjugated and reduced to slavery.

Queen Isabella, however, was animated by good intentions. In her will, written in 1503, one year before her death, she expressed her concern about the evangelization of the Indians and her rejection of violence: "Our principal design being to invite the peoples over there to convert to our holy faith . . . I supplicate the king my husband not to consent to the wronging of the Indians in their persons or in their goods." But under pressure from the colonists after her death, King Ferdinand authorized the general use of the *encomienda*.

The famous *Requerimento* ("requirement"), issued in 1513, defined the conditions of a "legitimate" war against the populations who refused to convert. Here is how Bartholoméw de Las Casas (see below) summarized the essence of it:

> The anticipated procedure was the following: interpreters were supposed to advance toward the Indians and read to them a brief narrative of the history of the world, speaking of the Christian revelation, the establishment of the papacy, and the donation made by Alexander VI to the kings of Spain. After this, the Indians would be "required" to recognize the church as sovereign and, in its name, the king of Spain. In consequence, they must then permit teachers to instruct them in the Christian faith. If they refused, fire and sword could justly be sent into their country.[128]

---

128 Bartholoméw de Las Casas, "L'evangile et de la force," trans. Marianne Mahn-Lot, in *Foi vivante*, 3rd ed., (Paris: Cerf, 1991), 20.

These arrangements legalized innumerable massacres.

By the seventeenth century all of South America was Christianized, with the exception of the Patagonia, some valleys of the Cordillera of the Andes, and the impenetrable forests of the Amazon.

Space does not permit a detailed presentation of how this enterprise unfolded. Two cases, however, are worthy of interest because, being more authentically inspired by the gospel, they stand in marked contrast to the brutal methods generally used: the struggle of Bartholoméw de Las Casas in the first half of the sixteenth century, and the *reductiones* ("reductions") of the Jesuits in Paraguay in the seventeenth and eighteenth centuries.

# BARTHOLOMÉW DE LAS CASAS

It would be an injustice to assert that all Catholic missionaries were without scruples and rallied to the brutal processes described above. Among those who resisted, the most eminent and the best known is Bartholoméw de Las Casas (1484–1566), known as "The Father and Protector of the Indians." He was a man of exceptional caliber who, in the name of the gospel, struggled with astonishing perseverance for justice and respect for the Indians against the countervailing current of ideas and interests of his compatriots.

Las Casas came from a less than wealthy family, probably the descendants of Jewish ancestors. After obtaining the degree of Bachelor of Arts, he received "minor orders," which is to say that he became a cleric without being ordained to the priesthood.

In 1502 at the age of eighteen, he followed the example of his father and joined the third voyage of Christopher Columbus, participating in the system of the *encomienda* without any apparent qualms. By his own account, he saw that the Indians were being treated in an inhumane fashion, but he was not overly troubled by this or even by the number of massacres that he heard about. He was leading a happy and easy life, enriching himself in a country in which he was much pleased. He returned to Europe and was ordained a priest in Rome in 1510. He later said his first Mass on the island of Haiti in the presence of his friend Diego Columbus, the son of the explorer.

In the same year some Dominicans, directed by Domingo de Mendoza, settled at Santa Domingo where they became conscious of the tragedy perpetrated on the Indian population. Most of the Dominicans declined to embrace the humanist and reformist tendencies of Iberian Catholicism that were largely inspired by the archbishop of Toledo, Cardinal Ximenez de Cisneros (1436–1517). A pre-Protestant return-to-the-Bible reform movement in the heart of the Spanish church, it did not survive the Inquisition. Some among the reformist Dominicans had sojourned in the monastery of Saint Mark at Florence where they were deeply impressed by the prior, Jerome Savonarola. The Florentine reformer, however, died on the pyre in 1498 after having preached repentance and a return to divine laws. In many respects the later reformist missionaries were his spiritual successors. One of them, Antonio de Montesinos, courageously denounced the cruelty of the conquistadors. Here is an extract from one of his sermons, given on Advent 1511. Its severe and impassioned tone suggests the spirit of Savonarola:

> This is the voice of one crying in the wilderness of this island, and for this reason you must hear me with attention, with all your heart and all your senses. This is a new voice that you have never heard, and it is the bitterest and the hardest, the most dreadful and the most dangerous . . . This voice says to you that you are all in a state of mortal sin, and that in sin you live and die because of the cruelty and tyranny by which you overwhelm this innocent race.

> I ask, what right and what justice authorizes you to maintain the Indians in such awful servitude? In the name of what authority have you started an atrocious war against these people who were living in their land in a meek and peaceful manner, where a considerable number among them have been annihilated by you and died in a manner never seen before, so much is it atrocious? Why do you leave them in such a state of oppression and exhaustion, without giving them anything to eat, without caring for them in their sicknesses that come from that excessive work with which you overwhelm them and of which they die? To speak more exactly, you kill them so that you will obtain more gold everyday.

> And what care do you take for their instruction in our religion so that they know God their creator, so that they are baptized? . . . Are they not men? Have they not reason and souls? Are you not obliged to love them as yourselves? Do you not understand this? Do you not feel this? How can you be plunged in so deep a slumber, how can you be sleeping so lethargically?

> Be very sure that, in the state where you find yourselves, you cannot save yourselves any more than the Moors or the Turks who have no faith in Jesus Christ and who refuse it.

Las Casas, who related this discourse, concluded: "Montesinos spoke to them in a manner that left them stunned. Many among them were out of their senses, others more hardened still, some a little moved, but no one, from what I have learned afterwards, was converted." According to his own admission, La Casas was then preoccupied "more with material profits than with spiritual progress." Though scarcely shaken by Montesinos' words, a seed had been sown in La Casas' heart that did not take long to germinate.

In the following year, in fact, while acting as the chaplain for an expedition of "pacification" in Cuba, he was greatly disturbed by the carnage that was committed before his own eyes. Now keenly aware of the problem, his conscience gradually came to grips with it until, during Pentecost in 1514 at the age of thirty, he underwent a "conversion" that he described in these terms:

In meditating on the texts of the Holy Scripture, I fell on this passage of Ecclesiastes: "The offering of one who commits iniquity is tainted . . . The one who offers a sacrifice tied to the substance of the poor acts as if he was sacrificing a son in the presence of his father." I then began to consider the misery and the servitude that the Indians were undergoing. My memory turned to the sermons that I had heard [from Montesinos and other Dominicans]. Until that present moment, I had not accepted these remarks . . . I then considered the ignorance in which I had lived and the spiritual peril there was in possessing the Indians . . . After having reflected for several days, and feeling myself more and more certain, a conviction established itself in me: Everything being done in the Indies vis-à-vis the Indians was unjust and tyrannical . . .

In the end I decided to preach on it. And finally, to be able to freely denounce [these practices] as unjust and tyrannical, I decided immediately to renounce the Indians that I possessed . . . I began to explain to the colonists their blindness, denouncing the injustices, tyrannies, cruelties that they were committing with regard to these innocent and defenseless Indians; to say to them that they could not obtain their salvation while continuing to keep them in their power; adding that they had an obligation to give them restitution, and that for myself, plainly conscious of the peril that my soul was running, I had given my Indians their freedom.[129]

From that time Las Casas had chosen his side and, speaking in the third person, he expressed his newfound convictions in these words: "He would no longer live except for the Indians, so that the love of Christ and his justice would be extended to them." He began everywhere to undertake the defense of the oppressed. He immediately encountered stiff resistance from the colonists and the representatives of the Spanish government. For this reason, he embarked for the first time in 1515 for the home country with Brother Antonio de Montesinos in order to plead the cause of the Indians before the authorities.

He stayed in Spain for one year, and it was then that he lent his support to the idea of replacing the deficient Indian labor with that of the more robust African slaves. The experiment had already been attempted for fifty years, more by the Spanish than the Portuguese, and no one had found fault with it. It was only much later that he became aware of the horror of this practice. Observing the tragic consequences in America, he was seized with remorse. Speaking again in the third person, he would explain his position in his partly autobiographic *Historia de las Indias* (*History of the Indies*):

Some Spanish of this island, seeing what Abbot Casas was claiming, and that the religious of Saint Domingo did not want to give absolution to those who owned Indians and refused to part with them, say to the abbot that if a royal authorization were reported to them allowing them to import a dozen black slaves from

---

129 Ibid., 21–24.

> Castile, they would renounce the Indians . . . This suggestion of authorizing the importation of black slaves in these countries was made by Abbot Casas, without him being aware of the injustice of their capture and of their reduction to slavery by the Portuguese; but after he was aware of it, he would not have countenanced it for anything in the world, for he always considered the blacks as unjustly and tyrannically reduced to slavery, neither more nor less than the Indians . . .

> The Abbott was not slow to repent of this solution that he had proposed . . . And indeed, it was not reasonable on his part to advise the importation of blacks so that Indians could be freed . . . He was never assured that his ignorance on this point, nor his good will, were excuses that would be sufficient before the tribunal of God.

Las Casas passed the two years between 1517 and 1519 in the court of the Spanish king, the future emperor Charles V, who charged him officially "to remedy the evils of the Indians." Through discussions, colloquiums, long and detailed writings, and even trials, he attempted to justify the cause that he was defending against the bishops and other dignitaries of the kingdom who were hostile to him. He wrote memorably to the king:

> These people of the New World are men very apt to receive the Christian doctrine, to practice all types of virtues, and to adopt virtuous customs. And these are free beings by nature, who have their kings and their natural lords, who police themselves . . . Our religion is destined for all the nations of the world; it welcomes them all; it deprives none of their liberty under the pretext that by nature they would be slaves. It is convenient therefore that Your Majesty banish from these regions the scandalous iniquity that plagues it, so that Our Lord Jesus Christ, who died for all men, will long render your royal state prosperous.

Accompanied by seventy Castilian peasants, he returned to the Americas in 1520 with the aim of founding a colony in Venezuela where the rights of the Indians would be entirely respected. He had already thought in detail about the organization of the colony. Sadly, the project sought to reconcile too many contradictory objectives, both spiritual and economic; and there were too many incompatible interests: those of the Indians, colonists, and king. And it also lacked means. Consequently, the experiment floundered after only a few months. Las Casas felt this failure to the bone. During the next ten years he fell silent, retreating into a time of study and reflection among the Dominicans. It was during this time that he took on the priestly habit, and was henceforth addressed as Father Bartholoméw. He formulated his missionary methods that would now involve peaceful evangelization through various sorts of economic partnership. He wrote:

Concerning the land already discovered but not yet explored, whose populations and secrets no one knows, it is necessary [for the missionaries] to begin by converting them [the Indians] and winning them to the aid of the religious with their sermons, good works and good example, and by making them gifts of trinkets on behalf of his Majesty. Once they have set aside the horror and fear they have of the cruelty and infamies of the Christians, the Christians will begin to trade with them . . . and sentiments of affection and amity will appear among them. Due to this conversion, preaching, and pacification, it will be possible in time to found Christian villages farther into the country, beginning from the province or the closest city.

After writing his monumental *History of the Indies*, a well-documented work thanks to the archives of the family of Christopher Columbus with whom he was close, La Casas also wrote *De único modo* (*Concerning the Only Way of Drawing All Peoples to the True Religion*), a treatise written in Latin and partially lost today. Despite the prejudices of his time, he did not cease to repeat that all peoples of the earth are capable of understanding the gospel. Moreover, he taught that the evangelization of the world could only be realized by the means employed by Christ himself, through the attractiveness of one's own life and the willingness to lay it down for others. On this score, he reproached Christians for having done exactly the opposite of what Christ prescribed: they behaved toward the Indians as wolves in the midst of sheep while Jesus sent the disciples out to be "as sheep in the midst of wolves" (Matt 10:16). The several brief extracts that follow give an idea of the objectives of the work:

We say that it is absolutely impossible that any race or nation, that any human being in whatever region, province, or kingdom to which he may belong, is so stupid and deprived of reason that he is not at least capable of receiving the evangelical doctrine . . .

Divine Providence has established through the entire world and for all times a single method of teaching men the true religion: namely, the persuasion of the mind by means of reasonable arguments, a gentle pressure or motion from the will. Indubitably, this method of proceeding must be applied to all men of the world, without any distinction by reason of sect, error, or corrupt morals . . .

It is absolutely evident that in preaching the kingdom of God the apostles used only persuasion . . .

It is evident that Christ never permitted a person to constrain or molest anyone else, in particular the pagans who refused to listen to preaching or to receive preachers [and Las Casas recalled the indignation of Jesus when he was confronted with the wish of the disciples to see a Samaritan village destroyed]. It is evident that it was never right to punish pagans who refused to receive the teaching of the faith. To act otherwise is to transgress the divine precept.

The evangelical nonconformism of Las Casas can best be seen by recalling some parallel contemporary events: the destruction of the Aztec civilization in Mexico by Cortés, the destruction a little later of the Incas in Peru by Francisco Pizarre, and the all-too-common pseudoevangelization that was a mere mask for deceit and cruelty. It was following these misdeeds that Pope Paul III (1534–1549) promulgated the bull *Sublimus Dei* in 1537, proclaiming solemnly that the Indians, being endowed with reason and dignity, were to be deprived of neither their liberty nor their goods, that they were perfectly capable of receiving the light of Christianity, and that they were to be invited to the faith through the preaching of the word of God and by good moral example. The impact of Father Bartholoméw's ideas is clearly manifest in the pope's message. Encouraged by this affirmation, Las Casas immediately translated and printed the text in Santiago de Guatemala.

He also integrated the text of the bull into his treatise noted above, *De único modo*. Here are several more lines from it:

> Man by his nature is capable of receiving the faith in Christ, and all those who share in this human nature have the aptitude to receive this same faith . . . Considering that these Indians, who by all evidence are true men, have not been found simply capable of receiving the Christian faith but, as we have learned, hurry to the faith with promptitude, desiring to make use of opportune remedies, we declare in virtue of our apostolic authority that these Indians, as well as all other peoples who in the future will arrive at a knowledge of Christianity, although they be still out of the Christian faith, must be deprived neither of their liberty nor of the enjoyment of their goods; that to the contrary, they must be able to use this liberty and these goods and to enjoy them freely and that they must not be reduced to servitude. These same Indians and the other nations must be invited to receive the Christian faith by the preaching of the Word of God and by the example of a virtuous life.[130]

In his *History of the Indies* Las Casas denounced the rapid, brutal, and superficial methods of Christianizing the Indians that were practiced by the Spanish conquistadors. For example, in Mexico, Father Martin de Valence (surnamed by the common people who loved him Motolinia, "the poor") followed the example of Saint Augustine: *Compelle Intrare* ("compel them to enter"), a policy he recommended against the Donatists. Similarly Martin advised that the Indians be compelled to enter *a palos*, by strokes of the cane. Alluding to Cortés, Las Casas denounced the absurdity of baptizing the Indians after only a few days and destroying their idols by force. He pleaded for a method infinitely more evangelical; and if the message of the following text had been accepted, South American Catholicism would doubtless not have taken the syncretistic and superstitious course that in many cases it still follows:

---

130 Ibid., 103–4.

What Christian teaching could the Spaniards bring to these people during the two, three, four, or ten days that they sojourn among them? It is evident that they speak to them of the true God in such a way as to cause them to abandon the erroneous confidence that they place in their gods, and that, as soon as they have gone from them, the people recommence their idolatry. First of all, the attachment they have to their idols must be erased from their hearts; that is to say, the faith that they have in them, holding them to be true gods, must be erased. Through daily teaching, with diligence and perseverance, it is necessary to impress on their hearts the veritable concept of the true God. Then, on their own, they will recognize their error and begin with their own hands and in all liberty to destroy the idols that they venerate as gods . . .

To erect the cross and to invite the Indians to give some marks of respect to it is a good thing, on condition that they can be made to understand the significance of the gesture. But if the necessary time is not available, or if one does not speak their language, it is a useless and superfluous thing, for the Indians may imagine a new idol is being presented to them, which they take to be the God of the Christians. Hence they are invited to adore a piece of wood as god, which is idolatrous. The surest approach, the only rule that is appropriate for Christians to observe when they find themselves in pagan territories, is to give them a good example of virtuous works. In this way, according to the words of our Redeemer, *seeing their works, they praise and glorify your Father* and recognize that a God who has such followers can only be good and true.[131]

Between 1539 and 1543, Las Casas sojourned in Spain, which he had not seen for twenty years. His influence with Charles V was then at its apogee. He recruited a number of missionaries whom he sent to evangelize a vast region that was called the "Land of Peace." At the request of Las Casas, the king of Spain took this territory from the colonists and conferred it exclusively on the Dominicans, who sought to apply their missionary methods there. They practiced a noncompulsory evangelism that received a great response from the Indians. Very much in love with music, according to one witness, "They were converted more by songs than by sermons." During this time in Spain, Las Casas obtained from the king in 1542 the famous *Leyes Nuevas* ("New Laws"), legislation that abolished slavery among the Indians and the *encomienda*, and declared all the indigenous people to be "free vassals of the king." Despite violent opposition, the "Protector of the Indians" seemed to have won his cause. But it was a paper victory; in fact, the colonists derided the laws with impunity. Moreover, insofar as the *encomiendas* were concerned, the New Laws were revoked after only three years, so great was the outcry that they had provoked among the colonists.

It was during this time in Spain that Las Casas wrote this poignant text, taken from the *Dedicatory Letter to the Prince of Asturies* (1542):

---

131 Ibid., 146–47.

Forgetting that they are men, the Spanish have treated these innocent creatures with a cruelty worthy of wolves, tigers, and
hungry lions. For forty-two years they have not ceased to pursue,
oppress, and destroy them with all the means already invented
by wicked humans and by others that these tyrants have come to
imagine. Also one today no longer remembers that two hundred
indigenous people in the Spanish island were feeding 3 million in
the past . . . One can guarantee as certain that the Spanish by their
inhumane and atrocious policy have caused 12 million persons,
men, women, and children, to die. But I estimate that the number
is closer to 15 million . . .

It is the avidity of the Spanish that has been the sole cause of this
horrible butchery: they have not known any god but gold; they
have not felt any other need than to gorge themselves with riches,
and as quickly as possible, at the expense of meek, peaceful, and
subjugated men, whom they have treated worse than animals and
with more scorn than vile filth, since they have caused them to
die in torment without being concerned to convert them to our
holy religion.

In 1543 Las Casas sailed again for South America and was designated bishop of
Chiapas, a Guatemalan territory extending from the Atlantic to the Pacific. Four years
later, however, he decided to return to Spain, conscious that the future of the Indians was to be played out in Europe. The principal Indian chiefs in Mexico, who had
encouraged this voyage, wrote to King Phillip II: "To bring about a remedy for our
difficulties, we need someone who can be our protector who resides permanently
in your court . . . the bishop of Chiapas, Father Bartholoméw de Las Casas." They described him as characterized by "a total Christianity and goodness."

Las Casas would spend the next nineteen years of his life in Europe, feeling himself to be invested with a prophetic mission, struggling without pause for the same
cause, so scandalizing the Dominicans that one man left the order rather than support Las Casas' position. He went as far as suggesting that the descendants of the
Incas in Peru be given a part of the empire of their ancestors. But he saw his influence diminish under Phillip II, who did not have the same openness of spirit as his
predecessor, Charles V. The "Father and Protector of the Indians" died in Madrid in
1566, being eighty-two years old.

# THE JESUITS IN PARAGUAY (1585–1756)

The Guarani tribe constituted the most populous ethnic group in a South America
that had already experienced numerous attempts at colonization in the sixteenth
century.[132] The Guarani were scattered among other tribes and spread over territories that were equal in area to that of Europe, from the equator at Uruguay to the
south, from the Atlantic to the Cordillera of the Andes. They were partially nomads

---

132 Very precise reports were written about them by the Calvinist Jean de Léry (cf. pp. 274ff of this work).

and rebelled assiduously against colonization. Living in great rectangular houses that were covered with palm leaves and gave shelter to as many as sixty families, they took to the hunt and to fishing, and cultivated corn and manioc. After five or six years when the land was exhausted and their houses were falling to ruins, they departed to settle elsewhere.

Among the Guarani, the chief of the tribe was often a shaman, or spiritual leader. It was his responsibility to organize the ritual ceremonies intended to conciliate the more or less malevolent spirits who ceaselessly interfered in their nomadic existence. The Guarani had a rather vague belief in a superior heavenly being whom they called *Tupan*. But, in fact, he had more to do with the demon of lightning, frightening by the effects of his anger, than a sovereign, benevolent, creator God. Their mythology also included a "civilizing hero," *Pay Zume*, who came from far away to accomplish great miracles and found their ethnic group. Some missionaries identified *Pay Zume* with Sao Tome, the Apostle Thomas, who was supposed to have come to evangelize the Indian peoples at the beginning of the Christian era.

The Guarani practiced polygamy, with men usually having three or four wives, though the chiefs could have as many as thirty or even fifty. The mortality was considerable among the men because of incessant and murderous tribal wars. These wars were also the occasion of ritual cannibalism, which Maxime Haubert describes:

> They bring back as many prisoners as possible. These are treated kindly, being allowed to take women and participate in all the tribal activities. But after a period of time, sometimes as much as several years, each of them is solemnly bludgeoned to death, dismembered, and eaten. It is considered, however, to be a glorious death; and the prisoner, who has enjoyed full freedom in the village, did not need to be guarded to be kept from flight. He confronts death rather well, with a joyous heart, and he derides his persecutors with the number of their tribe who have already been killed and eaten by his own, and by the vengeance that they will come to take for his death.[133]

The Jesuits in 1585 obtained from King Phillip II of Spain the administration of the Guarani territories, situated between land belonging to the Portuguese and that occupied by the Spanish, an area approximately covering present-day Paraguay. This territory was directly dependent on the Spanish crown, to whom its indigenous occupants were paying taxes. However, they were practically autonomous and forbade access to colonizers. Among the Jesuits engaged in this enterprise, most were of Spanish or Italian origin, but there were also a good number of Germans, Dutch, Austrians, and Hungarians. The most illustrious among them was Father Antonio Ruiz de Montoya, who was one of the creators of the famous communities known under the Latin-derived name of "reductions" (*reducti*).

---

133 Maxime Haubert, *La vie quotidienne des Indiens et des jésuites du Paraguay au temps des missions* (Paris: Hachette, 1967), 14.

*Map 11: Missions from 1500 to 1800 in South America*

During the first thirty years, the Jesuits were happy to carry out long missionary treks in the forest where they encountered populations marked by a fear of spirits and, it seemed, a thirst for the gospel. After rapidly baptizing whole villages, they discovered that soon after their departure the villagers' ancestral practices quickly reappeared. This led them to the conclusion that they needed to establish themselves in the midst of the population if the faith were to endure among them. They decided that the nomadic or seminomadic groups would have to become sedentary to achieve this, and hence they established the first reductions.[134] Claude Lugon explains, "The first community was Lorette. Founded in 1610, it consisted of a group of two hundred families that were baptized several years later by the Fathers Ortegá and Filds. The inhabitants of twenty-three other small villages in the area soon joined them, attracted by the guarantee of freedom that was given by the Fathers. As Lorette was soon overpopulated, the Fathers traveled a league and a half farther away to found San Ignacio-Miní, which was immediately populated by several hundred families."[135]

In general, in their concern for evangelization, the Jesuits sent "their" villagers to recruit others from farther away. This led to some reductions becoming large villages. Already by 1612 there were four or five localities that had more than two thousand Indians each, though for the most part they were still pagan. By 1623 there were thirteen reductions. By 1630, twenty years after this program had been launched, there were thirty-four reductions, totaling close to 100,000 inhabitants and spread over an area about half the size of France. In their period of greatest success, the reductions had four thousand to fifteen thousand inhabitants each, totaling close to 300,000 Indians. In general, when a reduction reached more than 1,500 families, division became necessary. If this was not done, the villagers would have to walk too far to their cultivated fields—a source of fatigue, dangers, and emancipation. After a century and a half of existence when the experiment had come to an end under Portuguese pressure, there were still hundreds of Jesuit priests spread over thirty-two reductions that together totaled about ninety thousand Indians.

In Bolivia other more ephemeral Jesuit reductions were organized that included about 115,000 Indians of the Mojos and Chiquitos tribes. Beginning in 1682, the mission to the Mojos established twenty-seven reductions in the tropical plains close to Paraguay. A dozen years later, the missions to the Chiquitos consisted of eleven reductions that were planted farther north in the region of the Amazon basin.

During the first period, missionaries had to confront numerous difficulties, mostly due to attacks from "uncontrolled" Europeans. This primarily involved the Paulist *banderiras*, groups of slave-hunting adventurers from among the Portuguese colonists coming from Sao Paulo. Hence in 1630, six reductions were attacked and fifteen thousand Guarani chained and led with their herds as slaves to Brazil. Between 1630

---

134 Ruiz de Montoya writes: "We call large towns reductions, where the diligence of the Fathers reduced the Indians to a political and human life in which they could cultivate cotton to clothe themselves." The term does not signify therefore that the Indians were supposed to be "reduced" in the sense of "reduced to slavery," or "imprisoned," but "reduced" (Latin: *reducti*) to the Christian faith and to the ordered life.

135 Claude Lugon, "Les missions de l'Amérique du Sud aux XVIIe et XVIIIe siècles et la république des Guaranis," in *Histoire universelle des missions catholiques* 2 (1957): 266.

and 1636 several other establishments were pillaged and burned, with massacres as well; but the Guarani were slowly organized and armed under the supervision of the Jesuits, and in 1641 they managed to beat the Paulists.

Paraguay became a sort of theocratic republic and the experiment continued for close to 150 years. It was in 1750 that the Portuguese, having concluded a treaty with the Spanish, demanded that the Jesuits cede the territory to them. The majority of the priests left, bowing to the political agreement that the two European kingdoms had made at their expense. The Guarani, however, launched an armed resistance that terminated in a bloodbath. There were 1,500 dead among the Indians in a single battle. The last remaining Jesuits were finally driven out of Paraguay in 1768. Deported to Buenos Aires and "treated as cattle," they were embarked for Spain, imprisoned, and exiled. In 1773 the pope suppressed the Society of Jesus throughout Christendom. The hostility of those who had experienced the reductions of Paraguay contributed in large measure to this decision.

This Jesuit missionary enterprise has been closely studied and is now well known. The principal sources are the correspondence and reports of the Jesuit Fathers, but also the narratives of observers, some enthusiastic and others reserved or even hostile. It is evident that the decision of the Jesuits to protect the Indians from the ravages of colonization and slavery produced strong opposition in the colony and even more so in Europe. Their success was undeniable, if not in the spiritual domain where the outcome was mixed, at least in the areas of economics, sanitation, and the political administration of the territories. All of this, of course, also raised jealousies and concerns.

In the early years of the mission, the missionaries paid a high price for their efforts. Their commitment to adapting themselves to the culture and conditions of the local people was incontestably remarkable. "They made themselves barbarians with these barbarians," according to the witness of Father Domingo Muriel, who visited them in the eighteenth century. For example, he wrote with regard to Father Barrace:

> He sat on the earth with them to talk; he imitated their least movement and the most ridiculous gestures that they used to express the affections of their hearts. He slept in the midst of them . . . There was a missionary who, in the beginning, painted his face like them in order to gain their trust. It was a type of preaching that began their conversion with the face, so that one day, when he would judge it apropos, he could continue on to God.[136]

The Indians' destitution was severe. They lived in rags, ate manioc and maize, and were powerless in the face of tropical diseases. Father Ruiz de Montoya recounts:

> The huts, the furniture, and the food would have been very appropriate for anchorites. We have not tasted bread, wine, or salt for many years. We were reduced to sow with our own hands the wheat necessary for the hosts; we survived on a half-arobe [about

---

136 Haubert, *La vie*, 91.

five liters] of wine for almost five years, for we think that it should be used only for the consecration.[137]

The Jesuits often came from the intellectual elite and from the nobility of the great cities of Europe. Yet here they were compelled to humble themselves to do arduous tasks: chopping down trees, dragging lumber, baking bricks, constructing their huts and their churches, making themselves laborers. And they did all of this, at least in the beginning, without the aid of animal labor. Some died of privations, others were killed during intertribal confrontations or, as in the case of Father Diego de Alfonso, in resisting slave hunters. Still others knew martyrdom while seeking to reach hostile populations. The case is cited of Father San Martin who, having lost his reason following privations and trials, was authorized to leave the Society. Father Ruiz de Montoya himself was plunged for a year into terrible agonies; to use his own terms, his soul became like "a desert in the night." It is true, however, that these extreme conditions were characteristic only of the pioneer period. Afterwards, economic prosperity and a flawless organization made the Jesuit Fathers powerful administrators, exercising everywhere an arbitrary and tyrannical authority. They are reproached for attempting to carve out for themselves a South American empire.

While the missionaries were evangelizing the Guarani, they also taught them to read and write. More measurable were the effects they had on the local economy. They taught them the cultivation of cereals, fruits, and vegetables; the breeding of animals; the exploitation of the forest; and various artisan trades. The introduction of iron tools was an enormous factor in their progress. One of the missionaries, Father Sepp, wrote: "When I arrived in Paraguay most of the poor people were cutting their wheat with cow ribs that took the place of scythes; reeds of a curious type that they chopped in the middle served as knives; they were employing thorns to sew their cloth."[138] The Indians were not slow to understand the advantages that they could acquire from the techniques brought by the priests, and the installation of a forge in the village sufficed to attract and keep many there. The economic organization was founded on a strict "evangelical communism," and some of these establishments were highly prosperous. For example, the reduction of Father Paucke, a German, twenty years after its foundation possessed 24,000 dairy cows, 8,300 calves, 500 oxen, 1,500 horses, 1,200 mares, and 1,700 sheep—for a population of 1,900 people. Each week, forty cows were slaughtered. According to Jacques Soustelle, "for the Indians, whose diet depended on the uncertain hunt, it was also a benevolent revolution that could provide an abundant source of meat . . . all the witnesses agree that the introduction of the raising and consuming of meat by the Indians was a determining factor in the success of the mission."[139] Father Paucke taught women to spin, dye, and weave wool, and soon each was producing wool products out of her own home. The communal

---

137  Ibid., 95.

138  Ibid., 262.

139  Jacques Soustelle, cited in ibid., vi. Haubert writes: "At the time of the expulsion of the Jesuits, the reduction certainly possessed more than 1 million cows, about 300,000 sheep and goats, 100,000 horses, fifty thousand mules, and twenty thousand donkeys" (ibid., 200). For a population of ninety thousand people, these numbers are impressive.

workshop produced covers and rugs whose sales contributed to the prosperity of the whole community.

The land and the houses were communally owned, and there were neither salaries nor money. No market existed since everything was distributed in the community shops according to need. As individual property did not exist, inheritance was practically unknown. In principle, therefore, there were neither rich nor poor. The different clan chiefs met at the reduction of Caciques to distribute the land between their vassals so that they could be farmed to feed individual families. Each farmer owned his own harvest but not the land that he worked. He was also required to do work for the common good, such as the construction of churches or other public buildings, and especially work on the collective land known as *tupambae* ("the things of God"). The harvest from this was used to help the poor and sick, to pay the king of Spain's tax, and as a reserve for bad years.

Some reductions even created small industries that included mills, sawmills, brick kilns, metal forges, and installations for the refining of sugarcane, among others. The Indians were taught various trades: carpentry, joinery, wheel making, cooperage, pottery, tannery, shoemaking, and tailoring. In 1700 the first small printing press was established, and others followed, producing books of excellent quality, though it was necessary to import the paper from Europe. Several works were translated and published in Guarani, but not the Bible or even a Gospel. The construction and decoration of immense and richly ornamented churches necessitated the training of various types of craftsmen: sculptors, gilders, bell founders, instrument makers, and makers of trumpets, horns, vats, chalices, rosaries, and other things as well. This production involved commercial exchanges between the reductions. Journeys were normally undertaken by river ways, but there were also some good roads between the reductions, some with bridges and barks at river crossings. Moreover, a small chapel was constructed every five leagues, with one or two waiting rooms. Though several Indians had the responsibility to guard and maintain these buildings, lodging there was free.

Here is an extract from a rule drafted by Father Vieira, Visitor of the Jesuit Missions between 1658 and 1661:

> The Fathers will exhort the Indians to engage in several industries for their profit, conforming to their capacities and those of the country. And because these Indians do not have the aptitude to sell what they make or buy what is necessary for them, each of the Fathers will seek to have in town a person approved by the Superior who, for the service of God and Christians, is willing to do this charity for the Indians. They will be given the products so that they can sell them in the name of the Indians and buy for them whatever they need . . . The Indians should apply themselves to the work with sufficient moderation so that service to their churches will not become a fatiguing chore, for God will be better served by altars modestly ornamented than by the malcontent of

those who must be constrained to work hard in order to decorate them sumptuously.[140]

The Guarani villages were all constructed on the same model, with a great space decorated with palm trees. The plan was like a checkerboard, with the streets laid out perfectly straight. This facilitated supervision by the missionaries; sometimes two priests alone would direct villages having as many as eight thousand inhabitants. The width of the streets (about fifteen meters for the great avenues) and the grouping of the houses by blocks of six or seven limited the danger of fire. The public area divided the locality into two very distinct parts. On one side was the domain of God and the Jesuits: church, presbytery, hospital, school, cemetery; on the other side was the living area of the Indians. Haubert observes, "On one side the authorities, on the other the subjects. The Jesuits were not and did not want to be 'in the center' of the village." The exact plan of the reduction of San Ignacio-Mini is known. The place measured 127 meters by 108 and was surrounded by communal buildings: a church of 63 by 30 meters, hospital, schools, house of the Fathers, house of the visitors, arsenal, and house of the people (fifty-two columns of red sandstone). Three straight, paved avenues of 13–20 meters in width served the living quarters and were crossed by other less important streets in the square.[141]

On arriving at the village, the Jesuits offered bells or rattles to mollify the Indians. They immediately discovered that the Guarani were very sensitive to music. Some priests, such as Jean Vassaux de Tournai, were reputed musicians in Europe before leaving for the mission. On arriving in Paraguay, they taught the Guarani the most developed musical notations of the period. As early as 1622 Father Louis Berge, an eminent violinist, introduced his art in the schools. "With a single violin, he converted numerous infidels," it was said of him. The Guarani instrument makers showed great virtuosity in making these instruments. After a few years, the churches were equipped with organs and possessed choirs of children singing and dancing to the sound of harps, guitars, citharas, bassoons, and pipes. In six months Father Paucke was able to perform some amazing feats with his children's choir. Attendance increased at the Mass, with parents bursting with pride. Even the nonbaptized came to hear this celestial music. "In a word," said Father Paucke, "the musicians are the decoys that the missionaries use to draw the parishioners to the church." Song was also helpful in teaching the catechism. The essential points of Christian doctrine were put to music, and the children learned them easily and were able to repeat them in any situation.

In the reductions of Bolivia, the Jesuits seem to have obtained the same remarkable results with the Chiquitos and the Mojos. Here is an extract from a letter of the Swiss Jesuit Martin Schmid, written in 1744:

---

140  Laurence Evons, "La république des Guaranis," in 2000 ans de christianisme, vol. 6 (Paris: Sociéte d'Histoire Chrétienne, 1976), 230.

141  For the plan of San Ignacio-Mini as well as various photographs of the vestiges of the imposing religious buildings of the reductions, see Lugon, "Les missions," 263ff.

> Our small Indians learn in an excellent fashion. You could see here yourself how boys that were taken from the densest forest hardly a year ago, and at the same time as their savage parents, are now singing with much ability. They follow the rules of music and enjoy harps, violins, and organs. They even dance, according to the prescribed rules, with so much exactitude that they could measure themselves against Europeans with success.

After the departure of the Jesuits, the Indians kept the music of the missionaries alive in their culture. At first it was transmitted by indigenous copyists. A pile of dismembered and difficult-to-decipher manuscripts was recently discovered in old sacks in a region of Mojos. With the passing of time, oral tradition supplanted these written scores. Old instruments in good condition and two centuries old have also been found in more or less dilapidated old churches: transverse flutes, violins, viols, and harps. And among the Mojos Indians they continue to be made today according to the techniques current at the time of the Jesuits. Lacking the modifications later introduced to the violin, the Mojos violin has remained unchanged since the style current in 1700—its handle not raised, its strings made of intestines.

In the reductions of Paraguay, other art forms such as painting and sculpture flourished as well. Moreover, they did not disdain to make some cultural adaptations: the performers dancing with feather capes in the manner of their traditional ancestral dances. The architecture of their sanctuaries became increasingly sophisticated and majestic. According to Pierre-François Charlevoix, historian of the American colonies (1682–1761), "these churches would compare well with the most beautiful of Spain and Peru, as much for the beauty of their structure as for the richness and good taste of their silverware and all types of ornaments." The church of San Juan possessed a mechanical clock comparable to the one in the cathedral of Strasbourg, with its twelve apostles who parade at the twelve strokes of noon.

This picture can be completed with the perhaps somewhat idealized description of Claude Lugon: "Leisure occupied a large place. The Guarani were passionate about sport and competition with prizes. The Jesuits used this innate penchant for purposes of education. The religious and the secular were mixed with a liberty that shocked no one. The children, at the sound of an orchestra of thirty to forty instruments, performed their dances before the altar. The stories of the Bible were also presented while completely guaranteeing [the authenticity of] the style and personages . . . The first theatrical pieces enjoyed by the Guarani were antislavery dramas . . . The Jesuits also favored secular games, comedies, and tournaments."[142]

The principal question to be posed is whether these activities led to a true evangelization of the people and an authentic spiritual life in the reductions. Of course this is not easy to answer. Without questioning either the dedication of the priests or the fervor of numerous Indian Christians, it is not difficult to recognize that the influence of the gospel remained in general rather superficial. The Jesuits seemed

---

142  Lugon, "Les missions," 273.

convinced that the Indians were and would remain incapable and infantile.[143] Their "feeble intelligence still being darkened by paganism," they believed that one must not hesitate to resort to force, or then to gifts, to obtain conversions. In fact, among the Jesuits there was an ongoing conflict between those who favored a strong hand and those who preferred evangelization by more charitable means. It bears repeating that the remarkable demographic growth of the reductions was not due simply to better sanitary conditions or a falling rate of mortality, but also to the numerous efforts undertaken from the very beginning by the Guarani themselves to attract their racial brothers to the reductions. Lugon writes: "The Fathers were too few in number and overburdened by the ministry in general, the sick, the innumerable confessions. The best of the Guarani continued, as their ancestors of the first period had, to organize missionary expeditions, redeeming sometimes in a single effort as many as sixty pagan families to whom they had explained 'the goodness that one tastes in the service of the true God and the pleasure that there is of living in society.' Though the population welcomed the catechumens with the most generous hospitality, the names of these lay apostles have largely been forgotten."[144]

As for the catechism, the learning of elementary formulas by heart seems to have been the only type of learning envisioned. At the beginning, the Jesuits baptized children in danger of death. Soon they began to baptize others without their parents knowing it and even against their will. It is known that some missionaries wetted their sleeves to baptize the dying without those nearby knowing it.

One of the greatest shortcomings of this undertaking was that it was tainted by paternalism from top to bottom. The Jesuits scarcely sought to lead the Indians toward more autonomy. Though the reductions functioned admirably, they were a protected world that left the Indians passive and submissive. Jacques Soustelle writes: "Though the missionaries had pure intentions, they can be reproached for having barred the Indians from access to adulthood."[145] Hence after 150 years, there were no Indian priests, no indigenous and autonomous churches. The Jesuits strove to maintain an intangible distance between European priests and the lay, child-like Indian population. For example, the Indian males (never women) were only admitted into Jesuit apartments in case of absolute necessity, or to receive orders. The missionaries never visited the Indians, and they entered their homes only to bring them the last rites. They did not engage them in conversation. The Jesuits were a minute minority among the mass of the indigenous population, and they were devoid of all means of coercion. Consequently, their authority was based on the essential difference between the priesthood and the laity, a difference that they believed was absolutely necessary to maintain.

Behind a Christian facade, many pagan practices survived. Despite a general appreciation of the enterprise of the reductions, Haubert writes: "It is questionable if the Guarani understood the sense of practices such as Communion, confession, the

---

143  Hence Father Jarque wrote: "To be a priest among the Guarani is equivalent to having six thousand children."
144  Lugon, "Les missions," 274.
145  Cited in Haubert, *La vie*, viii.

notion of individual sin, chastisement, flagellation. Their zeal on this point seems more inherited from pagan conceptions than due to a still immaculate Christian fervor."[146]

Despite these shortcomings and failings, the reductions had a number of positive aspects that should be pointed out. Certainly the activities in them suggest a striking contrast between the mentality of the Jesuits of the reductions and the Spanish conquistadors or the Portuguese colonizers of this period. Many philosophers were fascinated by the generally idealized stories that arrived in Europe, some wondering if they were not present at the birth of a sort of utopian kingdom. Others, in contrast, compared the reductions to slave labor camps. It is true that the discipline there was constraining, especially the schedule. But it could be plausibly argued that these conditions were necessary to deliver an effective education that would lead to a real prosperity. On the other hand, they introduced into a hitherto nomadic and independent population painful shackles: marriage at fifteen years, obligatory catechism, corporal punishments, and the rest.[147] However, at about thirty hours a week the work was not very demanding, and it was less during prosperous times. Also leisure, games, and sports occupied an important place in the life of the community, as noted above.

The reductions, as we have said, gave rise to opposing opinions, some in diametrical opposition to one another. There follow two particularly contrasting examples. Interpreting in his own special way the stories of Bougainville, which tell of a visit to the missions of Paraguay at the moment of the expulsion of the Jesuits, the philosopher Diderot wrote:

> These cruel Spartans in dark morning coats were using their Indian slaves as the Lacedemonians did the Helots [as slaves or serfs]; had condemned them to demanding work; drinking their sweat, had left them no property rights, were holding them under brutalizing superstition by requiring a profound veneration; were marching in the midst of them, whip in hand, and striking without distinction of age or sex.[148]

Idyllic by contrast is the description given by Father Florenin upon visiting Paraguay in 1716. Such accounts have contributed more than a little to the forging of the "myth" of the reductions of Paraguay:

> I came among the common people of Saint Francis Xavier and I went right to the church: it faces a great place where the principal streets lead, which are all very large and straight as a line . . . The [Jesuit] community was composed of seven priests full of virtue and merit . . . Here is the order that I observed among the people where I was, which is composed of about thirty thousand souls.

---

146  Ibid., 283.

147  The parents who neglected to correct their children were shipped with them. The death penalty did not exist because the Indians, supposed to be like children, were considered to have only limited responsibility. The ordinary chastisements were the dungeon and the whip, the latter accepted with submission and even gratitude insofar as it was seen as a means of contrition.

148  Denis Diderot, *Supplément au voyage de Bougainville* (1772; repr., Paris: GF-Flammarion, 1972), 144.

The bell is sounded at the beginning of the day to call the people to church; a missionary says the morning prayer, and the mass is then said, after which everyone retires to go about their business. The children, from seven or eight to twelve years of age, are obliged to go to school where the masters teach them to read and write, teaching the catechism and the prayers of the church, and instructing them in the duties of Christianity. The girls are also obliged to go to their schools until the age of twelve years. Here the mistresses teach them the prayers and catechism, and show them how to read, spin, and sow . . . At sunset, evening prayer is heard, after which the rosary is recited . . .

The unity and charity that reign between the faithful is perfect: as goods are held in common, ambition and avarice are unknown vices, and one does not see among them either division or trial. They have been taught so well of the horror of impurity that faults in this matter are very rare; they are occupied only with prayer, work, and the care of their families . . . Many things contribute to the innocent life that these new faithful people lead . . . the examples of those who govern them, in whom they see nothing but edification . . . [and there is] little communication with Europeans . . .

The people are divided into different quarters, and each quarter has a supervisor who is chosen from among the more fervent Christians . . . Before the Jesuit Fathers carried the light of the gospel to Paraguay, this country was inhabited by entirely barbarous peoples, without religion, law, society, fixed living places . . . It is not easy to conceive what work they [the missionaries] performed in order to assemble these barbarians together and make them reasonable men before trying to make them Christians . . . Neither the poor nor beggars are seen here, and all have an equal abundance of the things necessary for life.

## NORTH AMERICA

King Henry IV of France hoped that Acadia on the east coast of Canada would be a place where France's Catholics and Protestants could coexist in peace. In 1603 he sent the Protestant Pierre du Gast, master of Monts, to direct the first French settlers there. He was accompanied by two chaplains, a Protestant minister and a Catholic priest. Sadly, the experiment was scarcely peaceful. Champlain, the French colonizer and founder of Quebec (1567–1635), described a tragicomic scene:

I saw the [Protestant] minister and our priest fighting hand to hand over the difference of religion. I could not tell who was more valiant and who gave the better blows, but I know very well that the minister complained several times to the master of Monts of the fight, and avoided in this fashion the points of controversy. I leave you to consider if this was a pretty sight. The savages fight

> sometimes on one side, sometimes on another . . . These inso-
> lences were truly a means for the infidel to cling more tenaciously
> to his infidelity.

After establishing the colony of Quebec, Champlain summoned a Catholic missionary team there in 1615. These religious sought to reach the Huron Indians, but
they had scarcely any results. They believed that "Frenchified" Indians were alone capable of leading a "more humane and civil" life and would eventually convert. As for
the rest, "it seems that their sins, darkened by impiety and brutal morals, had spread
among them a blindness and insensitivity to any sort of religion, which historians
have not noticed in the other peoples of the world."

In 1625 five Jesuits arrived in Quebec. In 1637, twelve years later and under the
direction of Father Lejeune, this increased to twenty-nine. In this same year, they admitted the first adult to baptism. According to the method defined by Father Lejeune,
the missionaries were attempting to hold the seminomadic Hurons in permanent
villages. The village of Sillery, founded in 1637, was home to four hundred families
by 1648. Inspired by the reductions of Guarani in Paraguay, the missionaries tried to
inculcate the methods of European agriculture to induce the tribe to become sedentary. But the settlements were only seasonal, the villages emptying in the winter
as the Indians pursued the hunt for beaver. Moreover, it was not possible to isolate these villagers from European colonists or from the other Indians that remained
pagan, with the ill-fated influences that this involved. The missionaries found it impossible to prevent the selling of alcohol to the indigenous people, for their village
Indians threatened to leave if liquor were forbidden. Despite everything, the years
between 1639 and 1649 saw the work develop and become stronger. The Jesuits were
reinforced by the Ursuline Sisters from Tours (notably Marie de l'Incarnation) and
the Hospitalier Sisters of Dieppe. These sisters, the first female Catholic religious to
have been sent in mission, concerned themselves with the care of the sick and with
teaching women.

The Iroquois were a very intelligent people but unreachable because of their ferocity and hostility to all French colonists. Between 1649 and 1650 they launched
frequent attacks against the Christian villages, burning several villages and extermi-
nating or dispersing the majority of the Hurons. Several Jesuits died in the massacres.

Beginning in 1632 the Capuchins evangelized the Algonquin tribes of Acadia.
Their efforts focused on the creation of mixed Franco-Indian schools, permitting the
"Frenchifying in meekness" of a new generation of Indians. The Jesuits, for their part,
founded a seminary in Quebec. It was intended for the Indians and the French, so
that they could receive a common education.

There were some great explorers among the French missionaries, notably the Jesuits Marquette, Joliet, and Hennepin, who traveled through the region of the Great
Lakes and then in 1673 and 1674 traveled south to discover where the Mississippi
empties into the sea. Throughout the journey they preached the gospel. However, it
was only in 1682 that Cavelier de la Salle arrived at the mouth of the river. In contrast
to many Iberian explorers, the French refused to use force to constrain the Indians

to become Christians. The policy of the Jesuits in Canada was very different from that of the Jesuits in Latin America, for they did not live amidst as brutal a process of colonization. Jarry writes, "In Canada the French never used the Indians as a work-force: the Jesuits did not have to defend them. Moreover . . . they [the Jesuits] favored French expansion with all the strength that they had. Without doubt because they were good Frenchmen; but also because they knew every loss to France was a gain for the heretics [Protestants], first the Dutch, then the English."[149] British and Dutch colonists, of course, did not recognize the authority of the Roman pontiff and so denied Catholic claims to North America.

Despite the presence of more than three hundred Jesuits in New France, and without counting the other religious orders, by the end of the eighteenth century there would scarcely be six Christian Indian villages with a total population of about two thousand persons, a rather meager record.

---

149 Jarry, "Les missions," 293.

# CHAPTER 11

# Catholic Mission in Africa

W hile America was divided between the Spanish and Portuguese, Africa was reserved for the Portuguese alone, who had been the first to travel around the continent.

Because Africa was a difficult continent to enter, for a long time it remained a frightening and unknown territory. At first the Portuguese were interested in using the continent to establish relay stations along the route to the Indies. Only later did they realize that Africa was rich, and that the riches lay in the people themselves. The Iberians eventually noticed that in the regions of their Muslim neighbors the most effective workers were African slaves, while in comparison the constitution of the American Indians was much more fragile. Africa, therefore, became a huge reservoir from which to draw the hundreds of thousands of human beings needed to replace the Indian manpower that had been decimated by sickness or massacre. Pope Leo X (1513–1521) condemned the traffic in African slaves, but he was ignored.

## CONGO AND ANGOLA

As noted above (p. 139), the king of the Congo, Mani-Kongo Mbemba Nzienga Nkuwu, was baptized in 1492 along with the queen and his heir, the prince; and he took the Christian name of Joao (John). This did not lead him to exclude from his court either polygamy or the worship of ancestral gods. The successor of this king, Don Affonso I, reigned in the period of 1506–1545. Fervently Catholic and devoted to the Portuguese, he sought to Europeanize his court and the administration of his kingdom. He asked for other missionaries, for the first had been decimated by sickness and accidents. In 1513 he sent his son, Don Henrique, accompanied by an ambassador, to Pope Leo X, who received him solemnly. Henrique, who had done his studies in Portugal, addressed the Pope in Latin. In 1518 the Pope named him bishop of Sao Salvador—he was the first African Catholic bishop.

Affonso sent a number of young Congolese to Portugal to train for the priesthood. In accord with the wishes of King Emmanuel I of Portugal, he sought to endow the Congo with an indigenous clergy. But he did not have much success.

Great churches were constructed, but the commitment of the people to Christianity remained superficial.

In the middle of the sixteenth century, a large number of Franciscans and even more Jesuits disembarked, as many as forty-five religious on a single ship. Thousands of Africans were baptized in several months, often at the request of the king. But they had not been instructed in the Christian faith.

The traffic in slaves, in which the Portuguese missionaries were more or less accomplices, was a great obstacle to the progress of the gospel. In 1526 Affonso I wrote a letter to the king of Portugal, making a request that, unfortunately, was scarcely given any heed:

> Sire, there is a grave problem in our kingdom, which does not serve God. Many of our subjects covet the merchandise of your kingdom that is imported here by your subjects. They are concerned only for their commerce, to sell what they have unjustly acquired, and ruin by their treatment our kingdom and the Christianity that has been established for many years and that cost your predecessors much sacrifice . . . European merchandise exercises such a fascination on the simple and ignorant that they leave God to take it up. The remedy is the suppression of this merchandise, which is a trap of the devil for sellers and buyers. Cupidity and the lure of gain lead the people of the country to steal their compatriots, without consideration for whether they are Christians or not. To satisfy their desire to possess these riches, many of our subjects capture their compatriots, sell them, exchange them, free or freed, noble or the sons of nobles, to resell them to the whites who mark them immediately with a red iron. This abuse is so great that we cannot remedy it without striking hard and very hard. And we entreat your Highness to aid us and support us in this business by giving an order to send here no longer neither merchants nor merchandise, for it is our desire not to allow the commerce of slavery to be established in our kingdom.[150]

The tragedy of the slave trade, the superficiality of evangelization, the absence of financial resources, and the insufficiency of missionary organization and training led to a number of failures. King Affonso I was profoundly discouraged by it, and after his death in about 1547 the mission practically disappeared. Several Jesuits made renewed efforts between 1547 and 1555, and against wind and tide, the new king, Affonso II (1547–1614), persevered in the Christian way and in the alliance with Portugal.

At the end of the seventeenth century, Kimpa Vita, a Christian Congolese who was baptized Donna Beatrice, created in the name of the Virgin Mary and Saint Anthony a movement to restore the faith and return power to a Christian king, Pedro IV. She burned fetishes and crucifixes that had become fetishes, and she announced a black messiah. Beatrice wanted to free Christianity from its Portuguese envelopment

---

150 These extracts are taken in part from Ype Schaaf, *La Bible en Afrique*, ed. Groupes Missionnaires (Lavigny: 1995), 36, and from Georges Balandier, *La vie quotidienne au royaume de Kongo* (Paris: Hachette, 1965), 72ff.

and to reestablish the independence of the Kikongo kingdom. But she was put to death by Portuguese priests in 1706. A little later, a Congolese king decided to drive out the foreign missionaries.

By this time the Portuguese had long since lost interest in the kingdom of the Congo, it being too poor. Instead, they turned their attention southwards towards Angola, whose mineral riches appeared more promising. On the coast they founded the city of Luanda. Beginning in 1560 the Jesuits followed this movement and established churches and a monastery at Luanda. The king was hostile at first and expelled the first Portuguese Jesuits, but several years later he had himself baptized. New missionaries arrived in 1578, and baptisms multiplied. By 1590 there were twenty thousand Christians in the kingdom, and in 1596 the city of Massangano became the seat of a bishopric. In the seventeenth century, Christian penetration progressed apace. Between 1645 and 1700, there were 600,000 baptisms registered in the Congo though, unfortunately, of a very superficial nature.

Historian Ype Schaaf writes, "In 1650 the missionaries asked Rome if it is permitted to baptize, without instruction, 'stupid and backward people.' Rome responded that it could be done in *fide ecclesia*, that is to say, with the faith of the church guaranteeing it. Latin was used for the Mass, and in 1624, Father Cardozo translated the first catechism in Congolese . . . Some other books were printed, but there was no regular instruction in the language of the people and no biblical translation. The first to be baptized were the king and the elite, and only later the people—for the latter, few pains were taken to explain the true significance of baptism. The missionaries, who understood their role well, established no real contact with the women."[151]

The missionaries were highly compromised in the traffic of slaves in Angola, as they had been in the Congo—the monastery of Luanda possessed twelve thousand of them. With the blessing of the bishop, the port of Luanda became a center of the trade that sent slaves to Brazil. During the three centuries between 1536 and 1836, an annual average of about five thousand slaves passed through the port of Luanda. It is only fair to add that the Portuguese were not the only interested party; the Dutch sought to supplant them on the Angolan coast so that they could at least acquire the traffic intended for Surinam.

Portugal strove to maintain its hold in Angola, but, against so many difficulties, it no longer sought to develop an indigenous church. Most of the time the missionaries were content to minister only to the Portuguese population, huddled at several points along the west coast.

These first missionary efforts on the west coast of Africa led to failure and the practical disappearance of the church before the beginning of the nineteenth century. When David Livingstone arrived in Luanda in 1854, he found the cathedral and churches entirely abandoned, transformed into cowsheds and warehouses. The cathedral of Massangano was completely dilapidated, the crucifix and statues serving as fetishes for witches. Sao Salvador—the city of the Savior—was a ruin covered over by vegetation. Schaaf writes, "The first Christianity disappeared from the shores of

151 Schaaf, *La Bible*, 37.

the Congo because the Word had not been truly transmitted and because no teaching followed the baptisms of the masses."

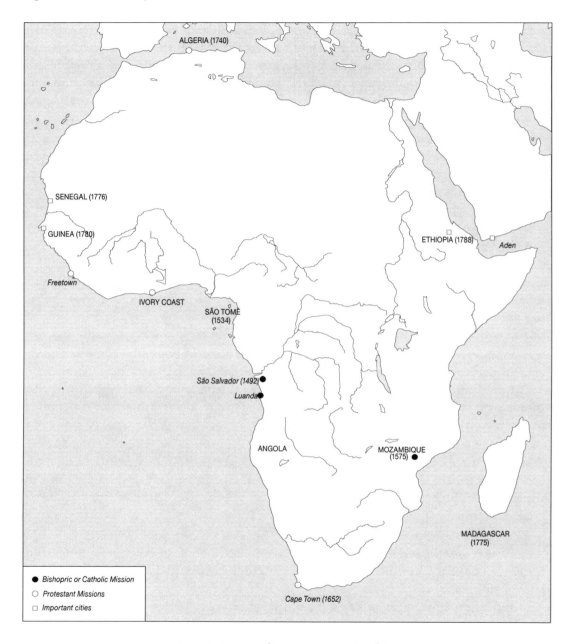

*Map 12: Missions from 1500 to 1800 in Africa*

# THE EAST COAST OF AFRICA

Later the envoys of various religious orders attempted to establish themselves in other places on the African coast, notably in the southeast of the continent and present-day Mozambique. Since 1509 the Portuguese had supplanted the Arabs on the east coast of Africa and, profiting from the rivalry between local sultans, were gaining a foothold in various African ports.

In 1560 the Jesuit Concalo de Silveria led to baptism the young chief of the Bantu kingdom of Zambezi, Nogoma Mapunzagatu; and he was followed by a great many of his subjects. But the Arabs would not allow themselves to be supplanted so easily. They spread the rumor that the Jesuits possessed evil powers, and in 1561 the missionary was assassinated.

About fifteen years later, the Dominicans and other Jesuits succeeded in gaining a toehold for Christianity in Mozambique, with Father Dos Santo baptizing 1,700 persons. In 1626 a Christian king seized power with the aid of the Portuguese, and another king of the same ethnic group was baptized in 1652. Despite these localized successes, at the end of the century there was almost no trace of a church presence remaining in these regions. Islam and local superstitions had offered strong resistance, and, moreover, Christianity had been much too tied to a Portuguese political power that was then on the decline.

# ETHIOPIA

In the sixteenth century, after the victorious intervention of the Portuguese soldiers that released the iron grip of the Arabs (see p. 132), the Roman church sought to bring back into its fold the ancient Abyssinian church of Ethiopia. The head of the Ethiopian church, the Father ("Abouna") was considered to be the fabled Prester John, who for many centuries was believed to be in the land of the Mongols in Asia. In 1545 the king (*negus*) of Ethiopia informed the king of Portugal that he and his subjects were disposed to recognize the authority of the pope. When Ignatius Loyola learned of this, he planned to go there himself. The pope, however, prevented him from doing this and sent in his stead three Portuguese priests.

In a letter dated 1555, the founder of the Society described without circumlocution the objective and the methods of the Jesuits who were to go:

> The patriarch [the Jesuit called to lead this enterprise of "recuperation"] and those who will be sent will employ their time in becoming close to the Father, and by all sorts of honest means to bring him to love us. When this has been done and he is very well disposed, they will bring him to understand that there is no hope of being saved outside of the Roman Catholic Church and that, to be saved, it is necessary to believe what she defines for faith and morals. If he can be convinced of this general truth, other minor points that depend on it and can be deduced from it will slowly be acquired.[152]

---

152 Ignatius Loyola, *Lettres*, no. 148.

Contrary to their hopes, at the moment in 1557 when the Jesuits presented themselves, the *negus* no longer had the same disposition towards Roman Catholicism and repulsed the missionaries. Among them, Father Andres de Oviedo alone remained behind, but he lived in miserable conditions and died after twenty years without seeing any fruit from his labors. After this unproductive attempt, the Jesuit Pedro Paez seemed to obtain a positive result when in 1622 King Susenyos announced his conversion to Catholicism. Paez, a remarkable personality, died a little later. The Jesuit sent to succeed him determined on a more forceful strategy. He imposed the Catholic liturgy, reconsecrated priests and churches, and rebaptized the faithful. A very disappointed king renounced Catholicism and expelled the Jesuits in 1632. The attempt to annex the Ethiopian church had failed.

## AFRICA: EVALUATION

Catholic missionaries had tried to gain a foothold on the African continent in the sixteenth and seventeenth centuries, but their efforts did not result in the planting of any durable church. After this, they would not take up the task again until the end of the eighteenth century. Historian Jean Delumeau writes: "It is not excessive to speak of Christian failure in Africa before 1800."[153]

It should be added that in the seventeenth century the French Lazarists founded a mission on the great island of Madagascar. This effort only endured for thirty-two years, 1642–1674. Here again is seen the ephemeral character of the missionary enterprise in this period.

---

153 Jean Delumeau, *Le catholicisme entre Luther and Voltaire*, in *Nouvelle Clio 30bis* (Paris: Presses Universitares de France, 1971, 3rd ed. 1985), 141.

# CHAPTER 12

# Catholic Mission in Asia and Oceania

## FRANCIS XAVIER

The first and one of the greatest Jesuit missionaries was Francis Xavier (1506–1552). Born of a Spanish noble family, Xavier came to Paris in 1525 to study philosophy at the College Saint Barbe. Ambitious for glory and reputation, he suffered from financial difficulties due to the death of his parents. He was aided by a rich, older compatriot who became his roommate, Ignatius Loyola—a fact that Xavier accepted reluctantly, finding Loyola excessively austere and pious. However, after several years of effort, Loyola brought the young man to the point of a profound religious experience, and later he became a part of the small group of friends who on August 15, 1534, at Montmartre founded the Society of Jesus. Xavier studied theology next and then dedicated himself to the service of the poor in Italy. In 1540 Loyola asked him to put himself at the disposal of the king of Portugal, John III, who by virtue of the system of the *Padroado* (see p. 140) would send him to preach the gospel beyond the seas.

John III sent Xavier to India. He disembarked at Goa on the west coast where the Portuguese had established their principal trading post. The young Jesuit did not find the missionaries who had preceded him to be very zealous, but he remained under their authority and applied their methods of evangelization to the poor classes of the population. He soon became the director of the College of St. Paul, founded the year preceding his arrival. His college work was a precursor to later Jesuit activity. If he took this college to heart, it was in the hope of seeing it become a training center for those with a missionary vocation. Conscious of the great urgency of mission, he wrote ceaselessly to Europe for reinforcements.

In his very soul an evangelist and pastor, he did not limit himself to teaching at the College of St. Paul. With zeal he visited the sick and imprisoned and catechized the children. He wrote:

> Here in Goa, I am lodged in a hospital. I hear the confessions of the sick who are found here and I give them Communion; there are so many that come to confess themselves that, if I divide myself

in ten pieces, each of them would have confession somewhere. When I have finished with the sick, I confess the well heeled who come looking for me in the morning . . . After having confessed the prisoners, I go to the chapel of Notre Dame, which is near to the hospital, and I begin to teach the children there the prayers, creed, and commandments.[154]

His impatience to make Goa a base of operations led to work on a larger scale. From 1542–1544 he carried the Christian faith to all the southeast of India, through which he tirelessly traveled. He spent much of his time on the coast between Malabar and Cape Comorin, the latter being at the extreme southern point of the continent where he evangelized the pearl divers, known as the *Paravas*. Among this vast population he found tens of thousands who had been baptized but then abandoned. Their language proved to be a serious obstacle, for he had to depend on less–than–proficient interpreters. He strove to teach the *Paravas* the rudiments of Christian faith and morals. Here is his witness:

> We passed by Christian villages; they must have become Christian eight years ago. There were no Portuguese living in these villages, for it is a country extremely infertile and very poor. Because there is no one to instruct them in our faith, the Christians in these villages know nothing more than to say that they are Christians.[155]

Even if he did better than his predecessors, his method of evangelization and catechetical teaching remained very superficial, for they consisted of having the people learn and recite Christian truths by heart. It should be kept in mind, however, that the population in which he operated was not very sophisticated.[156] He taught those under him every day in their own language, something that the Dutch Calvinists in Indonesia did not always do even a century later.

> On Sunday I assembled all the inhabitants of the village, men as well as women, large and small, to recite the prayers in their language; they came with much exhilaration and showed themselves ready to please. After having confessed a single God, triune and one, they recited the creed aloud in their language and what line-by-line I recited to them, all giving me responses . . . First we say the first article of the faith, and when we have finished saying it, I say in their language, and them with me: "Jesus Christ, Son of God, give us the grace to believe." After finishing the creed and

154  Hugues Didier, *Petite vie de saint François Xavier* (Paris: Desclée de Brouwer, 1992), 36.

155  Ibid., 40.

156  This is why, while asking that Europe send him priests, he pointed out that it was not necessary to supply instructed men or subtle minds. "Those who did not possess the necessary talent to confess, preach, and fulfill the subsidiary functions of the Society, after having served at the humble tasks for some months, were rendering great services in these countries, on condition that they had physical as well as spiritual strength. In effect, in these infidel countries, science is not necessary. It suffices to teach the prayers and visit the villages to baptize the children there," he wrote in January 1545 to Loyola (*Lettres*, no. 47). It will be observed later on that his subsequent experiences in the very different context of Japan will lead him to envision the problem very differently.

commandments, I repeat the Pater Noster and the Ave Maria to them, and as I recite, they all respond to me.[157]

Though the teaching was doubtless superficial, it was not syncretistic. Xavier had little more than scorn for Hinduism, which he knew only through its popular superstitions. Not knowing Sanskrit, he was ignorant of the sacred texts. He wrote:

> Among the gentry of this country, there is a group called the Brahmans. They are at the head of all the gentry groups. They are responsible for the houses where the idols are found: it is the most perverse race in the world . . . I reveal their deceptions and their balderdash to the poor, simple people who are their devotees only by fear, and I continue until I am tired of it.[158]

*The Spanish Jesuit Francis Xavier (1506–1552). In the course of his brief life, he engaged in intense missionary activity over a great part of Asia. He planted the cross, it is said, in fifty-two kingdoms and accomplished numerous miracles. During his lifetime, he had already become a legend. This engraving shows him baptizing Indians in Goa (Portuguese India).*

He also sought to restore to the bosom of the Roman Church the numerous Nestorian communities that had for several centuries survived there as best they could.

In the period from 1545–1547 he left India to plow the eastern part of the Indian Ocean. He had the profound conviction, acquired in nights of vigil and prayer, that God was calling him to go still farther:

157  Didier, *Petite vie*, 44.
158  Ibid., 50.

> By reason of his habitual mercifulness, God lavished an inner con-
> solation on me because he wanted me to remember and to make
> me feel and recognize that it was his will that I go to the coun-
> try of Malacca [present-day Malaysia], where people had recently
> been made Christians. This was to be so that I could give them
> information and teachings about our holy and true faith, at least
> insofar as supplying a translation in their own language of the ar-
> ticles and commandments of our holy law and faith, accompanied
> by some explanations.[159]

He left Goa, therefore, to visit the island of Malacca. Here he found a Christian population that had been baptized but not catechized. They had been waiting for him with growing impatience, for his reputation for holiness had preceded him, and a multitude of extraordinary miracles had been attributed to him. As in Goa, he went immediately to lodge at the hospital, among the poorest and sickest. He slept little because during the night he was assembling troops of children and going through the streets of the city sounding a bell and praying in a load voice for the souls in purgatory. Later he also traveled in the archipelago of present-day Indonesia, and continued on to the Moluccas, or Spice Islands, where he found a population recently and superficially Islamicized. "The gentiles [pagans] in Moluccas are more numerous than the Moors [Muslims]. They became Moors seventy years ago . . . What is good about these Moors is that they know nothing about their perverse sect. It is only for lack of someone to preach the truth to them that the Moors are not made Christians."

In July 1547 he returned to Malacca for several months. A little before continuing on to India, he encountered three young Japanese. One of them, Anjiro, was an outlaw who had had to flee his country to escape a conviction for homicide. But he had converted and spoke to Xavier of the immense spiritual needs of his country. This caused the missionary's heart to overflow: "If all the Japanese are as curious to know as Anjiro, they are, it seems to me, the most intellectually curious people of all the countries that have been discovered." This encounter disrupted his missionary projects. Henceforth he would give priority to the regions where Islam had not preceded the gospel, convinced that there the harvest would quickly become abundant. Inquiring further of Japan, he wrote:

> I asked Anjiro if, in case I should go to his country with him, the
> people of Japan would become Christians. He responded that they
> would not become Christians all at once, but that they would ask
> many questions of me, that they would see how I responded to
> them . . . And [they would] especially see if I practiced what I
> preached. If I do these two things well, it would only be a year and
> a half after having had this experience of me that the king, people,
> nobles, and all the other persons capable of discernment would
> become Christians.

---

159  Ibid., 59.

Before leaving for Japan, Xavier returned to Goa to inspect his mission among the Tamils as well as to see his Jesuit companions. He took Anjiro with him so that his friend could receive training at the College of Saint Paul. But Xavier was very disappointed by the state of the church in India, which he attributed to the passivity of the population and the poor image of Christianity presented by the Portuguese. A letter to Loyola revealed his thoughts:

> I want to make you particularly understand some things necessary for you to know. First of all regarding the people of this region, for as long as I have been here, they are, to speak in general terms, very barbarous and have no desire to know what is or is not in accordance with their pagan morals. They have no inclination to understand the things of God or their salvation. Their natural strengths have been corrupted regarding a great many virtues.[160]

This diagnosis confirmed him in his conviction that on reaching Japan with the gospel he would find a highly intelligent and active population where the gospel would prosper. "As for me, Lord," he said, "I am still not entirely decided on leaving for Japan; but slowly, it seems to me that it [my decision] is yes, because I scarcely believe that I am going to obtain the support necessary in India to allow our holy faith to grow, or even to maintain Christendom where it is already established."

Xavier, therefore, embarked for Japan, arriving in 1549 with six companions. He would reside there until 1551, finding himself at ease in a feudal society that reminded him of Spain. He discovered that his clerical clothing, which had opened so many doors to him among the deprived of the Portuguese east, was an obstacle to the Japanese. Consequently, he set aside his cotton clothes for the silk ceremonial clothing of the Japanese in order to better present himself before the dignitaries of the empire. He also presented them with rich gifts. He sought to learn about and to make contacts with the more elite and cultivated of the society, those who would scorn anyone not attired in all the signs of wealth and privilege. This was an entirely new approach for him, and it would be the strategy that the Jesuit Matthew Ricci and his successors would adopt to reach elite Chinese leaders about thirty years later. A letter that Xavier wrote to Loyola in 1552 after his return to Goa reveals the evolution of his thinking on this matter, and it is interesting to compare it to his "Letter 47," cited above (see p. 178-79, n. 156):

> It is necessary that they [the priests who would go to Japan] possess the knowledge to respond to the numerous questions posed by the Japanese. It would be good if they have mastered the arts, and it would not be a loss if they were also dialecticians. They should know something of the celestial sphere, for the Japanese take extreme pleasure in knowing the movement of the heavens, the ellipses of the sun, the waxing and waning of the moon, knowing how rainwater is produced, as well as storm and hail, thunder and lightning.

---

160 Ibid., 94.

At age forty-three Xavier began energetically to learn all the customs of daily life in Japan so that he could conform to local usage. He did not hide his sympathy and admiration for the Japanese people:

> From the beginning until now the people with whom we converse are the best among those who have so far been discovered. It seems to me that, among the infidel peoples, none have the advantage over the Japanese . . . They have something that no Christian countries seem to me to have: they esteem honor more than riches. They are a people who act courteously to one another . . . A considerable part of the people know how to read and write, which is a tremendous aid in their quickly learning the prayers and the things of God.[161]

The missionary, with the aid of Anjiro as interpreter, entered in conversation with the most cultivated people. He was struck by the lack of certitude in Buddhist teaching and how it presented vague answers to numerous fundamental questions.

> I have often had conversations with some of the most intelligent bonzes [Buddhist monks], principally with one of them . . . who is like a bishop among them, and if this title suits him, he would be pleased. In the course of the numerous conversations that we have had, I have felt that he is full of doubts and incapable of knowing how to determine if the soul is immortal or if it dies at the same time as the body. Sometimes he says to me yes, other times no.

One of the things that most astonished and shocked those who spoke with Xavier is the affirmation that there is only a single means of salvation and that this salvation involves a transformation in moral behavior.

> When we pass through the streets, some of the children and other people we followed were saying: "Here are those who say that we must adore God to be saved and that no one can save us except the Creator of all things." Others were saying: "These are those who preach that a man cannot have more than one woman." Still others were saying: "These are those who forbid the sin of sodomy," for this is very widespread among them.

With the several brothers who accompanied him, Xavier attempted to learn the Japanese language in an accelerated fashion under the guidance of Anjiro. However, there were numerous setbacks. For example, he was badly advised when he decided to translate "God" by the Buddhist term *Dainichi*. Later he discovered that in Buddhism there is no creator and that *Dainichi* is an immanent absolute–a being in each thing and the entire world at the same time! Consequently, the first texts translated had to be destroyed.

---

161 Francis Xavier, "Letter 110," cited in Comby, "Deux mille," 145.

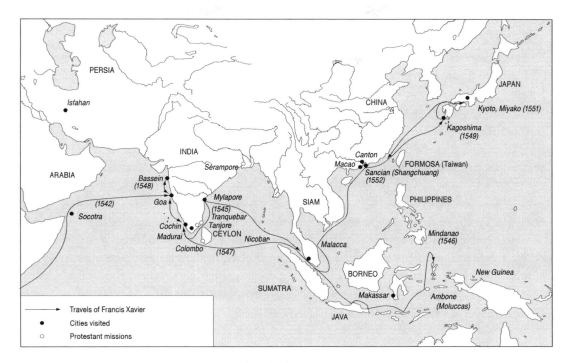

*Map 13: Evangelism in the Far East, 1500 to 1800*

Even if the enthusiastic prospects outlined by Anjiro were not confirmed by experience, Xavier obtained some success. He received land and official permission to preach the Christian faith. After scarcely more than two years of sojourning in Japan, he left behind a thousand converts scattered in three Christian communities. They would be in the care of two Jesuits, the Brothers Cosme de Torrès and John Fernandez, and later other missionaries would take over.[162]

After his departure from Japan, Xavier returned to Goa with numerous projects filling his mind. Despite the counsel of moderation given by his anxious companions because of his state of exhaustion, he was already prepared to embark on yet another long voyage. Always optimistic, he envisioned the evangelization of immense China where Christianity had once been established but since disappeared. He reckoned, in effect, that it would be in this extensive country that the key to the conversion of the entire Far East would be found, if one believes the lines written before his departure:

> China is a country vast, peaceful, and governed by great laws . . .
> These are generous people. There is no war among them. I hope
> to leave for China in order to accomplish the greatest service for
> our God . . . When the Japanese learn that the Chinese have ac-
> cepted the Law of God, they will quickly lose the faith that they
> have in their sects. I have great hope that the Chinese, as well as

---

162 See p. 188.

the Japanese, will leave their idolatries and adore God and Jesus Christ, the Savior of all men.[163]

The voyage was very trying. Terrible storms in the Gulf of Siam forced the passengers to lighten the small boat by casting into the water some of the presents intended for the emperor of China. Sickness broke out aboard, and the pilot did not know where they were. The ship finally reached the small barren island of Shangchuan, or Sancian (Saint John), off a section of the Chinese coast not far from Canton and known by the Portuguese as a way station for contraband. The wait to enter the mainland was prolonged, for foreigners did not have authorization to disembark on the continent, and Xavier could not find a way to overcome this obstacle, either officially or clandestinely. Exhausted by his travels and privations, his health quickly collapsed and he died on the small island on December 3, 1552, at the age of forty-six.

Francis Xavier has remained the model missionary of the Society of Jesus. Animated by an unshakable faith, he had a passionate love for Christ and was devoted to the Virgin Mary. He sometimes passed entire nights in prayer. His companions claimed that once during his hours of mystical contemplation his body levitated above the ground. He ate little and treated his body severely. In a time when sea travel was extremely dangerous and trying, especially in the climates that he knew, his incessant voyages are impressive. Also remarkable was his capacity to adapt to the different social and cultural contexts in which he found himself, from the fishers of pearls in the south of India to the nobles and scholars of Japan.

He would have wanted his enthusiasm to be communicated to all the church:

> I wish the time may come when I can go through the schools here below and cry out as if out of my senses in the University of Paris and also in the Sorbonne, cry to these doctors who keep all their science for themselves how the souls here, by their negligence, are missing heaven and going to hell.

Aside from such profoundly moving remarks, there is much in the account given here about Xavier's methods that is disconcerting. He said of himself, "I have made Christians" when he returned from collective baptisms of people who were not well informed about the faith. Among the records of his associates, these lines are found: "In the villages where you pass, assemble the men on some day and in some place; have them recite prayers in all their houses; baptize those who have not yet been baptized."

He had become a legend even during his own lifetime. His reputation for holiness was such that extraordinary miracles were attributed to him, and the fruitfulness of his ministry was exaggerated beyond all credibility. Prophecies and second sight were attributed to him as well as a million conversions, indeed more. Yet the currently accepted calculations correct this distortion of the record, settling on a number of baptisms in the neighborhood of thirty thousand. Though it was said that he had received a "gift of languages" as extraordinary as that received by the disciples on the

---

163 Comby, "Deux mille," 128.

day of Pentecost, Xavier often complained in his letters of the difficulty he had learning foreign languages. It is through his numerous and carefully preserved letters that the authentic Francis Xavier appears, and this is why we have cited several extracts from them. The man who emerges from these letters—a man "who planted the faith in fifty-two kingdoms" and whose motto was that of his Society, *Ad majorem Dei gloriam* ("For the greater glory of God")—remains an example of zeal and dedication that more evangelical missionaries might find inspiring.

## INDIA: ROBERT DE NOBILI

In the period following Xavier, the city of Goa became a great missionary center. But the Portuguese policy scarcely facilitated the progress of the church. In 1565 there were about 300,000 Catholics in the southern part of India, and the numbers of former Nestorians among them were not negligible.

Among the Catholic missionaries who worked in India in the seventeenth century, one of the most influential was the Jesuit Robert de Nobili (1578–1656), a member of an important Italian family. He arrived in 1605 in Madurai, a center of Tamil civilization in the southern part of the subcontinent. He discovered with consternation that the Christians in the area were considered as belonging to the caste of the *Parangi* (a word meaning "foreigner," but a distortion of the word "Franks," showing that it was derived from the time of the second Crusade undertaken by the Normans). He was especially shocked by the superficiality of the conversions often obtained in exchange for recompense, and by the sterility of missionary efforts. One of the reasons for this was the poor quality of the translations of the Gospels and catechism.

Distancing himself from the missionaries already in place who were complacent in their foreign status, he pinned a note to his door to affirm his distinctive beliefs:

> I am not a Parangi, but I preach the law of the true God who has already been proclaimed in these countries since ancient times . . . Whoever claims that there is a private law for the Parangi commits a grave sin, for the true God is not the God of a caste or of a race, but the God of all.

Nobili adopted the mode of his life to the holy men in the local religion, abandoning Western food and clothes. He expressed himself in Tamil and plunged himself into the study of Sanskrit literature—the first European known to do so. He strove to find correspondences between Indian and Christian wisdom, and composed numerous works in Tamil. He did not present himself as a Brahman, for this would have implied agreement with certain religious ideas. Rather, he adapted himself to the *sannyasi*, the penitents. He sat cross-legged, praying, reading, meditating, and enjoying few of the world's comforts. A contemporary witness recounts:

> Following the example of Saint Paul who was everything to everyone, and the example of the eternal Word, Father Nobili said of himself: I will make myself an Indian to save the Indians. He presented himself . . . as a Roman Radjah, a man of high nobility and a *sannyasi*, that is to say, a penitent who renounced the world and

all its pleasures . . . From this time the rice, milk, herbs, and water that he took once a day were all his food; a long robe of yellowish cloth, a white or red shawl on his shoulders, a hat on his head in the form of a turban . . . were his only clothes.[164]

For a time the Madura mission was gaining about a thousand converts per year. At the time of Nobili's death in 1656, there were four thousand converts, and among them were twenty-six Brahmans. By the end of the century, there were more than 100,000 Christians in this region.

Through all the time of his ministry, Nobili was admired by some and fiercely criticized by others. Missionaries from other orders accused him of compromising with the local religion and denounced him to Rome. Pope Gregory XV (1621–1623) decided in his favor, allowing Brahman converts to continue to wear their distinctive clothes and to use the sandalwood perfume of their caste, but this was on condition that these objects had not been consecrated or used in an idol temple. One of the principal obstacles that Nobili encountered was the caste system. Working among the people of superior castes, he assumed manners and customs to better associate himself with them, but by doing so he cut himself off from the other castes. It is said, however, that he went discreetly by night to work among the people of the lower castes and to give them bread.

After Nobili's death, the issue was taken up again, and Rome eventually decided to place strict limitations on the adoption of indigenous customs. The evolution of the debate that was known as the "Quarrel of the Malabar Rites" was similar to that of the better-known "Quarrel of the Chinese Rites," which will be presented shortly. Nobili remains a fine example of a missionary who truly sought a transcultural and de-Westernized evangelism, making himself "all things to all men so that by all possible means I might save some" (1 Cor 9:22). His strategy was not without risk, but at least it manifested an astonishing open-mindedness at a time when most missionaries did not recognize the extent to which they were conveying Christianity as bound up in a Western cultural straightjacket.

In a 1659 *Instruction* addressed to the apostolic vicars of the kingdoms of Tonkin and Cochin China, Pope Alexander VII (1655–1667) offered a practical and wise solution to the problem:

> Do not be zealous and do not advance arguments to convince these people to change their rites, customs, and manners, at least if they are not obviously matters contrary to morality and religion. What could be more absurd than to transport to China [the customs of] France, Italy, Spain, or any other European country? Do not introduce our countries to them, but the faith . . . It is, as it were, inscribed in the nature of all men to esteem, love, and elevate above everyone the traditions of their country and the country itself. There is, therefore, no more powerful way to create distance or hatred than to carry our own customs to another

---

164  Letter of Alberto Laerzio, provincial of Malabar, November 1609, cited in Comby, "Deux mille," 151.

nation . . . Therefore, never contrast the manners of these people with those of Europeans; far to the contrary, strive to accustom yourselves to them. Admire what merits praise. For what does not merit it, if it is inappropriate to praise it so as to deceive as flatterers do, be prudent enough not to pass judgment, or in any case not to carelessly or excessively condemn. As for usages that are frankly evil, you must change them by shaking your heads and remaining silent rather than by words . . .

You would not want to render yourselves odious over material questions. Remember the poverty of the apostles who gained by their hands what was necessary for them.[165]

# SOUTHEAST ASIA

In Southeast Asia, beginning in 1511, missionaries evangelized Malacca, preceding Francis Xavier by about thirty years. As for Indochina, it was reached in the following century: a Jesuit mission penetrated Annam in 1611 and Cochin China in 1615, soon counting two thousand baptized. The kingdom of Siam was only reached in 1662. The resistance to Christianity was very lively on the part of the great religions such as Buddhism and Hinduism. Many missionaries lived secretly and were periodically expelled, and a number of them knew martyrdom.

The best known among the missionaries to Vietnam is Alexander de Rhodes (1593–1660). Raised in Avignon, he did his studies in mathematics and then joined the Society of Jesus. He had intended to go to Japan, but persecution in 1623 prevented him from entering the country. From then on he dedicated himself to Vietnam. He began his work in the Portuguese port of Macao. On several occasions between 1625 and 1630 he sojourned in Cochin China and Tokin but endured several expulsions. Then for ten years he taught theology in Macao. Observing the makeup of the local clergy, he discerned the need for three hundred to four hundred indigenous priests for Cochin and Tonkin, since the foreign missionaries could not count on permanently staying in the region. Despite the obvious shortage of priests, he was not able to ordain priests because he was not a bishop. This is why he emphasized the training of catechists:

As I saw that I was the only priest who could preach, I suddenly realized that I had to take into my company Christians who were not married and who were full of zeal and of piety to aid me in the conversion of souls. During Mass they publicly vowed to employ themselves all their lives in service to the church, not to marry and to obey the Fathers who were coming to preach the gospel. Now there are more than a hundred in the seminary that the Christians undertook to finance.

---

165 Cited in Roux, *Missions*, 249; cited at greater length in Comby, "Deux mille," 168.

Father Rhodes returned to Cochin three times between 1640 and 1645, and then was expelled under penalty of death. He returned to Europe to publicize the missionary work in these regions, and his efforts resulted in the withdrawal of the *Padroado* system from Indochina. In 1649 this region came directly under the office of the Sacred Congregation for the Propaganda of the Faith in Rome, which sent three bishops as apostolic vicars in order to make possible the creation of a local clergy. We have cited above an extract from the interesting *Instruction* of the pope to those he sent in 1659.

Rhodes later returned to the mission field. This time, however, he traveled to Persia where he died at Ispahan at the age of sixty-seven.

He always strove to present Christianity in such a way that it would not appear as a foreign religion. He said in his *Catechism*: "Especially do not say that this law is from the Portuguese. For the holy law of God is a light greater and older than the sun itself . . . Although it appeared first to some kingdoms, it must not pass as a law of these kingdoms alone, but as the holy law of God."

Rhodes also contributed to the missionary effort by reducing the Vietnamese language to writing. He was passionate about the indigenous culture, and in his catechism he managed to allude to local poetry and religious spectacles.

In the islands of present-day Indonesia, Islam was well entrenched and opposed to Christian missions. However, the population on several islands converted. The Dutch, who had established themselves in the region during the seventeenth century, forbade Catholic missions. They undertook the work of evangelization themselves, but only pursued it sporadically.

The archipelago of the Philippines was conquered and occupied by the Spanish, and by the beginning of the seventeenth century it was entirely Catholic.

## JAPAN

In Japan the successors of Francis Xavier pursued his work with remarkable success, notably the Jesuit Alessandro Valignano, who exercised a fruitful ministry between 1578 and 1606. By reason of the scope of its success, the progress of Christianity raised fears and strong opposition. In 1597 for example, following a period of political tension with the Spanish, six Franciscans, three Japanese Jesuits, and seventeen of the faithful were crucified. This hostility, however, did not check the movement, as people were converting in all classes of society and even in the entourage of the *mikado* ("emperor"). By one count there were 300,000 Japanese Christians by the end of the sixteenth century.

Japan seemed on the verge of becoming Catholic when a violent anti-Christian reaction occurred. In January 1614 a government edict proscribed Christianity throughout Japan and unleashed a general persecution. Missionaries were brutally hunted down and Christians enjoined to abjure. The Japanese government took pitiless measures to eradicate Christianity. It is estimated that between 1624 and 1637 four thousand Christians died as martyrs to their faith. An uprising that was more political than religious took place between 1637 and 1638 in the southern Japanese province of Shimabara where Christians were numerous. The army crushed the population, but those who claimed that they were not Christians were able to save their lives. The others were massacred under particularly bloodthirsty and cruel conditions. There were at least thirty-five thousand victims—men, women, and children. Japan was then completely closed to foreigners, who were excluded from the country under pain of death. This continued until 1854.

# CHINA

## Matthew Ricci

The Jesuits, fulfilling the wish of Francis Xavier, installed themselves in China in 1581 and adopted the approach that he had inaugurated in Japan. Their success was both rapid and considerable.

The man who instigated this remarkable work among the Jesuits was Father Matthew Ricci (1552–1610). Born in Italy in the year of the death of Francis Xavier, he arrived in southern China in 1582. In twenty years of ministry, he gained the respect of the emperor and acquired a certain influence at the imperial court. He quickly mastered the language and wrote several treatises on various secular subjects, such as one on friendship, which won him much acclaim. He adopted indigenous clothes, customs, and language, taking the Chinese name of Li-ma-tou, and maintaining numerous personal relationships with those among the literati, who were impressed by his encyclopedic knowledge. The Chinese were passionate about astronomy, the physical sciences, and the technical achievements of the West that Ricci presented to them. He made clocks and maps of the world for them and translated Euclid's *Elements of Geometry*.

*The encyclopedic knowledge of the Jesuit missionaries in China, notably in physics and astronomy, impressed many of the Chinese elite.*
*At the left Matthew Ricci (1552–1610), to the right Schall von Bell (1591–1666).*
*Seventeenth century engraving.*

Since he spoke of God, he gladly made use of Chinese terms. For example, for "Supreme Being" he chose *Shang Ti*, and for "heaven" *t'ien*. The classic Christian expression for "God" would be *T'ien-Chu* ("the Lord of Heaven"). He also judged that Confucianism was a philosophy rather than a religion, and that it was therefore compatible with the Christian faith. Ricci and his companion, Father Trigault, wrote:

> Father Matthew [Ricci] wore the clothing of the literati but principally of those who called themselves preachers of the law . . . He proclaimed himself to be a preacher of the divine law not only by his clothing, but even more so by his discourses. For he was entirely occupied with testing the two idolatrous sects (the Buddhists and Taoists) and convincing them of error. But as for the sect of the literati, not only did he not attack them, he took Confucius to be a great man and praised him highly as a prince who preferred to be silent about what he did not know regarding the afterlife rather than speak of it. Also he applied the precepts of his law so that everyone's life would be better formed, so that each family and the kingdom would be well governed according to right and equity . . . The literati called the Father a true literati who, adoring a single God, did not want to sully true worship by honoring false gods.[166]

Ricci allowed certain Confucian ceremonies such as those that honored the dead. He judged that these were customs more social than religious in nature. Also, if Christians were to abstain from them, they would have been effectively banished from Chinese society. He conceded that some superstitions were attached to these customs, but he hoped to slowly secularize or even Christianize them. He also aspired to form a Chinese clergy and admit Chinese into the Society. The general of the Jesuits, however, refused to ordain Chinese to the priesthood. In 1605 Pope Paul V (1605–1621) authorized Ricci to celebrate the Mass in Chinese.

When Ricci died in 1610, he left 2,500 converts. Several of these were Mandarins and high personages close to the emperor.

### The Successors of Ricci: Schall von Bell and Verbiest

After the death of Matthew Ricci, other Jesuits successfully pursued the work, the most outstanding being the German astronomer Johann Adam Schall von Bell (1591–1666).[167] He arrived in Peking in 1622 and, due to fortunate circumstances, soon had an audience with the emperor, whom he sought to bring to the Christian faith. In 1623 and 1624 he announced eclipses that Chinese astronomers had not forecast, feats that helped to increase the number of his hearers.

One of the widows of the emperor and the prince and heir to the throne were baptized. The prince received the new name of Constantine, but there was not to be an emperor Constantine of China. In 1664 the Ming dynasty collapsed when the city of Peking fell into the hands of the Manchu. Despite several sporadic persecutions, the new masters of China were not generally hostile to Christians. Father Schall von Bell managed to convince them that he was indispensable to the intellectual life of

---

166 Matteo Ricci and Nicolas Trigault, *Histoire de l'expédition chrétienne au royaume de la Chine, 1582–1610* (Paris: Desclée de Brouwer, 1978), 421–22.

167 He is also often known as Schall von Bell.

the empire. In 1645 he was named to the Committee of Control of the Calendar, an institution especially prestigious in China. Because of jealousy caused by the recent success of the faith, in 1665 a rumor was spread that the Christians were involved in a conspiracy that was preparing the way for a Portuguese occupation. At age seventy-three, Schall von Bell was condemned to death. He was pardoned, but his five Chinese assistants were executed and several missionaries were expelled.

The successor to Father Schall von Bell, the Flemish Jesuit Ferdinand Verbiest (1617–1688), adopted the same knowing approach. He gained the friendship of the very young emperor K'ang-Hsi, who became the most illustrious representative of the Manchu dynasty. K'ang-Hsi named Verbiest president of the office of mathematics for the empire. At that time there were 117 Catholic missionaries in China, of which fifty-nine were Jesuits. Without deciding to become a Christian, in 1692 the emperor accorded liberty of worship throughout his empire to Christians.

The scope of the work of the Jesuits in the course of the seventeenth century should not be underestimated. There were churches in all the Chinese provinces with the exception of the regions farthest west. It is said that 150,000 were baptized by 1650, and nearly 300,000 by 1664. These numbers seem exaggerated and depend on misleading assumptions. The missionaries, for example, baptized a great number of infants at the moment of death.

### The Quarrel of the Chinese Rites

This work, however, was seriously undermined by the other Catholic religious orders. The Franciscans, Dominicans, and representatives of the Foreign Mission of Paris also came to China and, following the death of Ricci, began the long and ardent "Quarrel of the Chinese Rites." They accused the Jesuits of syncretism and compromising with Confucianism. The problem was referred to Rome where the discussion centered on three main issues: the use of Chinese in the liturgy, the use of Confucian terms to designate God, and the question of whether or not it was possible for Chinese Christians to participate in the official ceremonies that honored Confucius, the legislator, without at the same time giving him worship.

At first the Jesuits seemed to carry the day: in 1615 a brief by Pope Paul V gave authorization to Father Trigault to translate the holy books into Chinese and use them for the liturgy of the Mass. This was to be done "not in the common language, but in the scholarly language appropriate to literature." Moreover, "the Chinese who have come to the Catholic faith and have been canonically lifted as far as the dignity of holy orders could, in this same literary and scholarly language and according to the rite of the Roman church, celebrate the holy sacrament of the Mass, recite the divine office of the canonical hours, administer the sacrament, and perform all other ecclesiastical functions." In 1656 Rome also decreed that Chinese Christians could continue to render honor to Confucius and their deceased ancestors, but ceremonies would only be tolerated if they maintained a civil character.

The discussions later took a harsh and bitter turn. As the Jesuits attacked the Jansenists in Europe on the score of theology, the Jansenists responded by vigorously denouncing what they considered to be a laxity leading directly to syncretism. They strongly questioned the missionary methods of certain Jesuits in China, of which some examples were perhaps extreme cases or caricatures. But they were laid before the public anyway because the stakes were very high.

Here are some lines from Blaise Pascal, taken from *Provincials* (1656):

> It is by this obliging and accommodating conduct . . . that they [the Jesuits] embrace everyone . . . They respond so well to what one asks them that, when they find themselves in a country where a crucified God passes for folly, they suppress the scandal of the cross and preach only a glorious Jesus Christ, and not Jesus Christ suffering. They have done this in the Indies and China where they have permitted idolatry to the Christians even by the subtle invention of having them conceal under their clothes an image of Jesus Christ to which they teach them to mentally direct the public adorations that they render to the idol.

To attempt to justify themselves, the Jesuits asked Emperor K'ang-Hsi to confirm the civil character of these ceremonies, which he did. But the Roman doctors reckoned themselves more competent than him in matters of theology. In 1704, nearly a century after the death of Ricci, Rome finally decided to forbid the Chinese liturgy and its previous accommodations to Confucianism.

Immense China was sufficient unto itself and has always had isolationist—indeed, xenophobic—tendencies. This empire, so vast and so old, did not easily tolerate outside contributions to its culture. Christianity, as an imported religion, carried some undeniable and perennial risks. It was conveyed in a foreign culture, language, and rites. Worse still, it demanded obedience to a power established in the old capital of the distant West, Rome. The Catholic resistance to abandoning Latin and forming a Chinese clergy was felt to be proof positive of the imperialist tendency of the Roman power.

Emperor K'ang-Hsi, who was at first so favorable to the Christians, took the pontifical decision very badly. He wrote in August 1706:

> Here, therefore, is the manner in which the Westerners are content to speak of high Chinese doctrine, although none of them has been instructed in China . . . The Europeans cannot even penetrate to the sense of our books. It is therefore out of fear that the pope makes rules that, founded on false information, will infallibly bring about the ruin of Christianity in our empire. From now on, no Westerner will be permitted to propagate his religion in China.

Therefore, at the beginning of the seventeenth century, Christianity was once again rejected by China. From then on K'ang-Hsi forbade all new Catholic missionaries from entering his empire. Consequently, by 1717 there were only about forty-seven priests for all that immense country. In 1724 the emperor Yong-Tcheng further hardened Chinese opposition to Christian missions, as a decree from the tribunal of the rites demonstrates:

> The Europeans who are in the court are useful for the calendar and render other services there; but those who are in the provinces are of no use. They attract ignorant people to their law, both men and women. They raise up churches where, under pretext of prayer, they assemble indifferently, without distinction of sex. The empire does not obtain the least advantage from them . . . It is necessary to allow the useful ones in the court. As for those who are scattered in the provinces of the empire, if they can be useful, they should be taken to the court; the others should be driven to Macao [outside of the empire]. The temples that they have built should be converted into public buildings; their religion should be rigorously forbidden.

Responding to the Jesuits' pleas to be allowed to remain in China, the same emperor wrote:

> What would you say if I sent a troop of bonzes [Buddhist monks] and lamas [Lamaist monks] to your country to preach their law? How would you receive them? You want all the Chinese to become Christians; your law seeks it, I know it well. But if this happens, would we not become the subjects of your kings? The Christians that you make only recognize you. In a time of trouble, they would listen to no other voices but yours.

For 125 years following 1707, the persecution was so relentless that the missionary work almost entirely disappeared and the church became semiclandestine. By the beginning of the nineteenth century, it is estimated that there remained about eighty Chinese and thirty-one European priests. By 1850 there were only about 250,000 Catholics in China.

# OCEANIA

Several small islands in the South Seas, such as the Carolines and Marianas, were evangelized following their discovery in the seventeenth century. Other than these, however, the oceanic world of the Pacific was ignored until the eighteenth century.

On the whole, the missionary work of the Catholic religious orders in Asia achieved great initial success, yet in the long run Christianity was not successfully planted in this region of the world. The exceptions are the Philippines and some parts of India and Annam.

# SECTION IV

## THE EMERGENCE OF
## PROTESTANT MISSION

# CHAPTER 13

# *Protestant Missional Thought*

The Catholic missionary enterprise during the time of the Renaissance and Reformation resulted in a mixed outcome. The best was interwoven with the worst, especially in Latin America. There were many missionaries who were admirable for their dedication and capacity to immerse themselves into populations living in extreme conditions; but there were also questionable compromises with the political powers, and much scorn for the cultures and peoples encountered. Generalizations are not possible. As in all the periods of church history that precede and follow it, the missionary activity of this period is characterized by an inescapable ambiguity. It is by virtue of the great "despite all" of grace that God has acted.

Protestant historians do well to show humility in evaluating this history, for whatever the deficiencies of Catholic missions in the sixteenth and seventeenth centuries, they at least have the merit of existing. This is not the case for Protestants. In contrast to their Catholic contemporaries, the Reformers and their immediate successors were, in effect, scarcely attentive to the missionary question. The awakening of a Protestant conscience and sense of responsibility for unevangelized people came very late and very slowly to the scene. Nevertheless, Protestant missionary enterprises began to appear from the moment that Protestant nations first made "geographic" contact with non-Christians, either through the immigration of colonists to the New World or though the establishment of trading posts beyond the seas. This is the story that will be traced here.

## THE GREAT REFORMERS AND MISSION

Occurring in the midst of the Renaissance, the movement known as the Reformation was a gigantic upheaval throughout all of Western Christendom. Led principally by Martin Luther and John Calvin, it was in large measure a return to the source of Christianity, the Holy Scriptures whose authority was recognized by the Reformers as controlling. However, this return to the message of the church of the first centuries was in no way missionary. This is astonishing in as much as the Reformation coincided with the generation that marveled over the discovery of the New World. In effect, America had been discovered only twenty-five years before

Luther attached his Ninety-five Theses to the church door at Wittenberg. In contrast, the problem of the evangelization of the non-Christian peoples of the planet was a pressing concern to the theologians and authorities of the Catholic Church.

Do the Reformers merit a grave reproach? Though extenuating circumstances may not excuse this shortcoming, it is at least possible to explain it and to understand its causes.

Not only did the Reformers not send missionaries, but also it is especially remarkable—with some exceptions to be mentioned later—that they established no theological basis for an evangelical missiology. Why this lack of interest while, in the same period, Dominicans, Franciscans, and Jesuits were very active in Asia and the Americas?

Diverse reasons, tied to the particular circumstances of their lives and struggle, can explain this. Eight reasons are given below; four cultural-historical, four theological.

First, in each period the church has its priorities. All the Reformers were entirely engaged in the urgent struggle in which they found themselves. Luther named himself "the evangelist of the Germans." Conscious that the populations of Europe were plunged into real paganism, the Reformers believed that reform of their own lands must be given the highest priority. Their pressing duty was to lift up a church conformed to the word of God, as they understood it—for what good would it be to preach a distorted message, as the Catholic missionaries were doing, to the non-Christians in the newly discovered lands?

Second, the Reformers belonged for the most part to the continental peoples. For most of the sixteenth century the masters of the seas were the Iberian princes—at least until 1588 when the English fleet gained victory over the "Invincible Armada." According to the system of the *Padroado*, it was the Catholic kings who were entrusted with the responsibility of evangelizing the conquered territories. Consequently, any Protestant mission would have to clash with an insurmountable military opposition.

Third, the brutal procedures used by the Catholic colonizers to "Christianize" the conquered peoples had given Protestants a negative image of missions.

Fourth, for centuries the principal agents of Christian missions were the monastic orders. In suppressing all the monasteries, the Reformation deprived itself of an eminent means of propagating the faith.

The following explanations deal with theological concerns. These carry more weight, for they involve issues of greater permanence.

First, in the area of ecclesiology, the Reformers challenged the idea of a transmissible apostolic authority. In their eyes, the time of the founding apostles of the church had past. The Great Commission issued by the recently resurrected Christ no longer concerned the church of the later centuries to the same degree. They were, however, concerned with taking up the issue of the legitimate episcopate passed down by apostolic succession. (As we will see, this position was defended by Adrian Saravia, a Calvinist theologian who embraced Anglicanism.)

Second, in the field of eschatology, they believed that they had arrived at the end of time. The pope was the Antichrist; the Turks, who occupied a great part of central

Europe, were the beast of the Apocalypse; and the true church was reduced to a small flock. Hence it was no longer time to dream of new conquests beyond the seas.

Third, in terms of salvation history, the Reformers relied on certain texts of the New Testament that led them to believe that the gospel had already resounded throughout all the earth during the first century. All peoples had heard it, and if some remained pagan, it was because they had refused to accept the message. Deaf to the call of God, they were now irreversibly excluded from the new covenant.

Finally, one can say that the Lutheran concept of the "two-edged sword" allowed the Reformers to confer the responsibility for converting pagans to the princes who held the temporal sword. The idea that the propagation of the faith is the duty of the Christian magistrate was first advanced by Melachthon, the friend and disciple of Luther. At a time when the European states were launching far-flung colonies in places inhabited by non-Christian populations, this idea would have appeared promising. Zwingli, Bucer, and Calvin parted company with Luther and Melachthon on this issue, but there was scarcely any concern on either side as to whether or not the states and Protestant princes were ready or able to undertake such a task.

## MARTIN LUTHER

A great exegetical scholar, Martin Luther (1483–1546) well understood that the good news of Jesus Christ was supposed to be proclaimed to all the people of the earth. However, the idea that all the races had already heard it in the early centuries of the church and that some had refused it was clearly present in some of his remarks. This idea seems to have resolved the issue for the Reformer.

Luther's anachronistic ideas about world evangelization can be seen in his "Sermon on the Magi of the Orient": "the Magi represent the pagans, illuminated by the gospel, coming to the Christian church to find Christ . . . This has been accomplished since the pagans have accepted the gospel and have learned to know Christ." Or again in his "Sermon on the Ascension": "Even in this time one can find an island where there are pagans to whom no one has ever preached . . . However, the Scripture declares that their voice went out to all the earth." One feels the perplexity of the Reformer who, nevertheless, managed to be content with a rather vague conclusion: "The message has gone out in the same way as when one casts a stone in the water: it produces ripples and circles that spread farther and farther until they break upon the shore; in the center, all is already calm, while the ripples continue their regular movement. It is the same for the proclamation: it was begun by the apostles, and it advances without ceasing."[168] But Luther did not say how he supposed this would work in his own time, and he left scarcely any impression that he felt concerned about it.

According to Luther, as we have seen, Christ's imminent return no longer allowed for missions. It is recorded in his *Table Talk*: "The Last Day is at the door, the four empires of the prophet Daniel are past . . . Asia, Africa do not have the gospel, and in Europe most of the countries do not have it; it is not the small Electorate of Saxony

---

168 Martin Luther, *Prédications de l'année 1522*, no. 26.

that will prevent the end." On the other hand, the Dutch Reformed theologian Adrian Brouwer remarked that Luther, in light of the principle that every Christian is elect, thought that each was supposed to remain in the place where God had put him. In the course of the centuries that followed, the history of the Lutheran churches demonstrate in an irrefutable fashion the sad shortcomings of the missionary vision of Luther and his successors.

Finally, Luther has often been reproached for his extreme bellicosity in regard to the Turks, the Muslims with whom the Europeans of his time were the most directly and dramatically in conflict. This problem cannot be eluded. The Wittenberg Reformer drew the parallel many times between Muhammad and the pope, Islam and the papacy. However, he said: "I do not consider Muhammad as Antichrist: he is too crude. But the pope of our regions is the true Antichrist; like a devil, he is illustrious, subtle, attractive, dazzling . . . The Turk also seduces the world, but he has not introduced himself into the church of God and is not concerned with the name of Christ . . . He attacks Christendom from the exterior and is proud to be its enemy."

The Swiss Reformer Ulrich Zwingli advocated an evangelical mission among the infidels that would result in dissuading them from attacking Christendom. Luther, for his part, did not see any solution other than an interior mission; that is to say, the return of Christians to a life conforming to the gospel: "For Christians should not fight the Turks with arms as the pope and his followers teach; instead of raising their fists against them, Christians should recognize that the Turks are the lash of the whip and the anger of God, that they are necessary, or [they should] endure them as a test imposed by God because of their sins, or fight and hunt them solely by means of the arms of penitence, tears, and prayer."

If at first Luther opposed war against the Turks, he would later argue that the civil power has the responsibility to repel an invader and to defend his country against a threat to the existing civil order. For him, secular wars are sad but inevitable events in the context of this troubled and sinful world, but it is not necessary to mix considerations of religious order into these affairs, as the pope does. However, at the end of his life, Luther came, albeit provisionally, to envision war against the Turks as the fulfillment of biblical prophesies. His position, then, marked a change of mind: he accepted the idea that German Christians, allied to the Catholic emperor out of faithfulness to Christ and engaged in wars that were the supreme test of faith, would if they died become martyrs.

However, Luther always said that it would be better to preach to the Muslims than to undertake military crusades against them. He also maintained that to refute Islam it is necessary to know it. As noted above (p. 108-09), just a few years before his death he published Ricaldo da Monte de Croce's *Confutatio Alcorani* in 1542. In his introduction to the text, Luther wrote: "I would have loved to have read the Qur'an myself, and I ask myself how it is possible that no one has translated the Qur'an into Latin earlier, given that Muhammad has been a dominant figure for more than nine hundred years already and has caused so much harm. No one, strangely, is anxious to know what the beliefs of Muhammad are; and everyone is content with the sole certitude that Muhammad has been an enemy of the Christian faith. But where and how, point by point, this has not yet been revealed, and it is necessary to do so." Apparently the Reformer did not know all the works of the medieval theologians, among which is a Latin translation of the Qur'an that was completed in 1122 at the request of Peter the Venerable. Theodore Bibliander, the Zurich Reformer and successor to Zwingli, would nevertheless fulfill his wish (see pp. 207ff).

In any event, Luther believed in the necessity of a witness to the Turks and the pagans. In his eyes, the best preachers were the disciples of Jesus who lived in the midst of these distant peoples. They had the responsibility before God "to preach and teach the gospel to the pagans who are in error, even as to non-Christians, by a pure fraternal love, even if they have not been officially charged with this burden." Regarding Christian captives in the hands of the Turks, Luther said that they are the best messengers and witnesses of the gospel among the Muslims. He exhorted them in these terms: "As long as you behave yourselves in a faithful and diligent manner, you glorify the gospel and the name of Christ; your master and without doubt many others, if they are evil, are obliged hence to say: All the same, the Christians are a faithful, obedient, pious, humble, and merciful people. By your example, you can in this way cast discredit on the beliefs of the Turks and, who knows, convert many among them."

## JOHN CALVIN

The French Reformer John Calvin (1509–1564) interpreted the missionary texts of the Scriptures in the same fashion as Luther. The order of Christ to his apostles to go and preach the gospel to non-Christian peoples was no longer applicable. If there were still pagans, it was because they had previously refused the grace of God. Though he spoke "of antipodes and other distant peoples, which until today have heard no one even speak of Christ," he did not draw the conclusion that it was necessary to go to evangelize them.[169] Calvin also believed that he was living in the last days and, therefore, there was no longer time to evangelize the recalcitrant people of the world.

A text of Calvin can nevertheless be invoked as an explicit reference on his part to the responsibility that Christians have toward the representatives of other peoples and other cultures. This text clearly closes the door to racism:

> As far as the men that there are in the world, these are your neighbors . . . God has not chosen one race of men, he has not limited his service to a certain country, but the wall is broken, such that today there are neither Greek nor Jew . . . When I say: There is a man who is of a distant country, and even if we do not know how to speak a word to one another that can be understood, what contact might I have with him? Now when I have said all this, what have I to do? If I look at him, if I contemplate him, I will see in him a nature that he has in common with me . . . It is the same nature by which God has conjoined and united us all . . . Let us try to

---

169 Comm. Harm. Ev.; Matthew 24:14.

procure the salvation of their souls and the good of their bodies, insofar as we are able to do so.[170]

Another text of the French Reformer, taken from his commentary on Deuteronomy 33:18–19, should be cited:

> "They will call the peoples, etc." What we should retain from this passage is that we should try, insofar as we can, to attract all the men of the earth to God, so that, in one accord, he will be adored and served by all. And in fact, if we have some humanity in us, seeing that men go to perdition unless they have come to obey God, must we not be moved in pity to retrieve the poor souls from hell and bring them to the way of salvation?

It is important to note that in Calvin's thought the doctrine of predestination does not dampen the universality of God's call of salvation. In these texts the embryo of an evangelical missiology can be detected, but no such theology, let alone a concrete missionary project, would develop from them.

The other principal Reformers will adopt the same position, with the exception of the Strasbourgian Martin Bucer.

## MARTIN BUCER

Bucer (1491–1551) is the only one among the Reformers to have manifested a genuine openness regarding the church's missionary responsibility. He was more precise than most but fell short of advocating concrete initiatives to develop a missionary program.

His treatise, *Of the True Soul Cure and of the Just Ministry of Spiritual Guidance* (1538), witnesses to his interest in giving priority to ecclesiological questions. He perceived the church as "a spatial reality, a body that stretches to the ends of the earth," and affirmed that if the leaders of the churches seriously occupied themselves with those who were entrusted to them, the church would prosper. He wrote:

> Hence they could truly seek and bring to Christ those who are distant from him by birth and education, like the Jews, Turks, and other pagans. Ah! If they loved the rule of Christ and sought to extend it like they love and seek to extend their own temporal domains! But sadly we see that they covet rather the territory and goods of the Jews, Turks, and others pagans, and one feels that it is with much less seriousness that they try to gain souls for Christ our Savior.

Bucer continued by criticizing the conquest of the newly discovered lands and by severely attacking the extension of Christendom through the methods of colonization practiced by the Spanish:

---

170 *Opera XXVIII*, 16–17, cited in Emile Doumergue, *Jean Calvin*, vol. 4, *La pensée religieuse* (Lausanne: Bridel, 1910), 402.

> This advances nothing. First of all, observe that they kill the
> poor and strip them of their goods, and then they also kill their
> souls by the false superstitions taught by the monks of the
> mendicant orders.

He finished by addressing the elders of the evangelical church, urging them to accomplish their tasks with zeal and reminding them that the proclamation of the gospel of salvation had a universal dimension that directly concerned them:

> May these elders neglect no one, not even the Jews, Turks, and
> all the nonbelievers, to whom they should always have access. In
> this manner they will bring to Christ all those among them who
> belong to him.

Though this proposition remained theoretical, in the context of the Reformation it at least had the merit of having been proposed.

## THE ANABAPTIST COMMUNITIES

From their beginnings the Anabaptists were persecuted, both in the regions gained for the Reformation where they generally originated, and in the Catholic states where some hoped to find refuge. Did their desire for an unconditional faithfulness to the letter of the gospel lead them to an openness to the missionary responsibility of the church?

Their minority status, the necessity of living in secret, and even their initial settlement in the regions of continental Europe—Switzerland, the south of Germany, Austria, and Moravia—did not give them the possibility of envisioning a missionary effort to reach the non-Christianized countries. But the frequent expulsions they endured had the effect of dispersing them throughout the vast regions at the center of Europe. They saw in this forced itinerancy an effective means to spread the gospel message to populations that, by their own criteria, they considered to be pagan and ignorant of the good news of the kingdom of God.

Most being pacifists in principle, they were convinced that the faith must be the fruit of a free personal decision, and they could only envision evangelization under a form of preaching that called individuals to conversion. Some passages from the writings of sixteenth-century Anabaptist authors show their conviction that the gospel is intended for all peoples of the earth. An eminent intellectual among their number was Balthasar Hubmaier. The vice rector of the University of Ingolstadt, he was first attracted to Reformation teachings by the writings of Luther and later converted to Anabaptism. In 1524 he wrote: "A Turk or heretic can be convinced neither by the sword nor by the fire, but only by our patience and prayer . . . A law to burn the heretics is an invention of Satan. The truth is immortal." He died in Vienna in 1528, burned alive after being cruelly tortured. Hubmaier had organized communities practicing a sort of "evangelical communism" according to the principles of the church of Jerusalem after Pentecost.

Following his death, Jacob Hutter from Tirol in Northern Italy took up the torch. His communities included thousands of people who, though often pursued, ended up experiencing a certain prosperity. By one count there were 2,173 martyrs in their ranks. Hutter was himself put to death in 1536, but the Hutterite communities continued to develop. It was notably in the second half of the sixteenth century that they manifested a remarkable missionary zeal, sending their members two by two to preach the gospel in peril of their lives. These itinerant preachers bore their witness not only in Protestant and Catholic regions, but also in the territories occupied by the Turks, evangelizing those that the "Christian" princes had only envisioned combating by arms. The *Great Chronicle* of the Hutterites describes their motivation and methods:

> The Christian mission was instituted by the Lord and hence constituted a commandment. He said: "As the Father sent me, so I send you," and also, "I chose you and have established you so that you may go and bear fruit." This is why the servants of the gospel and their aides have been sent each year [at Easter and autumn] to the countries where we had some reason [to hope for success].

One of these numerous Hutterite evangelists, Claus Felbinger, wrote in 1560:

> Some have asked us why we came to the land of the duke of Bavaria to dissuade his people from being faithful. I respond to them: not only have we come to the land here, but to all the lands, as long as our language can be understood. For everywhere where God opens a door for us and shows us some zealous hearts that are ardently seeking the Lord . . . in all these places we foresee going, and for this we have some good biblical reasons.

Here are some extracts from the twenty-five verses of an Anabaptist hymn sung by Hutterite communities at the time of the biannual departure of their missionaries:

As Christ was sent by the Father,
So he has sent
His community of disciples.
And he has ordered that the gospel be announced to the peoples
So that they can know it.
It is still in this way that God sends
In these last days,
To turn the people from their evil ways,
And to say to men
That all will have to stand before God in the judgment,
Without any excuse to make.
We take leave of you,
Our dear brothers and sisters,
With the arms of the heart, we embrace you
In the pure love of Christ.
We bless you with faithful intentions,
For we must separate ourselves from you,
So here, even more persons may be found.

It is also appropriate to cite the words of the former Dutch minister Menno Simons (1496–1561) who, around the middle of the sixteenth century, gathered together many persecuted Anabaptists. In about 1540 he wrote:

> Here is my only joy and the single desire of my heart: that the kingdom of God be extended, that truth be lifted up, sin reproved, justice taught, famished souls fed by the Word of the Lord, that the scattered sheep be led on the right way, and many souls gained to the Lord by his Spirit, power, grace . . .

> I ardently desire, even at the price of my life and blood, that the holy gospel of Jesus Christ and of his apostles, which alone is the true doctrine and will remain such until Jesus Christ returns in the clouds, can be taught and preached in the entire world as the Lord Jesus Christ commanded his disciples and confided to them as his last wish on earth.

In terms that seem directly inspired by the writing of the Apostle Paul in his letters to the Corinthians, Simons elsewhere expressed his zeal and that of his brothers for evangelism:

> This is why we preach, as long as it is possible for us, during the day and during the night, in houses as in fields, in forests as in deserted places, here and there, in the mission and beyond, in the prisons and in the dungeons, in water and fire, on torture tables as on streets, before lords and princes, by voice and pen, with possessions and blood, with life and with death. We have done this during numerous years, and we are not ashamed of the gospel of the glory of Christ.

## ERASMUS OF ROTTERDAM

To tell the truth, although an ordained priest, the great humanist Desiderius Erasmus (1469–1536) was more a philosopher than a theologian or a man of the church. Moreover, he never embraced the ideas of Luther, though he considered them sympathetically. He should not be ranked, therefore, among the protagonists of the Reformation. His conception of evangelical mission, however, merits mention in this chapter.

Several months before his death in 1536 Erasmus published a book of Christian sermons in which his missionary thought is found. Here are some extracts from *Ecclesiastes sive concionator evangelicus* (*The Preacher*):

> Eternal Lord, how great are the fields of this world where the seed of the gospel has never been sown or where the tares occupy more space than the good grain! Europe is the smallest part of the globe. Greece and Asia Minor are the most fertile parts of it; in these countries the gospel was first introduced with great success when it came from Judea, but these regions are today totally in the hands of the Mohammedans who know not the name of

Christ. What do we possess in Asia, the largest continent? . . . What have we in Africa? In these vast spaces are without doubt found barbarians or simple tribes who could easily be attracted to Christ, if we would send among them men to sow the good seed. New regions, until now unknown, are discovered each day, and it is said that still more remain to be discovered . . .

Travelers return with gold and precious stones from these distant countries, but it would be more noble to carry to them the wisdom of Christ, which is more precious than gold, and the pearl of the gospel, which would show them the true value of the riches of this world . . . Christ gives us the order to pray to the Lord of the harvest to send workers, for the harvest is great and the laborers are few. Must we not pray to God so that He will send workers into these vast territories? But each declines to do so with fallacious pretexts . . .

It is much easier to oblige by force than to persuade by the word; it is easier to kill the body than to convert the soul to good. And however difficult this may be in itself, it is above all with the tongue that the preacher accomplishes it; for arms, he has sacred doctrine, tears, prayer, and a life without fault . . . Bodies may be forced, but souls, not being able to be forced, must be swayed . . . The priest does not have the right to kill; rather, he acts in such a way as to bring back to life, by the efficacy of his voice, souls that have long since been buried in vice . . .

After having shown the inanity of the excuses invoked to dispense with the missionary task and denounced the false motivations that animated the greater part of those who ventured abroad, Erasmus made a moving appeal. He charged the volunteers:

First therefore, you, the heroic and illustrious leaders of the army of Jesus Christ, put on the helmet of salvation . . . May your waists be belted with humility, may your feet be fitted with holy affections; in a word, be dressed in all the mystical armor to preach the gospel of peace. Give yourselves without any fear in this glorious work. Overturn, destroy, not men but ignorance, impiety, and the other sins. For to kill in this way is in reality to conserve. Never make terrestrial gain the purpose of your work, but strive to enrich the pagans with spiritual treasures. Consider it to be a great gain to save for the Redeemer souls snatched from the tyranny of Satan and to lead to Him in triumph in heaven souls by the thousands. Make not material goods the object of our work, but struggle to enrich the pagans in carrying spiritual treasures to them. Count as a great profit the souls that you redeem from the tyranny of Satan, in saving them through the Redeemer. Lead in triumph thousands of souls to heaven to be with him. I call you to a difficult task, but one that is noblest and highest of all. Oh! if God would judge me worthy to die in accomplishing a work so holy, rather than to be consumed by a slow death, in the tortures that I endure! No one is capable of preaching the gospel to the pagans if he has not renounced riches, pleasure, yes, even his own life . . . The cross will never be absent from the life of those who preach the gospel in truth.[171]

The great humanist Erasmus, as an advocate of mission, shows an aspect of himself that has largely been ignored! Yet despite his spiritual lucidity and the prestige of his voice, his call to mission scarcely caused a stir.

Concerning Islam, Erasmus shared the opinion of many theologians of this time. He saw its many borrowings from Judaism, Christianity, and especially from the Arian heresy, and that at its base this mixture was pagan. With Wycliffe and the Reformers, he was conscious that Christendom carried a large part of the responsibility for the ineffectiveness of proselytism among Muslims. Those who bear the name of Christians, Erasmus believed, are often scarcely better than infidels, and he wondered how any people could believe in Christianity if they could see what transpires in the countries claiming to be Christian. "I prefer a sincere Muslim to a Christian hypocrite!" he wrote, before concluding, "If we wish to lead the Turks to the religion of Christ, we must first be Christians ourselves."

## THEODORE BIBLIANDER

His true name was Theodor Buchmann (ca. 1504–1564). In addition to Heinrich Bullinger, Bibliander was Zwingli's successor in Zurich. In a more pronounced manner than Zwingli, he retained the humanist imprint of Erasmus. An eminent philologist and orientalist, he is without contest the Protestant theologian of the sixteenth century who most intensively studied Islam. He was, moreover, on the point of leaving as a missionary to Egypt. Between the years 1530 and 1540 he was dedicated to the translation of the Qur'an. His work was published in 1543 together with various other texts on Islam, written by the humanists of his time as well as by the Christian theologians of the preceding centuries (see pp. 104-15). Among others, these included Peter the Venerable and even Girolamo Savonarola. This publication of the Qur'an sparked lively reactions. Bibliander did not believe that the prohibition on the publication of the Qur'an would be of any help to Christians. Referring to the ban and destruction to which the writings of Judaism had been the object in the past, he wrote: "It was not in this way that the Jews became Christians, or the Christians better." Luther and Philipp Melanchthon, as well as the Strasbourg Reformers Bucer and Gaspard Hédion, vigorously encouraged this publication. At the same time that Bibliander was popularizing the Qur'an, he was also showing its shortcomings.

> The comparative study of the Qur'an and the Holy Scriptures is very useful; it makes clear the dignity, excellence, and grandeur of the Christian doctrine . . . For the truth itself is found throughout in the Holy Scriptures, while the Qur'an abounds in absurd

---

171 Erasme, "Oeuvres choisies," trans. Jacques Chomarat, in *Livre de poche classique* (Paris: Libraire Générale Française, 1991), 977–79.

lies. In the Holy Scriptures all texts are in agreement, even those written in different ages; at the time of the composition of the Qur'an, the small number of Muslim compilers could not come to agreement, so that they left numerous contradictions . . . In the Holy Scriptures, all is clear, simple, and conforms to the norms of the best proofs of the faith and of charity; in the Qur'an, things accumulate without order, all is thrown together pell-mell, in a veritable confusion.

For Bibliander, the Qur'an was a heresy that distorted the sense of the Bible. With the other Reformers, he focused his critique on the denial of the Trinity and the divinity of Jesus Christ, which he believed the disciples of Muhammad derived from a false understanding of monotheism. He also attacked polygamy and the five pillars of Islam, the latter he interpreted to be a theology of justification by works.

In contrast to other Reformers, the Zurich theologian was more positive in his critique of the Muslim social order. He praised Muslim discipline, ordered public life, and sense of family:

The father of the family is severe; the women are modest and zealous in the supervision of the house; the children are educated with care and good instruction in their religion. Excessive praise and pleasantries have little place among them, even so coarse games . . . They are simple but clean in their food and drink, in their clothing . . . For the most part the Turks have in their homes if not love, at least the cult of justice, and they are honest in commerce.[172]

And he asked Christians if they could not learn something from Muslims. In this he echoed the questions posed by his friends Zwingli and Bullinger. Zwingli asked, "What therefore is the difference between the Turk who, knowing nothing of the law of God, rises up against it, and the Christian who, knowing it, does not obey it? The answer is that the Christian will go, with much more certitude, to hell." Similarly, Bullinger wrote, "Christians are astonished and wonder with impatience why God permits the Saracens and the Turks to have so much success . . . and why He still tolerates their impure belief that is at odds with the just and true faith . . . These Christians, although they confess the true faith, little grasp how their evil and scandalous lives arouse the anger of God, who in consequence sends against them to subject them the armies of enemies whose power comes more from the sins of Christians than from the force of their own false beliefs."

Bibliander wrote in the same spirit:

There is no doubt that if our affairs had been regulated from the first according to the Word of God, and then if the clergy, Christian magistrates, and all the faithful people had put in common their zeal and effort to combat the impiety of the Muslims with spiritual arms, in a short time one would see the Muslims discredited

---

172 Segesvary, "L'Islam," 140.

and their doctrine degraded. The kingdom of Christ would be re-established in the regions that are today subjected to the prince of darkness, but which formerly sheltered the most remarkable churches of Christ.

Bibliander, however, distanced himself in an important theological point from the orthodoxy of the Reformers, particularly in his unedited writings in the last period of his life. He sharply attacked the doctrine of double predestination and manifested universalist tendencies that were closer to the humanist Cardinal Nicolas de Cusa than to Luther or Calvin.[173] His position appeared clearly in his *Relatio fidelis*, a book on the science of religion.

His thought was dominated by the conviction that God, whose love is infinite, wants to save each of his creatures and that, due to his immensity, his grace is universal. Indeed, he did not conceive that this grace could be independent of the person and work of Christ. He was convinced, however, that the effects of the Cross were available to all human beings: "Hence, the eternal and unique Son of God became man in order to obtain, as an expiatory victim, the forgiveness of God the Father for the entire world. One cannot limit this benefit to a chosen few and, consequently, limit the impact of the Redeemer, for he is the Redeemer of every type of human. Nor can it be restricted to a few due to a secret and eternal decree of God of which the sacred books do not witness."

He continued to affirm that God has deposited in all men the seed of religion and wisdom, which bears fruit in some while being lost or degrading into superstitions in others. But those in whom the seed germinates will be welcomed by the heavenly Father, whatever be the people in which they belong and the knowledge that they have or do not have of revealed truth. When the pagans follow the word of wisdom that leads to salvation, he said, they show by their life that they are sons of God and belong to an invisible church that knows borders in neither space nor time. God can "transform into very good Christians the Turks, Saracens, Tartars, Jews, like the stones from which he lifted up the sons of Abraham." Nevertheless, Bibliander pointed out that "no one obtains justification by his own works, since each is redeemed [by Christ]. God justifies men by faith, and faith is the act of the free will of man." A work of Bibliander, in manuscript form, opened with this salutation: "To all Christians, Jews, and Mohammedan Muslims, grace, peace, and many greetings in the name of God, our Lord."

This was a humanist approach that, though in some ways close to Calvin, clearly moved away from that of Bullinger and broke from the emerging orthodoxy that

---

173 The German cardinal Nicolas de Cusa (1401–1464), inspired by his religious universalism, made a very positive evaluation of Islam. Called to read and study the Qur'an, he sought to find evangelical truths hidden in it or truths difficult to recognize. "Whatever is beautiful, just, and transparent in the Qur'an necessarily comes from the luminous rays of the Gospels." Equipped with an approximate translation of the Qur'an, he sought to find in it a veiled notion of the Trinity and a tacit confession of the divinity of Christ. He was reminded that Muhammad had never wanted himself to be adored, and he greeted him as a prophet, great educator, and witness of the truth contained in Christianity. If Muhammad was deceived, it is because he sought his own glory more than that of God and because he allowed himself to be misled in his understanding of Christianity by the Nestorian heresy.

would settle in the second half of the sixteenth century on the churches issuing from the Calvinist Reformation.

# ADRIAN SARAVIA

One of the only Protestant authors of the sixteenth century who elaborated a missionary ecclesiology was a Belgian Reformed theologian whose ideas were most often rejected.

Adrian (or Hadrian) Saravia (1531–1613) was born in Hesdins of a Spanish father and a Flemish mother. At first a monk, he very early joined the Reformation. After having been well grounded in the study of theology at Oxford, he became a Reformed pastor in the church of Anvers and later in that of Brussels. He then departed for the Anglo-Norman islands of England. He was named, in 1582, professor of divinity at the Calvinist university of Leiden in the Low Countries. But accused of complicity in a dark conspiracy, he was obliged to return to England in 1587. He there became an Anglican minister and was occupied with important responsibilities before being named in 1601 prior of Westminster in London. In 1607 he was honored to be one of the translators of the famous English-language Bible known as the Authorized Version, but often referred to as the King James Version. At his death in 1613, he was widely respected and was interred in Canterbury Cathedral.

Saravia was not therefore an ordinary person, and his major work, published in 1590, attracted the attention of the theologians of his time. He treated the organization of the church under a complicated Latin title: *De diversis gradibus ministrorum . . .* (in English, a fuller version of the title is: *From Various Degrees of the Ministries of the Gospel Such as They Were Instituted by the Lord and Transmitted by the Apostles and Such as They Are Confirmed by the Perpetual Use That All the Churches Make . . .*). He stoutly defended the hierarchical episcopal system.

Chapters seventeen to nineteen of the book deal with the evangelization of non-Christians. Saravia's exegesis and arguments are solidly constructed. He responded in particular to the issue of whether the command of Christ to preach the gospel to all the nations is any longer valid. His response was that this commandment is addressed to all disciples until the end of the world; and following the death of the apostles, the early Christians demonstrated the ongoing validity of the command, often pouring out their blood to obey it. There being no time limit on the command, it will remain valid as long as human beings exist on the earth who do not know our Lord. Unfortunately Saravia added an addendum to this interpretation. The preachers of the gospel sent by the church, he argued, must have at their disposal an apostolic authority. Interpreting this in an espicopal manner, he believed that this authority should be conferred by a bishop at the outset of their mission, for missionaries sent by churches must have bishops at their head.

Saravia presented his position in these terms:

> After the death of the apostles, the command to preach the gospel
> in all nations remains valid for the church, just as does the prom-
> ise of the presence of Christ to which the command is indubitably

tied. The command of Christ obliges the church to accomplish it through the apostolic power, which in fact is needed for its fulfillment. The ministry and apostolic power have been given more to the church than to individuals . . . If the church today does not dream of carrying the gospel to pagan peoples, it is because its zeal and apostolic spirit have cooled. It is not individuals who must depart in mission on their own authority; the church alone possesses the apostolic authority necessary to send apt men in mission, and she has the duty to do so for as long as people exist who live in ignorance of God.[174]

Despite the carefully presented arguments of Saravia, Calvinist theologians seemed to focus only on his reference to an espiscopal structure springing from the apostles. Coming from a former professor of the strictly Calvinist University of Leiden, this was treason. At the same time they rejected his exegesis of the Great Commission found in Matthew 28:19–20. Theodore Beza himself took up the pen for a counterattack. In 1592 he published a Calvinist refutation of Saravia's treatise: *Ad tractatum de ministrorum gradibus ab Adriano Saravia Belga editam Theodori Bezae responsio . . .* (*Response of Theodore Beza to the Treatise Published by the Belgian Adrian Saravia on the Degrees of Ministries . . .*). Calvin's successor at Geneva defended the official position: the command of Christ was undertaken by the apostles and Christians of the first centuries, and they succeeded in reaching the extremities of the earth with the message of the gospel. The mission has therefore been accomplished.

> I believe [wrote Beza] that we must not out of curiosity seek to find out if the apostles reached all nations, neither should we greatly worry about a mission to the most distant nations, for there is among us and around us plenty of work for us and our descendants.

A little later the arguments of Saravia were also supposedly refuted by an illustrious Lutheran theologian, Johann Gerhard. In his famous *Loci theologici* (*Theological Commonplaces*), which appeared in 1617, he assailed Saravia's thesis in the same manner as Beza.

Hence it appears that the churches issuing from the Reformation, from their beginnings and for a long time afterwards, lacked a biblical theology of mission.

---

174 J. R. Brutsch, "Le fondement de la mission chez Hadrianus Saravia," in *Verbum caro*, vol. 1, no. 4, (Neuchatel: 1947), 169.

# CHAPTER 14

# The Beginnings of Protestant Mission

## THE CALVINIST VENTURE IN BRAZIL

In order to deny the missionary incompetence of the churches of the Reformation in the sixteenth century, the missionary enterprise of Coligny to Brazil (1556-1558) is sometimes set forth. It is a fascinating subject and one worthy of close examination. One of the participants, Jean de Léry, made a detailed and celebrated narrative of it that has been republished many times in subsequent centuries.[175]

The principal personage of this adventure was Nicolas Durant de Villegagnon (1510–1571).[176] Born in Provins in 1510, he studied at the University of Paris in 1530 at the same time as Calvin. A knight of the Order of Malta and a distinguished sailor, he embarked for the west of Algiers to combat the Barbary pirates. In 1548 he safely carried to France Mary Stuart, the queen of Scotland, and the talent he demonstrated in that affair gained for him the title of Vice Admiral of the Coast of Brittany. It was for these exploits that he came to the attention of Gaspard de Coligny (1519–1572), then a great admiral of France. Villegagnon seems to have been attracted to the ideas of the Reformation, for Jean de Léry wrote:

> He had a great desire to retire to some distant country where he could freely and purely serve God according to the Reformation['s interpretation] of the gospel; but he also desired to prepare a place there for all those who would want to retire to avoid persecution.

---

175 Between 1578 and 1611, Léry published five editions in French of his work in Geneva. There were during the same period three Latin editions, one Dutch, and one English (extracts only). Since 1880, at least eight editions in French, of which some are abridged, have been published. The most recent edition available, and the easiest to consult, was prepared by Frank Lestringant: Jean de Léry, *Histoire d'un voyage fait en la terre du Brésil 1557,* ed. Max Chaleil (Montpellier, France: Presses du Languedoc, 1992). The spelling is modernized, but the style of the author is preserved. The work is enriched by maps and engravings of the period, of which several are due to a companion of Léry, Jean Gardien, or to the author himself. The Library of Droz has published the facsimile of the edition of 1580, with the engravings of the author: Jean de Léry, "Histoire d'un voyage fait en la terre du Brésil," in *Les classiques de la pensée politique,* no. 9, ed. Jean-Claude Morisot (Geneva: Librarie Droz, 1975).

176 Sometimes written as Villegaignon.

It could never be proved, however, that Villegagnon was a Protestant. In any case, he died as a good Catholic. Géralde Nakam writes of this subject: "Villegagnon leaned, then, not towards the Reformation, but towards a sort of religious humanism held in the pre-Reformation period."[177]

## The Project of Admiral Coligny: A Huguenot Refugee in the New World

When Admiral Coligny (1519–1572) undertook this enterprise, he had still not openly declared himself for the Reformation—he would not do so until 1559. The purpose of this statesman was to make a place for France in the New World. He could not accept that the division of the New World's lands must be left to bold navigators alone. Had not sailors from Dieppe been discovering new shores in America since 1505? Coligny, in 1555, accepted the proposition of Villegagnon to organize an expedition. He revealed his plans to France's King Henry II, who gave his full approval. Though it cannot be known with certainty, it is probable that the admiral saw the possibility of killing two birds with one stone. Like many of his contemporaries, he believed that the religion of subjects was supposed to be that of the king, and that the political unity of the realm depended on its religious unity. He knew the value of the Protestant people, who were uncomfortable as dissenters in France. So why not create a Protestant France in the New World, separating the two realms by the Atlantic Ocean? Many, he reasoned, would hazard an Atlantic crossing to be able to profess their religion in freedom. Coligny never clearly expounded this great design, but events seem to confirm its existence. The Reverend Pierre Richier, one of the members of the expedition, wrote of the admiral to Calvin: "Coligny, by his authority, counsels, and even from his own financial resources, for as long as he has been able, has contributed to assure the foundations of our church; he is the leader and the head of our enterprise."[178]

Villegagnon left the port of Honfleur on May 6, 1555, with two ships. The three or four hundred passengers and crew included many Protestants, "people God-fearing, patient, and mild." It was, however, a strangely disparate group, where gentlemen Huguenots were next to monks and prominent Catholics, as well as a good number of people "rustic and without any instruction in honesty and civility, devoted to many vices and shameless dissolutions," if one believes the Acts of the Martyrs of Crespin (1564).

After a long and difficult crossing, the expedition arrived at the coast of Brazil. Villegagnon disembarked on an island in the Bay of Guanabara across from Rio de Janeiro, a place that the Portuguese had discovered a little before. He took possession of it in the name of King Henry II of France. The first settlement, protected by Fort Coligny, was christened Henryville in honor of the king. The colonists received the support of the Indians, who were hoping to find in the French an ally to help them in their struggle against the Portuguese then inflicting cruelties on them.

---

177 Géralde Nakam, "Au lendemain de la Saint-Barthélemy: Guerre civile et famine," introduction to Jean de Léry, *L'histoire memorable du siège de Sancerre (1573) de Jean de Léry* (Paris: Editions Anthropos, 1975), 17.

178 Olivier Reverdin, *Quatorze Calvinistes chez les Topinambous* (Geneva: Journal de Genève, 1957), 28.

Villegagnon, who was granted the title of "King of America," wrote a letter a few months later to the Reformed church of Geneva, which is preserved in the city's archives and dated in 1556. Villegagnon "was praying earnestly, not only that ministers of the word of God be sent to him . . . in order to better reform him and his people, and even to attract the savages to the knowledge of their salvation, [but also] that some numbers of other well-instructed personages in the Christian religion would accompany the said ministers." Jean de Léry, a Burgundian shoemaker who had come to Geneva in the hope of studying theology but then traveled to Brazil with Villegagnon, comments, "The church of Geneva, having received his letters and his news, first rendered thanks to God for the extension of the reign of God in a country so distant, even in a land so strange, and among a nation that was indeed entirely ignorant of the true God."[179]

Hence the Reverends Pierre Richier, at fifty years of age, and Guillaume Chartier, two years his junior, were sent, accompanied by twelve Huguenot volunteers. The latter included Léry, who by his outspoken passion for Brazil and its inhabitants and by his remarkable gift for observation (he took abundant notes and made numerous sketches), became one of the first modern ethnologists. Historian Frank Lestringant comments that Léry's book is "the first attempt at anthropology worthy of the name published in France." He gave precise descriptions of the morals of the Topinambous (or Tupinambas) Indians, who belonged to a large group called the Arawaks. Léry also described in highly colorful and detailed fashion the tropical flora and fauna. According to the ethnologist Claude Lévi-Strauss of the Académie Française, Léry's work is the "breviary of ethnology." In *Tristes tropiques*, he praises it as a "masterpiece of ethnographic literature" and writes, "I am astonished that no novelist or scriptwriter has yet seized upon it. What a movie [this history] would make!"[180]

The Huguenots left Geneva on September 9, 1556, and while in the process of departing, the travelers went to greet Admiral Coligny at Châtilon-sur-Loing. "He not only encouraged us to pursue our enterprise, but also, with promises to assist us through the navy, gave us hope that God would graciously allow us to see the fruits of our labor." In Paris, other Protestants joined the Genevans. The expedition left Honfleur on November 19, 1556, under the leadership of the Protestant Phillippe de Corguilleray, lord of Pont, "a man of indomitable faith and great firmness of character," and a refugee of Geneva since 1549. On March 7, 1557, Villegagnon cordially welcomed the new arrivals, who were not all Protestants, and after a service of thanksgiving, put them to work from the day of their arrival in making them carry stones for the construction of Fort Coligny! The first sermon took place March 10, 1557, and on March 31 the "King of America" addressed a second letter to the church of Geneva to give thanks for the good "advice" received from John Calvin and for the ministers the city had sent, whom he called "his brothers."

---

179 Léry, *Histoire d'un voyage*, 38 (citations refer to the edition established by Frank Lestringant).
180 Claude Lévi-Strauss, *Tristes tropiques*, 1st ed. (Paris: Pon, 1955). For our subject, see Claude Lévi-Strauss, "Tristes tropiques," in *Terre humaine* (1986), 87ff.

## Discovery of a Strange People

The Genevans immediately came into contact with the Topinambous Indians and did their best to communicate with them.[181] They discovered a people who seemed to be without religion. Not only did they have no knowledge of the true God, but "they confess to worship neither heavenly nor earthy gods; and consequently, they had no formulary or place set aside to assemble in order to have an ordinary service; they have no religious prayers either in public or in private."[182] If there is a superior being, it is Toupan, who manifests himself in the thunder and greatly frightens them, and a sort of devil, Aygnan, a demon who never ceases to torment them, either here below or after death. The Genevans noted their belief in the immortality of the soul and even in a notion of retribution: the souls "of those who have virtuously lived, that is to say, according to them, who are avenged and have much eaten of their enemies, go at last to the high mountains where they dance in beautiful gardens with their grandfathers."[183] They had itinerant prophets existing among them who occasionally visited them. These were the Caraibes, types of sorcerers whom the people honored with organized ceremonies that included drinks, threnodies, chants, ritual dances, and trances.

*Jean de Léry illustrated his narrative with precise sketches that display his keen sense of observation.*
*On the left: a Topinambous Indian couple with their child and a pineapple in the forefront.*
*To the right: two Indian women crying over a dead man lying in a hammock.*
*(Taken from Jean de Léry, "Histoire d'un voyage fait en la terre du Brésil," Librairie Droz, Geneva, 1975.)*

The Huguenot adventurers, who were in no way prepared to encounter a population so different from their own, were surprised by some aspects of the Indians'

---

181 In the lines that follow, close parallels can be seen between the descriptions given by Léry and those that will be made in the following centuries by the Jesuits working among the Guarani of Paraguay.

182 Léry, *Histoire d'un voyage*, 152.

183 Ibid.

morals. Richier experienced true culture shock. Here is an extract from one of his first letters:

> One thing that hampers us greatly, and we anguish over it, is the barbarity of the people, which is such that one would not know how to imagine anything greater. It is not just the fact that they are cannibals . . . What I must especially complain of is the crass stupor of their spirit . . . They do not distinguish between good and evil. The vices that nature renders other people conscious of, they hold for virtues . . . Finally, and it is the most fatal, having no idea that God exists, they can know neither his law, nor recognize his power and goodness. The result is that we are frustrated in our hope to reveal Christ to them. This is what above all appears to us grave and painful.

They discovered the Topinambous to be bellicose and ceaselessly on the path of war.

> These barbarians do not make war in order to conquer the countries and lands of one another, for they all have as much of these as they need; neither is it because the conquerors claim to enrich themselves from the spoils, ransom, and arms of the conquered; these are not, I say, what leads them on. For, as they themselves confess, they are not motivated by anything other than revenge for the relatives and friends on their side, who in the past have been taken and eaten . . . They are so fierce in encountering one another that whoever falls in the hands of his enemy awaits, without further reflection, to be treated the same, that is to say, to be knocked out and eaten . . . Their hatreds are so inveterate that they live perpetually irreconcilable.[184]

On the treatment reserved for prisoners, Léry notes: "Forthwith, therefore, upon their arrival, they are not only fed the better meat that can be found, but also women are given to the men (though not husbands to women); even someone holding a prisoner would have no trouble in giving him his daughter or sister in marriage . . . Nevertheless, after having fattened them up like pigs at the trough, they are finally struck down and eaten."[185] Moreover, they will not hesitate to eat the babies born of the unions between the prisoners and their women.

The Topinambous were polygamists: "It is permitted to the men," wrote Léry, "to have as many women as pleases them; making of vice a virtue, those who have the greatest number of them are esteemed the most valiant and hardy, having seen one who had eight of them." He noted that they were well treated and that there were few disputes between them. Moreover, he recognized that these people knew how to live in a pleasing and harmonious manner. He observed very little conflict between inhabitants of the same village; and when he inquired about it, they said that they left adversaries to fight among themselves according to the principle of "an eye for

184 Ibid., 135.
185 Ibid., 143.

an eye, and a tooth for a tooth." The Genevans were also able to discover remarkable qualities in these "savages":

> As for their natural charity, in distributing and making daily presents to one another of venison, fish, fruit, and other goods that they have in their country, they practice it in such a fashion that a savage, so to speak, would die of shame if he saw a fellow man or nearby neighbor lacking what was in his power to give, and also, as I have experienced, they practice this same liberality towards allied strangers. [Léry then cited several examples of the great generosity from which in several difficult circumstances he and his friends had benefited.][186]

## Léry: Precursor of Ethnology

Instead of satisfying himself with simply condemning the barbarous morals of the Indians, what is striking in the narrative of Jean de Léry is his capacity for reevaluation in the face of what he observes and his ability to integrate his European reading into his new understanding. Hence, after describing the extreme cruelty of their wars and their cannibal ceremonies, he sees a parallel between European and Indian ways:

> Nevertheless, so that those who shall read these horrible things practiced daily among these barbarian nations of the land of Brazil might also think a little more clearly of those who have done similar things among us . . . And does one need to go farther than France (I am French and angry to say it) during the bloody tragedy that began in Paris on August 24, 1572, of which I do not accuse those who were not the cause of it, among other horrible acts that could be recounted that were perpetrated throughout the kingdom . . . ? [He is referring to the massacres of Saint Bartholomew's Day, of which Admiral Coligny was the first victim. Six years later Léry wrote the definitive version these events.][187]

Léry also wrote of the total nudity of the Indians and especially of their women: "It has never been in our power to make them dress, for they were resolved not to wear anything whatever it might be." But to those who might think that "the relations between these entirely nude savages, and principally among the women, incite a lustfulness and bawdiness," he writes:

> In appearance, this might seem to serve as a lure to covetousness, however . . . I maintain that the get-ups, makeup, false wigs, hair twists, great neck ruffs, farthingales, dresses, and the other infinite number of trifles of which women and girls here [in Europe] disguise themselves and never have enough of, are without comparison the cause of more evils than is the ordinary nudity of

186  Ibid., 178–79.
187  Ibid., 150.

savage women who however, in reality, owe nothing to the others in beauty.[188]

Géralde Nakam writes in this regard: "The conclusion to which he [Léry] leads goes beyond that of a simple witness. Comparing the 'savages' to Europeans, he wondered, as Las Casas had, and as Montaigne would: 'What is civilization?' The problem haunts this transitional period in history. In 1599 Léry will formulate it with a particular neatness, in referring especially to Las Casas, whom he read in the edition of 1582 . . . In contrast to Brazilian morals, he sets out the scenes of cruelty by the Turks, French, or Spanish and easily concludes that in matters of atrocities the Europeans were superior."[189]

## Attempts at Evangelizing the Indians

Though Léry's narrative and the Huguenot expedition to Brazil are fascinating studies in ethnology, do they have a place in the history of mission? Certainly evangelism was not given priority in the project, neither on the part of Coligny, nor on the part of the other Protestant colonists. "'The French island' was not therefore a missionary center but rather an exotic mode of refuge," rightly noted Jean-Pierre Bastian.[190] Villegagnon spoke, in his letter to the ministers of Geneva, "of enticing the savages to [obtain] a knowledge of their salvation," but his actual behavior in Brazil showed that he was not concerned about it. All that he could say in a letter to Calvin about these "savages" was that they were people "far removed from all courtesy and humanity, living without religion or any knowledge of honesty." In short, they were "beasts with human faces." As for the Genevan members of the expedition, practically from the very beginning the Reverend Richier was frustrated in his attempts to share the gospel with them, and the others fared no better. However, with the passing of time, Léry wrote: "I am of the opinion that if Villegagnon had not rebelled from the Reformed religion, and if we could live for a longtime in this country, some of them might be drawn to and gained for Jesus Christ."

As for the rest, evangelistic opportunities occasionally presented themselves, and the Huguenots knew how to profit from them. Hence Léry recounted how he and his friends were welcomed in an Indian village. Before eating the food that was offered to them, they removed their hats and made a long prayer of thanksgiving. Their Indian hosts were greatly astonished at this performance. Using a translator, an old man asked whom they had addressed, and the Calvinists responded by speaking to them of God who created the heavens and the earth. They spoke also of the love of God, which they contrasted to their spirits who never ceased to torment them and leave them in fear. A conversation of more than two hours ensued in the course of which the Genevans tried to lead their pagan hosts to the discovery of the goodness of God the creator who takes care of his creatures. They also noted the perdition that awaited them if they did not receive the salvation offered in Jesus Christ. Through it

---

188  Ibid., 93–94.
189  Nakam, "Au lendemain," 29.
190  Jean-Pierre Bastian, *Le protestantisme en Amérique latine: Une approche socio-historique* (Geneva: Labor & Fides, 1994), 25.

all, they were careful "to always make comparisons to the things that were known to them."

Léry recounted, "Some of you have told us of marvels and things very good that we have scarcely understood, the Indians responded to them. They were so moved that not only did several promise henceforth to live as we would teach them, but some even promised to no longer eat the flesh of their enemies, and also . . . knelt down with us while one of our company gave thanks to God, saying the prayer in a loud voice in the midst of the people, which, afterwards, was explained to them by the Truchement [interpreter]." Léry continued, "Before we fell asleep, we heard them singing all together to the effect that to avenge themselves on their enemies it was no longer necessary to capture and eat them, an idea that had never occurred to them before."

On another occasion, Léry recounted a march in the forest in the company of several Indians with whom he was going on a hunt. Filled with wonder by the spectacle of the shimmering of the tropical vegetation that he was discovering, he began to sing Psalm 104 in a loud voice. His Topinambous companions took great pleasure in this and one of them, "all moved to joy and with a radiant face advanced and said to me: 'Truly, you have sung marvelously . . . But we do not understand your language; I implore you to tell us what the subject of your song was.' Hence I declared to him as best I could that I had only praised my God in general for the beauty and government of his creatures, and that in particular I had also attributed to him this: that it is He alone who feeds all men and animals, indeed, who makes the trees, fruit, and plants grow, which are everywhere in the broad world; and since the time that this song that I had sung had first been sung by one of our great prophets, who had left it to posterity to use even to the end, there had been more than ten thousand moons (for hence they count)."

Léry spoke to them in this way for more than half an hour without interruption; after that, "using their interjection of astonishment, Teh!, they said: 'O that you Frenchmen are happy to know so many such secrets that are all hidden from us, a puny and miserably poor people.'"

It is interesting to note Léry's underlying theology of evangelization. In the manner of Paul in confronting the pagans at Lystra and Athens, the principal angle of approach used to carry the pagans to repentance was an emphasis on monotheism and the doctrine of God the creator, who for all his creatures is sovereign and merciful. In reporting these events, Léry concluded with this commentary, which echoes the Reformed theologians of his time:

> I very forcefully and clearly made known to them the difference that lies between those who are illuminated by the Holy Spirit and by the Holy Scriptures, and those who are abandoned to their senses and left in their blindness. In this I have been strongly confirmed in the assurance of the truth of God.[191]

---

191  The narrative of these attempts of evangelization are found in Léry, *Histoire d'un voyage*, 159–63.

Evoking the permanent fear in which these pagans were living, Léry remembered that an Indian had said in addressing one of their number: "'Frenchman, my friend, I fear the Devil (Aygnan) or the evil spirit, more than any other thing.' The French colonist whom they addressed then responded: 'As for me, I do not fear Aygnan.' They responded by deploring their condition: 'Alas! Would that we could be as happy in being preserved from this evil as others!' It was only necessary, we assured them, to believe as we do in the one who is stronger and more powerful than Aygnan." Although they had often affirmed their desire to do so, notes the author, "all this soon vanished from their conscious thought."

## A Doomed Expedition

The Huguenot adventure to Brazil was sadly of a very short duration. The situation in which the Protestant colonists found themselves rapidly deteriorated, for Villegagnon and several Parisian colonists opposed the celebration of Holy Communion according to the Genevan liturgy and chose, instead, to defend the doctrine of transubstantiation. A sharp dispute broke out, and the Reverend Chartier even rushed to Geneva in June 1557 to elicit the arbitration of Calvin. During this time, Villegagnon forbade any Protestant services, which resulted in most of the Huguenot colonists deciding to return to Europe. This infuriated the "King of America," who then confiscated their goods, cut their supplies, and expelled them from the island of Seregipe. They had to take refuge in the Brazilian forest, where they benefited from the hospitality of the Topinambous with whom they had previously established excellent relations and who, according to Léry, "demonstrated incomparably more humanity."

It is hence that the Calvinists shared the life of the Topinambous for nearly three months, establishing themselves in a place called "the Brickyard," which corresponds to the central districts of present-day Rio de Janeiro. Finally, the captain of an enemy English vessel, the *James*, agreed to repatriate them through France. They left America on January 4, 1558, ten months after their arrival. Four among them, for fear of a shipwreck, decided to return to the land on a launch. Villegagnon required a confession of faith from them. "When this confession was sent to him, he reflected on it as seemed good to him and was led away by an evil disposition. He declared them heretics in regard to their views on the Sacrament, vows, and other things, viewing them with more horror than the plague-stricken."[192] They were condemned to death, and three among them were pushed off a high cliff after being tortured. These were Matthieu Verneuil, Pierre Bourdon, and Jean du Bordel.

The return passage on the rotting ship was dramatic. The voyage took place during an unfavorable season, and storms succeeded in gravely damaging the boat. It was necessary to throw all the cargo, including the provisions, into the sea to avoid a shipwreck. Then a flat calm prolonged the voyage to the point that several sailors died of hunger and thirst. "As for us passengers . . . not one died. But in truth we were little more than skin and bones, appearing to any observers as dead bodies disinterred." They disembarked at the port of Blavet in Brittany, where the captain of the

---

192 Jean Crespin, *Histoire des martyrs* (1619), cited in Nakam, "Au lendemain," 160.

boat had to inform the city tribunal of a letter written by Villegagnon that denounced the Huguenot passengers, accusing them of worse infamies and requiring that they be burned as heretics. Happily, the magistrates to whom the message was sent took pity on the Huguenots: "When they had seen what was commanded of them insofar as treating the passengers in the manner that Villegagnon desired, they decided on the contrary to provide us better food than was normally possible for them, and in addition, to those among us who had means, they even lent money."

Léry wrote later with a certain nostalgia: "In saying adieu to America, I confess how much in my particular case I have always loved and still love my own country . . . nevertheless I often regret that I am not among the savages, whom I knew with a more easy-going directness than some on this side of the sea, who, to their condemnation, bear the name of Christian."

On his return from America, Léry settled in his native Burgoyne and was briefly a preacher in Belleville-sur-Saône. He married in 1559 in Geneva and established himself among the middle class of the city in 1560. It was there that he drafted his first version of *Travel in the Land of Brazil*. He was next sent by the church of Geneva as a pastor to Nevers and then to La Charité-sur-Loire where he escaped the massacre of Saint Bartholomew's Day. He lived as a refugee in the citadel of Sancerre during the long and tragic siege in 1573, about which he wrote an account.[193] In the course of his misadventures, he lost the still-unpublished manuscript of his travels but later found it in Lyons in 1576. He would finally publish it in 1578, some twenty years after his return. The second edition appeared two years later. Beginning in 1589, Léry exercised a pastoral ministry in the canton of Vaud in French-speaking Switzerland. He was the second pastor of the parish of Aubonne, though actually in charge of the annex of Lavigny.[194] Then, beginning in 1595, he was the pastor of L'Isle, at the foot of Jura, where he died of the plague in 1613 at the age of seventy-seven.[195]

As for Villegagnon, he bears a heavy part of the responsibility for the failure of the expedition due to his own inconstancy. He returned to France at the end of 1559 and lived there until his death in 1571. In 1560 the Portuguese governor Mem de Sa took possession of the French island. After expelling the colonists who were still subsisting there under the direction of Bois-le-Comte, he destroyed Fort Coligny and Henryville and returned in triumph to Lisbon with their French canons.

In conclusion, if it is difficult to present this sad and ephemeral expedition as a true "Protestant mission," it did at least allow some Protestants of goodwill to encounter non-Christians, to become aware of another people's need of salvation, and to attempt to communicate some elements of the good news.

---

193 Published as Jean de Léry, *L'histoire memorable du siège de Sancerre (1573) de Jean de Léry* (Paris: Editions Anthropos, 1975), preceded by a presentation and analysis by Géralde Nakam: *Au lendemain de la Saint-Barthémey: Guerre civile et famine.*

194 According to the Archives Cantonales Vaudoises, catalog of the pastors and parish registers, as well as Eugène Mottaz, *Dictionnaire historique, géographique et statistique du canton de Vaud.*

195 Henri Vuilleumier, *Histoire de l'eglise réformée du pays de Vaud sous le régime bernois*, vol. 2 (1929) 1919, n. 1.

# OTHER CALVINIST MISSIONS

## *Huguenot Expedition to Florida*

Gaspard de Coligny made a second attempt in the period from 1562-1565 to create a viable colony. By this time he had publicly committed himself to the Reformation, but in terms of missions his new colony can be considered in the same light as his first. It was a Protestant expedition to Florida, which was discovered in 1512. The Spanish and French never succeeded in creating enduring colonies in this corner of North America; however, the enterprise seemed to begin in near-perfect conditions, being entirely constituted of Protestants who were very clear about their objectives. Jean de Ribaut, a Protestant seaman from Dieppe, took charge of the colonists. He managed to establish Charlesfort. A second fort, Fort Caroline, was established not far from the current location of Cape Canaveral by another Huguenot, Captain René de Laudonnière, who arrived a little later with three vessels. In the beginning, relations with the Indians were difficult as they had suffered from the preceding Spanish expeditions. Soon, however, better relations seemed to develop as can be seen from the fact that the hungry and destitute colonists only survived due to aid received from the Indians. Still later, they came to their aid again by hiding them when the Spanish, who claimed the same land, launched an attack against them. A Spanish admiral wrote of his astonishment: "It is admirable to see how these Lutherans enchant these poor savages," and he also observed that the French had undertaken to evangelize them.

When the colony seemed stable, Ribaut returned to France to enlist an additional group of nine hundred men for the colony. In addition to the men, the group that embarked included a number of women and children.

But the orders of King Phillip II of Spain were painfully clear: these colonists must be annihilated. The Spanish Captain Menendez, whose goal was to purify America of the Lutheran heresy, was charged with the work. Claire E. Engel tells the story:

> Laudonnière held Fort Caroline with about 150 men. There were also present women, children, and the sick. On September 20, 1565, Menendez launched the assault, carried the fort, and in cold blood cut the throats of 132 men, plus a further ten the next day. Laudonnière and the young brother of Ribaut, with one or two others, succeeded in fleeing. The lives of fifty women and children under fifteen years of age were spared, with this astonishing commentary by Menendez: "I would have feared Our Savior would chastise me if I had used cruelty towards them, especially the eight or ten children who were born there." Naturally, the fact that these French were Protestants justified the massacre in the eyes of Menendez.[196]

Ribaut fled to the sea with two hundred men, but unfortunately his boat sank. Menendez captured them but promised to spare their lives. However, according to

---

196  Claire Éliane Engel, *L'amiral de Coligny* (Geneva: Labor & Fides, 1967), 190.

his own words, "When these sad people surrendered themselves, I had Jean de Ribaut and all the others pass under the knife, as was appropriate to do in the service of God Our Savior and the Virgin Mary."[197] He spared only two ship's boys who were under eighteen years of age.

Among the survivors, Lord Dominique de Gourges reached England where he was able to tell the story of these tragic events. Such was the fate of this Protestant enterprise, which suggests that it was not yet time for Protestantism to launch missionary projects. In sum, of the approximately one thousand colonists, a third of the men were able to escape with Laudonnière, and twenty-four others saved their lives by abjuring the Protestant faith.

Some years later French Catholics embarked for the same place. Upon their arrival, the Indians, noticing that they were speaking French and not Spanish, had no fear and welcomed them warmly. They even asked them to sing psalms so that they could dance, but these French were evidently incapable of doing so. This anecdote from a subsequent period witnesses to the earlier good behavior of the Huguenots in regard to the Indians—and to their ability in this period to keep the beat while singing psalms.

### Failure in Lapland and an Attempt in North Africa

To complete this slim account of the Protestant missionary enterprise in the time of the Reformation, the expedition commanded by King Gustav I Vasa (1496–1560) of Sweden and the King Christian III of Denmark to evangelize the Lapp tribes to the north of their kingdoms must be included. Lapland is a region that includes parts of Norway, Sweden, and Finland, mostly within the Arctic Circle. The Lapps had been evangelized in the twelfth century but without much result. The primary obstacles were their nomadic existence and different language. For these same reasons, the new attempt did not enjoy greater success. It is also probable that the enterprise was no stranger to the annexationist aims of the king of Sweden with regard to the Great North. The Lapps themselves suspected as much. Consequently, it would not be until the eighteenth century that Protestant missionaries—this time the Moravian Brethren—once again undertook the evangelization of the Lapp people.

It only remains to note the efforts originating from Wurtemberg, inspired by Duke Ludwig (1568–1593), to introduce the Lutheran faith to North Africa. No trace of it, however, survives.

# THE SEVENTEENTH-CENTURY MISSIONARY PRECURSORS IN NORTH AMERICA

### Great Britain

King Edward VI of England (1547–1553) was faithful to the notion of *Padroado* that was also dear to the Catholic Church. He declared to his navigators, "The propagation of Christianity must be the principal interest of those who undertake the discovery of

---

197 Ibid.

new lands." His successors made similar pronouncements. Hence the great navigator Martin Frobisher (1535–1594), on the voyage in which he discovered the regions of
Greenland (1570), included among his crew a clergyman named Robert Wolfall, who
had left his wife and children in England as well as a good living, "so great was his
desire to save souls and reform infidels in leading them to Christ." Walter Raleigh
(1552–1618), for his part, embarked for North America in the period 1584–1585 to establish a colony that he called Virginia in honor of Queen Elizabeth. He was interested in
the Indians in the region, whose first convert was baptized on August 13, 1587.

After the destruction of Spain's "Invincible Armada" in 1588, English sailors no longer hesitated to plow the seas. The British East India Company was founded in 1600 in
London. From the outset, the ships of its fleet would each carry a chaplain.

### The Pilgrim Fathers

The first colonial charter granted to Virginia by King James I in 1606 stipulates that
one of the purposes of the enterprise would be to proclaim the Christian faith
"among the peoples who live in miserable darkness and ignorance"; and the second
charter of 1609 points out, "The principal result of this enterprise will be the conversion of these countries to the true worship of God and the Christian religion." James
I organized a public collection to create a Christian college in Virginia where Indian
children could be instructed in the Christian religion.

The first colonial charter for Massachusetts, issued in 1628, affirmed that the
desire of King Charles I was that the colonists "would win and invite the natives of
the country to the knowledge of the only true God and Savior of mankind and the
Christian faith."

Oliver Cromwell (1599–1658), the Lord Protector of England, seems to have understood the importance of the evangelization of non-Christian peoples. Responding to
a petition signed in 1644 by seventy English and Scottish clergymen asking that the
Parliament resolve to send missionaries to the American colonies, in 1649 his government established the Company for Propagating the Gospel in New England and Parts
Adjacent in North America. "Ministers," Cromwell urged, "should speak from the
pulpit to enlist contributions to finance it." The company also had the approbation
of the army and the universities of Cambridge and Oxford. The funds collected on its
behalf reached twelve thousand pounds. Such government sponsorship of mission is
not far removed from the Catholic system of the *Padroado*, which was also a missionary initiative supported by governments.

Since the restoration of the English monarchy in 1660, King Charles II wanted to
take possession of these funds by suppressing the company. He was dissuaded from
this by a courtier, Robert Boyle (1627–1691). Instead, he signed a royal charter in 1662
to institute the Corporation for the Propagation of the Gospel in New England. In 1701
this became the Society for the Propagation of the Gospel in Foreign Countries (SPG).
Representing the Anglo-Catholic tendency in the Church of England, it still continues
its work today in diverse regions of the world.

Boyle was the director of the Society for a period of nearly thirty years. Son of the
Earl of Cork, this young aristocrat studied at Eton and then in Geneva and other cities

of Europe. A disciple of Francis Bacon, he wrote numerous works of philosophy, but his passion was the evangelization of the North American Indians. He bequeathed the largest part of his fortune to the Society, and the revenues of this bequest were used for many years to pay for the studies of young Indians in the College of William and Mary in Virginia.

To tell the truth, the colonists who embarked for the New World had other interests on their minds than the evangelization of the Indians. In fact, the Pilgrim Fathers, as they are called in the United States, immigrated to New England to live out their faith in liberty. Leaving England, the Pilgrims were first refugees in Holland—in Amsterdam then in Leiden—under the leadership of the Reverend John Robinson. In 1620 a group of them embarked for New England on the famous *Mayflower*. After a dramatic crossing, they arrived on the coast of present-day Massachusetts at a place they named Plymouth. The region being largely unpopulated and the few Indians very hospitable, the colonists established a settlement and began to prepare for the winter.

Their contact with the native population proved difficult as they were semi-nomadic. Also the new arrivals were preoccupied with the demanding tasks of attempting to survive. They scarcely had time to encounter let alone think about evangelizing the Indians. It should be added that the Pilgrims were hardly the only ones to have set out for North America, for a small number of adventurers and merchants had preceded them. Soon many more would follow—and few were men of refined principles. It was necessary to clear the new land and cut down the forests that the local Indian tribes considered as their hunting grounds. When conflicts erupted between the English and the Indians, muskets proved to be more effective than bows and arrows. The traders soon discovered the disastrous effect of alcohol ("fire water") on the Indians and used it to deadly effect on those they wanted to exploit. The Indians, pacific and generous at first, reacted with violence, and the relations between the two races became hateful. One remembers the expression that was repeated by later Americans: "The only good Indian is a dead Indian."

Founded on Calvinist theology, the later Puritans, when they came to New England, insisted on the doctrines of the sovereignty of God and predestination. More optimistic than Calvin, they dreamed of establishing a theocracy in this land, in the expectation of the imminent victory of God over the Antichrist and the advance of the kingdom of God that the final expansion of the church was supposed to prepare. Their settlements in America would be the first glimmering of the realization of this dream. They envisioned the New World, therefore, as a promised land in which the Indians were the Canaanites to be displaced, indeed exterminated. This conception was consistent with the conviction, shared by the Reformers, that the non-Christian peoples of the world had already been evangelized in the time of the apostles. Since then, their refusal to accept the message of the gospel manifested that they were not the predestined people of the new covenant.

However, several among the Christian colonists were moved by the needs and sentiments of the Indians. Compassionate men and women discovered evangelistic missionary convictions, not in their books (which did not exist), but in their human contact with the Indians. The doctrine of predestination, in its positive dimensions, oriented them towards engagement in mission to the Indians, and they believed themselves to have been elected to spread the reign of God to the pagan peoples of America. Some among them, such as John Eliot, Roger Williams, and William Penn—whose stories will be told later—believed that the Indians were the descendants of the ten lost tribes of Israel that had disappeared in Assyria after the fall of Samaria, the Northern Kingdom of Israel that had separated from the Davidic dynasty at the time of Jeroboam.

One of the first events that contributed to the reversal of prejudice that assumed the Christianization of the Indians would be impossible was the conversion, following her marriage to John Rolfe in Virginia, of the celebrated Indian princess Pocahontas. She was a sensation upon her arrival in England in 1616 and was considered to be the first Christian representative of her race. Sadly, she could not endure the English climate and died early the next year. In Virginia, where a war was then about to break out between the colonists and Indians, Pocahontas was considered by her own people to be more a traitor to their cause than an ambassador of goodwill.

## The Mayhew Family

The Mayhews accomplished a remarkable work among the Indians of Martha's Vineyard and among the Indians on some of the neighboring islands off the New England shore. These lands were purchased from the crown of England by the patriarch of the family, Thomas Mayhew (1587–1680), a rich English merchant. After settling there with a group of immigrants, his son became the pastor of the small community of colonists. He soon dedicated himself to the evangelization of the native population. His first convert among the Indians, Hiacoomes, served as his interpreter. Later, after Thomas had recovered from an epidemic, he became a preacher himself, whose witness brought many to conversion. Despite the opposition of the powwows, indigenous witch doctors who inspired great fear in the population, there were soon three hundred native Christians. Sadly, Thomas Mayhew's son died prematurely in 1655 when his ship sank in the course of a voyage to England, undertaken to arouse interest in favor of the mission among the Indians. The father, the magistrate of the island, was then seventy-three years old. Nevertheless, he learned the Indian language so that he could continue the work begun by his son. When he died in 1680, at the age of ninety-three, there were close to two thousand converts on the island. This remarkable task of evangelizing and Christianizing the native population of the islands continued until 1806, having been pursued by five generations of Mayhews.

## Johann Campanius

Of Swedish origin, Johann Campanius worked with the aid of his son to evangelize the Indians of Delaware between 1643 and 1648. He succeeded in translating some of the biblical texts for them, but otherwise he believed that he had seen no fruit from his labor. Nevertheless, he had made a beginning that no doubt left an open door for William Penn, who later encountered the same population. The most eminent representative of this first generation of missionaries was John Eliot.

## John Eliot

Eliot (1604–1690) was born in England in the village of Widford where his pious parents raised him in the fear of the Lord. He studied in Cambridge and was very early distinguished by his gift for grammar and linguistics. He converted in this period under the influence of a famous Puritan, the Reverend Thomas Hooker. He decided to become a clergyman, but the Anglican Church was then closed to Puritans. Consequently, he resolved at the age of twenty-seven to embark for New England in the area of Massachusetts. He arrived in November 1631 and was followed two years later by his friend Hooker. Eliot soon replaced the absent pastor of a small church in the village of Roxbury, near Boston. He stayed there all his life.

This distinguished orientalist, who had shined in Cambridge, produced a new English translation of the Psalms, which was the first book printed in New England. He was a remarkable country pastor, known for his generosity, cordiality, and irrepressible energy. At the age of forty, when he was in the midst of a very active career, he was moved by compassion for the Algonquin Indians of New England. He decided at first to learn their language, which was a difficult undertaking. It took him two years, but he learned it so well that, on hearing him, one person believed that the miracle of Pentecost had occurred again. On October 28, 1646, he made his first tour of the Indian villages in the area. He was well received and preached his first sermon.

Based on the vision of dry bones found in chapter 37 of the prophet Ezekiel, Eliot's sermon was, in the usual Puritan manner, a two-hour-long doctrinal exposition. His listeners did not understand much of it, and Eliot experienced a strong sense of failure. The Indians, he wrote, "regarded it not." Not believing his message to be of value, they gave no "heed unto it, but were weary and despised what I said."[198] The missionary was not slow to adapt the message to the level of his audience, and soon the Indians began to pose all sorts of questions, such as: Why is the sea salty? Where does the sun go when it disappears on the horizon? These questions had scarcely any relevance to the content of his sermons, but his answers convinced the Indians that they had encountered an intelligent man. He rapidly won their confidence and was surprised to observe their reactions. He saw old warriors, known for their imperturbable impassivity, cry when he recounted the death of Christ to them.

They continued to press him with questions, but these became increasingly pertinent, as for example: "Why has no white man ever told us these things before?"[199]

The number of Eliot's listeners grew rapidly, and soon conversions began to take place. About one year after the beginning of his ministry, Eliot was able to write an encouraging report, of which this is an extract:

> The Indians have utterly forsaken their powwows. They have set
> up morning and evening prayers in their wigwams. They not only
> keep the Sabbath themselves, but have made a law to punish

---

198  Ruth Tucker, *From Jerusalem to Irian Jaya: A Biographical History of Christian Missions* (Grand Rapids: Academic Books, 1983), 85.

199  Tucker, *From Jerusalem*, 86.

those who do not. Whoever profanes it must pay twenty shillings. They begin to grow industrious and are making articles to sell all the year long. In winter, brooms, stoves, eelpots, baskets; in spring they sell cranberries, fish, strawberries. The women are learning to spin.[200]

Eliot taught his Indian friends to read and encouraged them to pursue a sedentary life. To the amazement of the colonists, a village was formed near Roxbury consisting of "Praying Indians."

The missionary quickly understood that it would be necessary to protect his flock from the pernicious influence of the white settlers. He decided to found Christian Indian villages deep in the forest. The first village, called Natick, was established in 1650 about forty-five kilometers southwest of Boston. He attempted to implement a political-religious program there that was inspired by the history of Israel. The Law of Moses was the basis of the theocratic constitution in which the Indians made a solemn covenant with God. Eliot created schools and trained Indian instructors and evangelists. He only founded the first Indian church after prudently submitting each neophyte to a meticulous examination. The first baptisms took place in 1651, five years after the first conversions. This work did not prevent Eliot from continuing to perform his pastoral ministry in Roxbury. Despite many obstacles and dangers, he undertook extensive missionary tours through the forest. During these days and weeks, he traveled on horseback and slept under the stars. In one of his letters, he wrote: "From Tuesday to Saturday, I have been dry neither day nor night for a single instant. When I want to take a rest, I remove my boots, wring out my stockings, replace them, and God assists and sustains me!"

Eliot's experience aroused a keen interest in England and gave added impetus to the movement to found the Company for Propagating the Gospel in New England and Parts Adjacent in North America, mentioned above. This company sent Eliot funds that permitted him to create an institution for the training of Indian pastors and instructors. By 1660 he had twenty-four Indian evangelists and several churches that were directed by indigenous, ordained pastors.

So many Indians were interested in wanting to live in Natick that it was necessary to found other villages on the same model. There were eventually fourteen such villages, each with its own thriving population. Each had a school, church, and magistrates. Other Massachusetts ministers imitated Eliot, and around 1675 there were more than 3,600 "Praying Indians."

Aside from these demanding tasks, Eliot found the time to produce an immense body of literary work. He translated the New Testament and then the Old Testament into the local language, works that were printed respectively in 1661 and 1663. In certain respects these Christian villages resembled the theocratic regimes established by the Jesuits in Paraguay and known as reductions. Yet the New England communities were distinguished from their Catholic counterparts by a concern that characterizes all Protestant mission: the desire to give the people the word of God in their mother

---

200 Tucker, *From Jerusalem*, 86.

tongue and to establish indigenous ministers. Besides the numerous books that Eliot published in English, he also composed books in the Mohegan language that include a catechism, grammar, book of math and natural sciences, and a songbook. These works are on display in a Boston museum, but no one can any longer read them, the Mohegan tribe being largely extinguished.

## King Phillip's War

Evangelistic work among the Indians was brutally stopped in full flight by an event that shook the colony: King Phillip's War (1675–1676). King Phillip, as he was known to the colonists, was the son of the chief who had generously welcomed the Pilgrims of the *Mayflower*. He was sickened to see the colonists slowly invade all his territory, in spite of promises and treaties; he was saddened by the traffic in alcohol that was physically and morally ruining his people; and he was ashamed to admit that the tribunals of the colonies considered the testimony of Indians to be of no value. He decided therefore to enter into war. However, before he had time to assemble his warriors, he was attacked by the English. The fierce combat that ensued ended in the victory of the colonists, whose arms were much more effective than those of the Indians. King Phillip was captured, drawn and quartered, and his head was sent as a trophy to Plymouth where it was put on display.

This confrontation was especially tragic for the Christian Indians. Most of them had stayed neutral, and some actually fought with the English. However, being caught in the middle of the conflict, they were mistreated by both their Indian brothers and the English colonists. Half of the villages were destroyed and the others seriously ravaged. The death of King Phillip was solemnly celebrated in the churches of the colony while the general public seemed to have forgotten the results of the mission work among them. Eliot and some of his friends, however, continued to visit the helpless Indians in the midst of the catastrophe.

When the war ended, the undaunted missionary attempted to raise up new communities out of the ruins. He set out to reassemble the distraught Indians, but this was not an easy task since all those who had not been massacred had fled deeper into the forest. Eliot, however, never forsook visiting them, though his missionary travels took him farther and farther from home. "I cannot do a great thing," he wrote. "However I am resolved that, by the grace of Christ, I will never abandon the work as long as I have legs to carry me." He made his last tour at the age of eighty-six. At the end of his long life, he had also begun to evangelize the African slaves that the English were importing in America.

The military drama of 1675–1676 largely destroyed Eliot's work among the Indians. His work and his example, however, had important repercussions. Eliot's biography was written by Cotton Mather, the well-known Puritan theologian and author, who also wrote the epic history of the Puritans in America, *Magnalia Christi Americana*: Or, *The Ecclesiastical History of New-England*.

For Mather and others, John Eliot was the pioneer *par excellence* of evangelistic Protestant missions; and his right to this title is unchallenged, especially in the light of later advances and the influence he would have on English-speaking Protestant churches. Though Eliot's Puritanism has since been caricatured and considered tainted with Old Testament legalism, his Christian compassion, zeal for the cause of God, and love for the Indian people is profoundly impressive and eclipses what, at first sight, appears rigid in his personality. At the very least, he stands out in the history of seventieth-century Protestant missions if only because Protestant missionaries were then so thin on the ground.

## Roger Williams

Roger Williams (1604–1684) is well known as a "pioneer in the liberty of conscience," for the principle of the separation of church and state, and as the founder, in 1638, of the first Baptist church in America. In contrast to the pioneers heretofore presented, he rejected the Puritan conception of a theocratic state. Resolved to refuse any salary from the established church because it was financed by the civil power, he undertook to provide for his needs, those of his family, and those of his ministry by engaging in trade with the Indians. His great facility in learning foreign languages eased his relations with the native population. Historian Robert Farelly writes, "From the beginning of his walks among the tepees and wigwams, he received a courteous and even warm welcome. His respect for the indigenous traditions, customs, and interests of the Indians, as well as his deference to Indian chiefs, left wide-open doors for him."[201] On several occasions he energetically took up the defense of the Indians, attempting to plead their cause before the colonists. This generated much animosity against him, especially when he dealt with the theft of Indian land by his compatriots who had forcibly seized land that the Indians had occupied since time immemorial.

Roger Williams (1604–1684), pioneer in the liberty of conscience and the separation of church and state. He was, among the Puritans, an ardent defender of the cause of the Indians, whom he evangelized in addition to his numerous political and ecclesiastical activities. Among the latter, he founded the first Baptist church in America in 1638. Statue from the Wall of the Reformation in Geneva. (Photo: J. Blandenier)

Due to the conflicts that Williams generated in Massachusetts, not the least being his opposition to the Puritans' goal of creating a Christian state, he was banished from the colony. He left Salem in 1636 and established a new settlement in what would eventually be the colony of Rhode Island, the first colony to inscribe liberty of conscience in its charter. Despite his numerous political and pastoral activities, he continued to dedicate himself to the Indians and to evangelize them with often-encouraging results. Williams, however, cannot be truly considered a figure in the history of missions.

---

201 Robert Farelly, "Roger Williams: Pionnier de la liberté de conscience," *Carnets de Croire et Servir* 95–97 (1989): 45.

### William Penn

Among the emulators of Eliot was the Englishman George Fox (1624–1691), founder of the Society of Friends, better known as the Quakers. Having had the occasion to visit New England, Fox was indignant about the fate he saw reserved there for Indians and slaves. In the rules of his society, *Christian Discipline*, he declared, "All the Friends, everywhere, when they encounter Indians or blacks, must preach the gospel to them, for the gospel of salvation must be preached to all creatures under heaven." One of his illustrious disciples was William Penn (1644–1718), who received from King Charles II of Great Britain in 1681 an immense territory in America in payment of a debt. This eventually became the state of Pennsylvania. Penn established in his colony the principles of religious liberty advocated by Fox. He also attempted to make his colony a place where Indians would be welcomed. Here their rights would be respected and they would be evangelized, a policy that soon bore fruit. As has been seen, Christian seed had been sown in this region thirty years earlier by Johann Campanius (p. 227).

# THE NETHERLANDS

The Netherlands was one of the jewels in the crown of Spain in the sixteenth century, but the northern provinces very early embraced the Reformation. The efforts of King Phillip II of Spain to restore his subjects to the bosom of the Roman Church set off a revolt by the seven Protestant provinces of the north, united in 1579 in the Union of Utrecht. The war continued over a period of eighty years and terminated in the independence of the United Provinces, recognized by the Spanish in 1648.

### The Merchant Companies

The Netherlands was a nation of merchants and shopkeepers. Under the domination of the Spanish, it was assured access to all European markets for the merchandise carried from America or the Far East by Portuguese or Spanish ships. Phillip II, the king of Spain and of Portugal, believed that, against the Dutch rebels who sought independence, economic weapons would be the most effective. Consequently in 1590, 1595, and 1599 he put an embargo on Dutch ships found in the ports of Spain and Portugal. This policy was very hard on the United Provinces, and the Dutch sailors reacted promptly. Instead of going first to Lisbon or Cadiz, where their cargos would be searched, why not go directly to their trading partners overseas? Especially after the fall of Anvers in 1585, which remained in the Spanish orbit, the way seemed free, despite the customs officials of Phillip II. The first Dutch navigators attempted the venture in 1595, and the merchandise brought back assured the investors of such profits that numerous competitors soon took the same risk. The Spanish strove to deny the oceans to the "smugglers of the sea," but the wide mesh of their net allowed many to pass through. The defeat of the Spanish Armada in 1588 had shown that the Spanish could no longer control the seas. In 1598 as many as twenty-two Dutch ships departed for the Far East. Dutch merchants soon engaged in fierce competition. In just a few years ten commercial societies were flourishing in the United

Provinces: four in Amsterdam, two in Rotterdam, two in Zeeland, one in Delft, and one in Enkhuizen.

Against the Spanish, this competition was suicidal, and the great statesman Johan van Oldenbarneveld understood the folly. He succeeded in persuading the societies to unite in a single vast organization, the Dutch East India Company (Vereenigde Oost-Indische Compagnie), commonly known by the initials VOC. The company was founded on March 20, 1602. The former rival societies now made up the "Provincial Chambers" that were ruled by a council of seventeen directors, of which eight were named by Amsterdam companies. The Council of Seventeen then held in its hands all the commerce of the Netherlands with overseas countries. The power of the Dutch East India Company was immense: it hired its own civil servants, recruited it own soldiers, even struck its own money. It had a monopoly of the commerce between the Cape of Good Hope and the Straights of Magellan.

In the beginning, the company was content to establish several trading posts in faraway counties, and it had twenty-eight by 1613. These posts rapidly became permanent establishments, veritable colonies that were occupied by soldiers, administered by civil servants, and ruled by governors. Above them all was a governor general assisted by the Council of the Indies.

All the personnel as well as the shareholders of the company belonged to the Reformed Church of the Netherlands, a strictly Calvinist institution. Most of the ship captains, who left for many months on the dangerous seas, found it advisable to take chaplains with them. This felt need was examined by the Council of Seventeen, which decided to assume the costs that would be occasioned by "consolers, admonishers, speakers, and pastors" embarking on the ships for the long voyages sponsored by the company. Some of these chaplains, being plunged into non-Christian populations, felt compelled to preach the gospel to them. Their activities eventually produced a clause to be found in the instructions given to the first governor general in 1609. It directs that "the civil servants of the VOC will supervise the activity of the preachers who must not occupy themselves solely with the Dutch but must also take care of the non-Christians so that the name of Christ will be extended and so that the work of the company will be accomplished as it should be."

## Petrus Plancius

To permit this missionary activity to progress, it was necessary that new Calvinist missionary thought be developed. Several Dutch theologians concerned themselves with this. One of the first was Pieter Platevoet, better known by his Latin name of Petrus Plancius (1552–1622). Born near Ypres into a Flemish family of rich merchants, he very early accepted the Reformation. He studied theology, science, and geography in Germany and England, and then became a pastor in Brussels in 1582. In 1585 he took refuge in Holland where he was called to the ministry by the Reformed Church of Amsterdam and chosen to be one of the translators of the famous "Bible of the States-General." This intellectual clergyman actively interested himself in the voyages to the Indies and became one of the important shareholders in one of the first commercial societies. He conceived the idea of opening the first school of scientific navigation in Amsterdam. No pilot could be hired to serve on the ships of the Dutch colonial fleet without first having received a certificate of competency awarded by Plancius.

He insisted that clergymen be sent to the Indies. In truth, few volunteers presented themselves. Consequently, it was necessary to exert strong pressure on two or three of the fellows studying theology at the University of Leiden. As a means of persuasion, Plancius assured them that the chaplains of the company would have "the opportunity to instruct in the true Christian religion the inhabitants of these regions who are sitting in the shadow of darkness."

The company, wanting to have only qualified personnel to send overseas, asked the authorities of the Reformed Church of Amsterdam to take responsibility for the training of these religious employees. After long discussions and much persuasion by Plancius, the church officials of Amsterdam decided to form an institution of higher education for chaplains and other "admonishers" of the company. The Seminarium Indicum was opened under the responsibility of the College of Reformed Theology of Leiden in 1622, the year of Plancius' death. The students, lodged in the house of professor Walaeus, were subjected to severe discipline and were never very numerous. The seminary furnished little more than a dozen chaplains for the company, which, on finding that the endeavor involved excessive expenses, closed the school after only ten years of operation.

### Justus Heurnius: One of the First Reformed Missionaries

It is incontestable that some of the chaplains of the Dutch East India Company discovered their missionary vocation simply by encountering non-Christians. One of the most remarkable among them was Jus Van Heurn, or Justus Heurnius (1587–1652). Son of a professor of medicine, he followed the example of his father and obtained his doctorate in 1611; then, abandoning medicine, he studied theology and became a minister. Convinced of having received a calling to evangelize pagans, he offered his services to the company, which sent him as a chaplain to the island of Java in 1624. Before leaving, he published a brochure entitled *A Call to Take Seriously the Protestant Mission to the Indians*, which caused some sensation in the church.

His ministry was far from easy, for, not limiting himself to the Dutch as a chaplain, he soon began to care for the indigenous sick and actively to defend their interests. This was too much for the governor, who sharply reproached him for his efforts. The missionary, however, did not back down, and so the governor had him placed in prison and threatened him with expulsion. At the last moment, the governor was replaced by a man who had more Christian sentiments and who gave Heurnius his liberty. Undaunted, he pursued specifically missionary work. He learned the Malaysian language and translated biblical passages for his converts. He quickly dedicated himself to the training of an indigenous church. Heurnius is considered to be one of the first missionaries in the Reformed tradition; and he was also, together with his colleague Cornelius Ruyl, a Protestant pioneer in the translation of biblical texts into non-European languages.

The first Protestant missionary theoretician was one of the professors of theology under whom Heurnius had been a student: Gisbertus Voetius.

## Gisbertus Voetius

Born in Heusden near Utrecht, Gisbertus Voetius (1589–1676) is considered to be the founder of Protestant missiology. He studied at the University of Leiden from 1604–1611, and then became a pastor in a small village. In 1617 he was appointed to be a pastor in his home village. Despite an absorbing pastoral ministry, his encyclopedic spirit led him to study diligently and give courses in theology, physics, and oriental languages. In 1618 he actively participated as a delegate in the famous Synod of Dordrecht where he was one of the representatives of orthodox Calvinism. He accepted the post of professor of theology and oriental languages in 1634 at the University of Utrecht, which had just been established. A man of profound piety and intellectual vigor, his influence was considerable. He is particularly known for his controversy with René Descartes, who dedicated a treatise to him in 1643: *Epistola ad celeberrimum virum Gisbertum Voetium.* In 1669 Voetius also attacked the mystics gravitating around Jean de Labadie. He was known as a man of profound piety.

He had a lively interest in the conversion of pagans and in the problems posed by the evangelization of the world. In studying Catholic missiology, he was impressed by the creation in Rome of the Sacred Congregation for the Propaganda of the Faith in 1622. He often made allusions to missions in his *Disputations* (instructive dialogues that were used in the universities since the Middle Ages), and he dedicated a chapter to mission—*De missionibus ecclesiasticis*—in one of his principal works of dogmatics.

The theology of mission elaborated by Voetius can be summarized in the following five points:

First, the foundation of Christian mission is the person of God himself. His universal sovereignty and his will to save are revealed in the Old Testament. The promises made to Abraham, and reasserted by the prophets of the Old Testament, affirm that God wants to appeal to all the peoples of the earth. In the New Testament, all depends on the order of Jesus given to his disciples at the time of his ascension: "Make disciples of all nations" (Matt 28:19). Voetius discussed at length the arguments of the Reformers. With them, he believed that the apostles accomplished the mission in a unique and unrepeatable way, being girded in an apostolic and nontransferable authority. However, in contrast to the Reformers, he argued forcefully that the apostles' mission had established the model of mission that must be pursued in every age in the long history of the church. The orders of Christ remain valid and relevant for each generation of Christians. Hence, the first cause of mission is the sovereign will of God, expressed by his decision out of time, command in the present, and promise for the future. If the church is to be obedient, it is imperative for it to preach the gospel and "to plant churches."

Second, mission has another cause in the vocation of the church. Voetius distinguished between two complementary vocations in the missionary service. The first, an internal vocation, is the work of the Holy Spirit in the heart of the one that God calls. The second, an external vocation, concerns the church. He based his case on the thirteenth chapter of the book of Acts, deducing from it that the power of the external vocation belongs to the local church, and not to the prince, state, ecclesiastic hierarchy, or even a synod. It is therefore out of the question to found a "Protestant Congregation for the Propaganda of the Faith." This is a task for the local church to fulfill. And it is to each believer, whether a merchant, soldier, or some other professional, to communicate his faith to all humanity.

Third, the task, above all others, is the preaching of the word of God. Consistent with the Reformed conception of the ministry, Voetius argued that the missionary is a servant of the Word. However, there are auxiliary ministries such as teaching and caring for the sick. The missionary must be clear that Christian faith begins with the consent of the heart; and, therefore, the preaching of the Word is the necessary and indispensable means of evangelism. All coercion must be unambiguously rejected. Voetius insisted on the qualifications necessary for a missionary ministry, and he excluded the sending of those incapable, poorly trained, or unwanted in Europe.

Fourth, the immediate purpose of mission is the conversion of individuals. Voetius conceived the proper progression of stages for pagans to become Christians to be the following: listeners, catechumens, candidates, and finally members of the church. The principal purpose of mission is the implantation of churches, and its ultimate end is the glory of God.

Fifth, Voetius treated in a remarkably lucid manner an issue that even modern missiologists have been at pains to address: the relation between missions and the churches born of their work. In contrast to Hadrian Saravia who had an episcopal—hence hierarchic—vision of the church, Voetius was a congregationalist. The local church may, like an infant, be brought to birth by its parents and afterwards receive nurture and guidance from them, but once it has reached maturity, it must be considered as an adult. As such, it is free and sovereign under the authority of the Lord. The young church will elaborate its own discipline, choose its own ministers, and decide if, and with whom, it may want to unite. Is the doctrine that it professes tied to the heart that has founded it? Yes, but only to the initial founders, the apostles, who alone are infallible and whose authority is nontransferable. The immediate founders, whatever blessings they may have brought, are fallible and have no right of ownership or domination over the church born of their work. It belongs to the Lord. All churches, therefore, are equal, and there is no right of paternity or presupposed hierarchy existing between them.

Hence, Voetius is the first Protestant theologian of mission. It is astonishing that over the centuries this aspect of his work has been almost entirely forgotten.

## Hugo Grotius

Another Dutchman should be mentioned here: Hugo de Groot, called Grotius (1583–1645). Accused of Arminianism in his country and condemned to life imprisonment, he fled and sought refuge in France, where he was protected by Louis XIII and named ambassador to Sweden. While he was still in Holland, he had written a treatise, *Mare Liberum (The Freedom of the Sea)*. He was contesting the pope's claim to have the right to give a monopoly of navigation on the oceans to Spain and Portugal, and his position supported the right of the Dutch East India Company to trade with the Indies over and against the exclusive claims of Portugal to this trade. Grotius was a renowned jurist and author of a code of international public law, *De jure belli ac pacis* (*The Law of War and Peace*, 1625). He also published *De veritate religionis Christianae* (*Of the True Christian Religion*), a book destined to aid and stimulate the zeal of those who wanted to evangelize non-Christians. The book was translated into several languages, including Arabic. Under the influence of Grotius, a student of German law, Peter Heyling, decided to leave for the Orient. His ministry will be presented a little later (see p. 239).

## The Missions of the Dutch East India Company

The work of mission performed by the Dutch East India Company cannot be passed by in silence. It is certain that much work was accomplished in Ceylon, Formosa, and in the islands of present-day Indonesia.

The work was organized in 1612, and by 1647 there were twenty-three pastoral posts: two in Ceylon, two in Malacca, one in the Indies, two in Formosa, three in Batavia in the island of Java, and thirteen in the archipelago of the Moluccas. In 1660 the number of posts was raised to thirty-six, but all the positions were rarely filled. The ministers only stayed overseas for three to five years, and they did not generally know the indigenous languages. According to Yves Krumenacker, "in total, from 1602 to 1800, the VOC sent eight hundred ministers and thousands of deacons and teachers to the colonies, and financed numerous books and the construction of buildings. Records show 43,748 Indonesians baptized between 1708 and 1771. This suggests, therefore, a mass evangelization to a strict Calvinism that did not distinguish between religion and politics; the results [of this approach] are often superficial and very fragile."[202]

It is surmised that conversion was demonstrated through the recitation in Dutch of several formulas found in the catechism, notably the Our Father, the Creed, and the Ten Commandments. In the relationship between the ministers and local population, commerce and the interests of the company were never supposed to be far from view. Some privileges were accorded to Christians, and the chaplains received bonuses proportional to the number of baptized. The result was that conversions could emerge from ambiguous motivations.

The superficial character of the conversions of the non-Christians of the Indies appears clearly in the records of the Dutch Reformed synods charged with resolving the problems raised by the chaplains of the company. The synods often discussed at length the question of baptism. They were concerned with the issue of whether or not the illegitimate infants of Dutchmen and Indian women should be baptized. The decision they came to, though it was not equally applied, was that children were not to be baptized systematically but only on condition that they receive instruction in the Christian religion. The synods also discussed the question of the admission to Holy Communion of the concubines of the colonists.

---

202 Yves Krumenacker, "Les missions protestantes au XVIIIè siècle (1690–1790)," in *Etudes théologiques et religieuses*, Vol. 73/1, (Montpellier 1998).

At the beginning in the eighteenth century the missionary efforts of the company collapsed. When the enterprise was dissolved in 1798, only seven pastoral posts remained, and the colonists had gained a reputation for immorality. In this period, however, the archives are mute.

This experience shows that, with some notable exceptions, missionary bureaucrats of a commercial company are scarcely qualified to preach an authentic gospel to the pagan people of a colony. The Dutch experience, however, was not entirely negative. It illustrated the complex problems of mission to theologians like Voetius; it led to several good translations of the Bible in Indonesian languages; and it no doubt facilitated the evangelization of these regions by the missionaries of the nineteenth century.

## Dutch Mission in the West Indies

The Dutch West India Company (*West-Indische Compagnie*, or WIC) was founded in the Netherlands in 1621 to trade with the Americas, and by 1624 Dutch colonists occupied a notable part of the northeast coast of Brazil. Though the Dutch colonization effort was of a short duration in Brazil due to the supremacy of the Portuguese in this region, the results of their evangelistic efforts were more positive than in the Far East.

The colony knew a real prosperity in the time of Prince John Maurice of Nassau-Siegen, a convinced Calvinist. By about the year 1640 the colony had a population of ninety thousand. One-third was Portuguese, one-third black slaves, one-sixth Indians, and one-sixth Dutch or other European nationality.[203] Some Catholic churches, such as those at Olinda and Récife, were transformed into Protestant churches. The well-organized Reformed Church included fifty pastors and twenty-two parishes. Following the model of the Dutch Reformed church, this Brazilian church was carefully organized into two "classes" (synods): Pernambouc, established in 1636; and Paraïba established in 1641.

Animated by a true missionary spirit, the governor made an appeal for preachers, and several began a study of the language of the Tupis. There was no systematic Christianization of the Indian and black populations, but individual evangelization was conducted, with those involved encouraged to make a personal decision. It was an evangelical conception of mission of the type that Las Casas had advocated that Catholics practice instead of the forced baptisms performed by the Spanish and Portuguese religious. The spiritual quality of this evangelization is attested by the fact that several converts remained faithful unto martyrdom when in 1654 the Portuguese supplanted the Dutch and forced the population to abjure its Protestant faith.

"During the Dutch period," according to historian Schalkwijk, "the political-religious situation favored the formation of a Reformed Christian theocracy that included a high degree of religious liberty, of worship as well as of conscience; after the expulsion of the Dutch, a Roman Catholic theocracy was reestablished, which no

---

203 Bastian, *Le protestantisme*, 30.

longer permitted religious liberty and felt obliged to take the lives of those who were not disposed to accept this thought."[204]

For example, Chief Peter Poty died after the poor treatment he received on being deported to Portugal for having refused to convert to Catholicism; and Chief Antony Paraupaba wrote a memoir that underscored the evangelical faithfulness of the Indian tribes of this region. The Portuguese destroyed all traces of this evangelically inspired missionary work.

Initially, the Dutch sought to eliminate slavery from the colony. Soon, however, writes historian Roger Bastide, due to the labor shortage on sugarcane plantations, "the pressure of economic interests was stronger than Calvinist morality." When the Portuguese regained control of the colony, they captured the previously emancipated black workers. Some chaplains explained the collapse of the Dutch colony in the face of the Portuguese in 1654 by invoking divine judgment:

> The Council inclines to consider that, among other reasons, God has shown himself irritated because in these lands we were not able to take the necessary measures to ensure that the existence of God and of his Son Jesus Christ were known among the blacks; for the souls of these poor creatures, whose bodies we employed to our service, should have been snatched from the slavery of the Devil.[205]

# GERMANY

Germany fell to a deplorable state in the seventeenth century. The destruction and massacres of the Thirty Years' War (1618–1648) wrought great anguish for the population of central Europe.

The Protestant church was reduced to a strictly orthodox Lutheranism in which the fiery soul of Luther had for the most part been extinguished.

In these nonmaritime regions of the European continent, nations were slower to develop a missionary conscience. However, it was during this troubled period that the first signs of a missionary awakening appeared in Protestantism. If the Pietist movement of the eighteenth century can be seen as the great impetus of modern Protestant missions, it is owed in part to several isolated and largely unknown precursors in the preceding century.

## Peter Heyling

At Lübeck seven "revivalist" students reacted against the low morals of their fellow students to form a group to study the Bible and pray together. Among them was Peter Heyling (1607–1652). He left Lübeck to study in Paris, far from the Thirty Years' War where he made the acquaintance of Hugo Grotius, the well-known scholarly genius spoken of above (see p. 236-37). He suggested to Heyling that he should attempt to inspire new life in the churches of the East.

---

204 Ibid., 31.
205 Ibid., 32.

Heyling left in 1632 for Abyssinia, via Malta and Egypt. He arrived there at the moment when the Jesuits were being driven from the country after their momentary success in having Roman Catholicism proclaimed as the state religion. His purpose was not so much to create a new church as to revivify this ancient Christian church by giving it access to the Bible in its own language. He worked for twenty years in Abyssinia and translated the New Testament in the Amharic language, the language spoken on the Ethiopian high plateaus. After this success, he traveled to Egypt where, in all likelihood, he experienced martyrdom while seeking to evangelize Muslims. In fact, little is known about the ministry of this isolated missionary, who, sadly, had no successor in Ethiopia. But Heyling can be considered as the first Lutheran missionary in history.

A little later an exceptional man appeared. Though unknown in his time, he was somewhat in the mode of Raymond Lull, a singularly clearheaded precursor of evangelical missions: Justinian von Weltz.

## Justinian von Weltz

Baron Gotthard von Weltz was a member of the Austrian nobility of Carinthia. A Catholic in a Lutheran country, he left his native land, abandoning his castle and properties to settle in Saxony, at Chemnitz, in 1628. He died two years later, leaving his title to his eldest son, Justinian (1621–1668).

In 1641, at twenty years of age, Justinian undertook his studies at the University of Leiden, in Holland. In the same year he published a treatise on tyranny and social justice. In 1643 he wrote against Spanish behavior in their colonies. Then from 1643–1663 he lived in Germany. During this time he read deeply and was converted. He was especially influenced by his reading of Saint Augustine, Martin Luther, and the mystics of the Middle Ages. Of the latter influence, he was particularly moved by Thomas à Kempis. He became a highly cultured man. In 1663 he published *De vita solitaria* (*The Life of Solitude*), a defense of the ascetic life according to the Bible wherein he witnessed to his faith and called others to conversion and a simple life. He exhorted his readers to live for the glory of God and emphasized the importance of reading and studying the Bible. This work appeared a dozen years before Philip Jacob Spener (1635–1705), the father of Pietism, published *Pia desideria* (*Pious Wishes*). The two books had much in common. Von Weltz then exerted himself in the production of a great literary outpouring. In 1663 and 1664 he published six treatises on several subjects, including a work urging the union of the Lutheran and Calvinist churches. Also notable was a revolutionary treatise on mission in 1664, *A Call to All Loyal and Faithful Christians to the Confession of Augsburg with a View to the Founding of a Special Society by Which, With the Aid of God, the Evangelical Religion Can Be Extended to All Hearts Loving Jesus Christ*. This work was addressed "to nobles, leaders, professors, pastors, students, and all hearts loving Jesus Christ." He discussed in it the traditional interpretation of the missionary orders given by Christ in the Great Commission. In his tightly woven argument, he affirmed that the proclamation of salvation to all men is, first of all, the will of God and the *raison d'être* of the church, and that the Christians of the first centuries understood it in this way. He invoked the energetic example of the Roman Church, arguing that Protestants for especially prideful reasons had kept the gospel to themselves as an exclusive privilege.

He posed three pertinent questions:

1. Is it right that we, evangelical Christians, keep the gospel for ourselves alone without ever trying to make it known to other peoples?

2. Is it right to have in our towns and cities many wise theologians without ever giving them the opportunity to work elsewhere in the vineyard of the Lord?

3. Is it right that we, evangelicals, spend all our money to clothe ourselves luxuriously, eat and drink copiously, and do other things as well, while until now we have never had the means to spread the gospel?

He added a second treatise in which he proposed some practical solutions: Christians must create a "Society of those who love Jesus" to spread Christianity and convert the pagans. Missionaries must be recruited, trained in special colleges, sent out, and a correspondence maintained with them. This society, whose members should belong to every social class and profession, would include several categories of members: the promoters who would give money and would pray; the conservators who would administrate and direct the society; and finally, the missionaries who would be sent. This is a rough sketch of what William Carey would propose a century later.

Von Weltz received some encouragement. Happily, he decided to propose his project to the *Corpus Evangelicorum*—the Protestant delegates of the imperial Diet that was going to sit at Ratisbon. He went, therefore, to this city and, to show his seriousness of purpose, deposited in a bank the considerable sum of 10,000 thalers to cover initial expenses. He also made the acquaintance of a young enthusiast, Johann George Gichtel (1638–1710), who already had a reputation for extreme mysticism. Becoming passionate about the formation of a missionary society, Gichtel deposited 18,000 thalers in a bank to finance the project.

Unfortunately, the authorities that von Weltz consulted discreetly discouraged him. He thought about abandoning the idea but then changed his mind. Instead, he published a new brochure, written in a caustic tone: *A Sincere and Serious Call and Recall to Take into Consideration the Conversion of Non-Christian Peoples* . . . He addressed it "to the most reverend and distinguished chaplains of the court, to the highly venerable ecclesiastical superintendents and doctoral professors" and asked them to support his project. He refined his plan, proposing that each Protestant prince possessing a university should found a missionary college *de propaganda fide* ("for the propagation of the faith"). He began by naming three professors who would teach linguistics, the best methods and means of converting pagans, and geography. He suggested, moreover, that in the church history course the work of the great missionaries, such as Paul or Anskar, be taught. The brochure was polemical and censorious. Consequently von Weltz could not find a German printer to publish it, and eventually it was published in Holland.

The poor author tried to appeal to Johann Heinrich Ursinus (1608–1667), superintendent of the Lutheran church of Ratisbon. He was considered to be among the "enlightened Lutheran" leadership of the time, having the reputation of being a theologian with generous ideas. But Ursinus expressed to the Protestant delegates of the Diet his most extreme reservations about von Weltz's proposals; and at the end of 1664 he even responded to von Weltz's brochure with an anonymous tract of his own: *A Sincere, Faithful and Serious Response to Justinian . . .* He astutely sidestepped von Weltz's biblical and theological arguments by simply pointing out that the duty of missions resided with the church. Moreover, he argued, the baron's proposals could not resolve this difficult problem. Finally, he rejected the ideas of one he considered to be "only a dreamer, a lively deceiver of an Anabaptist or Quaker spirit." As for a Protestant version of the Society of Jesus, "God preserve us from it!" He added, if pagans still exist who are susceptible to conversion, "They will only be savages who have nothing but the human form, such as the cannibals; they will be cruel or tyrannical, such as the Tartars in denying strangers access to their country, or as the Japanese or the American Indians; there is no necessity to cast before these swine and these dogs the sacred things of God." He concluded his pamphlet with this final and decisive note: "What should cause you [von Weltz] to reflect is that no theologian is with you."

Being discouraged by so much incomprehension, von Weltz decided to seek refuge in Holland, while in November 1664 Ursinus had Gichtel arrested.

Von Weltz was welcomed to the Netherlands by Fredric Breckling (1629–1711), a Lutheran minister of Zwolle and a creative individual who had written a treatise against Orthodox Lutheranism. He was thrilled by the attacks von Weltz had made on the German theologians and particularly against Ursinus, whom he thought of as "the high priest of the Pharisees." Breckling's support of von Weltz confirmed the adversaries of his projects in the belief that he was a fool. It is true, however, that von Weltz had the gift of attracting personalities who were sometimes a little marginal. Hence one of those who had furnished him with funds soon fell into bankruptcy and was led away to prison, a development that evidently did nothing to improve von Weltz's image.

Breckling suggested sending missionaries to the Dutch colony of Surinam (formerly known as Dutch Guiana) in South America. Due to the absence of candidates, von Weltz offered himself for this mission. Believing that it was necessary to make him a minister of the church, Breckling solemnly ordained him as an "apostle to the pagans." Following the service of ordination, the baron decided to abandon his noble title, a gesture that he confirmed in a brochure, *Justinian's Renouncement*.

He departed for Vienna to liquidate what remained of his patrimony. He then returned to Amsterdam where he attempted in vain to obtain theology students who would join him. Finally, he embarked alone in 1666 for Surinam. Little is known of what became of him. A ship was sent to search for him in 1668, but it found no trace. Some believed that wild beasts had devoured him, but this is unlikely. It is more probable that he was a victim of Indian hostility or tropical disease, Surinam having a climate that was then very dangerous for Europeans.

Hence was lost a visionary, completely misunderstood by his contemporaries. However, his message, which came with a burning missionary zeal, was not forgotten. In 1675 Philip Jacob Spener published von Weltz's works and recognized his debt to his missionary thought. Von Weltz was, undeniably, a man without much tact, as can be seen in his alliance with Breckling and the polemical character of some of his pamphlets. He was also a friend of Gichtel who was, more or less, a disciple of Jacob Böhme, the founder of strict communities known as the "Brethren of the Angelic Life," that professed unorthodox doctrines that approached pantheism. Nevertheless, in a time when the church was deaf to the missionary call, von Weltz's message had a prophetic dimension that merited a better reception. It is also appropriate to recognize in his solitary struggle a precursor of modern mission.

A number of Lutheran names can be cited in this period as participating in the embryonic missionary enterprise, but little information actually exists about them. The Reverend Joachim Dannenfeldt went to Gambia in 1654; and Wilhelm Johann Müller was a chaplain for the Danish Commercial Company on the Gold Coast between 1662 and 1670. Müller did not limit himself in his task of chaplain to his Lutheran parishioners since he elaborated a word list for the Twi language. Finally, some pleas in support of missions were published in the seventeenth century by theologians such as Balthasar Meisner, Ludwig Dunte, and George Calixt—the latter insisting on the necessity of the conversion of the pagans in order to remove all obstacles to the return of the Lord.[206]

---

206 Krumenacker, *Les missions*, 40.

# CHAPTER 15

# *The First Missionary Societies (1670–1800)*

## THE EVOLUTION OF BRITISH MISSION IN THE EIGHTEENTH CENTURY

The currents of theology, missionary thought, and the impetus to engage in the evangelization of the world were altered in the course of the eighteenth century. The change is particularly perceptible in the English-speaking world due to the influence of the Great Awakening in America (1725–1760) and the Methodist Revival in England following 1738. In Germany, the Pietist movement promoted mission to the nonevangelized people of the world, and this inspiration found a second wind in the Moravian communities of the eighteenth century. Indeed, beginning in 1732 the Moravians were the iron lance of Protestant missions.

Rooted in Puritanism and watered by a new evangelical spirit, the Great Awakening in America was a movement largely instigated by Jonathan Edwards and George Whitefield, among others. It helped to change the nature of colonial Christianity by making people more directly responsible for participating in the conversion of pagans through the proclamation of the message of salvation. Calvinists had typically insisted on the notion of a sovereign God who makes a covenant with select people by virtue of his eternal plan. With the Awakening, this position gave way to a more marked insistence on the notion of the glory of God in which believers, having experienced repentance, are able to contribute to the reorientation of their lives and work. Moreover, they are now to be consecrated to the task of world evangelization.

This new conception also came about, in part, due to the influence of Lutheran Pietism and the Moravian Brethren. A primary motivation for missionary action came to be the notion of the love of God for those who are lost. In this view, following in the steps of the Son of God incarnated and crucified, missionaries are called to identify themselves with the conditions in which pagan peoples exist—to the peril of their lives if they fail to do so. Moreover, Pietists and Moravians opposed the idea then current that present-day pagans are the victims of a definitive curse due to the rejection by their ancestors in antiquity of the message proclaimed by the apostles or their successors. This reaction went hand in hand with the insistence that conversion must be a personal decision, an idea that characterizes Pietism. It is not peoples but individuals who are called to convert. The eternal destiny of each person does not depend on ethnic origins but on the experience of the new birth. For the first time, perhaps since the missions of the first centuries following Christ, a priority was placed on obtaining personal conversions to the gospel. The dominant strategy was no longer to gain an entire people to Christianity.

It is also important to note that a generally millennialist eschatology enjoyed a great role in conferring on missions a sense of urgency, a tendency more true among British and American evangelicals than Lutheran Pietists. According to this view, the advance of the kingdom must be preceded by the conversion of the Jews, who will recognize their Messiah only after the totality of pagans have turned away from their false religions and turned to the gospel of salvation proclaimed by the emissaries of Christ.

## New Societies

At the threshold of the eighteenth century, some British missionary societies existed and were more or less active. The Society for Propagating the Gospel in New England and Parts Adjacent in North America, already mentioned, was founded in 1649. In 1662 this became the Corporation for the Propagation of the Gospel in New England. Finally, in 1701 it became the Society for the Propagation of the Gospel in Foreign Parts and was known by the abbreviation SPG. The Society for the Promoting of Christian Knowledge (SPCK) was founded in 1698, and there was also a Scottish branch of this organization.

In the course of the eighteenth century, about three hundred Anglican missionaries were sent to the thirteen American colonies. The term "missionary," however, does not apply to most of them, who above all considered themselves to be ministers to the British colonists.

## David Brainerd

Brainerd (1718–1747) is one of the better known among those who accomplished fruitful work among the Indians. His ministry is in continuity with that of John Eliot in the preceding century.

He was a missionary in his own country since he was born in America. Orphaned while very young, he was a tormented adolescent who experienced a profound conversion before being caught up in the Great Awakening. Abruptly interrupting his studies, Brainerd offered his services to the Scottish Society for the Diffusion of the Gospel, which appointed him a missionary to the Indians in the region to the east of the Hudson, close to the Delaware and Susquehanna rivers. At the start, his life in the forest was very difficult. His words give vent to a painful depression:

> My heart was sunk . . . It seemed to me I should never have any success among the Indians. My soul was weary of my life; I longed for death, beyond measure . . . I live in the most lonely melancholy desert . . . My diet consists mostly of hasty pudding, boiled corn, and bread baked in ashes

. . . My lodging is a little heap of straw laid upon some boards. My work is exceeding hard and difficult.[207]

He at least had the joy of seeing his work bear fruit. In a meeting on August 6, 1745, Brainerd witnessed the first time the Spirit of God was felt among the Indians. In the following extract, he recounted this event in a manner highly reminiscent of the Great Awakening:

> In the afternoon, they being returned to the place where I had usually preached among them . . . They seemed eager of hearing; but there appeared nothing very remarkable, except their attention, till near the close of my discourse. The divine truths were attended with a surprising influence, and produced a great concern among them. There were scarce three in forty that could refrain from tears and bitter cries. They all, as one, seemed in an agony of soul to obtain an interest in Christ; and the more I discoursed of the love and compassion of God in sending His Son to suffer for the sins of men; and the more I invited them to come and partake of His love, the more their distress was aggravated, because they felt themselves unable to come. It was surprising to see how their hearts seemed to be pierced with the tender and melting invitations of the gospel, when there was not a word of terror spoken to them. It was very affecting to see the poor Indians, who the other day were hallooing and yelling in their idolatrous feasts and drunken frolics, now crying to God with such importunity for an interest in His dear Son![208]

On August 25 he baptized twenty-five Indians and founded the village of Bethel for them, following the example of the villages of "Praying Indians" established earlier by John Eliot. Soon the revival spread like wildfire among the population.

With a little more perspective, he evaluated his revival ministry in these terms:

> Since my arrival among the Indians, the center of my message has been Christ crucified . . . I have also noticed with amazement that I am naturally and easily led to speak of Christ, whatever the subject treated.

The Great Awakening in North America was often characterized by dramatic psychic or physical manifestations on the part of the participants, who were entirely seized by the conviction of their sins. It is in this context that Brainerd's following lines should be placed:

> There was no "false religion," or corporal agonies, convulsions, hysterical crying, fainting, or analogous phenomenon, no trances, or visions . . . but the work of grace was done with great sobriety and purity . . . Despite great suffering and anguish for the salvation of their souls, they manifested no evil hopelessness.

---

207 Tucker, *From Jerusalem*, 91.
208 Ibid., 93.

Sadly, the young missionary could not endure the conditions of life in the outdoors. Three years after he was ordained as a minister, he was struck down by "galloping consumption" (tuberculosis). In the arms of his friend Jonathan Edwards, he died on October 9, 1747, at the age of twenty-seven. Edwards published his journal and biography. The *Journal of David Brainerd*, many times reprinted, has inspired numerous missionary careers. Despite his ephemeral ministry, Brainerd by his example played a considerable role in the history of evangelical missions.

### Methodist and Baptist Missions

John Wesley (1703–1791), accompanied by his brother Charles (1707–1788), embarked for America in 1735. He was moved to do so by reading *Narrative of the Captivity and Deliverance of Mrs. Mary Rowlandson*. Written in 1682, it related the author's experience of being captured by Indians. John Wesley remained in America for only two years, and he felt that his ministry, which was exclusively dedicated to the colonists, was a bitter failure. He said later that he had left for America compelled by the hope of "discovering the true sense of the gospel in preaching to the pagans." He wrote on his return, "I went to America to convert the pagans. Alas! who will convert me?" After this painful experience, he sought urgently needed spiritual aid among the Moravian Brethren. Following a long conversation with brother Peter Boehler, Wesley later discovered, in the course of the celebrated evening of May 24, 1738, the Lutheran message of free grace and the certainty of forgiveness available through the perfect work of Christ. John and Charles Wesley would become, with George Whitefield, the major promoters of the Methodist Revival in England. Whitefield would also travel to America seven times between 1738 and his death in 1770. He was, with Jonathan Edwards, one of the promoters of the Great Awakening in America, but his ministry was played out essentially among the colonists. The diverse American Methodist Societies, which began to be formed as early as 1760, had scarcely any interest in the evangelization of Indians or African slaves. Jonathan Edwards, in contrast, developed an important work among the Indians. He publicized it with a manifesto published in 1748: *A Humble Attempt to Promote an Explicit Agreement and Visible Union of God's People.*

Beginning in 1758, Methodist missionaries sent by Charles Wesley went to the Antilles to undertake a work parallel to that of the Moravian missions (see pp. 265-69). Their efforts were crowned with success and resulted in the foundation of several Methodist churches formed of African slaves. In 1769, at the prompting of John Wesley, two Methodists began a missionary work in North America: Richard Boardman and Joseph Pilmoor. In 1784 Wesley sent Thomas Coke (1747–1814) to convert the African slaves of the West Indies. Two years after his arrival he founded the first Methodist mission in the islands. From this work was born the African Methodist Episcopal Church in 1787 and the African Methodist Episcopal Zion Church in 1796. Both of these black Methodist churches would play a great role in the emancipation of the slaves.

In Europe, the Methodists and the Quakers were the first to rise up against the traffic in slaves. It is with their support that William Wilberforce and his friends persuaded the British Parliament to end the slave trade in 1807.

The Baptists in their turn were engaged in the evangelization of the African slaves. The first black church in America was established in 1758 by the Baptist William Byrd at Bluestone River. George Liele, a slave converted and baptized by the Reverend Matthew Moore in 1773, began to sing and preach the gospel among the slaves. He formed an African Baptist community in South Carolina and then, in 1777, another church in Savannah. Emigrating in 1783 to Jamaica, Liele founded the first Baptist community on the island in 1784: the Ethiopian Baptist Church, in Kingston. Hence, writes historian Yves Krumenacker, "beginning with a fortuitous event, the baptism of a black slave by a Baptist pastor, began the Christianization of the slaves by the slaves themselves and a symbiosis between Christianity and the African worldview."[209] In the following century, emancipated Jamaican slaves were among the pioneers of Protestant missions in various African countries, particularly in Cameroon where they founded the first Baptist churches.

## GERMAN PIETISM

The first overseas Protestant missionary efforts were undertaken by individuals or small groups of persons. In these can be seen the firstfruits of the Pietist movement, which was born in Germany in the second half of the seventeenth century.

The Reformers were wrong not to insist as much on personal piety as on correct theology. In Germany, in any case, the successors of Martin Luther seem to have accorded so much preference to doctrine that some said they had engendered a dead orthodoxy. Around the middle of the seventeenth century, a revival movement of considerable influence suddenly exploded: Pietism. This movement had at its origin a remarkable man, Philip Jacob Spener (1635–1705). He has sometimes been called the new Luther. This young Alsatian was the first free preacher in Strasbourg and was then named the first pastor of the Lutheran church of Frankfort. In the latter position, in his preaching and his private conversations, he insisted on the importance of personal conversion and sanctification. He organized meetings for prayer and Bible study in his house that he named *collegia pietatis* (schools of piety). It was from this Latinism that the sobriquet "Pietist" soon became attached to the movement.

Spener's approach responded to a profound need in the members of the German church. Numerous eager participants soon pressed themselves into his meetings, and his activities were imitated by many colleagues. The result was a veritable "revival." However, opponents of the movement quickly appeared. Spener responded to them with several works wherein he explained that he sought to conform to the doctrines of Luther at all points. He was aided by a remarkable colleague who knew how to organize the movement, August Francke (1663–1727). Francke made the city of Halle the center of German Pietism, where he founded an orphanage and schools, transformed the university, and established an evangelical printing house. The number of students grew, which spread the spirit of Pietism all over central Europe. Despite obstacles and even some persecution, the Pietists profoundly influenced German Lutheranism. Doubtless the most important contribution of Pietism to Protestantism in general

---

209 Krumenacker, *Les missions*, 50–51.

was the rediscovery of the missionary duty of all Christians. The printing house at Halle published a missionary review edited by Francke and republished the works of Justinian von Weltz.

In a treatise of 1693, Spener affirmed that missionary preaching was the duty of all Christians since it was clear that apostolic preaching had left no trace in numerous regions of the earth. Under the leadership of Francke, the Pietist center at Halle was animated from its conception by a missionary vision, a fact witnessed to by *Hallesch Correspondenz (Halle Correspondence)*, the first Protestant missionary journal. The Pietist conception of evangelization and missions demanded personal conversions; hence, missions could not in Pietists' eyes be left to governments or trading companies. Missionaries who were personally converted and convinced of the call of God were alone capable of being instruments for the propagation of the gospel. Such missionaries were often objects of mistrust and hostility by political powers. Colonial administrators and merchants feared the troubles that a Christian missionary enterprise could arouse among the priests of local religions.

However, as will be seen later, Pietists were not concerned only about the salvation of individual souls, as the caricatures of them might lead one to suppose. Rather, they believed that all aspects of existence were to be objects of regeneration in Jesus Christ. Consequently, the missionaries of Halle were among the first in the Indies to found open schools for girls and those belonging to inferior castes. They also undertook important medical work.

## The Tranquebar Mission of 1705

The Pietist movement also won over the Danish Lutherans. King Frederic IV (1671–1730) acceded to the throne of Denmark in 1699 and named as chaplain to the court the Reverend Franz Julius Lütkens, an intimate friend of Francke. The king experienced a Pietist conversion and then energetically supported the movement. Like Great Britain and the Netherlands, Denmark also sent trading ships to Asia and possessed several trading posts, in particular in the Indies. Lütkens spoke to the king of his duty towards the non-Christian populations living in Danish territories. Frederic was enthusiastic about the missionary prospects in his lands and decided to found a college in Copenhagen for the training of missionaries. Instead of waiting for candidates to be recruited and instructed, he asked Lütkens to hire youths already trained by Francke at the University of Halle. Volunteers among the students of the university were asked to go to India. Two presented themselves: Bartholomäus Ziegenbalg and Heinrich Plütschau.

## Bartholomäus Ziegenbalg

Ziegenbalg (1683–1719) was born in Saxony into a pious family. Orphaned while very young, all his life he held dear the memory of his mother, who had a great love for the Bible. Plütschau (1677–1746) was an instructor. The king intended that they should go to the small city of Tranquebar, which lies in the southeast of India, on the coast of Coromandel, to the south of Madras, India.

The two young people embarked on November 20, 1705, and arrived at their destination only in May 1706. Despite a letter of introduction from the king, they were received coldly by the governor, for, unknown to the missionaries, the trading company of the Danish Indies had imparted to the captain of their ship a letter instructing the governor to make things so difficult for them that they would soon return to Europe. The company's questionable meddling in such affairs could have had dreadful consequences. As things worked out, the two missionaries found no lodging available in the European quarter of the port. They were not long discouraged, for they soon discovered in the indigenous quarter, close to the wall, a vacant room where they were able to settle. It was an ideal place in which to learn the Tamil language spoken by the population. They had neither grammar nor dictionary, but Ziegenbalg showed himself to be a remarkable linguist. He began by playing in the street with children, and then found a Tamil who knew several English words. He very quickly mastered the language sufficiently to understand and communicate. At the end of a year, he began to translate Luther's catechism. Soon there were several conversions. A chapel was constructed, and schools were opened, the first girls' schools opening in 1707. Then he baptized the first five Christians. In 1708 he began to translate the New Testament. To achieve mastery of the language, he began a concentrated study of Malabar literature.

*Bartholomäus Ziegenbalg (1683–1719), one of the first missionaries sent to the Danish Indies by the Pietist missions of Halle. He founded the mission of Tranquebar and translated the Bible into the Tamil language.*

These efforts and successes were unendurable to the European merchants, even to some good Protestants, and especially to the governor, furious at having failed to discourage the young fanatics. The missionaries had to undergo all sorts of vexations and even an imprisonment of four months. Nothing, however, could dampen the zeal of these pioneers. They soon received reinforcements and extended the work in the environs of Tranquebar. They also evangelized the Muslims and Portuguese present in the city. Ziegenbalg completed his translation of the New Testament in 1711. He then undertook the editing of a dictionary, a liturgy, and hymns. He also composed thirty-three treatises, translated Spener's catechism, and began to produce a Tamil version of the Old Testament. These books were printed at Halle in Tamil characters. Unfortunately, some of these works, notably a *Collection of Malabar Morals Explained in a Christian Sense* (1708) and *The Malabar Paganism* (1711), aroused the disapprobation of the Pietists and were only published a century after Ziegenbalg's death. Though his efforts were criticized as syncretistic, he organized conferences for the Brahmans that accurately pointed out the doctrinal incompatibility between the Tamil religion and the Christian faith. To this end he discussed with them the problem of evil and sin, monotheism and resurrection, and argued against pantheism and the doctrine of reincarnation. His profound study of the languages and local religions made him one of the first German specialists of Indian civilization.

In 1711, after five years in India, Plütschau fell sick and was repatriated to Germany. Nothing is known of the end of his life. In 1712, Tranquebar had 245 baptized Christians and seventy-eight children in Christian schools.

In 1714 Ziegenbalg returned to Europe. Frederic IV, then engaged in war, was still ready to meet the missionary and hear from his own lips the story of his adventures. Ziegenbalg received an enthusiastic welcome everywhere, which surprised him. The duke of Wurtemberg organized a collection throughout the country to finance the mission. Ziegenbalg even visited the Netherlands and England where he aroused as much interest as he had in Germany. It is interesting to note that among those who received the news bulletin of the Tranquebar mission was the Anglican minister Samuel Wesley, whose son John developed a fascination in his childhood for the evangelization of the Indies, something he never forgot.

In 1716 Ziegenbalg returned to Tranquebar. During his absence, reinforcements had arrived and opened a normal school for the training of Tamil instructors. The chapel had become too small and been replaced by a beautiful church. The opposition from the Danish had ceased and the new governor, far from being hostile, encouraged the missionaries. Ziegenbalg had begun a translation of the Old Testament, but a serious illness confined him to bed before he could finish it. He died at the age of thirty-six on February 23, 1719. The work that he accomplished in thirteen years of ministry is all the more impressive for his having had no practical Protestant predecessor whose experiences might have guided him. The translation of the Bible and the Pietist hymns in the Tamil language that he had not yet finished were taken up by his colleague Benjamin Schultze, who otherwise dedicated himself to the evangelization of Muslims.

Despite the interest aroused by the Tamil mission in Germany, the authorities of the Lutheran Church refused to recognize it as an official extension of their work. The Pietist mission of Tranquebar was not the first in the history of Protestantism to move beyond the dimensions of an individual and ephemeral work; and it did not disappear with the death of Ziegenbalg, even if the successors to the pioneer lacked his caliber. Beginning in 1725, the work of the mission was extended beyond the Danish territories. During the first third of the eighteenth century, the Danish mission of Halle sent fifty-six missionaries, the majority being Germans. Collaborating with the English missionaries that SPCK sent into the same regions, the Danish opened schools, constructed chapels and, beginning in 1730, sent medical doctors. In 1733 a Tamil by the name of Aron was ordained a minister. Among the Pietist German missionaries, one of the most remarkable of this second generation was Johann Philip Fabricius (1711–1791), who worked principally in Madras. He undertook a new translation of the Bible in Tamil, published a grammar and dictionary, and engaged in extensive linguistic research. But his activities were disliked by the colonial powers, and he served several terms in prison.

About thirty years after his death, Ziegenbalg had a remarkable successor in the person of Christian Friedrich Schwartz.

### Christian Friedrich Schwartz

Schwartz (1726–1798) was born in Prussia. When his mother was at the point of death, she spoke to her husband about her four-year-old son: "I have prayed to have this child, and God has granted my prayer. Therefore, I want to give him to the Lord. He will teach him all through his life." At a young age, Schwartz felt himself called to the ministry. He did his studies in theology at Halle where he encountered a former colleague of Ziegenbalg. At this time the initial printing of the Tamil Bible had been completed at Halle, and Schwartz was asked to correct the proofs. When after eighteen months he had finished his work, he knew this Indian language quite well. When his studies were complete, despite his friends who implored him to take a parish in Germany, he offered his services to the mission of Tranquebar.

He was ordained in Copenhagen and left from London for the East in 1750. He stayed in India for five years. After only four months, he could preach his first sermon in Tamil. A fine linguist, he also knew English, Portuguese, and Persian. He immediately dedicated himself to the tasks of teaching and preaching, as well as the evangelization of the villages around Tranquebar. He traveled through the south of India, going as far as Colombo, on the island of Ceylon (present-day Sri Lanka). He concluded that his colleagues were wrong to restrict themselves only to the region of Tranquebar. As a single man, he lived in the simplest possible fashion, eating rice and vegetables cooked in the Indian style, and living in a small room that scarcely contained more than his bed and a table. He was seen to walk untiringly through the cities and villages, always dressed in clothes of black cotton. He knew how to win the hearts of those he encountered—officers, governors, proud Brahmans, majestic rajas, soldiers, untouchables—all attracted by his spiritual radiance and his total self-abnegation. Desirous to preach the gospel to a crowd, he decided to leave Tranquebar, which was only a small, unimportant port city, and to settle in one of the interior cities. In 1762 he moved to the important city of Trichinopoli and then, in 1772, to Tanjore. When he had the opportunity to evangelize the English soldiers, he succeeded so well that the British East India Company hired him as a chaplain. Visiting the villages of the region and carrying the Christian faith to numerous young people, he recruited several that he trained as evangelists and sent them through the diverse regions of South India.

He acquired such a reputation for goodness and wisdom that the raja of Tanjore did not hesitate to ask his advice when confronted with a difficult problem: "With you, my father, I have no fear of cupidity. I know that your advice will be disinterested." He had the joy of seeing an entire village turn to the gospel and transform its pagan temple into a church. In this period, the English government was frightened by the actions of Sultan Hyder Ali, who had allied himself to the French and was reigning over a large part of the state of Mysore. The British wanted to send an ambassador to him, but the sultan, who mistrusted diplomats but had come to trust Schwartz, responded: "If you want to send someone to me, I will accept only the Christian father." At first the missionary hesitated, but then he left for Seringapatam in the hope of being able to preach the gospel to new listeners. After six weeks of a perilous journey amidst feverish military preparations, he came to Hyder Ali. This Muslim leader, reputedly cruel and capricious, was won over by Schwartz's charm and invited him to stay in his palace. The missionary passed his time preaching the gospel not only to great lords and courtiers but also to servants and the population at large in the city. However, seeing that his efforts to avoid war were in vain, he returned to Tanjore. Hyder Ali gave him a safe-conduct: "Allow Father Schwartz to pass. Show him respect, for he is a holy man who has no bad intentions."

The war unleashed between the sultan and the raja of Tanjore, who was aided by the British, was hideously bloody and devastating. In these difficult circumstances, the influence of the missionary grew still greater. He had amassed abundant provisions of all sorts that he distributed to the hungry refugees. Inspiring confidence in all parties, he saved Tanjore from famine. In the neighboring countryside there was wheat and livestock, but the peasants withheld their goods for fear of not receiving payment. Schwartz announced that he would act as guarantor for the reimbursement, even if he had to pay out of his own pocket! Two days later, eighty thousand measures of wheat and some animals for slaughter were delivered to the city. Schwartz also took up a collection so that all might contribute.

Upon his personal intervention with Hyder Ali, another city was saved from destruction. When a peace accord was signed in 1784, the British placed the state of Tanjore under the supervision of a government committee that included the missionary.

More surprising were the events that followed the death of the raja of Tanjore, who, despite his evident sympathy for Schwartz, resolved never to become a Christian. Some hours before his death, he summoned Schwartz to his bedside to make him the guardian of his son, the prince and heir apparent Serfojee. Frightened that the intrigues in the palace threatened the assassination of the prince during his minority, Schwartz needed all of his spiritual authority to thwart the numerous palace plots and protect his pupil, who considered him as a second father.

When he sensed his strength declining, Schwartz summoned Serfojee in order to leave him a remarkable political testament. He then expired on February 13, 1798, at the age of seventy-one. His funeral was worthy of his life. In spite of protocol, a sobbing young raja followed the coffin while hymns could not be sung because of the loud lamentations issuing from the immense—and mostly pagan—crowd. To render the last honors to his friend, Serfojee composed an epitaph for his tutor. This was the first English poem composed by a Hindu:

> You were firm, humble, wise,
> Honest, pure and without fraud,
> You gave light to those who are in darkness
> Can I show myself worthy of you.

Schwartz's ministry shows that a missionary content to preach the gospel, with the Pietistic emphasis on individual salvation, can have a significant social, economic, and political influence on any people. The Christian is truly the salt of the earth.

Schwartz was considered a master of the Tamil language. He understood that it was impossible to evangelize a people while only knowing their culture in the abstract. He worked with relentless vigor to learn both the language and the remarkable civilization of the people of south India. When the Pietists of Halle did not approve of this approach, Schwartz disassociated himself from them and, in 1767, offered his services to the British Society for the Propagation of the Gospel.

As for the mission of Halle, it collapsed in the course of the eighteenth century. Most of the Pietists were swept away in the great deluge of rationalism that characterized the age of the Enlightenment. Becoming disciples of Jean-Jacques Rousseau, many concluded that it would be futile to send missionaries to convert "noble savages." It is curious to observe that in the space of a single century attitudes toward non-Christians in undeveloped countries could be so completely reversed, allowing European Christians to shirk their missionary responsibility. In his polemic against von Weltz, Ursinus had claimed that the "savages" were too degenerate to be worthy of hearing the gospel, but later the followers of Rousseau affirmed that these same "savages" were already too good to need it. Even those of Halle would question the need for missions. Several Protestant Indian churches in the Madras region converted to Catholicism. And the kings of Denmark ceased to be conscious of their missionary responsibility, no longer valuing the royal missionary organization established by their predecessors.

Two years after Schwartz's death, a Christian fervor broke out like wildfire in the north of India in the Danish colony at Serampore. It was a conflagration that would eventually engulf the planet. (See the work of William Carey in Book II.)

# THE LUTHERAN MISSION TO GREENLAND

The history of Lutheran missions in Greenland (1721–1736) is peculiar. It was begun by a man of exceptional perseverance, who was commonly taken for a visionary among his contemporaries and was greatly esteemed. Today, however, his work has been almost entirely forgotten and, in terms of the larger missionary enterprise, can scarcely be said to have changed the course of things.

## Hans Egede

The son of a high Danish bureaucrat, Hans Egede (1686–1758) was born and raised in a small Norwegian village. In a Lutheran environment influenced by Pietism, he converted in due course and did his theological studies at Copenhagen. At the age of twenty-three he became a minister in one of the Lofoten islands to the north of the country. During his childhood he had been moved by the history of the missionaries of Tranquebar and wondered if God did not want to send him overseas. He also happened upon a book about Eric the Red that fascinated him. It concerned a Viking group that had established a colony in Greenland in about the year 980. The small Scandinavian colony converted to Christianity in the twelfth century. Abandoning their pirating ways, the people tried to Christianize the local Inuit population. During the fourteenth century, the descendants of these immigrants, who by this time had considerably declined, were probably massacred by the Inuits. Then a veil of forgetfulness fell. Were there survivors? Had other tribes among the Inuit become Christians? These were the questions that haunted Egede's imagination. The unsuccessful efforts of Robert Wolfall in 1570 do not seem to have been known to him.[210] He was soon persuaded that God was asking him to find the answer to the questions that plagued him by visiting the forgotten shores of Greenland. He gathered all the documents he could find on the subject and learned that Dutch sailors had recently reached those regions. They had encountered peoples shy and difficult to get to know.

He decided to travel there to proclaim the gospel and revealed his thoughts to the bishop of Trondheim, who encouraged him. His family and friends, however, made every effort to dissuade him from it. In particular his wife, Gertrud, a mother of four children, energetically opposed this project over a period of several years. A nearly tragic accident, however, in which she almost lost her son, brought her to a complete change of heart. The child had imprudently ventured onto a rock on the seashore, not noticing the rising tide that soon cut off his retreat to the shore. During some dramatic moments, his mother saw the waves slowly rise until they completely engulfed the reef from which her son was calling for help. Powerless, she could only kneel and entreat God to save him—and her prayer was granted. This experience profoundly transformed her. From then on, she was more enthusiastic about the missionary project to Greenland than her husband. Egede decided to move forward with his plan. In 1718, with the agreement of his bishop, he resigned his position and dedicated himself to the task of finding the necessary financing for his enterprise, which proved to be more difficult than he had initially anticipated. The College of the Mission of Copenhagen, founded in 1714, concluded that the effort would be premature. After an anguished struggle, Egede listened to the counsel of those who told him of the missionary zeal of King Frederic IV of Denmark. He went to Copenhagen to explain the project personally to the king, who received him favorably and showed a definite interest in the evangelization of Greenland. He promised to grant a charter of monopoly for a trading company that Egede would organize, and he even promised to purchase shares in the enterprise.

Thanks to this royal support, he succeeded in gaining the participation of several merchants in the adventure and founded the Society of Danish Greenland. He chartered two ships. One would stay in Greenland as a fishing vessel while the other would sail back and forth between Greenland and Denmark, carrying the mail, bringing trading goods, and returning with fish in exchange. The king issued the promised charter and contributed three hundred *écus*, a sum renewable annually.

On May 3, 1721, Egede, with wife and children, finally embarked for Bergen on the vessel *Hope*, while his family and friends considered him to be a fool. Eleven years had passed since he had received his call and had begun the struggle to obey it. The voyage was appalling, and the passengers only just escaped shipwreck. At the end of a month, they arrived in sight of Greenland. This was not a verdant country, but a block of inaccessible ice. Navigating in the midst of icebergs, they sailed along the inhospitable coast before dropping anchor to the southeast of the peninsula at the mouth of a fjord. Here they discovered a valley without snow where willow and birch trees were growing, as well as a little grass. On the small island of Imeriksos, at the entrance to a fjord that they named Godthaab (now Nuuk and the capital of

---

210 For Wolfall see p. 225.

Greenland), they found a favorable location, disembarking there on July 3. After they came ashore with their supplies, one of the ships departed as had been agreed.

Now they would begin to settle in for an arctic winter. The summer would be very short, and they would begin to endure the rigors of the cold climate as early as September. The thirty colonists busied themselves with constructing shelters using the wood they had brought with them, for there were only stones in the area. They finished everything in two months. Then Egede took possession of the territory in the name of the king, read the charter in the course of a solemn service of inauguration, and remembered the law of the kingdom.

Sadly, the fish in these unknown waters were not plentiful, and there were scarcely any animals that might be hunted, with the exception of some polar rabbits and reindeer. As for trade with the Inuits, this proved illusionary. It was impossible to reach the shy nomads, who when the newcomers approached would immediately slip away. Moreover, their witch doctors warned them against the Europeans. In October, Egede discovered some of them living nearby in igloos. He made them a gift, but when he returned a little later, all had vanished.

Given this situation, the colonists decided to abandon the experiment and return to Europe by the next ship. Gertrud Egede was the only one to refuse to pack her bags. Finally the summer ship arrived, carrying numerous colonists and a warm letter from Frederic IV. He had even created a tax to subsidize the Greenland mission. Most of the colonists were bucked up by this news and decided to remain for another year. Although still difficult, the second year was easier. The fishing and hunting produced better results, but trade remained almost nonexistent. Egede despaired of the nomadic life of the ever-elusive Inuits. They spoke an agglutinative language that was very difficult for Europeans, and Egede was at great pains to learn even a few words. The children, however, began to play with the other Inuit children and slowly succeeded in communicating with them.

In the third summer of 1723, the Lutheran missionary Albert Top came as a reinforcement. He stayed with Egede until 1736, when he returned home.

After much patient endeavor, Egede finally found a means to enter into contact with the local people. He succeeded in gaining the confidence of several Inuit children, whom he instructed in his home and baptized, the first baptism being administered to a child in 1724. The catechumens made engravings and sculptures of various scenes and persons in the Bible. On several occasions, Egede visited the parents of these children in their igloos where he found the unhygienic conditions repulsive. He succeeded in gaining the confidence of several of them, but they remained impervious to the message of the gospel. An Inuit named Aaron, who seems to have been converted, did his best to translate for him. Two other missionaries arrived in 1725, Lange and Milzoug, but they did not persevere long. At this time, an Inuit named Poëh went to Norway and returned enthusiastic about what he had seen. However, he quickly returned to paganism and his nomadic life. Also in the same year, the eldest son of the family, Paul, left to study in Copenhagen.

As for the trading company, it was not making any return to the shareholders. In 1724 the ship, which shuttled between Denmark and the island, sank at sea, and the missionaries and colonists remained isolated and without news for some time. Recognizing that the trading company would never be a profitable affair, the directors dissolved it in 1727. At that point, King Frederic IV intervened and decided to make Greenland a colony of the Danish crown. He sent two warships with a governor and soldiers, who succeeded in constructing a fort. Emigrants were also recruited from the prisons. For the most part these ex-prisoners and women of ill repute were more or less "reformed." Their settlement, however, was a true disaster. Disagreements occurred between the soldiers and the colonists, and disorders became commonplace. Egede had to place a guard in front of his house. Several colonists fell sick and died. Seeing all this, the Inuits became still more distrustful and departed for lands farther north. Egede decided to resettle on the firm ground of Godthaab.

Yet another hard blow soon struck the mission: a ship arrived in 1730 carrying news of the death of King Frederic IV. His son, Christian VI, was a good Lutheran but did not share his father's missionary sentiments. He ordered the governor, soldiers, and colonists to return to Denmark. To those who wanted to remain, he promised only one year's worth of supplies. Everyone left for Europe except Egede, his family, and a small remnant of the faithful, which included Albert Top. For the first time, the Inuits showed some sensitivity to the missionary, saying, "Since you have chosen to remain with us with your wife and children, you will never lack for seal meat."

## Reinforcements from the Moravian Brethren

While Egede's family was fighting solitude in Greenland, one of the greatest missionary revivals in Protestant history was then coming to life in Germany amidst the Moravian Brethren of Herrnhut. The Moravians had received the erroneous information that Hans Egede was on the point of abandoning the mission to Greenland and returning to Europe. While they had just sent their first missionaries to the Antilles in 1732, the Brethren were convinced that they had heard the call of the Lord to continue the missionary effort in the icy and distant reaches of Greenland, which were being ignored by nearly everyone. Three of the Brethren were designated to go, among whom was Christian David, one of the earliest associates of Count Zinzendorf, the leader of the Moravians (see Book I, Chapter 16).

Without any supplies, they left in the spring of 1733 and arrived at the end of May in Godthaab. Egede welcomed them with joy . . . and surprise, for he had not been informed that they were coming. Not far from Egede's home, the Moravians constructed a small missionary post that they called New Herrnhut. Following the instructions of Zinzendorf, they offered their services to Egede. At the same time, Paul Egede, the missionary's eldest son, returned to Greenland, having finished his studies in theology in Denmark. He was the only one who really understood the Inuit language well, having learned it among them as a child. With the aid of the Moravians, he soon dedicated himself to the translation of the Bible. Was the work finally going to take flight? After twelve years in Greenland, Egede now had the pleasure of seeing a group of Inuits settle in his vicinity because of the material advantages that they gained from his presence, and because of the friendships that he had slowly forged with them. However, they still showed no interest in the Christian message.

Collaboration did not come easily between the old missionary and the newly arrived Moravians. Although influenced by Pietism, Egede was a strict Lutheran and very attached to orthodox views. Moreover, he was a strong character, without which he would never have been able to persevere in such adverse conditions. The Moravians, who were on fire for their Savior and heady with the enthusiasm of the Herrnhut revival, had difficulty understanding why Egede's faith seemed so sterile. They were living out their faith in a typically Moravian style, full of emotion and with little inclination to doctrinal precision, their training in this regard being rudimentary.

Despite the joy Egede no doubt felt to receive reinforcements, it is not difficult to imagine that he did not find it easy to make room for these new arrivals, who reproached him for being too rigid and intellectual. Rather than preach to the Inuits about justification by grace alone, they would have him appeal to their hearts in calling them to conversion.

A letter written by Matthew Stack to the Brethren at Herrnhut three weeks after his arrival in Greenland provides a good picture of Moravian religiosity:

> What we were looking for we have found: pagans who do not know God and who travel from one place to another, anxious only to know how many sealskins, fish, and reindeer they possess. It is to this people that we will announce God, Jesus Christ and the Holy Spirit. But how will we make them listen? How can we reach those who travel from island to island and who seem so dense as not to understand even our signs? . . . However, by the grace of God, we will not lose courage but will await the hour of the Lord . . . And if we should see no result from our work in Greenland, if all this should lead only to a supreme humiliation, we will bless Jesus and render honor to his name. May all to him be sacrificed: our goods, blood, life, to him who, by his death, has taken away our sins.[211]

A little later, a new and terrible trial struck the missionaries. A young Inuit, who had traveled to Denmark and returned, carried smallpox with him. The Inuits had no immunity to a disease unknown among them. Transported from place to place by the nomads, it ravaged and decimated the population of south Greenland. It is estimated that there were between two and three thousand deaths. And in Godthaab, of the three hundred Inuits—children and adults—who had consented to live close to the Egede family, only thirty survived. Most of these fled, leaving a great empty space around the missionaries' settlement. Egede, Top, and the Moravian Brethren expended themselves without stint to care for the sick and bury the dead. Despite their iron health, Hans and, more still, Gertrud were exhausted. They decided then to return to Norway. Their son Paul, who communicated easily with the Inuits, would continue the work as would the Moravians. But, sadly, some days before Christmas 1735, Gertrud, being at the end of her strength, suddenly died. Hans passed through a time of dismal despair, nearly losing his reason. Here is how he recalled this tragic time:

---

211 E. A. Senft, *Les missions moraves* (Neuchâtel: Delachaux & Niestlé, 1890), 84.

> My soul was plunged into the anguish of hell and enchained by ties to the dead. When I came a little to myself, the only thing that I was capable of expressing, with pains and groans, was that God had abandoned me. My companions and my dear children came to me and strove to console me with the Word of God. But I was not in a state to listen to any word of consolation. Then my conscience cursed me to have thought that no help would be accorded me on the part of God. I found no vent for this interior and exterior agony. I remained for two hours in this extreme state. But God, in his goodness, he who afflicts but does not reject forever, had pity on me and heard the cry of my supplications. He redeemed me from hell and made me reborn to life.

On August 9, 1736, he embarked with his colleague Albert Top on the return ship. He took for the text of his farewell sermon, "I have labored to no purpose" (Isa 49:4). It is not known if he commented on the end of the verse, "Yet what is due me is in the Lord's hand, and my reward is with my God." Egede had struggled for eleven years to launch his expedition and had left home with an almost total ignorance of the place to which he was going. For fourteen years in Greenland, in tears and almost total solitude, he witnessed and fought for his faith in trying climatic conditions, and this without any apparent spiritual fruit.

At Copenhagen the king welcomed him with great sympathy and encouraged him to found a Greenland Missionary Seminary. In 1740 Egede was named superintendent of the Missionary Church of Greenland. He wrote the story of his mission and translated a catechism and some psalms in the Inuit language. He died on November 5, 1758, at the age of seventy-two.

## The Birth of an Inuit Church

But the story does not end with the departure of Egede. The Inuits were even more resistant to the teachings of the Moravians than to those of Egede. Moreover, they made the Europeans the scapegoat for the evil that had struck them. The Brethren were the objects of harassment; indeed, cruel treatment. They were even threatened with death.

In 1738 the missionaries wrote to Herrnhut:

> Physically, we lack the strength to hold up well in this country; may God give it to us. Morally, all the natural goodwill and all the courage for language study that has been among us have disappeared. What alone remains is the grace that has operated in our hearts. God knows why he began this post, the weakest and least likely. Before us there are only impossibilities. But we will keep the faith until Jesus comes to help us, we the wretched; we will spare no effort so that we might please him.[212]

---

212 Ibid., 86.

At the same time, Count Nicolas von Zinzendorf received an angry letter from Copenhagen that characterized the Greenland missionaries as perfect incompetents. Shaken by this, the Count addressed an ardent and tearful supplication to the Lord that he would intervene with power in this apparently hopeless situation. When the Brethren received news of the victory of the gospel in the Moravian mission of the Antilles, they wrote: "It is among us alone that the Word of God produces no effect. But believe it, beloved brethren, the glory of the Lord will also rise in Greenland." Not too long after this, something did happen at New Herrnhut, an event entirely new and truly extraordinary.

On June 2, 1738, a band of furious nomads suddenly intruded into the Moravian house intending to wreck it, surprising brother Jean Beck, who was then occupied in recopying the translation of a text of the gospel. He succeeded in calming them by engaging them in conversation. He also had the presence of mind to ask them to listen to him read what he had been in the process of writing in their language. This was the story of Christ's passion in the garden of Gethsemane and his death on the Cross. "Do not any longer refuse this Savior!" concluded Jean Beck. Then Kajarnak, the chief of the Inuit band, showed some interest: "Repeat this story once more," he said with emotion. The passage had apparently made quite an impression on Kajarnak, and the missionary reread it several times for him.

*Left: Matthew Stack (1711–1787), the first Moravian missionary who arrived in Greenland in 1733 to aid Hans Egede. He remained until 1771. Right: Jean Beck (1706–1777). A Moravian missionary in Greenland who arrived in 1724, he was instrumental in the conversion of Kajarnak, the first Inuit to become a Christian. Beck remained in Greenland for fifty-three years, until his death in 1777.*

This was the first time that an Inuit had responded to the message of the gospel. But the entire band departed the next day.

Fifteen days later, they returned, and Kajarnak asked the Moravians to instruct him. He made rapid and prodigious progress, then left again. But he returned soon, professed an authentic conversion, and then went to witness to his family. On March 30, 1739, he was baptized with his wife, son, and daughter. About twenty of his relatives came to join him, and they also received the gospel. However, they soon had to flee before the threats of the other Inuits, who considered them as traitors.

The missionaries began to emphasize the love of God in their sermons and talks, and numerous conversions were produced. The sudden death of Kajarnak in 1741 did not slow the growth of the new Inuit community. The nomadic life itself became the means of rapid expansion, for in several years the gospel was being proclaimed even in the most distant encampments. The society was transformed. New villages were slowly constructed around chapels or churches. One among them carried the name of Egede: Egedesminde. It was founded in 1759, one year after the death of the intrepid pioneer whose untiring perseverance was now bearing fruit.

The eldest son of Hans Egede, Paul (1708–1789), became the superintendent of the Church of Greenland upon the death of his father in 1758. By 1766 he had translated the New Testament into Greenlanders. Another son of Hans, John, was also a missionary to Greenland, from 1770 to 1778.

# CHAPTER 16

# *The Moravians*

The mission initiatives of the Moravians were the most important missionary efforts of the eighteenth century. They were the direct fruit of German Pietism since their founder, Nicolas von Zindzendorf, was trained in the schools of Halle. But who were the Moravians? Above all they were a persecuted religious minority. To understand them one must look back further into the history of the church. As early as the eighteenth century Bohemia and Moravia in central Europe were lands of refuge for the Vaudois who were persecuted in France and Italy. Some even think that Pierre Valdo died in Bohemia.

John Huss (1370–1415), whose teachings were formative for the Moravians, was already rector of the University of Prague at the age of thirty-two. He was highly influenced by the evangelical theology of John Wycliffe, several of whose works he translated, and through him this teaching would have an immense influence among his compatriots, despite the opposition of the clergy. His excommunication and martyrdom in Constance in 1415 did not put an end to the diffusion of his ideas. His followers organized such an effective armed resistance that they were permitted to subsist if they would agree to respect a compromise. They accepted, and the Hussites survived in the mountains of central Europe. A number among them formed an independent church in 1467, the United Brethren (*Unitas Fratrum*). In the time of Luther, there were hundreds of Brethren churches that joined the nascent Reformation.

In the seventeenth century, the Counter-Reformation appeared in Moravia, in which evangelicals were persecuted with increasingly violence. The Hapsburgs, in particular, resolved to eliminate the Protestants in their states. And they succeeded. Small, isolated groups of inveterate Moravians hid themselves in the mountains, but they were pursued even in their refuges. Many escaped to Saxony, leaving behind all their possessions.

In 1722 a group of Brethren under the leadership of David Christian, a converted Catholic, fled the ruthless persecution in Moravia to seek refuge in Saxony where the refugees encountered Count Zinzendorf. Due to this apparently fortuitous event, the church and the mission of the Moravian Brethren were born.

## NICOLAS VON ZINZENDORF

The Zinzendorf family, being allied to most of the kings and princes of Europe, was one of the most illustrious in Germany. Nicolas von Zinzendorf (1700–1760) lost his father while he was still a child. He inherited the title of count of the empire, which in this period was one of the highest dignities possible, conferring on him almost sovereign rights. His relatives were very pious and, in order to embrace Lutheranism, had abandoned their considerable properties in Austria. Settling in Saxony, they were influenced by Pietism, and Nicolas was sent to Halle to be educated. The child showed remarkable talent. At Halle he heard talk of the mission of Tranquebar and became fascinated with the adventures of the missionaries in India. With his comrades, he founded an order of knights, the Mustard Seed, whose purpose was to preach the gospel to Jews and pagans.

His family wanted to make a diplomat of him or a minister of state, but he wanted to be a Christian minister. This was unthinkable for a count of the empire. Therefore, in order to dispel this apparently bizarre idea from his mind, he was sent to study law at the University of Wittenberg. He was scandalized by the debauchery of the students that he encountered there and did not come to change his mind. Instead, this experience reinforced his desire to dedicate his life to the service of God, even if his rank denied him a pastoral ministry. He was sent next on a journey through Europe, an indispensable step in the formation of a great lord. He sojourned for a long time in the court of Versailles where he made the acquaintance of Cardinal Louis-Antoine de Noailles, the archbishop of Paris, to whom he would remain very close. It is in the course of this journey that he came to the art gallery of the prince elector at Dusseldorf, where he saw a painting by the Italian Domenico Fett that changed his life. The painting depicted Jesus before Pilate and bore this inscription: "I have suffered this for you, what will you do for me?"[213] Deeply moved, he saw in this painting a personal call to total consecration. "The blood rose in my face because I could not find anything great to respond; and I prayed to my Savior to draw me by force into the communion of his suffering, if my spirit should refuse it."

On his return, he decided to marry a young girl who shared his views. It was in the course of his honeymoon on his property that, in 1722, he encountered the Moravian refugees. He decided to welcome and accommodate them on his lands by founding the village of Herrnhut, which means "In the keeping of God." Other Moravians came to expand the population, and by 1727 there were six hundred settlers whom the count had organized into a community. This was to be his life's work. For this, he left his position as counselor of state at Dresden and gave himself entirely to the leadership of the community of Brethren.

Zinzendorf, however, did not forget the passion he had in his youth for mission. In the celebration of the crowning of King Christian VI of Denmark, who was a close relative, he encountered several Inuits of Greenland, sent by Hans Egede,

---

213  Painted around 1600 by Domenico Fett, a student of Corrège, this rather mediocre work of art is on display in the Pinacothèque of Munich. The Latin text inscribed on it is the following: *"Ego pro te haec passus sum; Tu vero, quid fecisti pro me?"*

and a black slave from the Danish Antilles. On questioning them, he was amazed to observe their openness to dialogue. The Antillean was Anton Ulrich, a valet of a Danish count, who told Zinzendorf that he had for a long time desired to come to a knowledge of the true God. Zinzendorf invited him to come with him to Herrnhut. Ulrich spoke to the community of the distress of his black brothers, their hard work, nostalgia for their motherland of Africa, and ignorance of the message of salvation. When the assembly of the Brethren heard this testimony, as well as the report of the count on the difficulty of the task in Greenland, they were deeply moved by their plight and at the same time filled with enthusiasm. They immediately perceived the call of God to send missionaries.

The activities of Zinzendorf at Herrnhut, and of the several other groups that had formed communities on the model of this village, disturbed the authorities of the Lutheran Church. Zinzendorf, despite his position and his relations, was severely criticized, being accused of preparing a schism. He was finally condemned to banishment from Saxony but profited from this opportunity to travel and spread his ideas and the message of the revival, especially in the Netherlands. After some time, passions cooled and the judgment against him was rescinded. The government even asked him to establish other villages in Saxony on the model of Herrnhut. The influence of Zinzendorf and of the Moravian community was considerable, in particular in Lutheran countries.

Having listened to the news from the Antilles and Greenland, the conscience of the Herrnhut community had been stirred. Zinzendorf did not put any pressure on the Brethren to act but simply planted the question like a seed in their minds, leaving it to germinate on its own. He was conscious of the enormous physical difficulties that the missionaries would be sure to encounter, as well as the resistance that Satan was going to put up. He refrained from influencing them, convinced that only the Holy Spirit should give the mandate for such a task. These Moravians were a tough race, persecuted through the centuries, living hidden in the mountains, subsisting in danger and extreme poverty, inflexible, untamable. It would require a people of this temper to confront the risks to which such a mission would expose them. Introducing one of his candidates to the Dutch West India Company, Zinzendorf said, "I present to you a man used to suffering."

Concerning the missionary work of the Moravians, we have already seen that in 1733 they undertook the work alongside of Egede in Greenland, and what fruit it eventually bore.

## THE MORAVIAN MISSION IN THE ANTILLES

The other field where the Moravians decided to send workers was that of the Danish Antilles. The Virgin Islands are an archipelago to the east of Puerto Rico and the Dominican Republic, and to the north of Martinique. A young potter, Leonard Dober, felt called to go there. The assembly therefore sent him in the company of an "elder," David Nitschmann, who would later return to give an account of the beginnings of the work. The two left for Hamburg with almost no money and worked as laborers on the farms they encountered along the way in order meet their expenses. At Hamburg they were advised not to launch out on this perilous adventure, but they continued on their way undeterred. Historian A. J. Lewis has written that they "set out on foot for Copenhagen, bundles on their backs, thirty shillings in their pockets, and the invincible all-embracing love of Christ in their hearts. Thus the modern worldwide missionary movement was born."[214] No ship of the Danish Indies and Guinea Company wanted to embark with them, so they hired themselves out as seamen on a Dutch ship whose captain, perhaps something of a pirate, consented to take them aboard.

It was a difficult voyage. They disembarked at St. Thomas (one of the Virgin Islands) in December 1732. The island was small but included a significant number of slaves—more than three thousand—leading an exhausting life in the rich sugarcane plantations. A Danish planter consented to lodge the missionaries for several weeks. The two profited from this time by making contact with the slaves. They discovered how difficult it was to communicate with these Africans of highly diverse origins. They spoke Creole, a form of Dutch mixed with English, Spanish, and French words. Nitschmann, having led Dober safely to port, returned as planned to Herrnhut after three months of common labor.

Dober had quickly discovered that he would not be able to support himself by practicing his trade as he had anticipated, the clay on the island not being suited to pottery. Eventually, the governor took pity on him and offered him a position as an overseer. The missionary was well paid, but he soon learned that as a superior to the slaves he had almost no contact with them. He resigned his post in 1734 and hired himself out as a guard on the plantation, a miserable job but one that permitted him to live among the slaves, to speak with them, and to witness his love of Christ to them. He won hearts, and in short order a little nucleus of believers assembled around him. Anton Ulrich, a former West Indian slave, had said to him at the time of his visit to Herrnhut, "To reach them [slaves] you would most likely have to become slaves yourselves."

While Dober was making progress in the Antilles, he discovered that at Herrnhut he had been appointed one of the "elders" who would be responsible for the community. He therefore had to return home after a difficult two years' sojourn. Subsequently, in 1738, he traveled to Amsterdam to evangelize the Jews and establish a community of the Brethren in Holland.

Before his departure from St. Thomas, a group of eighteen volunteers had left from Herrnhut, without the full consent of Zinzendorf, to replace him. One party established itself on the neighboring island of St. Croix. Due to a lack of means to subsist, life became precarious and soon the enterprise experienced tragedy. Many fell sick, and after only six months ten among them were dead. Those who remained quarreled among themselves and before long returned to Europe.

---

214 A. J. Lewis, *Zinzendorf: The Ecumenical Pioneer* (London: SCM Press, 1962), 79–80. Cited in Michael Griffiths, *Envoyer, c'est partir un peu* (Lavigny: Groupes Missionaires, 1998), 132.

In December 1736, four years after the arrival of Dober and Nitschmann, thirty missionaries had come from Europe, but among them eighteen were buried on the islands. Among the survivors, several were sick. The announcement of the arrival of a missionary doctor was, therefore, a comfort. But the doctor scarcely had time to care for any of the Brethren, for he survived only six days after stepping ashore.

### Frederic Martin

Happily, in 1735 Frederic Martin arrived. A remarkable missionary, as soon as he could preach in Creole conversions began to multiply as did church assemblies, over which he exercised a strict discipline. Although the planters were all good "Protestants," they were furious at these developments, especially since their servants began to teach them moral lessons. Soon the planters forbade their slaves from speaking to the Brethren under threat of the lash. A veritable persecution was instituted. However, most of the converted remained faithful, and the work progressed in spite of obstacles. Then the planters turned on Martin himself. In order not to contravene the rule of the official churches, Martin was to refrain from baptizing the converted. The Brethren were to await the coming of August Gottlieb Spangenberg (1704–1792), who had been ordained a minister by Zinzendorf.

Nevertheless, Martin officiated at the marriage ceremony of Freundlich, a Brethren missionary, to a mulatto Christian woman. Informed of this fact, the Dutch pastor of the island, Berm, denounced him to the authorities. Martin had broken the law in blessing the marriage, for he had performed an ecclesiastical act without having received clerical ordination. Appearing before a colonial tribunal, Martin was given a heavy fine that he could not pay and so was placed in prison. Freundlich was condemned to forced labor, and his young wife sold as a slave. The Christians assembled themselves under the window of Martin's prison cell to listen to his exhortations, preached from behind bars. At this juncture the humor of God might be detected, for at this very moment Zinzendorf landed on the island. He had come to pay a visit on missionaries, but he had not been informed of the trials that they were then undergoing. He must have been astonished when, asking to meet Frederic Martin, he learned of his imprisonment. The governor was disquieted; he had never had the honor of a visit from such a high personage of the empire, a man ranked near the king. He could only make haste to free the missionary. Zinzendorf, for his part, quickly obtained a royal edict recognizing Martin's Moravian ordination.

The persecution slowly ceased, for the planters discovered that the slave converts not only no longer lied or stole, but worked harder. The Christian slaves even sold for higher prices in the slave market. With public opinion turned around completely, a true revival began. In 1741 Martin wrote, "Almost every day, some souls come to find me. If one goes through the plantations, one hears everywhere crying and praying." He recruited sixteen young people whom he trained as evangelists, and soon ninety converts were baptized on the same day. The work also took hold on the island of St. Croix, from which it was extended to the island of St. John. After fourteen years of fruitful ministry, Martin died in 1750.

In 1757, after twenty-five years of activity, the statistics for the work of the Moravians in the three islands of the Danish Antilles were the following: ninety-two missionaries (sixty-two men and thirty women) had come from Europe; seven among them had died due to shipwrecks on the passage over, forty-seven had died on the islands, and thirty-eight had survived—but not all of them had remained in the Antilles. More than 1,400 had been baptized. From the very beginning, the Brethren were anxious to train their Christian converts and give them church tasks to perform. In this way they hoped to shape a communal character in the churches they were establishing in the Antilles, following the model of Herrnhut. Moreover, the converts showed themselves to be extremely zealous. There was a Christian slave, for example, who, on receiving responsibility for several new converts, engraved their names on his baton to be certain not to forget a single one. A catechist named David addressed his racial brothers who were receiving instruction for baptism:

> I give thanks to my Savior for having led me from Guinea where I was free, through the seas, to this country of slavery; for here I can hear his gentle gospel that I did not know over there. Although I am a slave and I must work hard, I am not anxious, for by his death, the Savior has freed me from the terrible slavery of sin! Give him all your heart! And I will rejoice if you also, who are black like me, obtain his grace.[215]

*Baptism of African slaves in the Antilles at a Moravian community in the eighteenth century.*

---

215 Samuel Baudert, *Aux ordres du Seigneur: Deux siècles de mission morave, 1732–1932* (Lausanne: La Concorde, 1932), 21.

The work continued to develop over the years. At the time of the centenary of the mission to the Danish Antilles in 1832, a great thanksgiving celebration was held on the island of St. Croix in the presence of an immense crowd. In the previous century, 31,310 baptisms had been administered in the seven mission stations, and at that time the seven Christian communities on the three islands included 9,822 members.

Beginning in 1755, the Moravians also evangelized Jamaica and other islands in the Caribbean Sea, with varying results. In Antigua (the British Antilles) the early years were arduous, with only fourteen baptisms in thirteen years. But following 1769 there was an abundant harvest. This was especially due to the ministry of Peter Braun, a Brethren from North America, who entirely shared the slaves' poor living conditions. During the twenty-two years of his ministry, there were more than 7,400 conversions. Braun died in 1791, a man much esteemed and respected.

Churches were slowly planted on the islands throughout the Caribbean, and catechumens could be numbered in the thousands. But the price paid for success dramatically rose. By 1782, after fifty years of work, the Caribbean held 110 graves of the Moravian men and women who had come as part of the mission. Sixty-six Moravian missionaries were present in the Caribbean in 1800, and the church included twenty-one thousand baptized members.

By this time, the first Protestant missionary societies of the modern era were struggling to be born.

## IN THE FACE OF SLAVERY

It is appropriate to include a brief commentary on the attitude of the Moravian missionaries toward slavery. It is easy to see the extent to which they were in solidarity with this poor and despised population, often sharing the inhumane living conditions imposed on them. Despite this, it is surprising that the Moravians were not antislavery militants, in contrast to the Methodist missionaries who took, following John Wesley himself, a firm position against slavery. Zinzendorf's successor, August Spangenberg, even cited the epistles of Paul to affirm that slavery was not incompatible with the gospel. Perhaps they feared the negative repercussions an overly militant stance against the system might have invited. The colonists, after all, were highly influential while the Moravians were always in a precarious situation. If perceived as antiestablishment, they would eventually have been expelled. It seems, however, that the discreet report sent by the Moravian missionaries to the Society for the Abolition of Slavery, founded by William Wilberforce in England in 1787, contributed substantially to fleshing out the dossier presented to the Parliament that led to the abolition of slavery in the British Empire in 1807, three years after Denmark. Afterwards, the Moravians exerted a calming influence on the confrontations that threatened to become bloody when the slaves rose up in response to the refusal of the colonists to comply with the new law that mandated their freedom.

# MORAVIAN MISSION IN SOUTH AMERICA

After obtaining the agreement of the Dutch West India Company of Surinam, in 1735 the Moravians opened up a new field of activity in Surinam, or Dutch Guiana. They disembarked at Paramaribo (the capital of Surinam), but after experiencing repeated failures among the slaves working on the plantations, they abandoned the settlements. Instead, the missionaries decided to enter the dense tropical forest to seek out the Arawak Indians, a fearful and suspicious people whose language would be difficult to learn. The enterprise took time to bear fruit. In 1753, after eighteen years of effort, they had only baptized sixty people. The first woman who asked to be baptized expressed her desire in typically Moravian terms: "I want to be washed from head to foot in the blood of the Lamb."

The principal figure of this mission was Salomon Schumann, a professor of theology and linguistics, who arrived in 1748. He quickly learned the language and then taught his colleagues. They then founded the village of Pilgerhut, where missionaries and newly sedentary Indians lived together in a community modeled on Herrnhut. The work soon became so successful, attracting more and more aborigines, that it was necessary to plan for the creation of other similar villages.

Subsequently, the Arawaks were relentlessly driven more deeply into the forest. The harsh environment took a terrible death toll, not only among the missionaries but also among the indigenous people. The enterprise, too costly in human lives, was halted in 1808.

## The Evangelization of African Slaves

The Moravians had been trying to reach the slaves of the plantations since 1735, but they experienced only failure. In part this was because of the hostility of the planters, who eventually recognized their error. But the major reasons for the failure of the mission among these people were their poor living conditions and the inhumane work required of them. Nine in ten died so young that they did not have time to produce offspring. The numbers speak eloquently: from the sixteenth century until the middle of the nineteenth century, 350,000 Africans had been brought to Surinam. By 1850 the black population of the country came to only thirty-five thousand.

Three successive evangelistic attempts had no result, except the death of several missionaries. Later, in 1754 the Moravian community of Zeist, in Holland, took this work in hand. Several Brethren arrived in Surinam and opened much-appreciated tailoring shops, then a bakery, a watchmaking shop, and other craft shops. In 1756 Salomon Schumann described the mission: "Brother Kamm serves coffee, brother Wenzel repairs shoes, brother Schmidt makes dresses, brother Doerfer is a gardener, brother Brambly works in the canal." They also financed the missionary work of their colleagues who worked with Schumann among the Indians in the forest, giving a source of income to a number of freed slaves, and witnessing to Jesus Christ among the colonists as well as the slaves.

This mission eventually bore fruit, but this occurred only after more than twenty years when, in 1776, the first convert was baptized. This was a freed slave. There were soon other black converts, and even some from among the white colonists. A chapel was constructed two years later.

### The "Negroes of the Woods"

The Moravians also endeavored to reach the "Negroes of the Woods." These were escaped slaves who sought refuge in the forest. The plantations were generally established on the cleared fields that lay on the edge of the immense tropical forest. Consequently, the "Negroes of the Woods" did not have to go very far to escape their masters. From the fastness of the forest, they posed an ongoing threat to the planters by their continual raids on the colony for arms and alcohol. It is estimated that their numbers eventually reached seventy-five thousand. Being so numerous, they organized themselves as a veritable state, with their own chiefs, laws, and customs—in the African tradition. In 1765 the Dutch governor went so far as to accord them legal status in the hope of pacifying them. He asked the Moravian missionaries to meet them, reasoning that they were the only ones capable of establishing trusting and constructive relations with them. Very soon afterwards, Arabi, the witch doctor and chief of the tribe, converted and was baptized. Over the next fifty years he dedicated himself to the evangelization of his subjects, obtaining numerous conversions. Soon a church emerged in the forest.

Due to the debilitating climate, the work was extremely dangerous for the missionaries. The most well known among them was a man named Stoll. He quickly lost his young wife and then, successively, all his companions. Completely isolated, he wrote in a letter: "I am suffering from an evil eruption, my body is only one sore from head to foot. Moreover, my preaching is sterile."

He died after eleven years of effort. By 1813 fifteen Brethren, nine brothers, and six sisters, had died, sometimes before even having begun the work. In such conditions, it was evident that Europeans could not continue as missionaries. The mission, therefore, withdrew its members, leaving the Christian community to be directed by Chief Arabi, who pursued the evangelization of his own population.

After the abolition of slavery, the "Negroes of the Woods" melted into the general population of the country.

## THE MORAVIAN MISSION AMONG THE NORTH AMERICAN INDIANS

The first Moravians arrived in North America in 1734 and continued arriving in numbers during the ensuing years. They were immigrants, not missionaries. In effect, the restrictions that the German princes placed on the people in their territories led to a great number of them deciding to seek greener pastures in America.

Following the model of Herrnhut, the Moravians founded two villages in Pennsylvania, Bethlehem and Nazareth. And as soon as possible, they made friendly contact with the Indians.

Zinzendorf came to visit and encourage them in 1742. He journeyed into the forest to meet the chiefs of the tribes of the great Iroquois nation and signed a solemn treaty of alliance with them. On this occasion, the count himself baptized the first Indian converts.

Christian Heinrich Rauch was the first Moravian to come to North America as a missionary. Arriving in New York in 1740, he successfully evangelized the Mohican tribe. English clergymen, concerned about the traffic in alcohol, came to believe that the Moravians were spies in the pay of French Quebec and, therefore, opposed a ministry that they believed to be dangerous. A veritable persecution followed, during which missionaries were imprisoned by local authorities.

## David Zeisberger

The most imminent of these missionaries was David Zeisberger (1721–1808). Born in Moravia, he became a refugee in Herrnhut while still an adolescent. Zinzendorf, observing his intelligence and exceptional personality, encouraged him to pursue his studies. The discipline of Moravian education, however, quickly became so burdensome for this boisterous boy that he escaped to America. It was in the New World, in 1743, that the young man came to conversion and decided to dedicate his life to the evangelization of the Indians. He demonstrated himself to be an excellent linguist, quickly mastering several languages. The Iroquois and Delaware Indians soon considered him to be one of their own. He shared their lives in troubled times, first in the Franco-British wars, and then in the War of Independence waged by the colonists against the British. In each case, Native Americans were forced by the two belligerents to fight on their respective sides.

*David Zeisberger (1721–1808). This Moravian missionary dedicated his life to the evangelization of the Iroquois and Delaware Indians with whom he fully identified himself by sharing their forest life during the troubled times of the Franco-British wars and the War of Independence.*

Like the Indians, Zeisberger found himself constantly caught between the fires raging on either side of him. With the Indians, he withdrew ever more deeply into the forest, and like them, he lived by hunting deer and bear. He stubbornly continued to preach peace and attempted to protect the Christian Indians who were being attacked by one side or the other. But over the course of his long ministry, the same scenario played itself out again and again. He preached the gospel, achieved a great number of Indian conversions, and founded villages of Christian Indians with a chapel and school—as John Eliot had before him. When the villagers became prosperous, enemies in arms would attack them in order to seize the riches that they had acquired by long and patient labor. Zeisberger, together with the survivors, would then advance more deeply into the forest and begin all over again.

Zeisberger enjoyed several years of rest and serenity in the region of the Great Lakes before his death in November 1808 at the age of eighty-seven. He was completely identified with the Indian tribes in whose midst he lived, surrounded by numerous converts. The dauntless courage he demonstrated in defending his Indian brothers won him the respect even of his bitterest enemies. Yet it is largely his linguistic work on the Indian languages that has prevented his name from being completely lost in the forgotten pages of history. Though he accomplished a work of great scope as a missionary, there are few today who remember the name of David Zeisberger.

## THE MORAVIAN MISSION IN SOUTH AFRICA

The Moravian Georg Schmidt (1709–1785), a butcher born in Kunevalde, Moravia, was imprisoned for his faith for six years before abjuring in order to gain his freedom. As soon as he could, he fled to Herrnhut where, at the age of seventeen, he confessed his sin of apostasy and was integrated into the community. He offered his life as a missionary and was sent by the Brethren to South Africa to undertake a mission among the Hottentots, a people the white colonists generally refused to consider as human beings. They spoke of them as the *schepels*—"black livestock." That anyone would undertake the task of evangelizing them was considered by many to be an offense to human dignity.

Schmidt disembarked at Cape Town in 1737 and traveled two hundred kilometers into the interior of the country to an inhospitable region called Baviaanskloof—"the Monkey Hole." He constructed a hut, lived as an indigenous person, and planted a vegetable garden and several fruit trees. Soon some Hottentots came to construct their huts in his vicinity. They taught him to cultivate the land and to speak their language. He in turn taught them Dutch as well as reading and writing. He also preached the gospel to them, which resulted in some conversions. After Schmidt had lived among them for a year, he was visited by elder David Nitschmann, then *en route* to Ceylon. On this occasion, Nitschmann wrote a letter full of hope to Zinzendorf:

> Africa is an immense field ready to be harvested . . . Our brother Schmidt enjoys a great reputation not only among the Hottentots, but also as far as Cape Town. It is claimed that others have not succeeded in accomplishing in the space of thirty years what he has done in thirteen months, that is to teach the Hottentots to pray, and to pray alone with their God . . . I have the conviction that God will call some missionaries to these countries and that he will bless their work among this poor, despised, and miserable people.

Zinzendorf sent a letter of ordination to Schmidt that authorized him to administer baptism. The five first converts in his village were baptized in March 1742, three men and two women. (One of the women was Madeleine—also known as Lena—whom we shall encounter later.) This fragile little group of baptized Hottentots was the first church born of the Protestant mission in Africa. On this occasion, Schmidt wrote to Europe:

> I have baptized five Hottentots! What joy this is for me, since for five years I have not dared to leave my lost and solitary post. I have sworn fidelity to my Savior and I have promised him to pour out my blood for him until the last drop . . . There is no rest, not as long as I have the strength to walk. And if I must fall, death will be welcome to me. I am in the hands of my God who will dispose of me.[216]

Despite the remoteness of the Christian village, the news of these baptisms arrived in the Cape Colony where it was greeted with great indignation: one cannot baptize animals! A delegation of Reformed pastors came to make an inquiry and had to admit that the Hottentots confessed their faith as well as their own parishioners. They nevertheless accused Schmidt of having committed an illegal ecclesiastical act, and he had to explain himself before magistrates in a tribunal at Cape Town. He was ordered to cease all pastoral activity. In facing the intolerance of the authorities and the implacable hostility of the white colonists, as well as the extreme difficulty of his mission among the Hottentots, Schmidt was overcome with feelings of loneliness and despair. He wrote a letter to the church of Herrnhut in which he opened his heart to his people:

> The enemy, no thanks to me, works hard to make my life bitter; I have come very close to abandoning all and returning sometime to be with you, but the Lord has not yet permitted this . . . I make no case for my life; I am as one sold to this people, and I am bound by him [Christ]. But what a poor nation! If I did not know that Jesus came to save all men, I would say: here are those who have no part in salvation . . . They listen but are as reeds shaken by the wind. Even the baptized scarcely do better; therefore I have not yet been able to give them the [Lord's] Supper. May the Lord have pity on me, may he look at my tears and my anguish! I desire only one thing, that is to be able to persevere until the end. Better to perish than dishonor the gospel. Therefore, do not forget me, people of God! Break, break my brothers, the barrier that stands in the way to Africa!

---

216 Senft, *Les missions,* 204. Senft adds in a note this explication to Nitschmann's allusion to the preceding failures: "One of the rare persons of Cape Town to make some slight efforts to carry the gospel to the Hottentots recounts the story this way: 'I have brought together several Hottentots; I have offered them tobacco and brandy; then I have spoken to them of the true God. Alas! when my provisions were exhausted, all turned their backs on me. I judge it to be impossible to redeem this people from their superstitions; it is said that they are born full of aversion to the gospel and all religion.'"

Seeing the helplessness of their missionary and the inextricable judicial difficulties that the Cape authorities had created for him, in 1743 the leaders of the community of Herrnhut authorized him to return. He left a small community of fifty Hottentots, of whom seven were baptized. They took leave of him with tears, making him promise to return. Despite several insistent attempts by the leaders of the Moravian mission, the Dutch government placed insurmountable obstacles to the return of Schmidt to Africa. The former missionary to the Hottentots continued to occupy subordinate positions in the Herrnhut community until his death in 1785.

Despite its extreme fragility, the small group of Hottentot Christians did not disperse. They continued to sing, cultivate the earth, teach their children what they knew, and read the Bible. A traveler passing through the region twenty-one years after Schmidt's departure recounted seeing a Hottentot woman go twice daily to a spring to kneel, read the Bible, and converse in solitude with Jesus Christ.

It was in 1793, fifty years after Schmidt's departure, that three Moravian missionaries returned to South Africa. Finding the Christian village of Gnadental that Schmidt had established, they preached the gospel in the shadow of the pear trees that he had planted. Among the listeners was Lena, one of the few survivors of the community that Schmidt had gathered. When the old woman understood the missionaries to say that Jesus was made man and had died on the cross for all she cried, "Yes, what the Brethren are saying is good. And, God be blessed, it is this which touched my heart!" She showed them her great treasure, a Dutch New Testament, protected by goatskins, that Schmidt had given to her for her baptism in 1742 when she was a young girl. She had learned to read from this book and declared that she had been reading it regularly since her youth. Having become senile and almost blind, she was thankful to her granddaughter for reading to her the biblical texts she loved so well, for only the word of God was capable of lifting her from spiritual torpor.

The small Christian community sprung to life again and grew rapidly. The missionaries were concerned with both the economic and spiritual development of the Hottentot population. Each family, therefore, received a tract of ground to cultivate a vegetable garden, and the villagers opened a cutlery, mill, butchery, and tannery. The locality of Gnadental soon experienced a prosperity that earned it both astonishment and renown all over South Africa. These development projects were exemplary at a time when the modern era of evangelical missions was just beginning, for the year of the Moravians' return to Gnadental coincided with that of the departure of William Carey for the Indies.

## MORAVIAN MISSION IN THE EIGHTEENTH CENTURY: TAKING STOCK

It is appropriate to pause to consider the other outreach efforts that witness to the missionary zeal of the Moravians in the course of the first century of their movement. Some of these efforts, however, were ephemeral, especially because of the high mortality rate of the missionaries. Others resulted in failure because of the negative reaction of the local populations, among whom no church could be established.

Three Brethren left for Russia in 1742 and planned to go as far as China. They were arrested upon their arrival in Saint Petersburg and remained in prison for five years before being allowed to return to Germany. Particularly tragic was the missionary effort between 1768 and 1788 on the island of Nicobar, near to Sumatra. Among a primitive population and living in untenable conditions, missionaries remained entirely cut off from the world for several years without anyone knowing if they were dead or alive. Twenty-three missionaries were sent successively. Among these, thirteen died on the island, and another succumbed in Tranquebar, India, where they had had to withdraw due to illness. Some returned to Europe with their health irreversibly destroyed. And all this without any visible result.

Here is an impressive but probably not exhaustive list of the places where long-lasting missionary efforts were established in the course of the eighteenth century:

1. Leporine (1738–1736)
2. Ceylon (1738–1741)
3. Algiers (1740)
4. Guinea (1737–1741 and 1867–1870)
5. Persia (1747–1750)Egypt (1752–1783)
6. The East Indies (Indonesia) (1759–1796)
7. Mongolia (1768)
8. Labrador (1771)

At the time of the centenary of Moravian missions in 1832, 209 Brethren were settled in for long-term involvement, working in seven mission fields: the West Indies, Jamaica, Surinam, among the Indians of North America, Labrador, Greenland, and South Africa.

Meticulous in their statistics, the Moravians had by then baptized 44, 757 people: 39,003 Creoles, 349 Indians, 2,604 Eskimos, and 2,801 South Africans.

In the period of 1732–1832, 1,199 Moravians (740 men and 459 women) had left their home country for the mission field.

In 1882, after 150 years of existence, the Moravian community had sent two thousand missionaries into the world. This represents one missionary for every ninety-two members, while in the same period other Protestant churches were averaging one missionary for every five thousand members.

The numbers above speak for themselves. In a time when Europeans in general, and Protestants in particular, showed an almost total indifference to those ignorant of the gospel, the Moravians sent out emissaries of Jesus Christ in all directions, toward all races, while surmounting difficult obstacles and fully conscious that their chances of survival were often slim. They had the certitude of the Lord's presence with them and that it was he who was sending them; and they continued to found churches despite failures and setbacks, believing that the gospel was intended for all the peoples of the earth. Defying the prejudices that led good Christians everywhere to despise the "savages," the Moravian witness constitutes a legacy of the church that will endure for all times.

An objective evaluation of the Moravians' work, however, brings to light some negative aspects that limited their effectiveness and increased their sufferings. These are due to a large extent to the inexperience of these precursors, who had scarcely any predecessors whose example they might have studied. This is why even the Moravians' shortcomings should be considered and pondered by those who follow them.

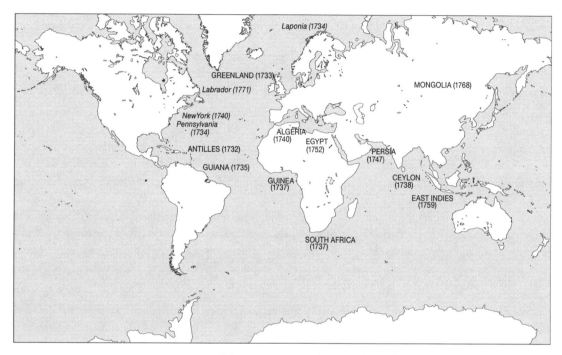

*Map 14: Missions of the Moravian Brethren, eighteenth century*

*First, the necessity of a missionary strategy.* The Moravians have shown that it was dangerous to allow themselves to be directed by circumstances or the apparent chances of fate. Indeed, God used the enthronement of Christian VI of Denmark to give a "missionary vision" to Zinzendorf, but the Antilles and Greenland were doubtlessly not the priority targets of this period. Before choosing a field of action, it would have been better if the Moravians had studied the number of inhabitants in a given country, its ports of access, its economic and political importance, its religious tradition, and its needs. In scattering their missionaries around the world, they no doubt wasted human resources.

*Second, the necessity of an organization for the work.* It is not wise policy to send missionaries far away, and then abandon them in their solitude. They need to be helped, sustained, and counseled. The Moravian missionaries had to find the means to sustain themselves in the field. Usually this meant that the one sent on alone was expected to work a separate job in addition to performing his ministry. This strategy was often very difficult to implement, as for example in the case of Dober in St. Thomas, who could not find clay for his pottery work. If there had been a team, one or two team members could have found employment in order to support all the rest.

But even selecting a few to provide subsistence for all the others often produces tensions and even serious conflicts. The example of the Moravians shows the necessity of a well-structured organization to provide support and maintain correspondence, so that expatriates will not suffer needlessly in their solitude.

The following quotation typifies Moravian attitudes towards mission. It relates a dialogue between Count Zinzendorf and Dr. Regnier, who wanted to go as a medical missionary to Surinam:

Zinzendorf: What is it your intention to do in Surinam?

Regnier: I will do my best to make my living and to bring sinners to Christ.

Zinzendorf: How do you intend to do this?

Regnier: I will simply have confidence in Christ to show me how to do it.

Zinzendorf: How long do you plan to stay there?

Regnier: I will stay there either until my death, or until the elders ask me to go to another missionary field.

This doctor's availability and confidence are impressive. All the same, the dialogue betrays an improvisational approach and a lack of rigor that, over time, compromised the continuity of the work.

*Third, the necessity of carefully training missionaries.* The Moravians were slow to become aware of the urgent need for missionary training. They discussed it in one of their synods, but at that time they had already sent numerous missionaries. Under the circumstances, they simply affirmed that it was sufficient for good missionaries "to love the Lamb" and principally preach "the love of the Lamb." This approach explains the failure of several of their attempts and even the considerable mortality rate among the missionaries. By the grace of God, the Moravians were fortunate in having sent out some first-rate personalities. Zinzendorf's device probably spoke for many of them: "I prefer one hundred fruitless attempts to none for the glory of God."

Whatever the shortcomings raised above, the epic of Moravian missions remains one of the most striking pages in the history of world evangelization. Since antiquity, the periods when a church was able to manifest such missionary dynamism have been rare. The Moravian story is rich in positive lessons and examples to inspire the church in all ages.

The Moravians were the first to envision mission, not as an individual or government-sponsored enterprise, but as a task for which the whole Christian community must feel responsible. Spiritual fruit, though sometimes gathered after long years of dedicated service and by men and women of high competence, is due above all to the prayers of the faithful. Since the revival of 1727 at Herrnhut and for more than one hundred years afterwards, a chain of uninterrupted prayer, seven days a week and twenty-four hours a day, carried aloft the missionary effort of the community. Even the debatable practice of drawing straws, to determine who would go, expressed the conviction that each member of the community should expect to be called and should be spiritually prepared.

The source of this missionary enthusiasm must not be looked for elsewhere than in an ardent love for the crucified Savior. Moravian piety could sometimes be a little surprising and certainly emotive—some would say mawkish. But this piety was nourished by the contemplation of the suffering of the Lamb who was sacrificed for the lost. This message touched Moravian hearts with such power that the faithful were truly dedicated, body and soul, to their Savior. In any event, there is more virility than mawkishness in the hardihood of these people. An anecdote impressively illustrates this spiritual state. August Gottlieb Spangenberg was in America when he learned that illness had tragically decimated the missionary teams at St. Thomas and St. Croix (see p. 266), and that some in the teams had immigrated to the American colonies. He wrote to Zinzendorf, "Since the community learned of the death of the witnesses in St. Thomas, all were enflamed with a desire to leave for the island, without fearing the danger that threatened them. If I had asked who was ready to go into this 'plague hole,' there would have been twenty to thirty Brethren and Sisters ready to leave immediately."

Their piety had its failings and exaggerations and, in some respects, seems hopelessly outmoded today. Nevertheless the exaltation of the suffering of Jesus and of his bloody sacrifice on the Cross produced among these men and women a sense of the need to make a gift of themselves, which remains exemplary. The Cross was not simply for them an orthodox doctrine, but an example of love to emulate. For them, the price to be paid for the evangelization of the whole world was only an extension of the price already paid by God the Creator in giving his beloved Son to save sinners.

The Moravians have been pioneers in many areas. History demonstrates that they had a considerable influence on the attitude of Christians regarding the evangelization of the world, and when Zinzendorf died in 1760 it was in an aura of general esteem. The extraordinary surge of evangelical missions in the nineteenth and twentieth centuries, which entirely changed the "spiritual geography" of the planet, is owed to an important extent to the Moravian community, a group that can be properly characterized as prophetic. For example, the missionary journal of the English Moravians, *Periodical Accounts*, had a strong influence on the young Baptist minister William Carey, considered the father of modern evangelical missions. Presenting some of the Moravian work discussed in this review to his highly skeptical colleagues at the time when he was pleading for the foundation of the Baptist Missionary Society in 1792, Carey declared to them: "You see what the Moravians have done. Can we not follow their example and, obeying our divine Master, venture to carry the gospel to the pagans?" Moreover, it was the teaching drawn from the Moravian missionary experience that permitted Carey to develop a veritable science of mission.

## CODA: AN EVALUATION OF PROTESTANT MISSION

Protestant missions were nonexistent in the sixteenth century. In the seventeenth century they were undertaken by individuals who were often marginal and highly criticized. If in the seventeenth century Protestant missions were handicapped by too great a dependence on European trading companies, Protestant missionaries of the eighteenth century were often in conflict with their colonial compatriots, administrators, and bureaucrats. The hostility that they encountered exempts them from any suspicion of complicity with the numerous abuses of the colonial period. Though

Protestant missions grew noticeably during the course of the eighteenth century, they still clearly remained in the shadow of the Catholic missions of the same period. In terms of the period studied in this work, the majority of the non-European population of Christianity was Catholic.

Protestant missions criticized Catholic missions for their superficiality, syncretistic tendencies, and tolerance for superstitious religiosity. Moreover, they denounced the use of violence practiced in some regions, particularly in Latin America. The Protestant approach to mission is marked by the theological radicalism of the Reformers who, rejecting a humanist point of view, considered human beings to be in their entirety corrupted by sin and incapable by nature of turning towards God. In this vision of humanity, there is no continuity between nature and grace, and, therefore, non-Christian religions cannot be considered as steps toward faith in the Christian God. In contrast, Catholic missionaries, especially the Jesuits, embraced the strategy of adapting their message to the local cultures. This was done at the risk of amalgamating religions, for which they were reproached even by some of their coreligionists. However, on the Protestant side, the eighteenth-century Pietist missionaries in the Indies also showed a great interest in the civilizations and religions of the local people among whom they worked. But this interest did not dampen either the Pietists' emphasis on the necessity of individual conversion or their suspicion of all mass movements to Christianity.

The radical and demanding requirement of individual conversion for acceptance as a Christian in part explains the low numbers of non-European Protestants during the three centuries following the Reformation. But in part only! During this long period, the absence of a missionary conscience in either Lutheran or Reformed Protestantism is, alas, an incontestable fact. The Moravians are the only true exception. Hence they are the precursors of the clear change in the understanding of mission that came about in the period beginning in the last decade of the eighteenth century. The great surge of Protestant missions in the nineteenth century would profoundly alter the history of Christianity, making it a world religion. The study of this period in mission history will be the subject of the second book.

BOOK II

# THE
# EVANGELIZATION
## OF THE WORLD

### A CONCISE HISTORY OF MISSION

### FROM 1792 TO 1945

JACQUES BLANDENIER

TRANSLATED BY MICHAEL PARKER

# Introduction to Book II

Book II of this history of missions invites the reader on a world tour over a period of a century and a half. It has more breadth than depth, and yet it constitutes only the visible part of the iceberg—and even a minute part at that. As the missiologist Lesslie Newbigin explains: "All of history is written by choosing from among the almost infinite amount of recorded or transmitted facts the miniscule portion among them that one believes important."

In the course of the first half of the twentieth century, numerous missionary stories and biographies were published in the French-speaking world. These were sources of firsthand information of great value, but many today are lost and cannot be replaced. A historical work as complete as possible is indispensable so that this heritage will not be lost forever.[1]

Book I of *The Evangelization of the World* deals with the history of mission from its origins through the eighteenth century. Until the sixteenth century, this history is part of a heritage that, for better or worse, Protestants have as much right to claim as their own as any other. For the period of the Reformation and for the two succeeding centuries, the work of Catholic missions were described as well as that of the then-embryonic Protestant missions. I would have wished to accord equal space to Catholic missions in this second volume, especially as they underwent much development in this period. Regrettably, however, both the complexity and the scope of the subject constrained me to set aside my personal preference in the interests of brevity. Readers interested in Catholic missions should consult more specialized studies.

The book is arranged geographically, being divided into four parts: Asia, the Pacific Islands, Africa, and Latin America. It is not restricted, however, to a country-by-country survey, although in general some parts from the history of each country

---

1    The last book of general Protestant missionary history written in French was published in 1929 by the Evangelical Missionary Society of Paris: *Petite histoire des missions chrétiennes par un laïque*. The translation from English to French that Vida published in 1989 of Ruth A. Tucker, *From Jerusalem to Irian Jaya: A Biographical History of Christian Missions* (Grand Rapids: Academie Books, 1983) presents a biographic history of Christian missions. This is a valuable and well-documented work, but it is limited to the Anglo-Saxon world and omits the missionary work in West Africa.

are given. In the introductory section, the births are noted of some of the principal missionary societies in the West to be encountered subsequently "on the field."

In the same way that notable theologians and ecclesiastical leaders are the "Fathers of the Church," so too are the great mission pioneers. Though it is fitting to recall their careers, there is little room to recount them beyond providing the broad outlines and pertinent details necessary to understand the decisive roles they played in the development of the church of Jesus Christ in the world. I have not hesitated to include some of the circumstances of their personal spiritual journeys and their family lives, and I have included extracts from their letters and intimate journals. It is through this personal dimension that the gospel to which they witnessed was incarnated. To leave this out would be, in effect, to betray the essence of mission, for the spread of Christianity cannot be understood simply by explaining the strategies of the major states, recounting the great missiological debates, or supplying statistics and lists of dates and places.

Readers might be astonished that no chapter deals with modern Europe as a mission field, especially since Protestant mission endeavors in Catholic and Orthodox nations are included in the narrative. This book, however, is limited to mission enterprises in the regions of the world that have not previously had contact with the gospel. Hence regions of the world that were already Christianized will not be discussed here, though their reevangelization is also of historical interest. Latin America is a partial exception to this rule for reasons that will be given in Section IV.

Finally, a technical detail: the names of some countries have changed over the years. I have adopted the convention of using the name that was in use at the time of the history being related.

# SECTION I

## THE BIRTH OF THE PRINCIPAL PROTESTANT SOCIETIES IN THE AGE OF MODERN MISSION

# CHAPTER 1

# Precursors and Founders

Two and a half centuries after the Reformation, Protestantism was only really established in Europe and among the immigrants of North America. The evangelization of non-Christian peoples was still not perceived to be necessary. During the seventeenth century, only a few happy exceptions can be cited, such as among the chaplains of the Dutch commercial companies. Among this group, Justus Heurnius (1587–ca. 1653), who arrived in Java in 1624, is considered to be the first Reformed missionary. He had been strongly encouraged by Gisbertus Voetius (1589–1676), a renowned Dutch theologian and precursor of Protestant missiologists. Among the Lutherans, the first known missionary is the German Peter Heyling (1607/8–ca. 1652), who left for Abyssinia in 1632 where he worked alone for a long time before dying as a martyr in Egypt. He had no successor. Another Lutheran precursor is Justinian von Weltz (1621–1668), a wealthy Austrian aristocrat with an original mind. His appeals to his German coreligionists, however, received no response. Finally, he left alone for Dutch Guiana (present-day Suriname) where he disappeared without leaving a trace in 1666.

As for Britain, the Puritan John Eliot, emigrant to New England in 1631, struggled admirably as a missionary among the Algonquians. His entire life's work was destroyed during King Phillip's War, a conflict between the colonists and Indians. It is in part thanks to the interest aroused by his newsletters that the oldest missionary society of Protestantism came to be in 1649, the period of Cromwell's commonwealth. Originally organized with the intention of evangelizing the Indians of New England, in 1701 the society took the name Society for the Propagation of the Gospel in Foreign Parts. In later years it was principally supported by the High Church party of the Anglican Church and exists still today under the name Society for the Propagation of the Gospel (SPG).

Protestant Europe in the seventeenth century had conserved the heritage of the Reformers in a strict but nearly moribund orthodoxy. Wars of religion, persecutions, and theological polemics had stifled the spiritual momentum of the preceding century. Moreover, the results of Protestant missionary efforts in these years were meager. The missionaries noted above, and others still less well known, were more precursors than pioneers, for they were not able to establish permanent missionary bases from which the work could be carried on by successors.

The Pietist revival, which appeared in the second half of the seventeenth century, was a new source of spiritual life. One consequence of the revival was the emergence of a missionary consciousness among the churches. From then on, a concern for the evangelization of the world was less dependent on a few isolated personalities. The Danish-Hallo Mission in Tranquebar, founded a little after the year 1700, was marked by the presence of such eminent figures as Bartholomäus Ziegenbalg and Christian Friedrich Schwartz, but the scope of its activities quickly went beyond the initiative of a few and became a community-based venture. However, even in this case, the effort was short lived and only pursued due to a revival. Pietism bore only one long-lived missionary effort in the eighteenth century, the luminous example of the Moravians, who would be an inspiration for nineteenth-century Protestant missionaries.

## THE BIRTH OF "SOCIETIES" IN THE WAKE OF REVIVAL

In the eighteenth century, the Wesleyan revival in England inspired many Christians to a renewed commitment, which crossed all denominational boundaries. At this time evangelism, defense of good morals, philanthropy, and social and political measures were proposed to combat the injustices and mitigate the tragedies of nascent industrialization or slavery. While institutional churches seemed immobilized by internal and external divisions, Christians from a variety of churches united to establish reform societies, such as the Society for the Abolition of the Slave Trade in 1787, in an attempt to find effective outlets for their heightened desire for activism.

William Wilberforce (1759–1833) was involved in the formation of many of these efforts. An eminent member of the British Parliament known for his eloquence, he had a decisive spiritual experience at the age of twenty-seven and became a disciple and friend of John Wesley (1703–1791). It was to him that Wesley wrote his last letter before dying, encouraging him in his struggle against slavery. Wilberforce fought with undaunted determination in the House of Commons until the law abolishing the slave trade was adopted in 1807, which made him a national hero. Many in the expanding British middle class followed his leadership. Some of the leaders who resided together in the London suburb of Clapham founded the Evangelical Movement,[2] which sponsored an astonishing number of societies that were dedicated to social reform as well as evangelism.

These societies became the instruments of choice for the propagation of the gospel throughout the world. Those dedicated to the translation, printing, and distribution of the Bible played a strategic role that aided all the other organizations. The most important among them was the British and Foreign Bible Society, founded in 1804, which soon sought to make its activities worldwide.[3] The societies that were dedicated to mission in the nonevangelized regions of the world are those of interest

---

2    Hence their adversaries dubbed them the Clapham Sect.
3    See the following: Ype Schaaf, *L'histoire et le role de la Bible en Afrique*, 2nd ed. (Lavigny: Les Groupes Missionnaires, 2000).

to us here. The first of these was the Baptist Missionary Society, formed in 1792. It came about due to the vision and tenacity of the English Baptist minister William Carey, who played a key role in reviving the missionary consciousness of Protestantism.

## FOUNDATION OF THE LONDON MISSIONARY SOCIETY

In the *Evangelical Magazine*, a periodical of the Evangelical Movement, Carey published letters that dramatically depicted the immense spiritual needs of the Indies (present-day India, Pakistan, Bangladesh, and Sri Lanka) and produced a strong current of intercessory prayer for mission. A campaign was launched to promote a great missionary society that could appeal across Protestant denominational lines. The goal of the new society would be to unite all the evangelical forces in the country to send out as many as twenty to thirty missionaries every year.

Many servants of the Lord responded to this appeal and came together for the first time at the end of 1794. In the early autumn of 1795, three years after the founding of the Baptist Missionary Society, several hundred ministers arrived in London at the invitation of the new organization, all animated by the spirit of revival. Afterwards these days were spoken of as a new Pentecost, so strong had been the conviction of the participants that, like the first Christians, they had heard an appeal inspired by the Holy Spirit to take the gospel to the ends of the earth. They decided to form a new organization, the London Missionary Society (LMS), whose first General Assembly took place on September 22, 1795. A committee of twenty-five members was formed to give direction to the work. The members agreed to the principle of recruiting only missionaries capable of preaching and teaching the gospel without imposing on converts either the theology or the church structure of their own denominations. In a few years, the society had sent out hundreds of missionaries to many different latitudes. Among their number were some of the great pioneers of mission who left a profound mark on the Christian history of three continents: Robert Moffat, David Livingstone, Robert Morrison, and John Williams, among others. The first LMS missionaries sent were a group of about thirty, who left on the same ship in 1797 for Tahiti and other Pacific islands.[4]

Other societies with the same apostolic objective were soon founded in the British Isles, the European continent, and North America. We will encounter many of them on the mission field in the chapters that follow. Below are the principal missionary societies formed in the last years of the eighteenth century and the first half of the nineteenth century:

1. 1792: Baptist Missionary Society
2. 1795: London Missionary Society
3. 1797: Dutch Society of Missions among the Pagans
4. 1799: Church Missionary Society for Africa and the East
5. 1810: American Board of Commissioners for Foreign Missions
6. 1813: Wesleyan Methodist Missionary Society

---

4    For the origins of the LMS, see Richard Lovette, *The History of the London Missionary Society, 1795–1895*, vol. 1 and 2 (London: Henri Trowede, 1899).

7. 1814: American Baptist Missionary Union (later the American Baptist Foreign Mission Society)
8. 1815: Basel Evangelical Missionary Society (later the Basel Mission)
9. 1821: Danish Missionary Society
10. 1822: Evangelical Missions Society of Paris (the Paris Mission)
11. 1824: Berlin Missionary Society
12. 1825: Church of Scotland, Board
13. 1826: Evangelical Missions Society of Lausanne (later the Mission Roman, and then the Swiss Mission in South Africa)
14. 1833: Swedish Missionary Society
15. 1835: Evangelical Lutheran Mission Society of Leipzig
16. 1836: North German Mission (succeeded the Danish-Hallo Mission that emerged from the Pietist movement of Halle)

In the second half of the nineteenth century, many other missionary societies appeared, often being international and interdenominational in character. One of the first and best known was the China Inland Mission, founded by Hudson Taylor in 1865. Some great missionary societies came to be formed at the end of the nineteenth century and the beginning of the twentieth century. The genesis of the most important of these organizations will be described in the following chapter.

# CHAPTER 2

# The Missionary Societies of the "Second Wave"

The first Protestant missionary societies of the modern era grew steadily over the course of the nineteenth century. In the last decades of the century, however, new mission organizations were founded that had innovative characteristics. Their appearance marked the "second wave" of evangelical missions.[5] Each organization had its own sensitivities and objectives, but certain characteristics are generally found among most of them, giving them a certain family resemblance.

In the area of theology, they were generally conservative and evangelical. In this they were scarcely different from the first societies formed in the era of Protestant mission, though of course these early societies continued to evolve in their theology and missiology. It was these latter developments that explain why the new mission organizations tended to keep their distance from the world missionary conferences of the International Council of Missions.[6] Moreover, the young missionaries of the "second wave," animated by an ardent zeal and a strong sense of urgency about the evangelization of the world, often had the impression, whether rightly or wrongly, that the older societies had lost their initial momentum. At the very least, they seemed to be more absorbed in the work of the churches that they had founded than in the ongoing task of proclaiming the gospel to those who had not yet heard it.

In reading the history of the pioneers of the first part of the nineteenth century, one is stunned by the number of deaths registered in the course of these heroic times. With time and experience, these missions became more cautious. On the other hand, missionary infrastructures were gradually put in place on the mission fields, which eased the missionaries' entry into countries and helped to spare many lives as well. The stories of the first missionaries of the "second wave" are often as dramatic as those of the first pioneers, though they occurred three-quarters of a century later. Imprudent and inexperienced? Perhaps, but they also had an inflexible will to reach, at whatever cost, the most inaccessible regions of the globe, those

---

5    We are noting here only the circumstances of their birth in their countries of origin without describing their development in their various fields of action. A number of the societies will appear in subsequent pages with regard to their work in Africa, Asia, and Latin America.

6    For the evolution of the missionary thought reflected by these conferences, see chapter 32.

where no one had yet dared to venture. By their courage and dedication, the pioneers of the "second wave" were worthy successors to the pioneers of the first half of the nineteenth century.

One characteristic marked several of the "new missions" following the example of Hudson Taylor, their forerunner and model, they strove to penetrate deeply into the interior of the continents. Several of them even incorporated the word "interior" in their titles. In contrast, those who had preceded them generally worked along coastal regions. Others among the new missions had specific objectives, such as medical work among lepers or the translation of the Bible into languages not yet written.[7]

The new missions defined themselves by evangelical confessions of faith rather than loyalty to a particular denomination. Almost all of them originated from English-speaking countries, though they quickly acquired an international dimension. In this chapter we will deal principally with those that were represented by an office or a committee in French-speaking Europe.[8] Otherwise the chapter will be limited to the more important among them, those whose fields of activity covered several countries, sometimes even several continents.

It is well to reiterate that the majority of these mission organizations strictly applied the principle of faith missions—at least in the beginning. Hudson Taylor's China Inland Mission, begun in 1865, was the precursor of this approach.[9] Faith mission organizations did not make a financial appeal; rather, they developed without assured revenues and did not contract any debts. The organizations were not employers in the sense of assuming responsibility for furnishing a regular and fixed salary to those they sent abroad. Potential missionaries could not leave for the mission field until they had found supporters ready to assure their livelihood—something that was an authenticating sign of their vocation. There were about forty missionary organizations that can be considered to have been faith missions. They generally emphasized direct evangelization but still engaged in medical work, education, and agricultural development.

## THE NORTH AFRICA MISSION

The North Africa Mission was established in 1881 at the initiative of three British Christians: H. Grattan Guinness, Edward Glenny, and George Pearse.

H. Grattan Guinness, born in Ireland in 1835, was a doctor in theology, renowned among British evangelicals, and a fervent supporter of mission. He founded the East London Training Institute, which trained hundreds of missionaries. Upon a visit to Algeria in 1879, he acquired the conviction that God was calling him to undertake evangelical work in that country, heretofore ignored by Protestant missions.

---

7   Although it is beyond the chronological limits of this work, we will note some missions that were more specialized still, as, for example, radio evangelism or aviation missions.

8   As for missions born during the same period in French-speaking Europe, such as the Evangelical Mission in Laos, the Philafrican Mission in Angola, or the Biblical Mission in Ivory Coast, they will be presented in the chapters dealing with the countries where they pursued their activities.

9   Though the China Inland Mission was a model for many mission organizations, its existence can only be touched on here. Its history is presented more fully in Book II: Chapter 6.

Edward Glenny, a layperson who often traveled for reasons of business, seized all occasions to preach the gospel in the countries through which he passed. He was influenced by the spirituality of one of the leading figures of the Plymouth Brethren, the philanthropist George Müller of Bristol. His business affairs led him to be interested in Algeria, and he joined a small team that in 1881 established the first mission station in Kabylie. After several years, he returned to London to become the secretary of the North Africa Mission, then in full bloom.

George Pearse had been one of the founding members of the Chinese Evangelization Society that sent Hudson Taylor to China in 1850. Later he was involved in the distribution of the Bible among French soldiers. It was this work that in 1876 took him to Algeria where French troops were quartered. Struck by the spiritual needs of the Berber people, he and his wife decided to serve God in Kabylie. At the time he was sixty-five years old. In 1881 he returned to Britain to found with Guinness and Glenny the "Mission among the Kabyles." In 1888 they changed the name to the North Africa Mission (NAM).

The work progressed quickly and, after nineteen years, it had 115 missionaries and seventeen centers in five countries: Algeria, Morocco, Tunisia, Libya, and Egypt. Medical work, crafts, and industrial activities went together with evangelization. Later, the mission experienced decline, recovery, and decline again. By 1913 there were only about sixty-three missionaries left, but by 1930 its numbers increased to about a hundred. The Second World War, however, intervened to retard its activities, and in 1947 there were a little more than sixty missionaries. During a century of activity, NAM sowed more than it reaped. The secretary of the American branch of NAM wrote a history of the mission whose title testifies more to the organization's faith than to its actual record of accomplishment: *Not in Vain*.[10]

## SERVING IN MISSION (SIM)

The organization was formed in 1982 from several existing mission organizations that were then about a hundred years old. They occupied regions of the world far from one another, but they had a common spirit and sought similar aims. The most important of these organizations was the Sudan Interior Mission (SIM, an acronym preserved when the society renamed itself), whose principal accomplishments will be presented in Chapters 16 and 19.

In 1893 two young Americans disembarked at Lagos, Nigeria, to meet their friend Walter Gowans. Gowans was the first to be convinced that it was his duty to go into the interior of the African continent to evangelize the sub-Saharan regions—then generally known as the Sudan. The 60 million people of this region had not yet had any contact with Christianity. The three friends were not able to persuade the other missions already present in Nigeria to extend their work to these reputedly difficult regions. In fact, everyone discouraged them, predicting their certain and

---

10  Francis Steele, *Not in Vain: The Story of North Africa Mission* (Pasadena, CA: William Carey Library, 1981).

swift deaths.[11] And in the event, less than one year later, Gowans was captured by a local chief and died of untreated dysentery; his colleague Thomas Kent succumbed to malaria; and the third was Rowland Bingham (1872–1942), an Englishmen from Canada, who had to return home for reasons of health. Here is his anguished reaction to the losses on the field:

> My faith has been shaken to its foundations . . . Why is it that people desirous to obey the commandments of the Lord and to carry his gospel to the millions of people in darkness have been cut down at the beginning of their careers? Such questions agitate me . . . Was the Bible simply a step in the evolution of human thought, stuffed with prejudice, or was it a divine revelation? A struggle stirred within me for months before I found myself on firm rock.[12]

In 1900 after having overcome this crisis and been married, Bingham tried again to enter the Sudan, but this resulted in as rapid a repatriation as his first attempt. Also, the two young people who accompanied him abandoned the work. But after a time of terrible discouragement, "the darkest period in all my existence," Bingham refused to admit defeat. His health had been too greatly damaged for him to engage in another African journey, so he began the Sudan Interior Mission. He formed a new team of four men, who left in 1901. They established a base that lay eight hundred kilometers from the site that would eventually be considered the birthplace of SIM in Africa. But from the beginning the enterprise experienced extreme difficulties. After two years only one man remained at Patigi, a mission station upstream on the Niger River; and one of his colleagues had died and the other two had had to return, laid low by disease. After a dozen years and despite many sacrifices, there were only a few converts. Nevertheless, new stations were gradually established. The mission was particularly active in an area where there were many lepers, most of whom were Muslims. After having evangelized several countries bordering Nigeria, in 1928 SIM entered Ethiopia.

Four other mission organizations would join together to form the modern SIM. In 1893 the Englishmen Benjamin Davidson, accompanied by three colleagues, began work in Ceylon (present-day Sri Lanka) among the Buddhist Cinghalais and Hindu Tamils. Adopting the name of Ceylon and India General Mission, the organization's work soon extended to the south of India and then to the Philippines. It was also in 1893 that the Australians Charles Reeves and M. E. Gavin undertook the evangelization of Poona (or Pune). This city of Maharasthra, India, lying two hundred kilometers southeast of Bombay (present-day Mumbai), is one of the principal centers of Jainism, a religion that sprang from Buddhism. Reeves and Gain also evangelized the neighboring rural areas. They called their organization the Poona and Indian Village Mission. In 1894 the South Africa General Mission was founded to continue the work that had begun five years earlier in the Cape at the initiative of several British and

---

11 The director of a Methodist mission warned them in these terms: "Young people, you will never see the Sudan, nor your children either, your grandchildren, perhaps."

12 Tucker, *From Jerusalem*, 373.

South African Christians. In 1907 the New Zealander George Allan began a ministry among the Quechua Indians of Bolivia. In the following years, he received the aid of several colleagues, and their work rapidly expanded. Both the Evangelical Mission of the Andes and the Evangelical Christian Union of Bolivia were the fruit of these efforts.

The promoters of these missions belonged to different denominations: Presbyterian, Congregational, Anglican, and Baptist. The works that they founded had an international and interdenominational character long before they united to form a single organization.

## THE CHURCH AND MISSIONARY ALLIANCE

Albert Simpson (1844–1919), founder of the Church and Missionary Alliance (CMA),

*Albert Simpson (1844–1919), founder of the Christian and Missionary Alliance.*

was a Canadian Presbyterian minister, well known for his gifts as a preacher. Despite his undeniable success, he passed through a profound spiritual crisis when he recognized that conformity to ecclesiastical traditions was limiting his ministry. He experienced a vision that to him was like Pentecost, which led him to a total consecration of his life to the world mission of the church. He planned to be a missionary to China, but the opposition of his wife, a mother of six children, prevented him from fulfilling the call that he believed he had discerned in his vision. Nevertheless, he left his New York parish in 1879 and began to address vast assemblies of listeners at missionary conferences. From these gatherings, small groups formed of those who had become responsive to the missionary cause and who shared Simpson's belief in the urgent need to evangelize non-Christian people—an urgency based above all on the expectation of Christ's imminent return.

He founded the Missionary Alliance in 1887, which became the Christian and Missionary Alliance (CMA) in 1897. Contrary to the other organizations of the same type, it did not concentrate on a particular region of the world but, rather, sent missionaries to several continents. After five years, it already had nearly 150 missionaries in fifteen countries.

The first to leave in 1884, even before the official birth of the Alliance, were five young people who entered the Congo. The others went a little later to the Sudan. Due to the climate, and no doubt also because of a lack of experience and not taking the necessary precautions, there were casualities among them. In the same way, members of the CMA in China suffered much in the Boxer Rebellion in 1900 when thirty-five people, including children, were put to death.

At the beginning of the work, Simpson created the Missionary Training Institute in New York City (now Nyack College), and soon several others followed the same model in various regions of the United States and Canada. Simpson had a considerable influence on numerous American evangelicals, and the founders of several other missions studied in the institute that he had started. He was a man of exceptional caliber, but it is also true that he lacked moderation. While he enjoyed spiritual experiences of great intensity, he also knew times of profound discouragement and even depression. When he died in 1919, CMA missionaries were working in twenty-four different languages. By 1940, 110 language or dialect groups had been reached. Following the Second World War, the mission once again experienced rapid growth. In 1945 it had 340 missionaries, and in 1949 it reached 590.

# THE AFRICA INLAND MISSION

*Peter Scott (1867–1896),*
*founder of the*
*Africa Inland Mission.*

Peter Scott (1867–1896), the founder of the Africa Inland Mission (AIM), was born in Scotland and at an early age immigrated with his family to the United States. He had intended to pursue a career as an opera singer when the conviction of a missionary vocation placed before him a difficult choice, one that would determine his entire future. He decided to obey the call of God and enrolled at the Missionary Training Institute directed by Simpson. He went as a CMA missionary in November 1890 to West Africa. His brother John soon joined him but died after several months. Scott left Africa a shaken man. It was in England, reading the text on the tomb of David Livingstone in Westminster Abbey, that he reconsecrated his life to the evangelization of Africa.

Upon his return to the United States, he developed with several friends, including C. E. Hurlburt, the strategy of a new mission organization whose primary objective would be to penetrate into the most inaccessible regions of the African continent—the new organization was the Africa Inland Mission (AIM). Scott disembarked at Zanzibar in August 1895 with a seven-member team that included his sister Margaret. The first station was established in Kenya, and then Scott traveled farther into the interior of the land to locate favorable places for other stations. After a year, he wrote an enthusiastic report. Four stations had been opened, houses were constructed, educational and medical programs were begun, and several missionaries had made good progress in learning the language. In the course of this first year, other volunteers filled out the team, which included one of Scott's sisters and some of his other relatives.

But the pioneer was not spared for the task. During this first year, he traveled four thousand kilometers on foot in a trying climate. Less than two months after drafting his report, he was brought down by malaria and died, having served for only fourteen months in Africa. Several other members of the team died a little later, and others returned to America. In 1899 there was only one missionary left on the field, William Gangert.

After a promising beginning, the AIM seemed about to collapse. Soon two new recruits arrived as reinforcements, and then in 1901 C. E. Hurlburt decided to reside in Africa with his family in order to better supervise the work.[13] One of the founders of the mission and now its director, his presence gave AIM a new impetus. In 1909 the mission was extended to Tanganyika, and due to rather peculiar circumstances, a little later it also entered the northeast section of the Congo. When former U.S. President Theodore Roosevelt was planning a safari in East Africa, he sought out Hurlburt for his counsel. Roosevelt was impressed by the achievements of the mission, and some years later he volunteered to intervene with the Belgian government to urge it to lift its opposition to the placement of AIM missionaries in the Congo.

Hurlburt was the first to begin schools for the children of missionaries in Africa, an idea that subsequently was further developed and became especially important for English-speaking missions. In 1913 he helped to sponsor a conference whose aim was to reorganize all the Protestant missions in East Africa in order to obtain better cooperation for the sake of their common goals. But this had little impact.

The French-speaking branch of AIM developed its own name, which preserved the society's acronym: *Association Internationale Missionaire*.

## THE SUDAN UNITED MISSION

This mission, known today as Vision Africa, was founded by Karl Kumm (1874–1930). An explorer, pioneer, and mission founder, he was generally known as the "the last of the Livingstones." Born in a well-to-do Lutheran family in Hanover, in northern Germany, he married a British woman and became a British subject. He discerned his missionary vocation upon attending a conference where he heard Edward Glenny, the director of the North Africa Mission (NAM). Kumm interrupted his studies in the natural sciences to pursue the two-year program of the East London Training Institute, directed by H. Grattan Guinness, another worker associated with the NAM.

In 1895 Kumm was sent by the NAM to Aswan in Upper Egypt, and married Lucy Guinness, the daughter of the NAM's director. The couple dedicated themselves to evangelization, education, and medical work among the Nubian population. Karl and Lucy very quickly formed the conviction that they must extend their work to the Sudan, the largest region of nonevangelized Africa, with 50–100 million habitants speaking more than a hundred different languages or dialects.

This project led Kumm to leave Egypt and the NAM organization. Returning to Germany in 1903 to find support for his new vision, he founded the Sudan Pioneer Mission (SPM) in Wiesbaden. The primary objective of the new organization was to reinforce the effort then being pursued in the Nile valley without becoming engaged

---

13    He was following the proposal, propounded by Hudson Taylor, that the directors of a mission should be in the place of its work.

in new regions.[14] For his exploration project, Kumm sought the support of the British branch of the mission established at the same time.

Karl and Lucy Kumm wanted to interest others in the mission to evangelize the Sudan. Not having the necessary means, Kumm proposed to send their missionaries under the auspices of the British SPM. The mission changed its name in 1904, becoming the Sudan United Mission (SUM). Several hundred ministers of the free churches of England, Scotland, and Ireland signed the following declaration: "We, the members and delegates of the free churches united in conference, desire to engage ourselves together in a United Mission for the peoples of the Sudan, where the name of Christ has never been proclaimed."[15] An American and then a Scandinavian branch of the SUM was created, and very soon their missionaries opened stations in northern Nigeria. In the United States, Kumm encountered Rowland Bingham, the founder of the Sudan Interior Mission. Sharing the same vision, they came to collaborate as far as possible in their mission activities, working in neighboring fields.

Kumm had hoped to travel up the Nile as far as Aswan and then set out for the Niger. The Anglo-Egyptian authorities, however, refused to authorize this undertaking for fear of a hostile reaction from the Muslim chiefs. Kumm, therefore, prepared for the same voyage but reversed his direction: now he planned to travel from the Niger to the Nile.

It was not until 1909 that Kumm was able to undertake this expedition, with a party of nearly seventy that included team members and African porters. In going up the Niger and then its tributary the Benue River, they visited SUM stations that were being established in northern Nigeria. Next, they continued on land, traveling through German-controlled Cameroon and French-controlled Chad where floods, fevers, and tribal hostility rendered the journey very dangerous. In exploring these unknown regions, Kumm wanted to evaluate the advance of Islam into Central Africa and to identify the regions that were still animistic. Among the latter he hoped it would be possible to establish missionary posts to check Muslim progress.

The convoy crossed the border into Anglo-Egyptian Sudan, traversing regions where no white person had ever gone. They finally reached the White Nile and found some Anglican mission stations established by CMS. A route north of the equator between West and East Africa, the dream of many pioneer missionaries, had finally been realized. The explorers reached Khartoum, the capital of Sudan, ten months after having set out from Nigeria. Despite the obstacles and dangers in unknown territory, they had only a single death to lament, a notable contrast to the missionary explorations of the nineteenth century.

Upon his return, Kumm profited from the popular acclaim that followed his expedition by writing a book, *From Haussaland to Egypt* (1910). His intention was to create public sentiment for mission that would reverse governmental policies, for the

---

14   Subsequently, the Sudan Pioneer Mission continued to grow and arouse the interest of German-speaking Christians for the mission in Egypt. A Swiss committee was also formed, which later became independent of Germany due to political and military circumstances, and took the name of Schweizerische Evangelische Nilland Mission.

15   Cited in P. J. Spartalis, *Karl Kumm: Last of the Livingstones* (Afem-Mission script, 1994), 38.

nations of the West had adopted unfavorable policies toward Christian missions in Muslim countries. At the same time he addressed the World Missionary Conference at Edinburgh in 1910, making a profound impression. In seven minutes, which each delegate was allowed, he named about thirty animistic tribes and recounted how they were refugees in the mountainous zones, resisting the advance of Islam. He concluded his address with these words: "It would be an eternal shame if our generation left these tribes to be conquered by Islam."

During the following years, Kumm traveled much to plead the cause of the Sudan, from South Africa to Australia and New Zealand. Everywhere national committees of the SUM sprung up, and the results of their appeals to evangelize the regions on the frontiers of Islam surpassed his expectations. The high degree of independence possessed by the national committees permitted them to capitalize on the clear dynamism of the movement to send missionaries to the diverse regions of the Sudan.

The growth of the SUM suddenly halted with the advent of the First World War, and the effects of the war were felt as far away as Africa, including the region of the Sudan where the warring nations had established colonies. Before the beginning of hostilities, however, the chain of stations from the Niger to the Nile had almost been completed. This was due to the contribution of the numerous national committees, which had been at work for only ten years.

Karl Kumm visited Nigeria one last time in 1923; then, weakened with age, he retired to California where he died in 1930.

## THE WORLDWIDE EVANGELIZATION CRUSADE

Charles T. Studd (1860–1931) was one of the "Cambridge Seven," a group of students well known in the sports world and in British high society. Possessed of a living faith due to the ministry of D. L. Moody, Studd responded to an appeal made by Hudson Taylor and embarked for China in 1885 (see p. 364). After ten years of ministry, Studd returned gravely ill.

Popular for being one of the best cricket players in the British Isles, he held innumerable student conferences both in Britain and the United States. His father had originally made his fortune in India, and it was there that he worked as a minister among the British settlers from 1900 to 1906. His ministry, however, was once again interrupted by illness.

In Liverpool in 1908 he was struck by the humor of a poster announcing a conference by the founder of the SUM, Karl Kumm: "Cannibals seek missionaries." He at-

*Charles T. Studd (1860–1931), missionary in China, India, and finally the Congo where he founded the Worldwide Evangelization Crusade.*

tended the conference, and it altered the course of his life. Despite the opinion of the doctors and the impossibility of his wife surviving due to her health, he left for Khartoum. After several exploratory expeditions in southern Sudan, he undertook a journey with Alfred Buxton. Studd was then fifty-two years old, and Buxton only twenty. They set out together on a march of 1,400 kilometers that was supposed to lead to the northeast border of the Belgian Congo. It was there in 1913 that he established the first bases of a new mission whose name gave expression to his expansive vision: Worldwide Evangelization Crusade. He wrote:

> The committee under whose orders I serve is agreeably small, but it is an extremely rich committee, extremely generous, and it sits permanently. It is the Committee of the Father, Son, and Holy Spirit. We are supported by a multimillionaire, by far the richest person in the world. I have had a conversation with him. He has freely given me an entire checkbook and has insisted that I place all on his account. He has assured me that it is the firm that clothes the lilies of the field, watches over the birds of the air, and counts the hairs of children."[16]

The text reveals a person endowed with an audacious faith, expressing itself in an original fashion, often with an exaggeration that would shock the British Christian public. And he was also an individualist in claiming a direct dependence on the Holy Spirit.

He returned to Britain to organize a mission headquarters and a committee to oversee it, of which his wife was the mainspring. He also recruited eight candidates before leaving in 1916. Despite declining health, he lived another fifteen years without ever returning to his country, and he only saw his wife for fifteen days when she came to visit him in 1928, one year before his death.

In 1921 the relations between part of the missionary team and the mission committee were strained. After a dozen years, only thirty-five of the eighty-eight new missionaries in the Congo agreed to remain under Studd's direction. Since his youth, Studd had been known as a "go-getter," but with age and the toughness that resulted from fighting many battles, his demanding leadership became difficult for his subordinates to bear. Disappointed by the defection of numerous African converts, he became excessively severe in his preaching. Norman Grubb, his son-in-law and successor, wrote: "What shocked me the most was his attitude vis-à-vis the African Christians." He reproached them often and brutally for being lazy, yet much of what he said was really intended for his fellow missionaries, even the members of his family. He himself, old and suffering, was content to sleep four hours a night and eat while working. He found it intolerable that others would not adopt the same rhythm of life. His teaching on absolute sanctification earned him the criticism that he was preaching salvation by works, and his financial principles rendered the missionaries' material life precariousness.

After the death of Studd's wife, his relations with the mission committee worsened. His son-in-law tried to lessen the shock of his virulent letters by numerous voyages back to Britain. The rupture came a little before Studd's death in 1931. A

---

16  N. Grubb, *Charles Studd: Champion de Dieu*, 5th ed. (La Bégude-de-Mazenc: Croisade du Livre Chrétien, 1977), 134.

number of his subordinates left him and, together with the committee, founded the Unevangelized Fields Mission (UFM). Eighteen missionaries, who had left for the Amazon under the auspices of the WEC, went over to the UFM.

Upon Studd's death, Grubb took over the direction of the WEC. Due to his commitment and competence though difficult times the mission experienced a remarkable resurgence. By 1934 it was occupying new fields in Colombia, Central Asia (notably in Tibet), Spanish Guinea, and the Ivory Coast. For his excellent leadership, Grubb should be considered as the refounder of the WEC. Inspired by Hudson Taylor, he and his wife were entirely confident that God would meet their growing financial needs and asked the Lord each year for more missionaries: first for ten, then fifteen, then twenty-five, and finally fifty new candidates.

Grubb was his father-in-law's biographer. Although he had suffered from Studd's difficult character and excesses, he was attached to the honor of his memory and wanted to underscore the remarkable qualities of this indefatigable pioneer whose love and entire dedication to the cause of world evangelization could leave no one indifferent. The biography enjoyed an immense success, was republished many times, and was translated into a dozen languages. One must deplore, however, that Grubb passed over in silence the less attractive aspects of Studd's leadership, the painful conflicts and the ruptures that his demanding personality caused.[17]

## THE EVANGELICAL MISSION AGAINST LEPROSY

The Mission to Lepers (later The Leprosy Mission) was founded in 1874 by Wellesley Bailey.[18] This young Irishman was converted on a ship carrying him to Australia where he dreamed of making his fortune. That was in 1866, and he was then twenty years old. Three years later, his illusions dispelled, he came to find his brother stationed with the British army in the Punjab. While there he offered his services as a teacher to the American Presbyterian Mission in Ambala and very quickly became disturbed by the situation of a large number of lepers, rejected by society and without hope. On returning to Ireland, he made his burden known, and a small group promised to give him material and spiritual support in his effort to bring aid to the sick. And so was born The Leprosy Mission, which worked first in the northwest of India, and then, between 1893 and 1913, in the whole of the Indian subcontinent as well as the Far East: Burma, Thailand, China, Japan, and Korea.

The purpose of The Leprosy Mission was to offer specialized services to other Protestant missions in the treatment to be given to the leprous and, wherever it was necessary, to establish its own hospitals. At the beginning of the twentieth century, national committees were formed in various countries. This was the case in Switzerland in 1905 when Hanna Meyer, a teacher in Zurich, took the initiative to form a support group for four former missionaries. After the Second World War, national committees were also formed in France and Belgium.

---

17   The biography of Norman Grubb, written by Steward Dinnen, *Faith on Fire*, is by contrast remarkably objective (Fearn, Scotland: Christian Focus Publications, 1997).

18   In English-speaking countries, the Mission to Lepers was later called Leprosy Mission International.

The objectives of The Leprosy Mission as formulated in its founding documents were: "To provide, in the name of Jesus Christ, for the physical, psychiatric, social, and spiritual needs of disadvantaged leprous persons and communities; to work with them to give them human dignity and to eradicate leprosy."

# THE WYCLIFFE BIBLE TRANSLATORS

*William Cameron Townsend (1896–1982), founder of the Wycliffe Bible Translators.*

The Wycliffe Bible Translators and the Summer Institute of Linguistics (SIL) were established by Cameron Townsend (1896–1982). At the age of twenty-one he went to Guatemala under the auspices of the Los Angeles Bible House to sell Spanish Bibles. It was not long before this young American recognized that his work was in vain, for the rural population of the Cakchiquel Indians could neither read nor understand Spanish. He began to study their language and to fix it in writing, though he had no training in linguistics. After ten years of effort, he completed the translation of the New Testament in 1928.

Townsend's vocation was not to plant churches but to translate the Bible into the languages of the Central American Indian groups who, up to that point, had no access to the word of God. He came to the conclusion that the only method that would lead to success was to immerse himself in a village population and share its life in order to capture the sounds of the language, create an alphabet, and begin a Bible translation.

In 1934 he returned to the United States and opened a school of linguistics, which he called "Camp Wycliffe," on an abandoned Arkansas farm where he proposed to initiate students into the work of Bible translation. In the first year he had only two students, and in the second year five. At the conclusion of the two-year program, he went with them to work in Mexico.

Townsend dedicated himself to his school of linguistics to which he gave the name *Instituto Lingüístico de Verano*. Later this became the Summer Institute of Linguistics (SIL).[19] In 1942 SIL was affiliated with the University of Oklahoma, and in this period, the number of those who were engaged in the translation of the Bible reached about a hundred. SIL soon sent its linguists to the Philippines, then the Pacific, and by 1953 they were also present in other continents.

Townsend, in many respects in the *avant-garde* of his profession, was not always understood by his contemporaries. Some criticized him for his willingness to work with questionable governments and any mission or church—even the Catholic

---

19 Beginning in 1942, Wycliffe was responsible for public relations and for the recruitment of the candidates, and SIL for linguistic training and activities on the ground.

*Kenneth L. Pike,
an eminent linguist
in the service of
Bible translation.*

Church—as long as they were interested in translating the Bible and making it available in vernacular languages.[20]

Kenneth L. Pike (1912–2000) was one of Townsend's first students. He lived for some time in a remote village in the state of Oaxaca in order to analyze the Mixtec language. He subsequently acquired a world reputation for his innovations in the area of phonetics and for his contributions to the science of linguistics. He became responsible for the development of linguistics at Wycliffe University. Professor at the University of Michigan, author of numerous works, and a conference lecturer who was much in demand, he maintained a passion for mission and communicated to thousands of students his enthusiasm for the translation of the Bible into unwritten languages.

---

20  Hence Townsend developed a relationship with Lazaro Càrdenas, the president of Mexico between 1934 and 1940. Càrdenas especially wanted linguistic work to be pursued among the Indian tribes of the country, but his socialist political program displeased numerous North American Christians. See the history of Wycliffe by Emily Wallis and Mary Bennett, *Two Thousand Tongues to Go: The Story of the Wycliffe Bible Translators* (New York: Harper & Brothers, 1959).

# SECTION II

## PROTESTANT MISSION IN ASIA

# CHAPTER 3

# William Carey:
## "Father of Modern Missions"

W hen the birth of modern Protestant missions is mentioned, the name of William Carey immediately arises. It is not an exaggeration to say that there is a "before Carey" and an "after Carey." Of course, he was not the first Protestant to have engaged in missiological reflection or to have paid a high personal price for proclaiming the gospel where it had never before been heard. But Carey, by his unstinting efforts, launched a movement that was a new departure for Protestant missions and resulted in evangelical churches being planted around the world. Carey's influence so profoundly influenced the heart of Protestantism that after him it was no longer possible to marginalize the missionary responsibility of the church, as had been the case for many years. For these reasons, we will present both his life and ministry at length.

Pioneer missionaries have everywhere been idealized, and one is tempted to do the same for Carey. For our part, we will not try to dissimulate his errors or weaknesses from which some members of his family, his young colleagues, and his mission committee sometimes suffered. In some ways, of course, his faults were the natural outcroppings of his virtues. But without doubt he was a man of rare caliber whose strong character made possible the opening of a new era in the history of mission.

## ORIGINS AND TRAINING

William Carey was born in 1761 in a small village in Northamptonshire, at the center of England, amidst an Anglican family of modest means. As a schoolboy he was so captivated by the adventures of the great explorers that his playmates nicknamed him Christopher Columbus. He was a boy with an insatiable curiosity and thirst for knowledge.

As evidence of his methodic spirit, he gathered specimens of plants found in the woods and systemically classified them with abundant documentation. He wanted to become a gardener, but his sensitivity to the sun prevented this. Instead, at the age of sixteen he became an apprentice shoemaker.

He said that at this time in his life he was indifferent to spiritual matters, but he nevertheless converted when he was eighteen years old.[21] His passion for distant

---

21  At the age of twenty-two he became a member of the Baptist Church and asked to be baptized.

countries was then enriched by a new element: prayer for the evangelization of non-Christian peoples. He began to gather all the materials he could to learn about the different regions of the world and their inhabitants. Andrew Fuller, the future director of the Baptist Missionary Society, preserved this remembrance:

> I recall that on entering his shoemaking shop, I saw, suspended on the wall, an immense map of the world formed from numerous chips of paper joined together, on which he had inscribed each known country with the information that he had been able to find on its population, religion, etc.

At the age of twenty, Carey married Dorothy Plackett, who was five years his senior. She was illiterate, as were three-quarters of the women in England in the eighteenth century, and she had signed with a cross in the state marriage register. Their first daughter died of a fever at an early age, but by the age of twenty-four, Carey was the father of three daughters. To augment his insufficient income, he opened a class in the village of Moulton where the family had just established itself—all the while pursuing his shoemaking career. The shoemaker and instructor united his two pursuits to make a leather map of the world in order to help communicate to the class his passion for distant lands.

Carey became a lay preacher in the small Baptist churches of the region. Here again, he engaged himself unstintingly, assigning himself the task of mastering the biblical languages to be assured that he understood the sense of the texts. He devoted himself to these studies by day while repairing shoes in his shop and, later in the evening, continued his studies by candlelight. The knowledge of the biblical languages and the astonishing linguistic capacity that this small craftsman and autodidact developed was of inestimable value for his future missionary ministry.

In 1787 when he was twenty-six, he was ordained a pastor of the Baptist Church of Moulton. From that point he had three careers: shoemaker, teacher, and pastor. Despite many responsibilities, Carey's pastoral work led the parish to experience a real renewal. Carey was disturbed upon reading the *Journal of David Brainerd* and learning about the new Moravian missionaries.[22] His passion for distant lands moved him deeply when he considered the eternal destiny of their habitants and the will of God for the salvation of the world.

Carey sought from then on to communicate his missionary vision to his colleagues in the church. Though he had only recently come to the Baptist pastorate in Northamptonshire, he took up the task of reflecting upon a question that appeared to him to be a Christian priority: Is it the responsibility of all successive generations of gospel ministers to attempt to fulfill the commandment of the Lord to the apostles to evangelize all the nation until the end of time? Upon presenting the cause of mission to his fellow ministers, Carey received a famous rebuff from the venerable dean

---

22  David Brainerd (1718–1747) was an American missionary among the Indian tribes. Carey possessed *Life of Brainerd*, written by Jonathan Edwards, the great American theologian (see p. 246). For a recent edition see Jonathan Edwards, *The Life and Diary of David Brainerd* (Grand Rapids: Baker Book House, 1989). In his *Enquiry*, to be presented a little later, Carey often cited the *Periodical Accounts of the Moravian Missions*.

of the pastorate, John Ryland, a strict Calvinist: "Sit down, sit down, young man. You are an enthusiast. When it pleases God to convert the pagans, he will do it without your advice and without mine. It would first of all be necessary that he produce a new gift of languages, as at the Pentecost."

The cause of mission was far from being won, even in the nonconforming churches. Carey did not allow himself to be discouraged, and he understood the necessity of bolstering his arguments to convince his colleagues. He did it with the methodical rigor that characterized him. The evidence he had patiently gathered over the course of years would now be put to great use. The fruit of his work was a book of ninety pages that he sent to his colleagues and then distributed more widely in 1792, the celebrated *Enquiry*—of which the complete title is: *An Enquiry into the Obligation of Christians to Use Means in the Conversion of Pagans and in Which Are Considered the Religious State of Different Nations of the World, the Success of the Missionary Enterprises of the Past, and the Possibility of New Attempts of This Type.*

( 48 )

ASIA.

| Countries. | EXTENT. | | Number of Inhabitants. | Religion. |
|---|---|---|---|---|
| | Length. Miles. | Breadth Miles. | | |
| Isle of Ceylon | 250 | 200 | 2,000,000 | Pagans, except the Dutch Christians. |
| —— Maldives | 1000 in number. | | 100,000 | Mahometans. |
| —— Sumatra | 1000 | 100 | 2,100,000 | Ditto, and Pagans. |
| —— Java | 580 | 100 | 2,700,000 | Ditto. |
| —— Timor | 2400 | 54 | 300,000 | Ditto, and a few Christians. |
| —— Borneo | 800 | 700 | 8.000,000 | Ditto. |
| —— Celebes | 510 | 240 | 2,000,000 | Ditto. |
| —— Boutam | 75 | 30 | 80,000 | Mahometans. |
| —— Carpentyn | 30 | 3 | 2,000 | Christian Protestants. |
| —— Ourature | 18 | 6 | 3,000 | Pagans. |
| —— Pullo Lout | 60 | 36 | 10,000 | Ditto. |

Besides the little Islands of Manaar, Aripen, Caradivia, Pengandiva, Analativa, Nainandiva. and Nindundiva, which are inhabited by Christian Protestants.

*Facsimile of one of the eighty-seven pages of the evidence assembled by William Carey in the* Enquiry *about the areas, populations, and religions of all the regions of the known world in 1792.*

In this work, Carey first presents the theology of mission and then the history of mission through the course of the centuries. Next, he presents a picture of the situation of the world in his period, from the demographic, political, social, cultural, and religious points of view—with charts and statistics to support his argument. One of his biographers writes:

> In an obscure village, far from a library . . . this shoemaker, still less than thirty years old, gives us a picture of the entire world, continent by continent, island by island, race by race, religion by religion, nationality by nationality, presenting summary charts so

precise, making the following general explications so pertinent and so logical that he still excites the admiration of scholars today.[23]

The fourth part of his book is a plea. What the explorers and merchants did for money, will Christians not do for the gospel? Are the pagan peoples barbarians? But in what state were the English before the coming of the first Christian missionaries? Indeed, there are obstacles, but Jesus calls us to carry our crosses and to follow him at the cost of suffering and even death. Here is an extract from the book:

> It has been objected that there are multitudes in our own nation, and within our immediate spheres of action, who are as igno-rant as the South-Sea savages, and that therefore we have work enough at home, without going into other countries. That there are thousands in our own land as far from God as possible, I read-ily grant, and that this ought to excite us to tenfold diligence in our work, and in attempts to spread divine knowledge amongst them is a certain fact; but that it ought to supersede all attempts to spread the gospel in foreign parts seems to want proof. in our own country men have means of grace, and may attend on the word preached if they chose it. They have the means of knowing the truth, and faithful ministers are placed in almost every part of the land, whole spheres of action might be much extended if their congregations were but more hearty and active in the cause: but with them the case is widely different, who have no Bible, no written language (which many of them have not), no ministers, no good civil government, nor any of those advantages which we have. Pity therefore, humanity, and much more Christianity, call loudly for every possible exertion to introduce the gospel amongst them.[24]

He concluded with a list of practical propositions:
1. May there be prayer for the work of the Lord among the pagans.
2. May each Christian be concerned with the affairs of his Master. May rich and poor practice the tithe, like the Israelites.
3. Finally, may the Baptist churches form a society directed by a committee for the realization of a concrete missionary project.

## FOUNDING THE BAPTIST MISSIONARY SOCIETY

Carey gradually became an orator known for his passion and force of conviction. He was not afraid to take on the burning questions of his day, becoming part of a group of militant Christians opposed to slavery, and calling for a boycott of sugar produced in the plantations using slaves.

In May 1792 he preached to a general assembly of Baptist pastors in Nottingham on the theme, "Enlarge the space of thy tent" (Isa 54:2,3). On this occasion he used

23   R. Farelly, *William Carey* (Paris: Société de Publications Baptistes, 1984), 30.
24   William Carey, *An Enquiry into the Obligation of Christians to Use Means for the Conversion of the Heathens,* fac-simile edition with an introduction by Ernest A. Payne (London: Carey Kingsgate, 1961), 13.

an expression that would become famous: "Expect great things from God, undertake great things for God." On his insistence, it was determined that a missionary committee would be formed. The organizing meeting of the Baptist Missionary Society (BMS) was held on October 2, 1792.[25] Carey announced that he was offering himself as the first to be sent.

After a period of study, Carey became convinced that he should leave for Tahiti. It was then that he met John Thomas, a doctor in the Royal Navy and a member of a Baptist church. Thomas had recently returned from Bengal where he had left his family and a great many debts. He spoke Bengali and even began to translate some of the books of the Bible into this language. Though his expectations later proved unrealistic, Thomas set out the many possibilities that presented themselves for the evangelization of the Indies and pleaded the cause of Bengal with Carey. Discerning the will of God in the doctor's proposition, Carey presented himself and Thomas as candidates on January 9, 1793, before the missionary committee founded three months before and presided over by the Rev. Andrew Fuller. Thomas would be a devoted colleague but a disastrous manager, causing Carey, who committed the purse strings to him, much anxiety.

There were numerous obstacles to overcome before departing for the mission field of the Indies, but Carey was not one to be easily discouraged: "If the Lord wants us in the Indies, what therefore will be able to prevent us?" First there were financial obstacles: the small society that had just been formed was scarcely in a position to provide the funds necessary to cover the costs of a voyage. Political obstacles came next: it was almost impossible to find a ship that would agree to take missionaries on board. All the British ships depended on the British East India Company, which did not want Christian preachers in its territories.[26] Finally there were family obstacles: Dorothy Carey, pregnant with her fourth child, categorically refused to leave England. Carey proposed, therefore, to depart only with his elder son, Felix, then eight years old, a decision to which Dorothy finally agreed.[27] From the ship that would take them to the Indies, he wrote to her these painful but determined lines:

> You wish to know my state of mind. If I possessed the entire world,
> I would be ready to give it up without reservation to have you and
> the children with me. But my sense of duty is so strong that it
> supplants all other considerations. I could not be diverted from
> my task without rendering myself guilty. Say to my dear children

25 The complete name of the Society is the Particular Baptist Society for the Propagation of the Gospel among the Heathens. Particular Baptists are those who profess a strict Calvinism regarding predestination. General Baptists, in contrast, follow Arminius, as did John Wesley, and affirm the liberty of each person to appropriate (or not) through his or her own faith the salvation accomplished by Jesus Christ.

26 "In the eighteenth century, it was a firmly established principle insisted upon by the commercial companies that in no case should the social customs and religions of the Indians be disturbed." C. H. Philips, *The East Indian Company 1784–1834* (Manchester: University Press, 1961).

27 During this period, the members of colonial administrations and the army left their families in Britain for the duration of their stays overseas. However, in light of Christian ethics, the situation was different for missionary families: a departure that caused the separation of a couple, even temporarily, risked being badly perceived by most of the churches.

that I love them tenderly and pray without ceasing for them. Be assured that I love you with all my heart.[28]

After a considerable search, room was finally found on a Danish ship, and they left England on June 13, 1793. The voyage took five months, during which Carey diligently studied Bengali with Thomas. Before arriving, the two travelers had succeeded in translating a large portion of the book of Genesis. This was Carey's first attempt at Bible translation, to which he would dedicate himself, making it his priority and pursuing it unremittingly for the forty-one years of his ministry in the Indies. When the ship dropped anchor in the Bay of Calcutta on November 11, 1793, the missionaries landed secretly, using a small and unofficial disembarkation point in order to avoid the police at the port whom they feared would turn them back.

## FIRST YEARS IN INDIA

Carey and Thomas were obviously not the first Christian missionaries in the Indies. Churches had been planted there in antiquity, and the Catholic Church had been present at least since the Middle Ages. More recently, the Danish-Halle mission of Tranquebar had arrived at the beginning of the eighteenth century. When Carey came ashore, the Pietist missionary C. F. Schwartz (1726–1798) was still living in Tanjore, in the southeast of the peninsula, 1,700 kilometers from Calcutta (see p. 253). But Bengal had not yet seen British Protestant missionaries.[29]

The beginning was extremely trying. The financial reserves on which the travelers were depending when they arrived were not sufficient. After several weeks of disastrous management by Thomas, their purses were completely empty, though they had imagined that they had had enough money for the first year. The Carey family had to change its living quarters three times and finally settled into a poor and insalubrious dwelling. Due to lack of properly prepared food, the entire family suffered from dysentery. During this time, Carey tried in vain to find employment in a botanical garden.

Finally, after three months, Carey and his family moved to the region of Debhatta, a three-day canoe journey from Calcutta where the government was offering land to those who were willing to clear land and farm it. William constructed a house with his own hands and planted a small field to feed his family. While waiting for the first harvest, the children suffered from malnutrition. Dorothy, afflicted by sunstroke, became gravely ill. All experienced malaria or dysentery to various degrees. The region was almost entirely deserted, as tigers had recently killed twenty people and the villagers had fled. Carey had to cultivate his garden with a rifle in hand. Evangelization under such conditions would have been a quixotic effort.

---

28   J. B. Myers, *William Carey: The Shoemaker Who Became the Father and Founder of Modern Missions* (Kilmarnock: 1887), 33.

29   A group of Moravian missionaries were established in 1777 in Serampore, a Dutch enclave near Calcutta and future base of the Baptist mission. But, following several deaths and repeated failure in their attempts to establish a church, they gave up after fifteen years, and the last of them abandoned the region in 1795. There was no longer any trace of their work, it seems, when Carey and his friends settled in Serampore in 1800.

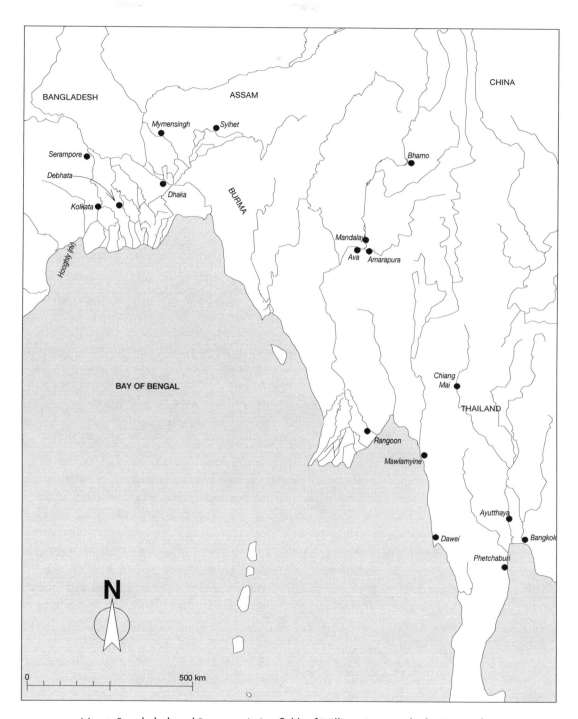

*Map 1: Bangladesh and Burma, mission fields of William Carey and Adoniram Judson*

Carey, however, soon discovered a solution to his financial problems. The position of foreman was offered to him in an indigo factory in Mudnabatti, 450 kilometers from Calcutta where the family settled about nine months after its arrival in the Indies. This post assured them of a sufficient income for six years. Carey wrote to his committee that it should no longer send him money and that his salary should be used for other missionaries. Carey's proposition was premature, but his new posi-

*William Carey (1761–1834), "The Father of Modern Missions."*

tion did help him deal with his malaise. The situation Carey found himself in was far from the one he had dreamed of in Britain when he imagined himself in the role of a missionary. Moreover, he was absorbed by the cares of the management and education of the children, his wife's health being too reduced for her to assume this responsibility.

For the mother of the family, these first months were far beyond what she could physically and psychologically endure. While still in Britain, she had anguished over the prospects of raising her young children in the Indies. And in this respect, the facts confirmed her worst fears. The successive moving, material destitution, anxieties for her health and that of her children, and so many strange novelties—the language, customs, climate, and food—proved to be a shock that would affect her to the end of her days.

Moreover, not long after settling in Mudnabatti, the family received a bitter blow: Peter, the third child, then only five years old, succumbed in several hours to an attack of dysentery. Since none of the workers in the indigo factory, neither Muslims nor Hindus, wanted to make a coffin and inter the child of an "infidel," Carey buried the boy himself.

Several months after the death of her son, Dorothy showed clear signs of being psychologically disturbed. She began to live in an unreal world, a victim of worry and hallucinations. She manifested a pathological jealousy in regard to her husband. On several occasions it was necessary to confine her, both to protect her from herself and to protect her family. In almost all of Carey's letters during this time are found words such as the following: "My poor wife is always very ill . . . her state worsens . . . after several signs of improvement, she is again profoundly fallen into dementia . . . poor Mrs. Carey is terribly tormented, a melancholy victim of mental derangement." This state continued for twelve years, and during the last years, she was semipermanently confined. This was a tragedy for William as well as for Dorothy. He came to the Indies in the hope of converting people, but how could he preach the gospel while being ceaselessly pursued by his own wife accusing him of adultery and immorality? He was also very anxious for his sons who were present at these traumatic scenes.

The mission passed over such incidents in silence. The first biographies of Carey, however, often treated Dorothy roughly. She was condemned as a weight of death, a shadow of an unhappy marriage on the life of a great man, a woman insensitive to the spiritual objectives to which her husband had dedicated his life, and more. Sometimes she was reproached for having refused to accompany her husband, sometimes for having accompanied him without a personal calling. In fairness, it should be noted that she had not married a missionary, but a shoemaker of central England. What could that strange life in the Indies have represented for this mother of four children who had never before left her county and had never attended school? What could it have meant to travel to a far and unknown land in order to accompany her husband in the pursuit of a project for which she had not heard a divine call?

More recently, psychiatrists have been inclined to be more sympathetic in the case of Dorothy Plackett Carey. In attempting to understand her tormented life, they have diagnosed the obvious signs of paranoia.[30] In the Indies, several factors came together to bring about this tragedy: climate, sickness, grief, feelings of abandonment (she had to wait fourteen months before the first letter arrived giving news of her family and friends), and fear of the environment (snakes and wild animals surrounding their home became a persistent fear). Her husband did not fully understand her anxieties or the adverse effects of her solitude. Unlike his wife, William was absorbed in the many aspects of his work and felt perfectly at ease in discovering new things about the country that fascinated him.

According to the son of one of Carey's colleagues, John Clark Marshman, "What illustrates the force and energy of Carey's character is that he was accomplishing the biblical and literary work to which he was fiercely dedicated . . . while an insane woman, agitated to a state of painful excitement, was living nearby."[31] No doubt Dorothy was a burden and hindrance to her husband's ministry. But at the same time, it is difficult to deny that William sacrificed her to the absolute priority he gave to his vocation and activities. He could then only stand by, helpless despite his ardent prayers, and observe the ravages of mental illness. James R. Beck, in his in-depth study, came to the following conclusion regarding Carey's responsibility for the tragedy:

> Carey's major fault could well be his limited capacity to establish relationships in the family setting.

Hence, one of the most glorious histories of modern missions also includes one of its greatest tragedies. While William was making an almost unparalleled contribution, Dorothy had to make the greatest of sacrifices. Death would have been easier for her. She made his life miserable, and he made her life miserable. In the Carey family home, we find a microcosm of the best and the worst of what can be encountered in missions: exceptional gifts and agony; magnificent accomplishments and dementia; divine blessing and prayers unanswered.[32]

---

30  A searching work about her was recently written: James R. Beck, *Dorothy Carey: The Tragic and Untold Story of Mrs. William Carey* (Grand Rapids: Baker Book House, 1992).

31  John Clark Marshman, *The Life and Time of Carey, Marshman and Ward*, vol. 1, (London, 1859), 301.

32  Beck, op. cit., resp. 138, 21.

Suffering from recurring fevers, Dorothy died in 1807 at the age of fifty-one, after fifteen days in a coma. She suffered from this terrible sickness for twelve of the fourteen years that she lived in the Indies.

Carey's journal—the only confidante he had in his solitude—often expressed feelings of helplessness. Whatever the prestige of this giant among pioneer missionaries, he found it necessary to mask the distress that often gripped him. After only a few weeks in the Indies, he wrote:

> I am very depressed. I find myself in a strange country, alone, without Christian friends, with a large family and incapable of granting their desires . . . I am depressed, not for myself, but for them . . . The other day, the time passed in prayer with God made me much better, but then, I was overwhelmed by the manner in which my wife has treated me, she who should be an aid to me. I was irritated by it, wounded, and shocked. I am sad for her who has never put her heart in this enterprise.[33]

His deep feelings of failure were scarcely assuaged by the intensity of his activities:

> Sometimes I walk in my garden and try to pray to God. Moreover if I succeed in prayer, it is only in the solitude of a walk. It seems to me that I was a little less beaten down today, but soon the darkness returns to me. I have exchanged several words with a Muslim on the subject of the things of God, but I also feel bad about it. (February 6, 1795)

> I have been truly unhappy. My soul was submerged in discouragement. (March 15, 1795)

> I have known of painful family trials for a trimester about which I do not want to speak. More than ever, I need faith and patience and I bless God not to have been completely deprived of his graces, although, alas! I have multiple subjects to complain of in my heart. (June 14, 1795)

Despite these first years of sadness, certain signs seemed to indicate that Carey's activities were not totally unfruitful. The meetings of the Baptist Church were attracting curious and always large crowds, often as many as six hundred people, Muslims for the most part. Carey was soon capable of addressing them in their own language, Hindustani.[34] "The name of Jesus Christ is no longer strange in this quarter," he informed his friends. During all the time he was in Mudnabatti, he left each Sunday, on foot or in a canoe, to preach the gospel in the villages of the region. He started two classes for a dozen students that he taught himself; one in Sanskrit, the other in Hindustani.

---

33  Journal of Carey, January 15–16, 1794, cited by Beck, op. cit., 95.

34  As soon as he thought he had mastered Bengali, he began to study Sanskrit and Hindustani. Less than two years after his arrival, he managed to converse and to preach in each of these three languages.

In general, the Muslims tended to be hostile to the gospel message while the Hindus listened with interest, without however showing even a vague interest in changing their religion. One of Carey's most concrete results was the completion of the translation of the New Testament in Bengali at the end of 1796, after less than four years of work. At this time John Fountain (1767–1800) arrived to join the work begun by Carey and Thomas. Young and single, he was the first Baptist missionary to join them and brought much-needed assistance, especially in the first printing of the New Testament in 1797. Fountain also showed himself highly adept in the translation into Bengali, and soon the entire Bible was ready for printing. After a four-year sojourn in India, Fountain died at the age of thirty-three, having married not long before.

The team's first translation of the Bible in Bengali was not of a high quality. Carey would make eight revisions of it during the course of his career, the last of which was printed posthumously.

Undaunted by the precariousness of the missionary life, Carey asked Andrew Fuller to send seven or eight additional couples to help in the work. Despite the painful experience that he was having with his wife, he knew that only female missionaries would be able to reach Indian women who were the key to winning over the new generation. At the end of the year 1799, four couples embarked from England.[35] Due to the opposition of British authorities, these new missionaries came to reside in Serampore, a Danish enclave about thirty kilometers upstream from Calcutta on the river Hooghly.[36] The governor of Serampore, Colonel Ole Bie, was well disposed to the missionaries and accorded them Danish passports, which assured them of protection when they traveled into British territory.[37] At the beginning of 1800, the Carey family joined them in the Danish region, bringing along all their baggage, the printing press, and a collection of translations in manuscript. (For the map of Bengal, see p. 332.)

## THE "SERAMPORE TRIO"

Among these new missionaries was a printer that Carey had found in Britain before his departure, anticipating that he would have need of his services. With William Ward (1764–1823), Carey set up a print shop whose primary purpose was the publication of the New Testament in an impressive number of languages. Several of these languages having never been printed, it was necessary to engrave and carve the molds before being able to cast the characters. Soon evangelistic tracts and books printed in Bengali left the presses, as well as scholarly books, dictionaries, grammars, and scientific studies in various Asian languages. In nine months, 31 million pages of the Bible were printed. It is calculated that—between 1801 and 1832—212,000 volumes left the Serampore presses, employing more than forty different languages.

---

35   In ten years, more than sixty missionaries would go to India thanks to the Baptist Missionary Society.

36   In the course of the second half of the seventeenth century, Serampore, under the aegis of the Danish, had greatly expanded and was transformed into an important center of commercial exchange with the West. Members of numerous ethnic groups came to work there.

37   Ole Bie (1726–1798), a disciple of C. F. Schwartz, was a pioneer Pietist in the Indies.

The building was entirely destroyed by fire in 1812. Translations in various languages still in manuscript form went up in smoke, molds specially engraved in these languages fell victim to the flames, and numerous texts already composed in lead melted. After the fire, three and a half tons of lead were found melted on the floor. Carey never again had the time to redo certain ethnological and linguistic works that had disappeared in the fire. He was informed of the tragedy while in Calcutta and returned in haste. With tears in his eyes, he declared on his arrival:

> In the space of a short evening, the work of several years has been consumed. I have recently carried them to the highest level of perfection possible and contemplated this missionary establishment with perhaps too much self-satisfaction. The Lord has brought me low so that I will look on him with more humility. How incomprehensible are the thoughts of God![38]

Incomprehensible, indeed. But in Britain the shock of the news of this catastrophe increased public interest in the mission and produced an unprecedented mobilization of effort among Christians, as much in prayer as in liberal giving. Consequently, after only a few months, the printers were producing publications in seven languages.

The Serampore mission's print shop played a key role not only in evangelization but also in the cultural and even industrial life of the country. It engendered several other crafts: the making of paper, ink, and molds. Thanks to this work, during the nineteenth century the city of Serampore became a great papermaking center, capable of competing with European production in all the markets of Asia.

Another person also arrived: Joshua Marshman (1768–1837), a schoolteacher. With the very effective assistance of his wife Hanna, he began a number of boarding schools and classes for children, first in English and then in vernacular languages. The objective was to give poor children a free education in their native language. Carey always considered popular education in the struggle against illiteracy as a primary task of the mission. The number of schools increased as finances allowed, and by 1818 Marshman had established about a hundred schools with some ten thousand students. In the villages, the schools were placed under the supervision of the villagers themselves, and religious teaching was not obligatory. An attempt at coeducational schools failed, for the population opposed it. Consequently, beginning in 1818 Hanna Marshman assumed responsibility for girls' primary schools, which had not existed in the country until then. By 1837, the year of Marshman's death, close to 130 boys' schools and twenty-seven girls' schools were operating in the region.

Marshman was also engaged in Bible translation, with more or less happy results. He went as far as to work for fifteen years on a version of the Bible in Chinese, relying on the counsel of a native speaker whom he later discovered to be incompetent. Thanks to the Serampore printing press, this Chinese edition was a masterpiece of typography, but, on the other hand, as an effort in linguistics it was a patent failure. The failure was more distressing than it might have been since it could have been avoided. The pioneer of Protestant missions in China, Robert Morrison, a missionary

---

38 Khirendra Kumar Sahu, "Serampore Then and Now," *Indian Journal of Theology* (1993): 9.

of the London Missionary Society (LMS), had simultaneously undertaken the same task, but he was working under infinitely better conditions because he was actually living in China (see p. 345). Despite Morrison's warnings about the "professor" whom he had had the occasion to test in England, Marshman obstinately continued to carry through to completion his redundant effort. This was a strange decision, given the huge burden of work that he was already bearing. Perhaps his impetuous zeal caused him to forget his limitations and to fail to respect the contributions that others were making. Sadly, this is not an isolated example in the history of missions of a waste of energy.

Carey, Ward, and Marshman worked with inexhaustible energy and were astonishingly complementary in their qualities. Over a period of twenty-three years, they formed what has been called the "Serampore trio." As Stephen Neill put it: they were "the most famous missionary team in the history of missions." Together with their associates, they created a Christian community similar to the early church in Jerusalem, a model they were inspired to follow by the Moravian Brethren. The tasks of each were well defined.[39] Each Saturday evening was dedicated to an exchange in which any source of tension or grief was expressed and mutual forgiveness practiced. Every member of the community was required to learn the local language and to take part regularly in the preaching done during the evangelistic tours in the villages. Their spouses were entirely integrated into the life of the community, but despite several attempts, it proved impossible to include Dorothy Carey.

Carey and his colleagues were imbued with the spirit of the evangelical revival of the eighteenth century. Though this spirit has often been characterized as individualistic, the Christian life and the ministry practiced by the Serampore trio and of the larger missionary community that surrounded it was marked by mutual support and shared values.

## BIRTH OF AN INDIAN CHURCH

Despite the competence and dedication of this missionary community, the birth of a church was neither easy nor rapid. The Hindus, often interested in the gospel, generally listened a long time before taking the decisive step and risk of a public commitment. And the Baptist mission did not baptize lightly. It was seven years after Carey's arrival in Bengali that the team was finally able to communicate in a circular letter the news of its first conversion. The baptism of Krishna Pal had taken place in the waters of the river Hooghly, a tributary of the Ganges, in the presence of a large, curious crowd. A carpenter of the artisan caste, he became a patient of Doctor Thomas following a work-related accident. Not long after this, Thomas suffered from a fever and died. During the last months of his life, he experienced moments of exaltation as well as rather painful times of mental imbalance.

---

39  Carey himself, while generally responsible for the supervision of the whole work, was specifically tasked with the "departments" of agriculture, medical care, translations, and finances. He was also the pastor of a small Baptist church.

In 1802 the missionaries recorded the first conversion among the caste of writers and among the Brahmans. They also celebrated the first Christian marriage. By 1804 they had established a small church composed of forty-eight baptized members from various castes. Two years later, there were about a hundred. In 1809, when Carey had been working in the Indies for sixteen years, the church included two hundred indigenous members, and the evangelistic work was by then largely overflowing the small Danish enclave of Serampore. By 1812, when Carey was fifty-two years old and had been a missionary for nearly twenty years, a dozen mission stations had been established in the vast territory. There were six hundred Indians baptized by 1818, and the number of stations by the time of Carey's death in 1834 was about thirty.

In 1806 the new British governor, Sir Georges Barlow, forbade the missionaries from engaging in any evangelistic activity in the territory of Bengal. Hindus hostile to Christianity had persuaded him that certain anticolonial riots were in reality directed against the missionaries whose proselytism, according to them, constituted aggression against the local religion. It was not until 1813 that Christians in the British Parliament intervened to lift the interdiction. The political debate on this occasion was closely followed in the British press and helped to make the work of the Serampore community known to the British public.

## A COHERENT AND BALANCED STRATEGY

The mission work of the Serampore trio took many forms, yet the vision that inspired it was simple, coherent, and comprehensive. It is summarized in six themes below.

### Evangelism

From first to last, Carey's greatest passion was to lead nonbelievers to the knowledge of Jesus Christ. This ardent desire was already apparent before his departure from Britain in his celebrated *Enquiry*. The urgency of evangelization determined all the great decisions of his life, including his commitment to learning languages and translating the Bible. Carey once wrote, "The outdoor meetings are the most interesting, for they are accompanied by conversations, questions, and responses. Tracts are put in circulation in Bengali. They deal especially with idolatry and presenting the message of the grace of God in Jesus Christ crucified."[40] Carey and his collaborators sought without respite to reach regions where the gospel had not yet been heard. This included the entire Ganges basin, the region of present-day Bangladesh, and even as far off as Burma.

The aridity of the first years and the church's slow growth over Carey's long life caused him some degree of suffering and even self-doubt. After he had been in India for many years, he expressed his thoughts in this way:

> When we see around us the multitudes who are not anxious about
> God and are given to vice and all sorts of covetousness, we are as-
> sailed by distress, and it happens that we momentarily succumb
> to discouragement. In passing these thousands of people in the

---

40   Farelly, op. cit., 65

street, one is filled with sadness at the thought that none of them
has a true knowledge of the grace of God.[41]

While the masses were slow to respond to the message of God's love, Carey's
initial enthusiasm and sense of the urgency for the task that animated him from the
beginning was slowly transformed. Over time his vision of mission became broader
and more realistic as he took into account man in his totality. He understood that one
cannot isolate the gospel message from an engagement in social justice and from an
interest in the cultural, economic, and scientific life of the country. Establishing the
church in Bengal remained his supreme goal, but he did not want this church to be
a foreign body, cut off from the realities of the life of the people. Despite the aridity
of the land, a small but solid church has persevered in India down to the present day.

## Bible Translation

Carey studied Sanskrit, the sacred language of India, for he had discovered that it
was the basis of almost all the Indian dialects. It was also necessary for his relations
with the high officials and cultured people of the country. But to reach the common
people, knowledge of the vernacular languages was indispensable.

Carey translated the entire Bible in Bengali, Sanskrit, and Marathi; Ward and
Marshman translated it into three other languages. Carey's translation of the New
Testament into Hindustani "presents a remarkable purity of style." He had indigenous
assistants as his coworkers in the translation of the New Testament in twenty-three
languages, and he supervised the publication of Bible texts into forty-four languages
or dialects spoken in the Indies and other parts of Asia. The British and Foreign Bible
Society cooperated with him and provided financial support. These translations were
the most remarkable aspect of the Serampore trio's work.

The mission historian John Foster notes that during eighteen centuries of Christianity the Bible had been translated in about thirty languages and that, in only one
generation, the Serampore missionary team had practically doubled that number, at
least insofar as the New Testament is concerned. Though the trio's numerous translations had the urgent objective of reaching the largest number of people possible,
not the perfection of the science of linguistics that was then taking its first faltering
steps, in 1807 Carey received a doctorate *honoris causa* in theology from the University of Providence in Rhode Island for his translation work.

## Educating Children, Training Indigenous Pastors

If the objective was the edification of an Indian church, the means of obtaining this
goal was to train national Christians as quickly as possible in order to entrust them
with the task of teaching. Carey wrote:

> One important part of our work is the training of our indigenous
> brothers so that they can be used, and to encourage all the differ-
> ent sorts of abilities that we discern in them. The gifts and graces
> that they have received must be developed. We never dedicate too

---

41   Beck, op. cit., 168.

much time to their perfection. It is only with indigenous preachers that we can hope to spread the gospel everywhere in this immense continent.

Making literacy more widespread in the population and educating children was part of this strategy; it was in fact the first step in achieving it. We have already mentioned the contribution of Hanna Marshman in this area.

Carey also reserved much of his time for higher education. The British governor of the period, Lord Wellesley, contrary to his predecessors, was entirely disposed to the missionary cause. Observing the low cultural level of the young British immigrants, he established the college of Fort William at Calcutta, which has been called "the Oxford of the East." Since it had need of a competent professor of Indian languages, Wellesley asked Carey to teach Bengali, Sanskrit and, later, Marathi. After consultation with his colleagues, Carey accepted the task, which was added to all his others. His salary at the college would allow him to acquire new missionaries and also give him an opportunity to become acquainted with several future government officials in the colonial administration. Furthermore, it initiated him into the social and cultural realities of the country, sensitizing him to the cruelties of certain customs that British authorities tolerated.

To attain the long-term objective of providing advanced education for Christian converts, in 1818 Carey established the "School of Higher Teaching of Oriental Literature and European Science"—later the College of Serampore. He began with thirty-seven students, nineteen of whom were Christians. The college was open to all, without distinction of caste, color of skin, or religion. Theological teaching was the principal concern, for Carey's first objective was to train a pastoral body of qualified indigenous people. The college was effectively a nursery for the Indian servants of God.

In 1827 the king of Denmark bestowed the rank of university on the College of Serampore, the first Asian institution to receive this honor. At that time it was offering diplomas in literature and theology. The college building, constructed in 1818 and financed entirely from the salaries and through the economy measures of Carey, Ward, and Marshman, still exists today, impressive in its imposing dimensions.[42]

### Development of a Poor Country

From his earliest days in the Indies, Carey asked his supporters in Britain to send garden tools as well as selected seeds for flowers, vegetables, and fruit trees. No foreigner so clearly perceived the needs of the Indian rural population as Carey. Already at Mudnabatti, thanks to his work in connection with the indigo plantations,

---

42  In the course of the nineteenth century, the college passed through a period of decline in which only the theological college survived. But in 1911 it had a new birth through the cooperation established between the theological college and the various Protestant denominations in Calcutta and Bangalore. In the course of the twentieth century, the College of Serampore granted more than ten thousand diplomas in theology. Eventually other colleges were established, such as those of the arts, sciences, and economics. This was done in the spirit of Carey, who wanted Christian theology to be in perpetual dialogue with the Western sciences and the culture of the East. In 1990 the college welcomed 2,750 students, of whom 111 were to study theology.

he encountered more than two hundred farmers in the region. After studying their methods, he soon proposed various reforms. Later, he continued to be interested in agricultural matters.

In 1820 he founded a cooperative institution to co-ordinate research into agricultural and horticultural techniques. He hoped to introduce more effective methods such as alternation of fields, fertilization, and irrigation in order to combat the malnutrition he observed among the poor population. Carey also introduced the new technique of drainage and set up a plan for the preservation of forests threatened by un-

*The College of Serampore, constructed by Carey in 1818, still notable today for its capaciousness.*

controlled clearing and exploitation. The government, however, ignored his ideas. Carey's discernment and foresight are perhaps better appreciated today than in his own time, especially in that he was among the first to be conscious of the need to preserve the environment and promote ecological balance.

The rural population of Bengal lived in difficult climatic conditions and was subjected to the rule of prominent and unscrupulous landowners. One of their chief problems was the indebtedness that followed every time there was a poor harvest, which did not allow them to recover in time for the next year's harvest. Banks generally refused to lend to the poor, and creditors charged high interest rates that were beyond the peasants' ability to pay. They were quickly being stripped of their land and falling into semislavery. The Serampore team began the first effort to help the poor farmers of the country, providing aid to the most destitute so that they could escape an otherwise endless indebtedness. The mission also organized an agricultural cooperative whose essential role was to manage a reserve of seeds for the following season.

Inspired by the gospel, the missionaries fought for the emancipation of women. Through his printing operation, Carey was able to furnish employment to numerous widows for the work of composition, which required a high level of training. His purpose was not only to aid them financially, but also to demonstrate that women were as capable as men to perform tasks requiring specialized skills. To employ women and to pay them was an entirely novel idea in India.

In the area of medicine, which was the personal domain of Doctor Thomas, the mission placed a special emphasis on the needs of the leprous. No medical treatment then existed for leprosy, and a large number of people suffered from it. One frequently adopted solution was to kill the sick, often burning them alive. Carey witnessed such scenes and described them in an open letter intended for the members of the British Parliament. He hoped that by publicizing the problem he would shape popular opinion and engender a militant movement to press for the interdiction of the practice. The mission opened a leprosarium on its own land in an attempt to respond to the moral and social needs of the leprous. It also established a dispensary to offer free medicines to the indigent sick.

Carey's eldest son, Felix, had an excellent knowledge of the country's languages. After completing medical studies, he inaugurated a department of medical science at the College of Serampore in 1822. Sadly, he died in the same year before being able to firmly establish this new departure.

## Overture to the Culture in the Languages of the Country

Carey is recognized as a great orientalist and a linguist of the first rank. With the aid of Marshman, he translated several texts of the ancient Hindu literature into English. He also translated the first books of the *Ramayana*, a poem in Sanskrit from about the fifteenth century B.C. that celebrated the exploits of Rama, the seventh reincarnation of Vishnu. Certain Christians reproached him for this work because of the religious character of the writing. They did not understand that his objective was to help missionaries to better grasp the worldview of those to whom they wanted to announce the God of Jesus Christ. Despite the admiration that he often expressed for Hindu civilization and tolerance for others, there is nothing in the record to suggest that Carey was a religious relativist or had a penchant for syncretism.

His contribution to the Bengali language is also remarkable. By 1801 he had already published a Bengali grammar. With Ward's help, he compiled a number of documents, dialogues, and stories that captured the daily life of the diverse social levels that made up the population of Bengal. His *Kathopakathan* became the first book in Bengali prose ever published. Written in clear and accessible language, it was intended to reach the greatest number of people possible. Today it is considered an irreplaceable source for the social history and morals of nineteenth-century northern India. For social and political reasons, written Bengali had all but disappeared in the course of the seventeenth century, having exploded into a number of dialects with few grammatical rules. Consequently, Carey's translations and editing of Bengali writings contributed to revivifying the Bengali language and uniting the various spoken dialects to form a single language capable of giving expression to a great literature. Carey might well be called the father of modern Bengali prose. The mystic Indian poet Rabindranath Tagore (1861–1941) wrote in 1923 that Carey was the pioneer of the renewal of interest in vernacular Indian languages, which, according to him, were well on their way to disappearing by the beginning of the nineteenth century.

Carey was a very active member of the Asiatic Society of Bengal, founded by British people anxious to save ancient Indian literature from extinction and promote oriental studies in Europe. The term "contextualization" was not yet in use at this time, but Carey and his colleagues instinctively practiced it due to the love and respect they had for those to whom the Lord had sent them.

Carey published a Sanskrit dictionary and grammar of more than a thousand pages, and he is considered to have been one of the best teachers of Sanskrit in this era. In fact, he developed and published grammars in six different languages, a tremendous cultural and linguistic contribution.

## Reforming the Society

Interaction with the local culture requires respect and understanding, but the witness of the gospel also leads to a struggle for the transformation of morals and customs in the light of a biblical vision of human beings and society. Consequently, missionaries often find themselves in confrontation with the societies they were sent to serve.

One of the first societal realities confronted by the Serampore mission was the caste system. In the church and every new institution created by the Serampore mission, the caste system was excluded as incompatible with the gospel message, for in Christ there is no longer "neither Jew nor Greek, neither slave nor free"—nor Brahman, nor outcast. The first Indian baptized by the mission church, Krishna Pal, belonged to the caste of artisans but his daughter married one of the first Brahmans to become a Christian. In Indian law, such a union was entirely illegal. When Krishna Pal died of cholera in 1822, his body was placed in the earth beside a Brahman, a converted Muslim, and two Europeans. It was a scandalous ceremony in the eyes of the Indians but a striking sign of the kingdom of God. The caste system played an enormous role in the structure and stability of society. The poorest knew that they could never, at least in their present existence, cross the barriers of their caste. To do so in large numbers would have been to launch a social revolution. Hence the gospel, as an agent of social change, could appear threatening to the members of the favored castes.

In order not to cause disturbances, the colonial authorities adopted the principle of noninterference with regard to the practice of religion within the population, even if its practices were inhumane by Western standards and illegal in British law. But the ethics of the gospel did not allow missionaries to remain silent before such a cruel custom as infanticide, which was frequently performed by throwing the children, especially young girls, into the Ganges River or the Bay of Bengal. At the request of Lord Wellesley, Carey studied the sacred Sanskrit writings to find the origin of this practice. As a result of his research, he could prove that infant sacrifice was foreign to the original Hindu teachings and had its origins in a popular superstition that sought to appease the anger of the goddess Ganga. A government decree, therefore, abolished infanticide, and the chief Hindu leaders were unable to cite religious texts to oppose this decision.

Local custom also prescribed that at the time of an annual religious holiday about a hundred widows and old people go to the mouth of the Ganges in the Bay of Bengal in order to drown themselves. They believed that by doing this they would obtain eternal salvation. This tradition distressed the missionaries, but their preaching made little progress in extirpating such beliefs, which had long been rooted in the popular mind.

The abolition of the terrible custom of *sati* (the cremation of widows with the bodies of their deceased husbands) was obtained after a difficult fight that lasted twenty years. Conferences and public debates were held, and alarming statistics and revealing articles were published in the Indian and British journals in the struggle against this widespread practice. In the whole of Bengal, it is estimated that ten thousand widows per year, often adolescents, were forced by religious laws to throw themselves alive on the funeral pyres of their husbands. It is also important to note that the fate of abandoned widows was generally so tragic that many continued to commit suicide even after the abolition of the *sati*.

Carey's research established that the sacred Hindu texts mentioned the practice of *sati*, but did not prescribe it. The opposition of conservative Hindus was nevertheless virulent. Happily, Carey and his friends could count on the support of Rajah Ram Mohan Roy (1772–1833), a well-educated and progressive Hindu prince. Roy placed all of his authority in the balance and enlisted a number of intellectuals in the cause. He was not a Christian but proclaimed that no ethic equaled that taught by Jesus Christ.[43] Above all, he was concerned to return Hinduism to the primitive teachings of the Vedas, purging it of superstitions. Attracted by monotheism, Roy had a number of passionate conversations with the missionaries and even engaged in a public religious controversy with Joshua Marshman—no doubt the first attempt at interreligious dialogue in the history of Protestant missions in India.

It was in 1829 that the British Parliament finally voted to abolish the *sati*, recognizing it as homicide. M. M. Thomas writes:

> Carey received the decree officially prohibiting the *sati* while he was preparing to preach on the Sunday morning of 5 December 1829 and decided to translate it. He immediately found a colleague to preach in his place while he translated the decree, for he did not want to delay a single hour, in the name of religion, the announcement of this decision. "The Sabbath was made for man."[44]

"If I delay the translation and publication of this decree a single instant," he added, "who knows how many widows will pay with their lives?" It may appear shocking today that the laws regulating the social life of a great Asian country were promulgated by a European parliament. Whatever the criticism of colonialism, Carey and his friends succeeded in bringing about the abolition of certain injustices that victimized the most vulnerable among the Indian population.

An Indian author gives much credit to Carey for the role he played in helping to bring about a renaissance in his country:

> Carey's primary objective was to preach Christianity, but he also played an important role in the development of Bengal, and the Bengalis were greatly benefited by it. The name of William Carey is remembered today more for this involvement and for his love of the Bengali language and literature than for his religious teachings. The influence that he exercised in this area has been generally recognized as an important contribution to the Indian Renaissance.[45]

---

43   Ram Mohan Roy published a bilingual magazine (Bengali-English) to defend Hinduism against the criticisms of the Christian missionaries, but he also published in 1820, with the intention of making known the teachings of Jesus to his compatriots, a book entitled *The Precepts of Jesus*. He founded the syncretistic movement Brahmosamaj, which sought a synthesis between the Hindu, Buddhist, Islamic, and Christian spirituality. He succeeded in influencing some intellectuals.

44   M. M. Thomas, "Bicentennial of Carey's Arrival in India, 1793–1993," *Indian Journal of Theology* (1993): 4.

45   M. Dewanji, *William Carey and the Indian Renaissance* (Delhi: The William Carey Study and Research Centre, 1996), 43.

Since Christian missions have often been denounced as cultural imperialism, Carey's role in revitalizing Bengali culture should not be overlooked, though no doubt the remarks above would not have been fully satisfying to Carey himself.

## THE RUPTURE WITH THE LONDON COMMITTEE

By 1827 there were no surviving members of the Baptist Missionary Society that had initially seen Carey off thirty-five years earlier. Andrew Fuller, Carey's closest friend, died in 1815. The new members knew Carey only by reputation, which was not entirely positive. Since he had never returned to Britain, many imagined him as having the tendencies of a tyrannical oriental potentate.

Reasons for conflict gradually accumulated over time. The London committee feared that there was too great an increase in the number of activities in which the mission engaged. Moreover, the committee reproved the mission for beginning these activities without its consent and for practicing the politics of *fait accompli*. From the mission's point of view, however, awaiting decisions from the committee risked paralyzing the work. In fact, it usually took more than six months to obtain a response to a letter. Waiting this long for decisions was simply intolerable to these enterprising men who took seriously the urgency of the task. Moreover, the members of the committee had only an approximate idea of the needs and possibilities for action in the Indies, a land they knew little or nothing about.

The committee could also appear overly fastidious in its relations with the missionaries, which at times was unnecessarily wounding to these men who had dedicated their lives to spreading the gospel in a foreign country. Occasionally members would forget that most of the expenses of the mission were self-financed due to the many profitable activities of the Serampore group. These missionary activities, according to Carey, embraced the spiritual, material, intellectual, and political needs of the country—a vision that was not always understood by all the diverse groups that supported the mission.

Over the years, some of the young missionaries experienced the older pioneers—especially Marshman—as authoritarian; indeed autocratic. The older generation seemed incapable of understanding that the new arrivals had neither their breadth of interests, nor their ability to live a simple lifestyle. The generation gap that was experienced between these two groups resulted in a serious conflict in which both sides no doubt shared some measure of the blame. The older generation was not prepared to change its habits and to recognize the need for gradual change over time. They welcomed new arrivals but expected them to consent to the sacrifices of the communitarian life practiced at Serampore.[46] Finally, in 1818 a group of young missionaries separated themselves from the Serampore mission and founded the Missionary Association of Calcutta. The older missionaries accused them of being schismatic and of creating an organization in competition with their own.

---

46   One young missionary, according to what the elders said, required since his arrival "an individual house, a stable, and servants."

Called to intervene in this conflict, the London committee felt closer to the younger group that it had sent out and placed all the blame on the elders. Ward and Marshman traveled to London in 1826 and 1829 respectively in order to seek a mutually acceptable solution, but despite these efforts, the Serampore mission broke with the Baptist Missionary Society in 1827. The veteran missionaries were deeply saddened by this. Carey ceded to the Society the mission's apartments, but he retained the college and moved the print shop there. The work of the mission was reunified in 1837, one year after the death of Marshman, the last surviving member of the celebrated Serampore trio.

## THE LAST YEARS

In May 1808, when Carey had been a widower for scarcely more than six months, he married a second time. His new wife was a contented and cultured Danish aristocrat, Lady Charlotte Rumohr, who had settled in Serampore several years earlier. Charlotte had been converted through Carey's ministry, and he became her pastor and baptized her in 1803. "I have a very affectionate and pious woman, whose mind has been remarkably cultivated by education and reading," wrote Carey. Particularly gifted as a linguist, she was a first-rate assistant to her husband; and for his children, she was the attentive mother of whom they had been deprived until then. After thirteen years of marriage, she died in 1821. Carey wrote of her:

> Few mortals could have enjoyed a conjugal happiness as great as ours . . . She lived entirely for me. Her solicitude for my happiness was incessant, and she was capable of interpreting the expression of my visage in each instant and with so much certitude that any attempt to hide my concerns or anxiety would have been in vain.[47]

*Carey's tomb in Serampore.*

Two years after this loss, when Carey was sixty-two, he married Grace Hughes, a forty-five-year-old widow. Grace was greatly devoted to him during the last years of his life when age and wear from overwork had much weakened him. Carey retired from his teaching responsibilities at Fort William at the age of sixty-nine. A little later, he was the victim of an accident while traveling and the aftereffects long stayed with him. Then he suffered from several cerebral attacks and lost his mobility. His greatest joy was when his friends came to walk with him in his botanical garden as he kept pace in his wheelchair. He passed the last months of his life entirely confined to bed.

At the age of seventy-three, Carey died on June 9, 1834, after forty-one years of ministry in India without ever returning to Britain. On the day of his interment, a great crowd of Hindus, Muslims, and Europeans followed the procession. His old friend Joshua Marshman presided over the funeral service. In addition to the loss of

---

47  Beck, op. cit., 166.

his two first wives, in 1822 Carey had also lost his son, Felix, who had become an indispensable assistant to his father after having been a missionary in Burma. His third wife survived him one year. His four sons married and gave him sixteen grandchildren, the last surviving until 1937.

Carey prepared his own epitaph:

William Carey

Born 17 August 1761

Died 9 June 1834

"A wretched, poor, and helpless worm,

On Thy kind arms I fall."

The lectern from which the Bible is read in Westminster Abbey in London, whether during the regular services or during a royal marriage or the enthronement of a king, preserves the memory of the humble shoemaker and Baptist pastor William Carey. On it is engraved the sentence that was the *leitmotiv* of his life: "Expect great things from God, undertake great things for God." In India, William Carey is considered even by non-Christians to be a historic personage. An Indian author says of him:

> Carey occupies still, one hundred years after his death, a venerable place in the hearts of Indians, although it may appear incredible that Indians can hence celebrate a foreigner in the sacred language of their ancestors.[48]

## AN EVALUATION

If the number of conversions obtained by Carey could be counted, it might be observed that he had well nigh established the record. Moreover, the sum of the work he accomplished and his influence in the history of mission is stunning. He would justly have been able to appropriate the words of Saint Paul for himself: "I have worked more than all of them." But, with the apostle, he would soon have added: "Yet not I, but the grace of God that was within me" (I Cor. 15:10). He loved to say, "Do not speak of Carey, but of Carey's Savior." And he recalled that he was "not even a shoemaker, but only a cobbler mending the shoes of others."

It is important to recall his example and profit from it without idealizing the man. There is no longer any question of servilely attempting to imitate his work, for the times have changed—and was he not one of the great artisans of these changes? He is remembered today not only as an autodidact with boundless energy and exceptional abilities but for this thought, his *avant-garde* missionary practices, and the coworkers that he attracted to his cause. He set the standard against which all those who would understand the dimensions of God's mission must measure themselves:

1. The insistence on the primary importance of the translation of the Bible and the training of indigenous workers for the churches;
2. The conception of a well-formed team, but one that is at the same time integrated into the church of the country;

---

48  S. K. Chatterjee, *William Carey and Serampore*, cited by Beck, op. cit., 173.

3. Taking seriously the culture of the country, but also having the courage to denounce aspects of it that are unacceptable;
4. Attention given to the whole person: spiritual, physical, and social.

The remarkably balanced understanding of the gospel that Carey exhibited provides a wide and comprehensive vision of the missionary task. A contemporary Indian theologian writes of Carey, "In all things, he sought to lift up the people, not only by preaching the gospel, but also by applying evangelical principles to daily life." Though Carey was an exceptional man, all Christians can practice his spiritual principles: "Let us give ourselves entirely to this glorious cause. Let us forbid ourselves to ever think that our time, our gifts, our strength, our families, and even the clothes that we wear belong to us."

# CHAPTER 4

# Protestant Mission in India and Neighboring Countries

I t is not possible here to take a complete inventory of the missionary initiatives undertaken by the many different Protestant mission societies that worked in the immense Indian subcontinent in the nineteenth and early twentieth centuries. This account, therefore, will be limited to the nineteenth century, to a few significant missionary experiences in the southern part of India, and to the region of Bengal where we have already seen the work of William Carey and his colleagues. Christianity had in fact been present in these areas for a number of centuries, and the Protestant missionaries of the nineteenth century found them to be fertile ground. In contrast, the north and center of the subcontinent were more difficult terrains, being closely held either by Hinduism or Islam.

We will add some details concerning nineteenth-century missions in the states of what are now Bangladesh, Pakistan, and Sri Lanka. We will also include several paragraphs about Persia (present-day Iran). It is, in fact, from nearby Pakistan that the first Protestant missionaries went to Persia.

## IN CALCUTTA AND BENGAL

In 1813 the British Parliament accorded full liberty to Christian missions in the Indies. Several Anglican societies soon took advantage of this opportunity, establishing themselves in Calcutta and its suburbs. Carey's notoriety had generated much interest in the region throughout Britain; therefore it was generally British missionaries who worked in this part of India. First came the interchurch LMS with two missionaries, and then the CMS, and soon other Anglican missions followed. The Anglicans were primarily concerned with reviving the faith in their British coreligionists, for the Anglican Church had been visibly present in Calcutta since the start of British domination. They also built schools and chapels in various quarters of the city. The Baptists who had separated from Carey were in the field as early as 1818, and the Independent Baptists were also active at the same time. The Methodists began to work in the area in 1819, and the Presbyterian Church of Scotland in 1823.

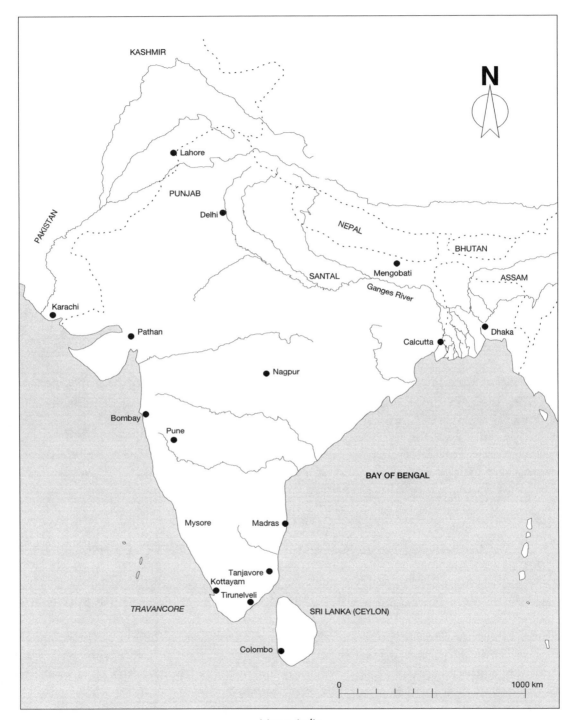

*Map 2: India*

Dr. Alexander Duff (1806–1878), a renowned orator in his native Scotland, offered his services to the Presbyterian Mission. Arriving in Calcutta in 1830, he was quickly convinced that the effort to teach literacy to children in the elementary schools in the local language was insufficient. He founded an English college of the same standards as that of Carey's in Serampore, where an hour of each day was dedicated to the study of the Bible. At its inauguration, three hundred students sought admission. Despite the determined opposition of the Brahmans, ten years later there were eight hundred students. Duff benefited from the support of Ram Mohan Roy, mentioned above (see p. 326). His institution was highly influential within the leading class of Calcutta, which henceforth included a number of Christians and many others sympathetic to Christianity, especially to its ethics and values.

From the city Christianity spread into the countryside. For example, the Swiss missionary Alphonse Lacroix, supported by the LMS, discovered a Christian community already existing in the plains region south of Calcutta. It had been founded by a villager who, on the occasion of a journey to Calcutta, had heard a sermon by a missionary. He returned home, replaced the temple of Shiva on his property with a Christian chapel, and proclaimed what he understood of the Christian message. Afterwards, missionaries occasionally visited, and his movement slowly grew in the region. Part of his message concerned the need for social reform, a position that resulted in bloody repression by the large property owners. Lacroix separated out those who were essentially motivated by political extremism and sought to found a solid Christian community that retained some typical local characteristics. A witness recalled:

> The chapel is soon filled with auditors; all are seated in place, the women on one side, the men on the other. A bizarre song is sung consisting of a prolonged rumble of voices, accompanied by unexpected flourishes, with the melody bawled out in full throat by one part of the assembly. The singing denotes a great fervor but is almost unendurable to European ears. This part of the worship service is followed by the reading of the Bible and the sermon.

In the early years of these missions, a terrible flood ravaged the country, producing a widespread famine. But the activities of the church saved numerous human lives. A similar famine occurred north of Calcutta in 1831. In contrast to the previous work of the church, the famine relief offered by the Anglican mission was badly managed. Massive distribution of rice led to thousands of people asking for baptism in the hope of receiving more generous aid. Despite having ulterior motives, baptism was administered to them without discernment, and the result was superficial Christianization.

## THE EVANGELIZATION OF SOUTH INDIA

The southern part of the Indian subcontinent had the deepest Christian roots. The Anglicans of the CMS came in 1816, animated by the desire to breathe new life into the old Syrian church that then numbered more than 100,000 members and claimed the Apostle Thomas as its founder. In 1599 it had been incorporated into the Roman Catholic Church, but in 1653 it rejected the Jesuit missionaries among them and reasserted its independence. It sought to be associated with the patriarch of the Orthodox churches of the East, from whence it had originally acquired the name "Syrian." In contrast, the Anglicans sought only to bring education to the local priests, which it achieved through the college at Kottayam. The collaboration between the two churches was at first harmonious, and a new translation of the Bible was made and printed in 1829. But then in 1836 the new metropolitan, Mar Dionysius IV, no longer accepted the interference of foreigners and asked the Anglicans to devote themselves exclusively to the evangelization of non-Christians.

A minority refused to separate themselves from the missionaries and continued to participate in the Anglican Church in the diocese of Travancore.[49] This church attracted many people from the lower castes, perhaps drawn mostly by the material and social opportunities it offered. The Anglican leaders, however, knew how to distinguish between authentic converts and those who came for nonspiritual reasons. In 1876 the mission numbered four thousand members and seventeen thousand adherents; and there were more than ten thousand members who had come from the Syrian church and were led by Syrian pastors. A seminary prepared the ministers for their work. A non-Christian of a higher caste bore testimony to the fruits of the word: "These people have marvelously changed," he said. "For ten years I was obliged to have my fields of rice guarded by armed men, and now the Christians bring me the harvest intact."

Abraham Malpan, a renowned Indian professor who had been educated in the Anglican college in the Reformed tradition, later brought pressure to bear on the Syrian church to be based exclusively on the Bible. In 1889 a rupture became inevitable. The Anglican missionaries wisely dissuaded the dissidents from continuing in the Anglican Church. Instead, they formed the Mar Thomas Syrian Church of Malabar, an independent Bible-based and Reformed church under the direction of one of their Syrian bishops.[50]

On the southeast coast of India in Tinnevelly (or Tiruneveli)—hundreds of kilometers from Travancore—a large number of people began to convert to Protestantism in the last years of the eighteenth century. For several years a Tamil villager had been regularly reading the Bible to Hindu listeners. Informed of this fact, C. F. Schwartz, then still living in Tanjor, asked an Indian minister to take an interest in them, and he sent them a missionary. Unfortunately the man died a little later in 1800, and these Christians were then left to themselves. A British military chaplain later discovered their church and asked the missions to take care of them. In 1820 the CMS sent Karl Rhenius, a German who had graduated from the Institute of Basel. In about fifteen years, thanks to an intensive method of training catechists in the villages, he breathed new life into this church and at least ten thousand new converts were added in about a hundred localities. He entrusted these multitudes to indigenous ministers, but this led to conflict with the bishop of the Anglican diocese of Madras regarding their ordination to the ministry. Although Rhenius was a Lutheran, he was

---

49  Travancore is a province on the west coast of India (the coast of Malabar), near to the far south of the subcontinent.

50  According to Barrett, *Encyclopedia*, 370, this church included 875,000 members in 1995.

strongly influenced by the Plymouth Brethren and despised all forms of clericalism. A rupture occurred in 1835, and he led many of his Indian colleagues out of the church. The veneration of Rhenius by Tinnevelly's indigenous ministry bore abundant fruit. After his death in 1838, a reunification took place, and in part unanimity was restored. In 1876 there were about fifty-five thousand Christians spread out through more than a thousand localities with seventeen principal stations. The work was performed by the CMS (evangelical Anglicans), and SPG (traditional Anglicans) who collaborated harmoniously.

At Tanjore itself and at Madras, the old Dutch-Danish Lutheran mission had become exhausted and handed the field over to the SPG in 1826. The church had grown accustomed to tolerating the caste system in its midst, and the Anglicans attacked the problem so energetically that their efforts led to a split. The Leipzig mission took the recalcitrant in hand, adopting a cautious approach in the hope that the dissolution of the caste system would result from the slow but inevitable work of the gospel in the hearts of the people.

A movement of Christian conversions came about in this region through peculiar circumstances. Vedamanikkam, a Travancore fakir who belonged to the lowest level of the society, made a long pilgrimage through the Indies in search for truth. Having visited the high places of Hinduism and been disappointed by the experience, he had a dream in which he saw a venerable old man who enjoined him to abandon his fruitless quest and return to his own province. While on his return journey, he stopped in Tanjore at the home of his relatives to whom he recounted his dream. They introduced him to an aged missionary named John Balthasar Kohlhof, who had been a colleague of C. F. Schwartz. Vedamanikkam believed that he was encountering the old man of his vision, and so he came to the end of his long quest. He converted and was baptized and then asked that a missionary accompany him to his country in South India. After several years, in 1809 the LMS missionary Walter Tobie Ringeltaube (1770–1820) responded positively to his earnest plea.

Ringeltaube was a former disciple of Immanuel Kant and had converted to Pietism through reading of Hans Poulsen Egede, the missionary to Greenland (see pp. 255ff). Arriving in India in 1797, he engaged in intensive but often misconceived activities that brought conflict and finally led to his expulsion. He returned in 1809 and concerned himself with the small groups that had been formed by Vedamanikkam. Generous but sometimes choleric, full of humor but solitary, spiritually alive but living and dressing poorly, he managed to win people who belonged to the most despised classes to the gospel. He was subject to bouts of depression, during which he was convinced that he had not accomplished anything valuable. Nevertheless, he was in charge of chapels, schools, and Christian communities in seven villages and saw as many as a thousand converts baptized. While *en route* to Europe in 1820, he died in the Cape in South Africa, probably murdered.

The LMS arrived in Madras in 1805, at first seeking to minister to the British and Eurasians in the area but in 1819 turning to the Tamils. The Anglicans of the CMS became involved in the work in Madras in 1814. The church they established very quickly became autonomous, and they soon had about forty schools in which there were more than two thousand students. The Wesleyan Methodist Missionary Society (WMMS) of Britain established a mission station in the region of Madras in 1817. It later erected elementary schools that were teaching about 3,800 students, and eventually it also established institutions of higher education. In contrast, its evangelistic efforts did not prove to be fruitful. The mission of the Free Church of Scotland created the Free Church Institution and Madras Christian College, an impressive college of high standards that in 1875 was teaching three thousand students. One of the striking characteristics of this institution was that sons of Brahmans and sons of Pariahs were sitting together on the same benches.

The American Board arrived in Madoura in 1834. Its activities were more successful in the villages than in the cities. By 1880 it was active in 250 villages and had about eight thousand Christians living in thirty-two different communities, the majority of them financially supporting their own pastors.

## SOME STATISTICS

According to Stephen Neill, the Protestant and Anglican population for the whole of India in 1858 came to about 100,000 members. There were at that time 2,400 indigenous workers and nearly one thousand missionaries. Fifty years later in 1907, the same churches counted 825,000 Christians in their ranks and an additional 3,600 missionaries. By 1914 the churches reached 1 million members, with about 5,500 missionaries.

Toward the end of the nineteenth century, many conferences were held and alliances formed with the intention of unifying the numerous missionary societies and denominations present in India. These included: Anglicans, Presbyterians, Lutherans, Methodists, and Baptists—with more Europeans than North Americans. According to J.-F. Zorn, "One of the artisans of the unity of the churches of India was Vedanayagam Samuel Azariah (1874–1945), sponsor of the Christian Union of Young People . . . At the time of the Edinburgh Missionary Conference of 1910, Azariah vigorously fought the paternalistic tendencies of the missionaries. In 1912 he was ordained the first Indian bishop of the Anglican Church."[51]

## THE MISSION TO BANGLADESH

Northeast of India, Bangladesh is one of the poorest countries in the world, a victim of repeated flooding. Its dense population is 85 percent Muslim. In 1947 at the time of India's independence, it formed a single state with Pakistan, the two regions being separated by 1,500 kilometers of Indian territory. Bangladesh seceded, becoming an independent state at the end of 1973.

Catholic missionaries came in the sixteenth century with the Portuguese merchants, but nothing remains of their work, and the first diocese of the country was not inaugurated until 1886. Catholicism was especially concentrated in the cities,

---

51  J.-F. Zorn, "Missions protestantes en Afrique australe," in *Histoire du christianisme,* vol. 11 (Paris: Desclée, 1995), 1056.

principally in the capital of Dhaka; and it was the religion of the racially mixed population descended from Portuguese and Bangladeshis.

When the Baptist mission of William Carey distributed its printed texts in Bengali in 1795, much of the literature was distributed in localities that are part of present-day Bangladesh. Though Dhaka heard the gospel as early as 1816, it was not until the end of the nineteenth century that a wave of conversions swept through the region of Mymensingh. The Baptist Union of Bangladesh was formed from the church founded by the British Baptists and those issued from the work of the Australian and New Zealand Baptists, reinforced later by the Southern Baptists of the United States.

Other Protestant churches were also formed. The Church of Bangladesh emerged from the union between the Presbyterian and Anglican missions, the latter present as early as 1805. The mission of Santal that opened in the north of India formed the Evangelical Lutheran churches in 1867. It received support from the Danish, Norwegian, and American Lutheran missionary societies. The church of Sylhet, two hundred kilometers to the northeast of Dhaka, was formed in about 1880 from the ministry of Welsh Presbyterians.

## THE MISSION TO PAKISTAN

When Great Britain granted independence to India in 1947 under pressure from the peaceful movement of Mahatma Gandhi, Pakistan detached itself from India to become an independent state. In 1956 the nation declared itself to be an Islamic republic.

Christianity penetrated the region of the Punjab in the eighth century through the work of Nestorian missionaries, but after several centuries nothing remained of their efforts. In 1594 Jesuit missionaries established contact with the court of the Mogul emperor Akbar in Lahore—also in the Punjab. The church made inroads at this time, and Augustinian and Carmelite missionaries made further forays later in the seventeenth century. Due to persecution, however, the Catholic Church withdrew in 1672, and it was not until 1842 in the era of British colonialism that Catholic missions regained a foothold in the country.

In 1849 American Presbyterian missionaries became the first Protestants to establish a mission base in Lahore. In 1855 they extended their activities to the regions west of the city. Two churches resulted from these efforts, with the United Presbyterian Church of Pakistan becoming the largest Protestant church in the country. In the nineteenth century it established three institutions of high education, and three more in the twentieth century.

Other missions were also present. The Anglicans of the CMS were in Karachi as early as 1850, and the diocese of Lahore was organized in 1877. The American Methodists, arriving in Karachi in 1873, were at the origin of a massive movement of conversions among the outcaste Hindus that occurred in the center of Punjab between 1902 and 1915, during which the number of Christians grew from 1,200 to fifteen thousand. In 1903 the Danish Lutheran Mission of Pathan undertook the evangelization of the northwest with the aid of Finnish Lutherans. The Salvation Army entered the field in 1883, the Churches of God in 1911, the Adventists in 1913, and the International Church of the Foursquare Gospel in 1928.

## PERSIA (IRAN)

Henry Martyn (1780–1812). In six years of ministry, he translated the New Testament into Arabic, Urdu, and Persian.

Two medical doctors from the Moravian Mission of Herrnhut, Friedrich Hocker and Johann Rüffer, worked in Persia between 1747 and 1750, but without success. If these two are set aside, the Englishman Henry Martyn (1780–1812) was the first Protestant missionary to undertake the evangelization of Persia.[52] Martyn was a brilliant mathematics student at Cambridge, England. Following his reading of the *Journal of David Brainerd* and learning of William Carey, he came to dedicate himself unreservedly to the service of God. He opted for a celibate and abstemious—even ascetic—life. In 1805 he was ordained into the ministry of the Anglican Church and, a little later, left for the Indies as a chaplain for the British East India Company. At a time when missionaries were judged undesirable by the British colonial administration, a chaplaincy was the surest means to obtain the authorization necessary to enter the country.

He met William Carey and his colleagues in Serampore. Carey discerned his intellectual capacities and encouraged him to undertake the work of Bible translation. He sojourned for five years in the Muslim region of northern India (present-day Pakistan). Knowing that he was an Anglican minister, the CMS proposed to assume responsibility for his salary in order to free him from his obligations to the British East India Company. Because of his ardent zeal, Martyn had been engaged in numerous missionary activities that were well beyond his responsibilities as a chaplain: he preached more to the Indians than to the Europeans; he opened schools; and he devoted himself to the translation of the New Testament in the languages spoken by the neighboring peoples of Persia and Arabia. In the latter work, he displayed remarkable linguistic gifts, as Carey had anticipated.

Though in precarious health, in 1811 Martyn decided to travel by sea to Persia in order to verify the accuracy of his translation and to promote its distribution. The climate being better, his health was restored. Soon he began to travel on foot or camel throughout the country, and he adopted the dress and lifestyle of the local population. He tried to gather the young people of the country around himself in order to instruct them in the Christian faith and also to further master their language to the end that he might perfect his translation. But the life of the common people in Persia was difficult, and without a respite, it was exhausting him. Consequently, his health once again began to decline. Sensing that his time was drawing to a close, he worked relentlessly at the revision of his translation in the hope of being able to personally offer the New Testament as a gift to the Shah of Persia. Sadly, his dream was not

---

52 Since 1935 the Persian kingdom has been called Iran.

realized. Gravely ill, he had to be evacuated to Britain and died in Asia Minor on his way home. He was only thirty-two years old and had spent the last year of his life in pain as he labored in Persia.

Despite the brevity of his ministry (six years in all), he produced excellent translations of the New Testament in Arabic, Urdu (the major language in Pakistan), and Persian. He remains an important figure in the history of mission, for he was one of the first Protestants to plead the cause of the evangelization of the Muslim world. Julius Richter writes, "The life of Martyn, marked by an extraordinary zeal, left a profound impression. But his death was a sermon even more powerful than his life."[53] In response to his pressing appeal for the evangelization of the Muslim populations, two missionaries traveled to Tabriz.

In 1832 the American Board sent two American missionaries, Dr. Eli Smith and Dr. Joseph Dwight, to work in Persia. Beginning in 1834, they concentrated their efforts on the Nestorian Christians who had been living in Persia for more than a thousand years.[54] In 1835 they settled at Urmia (present-day Rezaye, near the border of Azerbaijan). The spiritual life of this church was almost extinguished, and most of its people were illiterate. Moreover, the old translation of the Bible and the liturgy that they had were written in a language that had become incomprehensible to them.[55] Reinforced by two new missionaries, Justin Perkins and Dr. Asahel Grant, they established excellent relations with the Nestorians, but the leaders of the church resisted any idea of reform.[56] In 1838 a printing press was installed, and the New Testament appeared in the people's language in 1846, and then the entire Bible in 1852. Grant decided to live in the mountains of Kurdistan where he found numerous Nestorians. Welcomed by the patriarch, he established a mission station and, over the course of twenty years, performed medical work. But the conditions of life were so crude that the Western missionaries who succeeded him did not last long, and so this work was given to indigenous laborers. In 1855 the Evangelical Church of Persia (Presbyterian) was formally established, formed essentially of Nestorian converts.

After the brief career of Henry Martyn, the CMS was no longer active in Persia until 1871. Its renewed efforts came about without the church intending it. One of its missionaries in the Punjab, the Irishman Robert Bruce, asked to be allowed to remain for one year in Persia as he passed through the country on his journey to Europe for a vacation. He wished to study the language and to acquire a better knowledge of Persian Islam. Eventually he entirely declined his vacation and remained in Ispahan for two years. Although he was prepared to reassume his post in the Punjab, nine

---

53   Julius Richter, *Mission und evangelisation im Orient* (Gütersloh, Germany: Bertelsmann Verlag, 1930), 220.

54   One part of the Nestorians had been won to Roman Catholicism and its people were known as Chaldean Christians.

55   Their Bible was the Peschitto, an Aramean translation of the Gospels made in Edesse in the fifth century.

56   Perkins stayed in Persia until his death in 1869. As for Grant, he wrote a passionate narrative of his journey, praising the very warm welcome that the Nestorian Christians had for a Protestant missionary doctor. In the second part of his work he tried to demonstrate that the Nestorians of this region had been Christians since the second century, well before the coming of the disciples of Nestorius. He also believed that they had easily accepted the gospel. They were in effect monotheists and claimed descent from the Ten Lost Tribes of Israel: Asahel Grant, *Les Nestorians ou les tribus perdues* (Paris: Librairie Delay, 1843).

Muslims with whom he had had long discussions came to ask him for baptism, an extraordinary request for Muslims. It was evidence of a call for Bruce to live there, and the CMS agreed that its "hand had been forced by the Holy Spirit." Nevertheless Bruce wrote humbly of his new vocation: "I am not reaping the harvest; I can scarcely claim to be sowing the seed; I am hardly plowing the soil; *but I am gathering out the stones*. That, too, is missionary work; let it be supported by loving sympathy and fervent prayer."[57]

In 1875 Persia was recognized as a mission field by the CMS. Later, between 1897 and 1900, there were three stations in addition to that of Ispahan, with two hospitals and several dispensaries in the villages. The majority of the missionaries were doctors and nurses. Two schools were also opened, as well as a teaching institution for blind children; and various artisan shops were opened, producing traditional local crafts to provide a source of income for the poor women of the area. In contrast to other Protestant missions, the Anglicans did not try to reform the old Christian churches, whether Orthodox or Assyrian (Nestorian); rather, they sought conversions, with a small degree of success it is true, among the Jews, Muslims, and Parses (Zoroastrians).

In 1908 the Deutsche Blindenmission (German Mission to the Blind, later called Christoffel Blindemission to honor the founder, Ernst Jacob Christoffel) began to operate in Persia; and in 1909 some Persians who had emigrated to the United States and become Pentecostals returned to evangelize their home country, but their work was interrupted by the First World War. The American Assemblies of God continued in this effort beginning in 1924. In 1911 the Scandinavians of the Lutheran Mission to the East sent their first missionaries in the very year of their founding. The Adventists appeared in the country at the same time, and the Brethren Assemblies arrived in 1920. None of these undertakings, however, had a large impact on the country.

## THE MISSION TO CEYLON (SRI LANKA)

The island of Ceylon became independent at the same time as India in 1947. Its size is approximately that of Belgium and Holland combined. In 1900 the population was 60 percent Buddhist. The Hindus, who were then 23 percent, have since declined to about half their previous number due to the ethnic conflicts of the last decades of the twentieth century. The proportion of Christians was about 10 percent in 1900 and remained stable through the course of the twentieth century.[58] The Muslims, at 7 percent in 1900, came largely from Malaysia.

The Christian presence on this island goes back to antiquity. Cosmas Indicopleustes, a Nestorian traveler, reported discovering a church there in the year 537. Though purportedly founded by the Apostle Thomas, no direct evidence for this tradition remains today. The Portuguese occupied the island in 1505 and reintroduced Christianity. In 1544 the Jesuit missionary Francis Xavier sojourned in the north of the island, and his ministry bore lasting fruit among the pearl fishermen of the Paravar

---

57  Neill, *A History of Christian Missions*, 367.
58  Statistics furnished by Barrett, *Encyclopedia*, 694–698. (See 2001 edition.)

caste. He baptized seven hundred among them, and despite persecution, this church has endured until today. Other Jesuit missionaries introduced Christianity among the Hindu population, but their limited success was obtained through the toleration of syncretism and by procuring certain social advantages for the converts. The Buddhists, in contrast, were more refractory.

Between 1640 and 1658 the Dutch held the island. Reformed chaplains and missionaries disembarked in 1642 and soon obtained the expulsion of the Portuguese priests and seized the Catholic churches. The Reformed church grew rapidly, but in 1672 the Reformed minister Philippus Baldacus deplored that most of the Christians were only so in name, being still pagans in their hearts. Hope of gain or fear of chastisement had been the principal motivations for these "converts" to enter the church. At the end of the seventeenth century, the Reformed ministers had registered 300,000 baptisms, and by 1722 Protestants theoretically constituted 21 percent of the population. In Holland voices were raised against the recourse to compulsion to obtain conversions, a strategy judged to be totally incompatible with the gospel and the spirit of Protestantism.

Two Moravian Brethren arrived in 1740, but the Reformed consistory obtained their expulsion in little time. Nevertheless, by 1760 the Dutch ministers were few in number, there being not more than five, and only one of these spoke the Singhalese language. Consequently, they asked the help of C. F. Schwartz, who spent a year in Ceylon as an itinerant preacher. He tried to raise the spiritual level of the church but apparently without much success. When the British supplanted the Dutch in 1796 and refused to exercise governmental power in religious matters, many of the Reformed Christians on the island returned to Catholicism; thousands of others simply abandoned the Christian faith and began to frequent the Buddhist temples whose reopening the British had authorized. A greatly diminished Protestantism continued to be hindered throughout the nineteenth century by this somber heritage. In 1804 three Germans of the London Mission disembarked in Ceylon, but after ten years of fruitless effort they gave up.

At the insistence of William Carey, the Baptist Missionary Society opened an evangelism post in 1812 at Colombo and extended its work into the villages to the east and south of the city. The chief of the expedition, James Chater, worked assiduously, publishing a grammar of the local language and then a translation of the New Testament, and opening a dozen schools, two of which were for girls. He died in 1829, but Ebenezer Daniel, his successor, also energetically dedicated himself to evangelization. After ten years, Christian services were being celebrated in Colombo and in fifteen villages in the region. At his death in 1844, when the Baptist Missionary Society had been persevering in this work for more than thirty years, only two hundred converts had been baptized. In contrast, more than forty schools were then teaching some one thousand students.

The British Methodists sent six missionaries to Jaffna in 1814. It was with relief that they were received by the Tamil catechist who had been leading the community as well as he could. The Tanquebar Mission had founded the community in the preceding century, but it had been abandoned a dozen years before. Thanks to government funding, the Methodists developed an extensive educational system in Ceylon over a period of twenty years. In 1834 the state placed these schools under its direct responsibility. At that time there were six thousand students, of which 1,600 were girls. Two secondary schools were also then in operation.

The Congregationalists of the American Board, being forced by the British governor of Calcutta to leave Bengal, moved to Ceylon in 1816 to evangelize the Tamils. They exerted much effort but without a proportionate result. The majority of their converts came from the students of poor families who boarded at the schools they operated. Unfortunately, these Christians were cut off from their social milieu, and the mission had to provide work for them so that they would be assured of an income. In 1849 there were 480 converts out of the 680 former students of the boarding school, and most of them were dependent on the mission for employment. Nevertheless, the College of Jaffna, founded in 1823 by the American Board, over the course of the nineteenth century became the most prestigious English-language college in all of Asia.

The CMS decided in 1818 to evangelize the Tamils and Sinhalese who were living in a region where the population's chief source of income was from the production of copper idols. For this reason, the opposition to Christianity was intense, and sowing the seeds of faith very difficult. Later, in another part of the country, the numerous members of the Reformed Church of Holland joined the Anglican Church, which was then experiencing much growth. A census in 1883 furnished the following numbers: there were 35,000 Protestants, 358 churches, 115 mission stations, 36 missionaries, and 38,000 students in the schools. In 1900 there were 40,000 Protestants; about 1.1 percent of the population. At this time the Anglicans were 1.2 percent of the population, and the Catholics 8.3 percent.[59] These figures should be compared to those of 1722 cited earlier, at which time Protestants formed 21 percent of the population.

---

59  The numbers from 1883 are published in: Gustav Burckhardt and Reinhold Grundemann, *Les missions évangéliques*, vol. 1, *Amérique* (Lausanne: Bridel, 1884), 224; those of 1900 are in Barrett, *Encyclopedia*.

# CHAPTER 5

# *Protestant Pioneers in China:*
# *Robert Morrison and Karl Gützlaff*

Before modern times, Christians thrice came to penetrate the immense Chinese empire: first, the Nestorians in the seventh century; second, the Franciscans in the thirteenth century; and third, the Jesuits in the sixteenth century (see pp. 121-22, 126ff, chapter 12). But despite undeniable success, Christianity did not prove to be enduring. In all three cases it was seen as a foreign body that in the end was rejected. Hence by the beginning of the nineteenth century, the Catholic Church in China was small in number and existed in a semiclandestine state. The China of this period was highly xenophobic and seemed to be hermetically sealed to foreigners. Under pain of death the Chinese were forbidden to teach their language to interested foreigners. With these conditions prevailing, to envision the proclamation of the gospel in this country of 150 million people seemed a utopian fantasy. When one speaks of Robert Morrison as the "pioneer of Protestant missions in China," it is important to remember that he spent twenty-five years of his ministry bottled up in the port city of Canton (then the only city open to foreigners) or on the island-like Macao, a Portuguese dependent. Given these realities, Morrison's perseverance and the impact of his work are all the more striking.

## ROBERT MORRISON

Robert Morrison (1782–1834) was the eighth child of a humble Scottish family, his father being a farm worker. Morrison was a gifted adolescent, but in spite of a rigid education, he lacked discipline. At the age of fifteen, he converted and began to frequent a prayer circle in his Presbyterian Church. Some years later, he discerned the call of God and studied for two years in a Congregational theological college. By practicing economy, he paid for his lessons in Latin, Greek, and Hebrew. Then despite the opposition of his family, he offered himself as a candidate to the LMS. At first planning to go to Africa, he was eventually convinced that God wanted him in China, a land that then had no Protestant missionaries.

During his theological training, Morrison also acquired some knowledge of medicine and astronomy, and with the help of a well-read Chinese person living in Britain, he learned the first rudiments of the Chinese language. At the beginning of 1807,

Morrison was ordained to the ministry and left for China. He traveled via America as the British East India Company refused passage to missionaries. It took him almost twelve months to reach Canton.

Convinced that God had directed him to China, Morrison was prepared to confront the most seemingly insurmountable obstacles. He plunged into the work. Observing that due to the high costs in Canton it would be impossible for him to live in the quarter of the city reserved for foreigners, merchants, and diplomats, he found a place to lodge in a seamy district at the edge of the Chinese quarter. He adopted the clothes and lifestyle of the inhabitants so as to become inconspicuous in the neighborhood. He invited local people to visit him, first so that he could learn the language and later to help him in his first translation efforts. They did this at peril to their lives. In addition to police restrictions, the British East India Company engaged in close surveillance on British subjects. It did not want to see its fragile relations with the Chinese government compromised by imprudent expatriates.

Morrison worked relentlessly and used much of his meager income to purchase Chinese books. He soon possessed more than three hundred. But he lived in an insalubrious environment; moreover, he overworked himself and, because of his stringent economizing, was not eating enough. Consequently his health was seriously affected. Among other things, he began to suffer terrible headaches. He would certainly not have survived long in such conditions. What saved him was the need to flee from the onset of civil war. He left without his books, as foreigners throughout the region were forced to immediately depart in the face of the catastrophe. Morrison retreated to Macao, but the Portuguese Catholic priests maneuvered to expel him, and so he had to live in hiding, leaving his home only during the night for fear of being discovered.

Under these conditions, he decided to move temporarily to Indochina or Java where he found himself among Chinese immigrants. His stay proved short, for in 1809 he received an offer of employment from the British East India Company. Informed of his language skills, the company offered him a position as a translator. After two years of difficulties in China, Morrison believed that he detected the hand of God in a proposal that would allow him to return Canton with a good salary and under British protection. The work he would be paid to do would give him contact with numerous Chinese and, hence, the same opportunities to perfect his linguistic knowledge as he might otherwise have had. However, not knowing the nearly insurmountable obstacles that missionaries faced in China, many Christians in Britain did not understand his decision. Moreover, they were hardly familiar with the idea of a "tentmaking" ministry, an expression that Morrison was one of the first to use. It was the strategy of the Apostle Paul, who earned a living by secular employment while working as a missionary (Acts 18:3).

Before returning to Canton, Morrison married Mary Morton, the daughter of British doctor in Macao. They were separated for some time after their marriage, Mary being a foreign woman without authorization to reside in Canton. His new wife was of fragile health and subject to depression. One can imagine that she did not easily endure separation from her husband, who was dividing his time between

Canto and Macao. After little more than a year, to her woes were add the death of their newborn baby, their first child.

Despite the obstacles set up by the authorities, Morrison was engaged in a variety of activities in Canton. Most notably he organized a dispensary, which he soon transformed into a hospital. A doctor from the British East India Company worked there, established a pharmacy, and hired a Chinese doctor. The sick of this immense city, who until this time had no medical care, flocked there by the hundreds. This hospital was one of the first of the numerous Protestant missionary hospitals later established throughout the world.

*Robert Morrison (1782–1834), "the apostle of China."*

Aside from his profession as an interpreter, Morrison dedicated all of his free time to the translation of the Bible. The undertaking was complicated by the fact that the intended readers used several dialects according to their differing social and intellectual levels. He received good counsel about his possible choices as he moved toward a sound solution. He began with the Acts of the Apostles and was able to send a complete translation of it to Britain as early as 1810. Then he published the Gospel of Luke, and by 1812 he had completed Genesis. He also produced translations of a catechism, grammar, lexicon, and large dictionary. There were considerable risks in printing such works. In fact, the decision of an imperial criminal tribunal in 1812 had stipulated:

> Any European who secretly prints books written by preachers in order to corrupt the multitude, and any Chinese or Tartar sent by the Europeans to propagate his religion . . . will be executed.[60]

Unfortunately his translation and printing work were the occasion of a long and painful conflict with the mission of Serampore, which was previously presented (see p. 318-19). Morrison learned that Joshua Marshman, William Carey's colleague—the model of the missionary in Morrison's eyes—had begun the translation of the Bible in Chinese. This troubled him because he was convinced that God had called him to do this work; moreover, he knew that it would be virtually impossible to make a good translation without actually living in China. This waste of effort continued for seventeen years. In Britain, the LMS tried to intervene, but in vain. Marshman finished his work before Morrison, and his Chinese Bible, printed in Serampore, was presented in London in 1823. Morrison had finished the translation of the New Testament in 1813, and the Old Testament in 1819; but refusing to be rushed for the sake of winning a competition to be first, he took several more years to complete an additional revision. The printing was done in Malacca, and the first example of his translation arrived in

---

60 Jacques A. Blocher, *Robert Morrison: L'apôtre de la Chine, 1782–1834* (Paris: Les Bons Semeurs, 1938), 34.

Britain in 1824. The experts concluded that in regards to typography Marshman had done a remarkable job, but that Morrison had produced a linguistic masterpiece.

In reflecting on these unseemly circumstances, Morrison wrote these insightful words: "The great evil of our mission is that no one wants to be second." Perhaps there has been no time in the history of mission when doubtful motivations and the spirit of competition have not been a reality.

In 1813 Morrison welcomed a new arrival, William Milne, a Scotsman like himself. The mission committee had on first sight considered him to be an uneducated shepherd and had rejected him. It later reconsidered its decision on observing his remarkable prayer life and his brilliant record in missionary school.[61] Milne reached Canton by way of Macao, arriving secretly because he had no authorization to enter the country. He made rapid progress in Chinese, but the British East India Company, despite the pleading of Morrison, refused to grant him any legal cover or to offer him employment. After a year of difficulties and living in hiding, both in Canton and Macao, Milne and Morrison agreed that he should go to Malaysia. His principal objective was to find a place where he could establish a center for the mission—the "Ultra-Ganges" mission, as Morrison called it—that would be beyond the exclusionist laws of Canton and the obstructions of the Portuguese in Macao.

Morrison's plan was to establish a center that would serve not only China but also all of Southeast Asia. He believed, "The present situation in China makes the printing of holy books and other missionary work impossible. Since it is even difficult to reside there, it is desirable to establish a mission station near to China, in a country under the protection of some European Protestant government. This station would be the seat of our Chinese mission. Malacca seems to correspond to these conditions." In this place they could establish a school, edit a review, and publish books in Chinese, Malaysian, and English. They could also print a missionary bulletin in English that would help to link together all the Protestant missions working in Asia. An additional goal would be the evangelization of the numerous Chinese and immigrants as well as the Malaysian people.

Milne made the first trip there in 1814 and stayed for a period of seven months. He brought with him two thousand examples of the Chinese New Testament that Morrison had printed in Malacca, as well as thousands of tracks and catechetic manuals. Accompanied by his wife and their two-year-old son, he returned in 1815 to establish a mission base in Malacca.

After being in China for seven years, Morrison baptized the first Chinese convert, Tsae-A-Ko, in Canton on July 16, 1814. The baptism took place near a spring that flowed from a hill towards the ocean shore, far from human gaze, but under the sight of God. "Could this be," wrote Morrison, "the first fruits of a great harvest, among the millions who will believe in Jesus and will be saved by him from the wrath to come." Tsae-A-Ko died four years later, firm in the faith.

---

61  In the manner of Patrick, the evangelist of Ireland at the beginning of the fifth century, Milne passed some hours and even nights in prayer while guarding his sheep.

Mary Morrison's health was fragile, and at the beginning of 1815 it was decided that she should return to Europe for medical care. Morrison was separated from his wife and two children for six years. Not long after their return, in June 1821, Mary was struck down by cholera and died after two days. She left a nine-year-old daughter and a son of seven. The Catholic Church of Macao refused its cemetery to a heretic, as did the Portuguese authorities in the city. Morrison had to bury his wife in a common grave. When the British East India Company was informed of this sad event, it acquired land that became the British cemetery of Macao.

A year later, William Milne's wife also died. She was thirty-five years old and left four young children. Milne himself died less than two years later while in Singapore. He had spent nine years in Asia, and his death was a hard blow to the mission. His mastery of Chinese, as well as his zeal and piety, had made him an ideal missionary.

Desiring to honor its native son, in 1817 the University of Glasgow awarded Morrison the title of doctor *honoris causa* in recognition of the scientific value of his work in China. But the prize winner could scarcely rejoice, shunning any publicity that might alert the Chinese authorities to his work. Human praise had little value in his eyes as compared to the advancement of the work of God in China.

One of the great achievements of the Ultra-Ganges mission was the Anglo-Chinese college of Malacca. Similar to the college at Serampore established by Carey, the program included the study of Asian languages as well as English and Western sciences. Morrison hoped to train men to be living bridges between the cultures of the Orient and Occident. The center at Malacca soon attracted young European missionaries who came to study Chinese. Morrison saw in them the prospect of near-term reinforcements. The project was ambitious and could not be put fully into effect. Nevertheless, between 1818 and 1833, forty students completed the cycle of studies, and among them, fifteen received baptism.

Morrison had other reasons, perhaps less grandiose, to be encouraged. In 1823 in Canton the spouse of a Chinese Christian and their child asked for baptism. Her husband, Liang Fah, a printer, had preceded them in the faith and had courageously persevered despite physical abuse, which confirmed his faith. This was the first Chinese family to convert, the base cell of an embryonic church. Liang Fah would soon be the first Chinese to receive ordination to the ministry of evangelism in the Protestant church in China.

Having completed the sixth and last volume of his Chinese dictionary of 4,600 pages and forty thousand words, the fruit of sixteen years of labor financed by the British East India Company, at the end of the year 1823 Morrison returned to Britain for a stay of indeterminate length. Upon his arrival, he was received by King George IV, who named him a member of the Royal Society. Famous throughout the country, he preached to vast audiences, alerting Christians to their missionary responsibility. He put his notoriety to profitable use by eliciting support for the creation of a language institute in order to facilitate the promotion of the gospel in the world, and he remained in Britain until he was able to establish within the structure of this organization a School of Oriental Languages.[62] Morrison embarked in 1826 for a new sojourn in China after marrying a second wife, Elisabeth Armstrong of Liverpool.

On his return, Morrison stopped in Singapore where the seat of the Ultra-Ganges mission had been transferred. More or less abandoned, he tried to reorganize it, but after several years it proved insupportable. At Macao, he found his house and possessions in ruins: everything had been devoured by white ants (termites). Moreover, the Jesuits, trying to neutralize him because of their anxiety over his successes, succeeded in having the government confiscate the printing press at Macao, which had printed thousands of books and brochures. Due to the prohibition on foreigners venturing from Canton, these printed texts were Morrison's only means of introducing the message of the gospel into the interior of the country.

Before so many obstacles, trials, and hostility, how could he not be discouraged? But Morrison knew where to find the source from which to draw strength and hope. He witnessed to it in these lines that sprang from his heart during times of aridity: "O Golgotha, O Golgotha! when I see the blood of Jesus streaming from you, I am astonished at the coldness of my love and the cowardice of my zeal."

Having accorded a special status to Morrison, the British East India Company was not disposed to allow other British subjects to enter China under its protection for the cause of the gospel. From then on, only missionaries from other nationalities would have access to the country. This was the case with several young Americans in 1830 and 1832. After having worked for twenty-five years, most of the time in solitude, sadness, and adversity, Morrison could finally count on a missionary team; and though he had scarcely baptized more than a dozen believers, he had effectively prepared the ground for his successors through his translations and the men he had taught.

In 1833, after seven years in China, Elisabeth Morrison's health had deteriorated and she had to return to England to care for herself. She took five children with her from Robert Morrison's first and second marriages. Only John, Morrison's eldest son, who was already passionate about the translation work and hoped to walk in his father's footsteps, remained with him. At the age of sixteen, he was named translator for the British merchants of Canton. Morrison would never see his wife and other children again. Though only in his fifties, he had the body of an old man, used up by a superhuman task and an unhealthy climate. He no longer had the strength to face the assault of a fever. On August 1, 1834, he entered into his final rest at the age of fifty-two.

---

62  Unhappily, the school was in advance of its time and those who appreciated its strategic value were rare indeed. Consequently, it declined after several years due to lack of support.

# THE WORK THAT FOLLOWED

### Karl Gützlaff

In the portrait gallery of missionary pioneers, Karl Gützlaff (1803–1851) occupies a special and unusual place. Born in Germany in 1803, he studied at Basel and then went with his wife to Java in 1827 under the care of the Netherlands Society of Missions. After a year, he separated from this mission and established himself as an independent missionary in Bangkok with Jacob Tomlin, a colleague from the London Missionary Society. He soon made a good translation of several books of the Bible in Siamese. After the death of his wife in 1831, he began to travel from south to north along the China coast, venturing as far as Formosa (Taiwan), Manchuria, and Korea. His adventurous spirit led him to run considerable dangers while he was attempting to distribute Christian literature. Like Robert Morrison, he supplied himself with tracts and Chinese Bible texts and eventually even managed to enter into the interior of the continent—who knows how? He wrote the narrative of his productive travels, including spectacular incidents that helped to make his book a sensation in Europe and the United States.

*Karl Gützlaff's house in Bangkok.*

Gützlaff settled in Macao in 1834, the year of Morrison's death, and obtained a position as an interpreter at the British embassy. In 1842, profiting from his position in the diplomatic world and thanks to his German nationality, he was able to enjoy the role of a negotiator between the British and Chinese at the time of the Treaty of Nanking. The treaty brought an end to the Opium War and accorded free access to foreigners to five Chinese ports. Gützlaff became an administrator for a time in the city of Ningpo, and then once again dedicated himself entirely to his work as an evangelist. Next he resided in the city of Hong Kong, which became British due to the treaty. He made it the base of his many activities, and in six years he hired more than two hundred colporteurs. He quickly put them to work, assured of their zeal for having accorded them comfortable salaries. They were supposed to travel into each of the eighteen provinces of China where they would distribute hundreds of New Testaments. When they completed their task, they would have prepared the way for thousands of baptisms to occur over the next few years.

In 1849, Gützlaff made a tour of Europe in which he visited many churches to plead the cause of the evangelization of China. He raised the enthusiasm of numerous Christians and increased the already huge momentum in support of his ambitious projects. After several months, however, a disheartening report arrived from Hong Kong, transmitted by the missionary Theodore Hamberg, an employee of the Rhine Mission charged with the supervision of Gützlaff's work in his absence. The report said that all was moonshine. The colporteurs had practically never left Hong Kong and were leading comfortable lives with the salaries that Gützlaff had granted them; almost all were crooks, opium traffickers, indeed criminals.[63] Without the least concern for world evangelization or the distribution of the Bible, they were returning the literature to the printers from which Gützlaff was provisioning them and then buying the same merchandise a second time. As for the baptisms, they existed only in the fertile imagination of these "colleagues" who were exploiting Gützlaff's credulity. Informed of this chicanery, Gützlaff quickly returned to China. Despite his consternation, he energetically took up his work again, convinced that it was a well-founded enterprise. He died, however, the following year without having been able to recommence the distribution of New Testaments printed in China.

While it is generally recognized that his good faith was not in question, he had shown naïveté and enthusiasm touched with megalomania. Among his numerous friends and donors in Europe, no one seemed to be anxious about the credibility of an enterprise led by an individualist without supervision. Gützlaff was probably a superficial man, but one animated by audacity and astonishing energy and possessed of a prophetic vision about the importance of evangelization by means of the printed word. Commenting on this tragicomedy, Stephen Neill said of Gützlaff that one could see in him "a saint, an eccentric, a visionary, an authentic pioneer or a devoted fanatic." Hudson Taylor went so far as to accord him the title "Grandfather of the China Interior Mission."

## THE MULTIPLICATION OF PROTESTANT MISSIONS

The treaty of Nanking in 1842, which confirmed the victory of Great Britain in the First Opium War begun three years earlier, forced the Chinese to open their borders more widely to foreigners. The conflict erupted when the Chinese government determined to prohibit the British East India Company from acquiring opium and ordered the destruction of twenty thousand crates of this drug that had already been purchased by the British. Four coastal cities, in addition to the port of Canton, had from this time on to admit the presence of Westerners. There were then only about fifty

---

63   According to Hamberg, there were sixty  among the two hundred colporteurs who were opium smokers, fifty-five who were crooks, fifty who had disappeared without leaving a trace, fifteen who were incompetent, and twenty who were honest men.

Protestants in all of China. The LMS, which had already supported Morrison, Milne, and their colleagues in very difficult conditions, intensified its efforts. Other British and Americans missions—Anglicans, Methodists, Presbyterians, Congregationalists, and Baptists—profited from this opening and rushed in with large numbers. But they remained concentrated in these urban areas, not to say pent up. All this activity was due to a treaty in which Westerners had dictated conditions by the force of arms at the conclusion of a war it had started for a shameful motive—authorization of the opium trade. This placed mission in a false position with the Chinese population and its humiliated authorities. Those who arrived in this period had to be very dedicated, for their efforts were compromised through no fault of their own, and often they were not even conscious of it.

It is in this context that Hudson Taylor began his ministry, which extended through the second half of the nineteenth century.

# CHAPTER 6

# Hudson Taylor and the China Inland Mission

Hudson Taylor (1832–1905) incontestably occupies a place of eminence in the history of mission. At the time of his death the China Inland Mission, which had been founded forty years earlier, had 828 missionaries on the field and was the largest Protestant mission society of the age. Moreover, Taylor's manner of living out his faith and his engagement body and soul in the vocation to which he knew himself called have been a source of inspiration for generations of Christians. Other mission societies were formed according to his principle of "walking by faith," and it is impossible to know the number of missionary vocations that can be attributed to the reading of his biography, written by his son and his daughter-in-law.[64]

Especially important is that his conception of mission was in advance of his time. While retracing the outlines of his career at several crucial junctures, we will observe the innovative nature of his initiatives. When Taylor came of age, mission had enjoyed a half century of remarkable growth. Yet the first missionary societies, which were established as a result of the spiritual awakening that occurred in the last years of the eighteenth and the beginning of the nineteenth centuries, had become somewhat institutionalized. Taylor advocated and employed a new and dynamic understanding of what a mission society should be, a development that could not pass without notice among the mission-minded.

Taylor came to symbolize the heroic pioneer missionary, at once without fault and always triumphant. However, he would not have recognized himself in this image. Timid, short of stature, and limited by fragile health, he was subject to crises of discouragement. He also knew that his preparation as a missionary was incomplete, having arrived in China before finishing his medical studies or committing himself to any theological or missionary school.

---

64  The "great biography" of Hudson Taylor, written in 1918 by Mr. and Mrs. Howard Taylor, was published in two volumes in French in 1948 by the *Groupes Missionaires*, which reedited it as a single condensed volume in 1979. The abridged biography for youth was published in French in 1986 (same authors and editors) under the title *The Adventure of Faith*. The biography rewritten by Roger Steer, *Hudson Taylor: A Man in Christ*, was published in English in 1990 and French in 1996 under the title: *Hudson Taylor: L'evangile au coeur de la Chine* [The gospel in the heart of China] (Lavigny: Les Groupes Missionaires). See also K. S. Latourette, *A History of Christian Missions in China* (London: SPCK, 1929).

## YOUTH AND TRAINING

Taylor was born in Barnsley, in Yorkshire, England on May 21, 1832 in a strict and pious Methodist family of modest means. At the time of his birth, his parents dedicated him to missionary service in China, a country that would become familiar to him in childhood thorough the conversation and prayers of his father. His sister and most especially his mother played an important role in the development of his spiritual life. He converted at the age of seventeen, and this experience was accompanied by the conviction that God was calling him to China.[65]

The training that he acquired was that of an autodidact: personal systematic study of the Bible, visits to the poor quarter of town for purposes of evangelism, and training in the rudiments of the Chinese language. Lacking the means to acquire a dictionary, he made a word-to-word comparison of a Chinese version of the Gospel of Luke and his English Bible and thereby identified six hundred Chinese characters. To prepare himself for the difficult life of a pioneer missionary, he began to live as frugally as possible, sleeping on the bare ground, eating only black bread and apples for four months at a time, and all the while walking twelve kilometers a day to get to work. He eventually obtained a job as an assistant to a doctor and then pursued his medical studies in a hospital.

China occupied all his waking thoughts. These lines written to his mother reveal his state of mind:

> I do not know how to express the extent to which I long to be a missionary, to carry the Good News to sinners who are perishing, to expend myself for the One who died for me. Think of 12 million—a number that one can not grasp—12 million souls in China that, each year, enter into eternity, without God and without hope . . . Let us have compassion on this multitude![66]

Taylor offered his services to a recently formed and little-organized mission, the Chinese Evangelization Society (CES), this being the only one he could find that would accept a candidate without a university education. Much was spoken then of the Taiping movement and those areas of China where it had managed to impose itself. The founder, Hung-ch'üan, had originally been a Chinese evangelist trained by a Baptist missionary, but he suffered from mental instability and megalomania. He taught the existence of God the Father and of his Son Jesus, but he also said that he was the younger brother of Jesus, and he mixed Taoist oracles with biblical revelation. It is not surprising that the Taiping Rebellion (the term means "Great Peace") rapidly degenerated, disappointing the hopes of those who imagined that a large door had been

---

65  After his conversion, Taylor was influenced by the thought of the Brethren Assemblies who wanted churches to avoid all ecclesiastical and foreign structures in their forms of clericalism and, in effect, to apply strictly the principle of the priesthood of all believers. Later he would refuse to wear ecclesiastical garments, believing that the spirit of "denominationalism" is incompatible with biblical teachings. But contrary to the "Brethren," he never gave in to an isolationist tendency.

66  Howard Taylor, *L'aventure de la foi* [The abridged biography] (Lavigny: Les Groupes Missionaires, 1986), 25.

opened to Christian missions in China.[67] In response, the British and Foreign Bible Society printed a million New Testaments in the Chinese language; and the committee of the CES asked Taylor to conclude his medical studies and to embark without delay for China. It was the autumn of 1853, and he was then twenty-one years old.

## THE FIRST SOJOURN IN CHINA

At the time Taylor disembarked, various missionary societies were already present (see the preceding chapter) in the five port cities open to foreigners, which included Shanghai.[68] There were seventy Protestant missionaries then in China, two-thirds of them American and one-third British. The number of converts was extremely low. According to Leslie T. Lyall, in the ports open to foreigners there were 350 Chinese Protestants and 330,000 Catholics.[69]

After a voyage of five and a half months, Taylor arrived at Shanghai where the situation was extremely dangerous due to the insurrection. The cost of living was exorbitant and out of proportion to his meager resources. The committee of the CES, being inexperienced and lacking means, failed him at this point. But, fortunately, he was supported by a colleague from the London Missionary Society. This did not prevent the CES from sending the Scottish Doctor William Parker and his wife and children. With great difficulty Taylor was able to find lodging for them in a house rented by the CMS, an expression of the very real solidarity between Protestant mission organizations that then existed.

Despite the precariousness of his financial support and his intensive study of the language, Taylor undertook a dozen journeys for the purpose of evangelization during the first two years of his sojourn in China. He traveled in a junk on the nation's canals in the area around Shanghai where the population was dense. Sometimes he was accompanied by Parker and at other times by the Reverend J. S. Burdon, a colleague from the CMS who later became the bishop of Hong Kong. Several other missions were already at work in Shanghai, but Taylor wanted to reach those who were "beyond," those that the messengers of the gospel had not yet reached. He did it at great personal risk, for the settlement agreed to in the Treaty of Nanking authorized the Mandarins to incarcerate any foreigner found outside of the authorized zones. At the end of this period, he realized the extent to which his Western clothes in the countryside were exciting both the curiosity and the distrust of the inhabitants and preventing him from getting close to them. He was conscious of the fierce criticism that attempting to fit into the society would evoke among the missions established in Shanghai but decided nevertheless to dress in Chinese clothes and to cut his hair as a Chinese—that is, to shave the front of his head, dye his hair black, and wear a long braid of hair down the back of his neck. The reaction of his colleagues

---

67  After six years of bloodshed in which British troops aided the Imperial army, the insurrection ended in 1864.

68  Chinese politics with respect to foreigners was liberalized several years later thanks to the Treaty of Tientsin (1858).

69  Leslie T. Lyall, *Passion pour l'extraordinaire: Mission à l'intérieur de la Chine, 1865–1965* (Thune, Switzerland: Union Missionaire d'Outre-mer, 1965), 22. The author recalled that before the arrival of Robert Morrison in 1807, there was not a single Protestant Christian in China.

was as he feared, but the reaction of the population confirmed that his decision was well founded. If he lost the prestige of the foreigners, he gained the liberty to mix with the population.

After two and a half years, Taylor and Parker moved to the great city of Ningpo, two hundred kilometers farther to the south. There they found a CES colleague already in place, John Jones, and some Presbyterian, Baptist, and Anglican missionaries who had insisted on Parker opening a hospital in the city. It was during this period that Taylor made the decision to leave the Society for the Evangelization of China whose financial management and indebtedness had become unconscionable to him.

In January 1858, Taylor married Maria Dyer whose deceased parents had as early as 1827 been the colleagues of Robert Morrison, the pioneer of Protestant missions in China. Maria was living in Ningpo with her sister under the supervision of a very strict English matron. The woman put all her energy into blocking Maria's marriage to a young, nonconformist missionary. Thanks to the presence of his wife, who had spent all of her childhood in China, the missionaries were able to make contact with women and children; and the medical work in the hospital also provided many occasions to make known the love of God.

In August 1859, Parker's wife succumbed to cholera, and Parker had to return to Europe to entrust his five children to their grandparents.[70] Taylor was henceforth left alone to direct the hospital. Because this establishment was completely lacking in financial resources and had no mission to support it, the Christians of Ningpo came there to work without pay to the extent that they were available. The following anecdote is representative of dozens of others, which are sprinkled liberally throughout Taylor's biography. When the financial reserves of the hospital were totally exhausted, the cook came to warn that he was reaching the bottom of the last sack of rice. The missionary calmly responded: "Then the moment when the Lord is going to help us must be very near." Before the sack was entirely empty, a gift of fifty pounds sterling arrived with a letter from a British friend, saying that he had just inherited a fortune and was looking for the best way to use it for the work of God.[71]

The first floor of the Taylors' home was used as a meeting room and, opening onto the road, often attracted the curious. One of these was a cotton merchant, M. Nyi, a former Buddhist chief and president of a Confucianist society. He fortuitously entered one day and became engrossed in a Bible reading. He remained to listen to the foreign preacher who had perfectly mastered the local dialect. At the conclusion of Taylor's sermon, Nyi addressed the audience: "I have sought the truth near and far for a long time, but without ever discovering it. I have found rest neither

---

70  Steer (*L'evangile*, 175) notes on this subject that in fifty years, of the more than two hundred Protestant missionaries who had arrived since Morrison in 1807, more than forty had died on the mission field and fifty-one had lost their wives.

71  Many of these types of stories can also be found in the life of the British philanthropist George Müller, who collected thousands of orphans without having available regular financial resources. Müller was for Taylor an elder brother and a stimulating example of living by faith, and from the beginning of the China Inland Mission, Müller allocated large sums of money to him. As we have already indicated in Book II, Chapter 2, various Christian works, inspired by these examples and called faith missions, appeared in the last decades of the nineteenth and the first decades of the twentieth centuries.

in Confucianism nor in Buddhism nor in Taoism, but I find it in what you have been listening to this evening. This is why from now on, I believe in Jesus."[72] Becoming a passionate reader of the Bible, he soon went so far as to preach Jesus Christ at the Confucian society over which he had formerly presided.

The small Church of Ningpo grew slowly. In the winter of 1860, when the church had about thirty members, sixteen sick people from the hospital were admitted to baptism. At this time Hudson and Maria left to take a vacation in Britain for reasons of health.

*Hudson and Maria Taylor in 1861,
a little after their return to England.*

## "HIDDEN YEARS" IN ENGLAND

The Taylors' sojourn in China had lasted six years, and this is the same length of time that they would pass in Britain. Their first purpose was to reestablish Hudson's health, which had become gravely impaired. With his health restored, Hudson recommenced his medical studies, obtaining his doctorate in 1865. He then turned his attention to a revision of the New Testament in the Ningpo dialect. For this purpose a Christian Chinese, Wang Lae djün, had accompanied him to Britain. They soon set to work on a translation of various books of the New Testament and on some hymns.

These years of retreat were painful for Taylor. He felt with increasing urgency the need to evangelize the interior of China, which would necessarily require the engagement of numerous workers. Having left the CES, he went about the task of communicating his vision to all the British missionary organizations working in China, but everywhere he received the same response: the organizations lacked the means to do the job, and there were insurmountable obstacles to entering the interior of China.

In collaboration with his wife, Taylor wrote and published *China, its Spiritual Needs and its Rights,* a book that enjoyed a great influence on how British Christians perceived the needs of China. The first edition was exhausted in three weeks and the work was republished seven times in twenty years.

During this time that he passed while far away from China, Taylor often seemed sunk in an unhealthy guilt, and his spirit alternated between an audacious faith and prudent realism. "The millions of Chinese who were perishing," he wrote, "filled my heart and mind. I had no moment of respite during the day and did not sleep for most of the night. Then my health began to go."

In the winter of 1865, he enjoyed several days of repose on the shores of Brighton when suddenly he had the conviction that he was supposed to ask God for "twenty-four dedicated and qualified workers," two for each of the eleven provinces of China that were entirely without missionaries and two for Mongolia. He inscribed on a

---

72 Taylor, op. cit., 83.

page of his Bible (the precious note is still preserved) the date of his firm decision to await the granting of this prayer.

## THE FOUNDING OF THE CHINA INLAND MISSION

In the wake of this conviction, sustained by his wife and several friends, he conceived the idea of the China Inland Mission (CIM) and deposited in a bank account all the fortune this father of four children had. It came to, he declared, "Ten pounds, and all the promises of God." Summarized here are the six principles that would form the basis of his new work:

> Missionaries would be recruited from all Christian churches on condition that they sign a simple confession of faith that in essentials was evangelical.
>
> Missionaries would receive no fixed salary but wait upon the Lord for all their needs. Gifts received would be divided among all, and the mission would never contract debts.
>
> There would be neither appeals for funds nor collections taken, and the names of donors would not be divulged. Donors, however, would receive an annual accounting from the mission.
>
> To avoid the difficulties that Taylor had encountered with the CES, the first mission that employed him, the work in China would be directed by himself and the others working in China, not by a European committee.
>
> A plan to evangelize all of China was established, with the port cities being the strategic centers of the mission. The purpose would not be to obtain the largest number of conversions for the CIM, but to proclaim the gospel. "Knowing who brings in the harvest is secondary."
>
> The missionaries were to dress as Chinese, and worship services were to be conducted in Chinese-style buildings, not Gothic-style churches of which there were already a number of examples in China.

In general the rules established by British missionary societies required their candidates to be ordained into the ministry and, if possible, to have a university degree. Taylor accepted people who did not meet these standards, believing that the most important qualification was spiritual. "It was good," wrote Stephen Neill, "that one society was prepared to keep this door open; and cases were not lacking in which those who started with very little education grew to be notable scholars and sinologists."[73] Taylor also showed himself to be an innovator with regard to women. He strongly encouraged the ministry of women, including single women. R. Steer writes, "Hudson Taylor was convinced that Chinese women enjoyed a more determinant role than

---

73  Neill, *History*, 334.

men in their influence on the rising generation. The best way to reach Chinese women was to help them discover the gospel through Christian women."[74]

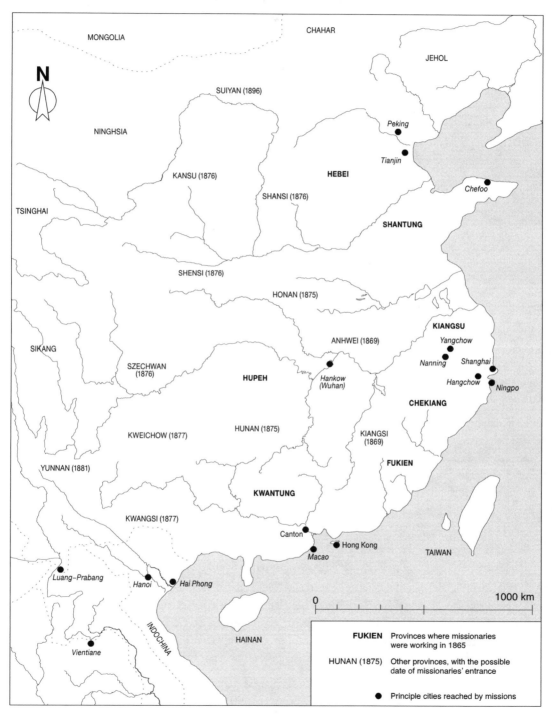

Map 3: The penetration of the gospel into China in the nineteenth century

74   Steer, op. cit., 301

## RETURN TO CHINA

In May 1866, Hudson and Maria Taylor embarked on the *Lammermuir* with their four children and sixteen new recruits from Scotland and England (as well as a French speaker, the Swiss schoolteacher Louis Desgraz). Apart from the Nicol couple, all were single, including eight young women. Before the end of the voyage, the majority of the members of the crew were converted through contact with this youthful team, which was full of faith and enthusiasm. Their four months of sailing time were dedicated to an intensive study of Chinese as well as biblical and spiritual preparation.

*One part of the "missionaries of Lammermuir," who embarked for China in 1866.*
*Sitting in the center is Hudson Taylor, and to his right is Maria Dyer Taylor.*

The arrival of this inexperienced group was greeted with contempt by the Chinese press. An English-language newspaper asked why their families had not confined these "fools and lunatics" in British asylums where they would have hurt neither themselves nor others. After some time in Shanghai, Taylor and his young recruits traveled to Hangchow, 250 kilometers to the southwest. This was an excellent site where there were already some missionaries and from which the CIM hoped to extend its work far and wide. The community life was not without some tensions, sometimes exacerbated by those from more traditional mission organizations who criticized this mixed group of unmarried, nonconformist youth who dressed like the Chinese.

The pettiness of these occasional conflicts hid profound differences of opinion that at heart were missiological in nature. Taylor had probably not made a long study of the history of missions in China, but he was passionate about Chinese history and knew that over the centuries Christianity, perceived to be a foreign religion, had been rejected three times by the Chinese. He expressed his insight in a remarkable text that revealed the acuity with which he perceived the stakes:

> [In China] we are in the presence of a population that retains many of its habits and customs because they are the result of centuries and of thousands of years of history. They are moreover not ill founded . . .

There exists perhaps no country in the world where religious tolerance can be pushed as far as in China; the sole objection that the princes and people raise against Christianity is that, in their eyes, it is seen to be a foreign religion.

I am not the only one to think that in preserving the manner of clothing and the manners of foreign nations, imposed by certain missionaries on their converts and on their children, in adopting a foreign style in the construction of chapels and in giving a really foreign air to all that touches the religion, the missionaries have considerably slowed the promotion of the truth among the Chinese. But why is it necessary to confer on Christianity such a foreign appearance? The word of God does not require it, and I see no compelling reason to justify it. We are not seeking the denationalization of the Chinese, but their Christianization.

We desire to train Chinese Christians, true Christians who remain authentically Chinese in all the senses of the term . . . Let us become therefore as the Chinese in all that is not bad, in order to save some by all means.[75]

It is well to remember that long before Protestants had arrived Catholic missionaries had been present. They had already spread out into the interior of the continent and had long since begun to live like the Chinese.

In June 1868, a year and a half after Taylor's arrival in Hangchow, he and his family with a team of colleagues and several Chinese Christians left to settle in Yangchow, several hundred kilometers farther to the north near the river Yang Tseu.[76] This was the first step in implementing the CIM's project of slowly moving away from the coastal regions. There was no missionary there, only a Catholic orphanage overseen by a Chinese director. The population had a reputation for violence and hostility to foreigners.

A full two months after their arrival, they were the target of a terrible riot. Certain prominent locals, fearing that the new religion would threaten their ancestral traditions, had posters made up and placed around the city accusing the missionaries of gouging out the eyes of the dead, eating children in the hospitals, and ripping open pregnant women to manufacture medicines. One went so far as to circulate the rumor that the "foreign devils" had stolen twenty-four children to make their food. An indignant and overexcited crowd, armed with knives and clubs, assaulted their house, breaking down the doors and destroying the walls, ransacking the rooms, and finally setting it on fire. When Taylor and his colleagues returned after having gone hastily in search of the authorities for help, they were informed that all the occupants had been killed, women and children included. In reality, they had escaped

---

75  Ibid., 225–26.

76  Yangchow is the city of which Marco Polo, in the thirteenth century, had been named governor by the emperor Kublai Khan.

by leaping out the windows and finding refuge in a neighboring house, but several were seriously hurt.

Not only was this event traumatizing for the missionaries, but it produced a lively debate in Britain. In the midst of the riot, Taylor had made an appeal for the aid of the local authorities; and after this aggression, he wanted to inform the British consul of all that had happened. Certain newspapers falsely claimed that Taylor had asked for the intervention of British gunboats, others that this mission was insanely imprudent in its actions. The CIM was the target of lively criticism, even on the part of certain friends who withdrew their financial aid. In the House of Lords, the Duke of Somerset engaged in a vehement diatribe: "What right do we have to endeavor to convert the Chinese who are in their own land? I am resolutely opposed to the protection of missionaries in the interior of China . . . A missionary is certainly inspired; if he is not, he is probably a mischief maker. No man would agree to go there to struggle upstream in preaching Christianity if he is not somewhat inspired. Now the inspired are always dangerous."

For the rest of the year 1868 and for part of 1869, Taylor suffered from nervous tension, irritability, and even depression. Several of his colleagues deserted due to personality conflicts and questions of power. But this difficult period was for him a step toward a profound spiritual experience in which he learned that the welfare of the CIM and even the salvation of China were not burdens that were to be borne on his shoulders alone. The letters in which he recounted the issue of this spiritual progress reveals a man at peace with himself, trusting no longer in his faith, but in the One who gives faith. He was a man now open to the work of the Holy Spirit within him.

Grace, the Taylors' eldest daughter, died at the age of eight in the year 1867. Two and a half years later, it was the turn of their five-year-old son, Samuel. The couple made the painful decision to send three of their four remaining children to Britain. The one who would stay with them was then only one year old. Several months later, Maria gave birth to a baby boy who lived only a few days. Two weeks after this, on July 23, 1870, it was she whom God took: she was thirty-three years old. These personal losses were terrible for Hudson, who remained in China with a small son at the tender age of two.

The following year, Taylor returned to England for a period of one year to consult with the mission committee that was engaged in reorganizing the work in order to promote better growth. In the course of this stay in his homeland, he married Jennie Faulding, one of the first CIM missionaries who arrived in China in 1866 with the *Lammermuir*. For the next thirty-five years she was his helper.

Upon his return to China, Taylor began to crisscross the country to visit the quickly growing number of mission stations. He was struck by the growth of the church and the engagement of the Chinese Christians. It was this that inspired the following thought, which was to become classic in missiology:

> European missionaries are as the temporary scaffolding raised
> around a building under construction. The faster this is completed,

the faster the scaffolding can be transported elsewhere, always with the same purpose, the interest of the work implanted and that of the regions not yet evangelized.

The fruit of evangelization, these churches were coming to be authentically indigenous, not projections of foreign denominations.

In 1874 on the occasion of another return to England, Taylor remained bedridden for several months following a fall on his back, which at the time was believed to have produced an irreversible paralysis. From his sickbed, Taylor launched a new appeal in the Christian press:

> China counts nine provinces as vast as a European country, each peopled with 17–19 million inhabitants entirely ignorant of the gospel. A number of Roman Catholic priests from Europe have settled in these provinces, but not a single Protestant missionary . . . Each of your readers would want, in reading these lines, to lift up his heart to God in prayer and ask of him, in a brief but immediate request, that he stir up eighteen men this year capable of dedicating themselves to the task?[77]

This number was quickly attained and even surpassed, and almost all traveled to China in the course of the year 1876. In this same year the treaty of Chefoo guaranteed that foreigners would be provided with a passport and given free access to all Chinese territory. In several months, the CIM would enter six new provinces, reaching regions that no foreigner had ever visited. There were then fifty-two CIM stations, and twenty-seven local churches.

## UNTO THE BORDERS OF THE EMPIRE

What is striking about Hudson Taylor is his capacity, despite seemingly insurmountable obstacles, to develop a strategy along with carefully thought-out plans for the methodical evangelization of an entire territory. In 1876 CIM missionaries journeyed twenty-two thousand kilometers around the country, most of the time on foot or in a junk. To reach the southwest of China, it was necessary to establish a base in Burma. Two members of the CIM obtained from the Burmese king authorization to settle in Bhamo. They were soon joined by the "Livingstone of China," the Scotsman James Cameron who, before arriving in Bhamo, traveled through the country making a vast circuit that notably included Tibet. Having crossed over a dozen mountain passes between 4,200 and 5,100 meters in altitude, Cameron became the first Protestant missionary to tread the soil of that country.[78] In the course of his brief career, he visited seventeen of the eighteen provinces of China as well as Chinese Turkestan, Mongolia, and Manchuria—most of the time on foot. The information that he furnished missionaries determined the course of Chinese evangelization as far as the borders of the empire.

---

77  Lyall, op. cit., 50.

78  It is true that in the next conference that Gützlaff held in Herrnhut in 1850 two Moravian missionaries were sent to Tibet; however, upon arriving at the border, they were not allowed to proceed.

In 1877 a general conference of Protestant missions in China was held in Shanghai. Seventy years had passed since the arrival of Morrison in Canton. Eighteen societies were represented, totaling more than five hundred missionaries. A survey was made there of the Christian publications in the Chinese language, revealing 520 books of theology and of spirituality, eighty-two catechisms, sixty-three hymn collections, fifty-four books of prayers, and forty-three Bible commentaries.[79] Despite notable differences on questions of theology and mission strategy, the atmosphere was serene. Thanks to the influence and spiritual authority of Taylor, the CIM garnered much respect from the more conventional missions that until then had been withheld.

In the course of the year 1878, a terrible famine struck China and millions of people perished. It occurred principally in the north of the country in the provinces of Honan and Shansi where only a few CIM pioneers were present. Among the thirty million inhabitants of the regions affected by this catastrophe, the women sold into slavery and the orphaned children especially suffered. Effective help could only be brought by female missionaries to this backward region, and it was Jennie Taylor who opened the way with three colleagues, two of whom were women. They became the first Westerners to risk their lives beyond the mountains in the interior of China.

In 1882 when the CIM already had close to a hundred missionaries, Taylor made a new call for an additional seventy, the number of large cities still lacking a Christian witness. This quota was attained in three years, and among the last to commit themselves were the "Cambridge Seven," a well-known team of college athletes who had converted during an evangelistic campaign conducted by the American preacher Dwight Moody and his song leader Ira Sankey.[80] Among them was C. T. Studd who, after several years in China, became a missionary in India and then the Congo; he also established a great missionary society, the Worldwide Evangelization Crusade (WEC; see pp. 299-301). Their number also included D. E. Hoste, future successor of Taylor as director of the CIM, and W. W. Cassels, who would be ordained in 1895 as the first Anglican bishop of western China. Stephen Neill, a missionary and Anglican bishop, praised the wisdom of Taylor in integrating missionaries from different ecclesiastical traditions. In 1886 the CIM divided the field of work into districts corresponding more or less to the denominations of the missionaries engaged. Hence, there were zones reserved for Anglicans, Methodists, and Presbyterians, and various districts were cobbled together to form a separate zone for the Baptists. During a stay in Europe, a questioner expressed astonishment at the CIM's lack of confessional coherence. Taylor responded in this way:

> China is so vast that the workers living in their different provinces can preserve the individual rules of their own churches . . . The great task that engages us overflows all the different theologies, and our watchword remains: "All one in Christ."[81]

---

79  According to Zorn, "Missions protestantes," 1078.

80  See John Pollock, *The Cambridge Seven* (London: InterVarsity, 1969); and Norman Grubb, *Charles Studd: Champion de Dieu* (La Bégude-de-Mazenc, France: Croisade du Livre Chrétien, 1977).

81  Steer, op. cit., 371.

The social and intellectual level of the "Cambridge Seven" differed from that of other members of the CIM, who were often of humble origin and lacking university degrees. The low social status of the CIM missionaries was in accord with the Chinese that the CIM were attracting to the gospel, for they too were generally from the lower social classes of the population. There were some exceptions such as Pastor Hsi, a renowned Confucianist and man of letters, but addicted to opium. He converted in 1879 through a Methodist missionary and was freed from his enslavement by faith in Christ. He accomplished a remarkable work in taking responsibility for more than forty victims of the drug; through faith, prayer, and the aid of medicines, their dignity was restored. When Taylor met Pastor Hsi, he proposed that he take over pastoral responsibility for the vast province of Shansi. After fasting and prayer, Hsi agreed.

During another visit to England at the beginning of 1887, Taylor published an appeal for an additional one hundred new missionaries. Before the end of the year, more than six hundred candidates presented themselves. One hundred and two among them were selected according to the required criteria, and the prayers for their financial support were granted.

## INTERNATIONAL EXTENSION OF CIM

At the insistent demand of an American Christian, Taylor agreed to return to China via the United States. He held a number of large meetings there, including one in Moody's vast auditorium in Chicago.[82] He made such a strong impression that about forty people presented themselves as candidates in the weeks that followed, and fourteen among them accompanied him to China. After a time of hesitation, Taylor agreed in 1888 that an American mission committee be formed. This decision

*Hudson Taylor in 1889 at the age of fifty-seven.*

represented an important departure, for soon the CIM became an international mission, with national committees established in the various countries where Taylor had urgently appealed for the evangelization of China. This was notably the case in Scandinavia, Germany, and Australia. The work continued to grow, and fifty years after these beginnings, it would count among its ranks thirty-five different nationalities.

In 1890 a great missionary conference was held in Shanghai, with delegates representing forty Protestant mission societies. The numerical weakness of Protestant Christianity became apparent to all at the meeting. It was commonly

---

82  He much surprised Moody and his audience by refusing to take up a collection at the end of the meeting in order not to deprive the other Christian workers of the gifts which would normally be given to them. He proposed instead that those who wanted to make a voluntary gift address it to him later, after reflection and prayer, in the form of a check. All his life, Taylor strictly held to his decision never to make an appeal for funds and never to take up a collection in his meetings.

agreed, therefore, that the societies would launch an appeal for a thousand additional missionaries. It was also decided to publish a common version of the Scriptures to replace the various translations then available.

Five years later in 1895, the Protestant missions in China had together enlisted 1,153 new missionaries. The CIM was then maintaining twenty-two principal mission stations, of which three-quarters were in the eleven provinces that had not been evangelized before Taylor's arrival in China.

Besides the numerous illnesses that his body regularly endured, and then the sadness of mourning his second wife, Jennie, who died in Switzerland in 1904, the last years of Taylor's life were overshadowed by two different problems, both causing him much sorrow. First, there was conflict between the mission committees of London and China. As we have seen, from the beginning Taylor opted for the new arrangement of a mission committee made up of the missionaries living in China. As good as this was, it was not enough. The expansion of the work, the examination of hundreds of candidates in Britain and other places, the necessary liaison with the sending churches, and the financial administration of such an enterprise had made a committee in Britain indispensable for the smooth operation of the mission. Unfortunately, the division of labor between the two committees was poorly defined, engendering a long and painful "constitutional crisis."

The other trial, much more dramatic, was the torment that swept across China at the dawn of the twentieth century. Among all the mission societies in China at this time there were about 1,500 Protestant missionaries in the country, who, for better or worse, were perceived by certain leading Chinese as agents of Western colonial imperialism. The Dowager Empress recruited a militia popularly known as the "Boxers," who adopted the slogan *mie yang*, "Death to foreigners!" In June 1900 an edict was published, ordering that all foreigners be put to death.

The missionaries were, of course, not the only foreigners living in China, but it is they who were the first targets, for they were the most numerous in the interior of the country. Hence, in Shansi, thirty-four Protestant and twelve Catholic missionaries were decapitated in the presence of the governor. The estimations generally advanced for the whole of the country are 135 Protestant missionaries killed, as well as fifty-three children. The CIM was affected the most, loosing fifty-eight workers and twenty-one children. The Boxer Rebellion was directed at foreigners, but Chinese Christians were accused of collaboration and treason and so also suffered as victims of violence. In the single region of Peking, there were fifteen thousand to twenty thousand Catholic martyrs, and nearly two thousand Protestant Chinese who were executed. Yet rare were those who abjured their faith.

During this period, Taylor was convalescing in the Swiss Alps, having entirely turned over the direction of the mission to D. E. Hoste. He had been suffering for some time with a loss of memory due to age and his state of exhaustion. As much as possible the drama that was playing out in China was hidden from him, but once he had recovered sufficient strength and was informed of it, he wrote hundreds of letters to console and encourage the missionaries.

When the situation was normalized in China, Western countries demanded enormous indemnities from the Chinese government as a matter of justice. After consulting with his committee, Taylor decided to ask for nothing and even to refuse all offers of reparation in order to manifest "the meekness and gentleness of Christ." Though the CIM had suffered much more than any other mission from this violence, Stephen Neill observes, "Few missions followed this example; but subsequent history suggests that the greater wisdom was that granted to Hudson Taylor."[83]

Taylor was able to return to China in the spring of 1905 after the death of his wife. He visited numerous churches and missionary stations, encountered some veterans of his China mission, and found himself surrounded by much veneration. Scarcely more than a month after this reunion, he died peacefully on the evening of June 3, 1905, after having participated throughout the day in a conference that included missionaries from six societies. His mortal remains were taken to Yangchow and interred in the cemetery where his first wife, Maria, and four of his children enjoyed their final rest. He was sixty-three years old.

*Hudson Taylor (left) several weeks before his death, with John Griffith of the London Missionary Society, and W. A. P. Martin of the American Presbyterian Mission. Taken together, these three veterans had worked a total 150 years as missionaries in China. (Ecumenical photo)*

---

83  Neill, *History*, 340.

## THE LESSONS OF A LIFE

Incontestably, Hudson Taylor left his own unique impression on the history of mission, not only by his missionary strategy, his gift for organization, and his *avant-garde* missiological vision, but also, and perhaps especially, by the example of his life of prayer and of unconditional confidence in the interventions of God. The deliverances and the extraordinary divine responses that mark the story of his life, forming a mythic "golden legend," are a stimulating example for every generation of Christians. In a time when rationalism was triumphing in the West, the miracles (for it is necessary to give them their proper name) accorded by God to the China Inland Mission were recognized as signs of his sovereign power.

Of course, Taylor had his weaknesses. He knew depression and times of anxiety, and he had some faults, which were the cause of conflicts and dismissals within his organization. Despite his meekness, he exercised strong authority over his mission, and his refusal to knowingly share power was due more to his concern for effectiveness than to a taste for power. He also committed some errors of strategy. He is especially reproached for his haste in preaching the gospel "to all creatures" (according to the devise that he adopted), which led him to disperse his missionary forces and overemphasize superficial evangelization to the detriment of training and pastoral care. Caring little for theological debates, he did not see the need to offer Chinese pastors an education that would have prepared them to develop an evangelical theology that was authentically Chinese.

Taking away the aura that he would never have recognized was part of him, one finds in Taylor a human dimension approaching the "average missionary," an eminent servant in whom one can feel more stimulated than overwhelmed.[84] He repeated ceaselessly that to accomplish his work God has no need of exceptional individuals but of men and women who take seriously his promises and who obey him by placing full confidence in him. To a questioner who declared to him at the end of his life, "You must take a legitimate pride in thinking of the work that you have accomplished," he responded, "This is not how I see things. I often think that God must have searched for someone rather weak, rather small, so that he could use him, and he found me."

## THE MISSION CONTINUES

The debacle of the Boxers was followed by a period of exceptional openness to the gospel in China. The imperial power was put down and a republic established. The Christian doctor Sun Yat-sen, who had been baptized in Hong Kong in 1884, took the oath as the provisional president in 1912. He attributed the success of his revolution "to the Christian faith, to its ideals of religious liberty, peace, and love, values that correspond well with the Chinese character."

In 1913 a third of the missionaries working in China were Chinese. They participated in the great missionary conference in Shanghai where it was decided to

---

84 One of the merits of the work of Roger Steer, besides providing a well-researched biography, is the presentation of an objective picture of Hudson Taylor's personality, more so than the preceding biographies written by the members of his family.

intensify the training of Chinese ministers and to work at a rapprochement with the churches founded by the many Western missionary societies. In 1914 there were 5,462 Protestant foreign missionaries in China, of which 1,652 were wives. The CIM had more than a thousand foreign missionaries and 2,500 Chinese workers in 1,200 centers. Twenty-seven doctors were practicing their art in nine hospitals and sixty-eight dispensaries. Following the example of Taylor, priority continued to be given to evangelization, but several Bible schools were established and more emphasis was given than in the past to the preparation of Chinese spiritual directors. Leslie Lyall noted that other missions slowly lost their spiritual emphasis and began to give greater attention to scientific and medical work; this was especially noticeable in the opening of five high-level Christian universities. Stephen Neill confirms: "The gospel was presented to the Chinese nation, less as the gospel of personal salvation in Jesus Christ than as a means of political and social salvation."

But simultaneously, some elite Chinese Christians contributed to the revival of the church. Among these was Dr. John Sung, who was both an intellectual and a gifted evangelist. He had a strong and uncompromising character and tended to operate in an individualistic manner, but he was able to accomplish much. And there is Watchman Nee who while still young became the head of a vast movement of independent churches, the "Small Flock." Several missionaries participated in this revival movement, which emphasized the confession of sins, repentance, reparation for mistakes, the sufficiency of the blood of Jesus Christ for purification, and the gifts of the Holy Spirit. Under the influence of Nee, many second- and third-generation Christians experienced profound personal conversions and some churches enjoyed a renewed zeal for evangelization.

In the course of the 1920s and 1930s, a Christian movement among the south China tribes developed in a remarkable fashion. It began in 1910 with the arrival in the Yunnan Province of James O. Fraser, a CIM missionary and an eminent musician. He dedicated himself to the Lisu ethnic group among whom the gospel spread like wildfire. The newly converted Christians proclaimed the faith among the members of their clan, resulting in churches springing up everywhere.[85] The church became entirely indigenous in 1943. Other tribes were also reached beginning in 1935. By 1940 forty CIM missionaries were working among six tribal groups.

We have seen above that James Cameron visited Tibet in 1877. It would be a long time before a mission could gain traction in this difficult and inaccessible region. Three CIM missionaries settled there in 1938, but the work was only just beginning.

## THE RISE OF COMMUNISM

The political situation in the new Republic of China was favorable to Christianity but only for a short time. The government of Sun Yat-sen had much difficulty maintaining its authority over all of the territories. After the First World War, China began to look to the triumph of communism in Russia as a model to follow. In 1921 the Communist

---

85  Cf. the biography of James O. Fraser: Eileen Crossman, *Fleuve de lumière* (Lavigny: Les Groupes Missionaires, 1985).

Party of China was founded. Sun Yat-sen died in 1925 as the communists were exerting ever greater pressure, and the country was practically cut in two. The antiforeigner reflex of the country regained its vigor and manifested itself even among Christians. Following China's military defeat in the middle of the nineteenth century, many missions had profited from treaties imposed at the time that allowed foreigners to travel into the interior of the country. Now many of the new churches that were the fruit of this period decided to break relations with their supporting missions.

Beginning in 1926 General Chiang Kai-Shek, himself a Christian, began to prepare the armed forces of the south to take the country from the communists. But he met heavy resistance. The ebb and flow of the two opposing armies resulted in the ravaging of the country over many long years. In 1935 in a city where the communists were entrenched, a young CIM missionary couple, John and Betty Stam, were captured, judged, and condemned as "imperialist enemies." They managed to hide their three-month-old baby who survived, taken in by Chinese Christians. A few hours before being decapitated, they were able to write these words: "All that we possess is in the hands of the communists, but we praise the Lord who fills our hearts with his peace. May the Lord bless and guide you. As for us, may God be glorified, either by our lives or by our deaths."

It was during this period that the communists undertook their "long march" in the course of which they captured a number of missionaries. Alfred Bosshardt, who had been a CIM missionary in China since 1922, was forced to march with the Red Army for 560 days. He was finally freed during the season of Lent in 1936.[86]

In addition to its internal divisions, in 1937 China was plunged into a protracted war with Japan, a conflict that concluded only with the end of the Second World War in 1945. After this period, the communist troops gained rapid victories throughout the country. Peking fell in November 1948; and then Shanghai, Canton, and other great centers quickly fell in turn. At the end of 1949, the CIM still had 737 missionaries in the country. One year later, the director of the mission concluded that cooperation with the Chinese churches was no longer possible, for indigenous Christians were suffering due to their relations with foreigners.[87]

---

86 The passionate narrative of the adventures of Bosshardt has been published in French: *Conduit par sa main* (Lavigny: Les Groupes Missionnaires, 1983). A film relating his saga was recently released in Britain.

87 In 1951 the remaining missionaries in China would be evacuated and redeployed to countries in Southeast Asia. The China Inland Mission would then change its name to Overseas Missionary Fellowship (OMF).

# CHAPTER 7

# *Protestant Mission in the Far East*

We must backtrack chronologically in order to review the first steps taken by Protestant missions in various countries of the Far East.

## THE FIRST AMERICAN MISSIONARY

### *Adoniram Judson in Burma*

Adoniram Judson (1788–1850) was born in the New England state of Massachusetts where his father was a minister in a Presbyterian-Congregational church. In reaction against the orthodoxy of his father, he was tempted by Deism and, at the end of his university studies, planned to study philosophy in a college in New York. The failure of this plan, added to other difficult experiences, was the cause of a spiritual crisis that led him to return to God. A little later he joined a small, student prayer group. It was the time of the Second Great Awakening, and the members of his group were all led to consider a missionary call. Eventually six youth among them left the United States at the same time to serve as missionaries, but Judson was the only one to complete a long-term missionary career. He is, therefore, correctly considered "the first Protestant American missionary."

The group of students with which Judson was associated comprised the first missionaries sent by the American Board of Commissioners for Foreign Missions, established in 1810. Primarily a movement of the Congregational churches, the mission committee of the American Board was at the outset largely lacking in the financial means necessary to support its missionaries. For this reason Judson went to England to solicit funds from the London Missionary Society. Fortunately, the American Board received some unexpected funds, and so it was under its aegis that Judson embarked for Calcutta with Anna Hasseltine, whom he had married several weeks before the departure. Judson was ordained to the pastoral ministry of the Congregationalist churches.

Knowing that he was going to encounter William Carey and his Baptist colleagues in India, Judson dedicated himself to the study of the doctrine of baptism during the long voyage. He came to the conclusion that the Baptists were more closely in conformity to biblical teaching than the Congregationalists and Presbyterians. So it was that in the course of their brief sojourn in Serampore, the Judsons were baptized by William Ward. The news was a shock to the members of the American Board, who did not share this conviction and separated themselves from their first missionary even before he had begun his work. Adoniram and Anna were provisionally supported by the Serampore mission, but the existence of Baptist missionaries soon engendered the creation of an American Baptist missionary society in 1814. This society joined with other mission groups within the Baptist denomination to form in 1817 the American Baptist Missionary Union. It would play a considerable role in the history of Protestant missions.

An intransigent British colonial government refused to allow the American missionaries to live in India. Immediately expelled from the country, Adoniram and Anna left on the first ship available, which happened to be bound for Burma (Myanmar). When Judson initially felt called to be a missionary, he had had the conviction that God intended him to serve in Burma; however, on hearing the stories describing the treatment foreigners were subjected to in the country, he had rejected this thought. On being expelled from India, he recognized the hand of God in circumstances that he had neither wanted nor foreseen. Consequently, he became absolutely certain that he was supposed to bring the gospel to Burma. Due to this conviction, he would find the energy to persevere through the terrible trials that he would encounter all through his long life as a missionary. Anna, already gravely ill during the voyage through the Gulf of Bengal, gave birth to a premature child who did not survive. It was a very weak woman who disembarked at Rangoon, Burma's principal port.

In Burma, "the country of pagodas," Buddhism was the religion of the king, who considered the population to be his personal property. Although several ethnic minorities (Chin, Karen, Kachin) were not Buddhist, promotion of any other religion was formally forbidden, and conversion was punished by death.

The Nestorians had reached Burma around the year one thousand and were the first to preach the gospel there, but no trace of their efforts remained when Judson arrived. The first Catholic attempt was made by Philippe de Brito, a sixteenth-century adventurer. He succeeded in bringing part of the country under the sovereignty of the king of Portugal, and 100,000 Burmese formally became Christians, willingly or forcibly. Brito destroyed the pagodas and oppressed the Buddhists, which led to an uprising. He was defeated and executed, and the Christians in their turn knew persecution. Nothing remained from this unfortunate episode. A Catholic mission closer to the Christian spirit undertook the evangelization of the country in 1722, eventually producing a small Burmese Catholic church.

At the beginning of the nineteenth century, the few foreigners residing in Burma were closely surveilled: several Protestant missionaries who had preceded Judson left after a short time, convinced of the impossibility of establishing a Christian church in a realm so inhospitable. It was truly an enterprise that awaited the pioneering young couple (see map 1, p. 313).

Judson believed that he would find Felix Carey waiting for him, the son of William Carey who had come to the Indies with two other missionaries in 1807. Judson was greatly disappointed when it appeared that Felix was in the process of renouncing his ministry. He found him not only cold and distant but disillusioned with regard to any possibility of evangelizing Burma. However, Felix's wife, Margaret, who was Burmese, welcomed the new missionaries into her home and was a great help to them in their first days in the country. Thanks to her, Anna Judson made quick progress in learning the Burmese language and a good number of the local customs and practices. Adoniram found a teacher who could instruct him in written Burmese, a language of extreme complexity. His progress was slow, but without mastering written Burmese he could not hope to accurately translate the Bible. Felix had already begun translating the Gospel of Matthew and had made good progress in writing a dictionary and grammar of the Burmese language. Though incomplete, these works enabled Judson to step immediately into the work.

Felix Carey had to leave Rangoon several months after the arrival of the Judsons. He had been called to serve as a doctor to the royal house in the capital Amarapura, in the north of the country. Because Burmese women were forbidden to leave their country, to avoid an expulsion that would have separated him from his family Felix was constrained to bow to the will of the king and abandon all missionary activity. But in the course of the voyage to the capital with his family, tragedy occurred on the river: the boat capsized, and his wife and two children drowned. Felix lost no time in returning to India.[88] As for Adoniram and Anna Judson, they felt terribly isolated from then on.

Their first attempts at evangelization were dangerous and unfruitful. Judson wrote: "You cannot imagine how very difficult it is to give them any idea of the true God and the way of salvation in Christ, since their present ideas of deity are so very low."[89] Every time a Burmese expressed an interest in the gospel, intimidation and threats prevented him from continuing to maintain relations with the missionary. Though Judson's first years had been used primarily in learning the language and translating the New Testament, it was no doubt a trial that he had to wait six years before being able to baptize his first convert.

Less than two years after the arrival of Judson in Rangoon, in this first period of solitude and dryness, Anna gave birth to a son. The couple's joy was short lived as

---

88 Felix Carey was converted in a time of enthusiasm at the tender age of sixteen and married Margaret when he was eighteen and she was only fifteen. At twenty-one, he was serving alone as missionary in Burma and returned to Serampore in 1807 at the time of his mother's death. He returned the same year to Burma, while his young wife of nineteen was pregnant with their third child. She died in bed. Felix remarried to a Burmese then became ambassador to the court of the Burmese king. Becoming a widower again due to the tragedy on the river, he embarked for India as a diplomat, living with ostentation on the strength of a series of doubtful letters of credit. Appearing to have arrived, his father would have said, "Felix is shriveled from a missionary into an ambassador" (Tucker, op. cit., 124). After having manifested the anxious signs of megalomania, he regained his footing thanks to the support of William Ward and pursued medical work. He also became an effective aide to his father in the area Bible translation. Felix died of a fever in 1822 at the age of thirty-seven, after marrying a third time. The trials that he knew in childhood due to the mental illness of his mother no doubt contributed to the lack of balance in his adult life.

89 Tucker, op. cit., 125.

the child did not survive more than eight months. For the parents, particularly for Anna, this death was profoundly unsettling, raising spiritually unanswerable questions about the life hereafter. Adoniram opened his heart to William Carey in a letter poignant in its sincerity:

> Our little Roger died last Saturday, May 16, 1816. We held a wake during the day, and in the twilight, laid him in his tomb. I am a novice in sadness . . . No other experience can cause such an agony that tortures the heart of a father, when he looks on the face of his only son, to listen if a last breath will still escape from him. And when the truth becomes obvious, when hope disappears with his life, he tries to summon prayer: "O God, I commit his spirit into your hands." Where has this spirit fled? To what mysterious place? Who can support and guide his steps through so dark a valley? Could this not have been spared us? He was all our comfort and our relaxation in this terrible place. Pray for us.[90]

## THE FIRST RESPONSE TO THE MESSAGE OF THE GOSPEL

At the end of 1816, almost four years after his arrival in Burma, Judson finally saw the arrival of a reinforcement in the person of George Hough, a printer by profession, who was sent with his wife by the American Baptist Mission. On a printing press that he brought with him, the Gospel of Matthew was soon produced. This was an important first step for the mission. Sadly, intimidated by the hostility of authorities and frightened by the threat of a cholera epidemic, the Houghs returned home after several months, sending their printing press to Serampore. A little while later two American Baptist ministers, James Colman and Edward Wheelock, arrived, accompanied by their wives. Wheelock was of fragile health and immediately fell ill. After a few months, it became obvious that he would not survive in such a climate, and he embarked more dead than alive on a ship *en route* to India. After a few days of sailing, despondent, he threw himself into the sea and disappeared under the waves.

Judson was increasingly conscious of the impossibility of the Burmese visiting the private residence of a missionary. He had noticed that the port city of Rangoon was filled with *zayats*, places of meditation and prayer where monks and priests explained the teachings of Buddha. *Zayats* were public places. Anyone who wanted to sit for a while, relax, or talk with or merely listen to a Buddhist master could freely come and go. Judson, aided by Colman, acquired a patch of land in 1819 to construct his own *zayat*. It was a small shack of eight by six meters with a great veranda where the Burmese would feel free to come without any commitment to listen to the missionary. It was near to small Buddhist monasteries, pagodas, and *zayats*. In strolling in front of the unpretentious building, passersby could hear the Bible read aloud. Some would willingly stop and listen and even enter, but few returned regularly. A few months after opening this Christian *zayat*, the first convert confessed his faith before a large Buddhist crowd. This was Maung Nau, and Judson baptized him in

---

90  H. W. Morrow, *Splendeur de Dieu* (Neuchâtel: Delachaux & Niestlé, 1963), 66.

June 1819 in a small lake on the banks of which stood an immense statue of Buddha. A little later Ma Min Laya, a woman from a distinguished Buddhist family, also asked for baptism. She became a missionary to her own people, founding the first Christian school in her house. By 1821 an embryonic Burmese church was in place with a dozen baptized members. Among them was Judson's language teacher, Maung Shway Gnong, an intellectual Buddhist and a seeker of truth who, while aiding Judson in the translation of the Bible, had contended against Christianity, opposing it in the name of his religion. Now, nothing could dissuade him from declaring the good news in the small Christian *zayat* in Rangoon, but later he would suffer much for his faith. His death in 1826 was a heavy lost for the nascent Christian community of Burma.

## THE GOSPEL PENETRATES THE ANIMISTIC ETHNIC GROUPS

These new Burmese Christians took an active part in the evangelization of the country immediately after their conversions, often distributing tracts. One of the first converts, Ko Tha Byn, was originally an animist and a member of the Karen ethnic group. He was a brigand and an assassin that Judson had nevertheless dared to welcome into his house as a servant, and he was won to the gospel by the love of his masters. He became an assistant pastor, the first Burmese servant of the Lord. The conversion of this Karen virtually opened the door to the evangelization of the country. Ko Tha Byn began to evangelize the Karens with a remarkable dynamism and found among them a surprising welcome to his message. Soon the majority of the members of the Burmese church were former animists of the mountain-dwelling ethnic groups, who tended to be more accessible than the Buddhists.

Stephen Neill has written:

> The Karens, though illiterate and despised by the Burmese, were far from being an uncivilized people; and they had traditions which seem to have served as a real *praeparatio evangelica*. They knew of the Creator God, and had a story of the fall through which they had lost the favor of God and been reduced to this quasi-servile position. They believed also that in times past they had had a sacred book which their fathers through carelessness had lost. When a preacher came, bearing a sacred book and telling them that God whose anger they had incurred had himself come to seek them in mercy in Jesus Christ, it seemed to them that their dreams and hopes had all been realized. Karens in their hundreds came forward to be instructed and to be baptized.[91]

Below is a brief extract from the oral tradition of the Karen, discovered and transcribed by a missionary:

---

91    Neill, *History*, 294. Neill notes, however, that certain aspects of these traditions are not very solidly attested. Don Richardson presents this case of "evangelical preparation" in his book *L'éternité dans leur coeur*, French translation (Lausanne: Jeunesse en Mission, 1982), 81–91.

God is immutable and eternal; he was in the beginning of the world. In former times, God created the world, and all things were carefully ordained by him . . .

He prescribed food and drink. He prescribed the fruit of testing. He gave exact orders.

Satan fooled two persons. He caused them to eat of a tree of testing, and they became subject to sickness, old age, and death.

If they had obeyed, if they had believed in God . . . We would be happy in our hearts. We would not have become as poor as we are.

Temptation, O fruit of temptation, it has poisoned our mother and killed her. In the beginning it killed our father and our mother. Through man the tree of life will come one day![92]

More than Judson, it was George Boardman (1801–1831) who dedicated himself to building up the church of the Karen and who opened the mission station of Tavoy among them.

## JUDSON BROKEN BY TRIAL

The medical missionary Jonathan Pierce was particularly helpful to Judson. The presence of a medical doctor was necessary given how often and how severely the missionaries' health were subject to tropical fevers and other illnesses due to the trying climate. In 1820, Anna traveled to Calcutta for much-needed rest, and in 1822 she left for a long stay in Britain and the United States in order to receive care that was indispensable for her health. Not long after her return, the Judsons settled farther north, in Ava where the king resided. At this time Judson and Pierce seemed to be held in favor at the court of the new sovereign.

Unfortunately, this situation lasted only a short time. Political relations between the British and the Burmese deteriorated and in 1824 war exploded on the scene. Although Judson and Pierce were Americans, they were soon arrested and imprisoned, suspected of espionage in the employ of the enemy. The conditions of incarceration were inhumane, and without the incessant intervention of his wife with the head of the prison, Adoniram would not have survived. Eight months after his arrest, Anna came to visit him in the prison with Maria, their small daughter born three weeks before.

In November 1825, after a year and a half of cruel detention, Judson was freed. His services were needed as an interpreter in the peace negotiations with the British. Judson retained some aftereffects of his imprisonment and suffered from fragile health for the rest of his days. His work as an interpreter kept him separated from his wife, and after a few months, he received news that she had died due to a severe attack of malaria. His pain was immense, but he consoled himself with his little

---

92  "Les missions évangéliques au XIX siècle," Journal publié par the Mission de Bâle, 2ème année, (published by the Basel Mission, second year) French edition (Neuchâtel: Delachaux, 1862), 365.

Maria, finding in her a tender reminder of his wife. Sadly, she was taken from him five months later.

The trial of this double bereavement was a terrible ordeal for Adoniram, who tried to lose himself in his work in order to cope with his grief. He plunged into the translation of the Bible, but even this task soon appeared to him arid and lacking in sense. Overworked and miserable, he soon fell into a deep depression. He had spent twelve years in Burma and had the feeling that everything was collapsing around him, that God had rejected him as an incompetent worker. For the next two years he lived in the depths of despair, sitting long hours with his dog before the tomb of his wife, reciting the Song of Songs, causing much anxiety in his colleagues Boardman and Wade. After some time, he retired into the jungle, a two-hour walk from the city of Moulmein. Here he constructed a hut and dug his own tomb, before which he passed many hours ruminating on his dark thoughts.[93] During the day he spent several hours at the mission, but the rest of the time he meditated in his jungle hermitage and permitted no one to approach. "God is for me a great unknown. I believe in him but cannot find him," he wrote.[94] While his missionary colleagues were no doubt consternated by what they interpreted as a psychological and spiritual shipwreck, the Burmese did not have the same reaction. Many considered his retreat into meditation and isolation as a sign of wisdom, in the manner of their monks.

Sarah, the wife of George Boardman, who was herself a remarkable personality, came to find him. She sought comfort as she was coming to grips with the realization that her husband's illness would shortly bring about his death. She reported their troubling conversation:

> Look your trouble in the face, Sarah, he said to her in a strong voice, until you are fully conscious of it. And when you will have it totally assimilated so that it is unceasingly present to you, ask God for the reason of this chastisement. [She then saw the open tomb that he had dug and asked him with dread what it was.] It is my effort to look death in the face. I sit there and I imagine my body overtaken by rotting . . . Since I have lived [during my imprisonment] for an entire week at the side of a man whom the executioner was killing a little each day, I consider the ignoble thing that death will make of my body. The slow putrefaction in the wet earth! I apply myself to imagining it until all love of my physical person dies in me. [Sarah responded to him:] What I dread for you is that Buddhism has influenced you too much . . .[95] All this [she indicated the hut and the tomb] proves that you are only concerned with the good of your soul and body and not with the

---

93 Since the arrival of the Judsons, the mission's center was at Rangoon, but in 1826, about one year after the death of Anna Judson, it was transferred to Moulmein, about two hundred kilometers farther to the south.

94 Tucker, op. cit., 153.

95 During this period, Judson was also influenced by an assiduous reading of the *Vie de Madame Guyon*. She was an eighteenth-century follower in France of Quietism, a mystical movement that drove her to excesses that bordered on the hysterical.

one who was lost on the cross to deliver us from all the doubts that now assail you.[96]

It is thanks to the prayers and affection of the little Burmese church and of his few missionary colleagues that Judson slowly recovered. He had never ceased his activities and had worked particularly hard on translating the Psalms. Paradoxically, the year of his deep depression, 1830, had been a fertile one for the young church, with fifty-six baptisms. Among the neophytes there were eight Karens, ten British soldiers, and thirty-eight former Buddhists—the conversion of the latter was entirely forbidden. In the same year Cephas Bennet, a printer and a man of good sense and robust health, was dispatched to Burma. The missionary society now seemed to grasp that the conditions of life in the country were such that only persons of strong mind and body could endure them. In 1833 three new missionary couples came as reinforcements.

While Judson was traveling the length of the river, people came to him from numerous villages. They had Bible pamphlets in hand, which they had received during previous visits, and were asking for baptism. In 1834 the translation of the Bible was completed and Bennett could begin the printing. Judson had also completed compiling linguistic material that he would need to edit an English-Burmese/Burmese-English dictionary, indispensable for the missionary work.

In the same year Adoniram married Sarah Boardman, who had become a widow years before and remained in Burma to pursue her husband's work among the Karen. She helped Adoniram to recover his psychological and spiritual equilibrium. In ten years she gave him eight children, two of whom died after a short time. One year after the birth of the last child, the couple took a vacation to the United States with three of their children. It was urgent that Sarah receive medical care, but she never arrived home, succumbing at sea.

A widower for the second time, Adoniram set out with three children to visit the homeland that he had not seen for thirty-three years. American Protestants were well informed about the terrible trials that their first missionary had undergone. They showed much veneration for him, and large crowds assembled to hear him.

Before returning to Burma, Adoniram married Emily Chubbock, a writer of well-known popular novels. He was then sixty years old, and she was thirty years his junior. He had sought her out to write the story of his wife, Sarah. They left alone, his three children remaining in America convinced they would never see their father again. Emily quickly learned about Burma and put her writing skill to the service of the missionary cause by composing stories that met with great success.

In 1850, three years after Judson's return to Burma, while Emily was waiting for her second child, he fell gravely ill. He undertook a sea voyage in the hope that the salt air would help him recover, but he died less than a week after setting sail. He was only sixty-two years old. The ocean served as his sepulchre, as it had for his first child born to Anna before their arrival in Rangoon, and as it had for his second wife, Sarah, *en route* to America. Emily's health also suffered, and she survived him by only thee years, dying at the age of thirty-six, not long after returning to the United States.

---

96   Reported by Morrow, op. cit., 308ff.

In the course of thirty-eight years of ministry that were subject to opposition, danger, incessant diseases, and several deaths, Judson witnessed to God's love for the Burmese people. So firm was he in the word of God and so giving of himself that his ministry succeeded in bearing much fruit. While many had warned him of the impossibility of bringing the gospel to the people of Burma, at the time of his death he left a church of close to ten thousand baptized members and at least thirty thousand adherents committed to the Christian faith. The church was led by more than 150 Burmese ministers and evangelists, and supported by several missionaries. As for the Protestant churches of America, they received a powerful stimulus to support missions from the example of one who knew profound struggles, suffering, spiritual crises, and doubt, and yet who was never abandoned by the One who had called him to his service.

Judson was certainly a missionary "out of the norm." His intellectual range was remarkable, as can be seen in his interest in philosophical questions, his open mind in regard to culture, and even his interest in the religion of his adopted country. But his heightened sensitivity, need for love, and ceaseless anxiety over questions of life after death made him a vulnerable and tormented man. At the same time, he was the touchstone and "father" of a mission and church that grew to an astonishing extent during the last part of his ministry. In this the grace of God intervened in his life to make him a powerful witness who left a unique mark on the history of mission.

## THE GROWTH OF THE BURMESE CHURCH

We have already seen that the church experienced much growth in Judson's time, especially amongst three animistic groups. The Karen were first reached in 1827, the Chin in 1845, and the Kachin in 1876. The latter were evangelized by the Karen and saw their first baptisms in 1882. The Buddhists, in contrast, remained unmoved by Christianity.

The entire Bible was made available in the language of the Karen in 1851. The Baptist churches had at that time 370 communities and eighteen thousand members, which were entrusted to 147 ministers. In 1865 the Baptist Missionary Convention of Burma was established. At the beginning of the twentieth century, the three ethnic groups noted above represented 75 percent of the Burmese Baptists.

The Society for the Propagation of the Gospel (SPG), the oldest English mission, arrived in 1859, a few years after the signing of the treaty of peace between Burma and Great Britain.[97] The head of the SPG in Burma was a man of great stature and energy, Dr. J. E. Marks, who made education the main focus of the mission. He quickly opened a school in Mandalay, and then in 1870 developed an education program in Rangoon. The value of this educational work was widely appreciated and even enjoyed the favor of the king. In 1877 the first Anglican bishop of Rangoon was ordained.

In 1879 American Methodist missionaries began in their turn the work of evangelizing India, and they were joined in 1886 by the British Methodists, who operated

---

97 There had been since 1825 an Anglican chaplain in Burma, but he was limited in his activities to British civil servants and traders.

in the north of the country. The work was further advanced in 1915 by the Salvation Army, in 1919 by the Seventh-day Adventists, and in 1930 by the Assemblies of God, a Pentecostal church.

In the course of the first third of the twentieth century, the CIM missionary James O. Fraser was dedicated to the evangelization of the Lisu and the Kachin, mountain-dwelling ethnic groups living close to the Karen in the territory of China and Burma (see above, p. 369). Fraser worked principally in China but also in Burma. His ministry had a notable influence on the development of the Burmese church, which grew appreciably when the Chinese communist revolution produced a large emigration of Christians from the mountain-dwelling ethnic groups near to Burma. Fraser died in China in 1938.[98]

# OTHER COUNTRIES OF THE FAR EAST

## The Origins of the Korean Church

The Korean population is nominally Buddhist, but the old shamanism of Central Asia was retained in the beliefs and sacrificial practices of a majority of Koreans. Catholicism entered Korea at the end of the eighteenth century thanks to a Korean who returned to his country after being baptized in China. He successfully evangelized many of his compatriots, and when the first missionaries made their appearance in 1794, four thousand Christians were waiting for them. These efforts, however, sometimes produced martyrs to the cause.

As with Catholicism, Protestantism also began to develop within the country before the arrival of Western missionaries. Beginning in 1830, examples of the Bible printed in China were distributed by Korean Christians who had been converted in foreign countries and wanted to witness to their faith in their homeland. They were encouraged in 1832 by the brief stay of a missionary, who came from China. In 1864 one of the rare Protestant missionaries who had attempted to establish himself in the country was martyred. Beginning in 1876, some Koreans went to be baptized in Manchuria where they had established relations with Scottish Presbyterian missionaries. Following a treaty with the United States, religious liberty was decreed in 1880, and the door was opened to Protestant missions.

In 1885 two Chinese evangelists settled in Pusan, having been introduced there by John Wolfe, an Anglican missionary in China. The preceding year, American, Canadian, and Australian Presbyterians undertook the establishment of churches in Korea, the best known among the pioneers being Horace Underwood. J.-F. Zorn writes, "This work developed and became in some ways a model for missionary stations in Korea: in addition to the ministers, there were several doctors for the hospitals and

---

98 In 1961 the Burmese declared Buddhism to be the state religion while proclaiming religious liberty. The church was then strongly established in the Karen, Chin, and Kachin ethnic groups. It is estimated that in 1981 Christians numbered 2 million in a population of 30 million, the majority of them being members of Baptist churches that were the result of the work of Judson and his colleagues. The rebirth of nationalism, at once both Burmese and Buddhist, carried with it great difficulties for Christians. Judson College in Rangoon was closed in an attempt to have the people forget the role of this pioneer in the history of their country.

dispensaries, and instructors for the colleges and orphanages."[99] These early efforts resulted in the birth of the Presbyterian Church of Korea in 1907. Two American Methodist missions were also at work in the country during these years. They eventually produced the Korean Methodist Church, which became independent in 1930.

In 1893 Dr. John L. Nevius, a missionary in Chefoo in northern China, made a visit that the Koreans consider to be a turning point in the history of the church in their country. At his instigation, a missionary council met to divide up the fields of activity in the country. In advance of the missiology of his time, Nevius was convinced that the young church could quickly become independent under the direction of the Holy Spirit. The missionaries in Korea took up the challenge and elaborated several guiding principles ("the Nevius plan") for the development of the work:

> Each Christian should remain in the social station in which he was found when called by God (1 Cor. 7:24). He should meet his material needs through his own work while at the same time witnessing to his faith in his social groups through his life and words.

The methods and facilities of the church should be developed only to the extent that the Korean church is capable of taking responsibility for them.

The church itself must address an appeal for full-time ministry to those it considers best qualified and insofar as it can financially support them.

Places of worship should be constructed according to local architectural styles and with the resources of the Christians living there.

In addition to these principles, the missionaries insisted on the evangelization of women and the translation of the Bible in the language spoken by the people, which was Hangul rather than the Chinese spoken by the elite. Bible teaching and the training of Christians were emphasized, and annual study sessions were organized.

*The first Korean ministers.*

Under these principles and emphases, the churches developed very quickly. During the single year of 1900, the number of members grew by 30 percent. In 1907 a revival occurred, giving the church new momentum in the life of prayer and piety, and its effects were felt as far away as Manchuria and China. In the same year, the Presbyterian Church became autonomous, and two years later it held its first general synod. In 1910 the Presbyterian and Methodist churches together included about thirty thousand communicants and an even larger number of believers and sympathizers.

When Korea was occupied by the Japanese in 1910, the Korean Protestants, who had forged a very independent character, were the natural allies of the movement that sought liberation for the country. When the influential Protestant laity was accused of having hatched a plot to assassinate the Japanese governor, many Christians

---

99   Zorn, "Missions protestantes," 1082.

were arrested. These events slowed the growth of the Protestant church but did not halt it. The repression continued through the 1930s and 1940s.

From the beginnings of the mission in the nineteenth century, Korea was the Asian country where the gospel was best received.[100] If a sociological explanation is sought for this, it has often been noted that Korea was strongly hierarchical due in part to its traditional religion; in this light, Christianity and especially Reformed Protestantism appealed to the less favored classes of the population as a force for liberation and equality.[101]

## The First Step of Protestantism in Japan

Protestant and Catholic missions were discreetly introduced into Japan in the middle of the nineteenth century, but this was not the first Christian attempt to evangelize the island of Nippon. Francis Xavier and his Jesuit companions arrived in Japan as the first missionaries in 1549. The Catholic mission was an undeniable success, for by 1614 there were 300,000 Christians on the island. But persecution began at this time. There were numerous martyrs, and the suppression of Christians continued for over two centuries. Several Protestant attempts were made in the first half of the nineteenth century, but all failed (see pp. 180-83 and 187-89).

It was not until 1858 that the history of modern missions in Japan began. Due to a treaty between the United States and Japan in that year, Americans who settled in Japan had the right to practice their faith and to construct places of worship; but the missionaries who tried to carry the gospel there did so at their peril, proselytizers being subject to severe penalties. This did not stop a succession of missionaries from coming between 1859 and 1869. These envoys were sent by the American Episcopal Protestant Church, the Presbyterian Board of Foreign Missions, and the Dutch Reformed Church. All were Americans, and some among them had previously worked in China. The Free Baptists entered in their turn in 1872, and the Church Missionary Alliance (CMA) in 1891.

The work in the first years went slowly, for it was necessary to be prudent for foreigners to win the confidence of a distrustful population. This was time put to good use by the development of grammars, dictionaries, and Bible translations. The first baptism was not celebrated until 1866.

In 1872 nine young men were baptized in Yokohama within the Reformed Church and began an underground organization, the Church of Christ in Japan. The same year the missionaries of various societies gathered for a conference in which it was agreed that they should avoiding using denominational labels in their work. In 1874 Shimeba Neesima, a Christian who had gone to the United States for training and had recently returned to the country, became the first ordained Japanese minister. At that time there were 565 Protestants divided into nine communities. In 1877 most of

---

100  Barrett, *Encyclopedia*, 558, 682, gives the following statistics: In 1900, Christians represented .5% of the population; in 1970, 1% in North Korea and 18% in South Korea. In 1900, 2% in North Korea and 40% in South Korea, of which the clear majority were Protestants (18%) and independent churches (16%), and the Catholics were 6% of the population (numbers are rounded).

101  Cf. Zorn, "Missions protestantes," 1083.

them joined together to establish the Tokyo College of Theology. The same year three Presbyterian missions merged with the tiny Church of Christ in Japan to become the Nippon Kirisuto Ichi Kyoukai—the United Church of Christ in Japan. The growth of the church was slow but steady: in 1878 Protestants had more than 1,700 members. At that time there were nine Japanese ministers, fifty-eight auxiliaries, and sixty-six missionaries. Using Latin characters, the missionary James Curtis Hepburn translated the New Testament into Japanese and saw it published in 1879.

From 1868 to 1912, the emperor Mutsuhito under the name of Meiji ruled Japan. The Meiji period was characterized by a quasimystic patriotism in which the emperor was considered to be more or less divine. The Japanese were supposed to render public homage to the gods of their ancestors, but Christians refused. Living under a cloud of suspicion, they especially endeavored during the Russo-Japanese War to prove their loyalty to the country.

Beginning in 1884 Buddhism and Shintoism ceased to be the only religions authorized and financed by the state.[102] The number of missionaries also increased during this period. From 155 in 1882, they reached about 450 by 1888. The number of Christians also increased appreciably, numbering some twenty-five thousand at the beginning of the 1890s. Numerous conversions occurred in the colleges, particularly at Doshisha College, which was founded in 1874 by the Reverend Joseph Hardy Neesima and soon achieved the status of a university. Due to institutions of this type, by the end of the nineteenth century a good number of Christians could be found within the nation's leading circles. Though the Christians continued as a small minority in the country, Christian influence in Japan generally exceeded what its numbers would suggest.

The agricultural school of Saporo, whose direction the government had conferred on an American Christian agronomist, experienced a revival. One of its students, Uchimura Kanzo (1861–1930), converted at this time and became an organizer of a large group of Christians who refused to align themselves with any of the denominational groups then present in Japan. Uchimura launched a movement called *Mukyokai*, which means "Nonchurch." According to the beliefs of this movement, the true temple of God has for its floor the earth that He created, for its ceiling the celestial vault, for its altar the heart of Christians, for its law the word of God, and for its pastor the Holy Spirit alone. Uchimura soon had thousands of listeners for his Bible studies in Tokyo, but each time a group of his followers was on the point of adopting an ecclesial form, he ordered its dissolution. This is one of the reasons that during the Meiji period an ever growing number of Japanese became Christians without being baptized or belonging to a specific church.

In 1889 a new constitution guaranteed religious liberty to all Japanese subjects "insofar as they do not compromise the public peace and order, and their practices do not conflict with their duties as subjects of the empire." Such a formulation left the door open to varied interpretations of what their "duties as subjects of the empire"

---

102 Buddhism and Shintoism are terms for the Japanese that signify "the voice of the gods." They use the terms Shinto or Shintoism to refer to a polytheism that often exalts the Japanese emperor and the Japanese race.

might involve. At certain times some wanted to make participation in the ceremonies at the tombs of the ancestors obligatory, especially in the colleges. Though a number of Christian colleges conspicuously yielded, numerous believers did not accept the interpretation offered by the state according to which it was necessary "to venerate" ancestors, but not "to worship" them. On this question and others, the small Christian community of Japan found itself divided between those who favored a strict approach and those who were more accommodating.

In 1901 a great evangelization campaign began that was called Taiky Dendo (Advance Movement), which had for its slogan "Our country for Christ." It met with considerable response, notably in the milieu of the universities. By 1902 there were close to forty-seven thousand Christians.

Masakisa Unemura, a Presbyterian ordained to the ministry in 1879, strongly insisted that foreigners withdraw from the direction of the churches and that the Japanese themselves undertake the evangelization of their own people. He took responsibility in 1904 for Tokyo Shingakusha, the first independent theological seminary in Japan. This was at the time of the Russo-Japanese War, which spurred the state to require that all religious communities unite in the defense of the country. The victory over Russia heightened Japanese nationalism, sometimes even in the churches. Several Japanese Christian leaders insisted on a strict application of the three-self rule and endeavored to present their churches as exclusively Japanese.[103] They believed that they alone were able to discern the implications of their fidelity to the gospel, and they emphasized the urgency of developing a Christianity in Japan that would be both loyal to the country and free of all foreign influence.

The concern for loyalty was legitimate but held certain dangers. The government decided in 1912 to officially recognize Christianity as one of the three religions of Japan, and it brought about the "Conference of the Three Religions": Buddhism, Shintoism, and Christianity. Many Christians were happy to benefit from an official status. Others, however, distanced themselves *vis-à-vis* the Movement of the Three Religions, whose avowed purpose was to promote the idea of progress as understood by the government. They perceived that the regime's underlying nationalist ideology and emphasis on militarism might lead them to a commitment incompatible with their Christian faith.

### The Protestant Implantation in the Philippines

The Treaty of Tordesillas (1494) gave the islands of the Philippines to Spain. At this time Islam was already present, having been introduced by Malay immigrants a little over a century before. The first Catholic missionaries belonged to the Augustinian order and were active in the country as early as 1565. Other religious orders followed in the sixteenth and seventeenth centuries: first the Franciscans and then the Spanish Jesuits, who established their first college in 1695. Their methods of evangelization were sometimes harsh and overbearing as was the case in Latin America in the same period. The Philippines became the only Asiatic country to have a majority Catholic

---

103 According to the famous formula of the three selves of the Anglican missiologist Henry Venn (1854), a church must be self-directing, self-financing, and assure by its own power the evangelization of its people.

population (see map 5, p. 400), and beginning in the mid-nineteenth century hundreds of Christian Filipinos would leave the islands to evangelize other Asian countries.

At the end of the nineteenth century the islands were generally considered to be Catholic, but the church was very Spanish. This inspired Father Gregory Aglipay, a Filipino priest, to organize an independent church in 1890 that would be free from the tutelage of the Spanish clergy. This became the Philippine Independent Church, which soon included 7 percent of the population. But the members the church, the Aglipayans as they were called, professed a Christianity that was far removed from Christian orthodoxy. They denied the Trinity, rejected the supernatural, and insisted on the superiority of science over the Bible. Yet they also retained a liturgy close to that of Roman Catholicism and established relations with various branches of American Anglicanism. By the time of the Second World War, the movement included close to a quarter of the Catholic population of the Philippines.

Following the American victory in the Spanish-American war of 1898, the United States supplanted Spain in the island and expelled four hundred Catholic missionaries. It also opened the door to Protestant missions, and at the beginning of the twentieth century numerous missionaries from a variety of traditions rushed in. They attached scarcely any importance to the Philippines being a traditionally Roman Catholic country and the people being at least nominally Christian.

Filipino ministers soon felt compelled to create independent churches in order to disengage from American tutelage. Like the Koreans, Filipino Christians quickly showed a spirit of independence, looking on the missionaries as colleagues and friends rather than as supervisors. A number of them were, in effect, discontented Catholics who came to Protestantism in reaction against their church, which they considered to be too subject to a foreign clergy. This is one of the reasons that the Protestant churches enjoyed such rapid growth from the outset, especially in the cities. Another explanation for this growth was the success of the Bible Society and Christian Unions, whose members in the first years of the twentieth century were largely made up of young people.

The American Presbyterians came to the Philippines in 1899 and by 1901 had already inaugurated Silliman University, which quickly acquired a reputation for excellence. In 1899 the American Methodists also sent missionaries. The church that was the fruit of their witness suffered successive divisions in 1905, 1909, and 1933. In 1907 Presbyterians and Methodists created the Manila Union Theological Seminary to train Filipino ministers. The Methodists also opened a hospital in Manila during the following year. And in 1929, Presbyterians and Congregationalists joined together to form the United Evangelical Church of the Philippines.

Other missions also came in the early years of the twentieth century. In 1900 the Baptists began to work on the islands of Panay and Negros, building hospitals, an industrial center, and a university. The first Baptist convention took place in 1935. Filipino Pentecostals who had immigrated to the United States and been converted there returned to their mother country in the late 1920s and formed an Assemblies of God church. The church of the United Brethren in Christ collaborated with the Disciples of Christ, which had arrived a little before them in 1901.

A CMA missionary settled on the great island of Mindanao in 1902 but became a victim of cholera after less than a year. The CMA mission took up the task anew in 1908 and worked among various tribes. The CMA reached out to ethnic groups that spoke about thirty different dialects and had never been evangelized by the Catholic Church. By the beginning of the Second World War there were nineteen CMA missionaries present, and they were soon joined by colleagues who had had to evacuate Indochina after the Japanese invasion. Unfortunately the island of Mindanao was in its turn occupied. Only a single CMA couple was not interred by the Japanese during the war. They remained hidden, protected by a tribal people among whom they continued to exercise their ministry (see map 5, p. 400).

In 1902 Charles Henry Brent (1862–1929), a Canadian of the American Episcopal Mission, also chose to work among the unreached tribes, in part to avoid entering into competition with the Catholic Church. He was a heroic pioneer in the mountainous regions in the interior of the island of Lucon, in the north of the archipelago. There he worked among the Igorot ethnic groups and soon developed a vibrant church. The Episcopal Mission also sought to evangelize other ethnic minorities, notably the Chinese of Manila and some Islamic tribes in the southern islands of Mindanao and Sulu.

The Evangelical Union, established in 1901, included a large number of the Protestant missions present in the archipelago. Its purpose was to divide the territory between the missions in order to avoid competition and to reach every region. On some of the islands languages were spoken in which the gospel had not yet been preached. During the period between the two World Wars, Protestantism experienced steady but modest numerical growth.[104] Around fifteen mission societies and many different Protestant denominations were engaged in the work.

# SOUTHEAST ASIA

## Siam (Thailand): Arduous Beginnings

The kingdom of Siam is one of the lands where Buddhism has been preserved in its most authentic form and has offered the most resistance to Christian missions.[105] However, in 1554 two Dominican chaplains of Portuguese troops, who were then engaged by the king of Siam, began to evangelize the population with some success. In just a few years they counted 1,500 conversions. In 1583 the Franciscans also decided to come, and then, in 1606, the Jesuits. They opened a seminary in the royal capital of Ayuthia where future priests were supposed to learn Latin in order to be able to say the mass. In the eighteenth century, opposition to Christianity took the form of a severe persecution. When Catholic missions began to gain new impetus in the nineteenth century, the missionaries practically had to start from scratch. They were busy principally in the central and northeastern sections of the country. The first Thai bishop would not be ordained until 1945.

---

104 According to the Barrett, *Encyclopedia*, 594, the Filipino population was 94% Christian in 1970. Among these, 15% were members of independent churches, and only 3% were Protestants.

105 The country took the name of Thailand in 1939, but between 1946 and 1949 it also used its former name of Siam.

The first Protestant missionaries were the German Karl Gützlaff (see also pp. 349-50) and his English companion Jacob Tomlin of the London Missionary Society. Upon arriving in 1828, they encountered much distrust. Only the Chinese immigrants seemed to show any interest, and Gützlaff baptized six of them. He also managed to translate several books of the New Testament into Siamese. But following the death of his wife in 1831, he left Siam discouraged. Tomlin had departed from the country a little before Gützlaff but returned several months later, being supported now by the Congregationalists of the American Board. After eighteen years, this mission withdrew without having baptized a single Thai.

Gützlaff appealed to American mission organizations on behalf of Siam. The American Baptist Mission, already present in Burma in the person of Judson, came to Siam in 1833. John Taylor Jones, one of their missionaries, completed the translation of the New Testament in 1843. Seeing the near impossibility of reaching the Thai people with the gospel, both the Baptists and Congregationalists concentrated their efforts on the Chinese immigrant population. When the Buddhist priests asked the king to forbid the new religion, the king responded: "Do not be anxious, no one will accept Christianity apart from some Chinese." Sadly, he was not far from the truth.

The American Presbyterians founded the Protestant Siamese Mission in 1840, which was the only mission to persevere in its efforts among the Thai population. They opened a chapel on a street in the center of Bangkok and slowly gathered a small community. But the first baptism, the one of Nar Chune, did not take place until 1859. On the coast two hundred kilometers to the southwest of Bangkok a mission station at Petchiburi was established 1861; a second was established one hundred kilometers to the north of Bangkok at Ayuthia in 1872. After thirty-five years, the Siamese Protestant mission had succeeded in establishing a church of only forty-five members, and among them were several Chinese. The most important mission station was developed at Chieng Mai in the northwest of the county where the Presbyterians concentrated on education and medicine.

When the Baptist Mission received authorization to work in China, it encouraged its missionaries in Siam, who had focused on Chinese immigrants, to extend their work there. Only one among them would remain in Siam, Dr. William Dean. The church born of his witness, a Chinese community of more than four hundred members, was inaugurated in 1874.

Other missions were active in Siam during the first half of the twentieth century. The Anglicans of the SPG established themselves there in 1903, and in the same year the Churches of Christ of Great Britain opened a coeducational school as well as a hospital in the region of Nakhon-Phanom. The communities founded by the Church of Christ were formed of Thais, Chinese, and members of the mountain ethnic groups. Several years later, Lutherans of the Marburg Mission also established a mission in the country.

CMA missionaries who had been active since 1923 in Battambang, in northwest Cambodia, crossed the border in 1929 and settled in the eastern provinces of Siam. Their first mission station was established at Ubon, where colporteurs of the Bible Society had previously undertaken a canvassing effort and subsequently asked the CMA for help in the area. The first convert was baptized in 1931, and a small Christian community was in place by 1934. The CMA gave priority to the evangelization of the fifteen eastern provinces of Siam. Seeing the importance of training church leaders, the CMA opened the first Bible school in the country. It established four new mission stations in the 1930s, but they were all evacuated due to the Japanese occupation during the war. With the cessation of hostilities in 1945, they soon picked up the work where they had left off.[106]

In 1934, the Presbyterian Church, the largest in the country, united with the Churches of Christ, the Baptists, and the Lutherans to form the Church of Christ in Thailand (CCT). Stephen Neill writes, in Thailand "all the missions had the same experience—friendliness, good will, and an almost unalterable repugnance to the idea of conversion; the progress in all the churches was very slow."[107]

## French Indochina

In the course of the second half of the nineteenth century, France slowly positioned itself in Indochina, a nearby island-like land formed of five regions: Cambodia, Laos, Tonkin, Annam, and Cochinchina—the last three constituting, from north to south, the three provinces of present-day Vietnam.

France settled in Cochinchina in 1858 to protect French missions and to secure a number of commercial trading posts. It occupied Saigon in 1859. Cochichina became a colony in 1867, and the two other coastal provinces of the South China Sea, Annam and Tonkin, became French protectorates in 1887. Cambodia had already obtained this status in 1863. At the request of King Oun Kham, who was seeking support to resist pressure from Siam, Laos became a French protectorate in 1893. In the beginning of the twentieth century, no Protestant mission was present in French Indochina. A report from the CMA written in the last years of the nineteenth century made this pressing appeal:

> In this part of our globe, there are 22 million human beings who live without Christ, and who, consequently, are without light in this world and without hope for the next. In China there is one missionary for about every 200,000 persons; India possesses one for every 150 individuals; in Africa and South America there is one for every 100,000 persons, but the Annam possesses not a single one for 22 million souls.[108]

## Laos

The appeal cited above resulted in the first Protestant missionaries being sent to Indochina in 1902. They established what was the only French-speaking, Protestant mission in all of Southeast Asia, the Evangelical Mission in Laos. For this reason, we will examine its history more fully than the other missions of the time.

---

106 A little later, the WEC and Finnish Pentecostals undertook the effort to evangelize the country.

107 Neill, *History*, 346.

108 J. Decorvet and G. Rochat, *L'appel du Laos* (Yverdon, Switzerland: Imprimerie H. Cornaz, 1946), 22. The number of twenty-two mission inhabitants, based on precise statistics, concerns both French Indochina and Siam (Thailand).

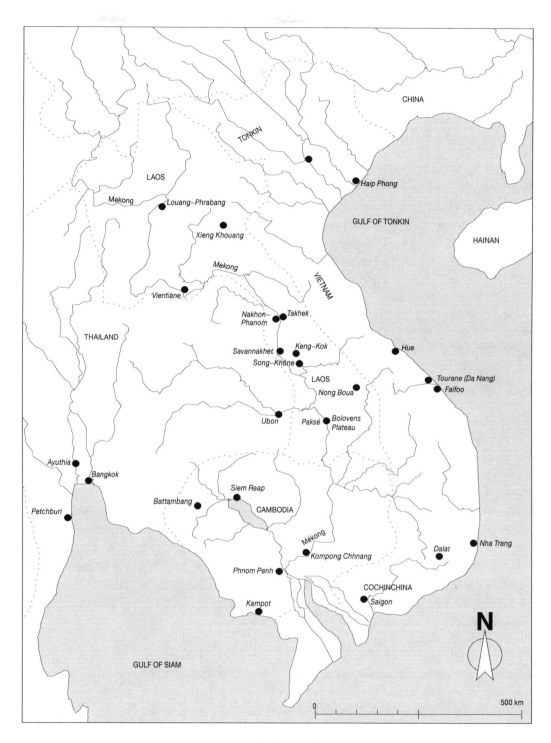

CHINA

TONKIN

LAOS

Mekong

● Haip Phong

GULF OF TONKIN

HAINAN

● Louang–Phrabang

● Xieng Khouang

Mekong

VIETNAM

● Vientiane

THAILAND

Nakhon–
Phanom ● ● Takhek

● Keng–Kok

Savannakhet ●

Song–Khône ●

LAOS

● Hue

● Tourane (Da Nang)
● Faifoo

● Nong Boua

● Ubon  Paksé ● ● Bolovens
Plateau

Ayuthia ●

● Bangkok

● Petchburi

Battambang ●

● Siem Reap

CAMBODIA

Mékong

● Dalat  ● Nha Trang

● Kompong Chhnang

Phnom Penh ●

COCHINCHINA

● Kampot

● Saigon

N

GULF OF SIAM

0                    500 km

*Map 4: Indochina and Siam*

## Gabriel Contesse and Maurice Willy: the Pioneers

Gabriel Contesse (1878–1908), eighth child in a family of traders in Vevey, Switzerland, converted through Unions Chretiennes de Jeunes Gen (Christian Union of Young People) and soon after became convinced of a missionary call. At that time he was seventeen years old and learning to become an architectural draftsman. His new vocation led him to leave architecture behind and take up the study of medicine at Livingstone College in London. Seeking to learn which region of the world God might lead him, he read the CMA's appeal for Indochina cited above. In his haste to respond, he interrupted his studies and presented himself to his church, the Evangelical Assemblies of French Switzerland (then known as the Assemblies of Big Brothers), rather than to an English-speaking mission. He had prayed to God, "Lord, send me to those to whom the gospel has never been proclaimed."

While searching for information on Indochina to prepare for his departure, Contesse discovered that Laos was the most disadvantaged and inaccessible region in that part of the world, which he took as a confirmation of his belief that God was calling him to serve there. Laos, which is about half the size of France, was then inhabited by 900,000 people. A little more than half of them were Buddhist and ethnic Lao; the others, belonging to various mountain-dwelling ethnic groups, were animists and spoke a large variety languages unrelated to Laotian.

Contesse lived for some time in Paris where he began the study of the Siamese language, which is close to that of Laotian. For a teammate he found a compatriot named Maurice Willy, who was familiar with Asian countries and had been a cook on a ship that plied the seas *en route* to Asia.

At the time of his departure Contesse was twenty-four years old. The two missionary adventurers disembarked at Saigon in early October 1902. They then undertook a tumultuous one thousand kilometer voyage up the Mekong that took them through Vietnam, Cambodia, and finally to southern Laos. After a month on the river, they arrived at the village of Song-Khône, which appeared strategic for being at the heart of an important region. They read the New Testament aloud in Siamese, and those who heard them seemed to understand. They also sang in public, accompanied by a small harmonium brought from Switzerland, in order to attract attention. Tit Pang, a sixty-year-old Siamese who had settled in Laos, soon gave his heart to Jesus Christ and was able to give an account of his faith to Laotians in their own language. In 1905 he became the first convert to receive baptism.

## A Predecessor to the North of Laos: David MacGilvary

Contesse and Willy were not actually the first Christian missionaries in Laos. In 1886 Catholic missionaries, who had come from Siam, succeeded in establishing a station in Tahkek on the shores of the Mekong.

As early as 1869 Dr. David MacGilvary, an American Presbyterian who was present in the beginning of the Siamese Protestant Mission, arrived in Louang-Phrabang, the royal capital in the north of the country. He came to be called the "Apostle of Laos." Already possessing a good understanding of the Siamese language, he was quickly able to learn Laotian and was well received by the population. A high-level bureaucrat trained by Buddhist priests soon accepted the gospel, and other converts followed. These conversions made a considerable impact. Many approached MacGilvary in the hope of learning to read and receiving an education. The king himself seemed favorable. Fearing, however, that Christianity might come to be generally embraced by the nation, he abruptly changed his mind and began to persecute Christians. Two martyrs were tortured and died without giving up the names of other Christians. One was a doctor; the other, Nan Tschai, was considered to be the wisest man among his people.

Not long after this, the king disappeared, and his son changed his father's policy, granting religious liberty to Christians. There were about twenty baptisms in 1877. Though MacGilvary soon had to leave, he had had time to establish the foundations of a Christian community. In 1902, the year in which Gabriel Contesse arrived in the south, Dr. Hugh Taylor and his wife made the first of several visits to the region of Louang-Phrabang. Presbyterians like MacGilvary, the Taylors worked for thirty-five years in northern Siam among a population similar to those in neighboring Laos. Taylor made several appeals to the Swiss missionaries to extend their activities to the north of the country. Despite these few attempts to explore and evangelize, no follow-up visits were made to Laos due to their apparent ineffectiveness. It was not until 1928 that another mission would respond to this need, as we will shortly see.

## An Avant-garde Strategy

A little after the arrival of Contesse and other Swiss missionaries in Song-Khône, the group received a visit from two Buddhist priests who were curious to learn about the new doctrine that they had come to teach. One of them was Chan Pan, a head *bonze* who had lived for eighty years in a Buddhist monastery. He offered to teach the language to the missionaries. Without hesitation Contesse enlisted his aid in the translation of the Gospels. In 1905 he sent the British Foreign Bible Society a manuscript of the Gospel of Matthew for publication.

Without any particular preparation in missiology, Contesse was "inspired by an astonishingly modern vision: to found as quickly as possible independent indigenous churches that would be materially and spiritually capable of doing without missionaries."[109] Not long after he arrived, he described his objective in these terms: "Our desire is that the Assemblies learn to finance themselves, and when the Lord saves Laotians who are called to be evangelists, the Assemblies will be able at least in part to provide for their expenses." To meet their own financial needs, Contesse and his colleagues adopted the principle of the faith missions, inspired by Hudson Taylor. Not only did they not have fixed salaries, but they refused to make their needs known to the churches that had sent them. Contesse wrote his brother, "Let us remember that we must not reveal our financial needs and all that concerns God alone and never expose it to publicity, for it is an outrage that we make our heavenly [Father] a banker."

In 1903 Charles Contesse, Gabriel's brother, joined the small missionary team at Song-Khône, and so did Willy's fiancée, Ethel Pomeroy, a nurse who had completed

---

109 S. Dupertuis, "L'evangile au pays du million d'elephants," in *Dossier vivre*, no. 20 (Geneva: Je Sème, 2002), 15.

her studies in Siam during the previous year. Upon her arrival, the medical work became a key element in the witness of the missionaries, permitting them to give expression to the compassion inspired by the gospel beyond the few words they had mastered. Soon they were in direct contact with all levels of the population, and their evangelistic meetings were attracting about fifty interested people.

*Gabriel and Marguerite Contesse.*

Returning to Switzerland in 1905 for a vacation, Gabriel married Marguerite Johnson, of the United Kingdom. The couple then sailed for Laos, accompanied by Ethel Pomeroy, Charles' fiancée. There were now three missionary couples in the southern part of the country.

Unfortunately this situation did not last long. In June 1908 a virulent cholera epidemic that had originated in Tibet reached Laos, emptying cities and villages of their inhabitants. Survivors often sought to escape the plague by fleeing into the bush. In a few days cholera reached Song-Khône. The missionary team did its best to care for the sick and inter the dead. After a few days, on the eve of Pentecost, Marguerite Contesse contracted the disease, and the next day her husband contracted it as well. In the midst of the crisis, he wrote:

> The undersigned, a sinner saved by grace . . . desires to answer several questions, for, as the hymn asks: Who knows if we will live tomorrow? Cholera made its appearance in Song-Khône on the morning of June 3. On the night of the next day my dear Marguerite was struck by the disease. She now hangs between life and death. Nothing has happened. One of her last words was: "Oh! It is good to rise in the morning in his presence." As for myself, I

am taken with diarrhea and vomiting. I am near to departing . . .
Thank you, Lord Jesus, for having saved a sinner such as I.

In case my wife and I should pass from this life to a better one, we
wish that our sister Marie would fill the place of mother for our
dear little Edouard.[110]

On June 8, 1908, the Monday following Pentecost, Gabriel Contesse expired several hours before his wife. They left behind their first born, Edouard, then only seven months old.[111]

At the time of their deaths, Charles and Ethel Contesse were the only missionaries in Laos. The Willys were on vacation during the tragedy and rushed back in order to fill the void.[112] Fritz Audétat, arriving as a reinforcement in 1909, dedicated himself over many years to the translation of the Bible. In 1924 he completed the typographic composition of the New Testament, and in 1926 five thousand copies were printed in Marseille under the watchful eye of Maurice Willy and then brought to Laos. The entire Bible, after constructing all the elements of the Laotian typographic characters, was printed in 1932 in Hanoi.[113]

Willy Brügger arrived in 1918, accompanied by his wife. She succumbed to a typhoid epidemic after only three years in the country. Her daughter, Suzy, just a few months old, soon followed her into the grave.

The Laotian church never experienced spectacular expansion but, rather, slow and steady growth. The enterprise was frustrated by the low number of missionaries present in the country, an average of less than four persons during the first four years. Those sent were often gravely ill, contracting diseases that in some cases required them to be evacuated; and there were several deaths to lament. Of the eighteen missionaries to serve between 1902 and 1939, five died as well as four of their children.

In 1911 there were twenty-five baptisms, the converts ranging from eighteen to seventy years of age. New stations were established during the second decade, most notably those of Ken-Kok and Nong Boua in 1917. In 1921 missionaries and Bible colporteurs visited seventy villages in which eleven different dialects were spoken. In the same year the Bible course taught at Song-Khône attracted a hundred participants. There were baptisms, and certain Laotian Christians demonstrated on this occasion a remarkable gift for preaching. Among these were Cita and Saly, who proved to be particularly gifted and dynamic evangelists. During the better part of twenty-five years, they traveled on foot around the country, preaching the gospel in all the villages through which they passed.

Between December 1923 and June 1924, forty baptisms were celebrated; and the Bible course in 1936 attracted more than two hundred Christians, with some

---

110 Decorvet and Rochat, op. cit., 46.

111 Edouard Contesse (1907–2000) became a key worker in the Evangelical Mission to Laos of the Swiss Assemblies.

112 Henriette Willy died in 1910, but her husband returned a little later to settle down permanently and dedicate himself to the printing of Bible texts in Laotian.

113 In contrast to Vietnamese, which was put to writing in Roman script by Jesuit missionaries in the seventeenth century, Laotian possesses its own alphabet, as do the languages of the Khmer and Thai peoples.

participants walking as many as three to six days to be present. Among the new Christians of this period there were a large number of "phi-pob." Veritable pariahs, these were people accused of being possessed by an evil spirit when a death occurred in their village. Hunted by the families of the deceased, it was only in Christian villages that they could find refuge.

Fritz Audétat served God during more than forty years in Laos. His wife died of typhoid fever in Song-Khône in 1920. He remarried in 1926 to Ida Steiner, and in 1938 the couple lost their son Daniel, a child born of their marriage. In 1928, after twenty years in Laos, Audétat rendered this witness: "Experience has taught us to sow with tears . . . The gospel has resounded in the ears of thousands of persons in hundreds of villages." In 1932 thirty years after the pioneers had arrived, there were only 180 baptized. Willy Brügger, who also remarried, remained in Laos until 1947. He was captured and tortured by the Japanese who occupied Laos in 1944.

In 1935 Audétat wrote a moving appeal to the Swiss Brethren Assembly on the occasion of their annual missionary meeting at Morges. Here is an extract:

> The several representatives of the Swiss Assemblies in Laos aged quickly and were used up under the tropical climate; they only reach about sixty. All have given a good number of years of service and will soon be at the end of their course, without young recruits appearing on the horizon . . . The young [Christians] gathered in Laos are soon going to find that they have been left to themselves . . . [or] at least that their Swiss fathers and mothers have decided not to send them reinforcements. In order to come here it is necessary to receive a very clear and sure personal call from the Lord of the harvest. Without this assurance, it is a thousand times preferable not to stir. But it appears very strange that God has not called anyone for nearly twenty years! In truth, several have professed to have received a call. Why have they not come? Have they recoiled before the difficulties? . . . Have they succumbed to soft indifference or to opposition from friends and family or to those who should have and could have encouraged and facilitated these things for them? . . . It would be good if numerous workers could come while the older ones are still here so that they might profit from the experience they have acquired and avoid the groping and errors that are so often fatal in the beginning.

This call was heard, and one year later in the autumn of 1936 Marie Dufour embarked for the Far East. A Swiss nurse, she opened a dispensary at Song-Khône and lived in Laos for almost forty years. And in 1939, when the war had already begun, Bernard Felix of Aubonne also departed for Laos, traveling with the Brüggers, who were returning after a vacation. He settled in 1940 at Paksé where he could have easy access to the mountain-dwelling tribes living on the plateau of the Bolovens. He was particularly attracted to the most marginalized, the lepers, to whom he gave himself body and soul. He became one of the key workers at the leprosarium opened in the region of Paksé, and he was one of the jewels in the crown of the Evangelical Mission in Laos.

By 1945 there were twelve organized churches, nine of them under the responsibility of Laotian spiritual leaders. There were also several annexes, about fifteen evangelist-colporteurs crisscrossing the country, and Christians to be found in about fifty villages.

The CMA established a presence in Annam in 1911 (see below). In 1928 the dean of this mission in Indochina, M. Cadman, visited the Swiss missionaries in Laos. In agreement with the CMA, it was decided that he would undertake the evangelization of the northern part of the country, which remained without missionaries despite the frequent appeals of the Presbyterian Mission in Siam mentioned above. Then in 1929 Geoffroy Edward Roffe came to settle in Louang-Phrabang, having received royal permission. He did not know the language and asked for help from those who had long proclaimed the gospel in the south of the country. Two of the most experienced Laotian evangelists were sent to him, Cita and Saly (see above). Their presence greatly enhanced the efforts being made in a number of locations where the gospel had not yet been proclaimed. In 1931 a station was opened at Vientiane, the administrative capital of the country located three hundred kilometers to the south of Louang-Phrabang. Another was opened in 1939 at Xieng Khouang, about five hundred kilometers to the east of Louang-Phrabang.

In the period immediately following the Second World War, a wave of conversions swept through the region. This followed the conversion of a shaman of a Montagnard ethnic group. The movement passed through several villages and continued to the limits of the territory, and this occurred without much assistance from the foreign missionaries. In less than four years, four thousand people turned to Jesus Christ.[114]

## Vietnam

The Catholic Church reappeared in this region of the world in the seventeenth century. Between 1625 and 1630 and then between 1640 and 1650, the Frenchman Father Alexandre de Rhodes directed Jesuit efforts. The missionaries persevered until everything came to a halt often due to brutal expulsions (see pp. 187-88). Over the years, however, their efforts bore fruit in more than 6,500 baptisms. In the eighteenth century, Christians were persecuted in the Northern province as they were in neighboring China. Conversely, the South was more peaceful, and it is estimated that at the end of the century there was a church of 200,000 members with about thirty foreign and fifty indigenous priests.

During the first period of French domination, Protestant missions were blocked from entering Vietnam. In 1893 the Reverend David Lelacheur of the CMA made a brief reconnaissance journey to Saigon, and then in 1895 two other CMA missionaries, Clarence H. Reeves and Robert Jaffray, went as far as Tonkin at the border of China but were not able to settle in the country. It was only in 1911 that the CMA obtained authorization to establish missionaries in Tourane (present-day Da Nang, in

---

114 For the development of the Laotian church during this period, see Dupertuis, op. cit.

the province of Annam). Jaffray then returned and quickly obtained success among a number of the influential personages there. This opening was due at least in part to the work of Bovet Bonnet, a French agent of the British and Foreign Bible Society.

In 1915 two other stations were opened at Faiffo in the province of Annam, and Haiphong in the delta of the Red River in Tonkin. A third was opened in Hanoi in 1916. The restrictions under which the missionaries worked in this French protectorate were severe. During the First World War, of nine missionaries only five were authorized to remain, and on the condition that they not engage in proselytism. They worked, therefore, at the translation of the Bible in Vietnamese, the first edition being completed in 1918. Nevertheless, churches were established in the province of Annam; and by 1928, after sixteen years of CMA's presence, there were seven thousand Christians there. Beginning in 1929, the religious policy of the French administration softened and some missionaries were able to settle in Hué, Nha Trang, and Dalat, the principal cities of Annam. There were sixteen churches organized there by 1939, and a dozen could be considered indigenous. Moreover, there were about twenty groups in the process of forming churches.

The CMA settled in Saigon in 1919 and from the beginning enjoyed liberty to engage in evangelistic activities in Indochina. In a few years, churches were established in the principal cities of the several districts. The CMA had forty-three indigenous churches by 1934, with a total of about five thousand members.

Despite obstacles erected by the French Administration, a Bible school was opened at Tourane in 1921. It played an important role in preparing a cadre of ministers for the three provinces, for about a hundred students passed through this school between 1930 and 1940. This was crucial for the church during the Japanese occupation when foreign missionaries were expelled or interned. Those who were interned translated or edited various theological works in Vietnamese, most notably producing a large Bible dictionary.

Mr. and Mrs. Jean Funé, a French couple who completed their studies at the Bible Institute of Nogent-sur-Marne in 1925, enjoyed a thirty-six-year ministry in Vietnam in the service of CMA. Beginning in 1930, various Montagnard tribes were evangelized by Jean Funé and others sent by the CMA. Several languages had first to be reduced to writing in order to permit the translation and printing of Bible texts. First in Tonkin and then Saigon, Jean Funé was responsible for printing evangelistic material. Later he directed the Bible Institute of Dalat. During the Second World War, he was interned in a Japanese concentration camp.[115]

By 1941 the CMA had established two hundred local churches, each being independent of the mission. They included about fourteen thousand baptized members, in three districts that coincided with the three provinces of Vietnam. Other than the Seventh Day Adventists, who arrived in 1929, the CMA was the only Protestant missionary society present in the country until the end of the French colonial era in Vietnam, which occurred with the fall of Dien Bien Phu in 1954.

---

115 Jean Funé's last sojourn in Cambodia occurred between 1970 and 1975 under the auspices of the CMA. His memoires were entitled *Feet Dipped in Oil*, published in Canada by his son George Funé in 1994.

## Cambodia

Jesuit and Dominican missionaries appeared for the first time in Cambodia in 1555, but there were no permanent mission stations before the seventeenth century. In this entirely Buddhist land, Christianity struggled to take root. By 1842 there were only four Catholic parishes to be found there, which included scarcely more than two hundred members.

Cambodia had no Protestant presence before 1923 when CMA missionaries first arrived; and until the Second World War, it remained the only mission in this country. It had to confront opposition from both the French administration and the Khmer king, who was determined to maintain Buddhism as the only religion in the country. The first CMA members chose to settle in the capital, Phnom Penh. They began by learning the language in order to be able to translate the Bible as quickly as possible, but they also sought to interact with the Chinese and Vietnamese immigrants. They baptized five Vietnamese and two Cambodians in the course of the first year of their work.

In 1923 a missionary couple came to live in Battambang, a large city in the northwest of the country, where they soon had the satisfaction of seeing conversions. A Bible school was opened in 1925, and in its second year it welcomed eleven students. In 1934 seven churches were organized in the district of Battambang.

The evangelization of the district of Kampot began in 1931. The missionaries, however, were not able to stay there long, so the task fell to Cambodian and Vietnamese Christians. In 1933 the king published a decree that authorized Christian activities only in those places where Christians were present before December 31 of the preceding year. Despite this, the mission discreetly pursued its work through several foreigners and especially through local evangelists. In 1939 two other districts were reached: Siem Reap and Kompong Chhang.

## The Gospel in Malaysia

The state known today as Malaysia, located in Southeast Asia, is a federation that includes the province of Malaysia (the area south of the Malaysian peninsula, sometimes called Malacca from the name of a principal city and from the strait that separates the peninsula from the island of Sumatra) and, on the island of Borneo, the province of Sabah (formerly North Borneo) as well as Sarawak (see map 5, p. 400).

In 1511 the first Roman Catholic priests were welcomed to Malacca. They were accompanying Portuguese explorers who sought to renew relations with China in order to establish maritime trade. The great Jesuit missionary Francis Xavier sojourned there between 1545 and 1547, discovering a population that had been baptized but that had remained totally ignorant of the content of the Christian faith (see p. 177). A diocese was established in 1557, but the Catholic Church then consisted only of Indians and Eurasians. The Dutch seized the Malaysian peninsula from Indonesia in 1605 and, forcing the Portuguese clergy to depart, occupied it in 1641. The Catholic missionaries would return, in 1841, two centuries later, and establish a bishopric in

Singapore in 1888.[116] The Reformed chaplains from Holland were generally content to minister to their compatriots and ignore the indigenous population.

The British arrived at the beginning of the nineteenth century. William Milne of the LMS, a colleague of Robert Morrison, disembarked at Malacca in 1814. He wanted to establish the headquarters of the Mission of Ultra-Ganges there, from which he could pursue the evangelization of China. This was necessary because at that time the imperial power refused to grant authorization to missionaries to enter into Chinese territory. Milne also sought to reach the numerous Chinese immigrants on the peninsula. He did not live there long, but in 1818 his initiative led to the establishment of the Anglo-Chinese college in Malacca (see p. 347). For various reasons, this institution did not thrive and closed its doors in 1833. Ten years later, the last representatives of the LMS left Malacca, as China was no longer widely open to foreign missions. The only member of the team left set out to evangelize the Islamic Malaysian population but found scant receptivity to his witness.

In 1847 the SPG undertook the evangelization of the Chinese and Tamil immigrants in the areas of Sarawak and northern Borneo. One of the first missionaries sent was Francis Thomas McDougall (1817–1886), an Anglican minister and doctor who enjoyed a long and fruitful career despite great difficulties. He and his wife lost successively five of their children. Daniel Wilson, bishop of Calcutta, declared after visiting the region: "There is not a mission field in all the earth that can be compared to Borneo." The first conversions occurred in 1851, and soon the Dyak, a tribe of fearsome headhunters, showed themselves to be surprisingly receptive to the gospel. After a few years, several missionaries joined MacDougall, who was consecrated a bishop in 1855. It was the first time that an Anglican received this charge while being in Asia rather than Britain.

It was only in the second half of the nineteenth century that Protestant missions became truly rooted in this part of the globe. Even so, they were not able to effectively reach the Malay Muslims, and, moreover, the government erected obstacles in every direction they sought to move. The Brethren Assemblies founded their first communities in 1865. The American Methodists arrived in 1885, establishing a church in Malacca that became the largest Malay Protestant denomination in the twentieth century. This mission relied on the ministry of pastors from India and Ceylon. The first annual Methodist conference was held in 1902, and its field of action was soon extended into the regions of Kuala Lumpur and Borneo.

An Evangelical Lutheran mission was established in 1907. The Evangelical Mission of Borneo, founded by the Australians in 1928, experienced much success in its undertakings, particularly in the evangelization of the Dusun ethnic group. This success is explained by the emphasis the mission placed from the beginning on the training of indigenous evangelists. It established the Central Bible College, which quickly grew. The Evangelical Church of Borneo, founded by this mission, is one of the largest of Malaysia.

---

116  By 1910 the Catholics had baptized thirty-two thousand, most of whom had originated from China.

Let us note, finally, the coming of the Assemblies of God in 1928 and the Salvation Army in 1935.

### Indonesia (The Dutch Indies)

The Indonesian archipelago is formed of thousands of islands among which the most important are Borneo (the two northern provinces belonging to the Malaysian federation), Sumatra, Java, Bali, Timor, the Celebes, the Moluccas, and western New Guinea (the eastern part constituting the independent state of Papua New Guinea). The distance between the east and west ends of the archipelago is greater than that between New York and Los Angeles.

Unlike most other countries in the Far East, Indonesia was in contact with Christianity as early as the seventh century. In the thirteenth century the Nestorians created a bishopric in Java, and in the fourteenth century the Franciscan mission reached Sumatra, Java, and Borneo. Between 1320 and 1530, the Portuguese sent priests to Moluccas, Celebes, and Timor. Francis Xavier, in 1546, discovered a population in the Moluccas that had recently been Islamicized but that was still open to the Christian message. At the end of the sixteenth century, eighteen Catholic missions were working in different parts of archipelago, which then had about twenty-five thousand Christians.

In 1605 the Dutch expelled the Catholic missions. In the beginning, the Dutch West India Company opposed contact between its chaplains and the indigenous population. The first Reformed missionary, Justus Heurnius, was even thrown in prison in Java a little before 1630.[117] Later the Dutch reversed this policy, even going so far as to grant their chaplains a bonus for each conversion obtained and conferring certain privileges on the converts, which fostered the growth of a superficial Christianity. At the end of the seventeenth century, there were 100,000 Christians in Java and forty thousand in Ambon—one of the Molucca Islands. The New Testament appeared in 1668, the translation having been started by Heurnius and his colleague Albert Cornelisz Ruyle in Javanese about thirty years earlier. This was the first time that the Bible had been printed in a Southeast Asian language. In the course of the eighteenth century as the interest of the Dutch in missions declined, there were no more than twenty-two ministers for all of Indonesia, of which only five spoke the local language. When Joseph Kam, the first missionary sent by Het Nederlandsche Zendeling-Genootschap (NZG, the Dutch Mission Society, founded in 1797) arrived in Indonesia in 1813, a single Dutch minister was living in Batavia. Kam settled in Ambon where the only active church established in the seventeenth century could be found. From there, the gospel spread to a great number of islands.

---

117  For Justus Heurnius, see pp. 234-35.

With the development of Protestant missions in the nineteenth century, interest in Indonesia grew.[118] The colonial administration did not oppose missions among the animists, but it set up obstacles to the evangelization of Muslims. Java was known as "a magnificent island, the principal source of revenue from the East Indies," and, therefore, the Dutch did not want their good relations with the local Muslim authorities to be disturbed.

A little after 1810, two European laymen established separate Christian communities in the eastern part of the island of Java. The communities were formed from Muslim converts and based on diametrically opposed models. The first was established by an orthodox German watchmaker of the Pietist tradition. His group of converts was totally cut off from their cultural roots and formed a church that functioned like a European one, isolated from non-Christian influences. The second community was formed by a Dutch planter who sought to maintain the Javanese heritage, going so far as to reject baptism for the faithful in order to avoid the suggestion of a rupture with the local culture.

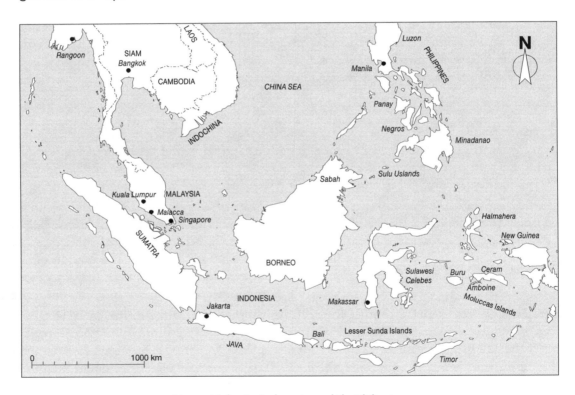

*Map 5: Malaysia, Indonesia, and the Philippines*

---

118 This was also the case with Catholic missions, present since 1807 and under the authority of the Apostolic Prefecture of Batavia. But by 1902, the Catholics had only 50,000 members, with 32 priests at 16 stations. At that time they were especially active in Borneo and on the south coast of New Guinea. They experienced much development in the twentieth century, notably in the area of medicine. In 1934 there were more than 400,000 Catholics, 26 hospitals, 23 dispensaries, 2 leprosariums, and 124 students enrolled in the Catholics schools.

When the Reverend John Garrett Jellesma, sent by the Netherlands Missionary Society, arrived in this region in which it was believed that the gospel had not yet been heard, he was surprised to discover that Christian communities were already well established and perplexed to observe their differences. He declined to live with either group. Locating his house in an area halfway between the two, he attempted to conciliate the two approaches by appealing to the better parts of both. In large measure he succeeded. Today, the Protestant Church of Java is the largest Christian community in the world made up of former Muslims; albeit, when Jellesma intervened, the Islamic population in the region was not well grounded in doctrine, and its beliefs were mixed with those of animism.

In 1827 the Dutch Mission Society began to work among the Celebes in Timor and Halmahera. The Dutch missionaries, however, exhibited many of the habits of colonizers. They waited a long time before consecrating Indonesians for the pastoral ministry, and when they did, the indigenous ministers had the status of assistants to the Dutch ministers and were denied the right to celebrate the sacraments. They did not have permission to stand before the baptismal font for fear that the sacred character of baptism would be devalued in the eyes of the population if indigenous ministers were allowed to administer it.

The German Lutherans of the Rhine Mission began to evangelize the Dayak ethnic group of Borneo in 1836. Following the German defeat in the First World War, they had to leave Borneo, and the Basel Mission took up their work.

## Ludwig Ingwer Nommensen among the Batak Cannibals of Sumatra

Beginning in 1861, the Germans were also engaged in Sumatra where they attempted to evangelize the formidable Batak cannibals. Two missionaries sent by the American Board in 1834 lived for several months among them but were then put to death and eaten.

*Batak Warriors.*

According to Stephen Neill, Ludwig Ingwer Nommensen (1834–1918), a missionary from the Rhineland, was "one of the most powerful missionaries of whom we have record anywhere . . . a man of sterling faith, indomitable resolution, and prophetic and poetic vision."[119] We shall see that this assessment is not exaggerated.

Nommensen was born in Nordstrand, now part of Germany but then Danish. Raised in a poor family, he experienced a difficult childhood. He was not able to go to school, being required to guard the geese and sheep of his village to earn money for his parents. His father, a lock guard, died when he was fourteen years old. During his adolescence, Ludwig was confined to bed for more than a year following an accident, but he profited from this time by extensive reading. His mother persevered in prayer to God for her son's health. When he recovered, he felt led to dedicate his life

---

119 Neill, *History*, 348.

to the evangelization of those who had never heard the gospel. He pursued training at the Rhenish Missionary Society seminary at Wuppertal-Barmen and left in 1862 for Sumatra.

Despite the advice of colleagues who had preceded him by a year, and even the formal interdiction of the Dutch colonial authorities,[120] Nommensen traveled to the valley of Silindung in the interior of the land, a region with a notorious population. He was convinced that he could learn the language faster by living among the local people and apart from his compatriots. Despite the Batak's threats and attempts at intimidation, he settled among them and even invited his fiancée to live in the village, where their marriage ceremony was soon held. During the first year, Nommensen and his wife experienced numerous difficulties and often suffered from poor health. Later, their two daughters succumbed to disease and their only sons were massacred at the time of an attack on the village by a neighboring clan. Ludwig escaped several murder attempts, which he attributed to the manifest intervention of God, and which bolstered his authority in the eyes of the local population.

The first baptisms took place in 1865 when four families converted, and several dozen others occurred in the following year. The courage and goodness of the missionary was evident to all. He resolved to render good for evil every time he was a victim of physical abuse, and his responses became eloquent sermons in action. Having gained the confidence of the people, he sought to lead them to Christian maturity as fast as possible. From the beginning, he imposed the responsibility of daily meditations on his young converts. "I was well disposed to preach the sermon myself," he wrote, "but for the good of the church, I limited myself to being an auditor." The Batak church became autonomous much more quickly than those on other mission fields, and it later showed a remarkable faithfulness and vitality.

The clan spirit was very strong among the Batak. The first converts, being unable any longer to take part in the sacrificial feasts dedicated to demons, were driven from their villages because they were considered to be a threat to the unity of the community. It was necessary, therefore, to found Christian villages for them. The good reputation and prosperity that these villages enjoyed soon led the chiefs of the neighboring villages to convert. Once a chief converted, the cohesion of the clan quickly led to the conversion of entire village communities. Between 1866 and 1876, the number of Christians rose from fifty-two to two thousand. By 1881 there were 7,500. Before they converted to Christianity the villages had been decimated by the wars between rival clans. Now, because they were living in peace, many throughout the land were referring to Nommensen as "the pacifier."

The team that worked with Nommensen was clearly insufficient to deal with the growth of the church. Consequently, after twenty uninterrupted years of living in Sumatra, Nommensen returned to Germany to look for new missionaries to help in the work. When he was ready to return to Sumatra, he decided to leave his wife

---

120 In the Dutch colony of Borneo, seven missionaries had been massacred in 1859, which led the colonial administration to forbid other Westerners to expose themselves to the same danger in territories under its jurisdiction.

behind in Hamburg because of her deteriorating health. He never saw her again, for she died not long before his next vacation.

Upon his return to Sumatra, Nommensen chose to settle as a pioneer in a new region, unsettled, nearly impenetrable, and ravaged by internecine war. While approaching it, he considered its mountain beauty and had a pleasant vision. He composed a poem in German to record what he believed this country would become, with schools and gardens, with cultivated hills and prosperous Christian villages. Here is a translation of an extract from the poem:

> When will this country bend the knee before Jesus, our King? I can already see Christian communities, schools, churches. I hear everywhere bells ringing, calling the people to the house of God. I see indigenous teachers and preachers standing in pulpits before them, showing the way of heaven to young and old . . . Does my imagination mislead me? No! It is not my imagination; it is my faith that sees all this. For all kingdoms must belong to God and his Son, and all tongues confess that Jesus Christ is Lord, to the glory of God the Father.[121]

And this is precisely what happened, though, albeit, after many years of difficult spiritual combat. Batak Christians numbered more than 100,000 in 1910. At the time of Nommensen's death in 1918, there were 170,000 Christians, eight hundred teachers, and forty indigenous pastors serving about a hundred local churches. Seventy-two missionaries were working among them, mostly Germans sent by the Rhine Mission. Overwhelmed by this rapid growth, Nommensen and his colleagues recognized that it would not be possible to organize the church on the European model. Therefore, they adopted the patriarchal structure practiced by the Batak. As communities were led by acknowledged elders and taught by local teachers, so the church would be led by lay elders and catechesis selected from among village teachers. "If we sow the country with a spiritual and disincarnated Christianity, we will never harvest men fashioned by the gospel in all the facets of their lives," said Nommensen. Since all the clans spoke the same language, a Bible translation suitable for everyone was soon available.

After fifty-six years of ministry in Sumatra, Ludwig Nommensen died in 1918 at the age of eighty-four.

Unlike the mission to Borneo, German missionaries were quickly able to return to Sumatra after the First World War. But they were slow to reckon with the demand of the Batak for more independence. Following the Nazi invasion of Holland in 1940, during the Second World War, German missionaries were interned by Dutch colonial authorities. It was only with this development that the leading indigenous Christians were finally able to assume the leadership of their own church.

---

121 L. I. Nommensen, *Cinquante-six ans parmi les cannibals*, trans. M.-L. Pilloud (Lausanne: La Concorde, 1960), 20–21.

# SECTION III

## THE EVANGELIZATION OF THE PACIFIC ISLANDS

From the perspective of the long view of human history or even the history of Protestant missions, what occurred in the little populated and isolated regions of the vast Pacific may appear to be of minor importance. In dedicating a section of this work to the Pacific islands, we are not indulging in a taste for exoticism for supposedly island paradises. Our motives are of another order. The mission work there is important because it was one of the first missionary efforts attempted by Protestants. Also, it is precisely because of their limited scope that these islands may be seen as a microcosm of the mission enterprise. The impact of the gospel on these human societies took place in a relatively brief period, making it more easily measurable than similar work on huge continents.

In a period of about thirty years, churches were planted on a considerable number of the islands. They were indigenous, having at their head indigenous ministers. In this brief period, writes mission historian J.-F. Zorn, "Protestantism became partly integrated into the culture, and a system of indigenous Christianity was already present."[122] Often, after an initial period of rejection, indeed of persecution or of ardent combat between rival factions, the population, following its chief, came to adhere en masse to the Christian faith. In this regard Zorn wrote of a "productive misunderstanding." The missionaries came with the religious purpose of sharing the gospel and encountered peoples with political aspirations: the desire through the missionaries to obtain economic, technological, and intellectual progress that would lead to prosperity and the establishment of modern states. Despite the ambiguous motives that lay behind the mass conversions of the population, the gospel produced a profound transformation not only on laws, mores, and religious practices, and beliefs, but also on hearts and consciences.

The best evidence for the authenticity of the mass conversions to a living and active gospel faith is the extraordinary missionary dynamism of these very young communities. When barely founded, they already had the vision to carry the gospel farther, sometimes much farther. The reader will discover in the narratives that follow that it was through recently converted Polynesians (some of whom had been

122 Zorn, in *Histoire du christianism*, vol. 11, 1100.

cannibals) that the name of Christ was first proclaimed in the majority of the archipelagoes of the South Pacific. Here is an example that world Christianity should take to heart.

Lacking space to relate all the missionary efforts in the Pacific islands, which number about three thousand, we will limit ourselves to a few islands. We will begin with Tahiti, one of the more important islands of the South Pacific where mission work began very early. We will also take a glimpse at the Marquesas Islands, Tonga, and Fiji, and then review the lives of two pioneer missionaries, eminent representatives of the missionaries of their generation, John Williams and John Paton. Finally, we will describe the beginnings of the evangelization of the Loyalty Islands and New Caledonia, where French Protestants were actively engaged after the forced withdrawl of the United Kingdom.

# CHAPTER 8

# Tahiti and the Society Islands

## BIRTH OF THE TAHITIAN CHURCH

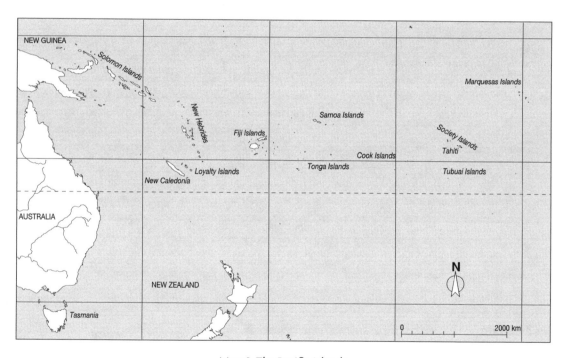

*Map 6: The Pacific Islands*

The Society Islands of the Polynesian archipelago were discovered by Samuel Wallis in 1767. The following year, the French navigator Louis-Antoine Bougain-ville (1729–1811) was the first European to land at Tahiti, the most populated island of the archipelago. He relates his discoveries in his *Voyage autour du monde* (Voyage Around the World) published in 1771. James Cook, the most famous British navigator of the era, sojourned for a long period in the archipelago, making three voyages there and staying for ten months in Tahiti between 1770 and 1780. His enthusiastic accounts filled the imaginations of his compatriots. Cook recorded that the king of Tahiti, Pomare I, desired good relations with Britain. Pomare succeeded in establishing his supremacy over the local chieftains thanks to the support of the famous mutineers of the Bounty, whom he took in his service as mercenaries in 1789.

When the London Missionary Society (LMS) was considering regions of the world where it might be judicious to begin new work, one of its founders, the Anglican Thomas Hawels, proposed Polynesia. He was aware of Cook's good opinion of the region and knew that no other mission had yet chosen this archipelago, which lay in a temperate zone well suited to Europeans.

## THE FIRST STERILE YEARS

*After seven months of sailing, the* Duff *carried the first thirty missionaries of the LMS to Tahiti and to the other islands of the Pacific.*

The LMS easily found the funds necessary to buy a three-master, the *Duff*. If one recalls the difficulties William Carey had in finding a ship acceptable to transport a missionary to India, the reasons for this investment are easily understandable.

The *Duff* left London on August 10, 1796, with thirty missionaries on board, which included six couples, three children, four ministers, a surgeon, and various types of tradesmen. They planned to divide themselves among Tahiti, the Marquesas Islands, and Tonga. As the *Duff* sailed down the Thames, a large crowd escorted the ship along the London quay, singing songs in an atmosphere of joy and revival.

In March 1797, after seven months of sailing, the *Duff* dropped anchored in Tahiti. The missionaries were welcomed by King Pomare I, who offered them land in Papeete, the principal island. On their second Sunday, the king attended the worship service and heard a sermon based on John 3:16. After listening attentively, he expressed astonishment: "Much time will be necessary before we understand this message; it is so different from all that we have heard until now." Several years would pass before the British missionaries mastered the language sufficiently to communicate effectively with the population, the interpreters found there being generally inadequate for the task.

*Papeete, the principal city of Tahiti, located on the northwest coast*

Although favorable to the presence of the missionaries, Pomare I would always remain attached to his own religion and indifferent to the gospel. The tools and techniques of the artisans greatly impressed him, but he seemed to be disappointed that his guests refused the generous advances of the women of the country. The sailors passing through had given him an entirely different image of the sexual behavior to be expected of

Europeans *vis-à-vis* the beautiful Tahitian women. For those sent by the LMS, it was in this unanticipated area that they became aware of what might be called a culture gap.

The romantic illusions that had so inspired the first missionaries were quickly dispelled. They soon realized that they had encountered a reality less idyllic than that depicted by explorers such as Louis-Antoine Bougainville, who had only stopped for a short while. Moreover, Bougainville was influenced by the theories of Jean-Jacques Rousseau as set forth in the *Discours sur l'origine de l'inégalite* (Discourse on the Origins of Inequality), written in 1771. Of Tahiti he wrote: "I say that there are no people in the world happier than the nation of which the New Cythera is the homeland."[123]

The reality was far different. The people's morals were brutish, their intertribal wars incessant, and their cannibalism frequent—the latter especially so in the court of the king. Also, the entire archipelago suffered cruelly from epidemics brought by the European crews passing through: venereal diseases, smallpox, measles, and scarlet fever. Their women held an inferior status to that of the men and were generally considered to be "profane" beings. To maintain demographic stability, infanticide was frequent. It is estimated that two-thirds of the children were killed immediately upon their births: crushed, suffocated, or buried alive. On the other hand, those that lived were adulated, considered as quasi-sacred, and never punished. Fathers were subordinated to their sons as bearers of the family name and wealth. The elders were ignored, and those who became invalids were interred alive. The worship given to their protector gods consisted of food, material, and animal sacrifices; and, during feasts, human sacrifices were also made. The French Protestant missionary Thomas Arbousset arrived in 1862 and, upon learning of the difficulties encountered by the pioneer missionaries, wrote: "In the face of such scenes, how could anyone dare to say that man is good by nature and that he has no need of Christianity to enlighten, purify, and regenerate him?"

Despite their deficiencies, the Tahitians had developed their culture to an astonishing degree. They possessed a system of advanced calculus, an extensive knowledge of astronomy, and a precise measure of time. They had also developed the art of navigation and possessed an extraordinary sense of direction.

The reality the missionaries encountered was so different from what they had imagined that some, after less than a year, became depressed and decided to abandon their posts and return to Britain. The dozen in the expedition who agreed to remain were sent to the islands Toga and Marquise. In the end, after less than two years, there were no more than seven missionaries in Tahiti. One missionary married a pagan wife, lost his faith, and soon after was murdered. Another, named Broomhall, succumbed to alcoholism, left the island to lead a life of adventure, and finally ended up in Calcutta. William Ward, the colleague of William Carey, found him there. Broomhall repented, decided to become a missionary again, but was lost a little later in a shipwreck.

---

123 In spite of all evidence to the contrary, more than a century later the painter Paul Gauguin wrote, "Under a heaven without winter, the Tahitian has only to lift his arm to pick his food . . . For them, to live is to sing and love."

Hostility against Christianity arose in Tahiti among the general population, and despite the protection of the king, three missionaries were massacred in Toga. The wavering morale of the missionaries was further shaken in 1799 when the *Duff* was captured by a French fleet off the coast of Rio de Janeiro, with twenty-nine missionaries and much material on board. Eight new missionaries arrived in Papeete in 1801, bringing with them many types of seeds. Pineapple and melon, among others, prospered magnificently, which helped to create a more favorable disposition among the indigenous population toward the missionaries.

*Pomare II*

King Pomare I died in 1803, and his son succeeded him under the name of Pomare II. In the beginning, he had the same attitude as his father: he was uninterested in the gospel but favorable to the missionaries. Nevertheless, when the president of the mission in Tahiti, the Reverend John Clark Jefferson, died in 1807 after ten years of ministry, there was scarcely any fruit from his labors or that of his colleagues to be noted. The following year, Pomare II was defeated in battle by a rival clan and had to flee to the neighboring island of Moorea.[124] The missionaries, deprived of his protection and seeing their houses ransacked, retreated to other islands and even Australia. The missionary experience at Tahiti seemed to come up short. But at Moorea, where several teams of LMS missionaries had followed the king, there were some significant conversions, including that of a prince and the high priest, Patii. After four years of exile, Pomare II asked to be baptized, "desiring to be happy after death and to escape the judgment." Because the missionaries suspected that his conversion was due to political opportunism, they delayed his baptism for seven years, during which time he was catechized and carefully tested.

The evangelization of the people proceeded apace. Chapels, village schools, a Bible school, and a beautiful octagonal temple were erected. In 1815 at Moorea, six hundred people converted, including several clan chiefs. The LMS purchased a boat to reach the other islands, and soon LMS missionaries succeeded in establishing themselves on the island of Raiatea, where they left several indigenous catechists. It was there that the pioneer missionary John Williams would settle several years later (see below).[125]

Due to a reversal in alliances, Pomare II was able to return to Tahiti in 1813. Informed of the progress of the gospel at Moorea, he asked with great insistence that missionaries come to Papeete so that the island's people would come to the true God. He was heard.

---

124 Tahiti, Makatea, and Moorea form the Windward Islands, part of the archipelago of the Society Islands. Moorea is separated from Tahiti by twenty kilometers of ocean.

125 Raiatea is one of the Leeward Islands, lying west of the Society Islands.

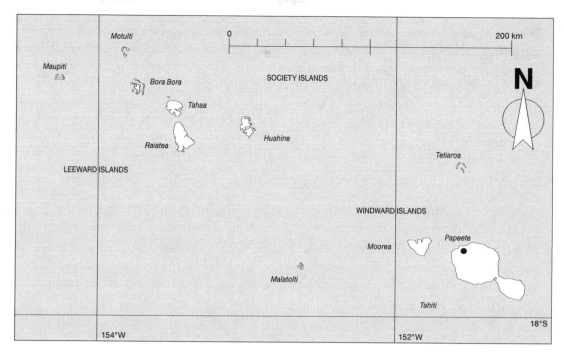

*Map 7a: Tahiti and the Society Islands*

Soon numerous conversions occurred in Tahiti, creating animosity among the non-Christians. Several Christians were captured and sacrificed to idols. During this time, Pomare II waged war in an attempt to reestablish his power. In 1815 a battle took place in which the chief of the enemy clan was killed and his troops dispersed. Pomare II took the opportunity to destroy the traditional temple and cut down the idol of Oro, the national god. But, departing from cultural expectations, he forbade the capture of the conquered, the pillaging of their goods, and the massacring of their women and children. Instead, he organized a thanksgiving service. His adversaries were impressed and decided to recognize Pomare II as king and to rally to a faith capable of inspiring so much magnanimity.

The French navigator Dumont d'Urville (1790–1842) commented on these developments in his *Voyage autour du monde* (Voyage Around the World):

> Pomare's conduct, which seemed so strange in this country, gained for him and his God a large following. The people compared the two religions: one full of sweetness and clemency, shedding blood only in defense; the other fierce and unpitying, asking for new victims every hour. The comparison was a beautiful argument for Christianity, which on this day achieved the conquest of Tahiti.

At Rarotonga, another Pacific island, a similar event took place several years later. The defeated pagan chiefs marveled at the conduct of the Christians: "They are less numerous than us, but they have been victorious. If we had won, we would have massacred them to the last, and yet they invite us to their table. We want their religion."

413

## A SOCIETY REFORMED BY THE GOSPEL

Soon, pagan customs were abolished; Pomare II received baptism in 1819; and the Christian faith became the national religion. The king promulgated new civil laws inspired by the Mosaic law: the Pomare Code. A temple was erected at Papeete that held six thousand people (the island then had a population of about sixteen thousand), and chapels were erected in the villages. As we will see later, various books of the New and then the Old Testament were translated into the local language and printed in Moorea. On the other islands, the work of evangelization was also highly fruitful.

A significant development occurred in 1818 with the founding of the Tahitian Mission Society. Its first goal was the evangelization of the Leeward Islands,[126] which constitute the western part of the archipelago of the Society Islands and lie several hundred kilometers from Tahiti. The Tahitian Mission organized a collection of palm oil among the Christians in 1819. This was sent to London and sold, the profits going to support the missionary effort of the LMS, which, for the period, reported a considerable sum received. This was seen as a remarkable application of the principles of generosity and reciprocity extolled in the epistles of the New Testament (Rom 15:25–27; 1 Cor 16:1–4; and others).

After so many years of meager progress, the success of Christianity in Tahiti was considered to be a veritable miracle. But much remained to be done if the inhabitants were to avoid falling into a superficial Christianity and move toward personal conversion and a knowledge of the Scriptures—with the ethical choices that this implied.

In 1821 King Pomare II died, and after a regency, his eldest daughter acceded to the throne in 1829 under the name of Pomare Vahine IV. She followed the path set out by her father, governing the country according to laws inspired by the Bible. She had to confront opposition from the adherents of the former religion who rejected the new rules and wanted to reinstate honor dances, tattooing, and other traditional customs. During these years, the church grew and bore fruit. Many schools opened, teaching general literacy and training teachers. A printing press was also operated, and Christian literature in the local language was made available throughout the country. Public worship was frequent, and family worship at home was practiced on a large scale. There was much social progress as homes, sanitary conditions, and food improved while alcoholism declined and was eventually to be found on the island almost exclusively among British sailors. The culture was also enriched by contact with European countries.

Witnesses from various backgrounds and perspectives agreed that in a dozen years Tahiti had undergone a profound transformation as a result of the influence of the Christian message. For example, the explorer Louis Duperry, charged by the French government with making a fact-finding voyage around the world, learned that marvelous things were taking place on this previously infamous island and decided to stop at Tahiti to see for himself. What he saw amazed him:

---

126 In addition to Raiatea, they include the islands of Tahaa, Huahine, and Bora Bora.

[On his arrival on May 3, 1824, neither dugout canoes nor Tahitian women welcomed him.] We soon understood why: it was the time when everyone was listening to the sermon at church; but the next morning, islanders in great number brought us all sorts of provisions . . . The island of Tahiti is very different today from what it was in the time of Cook. The missionaries have totally changed the morals and customs of its inhabitants . . . The women no longer come aboard the ships; they are even extremely reserved when encountered on land. Marriages are made as in Europe . . . bloody wars and human sacrifices no longer take place . . . All the natives know how to read and write; they have in their hands religious books translated in their language and printed in Tahiti . . . Beautiful churches have been built and all the people go with great devotion to them twice a week to hear the preacher. Individuals are often seen taking notes of the more interesting parts of the talks.[127]

François-René Chateaubriand, on the other hand, was less kind and rather ironic:

Tahiti has lost its dances, singers, voluptuous customs. The beautiful inhabitants . . . perhaps too praised by Bougainville, sit today under their bread trees and their elegant palm trees like Puritans. They listen to sermons, read the Scripture with Methodist missionaries, argue from morning to evening, and so in this tiresome way expiate the overly beautiful gaiety of their mothers. Bibles and ascetic works are printed in Tahiti.

## HENRY NOTT (1774–1844)

Among the missionaries in this early period, Henry Nott played an outstanding role. He was twenty-two years old in 1797 when he embarked for Tahiti as one of the first sent by the LMS. As a mason who had not completed his schooling, he was sent as an artisan. Amidst dramatic events and moments of general discouragement, he remained steadfast, absolutely refusing to leave the archipelago. Eventually he had a decisive influence on King Pomare II and became the principal drafter of the Pomare Code. He carefully studied the language and local customs, and his preaching quickly bore fruit.

*Henry Nott (1774–1844),*

His major work was the translation of the Bible. He printed the Gospel of Luke in 1818 on the island of Moorea. Between 1819 and 1823, the Gospels of Matthew and John as well as the Acts of the Apostles were also translated and published. And in 1829 the entire New Testament left the press. In the meantime, aided by several colleagues, Nott made progress in the translation of the Old Testament. He returned to Britain in 1836 to print the entire Bible, which he presented to Queen Victoria and, on

---

127 Cited by H. Clavier, *Thomas Arbousset pionnier* (SMEP, 1963), 164.

his return to Tahiti, to Queen Pomare Vahine. In spite of his lack of formal training, Nott succeed in translating the Bible into the Tahitian language. His success must be attributed to twenty years of persistent effort.

Like others sent by the LMS to Tahiti, Nott had arrived as a bachelor. After a few years the mission decided to send several "pious women" to the island in order that they might marry the single missionaries and establish homes. Nott's marriage proved to be unhappy, his wife having very quickly lost all interest in the mission and in enduring the difficulties of Tahitian life. One of Nott's colleagues said of her, "Her Tong[ue] is daily employed in abusing her Husband in the most cruel manner and to slander others with the lest [sic] just cause . . . Her Feet of late are never directed to the place where prayer is wont to be made but daily she joins with those who are studious in their design to perplex and thwart us."[128] She died after less than a year, probably due to alcohol abuse.

Nott passed the last years of his life among the Tahitian people in conditions that were difficult for the British due to the French protectorate. Unlike other more militant colleagues, he always sought to quell conflict, valuing as he did respect for the French government. He died in 1844, wept over by all those who had been profoundly impressed by his love and perseverance. Henri Vernier writes, "After forty-seven years of uninterrupted labor, one of the great figures of the first missionary enterprise of the LMS disappeared from the earth. Without formal educational preparation, he undertook a considerable literary work: with the aid of his colleagues, he fixed the Tahitian language in writing, and (as Charles Vernier said), it was always necessary to have recourse to 'Nott's Bible' to discover the original and pure Tahitian dialect."[129]

## THE ARRIVAL OF CATHOLICS PRIESTS

Despite the conversion of Pomare II, the climate of peace that reigned in Tahiti came to an end in about 1836. French Catholics and British Protestants then engaged in a struggle for influence in the Pacific region. Jesuits of the Society of the Picpus Fathers established themselves in 1834 on neighboring archipelagos where they encountered much success. In November 1836, the Catholic priests Honoré Laval and François Caret, claiming to be the bearers of the true religion, arrived on a French frigate from the Gambier Islands. Denied the right by the queen to settle in Tahiti, they made a clandestine attempt to do so. When the Jesuits were discovered, they were reembarked by force.

France cited this incident as a pretext for the use of force. In August 1838 a French ship of war, commanded by Captain Dupetit-Thouars, docked at Papeete.[130] Under threat of canon fire, Pomare Vahine was constrained to sign a *convention de bonne amitié* (treaty of friendship) between France and Tahiti. In the terms of the text, "the French, whatever be their profession, will be able to come and go freely, to establish themselves in all the islands under the government of Tahiti . . . The free exercise of

---

128 Reported by Tucker, op. cit., 202.

129 Henri Vernier, "Au vent des cyclones," *The Bergers et les Mages* (Paris, 1986), 42.

130 Dupetit-Thouars received a clear mandate from the French government to promote the establishment of French Catholics Missions in the Pacific. Cf. J. P. Faivre, *L'Expansion Française dans le Pacifique, 1800-1842* ( Paris: Nouvelles Éditions Latines, 1953).

the Catholic religion is permitted in the island of Tahiti."[131] The Catholic missionaries already in place were given official recognition in 1841.

Henceforth, France would supplant Britain in the administration of Tahiti. Between 1843 and 1847, the island was plagued by disruptions. In July 1844, seven of the ten LMS missionaries present on the islands left, concluding that they were in danger and subjected to too much harassment to be useful. Moreover, they believed that their presence was more of a handicap than an aid to the indigenous Protestants.

In 1847 Queen Pomare Vahine, who was a refugee on the island of Raiatea (the archipelago of the Leeward Islands), returned to Tahiti, having consented to submit herself to the authority of the French protectorate. William Howe, one of the British missionaries who had left the island in 1844, returned at this time to serve as the pastor of the small English-speaking community. He exercised a discrete ministry, training the laity, publishing books, and revising the translation of the Bible.

## THE PARIS MISSION CALLED TO HELP

As early as 1843 the committee of the Paris Mission was aware of the tensions arising from French supremacy in Tahiti and made the decision to warn the Protestant churches of France of the danger to Tahitian Protestantism. It then attempted to raise funds to employ French missionaries to work alongside their British counterparts. Its intention was to prepare these men to replace the British missionaries in case the day should come when they would be forced to leave the island.

The LMS, however, judged it inopportune to send French Protestant missionaries to Tahiti because of the anti-French sentiments of the inhabitants. Twelve years later in 1857, the LMS saw things differently. France had applied the policy of the concordat to its Polynesian protectorate, granting to Tahitian Protestantism the status of a state church. The British missionaries could not agree to this, and so the LMS asked the Paris Mission to come to its aid.

*Queen Pomare
Vahine IV*

The committee of the Paris Mission then approached Prince Napoleon, the minister of the French colonies who was known for his anti-Catholicism. He welcomed its advances and declared that not only was he not opposed to sending French Protestant ministers and teachers to Tahiti but that he would even help to facilitate it. By 1860, when the Paris Mission had not yet been able to send missionaries as intended, the legislative assembly of Tahiti sent a letter to Napoleon III, asking him to choose "two Protestant missionaries from among our coreligionists in France." The letter declared:

> It is the Protestant ministers who lifted us out of our primitive state; our religion is good; it has inspired us with a love for France, which protects us. We ardently desire that our children learn

---

131 Cited by J. Zorn, *Le grand siècle d'une Mission protestante* (Paris: Les Bergers & Mages et Karthala, 1993), 154.

French, but we do not want them to learn this language for the purpose of changing their religion.[132]

It was not until November 1862 that the Paris Mission could inform the churches of Tahiti that it was sending two missionaries: Thomas Arbousset, previously a missionary to Lessouto, and the Reverend François Atger, Arbousset's son-in-law. There had been an interval of twenty years between the beginning of the French protectorate in Tahiti in March 1843 and the arrival of the first French Protestant missionaries.

Upon his arrival in Tahiti, Arbousset attempted to counsel the church in its relations with the French administration. He also sought to clarify the structures of the church, assembling together the twenty ministers and forty deacons of Tahiti and Morrea and encouraging greater cohesion between the various parishes.

Atger arrived several months after Arbousset and was directed to concentrate his efforts on education, an area the British had not been able to pursue. The Catholic mission's control of most of the schools was a threat to the future of Tahitian Protestantism. In June 1864 the first French Protestant school was inaugurated in the church of Papeete. Arbousset returned to France after two years of intense labor to rebuild, train, and encourage the church. In Paris he remained a faithful advocate of the mission to Tahiti.

At the beginning of 1866, Atger's efforts in education were reinforced by Charles Viénot, a teacher from the country of Montbeliard who would remain in Tahiti until his death in 1903. From the beginning he showed himself to be very enterprising, striving to obtain, in his words, "with the support of the queen and the entire people . . . the simultaneous development of heart and mind in the faith of the Savior." But he was soon forced to lower his goals, the number of students in his classes having declined as the number of the Catholic schools increased. He had wanted to put in place the monitorial system, following the principles of the English pedagogue Joseph Lancaster (1778–1838). In his system, only the most advanced students were trained directly by the teachers. The method was supposed to permit a multiplication of the teachers' work as younger students sought to emulate older students while also developing a sense of personal responsibility. In contrast, the Catholics continued to use the traditional method, with large classes taught by a single teacher, inculcating discipline and training through memorization. The Catholic approach seemed more advisable to the Tahitian parents who did not wish to see their children instructed by other children. Moreover, the Catholics had a larger number of teachers at their disposal as well as financial backing from the state for their schools. Viénot dedicated most of his resources to forming a normal school intended to prepare Tahitian teachers. In forty years of ministry, he enjoyed a major role in the history of Tahitian Protestantism but largely in the area of education rather than pastoral care. He was also important in the struggle for religious liberty during a time when Catholicism predominated. He received various distinctions, including the title of Knight of the Legion of Honor (1883) and, a little before his death, that of Officer of Public Instruction.

---

132  Cited by Zorn, op. cit., 175.

Frédéric Vernier, another Frenchman, came to Tahiti a year after Viénot and was named pastor of the Church of Papeete. Both men worked closely together, with Vernier engaging in ministry in Tahiti for forty years.

It is not possible here to present in detail the evolution of the relations between the church of Tahiti and the French state, which in general reflected the relationship between church and state in France before its formal separation in 1905.[133] An independent synod was constituted in 1873. Suspected of being a force in the political opposition, it was replaced in 1879 by a high council in which the government had representatives who could express their reservations to decisions taken.

*A missionary house in Tahiti.*

Now firmly established in Tahiti, France had designs on the neighboring archipelagos. All these islands having already been evangelized by the LMS, the French Protestant missionaries strove to avoid having their faith appear to be foreign and pro-British. Therefore they encouraged the Tahitian church to array itself on the side of France. In 1887 the French gained possession of the Leeward Islands but had to evacuate the New Hebrides in favor of the British.[134] At the end of 1888, the committee of the Paris Mission decided to work on the Leeward and Australian Islands. The first French

---

133  For more ample documentation, we direct our readers to the work of Zorn, op. cit., 217–225.

134  It is necessary to keep in mind that this happened just two years after the "the scramble for Africa" between the colonial powers at the time of the Congress of Berlin in 1885. The European states disposed of territories without seeking the consent of the populations concerned.

missionary to Raiatea of the Leeward Islands was Gaston Brunel. The church he found there was already old and well established, and he lived on the island until 1911.[135]

The small team sent by the Paris Mission experienced a difficult period due to personal conflicts among themselves and to ecclesial and theological conflicts then vexing Protestantism in the city. Alfred Boegner, the director of the mission, upon his visit to Raiatea helped to resolve the personal conflicts by a better division of labor and by sending home some who had only recently arrived. After this unpromising beginning, the effort gained new momentum in the middle of the 1890s. One of those most responsible for this renewal was Gaston Brunel who, despite arriving only in 1893, set about crisscrossing the entire archipelago, greatly contributing to the unity of Polynesian Protestantism. He published a French/Tahitian journal of religion and culture, and he wrote a great deal of material that he printed on a press he brought with him. He also organized numerous evangelistic conferences as well as chapters of the Blue Cross that waged campaigns against alcoholism. In his eyes, the reevangelization of Polynesia was indispensable if the Christian faith was to be integrated into the local culture.

One of Brunel's principal concerns was to improve the rudimentary education established for the Christian ministers, an effort he began in 1888. It was urgent to reinvigorate the ministerial body put in place by the British missionaries, which was poorly adapted to the rapidly developing Tahitian society. Moreover, it was necessary to reform the processes by which the indigenous ministry was recruited so that it would be taken up by those with an authentic vocation who could then be trained and anchored in evangelical religion.

In 1895 Charles Viénot took the opportunity of a vacation in France to plea for the purchase of a ship, which he considered necessary because of the extension of the Paris Mission's work in the Pacific—the most distant of the Australian Islands—was 1,200 kilometers from Tahiti. In effect, many islands, which had rarely been visited by French Protestants, had been won over by the Catholics, Adventists, or even Mormons who had a good ship at their disposal. Thanks to a private subscription, Viénot soon had enough money to purchase a schooner, christened the *Croix du Sud* (Southern Cross). This ship was put to good use in the missionary work of the archipelagos and also allowed for the enlargement of the field of action. Paul-Louis Vernier, the son of Frédéric Vernier, was able to begin his ministry in the Marquises Islands in 1898 due to the availability of the schooner. Unfortunately, because of high maintenance costs the *Croix du Sud* was sold in 1912.

## A SUMMARY VIEW

Charles Viénot died in 1903, Frédéric Vernier returned to France in 1908, and Baston Brunel returned in 1911. These three personalities, differing in character and theological orientation, each in his own way left an important mark on the history of the mission to

---

135 After the return of Gaston Brunel to France, his wife wrote a well-documented biography of John Williams, the pioneer of the evangelization of Raiatea that began in 1818. Williams, an emblematic figure of the mission in the South Seas, will be one of the subjects of the following chapter.

Tahiti. They served during a long and delicate period, one that differed greatly from that experienced by the pioneers of the LMS during the first half of the nineteenth century.

The work of the Paris Mission in Tahiti during the second half of the nineteenth and first part of the twentieth centuries was threatened by the unrelieved pressure from Catholicism, the relentless assault from certain sects, the tensions within the missionary team, the difficult balance to be maintained between the needs of education and the building of the church, and the lack of a well-trained indigenous clergy able to meet the challenges of a rapidly changing society. Yet, through it all the mission remained an active partner in the Polynesian church.

## THE MARQUESAS ISLANDS

The group of islands known as the Marquesas are located among the eastern most part of the Pacific islands, some 1,500 kilometers from the archipelago of the Society Islands. In June 1797, not long after the *Duff* had stopped in Tahiti it continued on to the Marquesas Islands, following the plan made in London before its departure. The LMS missionaries William Pascoe Crook and John Harris then embarked for the shore. During their first night, Harris was assailed by the wife of the local chief. When he resisted, she enlisted other Tahitian women to hound him, which they did, being irritated by what they considered unusual behavior for a white person disembarking from a ship. Profoundly perturbed, the next day Harris persuaded the captain of the *Duff* to take him from Tahiti. Crook remained alone, but after little more than a year he too left the archipelago, discouraged that his preaching had not engendered any response. He returned to the Marquesas twenty-five years later with four Polynesian evangelists, but once again the attempt ended in failure.

The LMS sent more missionaries and indigenous evangelists in 1834, and this time there were more tangible results. In 1838 the French conquest led to the Catholic priests present on the island being protected by the national navy. The Catholic missionaries pressured the king of the principal island to expel the LMS missionaries, who, recognizing the impossibility of their position, withdrew to Tahiti in 1842. Forty-five years after the disembarkation of the first Protestant missionaries all appeared to be in vain.

But a dozen years later, a Christian sailor from Hawaii married the daughter of a local Marquesas chief. His witness impressed his father-in-law, who asked the Hawaiian Evangelical Association to send a missionary. Accompanied by several Hawaiian evangelists, the Reverend B. W. Parker disembarked in the Marquesas in 1853. Despite the opposition of the Catholic clergy, in 1870 seven mission stations were established on three islands of the archipelago, forming an evangelical community of a hundred communicants as well as several schools and a boarding school for young people. Since the French colonial administration was not interested in the Marquesas, it left only a small garrison there. In the anarchy that resulted from the lack of effective government, the development of the church was sometimes thwarted by tribal conflicts that often resulted in deaths, pillaging, and displacement of populations. In 1898, Paul-Louis Vernier from the Paris Mission arrived on the *Croix du Sud* to begin his ministry, as noted.

# THE ISLANDS OF TONGA AND FIJI

## *The Islands of Tonga (The Friendly Islands)*

This archipelago consists of three groups of islands (some of the islands or islets are uninhabited), on which a Polynesian population resides. The first explorers were so struck by the peaceful and hospitable character of the people that these islands were also called the Friendly Islands. The friendly character of the population did not make the evangelization of the archipelago of Tonga any easier than elsewhere. On the contrary, the mission there experienced several failures, and it was not until thirty years after the appearance of the first missionaries that a church was founded.

The first missionaries were the ten Britons of the first expedition of the *Duff* who had continued on their way after having left their colleagues in Tahiti in April 1797. Several British sailors had previously settled on Tongatabou, the principal island of the southern group, and now served as the missionaries' interpreters. However, their lifestyles and their questionable business affairs soon set them against the missionaries, and they succeeded in setting the king and population against them. George Veeson, one of the LMS missionaries, made common cause with the sailors, adopted their dissolute behavior, and married a local woman.

Though King Mouaini had generously welcomed them, he soon distrusted the missionaries, accusing them of being responsible for the disease and deaths that had occurred in the tribe since their arrival. Hence, the missionaries were not successful in this first attempt. Two years after their arrival, a civil war broke out, and amidst the general anarchy, their houses were pillaged. Three among them were murdered, and the rest threatened with death. Finally, in January 1800, they were picked up by a British ship, which they had rowed out to meet in small boats when it had dropped anchor in the area.

It was twenty-two years before a new attempt was made by Walter Lawry of the British Wesleyan Mission, who was accompanied by two artisans. Their ministry began with greater success as there were soon conversions, and one of the new believers was even the first to announce the name of Jesus Christ in the islands of Fiji. Unfortunately, the departure of Lawry due to poor health put an end to this second attempt to proclaim the gospel.

In 1826 the Wesleyan Mission made a new attempt in Tongatabou, sending John Thomas, a British blacksmith, and J. Hutchinson. They discovered that the two artisans left by Lawry four years earlier had scarcely undertaken any gospel work. Once again the honeymoon was of short duration as the island chief soon accused the strangers of provoking the anger of the local deities.

Just when failure seemed certain, Polynesian evangelists from Tahiti and Fiji suddenly appeared at the other end of the island. They soon experienced conversions, including that of the king of the region. Though the king did not persevere, other members of the royal family held firmly to the faith. One of these made an appeal to the missionaries to come and help. The gospel spread quickly among the islands located at this end of the archipelago. The most effective evangelists were the new converts, and the worship services attracted large crowds. The church counted more than eighty baptized in 1829. Schools were established and a printing press set up to publish the first translations of the Bible.

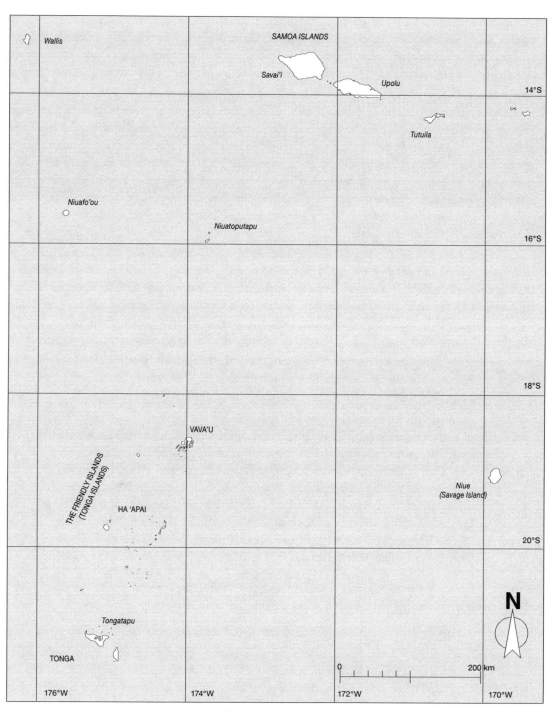

*Map 7b: The islands of Tonga and Samoa*

A Samoan Tonga was converted and became the first one to take the gospel to his compatriots. When John Williams visited the Samoan islands in 1831, he received a warm welcome from a group of Christians who had been anxiously awaiting the arrival of missionaries to teach them (see below, p. 434–35).

In 1830 Thomas chose to live at Hapai, the principal island of the central group of the archipelago. The king of the islands, Taufaa-Hau, had already taken the initiative to eliminate pagan practices and to teach the boys and men, while his wife did the same for the young girls. In the first year, Thomas baptized 150 of the inhabitants of Hapai, including the king himself, who took the name of George. In 1833, seven years after the arrival of Thomas and Hutchinson, the worship services on the archipelago were attended by eight thousand people, and thirty thousand books had been printed—the gospel and portions of the Bible, hymns, catechism, and more. But as often happens when conversions occur quickly and en masse, especially following that of the ruler, the faith lacked depth and the break from the previous religion was not always clear.

## Outbreak of Revival

During a worship service on July 23, 1834, on the northern island of Vavaou, while the preacher was commenting on the passage of the gospel where Jesus wept over the city of Jerusalem, a revival began. Under the action of the Spirit, listeners began to confess their sins and to ardently desire to be entirely free of all their remaining ties to paganism. The following Sunday, the same phenomenon repeated itself in another village and then was repeated in numerous other villages throughout the island. At this time the same experience occurred on a small island close to Hapal but before news of the revival could have reached there. L. Nagel writes:

> This time it was not just a matter of a more or less superficial conversion from paganism to Christianity, or from idols to the one unique and spiritual God, but a conversion of the heart, escaping from the power of Satan and giving itself entirely to God. Prayer and the search for grace so completely absorbed their thoughts that it was necessary to close schools and suspend ordinary work in order to hold five to six prayer meetings everyday in their place. From the time the missionaries or indigenous ministers began to preach, the people melted in tears, and several fell to their knees to invoke the name of the Lord, and they were not slow to cry out in the transport of a wholly new joy: "The Lord be praised! Until now I have not known Jesus; today, I know him! He has delivered me from my sins. I love Jesus Christ!"[136]

It is striking that in a time when the work of God was accomplished in so dramatic a manner, trials seemed to multiply. Terrible storms, various diseases, devastating famines, and fires in several chapels struck these young communities. But while in the past these types of disasters were attributed to the anger of the ancestral gods

---

136 L. Nagel, *Les Missions évangéliques au XIXe siècle,* journal published by the Basel Mission.

and brought the population's hostility down upon the Christians, now these calamities served to affirm their faith and secure their closer attachment to Jesus Christ.

On the island of Vavaou alone, 2,200 people accepted the gospel and were received as members of the church, and this in less than six weeks. Many, however, resisted the gospel, especially on the island of Tongatabou where the message seem to be blocked from the first. Some pagan chiefs even fomented civil war and massacred Christians. These troubles continued until 1839 when King George, who was reigning in Hapai, was recognized as the sovereign by everyone on the Friendly Islands and promulgated laws inspired by the Bible. This king, it was said, died at more than a hundred years old, having led his people to a profoundly evangelical spirit.

The extraordinary momentum of the revival led to the rapid transfer of responsibilities to local Christians not only for the ongoing evangelization of the islands but also for the direction of the church. A new revival exploded in 1846, and on some islands it was said that practically the whole population was manifestly caught up in the faith under the leading of the Spirit.

Among the Wesleyan missionaries, John Thomas enjoyed an eminent role and was considered the apostle of the Tonga, among whom twenty-five years of his life was passed. At the beginning of his ministry, the entirely pagan population was hostile; at his departure, the island was almost entirely Christian, and the gospel was clearly bearing fruit in the lives of a great many of the members of the church. However, whatever the importance of the role and the value of the dedication of Thomas and his colleagues, it was the Polynesian preachers themselves to whom God accorded the grace to be at the heart of this movement of conversions and revival.

The statistics of the Wesleyan Mission Society for the entire archipelago were gathered in 1857. At that time there were twelve European missionaries, five catechists, 208 teachers, 522 indigenous preachers, 6,500 communicants, fifteen thousand attendees in the worship, and seven thousand students in the schools. The development of the church continued, but it was slowed down by an epidemic that constrained all the missionaries, at least temporarily, to leave after fifty years of toil.

In 1860 the Australian Methodist missionary S.W. Baker enjoyed an important role as a counselor to King Tupu in the editing of a constitution that sought to free the archipelago from British authority. He also encouraged the church to take greater responsibility for itself. Coming to Tongo several years later, his colleague J. E. Moulton founded a college and translated the Bible. Soon the two missionaries entered into conflict; the Australian Methodist conference took Moulton's side, but King Tupu supported Baker. The latter founded a free church, which became the official Tongan church that was completely independent of the mission. Moulton withdrew in order to bring an end to the conflict. Returning in 1893 upon the death of King Tupu, he presided over the church that remained faithful to the Australian Methodist Conference. The two churches were unified in 1924. By 1900 the twenty thousand inhabitants of the archipelago were considered to be Christians, and by 1970, 98.7 percent of the Tongan population of eighty thousand were Christian.[137]

---

137 Numbers furnished by Barrett, *Encyclopedia*.

## THE FIJI ISLANDS

The Fiji Islands (then called Viti) are close neighbors to the archipelago of the Friendly Islands but are peopled by Malaysians, who were feared for their warlike character and cannibalism. It has already been noted that in 1823 the Fiji Islands were the home of one of the first Tongan Christians. Tahitian teachers were dispatched by the LMS in 1830, and in 1835 two Wesleyan missionaries also sojourned there along with several Tongan evangelists. Despite a number of conversions during the first decade, paganism continued to predominate and life remained extremely brutal. But then in 1845 a large number of conversions began to occur. A local king, who until then had led the opposition to Christianity, accepted Jesus Christ following a dream in which he saw the divinities of his religion prostate themselves before the God of the Christians. He was baptized in 1854.

Australian Methodists took up the task of evangelizing the Fiji Islands in 1855. At this time Joeli Bulu, an evangelist from Tonga Island who had arrived in 1823, played an important role in the organization of the churches and the training of the Fijian ministers. He served in full cooperation with the Methodist missionary Joseph Waterhouse, who pleaded for a perfect equality between the missionaries and the local ministers.

Numerous Indian migrants from Madras and Kerala began to be employed as common laborers on the islands' plantations in 1880. Consequently, Hinduism became the second most popular religion on the island, following Christianity. By 1900, 86 percent of the inhabitants of the Fiji islands were professing Christians.

# CHAPTER 9

# Two Pioneers of the Pacific: John Williams and John Paton

We must go back several dozen years to the period of the early nineteenth-century pioneers in order to review the career of an eminent servant of God in the mission history of Polynesia.[138] John Williams' (1796–1839) work in the South Pacific occurred on three successive bases: the island of Raiatea (1818–1827), the island of Rarotonga (1827–1834), and then, after four years in Britain, the Samoan Islands (1838). In 1839 he went to the New Hebrides where he died.

## JOHN WILLIAMS: THE DISCOVERY OF POLYNESIA

The missionary meetings organized in Williams' church engendered a lively interest in him, and he soon felt oppressed "at the thought that thousands were dying every day in darkness." At the age of twenty, he offered his services to the London Missionary Society in 1816. Faced with urgent needs, the mission ordained Williams two months later. He married Mary Chauner, a nineteen-year-old girl in his church, and without any formal biblical training, left three weeks later in November 1816. This was the period when, after years of aridity, the Polynesian church experienced rapid growth.

John Williams (1796–1839), at the beginning of his mission.

John and Mary Williams landed in 1817 at the island of Moorea where the fate of the mission was intertwined with that of King Pomare II. It had been twenty years since the first LMS missionaries had arrived. After attending a worship service on the island for the first time, Williams wrote:

---

138  A two-volume biography of Williams was written by Madame I. Brunel, wife of G. Brunel, mentioned in the preceding chapter as a missionary on the island where Williams worked: *John Williams, l'Apôtre des mers du Sud; the martyr d'Erromanga*, volumes 1 and 2 (Cahors: Coueslant, 1929).

> There, gathered in the church, I saw seven to eight hundred indigenous people who, five years before, were devoted to the worship of idols and to all the horrible practices that went with idolatry. Surely, I dreamed, the work here is completed: our coming will not be very useful . . . We asked ourselves if it was possible that those parents, surrounding their babies today with so much affection, be those who before were putting them to death. Is it truly they who—just a few years before—offered human sacrifices to appease their gods and seek their favors? Today, they begin to benefit from the sacrifice of the Lord for the forgiveness of their sins. All that we saw here filled our hearts with gratefulness, and we rejoiced. It is a complete reversal toward Christianity, and we hope that, in this crowd that had rejected idols, many are now truly converted and given to God.[139]

The last sentence seems to temper the enthusiasm shown at the beginning of the letter, demonstrating a cautious realism. Williams was soon conscious that the work was only just beginning. The people had a thirst to be taught about the worship of the true God, but at the same time, they continued to serve their idols. Seeing this, Williams was discouraged but moved to redouble his efforts.

## WORK OF THE PIONEER TO RAIATEA

In June 1818 the king of Raiatea, the predominant leader of the Leeward Islands, called for missionaries to come. He was profoundly troubled by the practice of human sacrifice that could be seen everywhere in Raiatea, the true capital of Polynesian paganism. Here was supposedly found the seat of Oro, the god of the South Seas, the Moloch of the archipelago. John and Mary Williams decided to confront this bloodthirsty sanctuary, leaving Moorea for Raiatea several months after their first contact with the Polynesians.

They stayed for nine years in Raiatea, making it a base from which to travel to the other islands. They found several Raiateens who were already Christians, converted through the ministry of Tahitian evangelists who had arrived several years before. Despite the warm welcome accorded to the two missionary families, the general climate of the island was dominated by violence and the depravation due to low sexual morals. Conscious of the difficulty of communicating the gospel by word alone to a population that differed from him in every way, Williams concluded that he would have to establish contact with them through his lifestyle while living among them. The example of the missionary and the visible results of his work in farming and building construction so impressed the population that, when he organized a school, both adults and children wanted to attend.

Williams did not hesitate to disrupt the culture and the lifestyle of the islanders. He was especially attentive to their moral and spiritual development, which seems to have undergone a rapid reformation:

---

139  Cited by Mme. G. Burnel, op. cit., vol. 1, 51f.

What marvels and profound transformation the preaching of the gospel has accomplished in just a few months! This is what inclined the heart of the king—though the pagan religion accorded him divine honors—to turn from idolatry to serve God. It is the gospel that led the priests of Oro to abandon their bloodthirsty worship through which they had gained their living. It is the gospel, the gospel lived by its servants who persuade the people, those given up from time immemorial to pleasure, vice, laziness, to leave their indolence to begin to work and to do what—several months before—they considered to be impossible, unendurable![140]

They soon began to bring their idols to the missionaries to be burned. According to Williams, these spectacular conversions could only be explained as demonstrations of a real spiritual thirst and the progressive work of God in their hearts. Travelers who had known the island before the proclamation of the gospel there would marvel, upon returning several years later, at the extent to which the life and morals of the inhabitants had changed.

*On the island of Rarotonga in 1819 the inhabitants threw their idols in the fire*
*after hearing the gospel preached.*

In May 1820 a church of sixty-four by fifteen meters, able to hold as many as three thousand people, was inaugurated. In 1821, three years after the arrival of the mission, the church was officially established: "an independent spiritual fraternity but open to other churches." Williams and his colleagues, cautious not to confuse a fleeting and superficial infatuation with true regeneration, would rejoice to see over the years a growing number of profoundly transformed lives. Williams wrote:

---

140 Cited by Mme G. Brunel, op. cit., volume 1, 77f.

> As for the children, we think that if the gospel had not been preached most of them would not have lived and that they would have been killed at the hands of their own parents. Almost all the women less than thirty years old are guilty of this horrible crime. I know a poor Raiatean, dying today, who has had fifteen children. Soon after their births, they were all victims of her cruelty. Today, she repents with tears. She was among the first of the indigenous people to ask for baptism. Since then she has remained firm; she has behaved well and shown her affection for spiritual things. "Now," she says, "I no longer believe in killing. Although my sins be very great, I trust in Jesus, and I believe that he loves me."

Williams' strategy, which he began to implement from the beginning, was to convert indigenous people and then give them the task of evangelizing their own people. Moreover, he hastened to send them out in mission. An auxiliary missionary society was in place in 1819, even before the official birth of the church. It was similar to the one in Tahiti and was affiliated with the LMS. Its purpose was to train Polynesian evangelists and send them to the South Pacific islands, even those farthest away with totally isolated populations. There they would hold school classes and proclaim the gospel. In his *A History of Christian Missions*, Stephen Neill records this episode warmly:

> But few marvels in Christian history can equal the faithfulness of these men and women, left behind among peoples of unknown speech and often in danger of their lives, to plant and build churches out of their own limited stock of faith and knowledge, supported only by the invigorating power of the Holy Spirit and the prayers of their friends. Many watered the seed with their own blood; but the churches grew, and far more widely than if reliance had been placed first and foremost on the European missionary.[141]

Here is an extract from a speech given by King Tamatoa at the religious service that inaugurated the missionary society:

> Remember what you were doing for your lying gods. You were giving them what they asked for: your strength, your possessions, and even your lives . . . And our eyes being open, we know that our former religion was only a lie. Let us act according to what we have learned. Let us have pity on the lands that still lie in darkness. Let us give joyously what we possess; let us give with our whole hearts so that we can also send them missionaries. It is well that there are a few things we can do for the true God. However, if you give nothing, you should have no fear of being punished or killed as you would have certainly been before. Let each act as he wants.[142]

The Polynesian missionaries would go as far as the Loyalty Islands and even to New Guinea: "I never considered," wrote Williams, "that the Mission of Tahiti and its

---

141 Neill, *History*, 298–299.
142 Cited by Mme. G. Brunel, op. cit., volume 1, 88f.

neighboring islands would be like a fountain from which waters would flow to the other lands and water them."

Needing ocean transport, Williams went to Sydney in 1821 to buy the *Enterprise*, a ship that would allow for easy travel between the islands. In order to pay for its expense, the ship was also to be used for commercial activities, which would also contribute to the prosperity of the insular population. Due to the *Enterprise*, Williams was able to explore with indigenous teams—generally young couples—numerous islands that had not yet been evangelized.[143]

In general he was well received wherever he went and left behind Polynesian evangelists to continue the work. One evangelist among them was particularly effective, Papeiha. As a pioneer he was gifted with extraordinary courage, both for being willing and able to swim in the enormous waves that broke on coral barriers, as well as for his reconnaissance on possibly hostile shores where small armies of unpredictable island people awaited them. Unfortunately, after several years financial causes necessitated selling the *Enterprise*.

*The Polynesian evangelist Papeiha, the courageous and effective coworker of John Williams.*

Despite his thirst for ever-expanding horizons, Williams did not neglect the work on Raiatea. He invested much of his time in completing the translation of the Bible in the local language, notably the books of the Old Testament; and his ministry encompassed a variety of activities, beginning with the instruction of believers.

## RAPID PROGRESS ON RAROTONGA

John and Mary Williams and Charles and Elizabeth Pitman left Raiatea in 1827, entrusting their pastoral work to Tuahine, one of the first Tahitian converts. They went to Rarotonga, one of the Cook Islands that lay outside of the shipping lanes. Williams had discovered the island himself in 1823 after a long search. The evangelist Papeila lived alone there, courageously refusing to abandon its people.

After several years of fruitful witnessing, Papeiha sent out an urgent request for help as thousands of Rarotongans were then asking to be instructed in the gospel. It was in response to his request that the Williamses came. One of the first to hear the message of salvation and destroy his idol was a pagan priest. The population had been terrified to see his idol cut down and then burned, convinced that the demons attached to it would swoop down and rain evil upon them. When nothing happened, the chief approached Papeiha, expressed his desire to become a Christian, and then burned his fetishes in turn. Nevertheless, some violent reactions of an occult nature occurred, perpetrated by the partisans of the traditional religion. The confrontations escalated into a civil war in which the Christians gained the victory, having succeeded in winning the hearts of their adversaries through the giving of thanks.[144] Without

---

143 In 1834 at the time of his vacation in England after eighteen years in the South Pacific, Williams could affirm: "No group of islands, not an isolated island of some importance in a radius of 3,000 kilometers around Tahiti, has been deprived of a visit from our evangelists."

144 It is this event that we have alluded to above, 413.

the intervention of European missionaries, by 1826 Rarotonga could be said to have been won to the gospel. At that time the chiefs decided, with the agreement of the population, to build a church where they could worship the true God. Williams came to the island for the first time for the consecration of the new building.

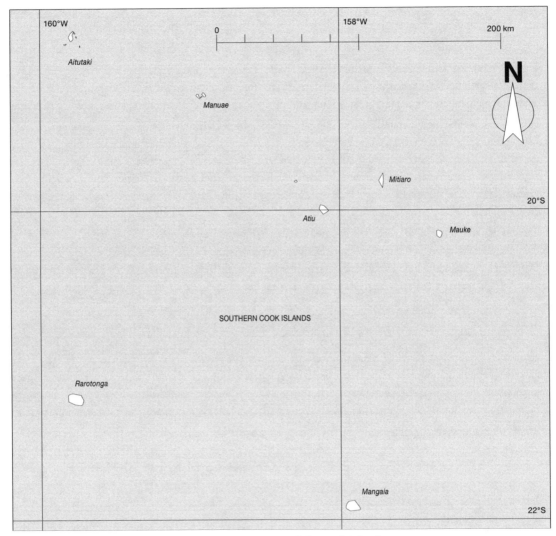

*Map 7c: Rarotonga and the Cook Islands*

The Polynesian dialect of Rarotonga differed substantially from that of Raiatea. Williams studied it relentlessly in order to fix the language in writing and produce a New Testament in it as soon as possible.

Life on Rarotonga was clearly more precarious than on the other islands: the arable soil there was rarer, the climate more trying, and the rats so numerous that they destroyed much of the harvest and attacked all sorts of objects, especially leather ones such as shoes brought from Europe that were impossible to replace. The missionaries could not eat a meal without the aid of one or two servants to hold the rodents at bay, and the rats attacked them even when knelling for their family worship. Some nights, Williams wrote, he found as many as four under his pillow. The cats brought by the missionaries were ineffective against this onslaught, and finally only some very voracious pigs were able to vanquish the rodents.

With little preparation, the pioneer missionaries of this generation struggled to master the numerous problems posed by local customs. In the Pacific islands, the temptation was strong not only for the white missionaries but even for the clan chiefs to simply replace the traditional civilization with a European one, which would allow the island people to move quickly toward material prosperity. Williams was conscious of the stakes and of the difficulties Polynesian culture presented. Notably with regard to polygamy, he is said to have been perplexed a longtime, knowing that any decision made would result in suffering and misunderstanding. On Rarotonga, the Polynesian evangelists required that the male candidates for baptism choose one of their wives and marry her in a public ceremony; the others he would send away but continue to be obliged to provide for their needs and that of their children. Williams wrote:

> I know that there are differing opinions on this delicate subject . . .
> In reading missionary narratives, I have often regretted that their authors remained silent about the difficulties they encountered and the decisions they made . . . It seems to me that these stories should not defer to the opinion of people who have never left their countries but explain the complex situations they encountered and the manner in which they were resolved.[145]

*John Williams disembarking on an island not yet evangelized.*
*His companions present gifts to the armed inhabitants to express their friendliness.*
*Engraving of the nineteenth century. (Ecumenical document.)*

---

145 Cited by Mme. G. Brunel, op. cit., volume 1, 260f.

When the customs were irrefutably opposed to the teaching of the gospel, Williams did not hesitate to eradicate them. One such custom was *kukumi anga*: the custom of a boy coming of age and having to hunt and fight his father. If he gained the victory, he took possession of his parents' goods, leaving them entirely destitute. Another example was *ao anga*: the custom of a widow's in-laws having the right to seize their deceased son's possessions. Rather than consoling and supporting her, they took away her lands, food reserves, and home, from which the mother and children were expelled.

With the agreement of the chiefs of the island, Williams and Charles Pitman tried to adapt the code of Raiatea in the language of Rarotonga. The missionaries endured the reproach of European critics who accused them of being preoccupied with the civil affairs of the people. Williams took a different view:

> We do not believe that the missionary must assume no political authority . . . The missionaries of the South Seas have been accused of arrogating to themselves royal rights. In this I will respond that no missionary of these regions has assumed such authority, and that the influence exercised by them is purely moral. Finally, I can say that I do not know of missionaries who have exercised this moral influence less in their own interest, and more for the public good.[146]

## ALWAYS FARTHER

In the course of this first period in Rarotonga, Williams constructed a ship of twenty by six meters, the *Messenger of Peace*. He accomplished this with his own hands, without saw or nail, and practically without any material other than wood, so dedicated was he to the extension of the gospel's reach. With this boat he was able to discover several groups of islands where, no doubt because his reputation preceded him, his preaching was well received. He often found that Christians were already present, having been converted during some prior trip to the islands when the gospel message, with its extraordinary power to transform, had taken hold of them. For example, the missionaries were received with great honors and their message heard with respect on the Samoan islands. The gospel had already been carried there by a Samoan, converted on the island of Tonga under the ministry of Methodist missionaries (see the preceding chapter, p. 424). When the first European missionaries settled there several years later, a church of two thousand members had already been formed.

It is doubtful if there is another people on the face of the earth who, in proportion to their numbers, have given so many missionaries to the Church, or have paid so great a price in sacrifice and martyrdom. At home not only do they build and maintain their own churches, schools, and other institutions, but they sustain

---

146 Ibid, 262.

their missionary guests as well. They regularly support the worldwide work of their churches.[147]

Williams returned to Britain, staying from 1834 to 1838. One of the reasons for this sojourn was the necessity of clarifying his relations with the committee of the LMS. Several of Williams' colleagues complained that he was behaving as if he were the patron saint of the South Seas missions.

But Williams' principal motive for being in Britain was to recruit new missionaries in order to respond to the urgent needs of Polynesia. The British assembled in large crowds in their churches to hear his testimony.[148] Williams also used his time to write a book on the progress of evangelization in Polynesia. His passionate appeals profoundly moved the Christians of Britain, and in 1836, six young people responded positively. When John and Mary Williams returned to Polynesia in 1838, they chose the islands of Samoa as the base of their future expeditions in the South Seas (see maps 6, p. 409, and 7b, p. 423), and the new missionaries dispersed themselves throughout the islands of the archipelago.

In November 1839, Williams had the conviction that God was asking him to proclaim the gospel in the New Hebrides,[149] an archipelago of which the inhabitants were reputed to be highly bellicose and particularly hostile to Europeans (see maps 6, p. 409, and 8, p. 446). But the island people's reputation aroused the compassion of this man of God, for it demonstrated how much these people needed to know the love of the Savoir that would change their lives. Conscious of the danger of the enterprise, upon his arrival Williams preached to the Samoans on the text of Acts 20:37, 38: "And they all wept sore, and fell on Paul's neck, and kissed him, sorrowing most of all for the words he spake, that they should see his face no more" (KJV).

On November 20, 1839 Williams went from this ship into a canoe in order to land on the shore of the island of Erromanga. He traveled with two European missionaries, James Harris and a man named Cunningham, as well as Robert Morgan, the captain of the ship. When the inhabitants approached the shore, Williams and his companions tried to communicate their goodwill by presenting them with pieces of cloth and by saying several words in their own language. Surreptitiously, they were

---

147 The fourteen Samoan Islands are a volcanic archipelago that were discovered by Dutch sailors in the eighteenth century; H. P. Van Dusen, *They Founded the Church There*, 99, cited by Neill, op. cit., 299.

148 His talks, however, did not always have the desired effect. He wrote of one incident, "I tried to play on their sympathies by offering them moving stories of pagan cruelty. I caused many tears to flow but did not succeed in drawing even four pounds sterling from their pockets. They are truly without pity."

149 The archipelago of the New Hebrides consists of about forty islands, for the most part mountainous and volcanic. It is situated in the western Pacific Ocean, 2,300 kilometers northeast of Australia and 450 kilometers from New Caledonia. The existence of these islands was noted as early as 1606 by a Spanish navigator who located them in an imprecise fashion. They were rediscovered and described a century and a half later by Bougainville (1768), and then by Captain Cook (1773). The archipelago was claimed by both France and Britain. In 1887, the two countries signed a convention placing them under the control of a mixed commission. France withdrew from this arrangement in 1889 in exchange for the sovereignty over the Leeward Islands. At the time of the arrival of the missionaries, the population was in sharp decline because of Western merchants who, while seeking sandalwood, the principal wealth of these islands, brought various contagious diseases, firearms, and munitions. About the year 1850, the population had dropped below 100,000 inhabitants, and it was just 50,000 in 1920. Today as an independent state, it bears the name of Vanuatu.

encircled, separated from one another, and cut off from the shore. One of them recognized the trap and alerted the others. Morgan and Cunningham ran and only just regained the canoe. They saw Williams slip on the riprap just as he stepped into the sea. Caught by one of his pursuers, his skull was smashed in and his body was soon pierced by arrows. His young colleague Harris was also struck down and killed on the shore.

*The warriors of Erromanga rushed on the missionaries to massacre them.*
*Slipping on the riprap, John Williams could not escape them.*
*Engraved in the nineteenth century. (Ecumenical document)*

The news of Williams' tragic death was a great shock to the churches of Britain in which his recent visit had made such a marked impression. Numerous young people spontaneously offered themselves to the LMS to take up the missionary work in this archipelago of the New Hebrides, where the population seemed to be living in a permanent state of violence.

# ERROMANGO: LAND OF MARTYRS

In 1842 three years after the death of Williams and Harris, the LMS sent George Turner and Henry Nisbet to the island of Tanna, the closest to that of Erromanga (about eighty kilometers to the south). Six months after their arrival, persecution became unendurable and the two men had no choice but to flee in the night on a small boat, taking nothing with them. From the human perspective, the frail craft did not seem capable of surviving long on the high seas, and the two missionaries contemplated a watery martyrdom. However, they were welcomed the next day by a whaler that was unexpectedly passing through the area. They were dropped off in the Samoan islands, where they pursued their ministry. (The island of Tanna will be further discussed below with regard to John Paton.)

The LMS did not attempt to send more missionaries to Erromango, and it would be eighteen years after the death of Williams before another mission would risk it. In 1857 the Reverend George Gordon and his wife courageously chose this place to work despite the terrible memories it evoked. Canadians supported by a Presbyterian mission, they began an intensive study of the language, making their priority the translation of the Bible. Soon a large number of youth were attracted to them and showed a desire to be instructed in the Christian faith. The couple taught them to read and write and prepared them to become teachers. Their worship services were attended by large numbers, and some among them declared their desire to renounce their idols. After four years, the foundations of a Christian community were solidly laid.

European and Australian sandalwood traders looked askance at the growing influence of the gospel on the island, and they kindled the hostility of a part of the inhabitants against the missionaries. When an epidemic of measles decimated the population[150] and a succession of violent storms wreaked havoc, the merchants convinced the people that the cause of these calamities was to be found among those who had persuaded them to turn from their ancestral gods. In May 1861 while Gordon was working on the construction of his printing press, he was drawn into the bush by a ruse, knocked out, and decapitated. Hearing his cries, Mrs. Gordon ran out of her house, and a man lying in ambush struck her with his hatchet, breaking her neck. Twenty-two years after the martyrdoms of Williams and Harris, and almost at the same place, two other witnesses to the love of God authenticated their message by the gift of their lives. But the work they had begun did not end with their deaths. A small church was formed and other ministers of the gospel took up the challenge.

In 1889 fifty years after the death of Williams, one of the sons of his murderer placed at the side of the church of Erromanga the first rock of a monument to the memory of the martyred missionary. Another became the pastor on the same land where the first messenger of the gospel had been massacred by his own father. The witness of the love of God had not been in vain. John Williams had rightly discerned that the more a people were plunged into violence and blood, the more they had need of the gospel. He had shown his love in the most authentically evangelical sense, for he had laid down his life for his enemies. This message of love, given in more than mere words, was soon accepted in all its transformative power by the people of the New Hebrides.

---

150 As we will see below, it was deliberately introduced into Erromanga and other islands of the archipelago by the traffickers themselves.

# THE FIRST CHURCH OF THE NEW HEBRIDES

## John Geddie

Aside from the brief attempt by Turner and Nisbet in Tanna, it was a dozen years after the death of John Williams before a new and lasting missionary effort was launched in the New Hebrides by the mission of the Scottish Presbyterian Church of Nova Scotia. In 1848 the Canadian John Geddie settled with his wife in Aneityum, at the southern end of the archipelago (see map 8, p. 446). The welcome they received was very different from that given by the other islands of the Hebrides. In this pleasant climate, they were able to teach, evangelize, translate the Scriptures, and train evangelist-teachers. The latter carried the gospel throughout the island, preparing the ground for the arrival of missionaries. A number of them did this work at the cost of their lives, as we will have occasion to observe in relating the ministry of John Paton in Tanna.

In a few years, 3,500 Anetymesians abandoned their idols and accepted Jesus Christ. Daily family worship became common as did cleanliness, which greatly improved the general health of the population. The Bible had been translated in fifteen years and its printing was entirely financed by the people of Anetyum. This was made possible by Christians who intensified the cultivation of the various products on their land, which allowed them to sell their crops at a good price in Australia.

A church constructed by Geddie contains an inscription that sums up the success of his ministry: "When he landed in 1848, there were no Christians; when he left in 1872, there were no heathen."[151]

# THE GOSPEL IN THE FACE OF VIOLENCE

## John Paton

The Scottish Presbyterian John Paton (1824–1907) began his ministry in the New Hebrides in 1858. He is, with John Williams and John Geddie, one of the great figures in the history of the evangelization of the islands of the South Pacific, and the autobiography he wrote at the end of his life had a considerable impact throughout the Christian world.[152]

Paton was born in 1824 in Scotland in a pious Presbyterian family. He left school at the age of twelve to work in a factory in the region, and then taught school to finance his studies in a Glasgow evangelism school. From 1846 to 1856, he gave himself to the evangelization of the poorest quarter of the city. To live amidst the permanent violence of these slums was a singular preparation for the work to which God was calling him in the New Hebrides. He took from this experience an important lesson:

---

151 Tucker, *From Jerusalem*, 214.

152 John G. Paton, *Missionary to the New Hebrides, an Autobiography* (London: Hodder and Stoughton, 1891). A French abridgement was published in 1898 in Geneva by Charles Challand, the editor-translator: *John G. Paton, le grand apôtre des cannibales*. Our citations are taken from this work. The Rev. N. Poivre has reprised the principal elements in a *Cahier Missionaire* (no. 15, 1929) from the Society of Evangelistic Mission of Paris: *John Paton, l'apôtre des cannibales*.

"Allow them to see that brutality makes you afraid, and they will mistreat you with violence and cruelty; but resist them without fear, and you will see them fall at your feet like small dogs." This is the method that he adopted much later in facing the cannibals of the Pacific Islands. No doubt it saved his life many times, but his approach also incurred the criticism of his colleagues.

When the Scottish Presbyterian Mission sought to send additional missionaries to the New Hebrides, Paton felt obliged to offer his services.

### Departure for the South Seas and the First Culture Shock

Paton studied for an additional year, taking courses in a college of medicine and in a professional school; then, at the age of thirty-four, he was ordained as a missionary in March 1858 by the Presbyterian Church of Scotland. Several months later, accompanied by his wife Mary Ann and the Reverend J. W. Mathieson and his wife Mary of Canada, he disembarked on the island of Tanna, the same place where about fifteen years before Turner and Nisbet had not been able to remain due to the hostility of the population (see map 8, p. 446). The culture shock they experienced was enormous.

> I must confess that my first impressions were such that I was soon seized with fright. When I saw these savage cannibals entirely nude, painted from head to foot, horror and pity filled my heart . . . Would it be possible to teach them of truth and justice, to Christianize them or even to civilize them? But these were only passing thoughts. I was soon as concerned for them and their salvation as I would have been for my own countrymen.[153]

The first shock due to the physical appearance of the people of Tanna was nothing compared to the shock of the discovery of their bellicose culture. Superstition was the major reason for the incessant confrontations that set one village against another. For them, the phenomena of sickness, death, and bad weather were not due to natural causes but to sorcery. It was always necessary, therefore, to find the guilty person, who invariably lived outside the village community. This was the pretext for attacks and raids, which in turn brought about reprisals and revenge. The missionaries discovered that fear and hate were the daily bread of this cursed population.

Six months after their arrival, Mary Ann Paton gave birth to a baby boy. Already weakened by the climate, she died fifteen days later. Three weeks after this, the baby followed her into the tomb. John was left in painful solitude, for his colleagues resided in another part of the island and communications were difficult.

Paton would have been sorely handicapped without the aid of the teacher-evangelists of Aneityum, who had been trained by John Geddie. There were a dozen of them, and they taught at six schools all around Tanna. The family life of these Christian teachers bore eloquent testimony to the transformative power of the gospel but also set off waves of hostility. Polygamy was commonly practiced in this culture, and wives were considered as slaves who could be beaten and sometimes even killed

---

153 Paton, op. cit., 26f.

by their husbands on the slimmest of pretexts. When a man died, his wives were commonly strangled so that they could continue to serve him in the afterlife. Paton opposed these customs with all his might, and his pleas saved numerous lives.

When two clans concluded a pact following a war, they celebrated it with a great meal. The main course consisted of two women, with each clan furnishing one of them. All sorts of holidays and special ceremonies called for the eating of human flesh, which was always much appreciated. Paton reported that cadavers that had been in the ground for several days were sometimes disinterred in order to serve as a meal. Once some Tannasians who showed an interest in the gospel confided to him, in all candor, that they were particularly fond of the tender flesh of children.

The "sacred men" were quick to accuse the missionaries and the new ideas they introduced as the cause of all the calamities that seemed to beset the islanders of Tanna. There is not enough space to describe in detail the many times that Paton was threatened, insulted, robbed, wounded, and his house ransacked. His moral authority, however, slowly grew, and thanks to some sympathizers, he quickly mastered the language. During those times when there was warfare between enemy clans, he showed striking evidence of his physical courage, interposing himself between adversaries at the risk of being wounded by the opposing camps—which is what actually happened in several instances.

A Scottish friend sent Paton a printing press and all the characters necessary to print a book. He was hesitant to print his translations of Bible texts into a Tannesian that he knew was only approximately correct. He also had difficulty operating the press, which he finally succeeded in mastering after much perseverance. The scene that Paton described of his first success reveals something of his character and commitment:

> One could hardly believe the joy I felt when I finally completed my first successful page. It was one o'clock in the morning; I was the only white on the island; all the inhabitants had been asleep for several hours; and I was truly in ecstasy. I was singing; I was throwing my hat in the air; I was dancing around my machine in such a way that I began to wonder if I was losing my reason. Would I have been worthy of being a missionary if I had not knelt and given thanks? Reader, believe me, it was as true a worship service as the one that David rendered to God when he was dancing before the ark.[154]

Paton's hopes were somewhat dampened when he perceived that the Tannesians had a fear of books, and their superstitious fears increased when they learned that the book he intended to present to them contained words that came from God himself.

During the four years that Paton was in Tanna, he endured the hatred of a majority of the population, which rejected him because of his race, religion, and ethical values. However, his worst adversaries were his own compatriots—traders, traffickers and, of course, proslavers whose odious practices he denounced.

---

154 Paton, op. cit., 76f.

At the end of the year 1860, a ship captain sought out Paton to inform him of something unimaginable and criminal:

> We have found the means to bring the resistance of your Tannesians to an end. We have sent measles among them, which is going to kill them by scores; for we have landed four young men infected with the disease in different ports of the island and, I assure you, this is going to expedite things without delay.[155]

The resulting epidemic ravaged the people. A third of the population died, and almost all the Christian teachers who were taking care of the sick followed them to the grave. The Tannaisans were enraged against the missionaries, equating them with the whites who were responsible for the plague.

Despite some encouraging signs, the year 1861 was marked by an irremediable deterioration in the relations between the missionaries and the general population. After having burned the church, one night someone attempted to torch Paton's house. In several instances, he saved himself by fleeing away, sometimes by land, sometimes by sea. Because it is often said that Paton was at once fascinating and colorless, his often dramatic and sometimes fantastic adventures bear repeating. He was conscious that survival under these conditions was an ongoing miracle, and he had no difficulty identifying with David's psalms of deliverance.

Paton and Mr. and Mrs. Mathieson were finally forced to admit that their presence had lost its purpose and, at the end of February 1862, agreed to be evacuated. After three and a half years of unbelievable trials in Tanna and no tangible results to show for it, Paton took ship with a leaden soul. He carried with him all of his material possessions: the clothes on his back, his Bible, and portions of the Scriptures translated into the local language. He left behind him in Tanna the graves of his wife and child, that of a colleague,[156] and those of a dozen teacher-evangelists, martyred or infected by disease while caring for the sick. The church he had built with his own hands was now in ashes; his house and small printing press were ransacked; and all the spiritual seeds he had sown appeared to be barren.

The story of these years of Christian witness in Tanna cannot leave one indifferent. How many times had Paton endangered his life to save others, often the lives of those who were his implacable foes? Still, he was firmly convinced that God loved this people and wanted to save them. Through it all, his faith in the help of God, even in the most extreme situations, is impressive.

Paton was a man gifted with a rock-steady character. That he would be left unharmed amidst so many furious men, armed with sledgehammers and firebrands,

---

155 Paton, op. cit., 103.

156 The colleague was Mr. Johnston, who had arrived in September 1860. During the time of troubles following the measles epidemic, he was seriously wounded. Overworked and full of anguish, he was overwhelmed by the trial. Gulping down a large dose of sleeping pills, he lapsed into a coma and died two days later, just four months after his arrival. Following a period of bereavement, his widow left Tanna and became a teacher in a school founded by John Geddie at Aneityum. She later married a Scottish missionary, and they spent the remainder of their lives in the service of the Mission on the small island of Fotuna, the westernmost island of the archipelago.

was indeed a miracle. But it is important to recall that he was of an exceptional stature: his word and his look were often more frightful than a weapon; and his physical courage gave those given to a belief in superstition the impression that it sprung from magical protection. Moreover, especially in the last period of his stay on the island, Paton stooped to threatening those who would attempt to take his life with divine chastisements—even suggesting that reprisals would come from Queen Victoria's navy. He was denounced from many quarters when, following his departure from Tanna, a British warship engaged in a punitive expedition against Tanna. Happily its cannonade resulted in no human causalities, but Paton was vehemently criticized by his colleagues, including his dear friend Geddie.

*John Paton (1824–1907), indomitable pioneer among the cannibals of the New Hebrides.*

## Aniwa: From Cannibalism to the Gospel

After a two-year hiatus in Britain during which he married Margaret Whitecross, Paton returned to the New Hebrides in 1866. The mission sent the couple to Aniwa, a small island of eleven by ten kilometers, neighboring Tanna. In the following years he visited Tanna several times but never stayed very long.

John and Margaret remained at Aniwa for more than fifteen years, and several of their children were born there. The population was less violent than at Tanna, and for his part, Paton was more flexible than before. His relationships with the chiefs developed in an atmosphere of mutual respect, and his family life spoke eloquently of his religion. After some time, a chief entrusted him with the education of his daughter and niece, each of whom had lost her mother. Soon the Patons opened an orphanage for girls and another for boys. Nevertheless, after three years, the general results seemed to be as discouraging as they had been in Tanna, even if the missionaries faced less peril. However, something occurred that suddenly and completely reversed this situation.

Since the island was completely without water sources, Paton decided to dig a well near his house. When the islanders observed him digging, he explained that he was seeking to discover "the rain below" that God wanted to give them. The islanders scoffed at this response and treated him like a fool. Finally, after weeks of effort, he discovered a source of deliciously fresh water at a depth of eleven meters. This created a sensation on the island, the effect being more striking than three years of evangelical preaching.

The next day, the old chief of the village came to find Paton to ask his permission to speak of the well during the worship service the following Sunday. Although the man was not a Christian, Paton agreed, feeling sure that the man would deliver a true sermon. In the cultural context of the island of Aniwa, the discovery of this water was naturally interpreted as a parable addressed by God to the people. The essential thrust of the old man's sermon may be judged from the several extracts below, recorded by Paton:

> People of Aniwa, since this missionary has come here, he has said many strange things to us . . . Now, we thought the strangest thing was his thought of digging into the earth to find the rain. But the missionary said to us that his God sees and hears, and that he would give him "the rain below." Was he a fool? Has he not obtained the water deep in the earth? We have laughed about other things that he announced to us. But beginning today, I believe that all that the missionary has said to us of his God is true. One day our eyes will see it, even as they have seen today the water that has come from the earth.
>
> Here in my heart several things tell me that the one who is invisible exists. This one that we have never seen and of whom we would have never heard spoken of had the missionary not made him known to us. Invisible until this day, the water existed even as it is now. It was our eyes that were too weak to see it. Well, in the same way, for me, your chief, I firmly believe that when I die I will see this one who is invisible, God, the Eternal. I will see him as surely as I have also seen the water that comes from the earth.
>
> May all men who think as I go to seek the idols of Aniwa, these gods that our fathers feared, and come back to break them here. What we rejected before, we will now believe.[157]

---

157 Cited, and without doubt put in form, by Paton, op. cit., 243f.

This discourse overthrew the traditional religion of Aniwa. The same day, the old chief and several of his men returned with their idols and destroyed them. During the following weeks, this scene was repeated many times over. If not a revival, this was at least a springboard to an awakening of faith, for all the inhabitants of the island began to come to hear the preaching of the gospel and to listen with an openness previously unknown.

Also striking was the profound transformation of the social order. Three generations enthusiastically frequented the school together in order to learn to read and to begin to learn from the "book that speaks." Personal vengeance and reprisals were now frowned upon, which broke the vicious cycle of violence in which the society had previously been trapped. The new order encouraged the cultivation of the soil, for farmers were now able to harvest their crops without fear that they would be stolen.

A church of twenty by eight meters and four meters high was erected and immediately became the pride of the benevolent villagers who had raised it. Soon after the work was completed, the church was blown down by a storm and nothing of it remained. Remarkably, these new Christians, neither troubled nor discouraged by this adversity, soon set about raising an even more solid edifice, which, like the first, did not cost the mission a single dime. In October 1869, after less than four years of missionary presence, a dozen people were baptized after a thorough examination, and Holy Communion was given to them. Paton wrote movingly of this event:

> At the moment I put the bread and wine into those dark hands, once stained with the blood of cannibalism, now stretched out to receive and partake of the emblems and seals of the Redeemer's love, I had a foretaste of the joy of Glory that well nigh broke my heart to pieces. I shall never taste a deeper bliss till I gaze on the glorified face of Jesus himself.[158]

In thinking of Paton's years of suffering and especially his failure in Tanna, one can begin to understand the intensity of the emotion expressed in these lines. Following this event, a catechetical period of two years was set for baptismal candidates, whose numbers grew increasingly voluminous in the fifteen years that remained to Paton in Aniwa. During this time, Paton's priority was the translation of the Bible in the language of Aniwa, as well as the publication of a collection of hymns, which he printed there.

The mission in the New Hebrides developed remarkably in the last decades of the nineteenth century. At the dawn of the twentieth century, nearly the entire population of the thirty inhabited islands of the archipelago had accepted the gospel, including Tanna. In appearance at least, paganism had disappeared. Several dozen missionaries were dedicated to this task, including two of Paton's sons, who had become his colleagues in the work. In 1925 the Presbyterian mission to the New Hebrides assumed sole responsibility for nineteen missionaries, three ministers, and

---

158  Tucker, *From Jerusalem to Irian Jaya,* 217.

150 indigenous teachers. By then church membership had reached more than twenty thousand.

## WILLIAMS AND PATON: AN EVALUATION OF THEIR MINISTRIES

Despite the obvious differences of personality between these two pioneers, Paton's ministry compares nicely with that of Williams'. They struggled in similar cultural contexts, and both had to work with recalcitrant and isolated populations.[159] It is not surprising that Christianity produced a veritable earthquake in these homogenous communities, with its radically new message, and with the improvement of the conditions of life introduced through efficient tools and techniques that seemed inextricably tied to the new faith.

This explains much of the ambiguity of the populations in receiving what the missionaries had to offer. The possessors of traditional authority were more hesitant than most because they had more to lose, the threat that Christianity posed to the structure of the societies they controlled being very real. It is difficult to imagine that these small communities could have sustained two entirely different and incompatible worldviews; hence, in general, the conversion of a king or chief led the way to mass conversions.

Stephen Neill reflected on this episode in his *A History of Christian Missions*:

> Missionaries have often been accused of destroying simple peoples by changing their age-old customs, and introducing such purely western habits as the wearing of clothes. It has to be admitted that missionaries have made many mistakes and have not always been wise in their handling of their converts. But on the whole the weight of evidence tells heavily against their critics. The missionaries from the start found themselves in bitter opposition to the white traders and exploiters, whose attitude was expressed by one of them to John G. Paton in the words "our watchword is 'Sweep these creatures away, and let white men occupy the soil,'" and who, in pursuance of their aim, placed men sick with measles on various islands in order to destroy the population through disease.[160]

It is appropriate to complete the picture by citing the opinion of the famous Scottish novelist Robert Louis Stevenson (1850–1894), author of *Treasure Island* and *Dr. Jekyll and Mr. Hyde*:

> I maintained strong prejudges against missions in the South Seas. But once I went there myself, these prejudges began to diminish, and then totally disappeared. Those who criticize the missionaries should simply come to the place to see them work.

---

159  The ministry of Paton is however more late than that of Williams: forty years separate their departures for Polynesia.

160  Neill, *History*, 355.

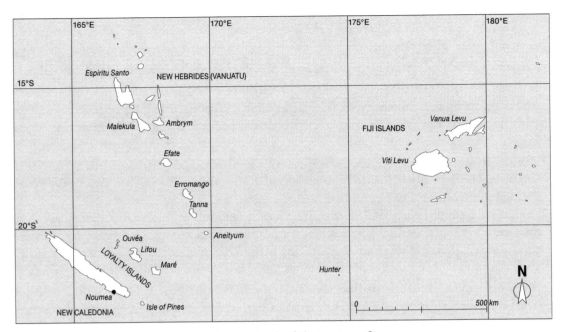

*Map 8: The islands of the West Pacific*

# CHAPTER 10

# The Loyalty Islands and New Caledonia

New Caledonia is an island in the South Pacific that is 450 kilometers in length by forty to fifty in width. About a hundred kilometers from the northeast coast of New Caledonia are three other islands lying close together and known as the Loyalty Islands: Lifou, Ouvea, and Mare. The population of the archipelago is largely Melanesian in origin, but immigration from Polynesia also occurred, especially in the eighteenth century. In the second part of the nineteenth century, there were about eleven thousand inhabitants of the Loyalty Islands and sixteen thousand of New Caledonia.

## THE LOYALTY ISLANDS

The Loyalty Islands were discovered in 1803 but were not visited by Europeans until 1840 when whalers and other foreigners began to come, though very slowly. Maurice Leenhardt affirms that "missionaries were the pioneers of civilization in the Caledonian archipelago."[161]

### A Church Founded by Polynesians: Mare, Lifou, and Ouvea

Though the initial evangelization of the islands was by the LMS, in 1824 the British missionaries entrusted the evangelization of Mare to two Polynesians from Samoa, Tanielo and Tataio. They were well received by an old chief of the island. At his death, his son showed favor to the Samonan evangelists by protecting them from witches. He soon converted and sent away all but one of his twenty-five wives, destroyed the objects dedicated to pagan worship, called his subjects to reform their morals, and ordered the construction of churches and schools. He engaged in several evangelistic expeditions to neighboring tribes, and though his life was imperiled, he never had recourse to the violence common among the chiefs of the Kanak tribes.

In 1842 a whaler from Rarotonga named Fao became an evangelist on the island of Lifou. He quickly gained the confidence and friendship of the population by joining in their activities of hunting, fishing, and farming. But he refused to carry arms during an expedition of war, and when his companions assembled themselves for

---

161  Maurice Leenhardt, *La Grande-Terre* (SMEP, 1922), 14.

the cannibal feast that usually followed a battle, he energetically preached on the respect due to human life. The tribal chief was impressed and, afterwards, assembled his men, not for a cannibal meal but to listen to Fao explain the biblical message. Other evangelist-teachers came to help, but despite the sympathy of the tribal chief, the people stubbornly resisted Christianity. Some of those who showed an interest in the gospel were put to death. In 1847 the evangelists had to flee to Mare, but two years later, the first conversions took place at Lifou in their absence. On his return, Fao opened schools that were soon packed with adult students, avid to learn to read in order to discover the message of the Bible.

Evangelists from Mare did not reach the island of Ouvea until 1856. The work was progressing quickly when Catholic missionaries appeared. The first among these was Father Bernard, who was well-disposed to the Protestants and concluded an accord with them. Ouvea being formed of two islands linked by a narrow tongue of land, the Catholics agreed to take the northern part and the Protestants the southern. Each side respected the agreement for three years, but then Father Barriol broke it by erecting a chapel on the southern part of the island that was beside the Protestant church, which he had closed. For the Protestants, the work of evangelism was entirely in the hands of the local people, while the Catholic priests, who were French, benefited from the support of the colonial administration. During the period that followed, a Protestant church was burned and some of the faithful were lost in the flames; other Protestants were exiled and had their land confiscated. One suspects that some of the Marist Fathers were behind the fanaticism of the tribal chiefs' anti-Protestantism. In 1865 all the Protestant churches were given to the Marists. Despite these trials, the evangelistic work continued apace.

## Missionary Planting

It was not until 1854 that the first European missionary families came to live at Mare, then at Lifou. This was the case of the LMS missionary John Jones, who sent the first evangelists to Mare thirteen years before. When he arrived, he had the magnificent surprise of being welcomed by six hundred Christians and discovering already-established churches and schools under the responsibility of catechist-teachers. Moreover, he rejoiced to observe the clear influence of the biblical message on the morals of the population. Many were literate, being able to read the Bible texts that had been translated and printed in their language. The role of the missionaries, therefore, consisted of strengthening the church and training its preachers. A press was put to use, and in 1863 a Bible school was opened with a first class of eleven students.

In 1857 fifteen years after Fao had come to Lifou, the first European Protestant missionary, John Coleridge Patterson, came to settle. Upon his arrival, a great assembly of Christians from eight different tribes came together for a service of Holy Communion. Patterson hastened to translate and print the Gospel of Mark in the local language, but he withdrew soon after he completed this work when he learned that LMS missionaries had arrived at Lifou. Having been sent by the Melanesian mission, he decided that he did not want to enter into competition with those who had introduced the gospel to the Loyalty Islands.

The situation quickly degenerated for the mission and the Protestant churches on the Loyalty Islands. When the first British missionaries disembarked in 1854, the archipelago was already coming under French colonial authority. And even though an entirely indigenous Protestantism had been established and been flourishing for fifteen years at Mare and Lifou, the French considered it a foreign intrusion. As in Tahiti, the Franco-British rivalry produced distrust, indeed hostility, in the French authorities towards the Protestants, whom they assumed would favor the British.

## The Arrival of French Protestants

The French government suspected the British missionary John Jones of being anti-French and, in 1881, called for a French minister to replace him. Jean Bernard Jauré-guiberry, the minister of the colonies and a Protestant, pressed the Reformed French church to find a candidate, giving assurances that the expense of his salary would be borne by the state. The Reverend Louis Cru from Ardèche, France, was chosen at the beginning of 1884. His status, however, was unclear because it was not the Paris Mission that was sending him to Mare. Moreover, Cru's presence inflamed the situation, for the majority of the Kanak Protestants were pro-British and saw him as a competitor to the Reverend Jones, to whom they were very attached. The governor expelled Jones in 1887.

Other British missionaries, more circumspect than Jones, found that they could live in the Loyalty Islands. The missionary James Hadfield, for example, would remain at Lifou from 1887 to 1920. During thirty-three years, he marveled at the soundness of the church as it regularly recruited pastors and catechists and urged them to evangelize the population, as well as study, reflect, and lead in the area of social action. For the first time an organization took responsibility for the care of the lepers on the islands, sought government help to combat alcoholism, and recognized the ministry of women in the church. The need was also conceived at this time to evangelize New Caledonia, an effort that will be reviewed below.

But there was much tension between those who remained attached to the British founders and those who wanted to prepare for the future of Loyalian Protestantism by favoring France. The hope of clarification came with the transfer of the work from the LMS to the Paris Mission. The committee of the Paris Mission, meeting in the Oratoire of the Louvre in Paris on February 12, 1890, unanimously agreed to assume this responsibility. The following year, the Reverend Edmond Langereau[162] took over for Louis Cru in the Loyalty Islands.

# NEW CALEDONIA

At the request of Catholic missionaries, New Caledonia was declared a possession of France in 1844. But the hostility of the population to this foreign intrusion led to violence, which caused France in 1853 to proceed to annex the island by force of arms. In the same year the French government installed a penitentiary on the little island off

---

162 Edmond Langereau had just completed his studies in theology. His father, François Langereau (mentioned below) was the chaplain of the penal colony of Nouméa.

of Noumèa, the capital. The convicts, once their time was served, were to remain in the colony for twice the time they had already served in the penal colony. Needless to say, most of them finished their days there, with consequences that one can well imagine for the local population.[163]

## Kanak Pioneers

The Christians of the Loyalty Islands prayed that the gospel would be propagated on the island of New Caledonia. The first Protestant missionary, who happened to be an Englishman, arrived there a little after 1860 with several Samoan ministers. He was expelled. Later, Christians from the Loyalty Islands who came to search for employment in New Caledonia would succeed in opening the door to missionaries by their witness. The quality of their work, their sobriety, and the fact that they had been educated was in stark contrast to the typical Kanak of New Caledonia. Observing the difference, the population developed a desire to hear the gospel message.

In 1894 about thirty years after the failure of the British missionaries and Samoan ministers, a Kanak minister from Ouvea named Mathaia came to New Caledonia in the hope of finding a tribe disposed to hear the gospel. He soon had the joy of seeing several conversions, including that of a drunkard by the name of Kapéa whose life was completely transformed. When Mathaia was expelled by the local authorities after only twenty months, Kapéa appealed to the French administrator of Nouméa. Accompanied by 250 members of his tribe, he demanded that Protestant ministers be allowed on the island. From then on the evangelists of the three Loyalty Islands could travel freely in New Caledonia and preach the gospel there. Hence this young Kanak church of the Mare, Ouvea, and Lifou islands, which in this period had only about nine thousand baptized members, quickly became a missionary church. Several parishes relinquished their ministers so that they could evangelize New Caledonia. In 1897, 150 Kanaks were baptized in Hauaïlou, the territory of Kapéa.

## The Paris Mission is Reinforced

Informed of the needs of New Caledonia and of the possibilities it presented, the Paris Mission in the following year asked Philadelphe Delord, a missionary who had spent some time in Mare, to explore the possibilities of work there. His report, dated January 1899, entreated the Paris Mission to dispatch a missionary to New Caledonia with all urgency:

> Take this to heart: there is something there so heroically saint-
> ly, so great in its simplicity that one feels filled with respect for
> "these poor Kanaks" in whose hearts the gospel produces such

163 Leenhardt wrote of the former prisoners: "His penal time completed, the condemned became 'free.' . . . He threw himself into the adventure and received an easy welcome from the indigenous tribes in which he found several former police [Kanak prison guards] . . . He sold alcohol to the tribe that had received him, he poisoned them, he encouraged there much ill-feeling and all the vices. He is a son of Satan reigning in a village of trusting Kanaks, and soon one could say that every seed of hope and life are forever crushed out in the hearts of these children. For fifty years, thousands of freed men were widespread throughout the island, dispersed in little-known regions, and accomplishing there almost unconsciously their work of death." *De la mort à la vie*, *l'Evangile en Nouvelle-Calédonie* (Paris: SMEP, 1922), 8f.

fruit. What a reproach for those Christians who bargain away their affection for the cause of missions! France has sent alcohol and convicts to these people, and now, close to the eleventh hour, exhausted from brandy and sullied by the luxury of freedom, they are going to disappear, while their brothers from the Loyalty Islands are going to them, carrying the light of the gospel. But, you understand . . . they can not remain alone.[164]

Delord was succeeding well as a missionary in Mare; nevertheless, he visited New Caledonia several times in order to encourage the Christians there, whose numbers were increasing. He brought back to Mare a Kanak chief who had been released from his position and driven out due to drunkenness. Delord taught him the gospel, and the chief signed a temperance promise before returning to New Caledonia. The transformative power that had acted in his life was so apparent that the French administration could not help but notice the social benefits of preaching the simple gospel message.

It was three years before the Paris Mission could respond to Delord's request. With the exceptions of François Langereau, chaplain of the convicts during the decade of the 1880s,[165] and the occasional presence of Delord, it was only at the beginning of the twentieth century that a Protestant missionary was sent to New Caledonia, preceded of course by the evangelists from the Loyalty Islands who had been coming for a dozen years. The new missionary was Maurice Leenhardt (1878–1954), who arrived in 1902.

Leenhardt lived there for twenty-four years. He received his ministrial charge from the hands of an old pastor named Haxen, who had come from the Loyalty Islands years before. Exhausted from work and wanting to return to his own island to live out the remainder of his days, he made the acquaintance of Leenhardt, called the elders of his church together, and said, "I have now seen the missionary. Listen to him. I have finished my work, but I will not return to rest in the country of my fathers; rather, I am going up there, to the house of my father." And having said these words, he died. It is therefore from the hands of the islands' own faithful servants that French Protestants inherited the mission in New Caledonia. A little after his arrival, Leenhardt observed: "The Mission of Caledonia is founded. There was neither white, nor missionary, nor pastor to arouse enthusiasm and guide hearts. This all happened calmly, from hut to hut."

The principal obstacle Leenhardt faced was the diversity of dialects, and he was also often alone, for few missionaries remained for long in New Caledonia. He was an indefatigable worker, traveling considerable distances and tirelessly visiting the small groups of Christians that were dispersed throughout the length of the island.

Leenhardt returned to France in 1926, having acquired a priceless knowledge of the customs and languages of the Kanaks. With a well-earned reputation as a missionary-ethnologist, he continued his missionary efforts on behalf of the Kanak

---

164 Cited by M. Leenhardt, *La Grande-Terre, Mission de Nouvelle-Calédonie* (Paris: SMEP, 1922), 40–41.

165 After having left the chaplaincy of the penal colony, François Langereau pursued his ministry in the Loyalty Islands for a dozen years.

population through his writing, helping to convince the colonial authorities to take a more enlightened approach toward the populations of the Pacific islands.

*Maurice Leenhardt (1878–1954), missionary and ethnologist. (Service Protestant de Mission, Paris)*

The gospel had a profound effect on the social life of the country. Alcohol brought by the Westerners had ravaged the population to the point that many were predicting the disappearance of the Kanak people. "Nothing can any longer be done to lift them up from their humiliation," a magistrate wrote in 1900 in an official report. "Every effort in their favor is henceforth useless. They are resigned to die."[166] At the beginning of Leenhardt's ministry in 1902, an administrator declared: "What have you come here to do, Reverend? In ten years there will no longer be any Kanaks!" This prediction was false. Soon a rapid demographic recovery began, in which the Blue Cross played an important role, as the number of inhabitants grew from fourteen thousand at the beginning of the century to seventeen thousand by 1912.[167] Throughout the island drunkards put down their bottles and never returned to them. Once again, the impact of the gospel on the destiny of an entire society was clearly demonstrated.

Leenhardt, now considered a great anthropologist, wrote at the time of his return to France in 1926:

> In all meekness the Caledonian churches [then numbering about five thousand adherents and fifty ministers] were conscious of their task. They were not slow to exercise a fruitful and no

---

166 Cited by M. Leenhardt, *De la mort à la vie*, 13f.
167 Towards 1970, 42,000 inhabitants (of which there were 16,000 Protestants).

doubt beneficial influence in the island . . . For the gospel desired by the indigenous people of Caledonia acted as a leaven among them. Until now they have avoided a compartmentalization of the conscience encountered elsewhere, in which one separates the religious life from the practical life. Among them, all facets of life are one. The result is that the Christians, by the character they acquired through contact with the gospel, had a slow but real and decisive effect on the indigenous society . . . The gospel appeared as a social leaven, giving vitality to the family. It encouraged work and, through this, indirectly created a new economic reality. In a word, the gospel arouses individuals to teach and improve themselves in every way.[168]

The following lines from the same author, written in 1922, have lost none of their relevance:

Some say the gospel is outdated and quaint. What purpose, therefore, do missions serve? The imperious and troubling question is posed by those who refuse to admit the gospel's power or to give their sympathy to missions. But in thinking of our responsibility and our immense task among so many peoples and souls who feel lost and are waiting to learn from Christians of their Savior and God, in thinking of so many injustices and of a poverty that simple efforts motivated by our love can contribute to relieve, in thinking of the goodness that brightens so many faces . . . in thinking of the life and moral beauty that come in response to our simple sacrifices, how can we still hesitate before the privilege of being able to contribute to this cause, the joy of giving ourselves completely to the work of God! And how incisive and profound remains this testament [of a Kanak Christian who died in France on a battlefield of the First World War]: "Life for us is the gospel!"[169]

---

168 M. Leenhardt, op. cit., 28–30.
169 Ibid., 40.

# SECTION IV

## THE EVANGELIZATION OF AFRICA

For many European Christians, the term "mission" immediately evokes an image of Africa. However, in the course of the last ten centuries of Christian history, the church has only recently become interested in this continent.[170] For many of these latter years Latin America and Asia were the lands of mission. It was only at the beginning of the nineteenth century that missionaries, more often Protestant than Catholic, set foot in Africa and stayed there—prior attempts not having been followed up. In the beginning, progress was slow and costly in human lives.

From the second half of the nineteenth century to the beginning of the twentieth century, the evangelization of Africa experienced considerable progress, with the exception of the Islamic regions of the North. At first mission stations were established on the coasts, often at the mouth of rivers, as missionaries sought ways to penetrate the continent to reach the populations of the interior.

For various reasons, African traditional religions generally offered less resistance to Christian missions than the "great religions" that originated principally in Asia: Hinduism, Buddhism, Shinto, and Islam. The estimation of the Christian population of Africa through the centuries illustrates this phenomenon. Between the fourth and the nineteenth centuries, Christians were approximately a third of the population of Africa: in the year 300, there were 6 million out of the 18.5 million inhabitants; in the year 800, 8 million out of 25 million. In subsequent years the Christian presence quickly declined. By the year 1200, it is estimated that the number of Christians was 2.5 million out of a population of 37 million inhabitants, or about one in fifteen. By the year 1800 it was 1 million out of a population of 70 million. But at this point the trend reverses. In 1850 there were 2.8 million Christians out of a population of 81 million, or one out of thirty. In 1900 there were 10 million Christians out of a population of 108 million, or about one out of ten. We do not possess the number for the beginning of the decade of the 1940s, the end of the period analyzed in this work; however, it is estimated that in 1970 there were 143 million Christians out of a population of

---

170 The first centuries, which were pre-Islamic, present on the contrary a different scenario (see Book I, Section I).

352 million inhabitants, or 40.3 percent of the inhabitants of the continent.[171] One can therefore speak of the success of Christian missions in Africa during the nineteenth and twentieth centuries, a success built in large measure on the foundations established by the pioneer missionaries at the cost of great personal sacrifice.

It is generally understood by those working with these statistics that they must be used cautiously. The 2001 edition of Barrett's *World Christian Encyclopedia*, which confirms them, notes that they concern only "the adherents to the Christian religion"; the census of actual "church members" reduces these numbers by half in most instances. For 1970 there were 63,200,000 church members in Africa. Among them, the Orthodox (Coptics) had 10,700,000 and the Roman Catholics 25,700,000 members; the Protestants, Anglicans, and independents together comprised 26,500,000 members.

The map of Africa at the time in which this account begins does not correspond to what we know today, for then vast regions of the interior were unknown to Europeans.[172] Also, the population was much less dense, having increased seven times since the beginning of the nineteenth century. Most of the important national borders were fixed at the time of the Congress of Berlin (1884–1885), which divided Africa among the colonial powers of Europe. Though it is recognized that these lines are often artificial and do not reflect ethnic realities, today there are fifty-four sovereign African states that are endeavoring to maintain the borders they inherited from the period of colonization. Naturally this is the origin of much of the fragility of the lines that demarcate the states of Africa.

In each part of this section, we will begin by examining the work of the pioneer missionaries. The regions in which they worked were not then constituted as states in the modern sense of the term. For the period of the twentieth century, we will review most of the African countries as they exist today (even if their names have been modified), and we will focus particularly on those of French-speaking Africa. Of course, our survey must remain partial and cannot claim to present an exhaustive tableau of the evangelization of Africa that occurred over the course of a century and a half of intensive missional effort.[173]

---

171  This number passed 45 percent in 1990.

172  In general we will use the name given to the country at the time of the facts related.

173  For a more complete history of missions in Africa, we refer the reader to the work of Peter Falk, *La croissance de l'église en Afrique* (Kinshasa: Institut Supérieur Théologique de Kinshasa, 1985), and P. Johnstone, *Flashes sur le monde*, 2nd ed. (Fontenay-sous-Bois, France: Éditions Farel, 1994).

*Part One*

# SOUTHERN AFRICA

# CHAPTER 11

# The First Missionaries in South Africa

South Africa enjoys a climate appreciably more pleasant than West Africa, which made acclimation for European missionaries less difficult. The populations were frequently displaced and cut off from their roots by tribal wars and, hence, were more receptive to the Christian message than in the other regions of Africa. In several instances, on the other hand, these incessant wars undermined the work of establishing churches due to the exodus of entire populations and the necessity of the missionaries withdrawing to less disrupted regions.

It is necessary, moreover, to take into account the European immigration in South Africa. The Portuguese discovered its shores at the end of the fifteenth century but did not want to live there. The first Dutch colonists, generally of the Reformed tradition, arrived in 1652 and began to occupy quasi-inhabited regions. At the end of the seventeenth century, they were joined by several hundred French Huguenots—their first refuge after the revocation of the Edict of Nantes (1686) had been Holland. British colonists arrived in their turn, mostly Puritans who envisioned colonies ruled by biblical laws as did their coreligionists in America. From the beginning, the colonists, whatever their origin, showed themselves to be rather cold, if not hostile, to the missionary enterprise, revealing the missional deficiency of Calvinism in the seventeenth century. It was at the time of the Great Trek (1834–1839) that the greatest tensions existed between the missionaries and the Boers (those of Dutch origin). We will see that later some among them changed their minds upon witnessing the remarkable transformations brought about by the gospel among primitive and violent tribes.

## THE MORAVIAN MISSION

In the eighteenth century, Georg Schmidt, an admirable Moravian pioneer among the Hottentots, was called to appear before a tribunal when the Reformed minister of the Cape learned that he had baptized the first Hottentot converts.[174] Not having received ordination as a minister, he appeared in their eyes not only as an unauthorized minister but as one totally lacking in discernment for having baptized "savages." He was forced to return to Europe in 1743.

---

174 See pp. 273ff.

In 1792 Moravian missionaries attempted to take up this task once again. Christian Kühnel, Hendrik Marsveld, and Daniel Schwinn took over where Schmidt had left off in the Hottentot village that he had founded fifty years earlier. They established a school and opened workshops to teach the inhabitants trades that would contribute to their prosperity. These included forging, cutlery, and printing. At first the governor was hostile, but he changed his mind after observing the success of the enterprise. He named the village Gnadental, the Valley of Grace, when he came to visit it. During the following twenty years, four other stations were added, as well as a project among the lepers. By 1850 the mission, then under the direction of a Swiss Moravian bishop named Hallbeck, had seven stations. The undertaking boasted twenty-eight missionaries, about fifteen Hottentot evangelists, and 7,100 baptized. Moreover, it had prepared the field for the missionaries of other societies who would arrive some years later.

The memory of the Moravians in South Africa lives on in the name of the residence of the chief of state, Gnadental. Also, during his term as president, Nelson Mandela participated in a synod of the Moravian Church of South Africa, at which time he declared:

> One thing has impressed me in the history of Gnadental. During the dark period when we were denied our native land, Gnadental and its missionaries deliberately took another direction, as a light in the night. They proclaimed the equality of men before God . . . I am also a product of the mission. We owe to the different churches the establishment of schools, while the government demonstrated no interest in the education of the Africans, half-castes, and Indians. To appreciate this fact, it is necessary to find oneself enclosed in a South African prison, held in the grip of human cruelty. Church leaders visited us there every Sunday, and they were our contacts between communities as well as with our families.[175]

## JOHANNES THEODORE VANDERKEMP

Among the Protestant missions active in South Africa in the nineteenth century, it was the London Missionary Society that created the most widespread and enduring work. Its first missionary was a Dutch aristocrat trained in Britain. To his great credit, he was able to make the colonists acknowledge the need to evangelize the black population.

Doctor Johannes Theodore Vanderkemp (1748–1811) was born in Rotterdam. His professional and spiritual journey followed a winding path during the first part of his life. After brilliant literary studies at Leyden, in which he learned an impressive number of ancient and modern languages, Vanderkemp opted for a more active existence. He became a cavalry officer. Later, his career took another dramatic turn when he undertook medical studies at Edinburgh. The son of a minister, he at first rejected

---

175 Klauspeter Blaser, ed., *Le fait missionaire*, no. 10, "Mission et photographie" (Lausanne, 2001), 64.

faith and then was content with a superficial religiosity. His life changed yet again in 1791 when he saw his wife and daughter drown in a shipwreck on the River Escaut, a tragedy he himself only just survived. He then experienced a true conversion, and he became one of the founders of the Netherlands Missionary Society in 1797. However, since the Dutch mission was not yet able to send missionaries, he offered his services to the LMS, which was established two years before. He was already fifty-one years old when he left for the Cape in 1799 as a medical missionary.

When Vanderkemp arrived, he barely escaped an attempted assassination by a group of colonists hostile to the presence of missionaries among their slaves. He gave himself to the most destitute and despised, the Hottentot nomads. He wanted to share the living conditions of this primitive population, which lived in the hollows of rocks and in the bush. He also adopted their eating habits, eating very simply and enduring nutritional deficiency. Following the Moravian example, he taught them to read and showed them how to cultivate the land, construct houses, and practice a trade. Soon a large community of stone houses and more than a thousands inhabitants formed around his house. He called the village Bethelsdorf.[176] Drawing on his personal fortune, he set numerous slaves free. He also married a second time to a young illiterate Malagasy slave whom he had redeemed.

The white population was surprised at the spectacular transformation of the Hottentots. Informed of the progress of this work, the LMS sent other missionaries to help. They also lived the simple life, like Vanderkemp. Thanks to the efforts of the Moravians and the LMS missionaries, a third of the Hottentot population was living in Christian villages. The missionaries never ceased to plead the cause of the Hottentots among the white farmers.

Vanderkemp envisioned going next to Madagascar, this great island without a church. As he was beginning to put his plans in motion, he died. The population of the city of the Cape assembled to show its respect and pay homage to this man who, twelve years earlier, some had wanted to murder upon his arrival.

## ROBERT MOFFAT

Among the most eminent of the missionary pioneers of South Africa is the Scotsman Robert Moffat (1795–1883). He converted in a Methodist meeting but remained a member of the Presbyterian Church of Scotland. Later, he presented his candidature to the LMS, which hesitated to hire him, for his only training was as an apprentice gardener. He was accepted on condition of receiving some brief additional training. He left for South Africa in 1817 at the age of twenty-three. Mary Smith, his Scottish fiancée, met him in the Cape in 1819, and the couple was married.

Though impeded by the white population, Moffat was soon able to leave the region of the Cape to advance more deeply into the continent. He went as far as the River Orange to a region called the Namaqualand.[177] Less than two years later,

---

176 This was to give homage to the Moravian Brethren, Bethelsdorf being the name of the locality in which the first Moravian community of Herrnhut was founded in 1722.

177 The Namaqualand had already been reached by Barnabas Shaw of the Wesleyan Methodist Missionary Society (WMMS).

in 1819, he was the instrument of the conversion of a formidable Hottentot guerilla chief, Jonker Afrikaner. He was a biracial man with a price on his head, for he was in revolt from the Boer and regularly pillaged their farms. He tolerated the presence of a missionary in his region because, when hard pressed, he counted on using him as a shield against the reprisals that his raids would inevitably produce. With his direct and colorful ways, Moffat knew how to gain his sympathy. Soon Moffat brought Afrikaner, as well as his two sons and nearly 150 of his subjects, to accept the gospel. Afrikaner accompanied Moffat to the Cape in 1820, where the authorities and population were profoundly struck by the transformation of this reputedly violent man. The historian J.-F. Zorn writes, "He became the first African chief to accept the 'gospel and civilization' . . . He represented the model of the indigenous nationalist chief whose friendship the missionaries sought and on whom they founded their hopes of establishing in Africa and elsewhere republics of free men who accepted the gospel."[178]

Thanks to Afrikaner, Moffat founded the missionary station of Kuruman in Bechuanaland (present-day Botswana; see map 9, p. 470). At this time bloody tribal wars were common, and the Betchouana (or Tswana) in particular showed themselves to be capable of merciless cruelty. Moffat encountered a people who seemed to be entirely resistant to the gospel and who presented an implacable opposition to his mission. One day a group of armed men forced his door and raged that he must choose between departure and death. Without losing his composure, Moffat responded that he was ready to die since he had been called by his God to be a witness in this place. He heard the bandits say among themselves: "This man must possess several lives since he can speak in this way . . . There is surely some truth in the stories he recounts to us about the resurrection!" Then they withdrew without having touched him.

After several unfruitful years,[179] Moffat recognized that the population understood Dutch much less well than the Namaqua people whom he had encountered at the beginning of his ministry. This constituted an insurmountable obstacle to communicating the Christian message. He began, therefore, to study the Setchouana spoken by the Betchuana. He also organized a school and translated the gospel as well as some hymns. His patience was recompensed in 1829, after ten years of effort. At that time a wave of conversions swept through the region, and by 1834 the church included 350 people.

To prepare himself for the task of translation, Moffat learned both Greek and German, the latter in order to consult exegetical commentaries. He adopted a method that latter became a common approach among Bible translators. He tested his translations by first circulating a small sample of them. This provided an opportunity to determine how indigenous readers understood the text and to profit from their remarks, with the result that the clarity of the text became progressively better. A Setchouana New Testament was printed in 1840, and the entire Bible was completed

---

178 Zorn, "Missions protestantes," 1011.
179 The first conversion took place eight years after his arrival in Kuruman.

in 1857 and published as a single volume in 1872. According to Y. Schaaf, the final product rendered by this autodidact gardener was the one of the best African translations of the Bible.[180]

*Robert Moffat (1795–1883).*

A gardener by training, Moffat was much interested in agricultural work. His principle, he used to say, was "to bring the Bible and the plow to the African population." Peter Falk has written of him: "He taught them how best to cultivate their gardens, obtain good harvests, work as masons, care for their children, and believe in Christ."

After fifty-three years of ministry, Robert and Mary Moffat retired in England. Robert was then seventy-five years old. He died in 1883 at the age of eighty-eight.

During one of his vacations in London, Moffat had encountered David Livingstone, a Scottish compatriot who was just about to leave as a missionary for China. He challenged him to consider a call to Africa, evoking "the smoke that rises from the morning sun on a thousand villages in the interior of Africa where no missionary has ever gone to proclaim the gospel." This image spoke to Livingstone's heart, and he resolved to go to South Africa. He arrived in 1840 and soon married Moffat's daughter.

---

180 Schaaf, op. cit., 92.

## John Philip

Alongside of Vanderkemp, Moffat, and later Livingstone, the name of John Philip also figures highly among the English-speaking missionaries in the southern part of the African continent. He personified the struggle of those rare European Christians who sought to help oppressed blacks to live as free men.

Arriving in Africa in 1817, the same year as Moffat,[181] Philip became superintendent of the LMS in the Cape in 1819. He undertook a campaign to improve conditions for the indigenous population, which was reduced to quasi slavery by white farmers. This work engendered much hostility against him in the Cape Colony while obtaining few immediate results. It was not until 1834 that slavery was abolished in South Africa.

*John Philip, superintendent of the LMS in the Cape, 1819–1851.*
*(Service Protestant de Mission, Paris)*

One of the important tasks Philip took up as a missionary was, as Louis Joubert writes, "to organize the work of the various Protestant missions, distributing the work among them, so that their efforts would be coordinated to the end of helping the African states to avoid colonial subjugation and accept the presence of missionaries so as to create a Christian Africa that would have a relationship of equality with Europe."[182]

Philip's name is also important in the history of the French Protestant churches. During a visit to Paris in 1828, he counseled the committee of the Paris Mission to send South Africa the first missionaries it could commission. The mission had several potential candidates, but it hesitated to make appointments. Philip offered to go with them and introduce them to experienced missionaries like Moffat, who could train and orient them for work in those regions where numerous ethnic groups were living that had not yet been reached. In retrospect, it is regrettable that the first French-speaking Protestant missionaries were sent to regions where British missions were already well established, while African regions under the French influence languished for many years before seeing Protestant missionaries. On the other hand, this approach removed French Protestant missions from the suspicion of profiting from French colonial power.

181 This was the general period in which a wave of new British immigrants arrived in the colony. Defended by British troops, they aimed to supplant the Dutch in the coastal regions.

182 Louis Joubert, "Mission et colonization en Afrique noire," in *Les missions protestantes et l'histoire* (Montpellier, France: Actes du IIe Colloque, 1971), 88.

# CHAPTER 12

# David Livingstone: Missionary and Explorer

The name of David Livingstone (1813–1873) is famous, but the missionary is often eclipsed by the explorer. He was certainly one of the great explorers of the nineteenth century, but his motivations differed from those of other explorers. Such men as John Speke (1827–1864), Richard Burton (1841–1890), and Cecil Rhodes (1853–1902), to cite only British examples, were above all else motivated by their interest in geography or their patriotism. What propelled Livingstone was and remained the service of God and the good of the African people. He wrote:

> I work for a goal that some understand at once while others lift their arms to heaven. But perhaps my God, in his mercy, will permit me to be a benefit to Africa and Britain more than one might at first believe possible. Some poor sillys attribute all that I do to my love of exploration and the search for glory in this world. Let us await the Day of Judgment when the secrets of hearts will be revealed. However, may God Almighty purify my motives, may he sanctify my designs!

When he undertook his first great journey of exploration, Livingstone wrote: "I am a missionary in my soul. God had an only son, who was a missionary and doctor. I am, or at least I desire to be, his poor and miserable imitator. In his service I hope to live, in his service I want to die." Rob Mackenzie characterized his beliefs in three words: evangelization, exploration, and emancipation.[183]

In a conference dedicated to Livingstone on the occasion of the centenary of his death. Stephen Neill declared:

> There are few persons in ancient or modern history whom we know as well as Livingstone . . . And I must clearly affirm and straightaway admit that without understanding that he was from first to last a missionary, it is absolutely impossible to understand his career.[184]

---

183  Rob Mackenzie, *David Livingstone: The Truth behind the Legend* (Feam, Scotland: Christian Focus, 2000), 29.

184  Stephen Neill, *Livingstone Memorial Lecture, 30th April 1973* (Malawi: Livingstone Centenary Committee, 1973), 3, 15.

## YOUTH AND TRAINING

Born in Blantyre near Glasgow, Scotland, Livingstone came from a poor family. He entered a textile mill at the age of ten and remained there for thirteen years. Endowed with uncommon strength of will and animated by an insatiable desire to learn, he kept a Latin grammar at hand while also keeping an eye on the shuttle of the trade, and he did this from six o'clock in the morning until eight o'clock in the evening, a seventy-five-hour work week. During this time he also took courses in the evening. At the end of his life, recounts Henry Morton Stanley, he was still able to recite by heart entire poems by Byron, Tennyson, and Burns, and even some Latin texts from Virgil. He was, however, more a man of action than a refined intellectual.

Despite his humble origins, Livingstone delved deeply into the studies of theology and medicine; and he showed himself remarkably competent as a geographer, geologist, and naturalist. He was, moreover, a gifted writer who recounted his discoveries in fascinating narratives of his journeys, which were an immense success among the book-buying public and acquired for him a notoriety that reached well beyond mission circles.

Livingstone was a member of an independent church, and it was the London Missionary Society (LMS) that sent him to Africa, following the intervention of Robert Moffat mentioned in a preceding chapter. Later on, the LMS decided not to support him, concluding that it could not justify to its donors the financing of a man known essentially as an explorer. From then on he lived on grants from the London Geographical Society and from the sale of his books, but he refused to believe that this rupture should be interpreted as an abandonment of his missionary vocation. Nevertheless, it is certainly true that he did not conform to the traditional image of the nineteenth-century missionary.[185] He wrote of himself:

> Nothing has more importance for me than human relations, than the help that I can bring [to the Africans] in shedding light on the slave trade and in giving them a glimpse of our religion. What I can do there is without doubt not a great thing, but at least this gives me the feeling of not journeying for nothing . . . When one works for God, the sweat that runs down the brow is no longer a chastisement. It is invigorating and changes itself into a blessing.

## FIRST MISSIONARY JOURNEY

Livingstone departed for Africa at the end of December 1840. Upon arriving at the Cape in 1841, he traveled to Moffat's mission station at Kuruman. In 1845 he married Moffat's daughter, Mary, who would give him four children.

He lived in this region of Betchuanaland for eleven years where he pursued a "classic" missionary ministry. Though he established three mission stations in this time, he was "champing at the bit" at the thought of the immense regions farther to the north where the gospel had never yet been preached. It chafed him too that these

---

185  His speech at the University of Cambridge (see p. 479) illustrates his unconventional approach.

fields were left untended while so many missionaries were content to live comfortably (by his standards) in well-established stations.

From the first, he was able to form relationships of friendship and confidence with Africans that were deeper than that experienced by most his colleagues. This was due in large part to his medical work, which absorbed much of his time. He wrote to a medical colleague in London: "My medical practice is immense. I have treated some sick people who have had to travel 130 miles (210 kilometers) on foot to be cared for. It is a medical paradise here as far as the practice is considered—as for fees, that is another matter."

He immediately saw the importance of entrusting the preaching of the gospel to African Christians:

> I do not hesitate to declare that one or two indigenous preachers can accomplish this work with a success equal, if not superior, to one of the whites. The indigenous people are so inclined to see only the habits and customs of the whites in the gospel that the latter make little progress in producing an impression on their souls, while if the truth is communicated by one among them, it touches them immediately.[186]

## AT THE HEART OF THE AFRICAN CONTINENT

The last twenty years of his life were dedicated to three great expeditions of exploration. Between 1853 and 1856 Livingston made his most spectacular journey. From the Cape, he traveled far into the interior of the continent heading north before cutting across to the northwest, going as far as the Atlantic coast at Luanda, Angola. Then he returned in an eastern direction, and traversed the continent to arrive at the mouth of the Zambezi at Quilimane on the Indian Ocean. This was an expedition of three thousand kilometers through as yet unexplored regions. It was the first time that anyone had attempted to cross the African continent from one ocean to another.

During his second long and costly expedition (1858–1864), Livingston explored the basin of the Zambezi, becoming the first European to see the famous Victoria Falls, then the region of Lake Nyasa. The dream that he hoped to achieve was the discovery of a navigable way into the heart of Africa through the Zambezi and its numerous tributaries. He persisted for a long time in pursuing this hopeless quest. This was one of his two great geographical errors, the second being his confusion as to the sources of the Nile. His wife, Mary, rejoined him in 1862 in the course of this journey, but she died on the banks of the Zambezi a few months later.

When he returned to Britain, he was celebrated as a national hero. He then attempted his third great journey, this time without a European companion. Indefatigable as always, he traveled east to the present-day Congo, passing through vast territories that were then entirely blank on the maps of Africa and all the while minutely describing in his journal all that he saw. The great mystery that he sought in vain to solve was the connection between the waters of the Congo basin that flowed

---

186 C. Northcott, *Livingstone en Afrique* (Neuchâtel: Delachaux & Niestlé, 1960), 30.

toward the Atlantic and those of the Nile that followed their course toward the Mediterranean. For several years there was no news of him, and rumors spread of his disappearance or murder. Finally, the *New York Herald* sent the American journalist Henry Morton Stanley to search for him. He found him skeletal, exhausted, dressed in worn and patched clothes, having lost almost all his teeth, covered in ulcers, and long lacking in medicines. Still, he was dignified, shaved, and clean. He had been attacked by brigands several months before and, relieved of his supplies, no longer had the means to contact the outside world.

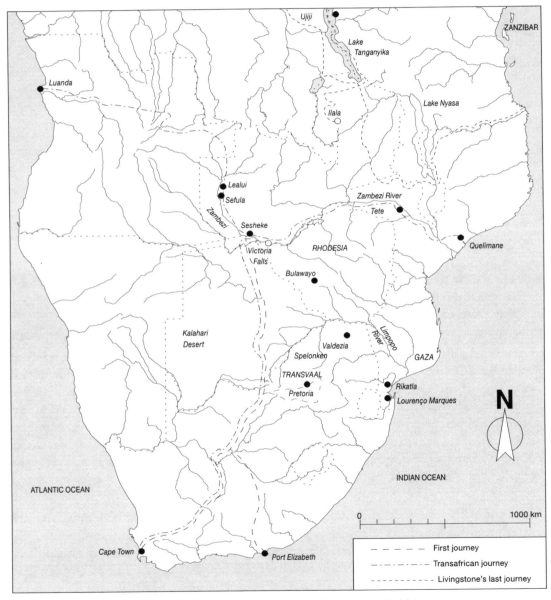

*Map 9: David Livingstone's journeys of exploration in Africa*

Stanley had set out at the beginning of 1871 with about two hundred people. He found Livingstone eight months later at Ujiji, on the east bank of the Tanganyika. The picture he painted of this encounter has passed into legend. Here is an extract:

> "I see the doctor, Sir," said Selim to me [a chief porter at the head of the caravan]. "How he has aged!" What would I not have given to have a small corner of the wilderness where, without being seen, I could have performed some folly: to bite my hands, roll over, whip the trees; finally to give vent to the joy that was suffocating me! My heart was beating hard enough to break; but I did not allow my face to betray my emotions for fear of harming the dignity of my race . . .
>
> While I slowly advanced, I noticed his pallor and air of fatigue. He had on grey pants, a red jacket and a blue cap with faded gold stripes. I wanted to run to him, but I was cowardly in the presence of this crowd. I wanted to kiss him, but he was British, and I did not know how I would be welcomed.
>
> I did, therefore, what my cowardice and false pride inspired: I approach in a deliberate step and said, while removing my hat: "Doctor Livingstone, I presume?"
>
> "Yes," he responded and removed his cap, with a kindly smile.
>
> With our heads recovered, we shook hands. "I give thanks to God," I said, "that he has permitted me to find you."
>
> "I am happy," he responded, "to be here to receive you."[187]

Stanley hurriedly sent messengers to the coast to deliver the news of their encounter to the newspaper that had financed his expedition. This was, if one dares the anachronism, the "scoop" of the century. The journalist remained several months with Livingstone, exploring the banks of Lake Tanganyika with him in an attempt to discover where its waters flowed.[188] At this time Stanley felt himself called to be an explorer (see pp. 561ff), but first he had to return to give an account to his backers. Livingstone also pressed him to leave so that, due to his notoriety, he could raise awareness in Europe and especially America of the treatment of blacks in Africa by telling the story that he had witnessed first hand. Livingstone did not want to accompany him, for he hoped that in several months he would be able to resolve the enigma of the sources of the Nile—a matter that had become almost an obsession with him. Together with several faithful African companions he took up his search again in August 1872 in the regions north of present-day Zambia. But soon his health deteriorated and, finding it difficult to walk, he often had to be carried. Nevertheless, he refused to abandon his quest and was determined to reach the Lualaba River,

---

187 Henry Morton Stanley, "Comment j'ai retrouvé Livingstone," in D. Livingstone and H. M. Stanley, *Du Zambèze au Tanganyika* (Paris: Gheerbrant, 1969), 401–2.

188 At that time it was believed to flow toward the north until it reached the Nile.

which he wrongly believed to be one of the sources of the Nile. Actually, it flowed westward toward the Congo basin.

Due to Livingstone's poor health, the little group stopped on April 30 at Llala, in the territory of Chief Chitambo. The next morning, May 1, 1873, his friends found him dead, kneeling at the side of his bed as he normally did while praying. He was sixty years old. They buried his heart in the African soil and then wrapped his body to be carried to the coast, from whence it was sent to Europe. He was buried in Westminster Abbey, and a year after his death, April 18, 1874, he was given a national memorial service.

His motto was: "I am ready to go anywhere, providing it be forward," and the question that he always posed to himself before making a decision was, "Is this for the good of Africa?"

## ABOLISHING THE SLAVE TRADE

Livingstone's great aim was to understand the topography and the hydrology of central and east Africa in order to discover deep, navigable water routes that would make journeys into the interior of the continent possible. Such routes, he hoped, would lead to Africans exporting the natural riches that lay in the interior of the land. Since international laws against the slave trade had proven to be ineffective in the struggle to end this commerce, he concluded that the African chiefs would have to be persuaded to end the trade by offering them another source of revenue.[189] Livingstone wrote:

> By encouraging the Africans to develop the resources of their countries, one can hope for a significant advance in direction towards the extinction of the slave trade. For it will quickly appear that these exports will constitute a source of profit superior to that trade.[190]

The hope of discovering such a route proved to be unfounded, for the courses of almost all the rivers in this region were punctuated either by cataracts or rapids. After many years of exploration, he concluded, "My hope of utilizing water courses as trade routes faded away a little at a time until I knew better."

While Livingstone proceeded ever deeper into the interior of Africa, he became increasingly distressed by the barbarous evidence of the traffic in slaves. In the story of his expedition to the Zambezi, he gave vent in many places to his mounting anger. The following are a few extracts that reveal the ignominy of the trade:

> May we be able to tell the exact story of the horrors in the trade of men and to give the approximate total of the lives that it destroys every year!

---

189 Several missions in West Africa, notably in the basin of the Niger, shared this conviction. It was Thomas Fowell Buxton, an English politician and successor of Wilberforce, who was the first to defend this idea.

190 David Livingstone and Charles Livingstone, *Narrative of an Expedition to the Zambezi and Its Tributaries* (London, 1865). Cited in Bridglal Pachai, ed., *Livingstone: Man of Africa* (London: Longman Group, 1973), 31.

The custom records of Zanzibar reveal that from the region of Nyasa alone there are nineteen thousand slaves per year. It should be understood that the slaves sent to the Portuguese harbor are not included in this number.

And can one conclude that the number 19 million represents all the unfortunates created by this annual trade in the market of Zanzibar. The captives that one redeems from the country form only a slight fraction of the victims of the trade. We can only gain a realistic estimate of this atrocious commerce by seeing it at the source; it is surely there that Satan lives.

Out of the hundreds of individuals who are procured by one of these expeditions, thousands of men are killed or die of their wounds, while others, set to flight, expire of hunger and despair.[191]

Further on:

Words cannot describe the desolation in this formally happy valley. Everywhere the same scenes of death; everywhere the solitude . . . And when by chance you should happen upon an indigenous person, his body emaciated and bearing the marks of hunger, his look expresses fear or despondency.

Drought followed the panic caused by the slave hunters . . . They were fleeing without provision, leaving their lofts in the mountains, and the famine became so great that not enough people remained to bury the dead. The cadavers that we have seen as we passed by were only the remnant of those unfortunates whose friends were too weak to dig a grave, or that the crocodiles, no longer being hungry, could not devour.

Wherever we directed our steps, we encountered skeletons . . . Many had reached the end of their misery on the floor of their huts, behind closed doors; cadavers were found there, having poor rags around their hips, the skull fallen to the side of a pillow; and between two large skeletons, a small body rolled carefully in a mat . . .

We understood that it would be impossible to establish regular commerce in this region as long as the selling of men, this monstrous iniquity that has so long weighed on Africa, has not yet disappeared.[192]

Though distressing to read, Livingstone felt compelled to testify to what he had seen. Wanting to shake public opinion, he did not attempt to tone down its shocking character. And his cry of alarm was not in vain. A month after his death, the great

---

191 David Livingstone, "Explorations du Zambèze et de ses affluents," in Livingstone and Stanley, *Du Zambèze*, 170–71. The most significant stories of Livingstone's journey have been published in French by Elikia M'Bokolo, *David Livingstone: Explorations dans l'Afrique australe et le bassin du Zambèze, 1840–1864* (Paris: Karthala, 1981).
192 Livingstone, op. cit., 169–70.

slave market in Zanzibar was closed, and in 1875, the Sultan of Zanzibar, under the influence of the Consul John Kirk, one of Livingstone's former companions, forbade "all transport of slaves by way of land and in whatever condition." Livingstone had achieved a posthumous victory.

## A SCOUT FOR THE MISSIONARIES

Before Livingstone, the only travelers who penetrated into the heart of Africa were the slave traders, the missionaries having generally limited themselves to the coastal regions or to the zones where white colonists were already found. Livingstone's explorations opened the way for the gospel into the numerous regions of the continent's interior.

Through his writings on Africa and his advocacy on its behalf, Livingstone had a decisive and enduring influence on British Christians. His numerous topographical and ethnological observations, albeit not well developed, suggested the pursuit of multiple missionary projects. His native Scotland became a nursery of missionaries, who were sent to the regions described in his writing, notably to the area of Lake Nyasa. It is on the basis of his discoveries regarding the linguistic relationship between tribes that were geographically distant from one another that the church and the Mission of Lesotho undertook the support of François Coillard's expeditions, which resulted in the Zambezi Mission. In 1877 when Livingstone had been dead for five years, the London Missionary Society followed the routes south to Lake Tanganyika and north to Rhodesia (present-day Zimbabwe) that Livingstone had discovered. The Church Missionary Society, for its part, pursued the regions still farther north as far as Uganda, while the Baptist Missionary Society established itself in the Congo.

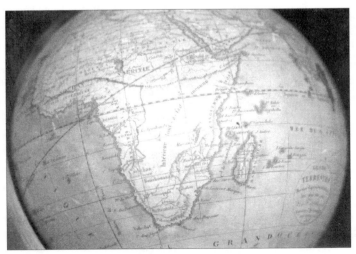

*Africa before Livingstone. A world map from 1821 leaves the vast regions of the continent blank with the explanation, "interior entirely unknown."*

Before Livingstone, Europeans were largely ignorant of Africa and had feelings about it that were mixtures of fear, wonder, and contempt. Livingstone had a profound respect for Africa and was capable of establishing with its people, particularly the tribal chiefs, relationships based on confidence and amity. His attitude toward his African guides, for example, contrasts sharply with that of other explorers. He wrote:

> It is rare that we walk more than five or six hours per day. In a hot country, it is as much as a man can do without exhausting himself; and we desire that the journey be rather a pleasure than a strain. To press the pace, to cast furious looks on his people, to say injurious things to them, to boast later of the rapidity with which one has made the journey is a stupidity in which the odious quarrels with the absurd. While the benevolence that one witnesses in his companions, the regard that one has for them . . . The pleasure of looking at the country, of observing as many new things as one can, comes best when one walks at an ordinary pace. Finally, the charm of rest breaks render the journey delicious.[193]

He knew how to laugh at cultural differences, being perfectly aware that the causes of astonishment or even dread are reciprocal:

> There is something in the aspects of whites that, at first sight, is dreadful for blacks. When we enter a village that a European has not yet visited, the first child who glimpses the men "sewn in sacks" girds up his loins and flees as fast as a London kid would if he saw a living mummy leave the British Museum. Alarmed by the wild cries of the infant, mother runs out of the hut; but she quickly withdraws once she sees the frightful apparition . . . The village, formerly so peaceful, now offers only disorder and racket from the moment when our Makololo [his African companion] causes them to laugh by affirming that whites do not eat blacks; for in Africa, a pleasantry often has more influence than the gravest words. Some of our dandies would perhaps lose a little of the good opinion they have of themselves if they could see all the pretty girls of a village flee at their approach, as well as the horrible cannibals; or if they heard, as has happened to us, the mommies transform them into bogeymen, saying to their kids: "If you are not good, I will call the white man to come and bite you."

As Livingstone dramatically described the Africans as victims of slavery, he did not hesitate to decry their traditional lifestyles, customs, and social structures, which he studied and described with empathy. He did not equate paganism with "darkness," taking a more nuanced approach.

> The African population is generally superstitious . . . [But] those Africans whose minds are free of these stupidities believe in a supreme being who has created everything. They know nothing of the relationship they have with the Great Spirit, nor the interest that he has in men . . .

193 Ibid., 78.

> All the Africans that we have seen were no less certain of their future life than of their present existence, and we have not encountered any among them whose belief in a Supreme Being did not have deep roots. But when they pass from this world to the other, they do not seem to dread any chastisement. Although rather sad in the eyes of a Christian, African religion is naturally mild.[194]

> It is possible, we believe, to rehabilitate the African; we do not doubt either his heart, or his intelligence . . . As for the place that he will one day occupy among the nations, we have seen nothing that justifies the hypothesis of his natural inferiority, nothing which proves that he be of any species but the most civilized . . . The African is not classed by ethnologists in the last place of the human species; physically, he is almost as strong as the civilized; and as a race, he is endowed with surprising vitality . . . The African has triumphed over an extreme climate that would have caused most of the human races to disappear.[195]

It should not be forgotten that when Livingstone wrote these lines there were still some Westerners who doubted that these "savages" had a soul and should be considered as fully human.

## LIVINGSTONE: A LEGENDARY HERO?

More than most pioneers of modern missions, Livingstone has been venerated as a hero. The enthusiasm that some of his biographers have shown in this regard may make some modern readers uncomfortable, especially as writers have idealized not only his spirituality but also his belief in the benefits of Western culture.

Livingstone was a pious Christian, who spent much time in reading the Bible and practicing intercessory prayer for Africa. He believed that the African had need of Jesus Christ, not because he was black or pagan, but because he was human. As such, the African needed to discover Christ in order to live in peace and dignity, just as Livingstone had discovered him in his youth while living in Blantyre. These lines, written several weeks before his death when he was quite weak, without medicines, and completely isolated, profoundly reveal the man:

> I have read the Bible four times, from one end to the other, while I was among the Manyema . . . I feel the acute desire to finish it [his life] . . . But I commit myself into the hands of the One who disposes of all things . . . If I die, I want to fall while doing my duty. My desire is to give to the youth of my country the example of a virile perseverance.

He shocked some of his British colleagues by his unconventionality. This was especially so in his failure to embrace the strict Sabbath rest that many in his day

---

194 Ibid., 20–21.
195 Ibid., 248–49.

observed, being inspired by a Puritanism that still enjoyed much influence in the British Isles. Also, Livingstone's expeditions were not "tours of evangelization," though his compassion for human beings and his dedication to serving God appeared throughout his narratives, as previously noted.

*David Livingstone with his daughter in 1864. The explorer was criticized for according more importance to his journeys than to his family.*

Henry Morton Stanley contributed to the idealization of Livingstone's image. Undeniably, Stanley's experience in searching for the explorer and the time passed in his company profoundly affected him. Stanley, a journalist with a troubled past, remained with Livingstone for four months, during which time he had an acute experience of faith. Until then he had lived most of his life in a milieu of violence and delinquency. The contrast between his past and the time spent with this man of God could not have been greater. He had expected to find a "hard" man, indeed a misanthrope. Instead he found a man with a tender heart whose scruples prevented him from quickly severing a relationship even when he had clearly been swindled. He said of Livingstone:

> I went to Africa with more prejudges against religion than the worst miscreant . . . When I saw this solitary man, I asked myself: What is it that inspires him? Little by little, through his piety, gentleness, zeal, seriousness, he brought me to the point of conversion without having tried to do it . . . I spent four months with him in the same hut, the same boat, under the same tent: in him appearance and reality were one and the same . . . His religion does not consist in theories, but in a constant, serious, and sincere practice of the gospel. It is not aggressive, it is not noisy, but shows itself in his every act. It governs his conduct in regard to his servants, in regard to the indigenous people as well as the sanctimonious Muslims—and finally in regard to all those who come in contact with him.[196]

And again: "He has an inexhaustible source of gaiety. His gaiety is delightful. His laugh is contagious; once he bursts out, you imitate him strongly; everyone joins in with him; he laughs from head to foot."[197] Stanley, however, had reason to dread the great man. Before beginning his search, he had encountered one of Livingstone's acquaintances, the British consul of Zanzibar John Kirk, and had this conversation:

> "What kind of man is he?
>
> "In general he is very difficult to live with. I have never had anyone complain to me about him, but from time to time I have seen him get angry with others! This comes, I presume, from detesting to have companions."
>
> "I have heard second hand that he is very modest," I responded. "Is that true?"
>
> "Oh! He knows perfectly what his discoveries are worth; no one knows it better than him. He is not an angel, not truly," the consul added with a smile.[198]

Rob Mackenzie, who has dedicated himself to deepening our understanding of Livingstone's character, remarked:

> Livingstone, despite his many human failings, strove to carry the gospel to all men. He never despised the indigenous people; he saw each person in accordance with his status before God . . . He endeavored to make friends among the people whom he sought to win to the gospel. He treated Africans with tact and patience, and seemed to have a sort of instinctive capacity to understand

---

196 Melvin E. Page, "The Arabs and the Slave Trade" in Briglal Pachai, ed., *Livingstone: Man of Africa: Memorial Essays 1873–1973* (London/New York: Longmans, 1973), 147.

197 Stanley, "Comment," 409–10.

198 Ibid., 271.

them. This, together with his calm, courage, and perseverance, explains why he found a ready access to all Africans. Among Europeans, however, he often lacked tact and, in certain cases, was even hostile.[199]

Livingstone was clearly happiest when he found himself to be the only European among Africans, which was frequently the case. He made his decisions alone and communicated little, which often led to strained relationships with his British companions. But the causes for frustration could be many: several days of difficult walking that led to nowhere, fevers and dysentery, porters who slipped away with precious supplies. All these things could easily get on people's nerves. Perhaps the greatest source of conflict was Livingstone's persistence—or was it obstinacy?—when, in some inextricable situation, everyone but him was in favor of turning back.

In a speech given at the University of Cambridge during his travels through Europe in 1865 Livingstone gave the clearest explanation ever of how he viewed his work and objectives. The following extract concisely states the goal of his missionary work:

> Spreading the gospel among the pagans is no longer consistent with the current image of the missionary; that is to say, a man going here and there with the Bible under his arm. The promotion of trade must become the object of special attention, for trade, more than other things, destroys the spirit of isolation that paganism engenders and that leads the tribes to feel dependant on one another and use one another . . . It is not enough that we put an end to the slave trade. We still have to introduce the African family into the body of nations in which no member can suffer without the others suffering with it.[200]

More than any of his contemporaries, Livingstone helped Africa to leave behind its isolation and to enter the modern world—for better or worse, we are tempted to add. But Livingstone could not know the best or the worst that was to follow. As previously noted, the question that determined all his decisions, "Is it for the good of Africa?" could not be answered with the knowledge of hindsight. Louis Joubert writes of Livingstone: "The most serious [paradox] is that when he died, having sacrificed everything to his dream of liberation, he had contributed so broadly to modern knowledge of southern Africa that it was then open for colonization."[201]

---

199 Mackenzie, op. cit., 83.

200 David Livingstone, "Discourse a l'université de Cambridge," in M'Bokolo, op. cit. Cited in Klauspeter Blaser, ed., *Repères pour la mission: Cinq siècles de tradition missionaire; Perspectives oecuméniques* (Paris: Cerf, 2000), 44.

201 L. Joubert, "Mission et colonization en Afrique noire," in *Les missions protestantes et l'histoire* (Paris: Société d'Histoire du Protestantisme Francais, 1971).

# CHAPTER 13

# *François Coillard:*
# *Founder of the Zambezi Mission*

Among the French Protestant missionaries of the nineteenth century, François Coillard (1834–1904) is no doubt the most famous. More than all the others, he helped to form the image of the pioneer missionary in the public mind.[202] It was an admirable image, but also one marked by its time: the outset of the age of colonization.

Born in 1834 in Berry, Asnières-lès-Bourges, he was the youngest in a family of eight children, and his father died when he was only two years old. He had an impoverished childhood but one marked by the piety of his mother, whose nickname in the village was "the kind mother." The village pastor was Ami Bost, a promoter of the evangelical revival in Geneva at the beginning of the nineteenth century. Coillard's childhood and youth were influenced by the faith and piety of the revival, a memory he treasured throughout his life. He received a scholarship to study at the Protestant Institution of Glay (Doubs), which happened at a time of personal crisis when he felt crushed by feelings of guilt. This led to a conversion experience that left him transformed.

Convinced that God was calling him to serve in Africa, Coillard presented himself in 1852 to the committee of the Paris Mission. Since he was only eighteen years old, the committee urged him to complete his studies. Without great success he took courses at the Faculté de Théologie de Strasbourg and in 1856 entered the Maison des Missions de Paris, whose director, Eugène Casalis, had recently returned from Lesotho. When Casalis explained to him the urgent needs of the region, Coillard regretfully shortened his time of study in order to follow the missionary François Daumas, who was soon to leave for Lesotho. In May 1857, he was ordained a minister in the church of Oratoire du Louvre in Paris and embarked for Africa in September of the same year, at the age of twenty-three.

---

202 The life of Coillard is well known, thanks to the large three-volume biography of Edouard Favre, published by the Société des Missions Evangéliques de Paris: *François Coillard: Enfance et jeunesse* (1908); *François Coillard: Missionaire au Lessouto* (1912); and *François Coillard au Zambèze* (1913). The same author and publisher have published an abbreviated version: *La vie d'un missionnaire français: François Coillard* (1922). Finally, for the centenary of the Mission to Lessouto, Favre published with the same publisher: *Les vingt-cinq ans de Coillard au Lessouto* (1933). References to these works in the following citations will be made by giving the year of publication.

# MISSIONARY IN SOUTH AFRICA

After arriving at the Cape, Coillard set out for the interior with the French missionary Jean Pierre Pellissier, who was returning to Bethulie.[203] When they came to the stations neighboring Lesotho, they found them pillaged and burned due to the war that had exploded between the Boers of the Orange State and the Basuto. The destruction was impressive and traumatizing for one so newly arrived.[204] At the end of May 1858, the travelers finally reached Thaba Bossiou, which had resisted the assault of the Boers.

Several months later, Coillard had an opportunity to better integrate himself into the life of the Mission of Lesotho by participating in a missionary conference. In response to the catastrophes of war and the resulting modification of the borders, the missionaries decided on a new strategy: the establishment of two new stations, Bethlehem and Leribe. Coillard was selected to take charge of the one at Leribe, which lay on the northern border of Lesotho and was their forward post.

In February 1859 Coillard arrived in Leribe where he was received with joy and curiosity by the population and its chief, Molapo. This second son of Moshesh was converted at Morija and had been baptized. His father had given him the rule of the northern region of the country, but once there, deprived of all Christian fellowship, the young king had abandoned the faith.

After one and a half years, Coillard traveled from Leribe to the Cape in order to welcome Christina Mackintosh. She was a young Scotswoman whom, shortly before his departure from France, he had encountered in one of those Parisian salons where the "Dames du Réveil" (ladies of the Revival) were holding prayer meetings for the mission. Christina, five years François' senior, was then teaching English in Paris. A zealous Christian, she had a great interest in the mission. Coillard made his heart known to her in a letter he sent from Africa. Christina at first refused him, but after a time of struggle, she wrote to him that she would be arriving in the Cape. She remained faithful to her commitment to him until her death on the shores of the Zambezi, thirty years later. She was a cultured woman who had a more positive and optimistic view of society and the Christian world than her husband. As such she complemented him and helped him to broaden his horizons.

Coillard returned to Leribe with his young wife. Being married turned out to be an asset to his ministry, indeed a necessity. For upon his arrival, being frail and small in stature, beardless and single, Coillard had scarcely been taken seriously by the local population.

The evangelization of Leribe proved difficult, the population showing little interest in religious meetings. The tours through the bush country, which he made on horseback with his wife, seemed to accomplish little. The focus of his efforts eventually became education. Coillard established a school where he taught reading, writing, math, calculating, geography, and religion. Hence, the school became his primary venue for evangelization. It was not until August 1862 that Coillard celebrated

---

203 The station, which was close to the border between Betchuanaland and Lesotho, was called Carmel.
204 See Edouard Favre, op. cit. (1933), 31.

the baptisms of a man and woman in Leribe.[205] These first members of the church bore the brunt of the hostility of their families and of chief Molapo. However, in the villages that were regularly visited, the mockers were slowly giving way to those showing a real spiritual thirst, and asking for schools.

*François and Christina Coillard in 1861. (Service Protestant de Mission, Paris)*

205 Ibid., 114.

Despite Coillard's efforts to establish reconciliation, war was waged between the Orange Free State and the Basuto, with its procession of massacres, villages burned, flocks pillaged, and refugees fleeing for their lives. And all this occurred in snowy winter. In March 1866 François and Christina retreated eastward to the British colony of the Natal. Coillard gave vent to his feelings of sadness and injustice:

> From the moment it was known that we were going to be chased out of the country, our poor Basutos, taking advantage of our circumstances, fell on us like a flock of vultures. They sought the food in our kitchen at all hours of the day and seized anything that might fall from our hands. They flew around us until the last of our horses [were packed] . . . I made my sad adieus to the tribe and distributed Holy Communion for the last time to the members of our flock.[206]

During the Coillards' exile in Natal, they served at an American mission among the Zulus. Eventually they received encouraging news from Leribe of a small revival.[207] When Lesotho was proclaimed a British protectorate, the Coillards were able to return to Leribe after an absence of three years. The church, though not very large, still enjoyed the momentum of the revival, and thirty-two candidates immediately announced that they were ready to prepare themselves for baptism. Two years later, the inauguration of a new church became the occasion to baptize fifty believers from Leribe and other neighboring villages.

In April 1872, at the time of the annual missionary conference, the decision was made to form a synod of the Lesotho churches. Until that time the churches had been connected to each other only through the missionaries. The first synod was formed in September 1872, the second in 1874. They were both directed by missionaries. At the time these synods were formed, long-simmering tensions suddenly boiled over into a full-blown crisis. Crucial questions were posed about the relationship between the new Christians and their ancient customs. Hermann Dieterlen, a missionary in Lesotho, wrote that the missionaries, "carried away by an exaggerated sense of their own authority," overreached by imposing too many rules on these new Christians.[208] It is not certain that the Lesotho missionaries perceived what was at stake missiologically. Coillard, in any event, scarcely noted it in his letters. He did see the harmful influence of Molapo, who exerted outside pressure on the participants of the synods.

Coillard envisioned the creation of new mission outposts in the mountainous regions within the country, which led to numerous and tiring journeys. He often found himself alone in vast territories, the evangelists being so few in number. François and Christina lived for about twenty years in Leribe, which became their adopted country. He wrote fables in the local language that he mastered like his mother tongue, and they remain classics in the culture of the country and are still taught in school. In spite of difficult circumstances and his many travels, Dieterlen summarized Coillard's

---

206 Ibid., 154–55.
207 Ibid., 158–59.
208 H. Dieterlen, "François Coillard," in *Récits missionnaires illustré*, no. 13 (Paris: SMEP, 1926), 33.

twenty years in Leribe as highly successful: he established eight annexes, each with its primary school. He received in the church 120 members, and numerous catechumens regularly received solid religious instruction."[209]

*François Coillard (1834–1904), missionary in Lesotho and founder of the Zambezi Mission.*
*(Service Protestant de Mission, Paris)*

## FIRST EXPEDITIONS TO THE NORTH

Coillard's colleagues called upon him to take the lead in an expedition towards the North Transvaal in order to reach regions that had not yet heard the proclamation of the gospel (see map 9, p. 470). This desire to break through to the north was not new.

---

209 Leribe soon had to be divided into five parishes.

Adolphe Mabille,[210] a former student with Coillard in the Maison des Missions (House of Missions) in Paris in 1856, had taken this desire to heart. Beginning in 1873, several expeditions undertook the task. The first was led by Mabille and Paul Berthoud,[211] who were accompanied by several African evangelists. They were turned back by the Bapedi but succeeded in leaving behind the evangelist Asser and several Basutos in the region. A few years later, this would be where Berthoud and his colleague Ernest Creux would found the Swiss Mission in the Transvaal. According to Coillard, Asser's return several months later had "the effect of an electric spark. It would be difficult to exaggerate the profound impression that his story had everywhere. A large wave of enthusiasm swept through all our churches."

Dieterlen headed a new expedition in 1876. But it suffered a serious setback upon arriving at Pretoria: the Boers threw Asser and the other African evangelists in prison and required a large ransom for freeing Dieterlen. After twenty years in Africa, François and Christina were planning a vacation in Europe. But then they heard the call to establish a missionary station in the North Transvaal, which struck them like "a bolt of lightening." During the next ten days Coillard and his wife struggled "to quiet the counsels of flesh and blood," and then they said once more to God: "Here we are, Lord, do with us what seems good to you."

Hence, in 1877 when Coillard was forty-three and had already spent two decades in Africa, he began a new stage in his missionary career. During the next ten years, he undertook regular and extensive expeditions until the Zambezi Mission was finally established. He was accompanied by his wife, his niece Elise Coillard (who had recently arrived from Europe), and four local evangelists and their families. After a year and a half of eventful wandering, their caravan arrived at the shores of the Zambezi. Coillard rejoiced, for he had been dreaming for a longtime of establishing a mission beyond the great river. There he encountered the Barotse tribe, which, according to Livingstone, spoke a language related to Sessouto. Since the Barotseland was about 1,500 kilometers from Lesotho, tribal wars had probably induced part of the Basuto people to migrate to the north. Two and a half years after they had left, the travelers returned to Leribe.

## SOJOURN IN FRANCE

Coillard submitted a report of his journeys of exploration to the executive commission of the Synod of the Churches of Lesotho, but due to the distance involved and other difficulties, it declined to undertake the project. The Churches of Lesotho were adamant about this, passing on the responsibility to the Paris Mission. This necessitated Coillard's return to France so that he could officially arrange for a new mission.

---

210 Adolphe Mabille (1836–1898), an intimate friend of François Coillard, was the son of a Swiss teacher in Yverdon. In 1859 he married Adèle Casalis, the daughter of the missionary Eugène Casalis, and left the same year for Africa. The year following, he became responsible for the station of Morija, in Lesotho. His biography was written by Hermann Dieterlen: *Adolphe Mabille: Missionnaire* (Société des Missions Évangéliques de Paris, 1898). In 1933 the Reverend J. E. Siordet wrote *Adolphe Mabille née Casalis (1840–1923)* (same publisher) from Mabille's *Souvenirs* and his correspondence.

211 Paul Berthoud, sent by the Free Church of the canton of Vaud, had just arrived in Lesotho.

The Coillards made the trip from Leribe to Paris between November 1879 and March 1880. They remained in Europe for two years, pleading the cause of the Borotse. Coillard refused to hide the difficulty and the cost of the enterprise. While seeking to enlist two missionaries and one or two artisans, he also openly sought to recruit some of their replacements in advance, for he knew that at least some among them would succumb "in this post of honor." Demonstrating a tireless commitment over a period of a year and a half, he visited churches in France, Switzerland, Belgium, the Low Countries, the British Isles (especially Scotland), and the churches in the Swiss canton of Vaud in the Piémont. His reputation as an explorer preceded him, and it saddened him that people wanted to hear him speak more of travels and adventures than of the evangelization of Africa. Coillard was honored by respected geographical societies and ranked by the press among the heroes of the day, but the missionary was more embarrassed than flattered by this adulation.

The funding that Coillard sought was secured, but all the same he was disillusioned, for French Protestantism had not unanimously supported the project of the Zambezi, finding it too ambitious, costly, and unrealistic. He returned with his wife and only one recruit, Frédéric Christol. As they had two young children, Coillard counseled them not to accompany him to the Zambezi; rather, he proposed that Christol take up a position at the station in Lesotho. Happily, another candidate joined Coillard a little later, Dorwald Jeanmairet from Switerland. A member of the Free Church of the canton of Neuchâtel, he was a watchmaker turned evangelist, who soon married Elise Coillard, François' niece.

Two Britons and around fifteen young African Christians accompanied the Coillards on this new adventure. Because organizing the expedition was more complex than they had anticipated, they did not leave Leribe until 1884. Including ox herders and all the other members of the group, there were more than thirty persons who set out. Their caravan included five wagons that were four meters in length, pulled by a dozen to eighteen oxen, followed by herds of cattle, goats, and sheep. The animals were to assure a food supply should hunting prove unsuccessful. They endured disease, hunger, attacks by local chiefs, and the revolt of some of their companions. It was one year before they reached the banks of the Zambezi River. King Lewanika granted Coillard the right to cross the river and settle in his territory in August 1885, which is considered the founding date of the Zambezi Mission. Ten years after this beginning, the mission experienced its first success.

## THE ZAMBEZI MISSION

At first Coillard worked with Dorwald and Elise Jeanmairet at Sesheke, but then he traveled three hundred kilometers farther north and upstream in order to found the station of Sefula. In 1887 more workers arrived: the Reverend Louis Jalla and his wife from the Vaud valley in Italy,[212] the Genevan doctor Henri Dardier, and a Swiss artisan. J.-F. Zorn writes, "With these new recruits, the expedition to the Zambezi came to an end, and, at the request of François Coillard, in December 1887 the com-

---

212 Three years later, his brother Adolphe would come to be with him.

mittee [of the Paris Mission] by a unanimous vote took the decisive step of officially including the Zambezi Mission in the list of the works that it was supporting."[213] With the subsequent development of the Zambezi Mission, the Paris Mission decided in 1893 to create a special commission to take charge of it. Though not an independent project, the Zambezi Mission acquired a unique status.

King Lewanika pressed Coillard to intervene with the British government to obtain the protection of her majesty's troops against the Boers and certain threatening neighboring tribes. Coillard, who was anything but a diplomat, responded at first by refusing to involve himself. Later, however, he pled the king's cause, advocating that Lewanika's realm become a British protectorate. He seems to have had a naïve confidence in the disinterested character of British politics.[214] In the end, he would reproach himself "for having sold the country to foreigners," to the detriment of its well being.

The relations between Coillard and the king were often difficult. Lewanika sometimes did his best to advance the work of the missionaries, but then one minor annoyance would be sufficient for him to overturn all that had been achieved, eliminating schools and dispensaries. Nevertheless, the king entrusted the education of his sons to the missionaries. One of these, Litia, converted, but his father quickly took him back under his influence, and he was not able to persevere in the faith. At the Pentecost of 1891, after six years of patient effort, the first baptism of a Barotse took place. The convert was a very capable young person who took the Christian name of André. Unfortunately, some time later the king was also successful in seducing him with tempting offers of taking him into his service. Occurring three months after the death of Colliard's wife, this was a great disappointment to the missionary, who had placed much hope in this first convert and had made him his assistant.

In September 1892, a Zambezi missionary conference brought together a handful of workers from three stations. They decided to establish a fourth station at the capital, Lealuyi, which was twenty kilometers from Sefula. Coillard and two Basuto evangelists took responsibility for it. In March 1894 the inauguration of the church of Lealuyi took place in the presence of the king, his numerous wives, and much of the local population. A Bible school also soon opened its doors in Lealuyi where Adolphe Jalla and his wife joined Coillard. A short time later, the missionary conference resolved to establish yet another station, the objective being to form a chain of stations through the valley of the Zambezi that would gradually be entirely entrusted

---

213 Zorn, "Missions protestantes," 461.

214 About forty years earlier, Moffat in Betchuanaland and then Casalis in Lesotho had already called for British protection against the military pressure of the Boers. But meanwhile the politics of colonization had modified the manner in which European governments envisioned interventions in Africa, a fact about which Coillard had not been sufficiently aware. In the May 1948 edition of *Foi et vie*, Louis Joubert drew this conclusion, with the benefit of more than half a century of hindsight: "If the civilized states . . . have considered it a duty for them to intervene in the rest of the world 'to watch over the preservation of indigenous populations and the amelioration of their moral and material conditions of existence' and 'to work toward the suppression of slavery . . .', it is clear that a grave accusation can be brought against them to the extent that they have transformed this benevolent role into one that advances their economies or their military preoccupations."

to African evangelists. Though a beautiful vision, the missionaries probably erred by dispersing their resources.[215]

To its credit the Church of Lesotho became a missionary-sending organization soon after its founding, but unfortunately it was not able alone to bear the burden of supporting the work in this distant field. Still it supported several missionaries who were, like all the Europeans, well-tested in their health and acquainted with grief.

The work on the Zambezi in Barotseland was finally showing some signs of progress. In the beginning of 1895, Coillard noted:

> The work has become very encouraging. About sixty young men and women have made a profession to serve the Lord and several others, men and women, are well disposed. It is the same thing in all our missionary stations. Litia, the son of the king who was lost, has returned to the good way and has returned the second wife whom he had taken. He is full of zeal that is beautiful to see. Yesterday, in the morning service, where we generally have more than 350 persons, three more have again declared for the Lord. We wait for the others. Their consciences are being stirred. As the faith replaces superstition, there are many things to redress.[216]

*François Coillard on the Zambezi at the time of an evangelism expedition along the river.*
*(Service Protestant de Mission, Paris)*

Just as the work seemed to be developing well, Coillard's health was deteriorating. Though his presence was more necessary than ever, his growing fatigue lent

---

215 The report of the August 1889 missionary conference, written while the participants were awaiting the return of Coillard and the additional reinforcements that he was bringing from Europe, states: "The fact that we are few and far removed from one another has until now been a weapon in the hand of Satan. Today our little phalanx is enlarged, the chain of our stations is composed of links less strained, and we will rejoin the struggle with more courage and ardor. God willing, this will be with greater success!" (Zorn, "Missions protestantes," 485.)

216 Edouard Favre, op. cit. (1922), 228.

weight to his arguments presented to the committee that he be allowed to return to France to care for this health and search for new candidates. Coillard, it should be noted, rose regularly at four o'clock in the morning to pray and read the Bible for two hours, and he drove himself to remain awake until late into the evening.

The old wrestler would not easily let go of his hold on life. In May 1895, he organized a reconnaissance and evangelism expedition that traveled up the Zambezi in the direction of its sources. During this six-week trip, Coillard was accompanied by several experienced Christians and catechumens. They moved from village to village where one of the members sang, the young witnessed to their faith, another preached the gospel, and still another continued on in a canoe to the next stop. They returned only when faced with massacre by a tribe hostile to foreigners.

In September 1895 Coillard suffered a serious kidney infection, and his colleagues decided that he should be immediately repatriated to Europe. He reluctantly agreed, leaving the station on a stretcher for the difficult journey.

## THE SECOND SOJOURN IN FRANCE

On May 21, 1896, Coillard embarked from the Cape bound for Europe. As he approached the coast of France, he felt a pang of anguish, remembering the triumphant welcome that had been prepared for him at the time of his first return. He wrote of disembarking from the train in Paris on June 18:

> Arrived in Paris at seven o'clock in the evening. A true ovation! I was entirely stunned. I had believed that I was held in contempt and that I had been mistaken for another. I was a log of wood that was passed around to hug and kiss. I thought I was dreaming. Why all these testimonies of affection? It is good proof that I am not well known.[217]

*Twenty-one wagons, 330 oxen directed by sixty ox herders: the great expedition to the Zambezi in 1899. (Service Protestant de Mission, Paris)*

217  Ibid.

Although still convalescing, he immediately began to work and became part of a committee to promote his goal of returning with a team of fifteen fully funded persons. He launched his campaign in France and in the neighboring countries. Conferences, meetings, and conversations in the midst of other activities left him no time for rest.

He was joined by Alfred Bertrand, a Genevan layman and explorer who had traveled north of the Zambezi and had been excited by the quality of the work and the dedication of the missionary team. Together, they started the Zambezians, groups that met to pray and financially support Coillard's ambitious work on the Zambezi, replacing the Paris Mission. At the time of his return to Africa, there were Zambezians in fourteen European countries. Before Coillard's death in 1904 there would be one hundred.[218] These groups were linked by a corresponding secretary in Geneva, Edouard Favre, who would also become Coillard's biographer.

On November 23, 1898, Coillard left Paris following a crowded meeting at the Oratoire. A group of friends accompanied him as far as the train station and sent him away with a warm ovation. He had not, however, obtained from the French Protestant churches all the support for which he had hoped. Nevertheless, the work of the mission was now on a solid foundation, for Coillard left Paris having secured the men he needed, notably Jacques Liénard, a minister in the Reformed Church of France whom Coillard hoped to make his successor as the head of the Zambezi work.

## THE TRAGIC RETURN EXPEDITION

During Coillard's absence, the work was carried on with several additional missionaries. Two new stations had been established, one being downstream at Livingstone, near to Victoria Falls. But tragedy struck again. Two evangelists returned to Lesotho, having lost their wives; and then Louis Jolla became a widower in his turn, having already lost three children in Africa. His wife, Marie, was only thirty-five.

Coillard returned to the Cape in the last days of 1898. His caravan assembled in Bulawayo at the railroad terminal and started out on its two-month journey on March 22, 1899. The caravan was large: twenty-one wagons, 330 oxen, and sixty ox herders. The fifteen newly arrived workers included eight from France and seven from Switzerland. In addition to Jacques Liénard mentioned above, there were four Swiss ministers and a Genevan doctor, Rodrich de Prosch. The majority came from the Free Church. One month later, while fording the Zambezi River, the youngest participant died: Marie, the nineteen-year-old wife of the Reverend Juste Bouchet. But this was only the beginning of misfortunes. In the two years that followed, six deaths and six health evacuations occurred among the fifteen newly arrived missionaries. This profoundly disrupted the work as some recent, hard-won victories had to be set aside, and several stations remained temporarily unoccupied.

The disturbing news of the successive deaths of young people was taken even harder in France. The mission committee was accused of imprudence, and accusations

---

218 In 1980 the author knew three people in Geneva who were still meeting as members of a Zambezian group.

against it filled the Protestant press.[219] This reaction was symptomatic of the new times. At the threshold of the twentieth century, sensibilities had changed and were evolving in a new direction, for the conditions of life were better and the mortality rate of the young was much lower than in the past. Consequently, large numbers of dead among those in the bloom of youth was no longer accepted as inevitable. In sending young missionaries into the field, the mission accommodated itself to the new reality. Candidates were given medical examinations, and the health of the missionaries was taken into consideration. Better provisions for food were made. Hygiene was improved through the construction of more salubrious houses. Terms were limited to six years, and a period for acclimation was provided, as was a period for convalescence in cases of illness. And henceforth the sending out of young, recently married women was avoided so that the lives of firstborns would not be at risk.

## THE VETERAN'S LAST BATTLE

This was not the only difficulty that Coillard had to confront during his last years on the Zambezi. Some Basuto evangelists who worked for the mission began to advocate for autonomy. One of these was Willie Mokalapa, who worked closely with Coillard and was his spiritual son. Mokalapa led the movement to found an Ethiopian church on the Zambezi—Ethiopian connoting an entirely African institution without any relationship to the mission. According to the analysis of the missiologist Maurice Leenhardt, the success of Ethiopianism in 1902 was due mostly to the lack of flexibility and pedagogic skill on the part of certain missionaries, and to a paternalism that too often relegated African ministers to a subordinate status that deprived them of authority over their own people.[220]

Colliard, perhaps because of his past as a pioneer or because of an inability to adapt to a new age, did not know how to respond to his discontented African brothers. For example, he refused to allow himself to be called "brother." He insisted that he was a "father" and his African colleagues "sons." Whatever his spiritual status, Coillard was free of all the prejudices that then characterized the European attitude towards Africans.

There were difficulties at the Lealuyi Bible School, and the evangelists began to go on strike. After many discussions, the missionaries felt constrained to accept that the "Ethiopians" would undertake the evangelization of regions that were heretofore unreached, but they opposed the founding of churches where the mission had already

---

219 For a typical article at the time opposed to the apparent recklessness in missions see Zorn, "Missions protestantes," 489. It is striking to note the contrast between this reasoning and that of Coillard's regarding the same tragedy, which suggests a very different spiritual understanding: "In the lugubrious light of the events of these last dozen months, our expedition of seventeen could only appear to some of our friends as a foolhardy enterprise, or even a grave mistake. . . . For my part, the more I reflect on this, the more my conviction is affirmed that it is God who has inspired us to undertake this courageous enterprise and that it is he who has led us. We can without ostentation testify that this is a work of prayer, love, and faith. . . . One year has hardly passed since our arrival at the Zambezi, and already our ranks are lightened. Why? What good has this loss done? Let us leave it to God to respond." Cited by Favre, op. cit. (1922), 275.

220 Maurice Leenhardt, *Le mouvement éthiopien au sud de l'Afrique de 1896 à 1899* (Cahors, France: Couesiant, 1902).

been established. Mokalapa, after making a surprising about-face, eventually bowed to pressure from Coillard with the result that the Ethiopian Church moved several dozen kilometers to the north. The movement, however, was short lived. Not long before his death Coillard employed his personal authority to restore calm among the evangelists and avoid a schism. This was his last battle.

In May 1904 Coillard was beset by a recurring fever. When he seemed to be recovering, his tired body finally succumbed to internal hemorrhaging. He died in his seventieth year on May 27. His friends buried him beside Christiana under a large sefula tree where the couple had often prayed together for the Barotse. His death was widely reported in the press, more so in France than in Britain or South Africa. *Le Figaro*'s headline paid special tribute to Coillard: "The death of the French Livingstone."

The accomplishments of the mission begun by Coillard were real if not spectacular. Twenty years after the foundation of the mission, the number of those baptized was still small. But eight stations had been established along the upper Zambezi, and the worship services were well attended. The mission schools were educating hundreds of children from the primary to the secondary levels, as well as preparing teachers. The medical work was well under way. And under the influence of a prime minister trained by the missionaries, the country was experiencing appreciable transformation.

When asked for a detailed report on the country by the committee of the Paris Mission, the missionary conference of 1906 described the remarkable changes that had occurred: "Since the mission was established there has been no civil war, and the last raid was in 1892; the tributes paid in children and the raids on children are set in the course of extinction; the slaves are emancipated. The status of women has improved, and young girls who have been violated have the right of recourse to the king. Poisoning and murder are severely punished, but the death penalty has been abolished. People feel secure, Africans as well as Europeans."[221]

With Coillard no longer on the scene, the Zambezi Mission was deprived of its emblematic figure. But the mission had already learned how to function without him during his long sojourns in Europe and times of illness. Adolphe Jalla became president of the missionary conference in September 1904. Between 1901 and 1906, twenty-five new missionaries were sent, three being ministers. A teacher, a deacon, and an artisan were French, and the others were Swiss or Italian. During these five years there was only one death among the missionaries, that of François Coillard himself.

In the first ten years of the mission, twenty-three missionaries came to the Zambezi. Few among them, it is true, stayed very long, but many later followed, the majority coming from Switzerland where the Zambezians were still very active.[222] Though the influence that Christianity had on the social aspects of the society was manifest, for various reasons the growth of the church continued to be slow. One reason for this was an excessively severe ecclesiastical discipline. This is evident in the

---

221 See Zorn, "Missions protestantes," 505.
222 In the twentieth century there were about a hundred.

small number of people accepted for baptism, hardly more than two hundred after thirty years. Another factor was the use of the Sessouto language of Lesotho, which was very different from the dialects in Barotseland and was only easily understood by the educated. Also, too much emphasis was placed on the work of the mission stations rather than on the evangelization of the villages where the bulk of the population lived. In short, a form of Christianity developed that was too demanding and insufficiently integrated into the social fabric of the culture. Nevertheless, in the course of the twentieth century the Presbyterian Church enjoyed an important role in the life of the country that was first named Northern Rhodesia and later Zambia.

*Part Two*

# WEST AFRICA

# CHAPTER 14

# *Dramatic Beginnings*

## THE FIRST AFRICAN MINISTERS

To understand the beginnings of the Christian movement in West Africa we must first take a brief look at several attempts at establishing it that preceded the period of modern missions presented in this work but that prepared the field for it (see map 10, p. 498).

The first African Protestant minister was originally of the Gold Coast (Ghana). Born around 1715, he was purchased as a young boy by a Dutch merchant ship captain, who gave him to a compatriot at El Mina, a Dutch fort on the west coast of Africa. The child was called Jacob Capitein by his first master. When he was eleven years old, he was brought to the Low Countries to be educated. Capitein was admitted to the Theological Seminary of Leiden in 1737. Five years later he left with a diploma, having won great success for presenting a thesis in Latin on the biblical justification of slavery.

Ordained a minister in the Reformed Church of the Low Countries, Capitein was sent to El Mina in 1742 by the consistory of Amsterdam. At first he sought to win over his compatriots, translating the creed for them into the Fanti language, which was printed in 1744. But it was very difficult for either the Africans or the Dutch to accept him, and in 1747 he died prematurely and alone at the age of about thirty. The ministry of the first African minister was therefore brief and, one might say, a gilded deception.

The trading companies of the Protestant European nations employed chaplains to minister to the sailors, staff, and administrators of their far-flung trading posts. Few among these were concerned with indigenous populations. Among the exceptions was an Anglican minister in West Africa, the Reverend Thomas Thompson, who formerly served as a missionary among New England slaves for the Society for the Propagation of the gospel (SPG). Sent in 1751 to Cape Coast, on the Gold Coast, he did not limit his chaplaincy to work among Europeans; rather, he developed a relationship with a local Fanti chief in order to learn the language. When forced to return to Britain for reasons of health, he brought with him three young, serious, and gifted Africans with the intention of giving them an education. One of them, Philippe Kwaku (also called Quaque), converted to Christianity. Ordained to the pastorate at the end of his studies, he returned to his native country in about 1765 and pursued a ministry that lasted fifty years, concluding only with his death in 1816. He founded a school that survived him and, in 1834, was employed by the Methodist Mission.

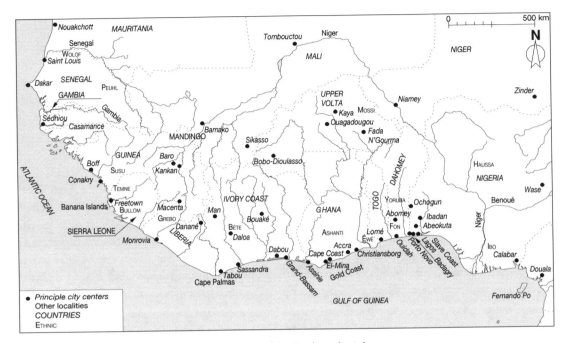

*Map 10: West Africa in the colonial era*

Hence there were two attempts made by Africans in the eighteenth century to establish Christianity on the west coast of Africa. But Capitein's and Kwaku's attempts to widen the ministry of the church beyond the colonial trading posts achieved minimal results.

## THE FIRST MORAVIAN MISSIONARIES ON THE GOLD COAST

The Moravians entered the mission field of the Gold Coast in 1737. It was generally called the Coast of Guinea and sometimes, because of the prevalence of the slave trade, was also called the Slave Coast. This most intensive of all the Moravian missionary efforts began when Count Nicolas von Zinzendorf was in Copenhagen and encountered a biracial person by the name of Jacob Protten. He was the son of an African princess and a Danish soldier posted at Christiansburg, a Danish trading post in West Africa. Protten was invited by Zinzendorf to join the community of Herrnhut, the cradle of Moravian missions located in Germany. He converted and agreed to prepare a missionary team to settle in the Gold Coast.

He left in 1737 with Brother Huckhoff, who fell sick and succumbed three months after his arrival. For linguistic reasons, Protten chose to live in Accra, his village of origin, where he became a tutor to the children of a local personage. He returned to

Europe in 1741, and it was not until a dozen years later, in 1757, that he would voyage again to Africa, this time as a chaplain to the Danish in Christiansburg. He opened a grammar school for biracial children and, with the aid of his wife, also a biracial person, he directed the school and translated Bible texts. As these efforts seemed to meet with success, the Danish authorized the Moravian Brethren to extend Protten's work to Nigo, near to the Danish trading post of Driesdenburg. In 1768 five Moravians took advantage of this opportunity, but Protten and two others died there after only a few months. The other two did not survive much longer. Four more Brethren, led by a man named Westmann, took up the challenge at the beginning of 1770. In July of the same year, Westmann abandoned the effort when all three of his companions died in less than six months. Five days later he too succumbed on the return ship. Having left eleven graves and not a single survivor, the Moravians abandoned the effort.

Apart from Kwaku, there were no Protestant missionaries along the West African coast at the beginning of the nineteenth century when the recently founded missionary societies attempted to establish themselves there. Nevertheless, Protten and the Moravians had sown the first seeds and, fifty years after the departure of Westmann, a number of Africans were again frequenting Danish worship services at Christianborg. Later on in 1828, additional missionaries were sent by the Basel Mission; hence in 1838 the Methodist Thomas Birch Freeman would benefit from the efforts of an earlier generation.

## FREED SLAVES IN SIERRA LEONE

In 1772 philanthropists obtained the abolition of slavery in Britain. In a single stroke, fifteen thousand Africans became free. But what was to be done with them? The first attempt to return the freed slaves to their continent of origin was made in 1787. With an astonishingly naïve idealism, the Antislavery Society, which had just been founded, organized an expedition of "repatriation" to Sierra Leone. They established Freetown, a colony of 350 freedmen and an additional sixty white women, petty criminals who had been forcibly married while intoxicated.

After a few years, only 130 survived in the colony. The failure of the Freetown colony had various causes: lack of preparation and organization, absence of social cohesion (the freed originating from very different African regions), and the hostility of the local tribal chiefs. The latter were Temne and Bullom, accomplices in the slave trade. The Society for the Propagation of the Gospel (SPG) sent a minister to accompany the colonists, but he returned after a year for reasons of health. In 1792, five years later, about 1,200 new arrivals came from America. These were former slaves who had been freed for having aided the British in the American War of Independence, in which the British had promised them liberty.

At the outset the philanthropists who started Freetown had no missionary aim. There were a good number of Christians of various denominations among the freed Africans, and there were also some "crude but powerful" preachers among them, according to a witness of the period who was concerned about the spiritual life of the colony. The British chaplain Melville Horne arrived with the contingent of 1792. He was concerned about the fate of the indigenous population, whom he sought to reach. His letters to British ministers helped to encourage the founding of the London Missionary Society in 1795.

## FAILURE OF THE FIRST ARRIVALS

When the newly created mission societies in Britain interested themselves in Africa, they thought first of Sierra Leone where they had preexisting contacts with the colony. Consistent with Horne's view, the first expeditions were directed towards the indigenous population rather than the freed colonists. Six missionaries arrived in 1797, two from the London Missionary Society (LMS) and four from the Scottish Presbyterian missionary societies of Edinburgh and Glasgow.

The two missionaries from Edinburgh, Greig and Burton, settled in the interior of the land, about a hundred kilometers north of Freetown. This was the region of present-day Guinea where the Soussou tribe lived on the Rio Pongas. They began a school there, but their work was interrupted when they returned to Freetown during the rainy season. Their work was also hindered by health problems and conflicts between tribal chiefs. The following year, Burton declined to continue in conditions that were so difficult. Greig returned alone, made progress in his study of the local language, and began to establish friendly relations with the population. As the work advanced and a small group of regular listeners was forming, Greig was murdered by a Peuhl thief whom he had taken into his home. Burton, who had remained as a chaplain in Freetown, was soon repatriated to Europe for reasons of health.

The fate of the two Glasgow missionaries was even more tragic. Having established themselves on Banana Island, they soon died one after the other. They were succeeded in 1798 by two others from the same mission, but one lost his faith and deserted while the other became a slave trader. As the LMS had before, the Scottish missions withdrew from the region.

## THE ANGLICAN MISSION PERSEVERES DESPITE DIFFICULTIES

The Church Missionary Society (CMS) took up the task, with more tenacity and better results. Due to the difficulty of finding good candidates in Britain, it appealed to the missionary institute of Berlin.[223] German candidates were accepted, and they succeeded in opening several schools in Sierra Leone. Between 1804 and 1816, the CMS sent out twenty-six missionaries. They emphasized education rather than direct evangelization. Though a slow means, it seemed to them the surest way to introduce the good news to the hearts of the young. The secretary of the mission, however, did not cease to encourage the missionaries also to preach, as this extract from a letter to them shows:

> The schools are the foundation, but this foundation is made with
> the intent of further construction. The time has come. Now the

---

223 Founded in 1800 by Jänike, it was an independent school in the Pietist tradition that became the cradle of the future Missionary Society of Berlin, created in 1824.

indigenous people know you to be honest. Visit them and preach Christ! . . . It is our first and greatest work. Everything else must be subordinated to it. Go regularly in the dry season to the homes of the Soussou and Bullom. Bring the children of your schools with you if you judge it useful. Have them sing a hymn in Soussou or Bullom. Proclaim the gospel and God will bless you![224]

The results were minimal due to disease and the frightful mortality rate of the Europeans. Few among them had the time to learn the language and to see a church born of their labor.

William Johnson, a Lutheran from Hanover who was sent to Sierra Leone by the CMS, had a profound effect on the work though he spent only a brief time there. With his compatriot, During, he worked in the freedmen's colony of Regents Town, about twenty kilometers from the coast. His description of the state of the colony upon his arrival gives evidence of the struggle of these people:

> Having originated from twenty-two different tribes, all of them having been freed from the chains of slavery, not having any means to communicate with each other but a few phrases of English that they remembered, they lived in continual hostility. Striped even of the idea that marriage was a bond, they gave themselves over to shameful debaucheries. Crammed into miserable huts, they contracted various diseases. Every day several died; whereas, during the first years, there were only six births in a population of 1,100 people. Deplorable superstition reigned in their midst. They raised up numerous chapels to honor the evil spirit. It was not possible to persuade them to devote themselves to farming the fields, and if some of them began to work the land, they soon gave it up because their companions would spoil the ground they had sown. Most of them were wandering in the woods, living on roots, and emerging only to engage in pillage.[225]

Following Johnson's arrival, a revival soon broke out from the prayer and hymn meetings held in his hut. The Spirit acted with power: not only were hearts changed, but the city itself was transformed. Even the official reports of government bureaucrats employed the term "miracle" to describe what had happened in the colony of Regents. In place of ruin and rapine, a society of mutual help appeared. In 1819 after only three years, the church had 258 communicants. The revival was slowly extended to other colonies, especially Gloucester where During was working. Sadly, Johnson and During, who had arrived together in 1816, were both evacuated one after other in 1823, having contracted yellow fever. Both succumbed on shipboard, homeward bound to Europe.

The revival that took place in Regents was no flash in the pan. Several "Johnson men," as the converts of the revival were called, were soon engaged in the educational

---

224 Jean Faure, *Histoire des missions et églises protestantes en Afrique occidentale des origines à 1844* (Yaoundé: CLE, 1978), 42–43.
225 Ibid., 52.

work in Sierra Leone. One of them, James Johnson, became a minister in Freetown. He also participated in meetings held in Britain in 1873 and eventually became responsible for one of the largest Anglican parishes of Lagos.

In 1827 Charles Haensel, another CMS missionary, became the first director of the famous college of Fourah Bay in Freetown. The pride of the CMS, the college played a decisive part in the birth of an indigenous church in West Africa. Over the years, it provided excellent education and became a veritable nursery of servants of God. The course of instruction included: Hebrew and Greek (due to the pressing need for Bible translators), exegesis and dogmatics, and Islam and African civilizations. Among the six students of the first class, a freedman from Yoruba, Samuel Crowther, would become the most prominent (his career will be examined below; see p. 508). Haensel benefited from collaboration with his colleague J. T. Schön, who had been a student like him at the Institute of the Basel Mission, in Blumhardt. Thanks to his robust constitution, Schön stayed for twenty years in West Africa, an exceptionally long period for a European expatriate in West Africa during the first half of the nineteenth century.

## THE WESLEYAN METHODIST MISSION

The freedmen of Sierra Leone included a number of Methodists, and one of the African ministers among them made an appeal for missionaries to the Wesleyan Methodist Missionary Society (WMMS). The society responded in the very year of its founding, 1811, by sending out its first missionary team, composed of three teachers and a pastor. Methodists and Anglicans collaborated harmoniously in Sierra Leone. The Methodist mission prioritized schools, and by 1837 it was teaching more than 1,100 students. Two among these students became ordained ministers in 1840. One, Charles Knight, ministered for thirty-five years in Sierra Leone.

By 1821 the Methodist mission had already extended its work into Gambia, a narrow country located on the west coast of the continent along the river of the same name. Britain had recently adopted it as one of its colonies. Nineteenth-century missionaries typically sought to establish mission stations along rivers, a strategy that appeared to be the best way of penetrating into the interior of the continent. After several years, the work in Gambia was reexamined by the mission committee. In 1842 the missionary W. F. Fox pleaded for an expansion of the work:

> I maintain that the Gambia River is one of the largest, most direct and surest ways into the interior . . . I am sure that if you send us sufficient means in a very short while you will have a missionary station at the great center of Africa: Timbuktu.

The principal obstacle to evangelization in this region was the presence of the Islamic populations of Peuhl, Mandingue, and Wolof. The missionaries achieved tangible results only on the islands of the river. Their work was greatly aided by two zealous Africans: John Cupidon, an escaped slave; and Pierre Salah, a slave redeemed by the mission from a Muslim chief. They served over a period of twenty years and came to work closely with the missionaries who were struggling to subsist in this difficult region. It was in Gambia in 1836 that the Methodist missionary McBraid produced the first translation of the Bible in West Africa: the Gospel of Matthew in Mandingue. In 1837 after twenty-six years of effort, the Methodist churches included about 1,300 members in Sierra Leone, and a little more than five hundred on two islands in the Gambia River.

## THE WEST AFRICA MISSION: HIGH PRICE, MEAGER RESULTS

In evaluating this first period of mission history in West Africa, one staggers at the high mortality rate. Between 1815 and 1840, the CMS in Sierra Leone lost 129 missionaries. The other missions that ventured into these countries also had to accept hard sacrifices. According to Jean Faure, more than two hundred missionaries died there before 1840. On average, the life expectancy of a missionary living in this period on the west coast of Africa was about two and a half to three years. Rare were those who lived long enough on this earth to enjoy seeing the fruit of their obedience. Most of those who went were very young: it is estimated that at the time of departure their average age was twenty-two or twenty-three years old.

During the first half of the nineteenth century, it was only South Africa—described in the preceding chapter—and the coastal region of West Africa to which Protestant missions had access. And even by 1840, the great majority of the ten thousand African Christians were those who had emerged from slavery and had been repatriated from Europe or America. According to Jean Faure:

> It is estimated that scarcely more than a few hundred Africans had left their traditional faith while living amidst their tribe . . . The schools included perhaps nine thousand children, of which six thousand were attending Anglican churches in Sierra Leone.[226]

What were the causes for so much failure, and at such a high price? A third of the missionaries succumbed within a few weeks or at most several months of their arrival. Most died through ignorance of the dangers present in the warm, humid climate of the coastal regions: sunstroke, yellow fever, malaria, dysentery, nutritional deficiency, and deplorable living conditions. Vaccines and quinine were not yet a part of the medical techniques available.[227] Moreover, instead of remaining close to one another in order to provide mutual aid and encouragement, the missionaries dispersed themselves as widely as possible. They were no doubt moved by the urgency of evangelizing as many as possible in the region. Many, however, discouraged and lonely, returned prematurely to Europe. The mission societies also share in the blame. In their haste and zeal to obey the Great Commission, candidates were sometimes accepted without undergoing serious medical exams, meeting sufficient criteria for selection, or receiving individual training. And once they arrived, they were not met by missionaries from whose experience they might have benefited. One can easily imagine their helpless confusion and the mistakes they made, one after another. In

---

226 Ibid., 81–82.

227 It was only after 1860 that quinine was available to treat malaria, and this resulted in the downward trend of mortality that occurred from this time forward.

these difficult conditions, the results were naturally meager. "Africa is a fortress," said one missionary, "and to be conquered, the moat must be filled up with the bodies of the missionaries who have laid down their lives that the gospel might be proclaimed here." A comparable rate of missionary mortality in our day would produce an outcry in the press and even the churches—and few candidates would press forward to offer their services. In the last 150 years our outlook has undergone substantial change: revival zeal has waned and, in a time of ease and abundance, notions of sacrifice, courage, and laying down one's life have dropped from the evangelical vocabulary. However, to put this in historical perspective, it is necessary to remember that life expectancy in the West was then much shorter than it is today. To die young was not exceptional, and epidemics that were then quite common in Europe are today largely forgotten. Without minimizing the sacrifices of this pioneering generation, one needs to see them in context. The death of so many young people was not any less sad than it would be today, but it did appear less scandalous.

## THE CHURCH IN THE COLONIES OF THE FREED: SIERRA LEONE

The population of the colony of Freetown grew rapidly due to the repatriation of former slaves who were freed by law or liberated from intercepted slave ships. In 1807 the number of inhabitants was one thousand inhabitants, in 1814 it grew to five thousand, and in 1822 it reached fifteen thousand. From 1800 to 1840 about fifteen colonies of freedmen were established, spread out between Freetown and the Niger delta. Often these were simply enclaves organized around a trading post that had been authorized by a local sovereign. These areas were under constant threat; and under pressure from slave traders, the indigenous neighboring populations were tempted to capture the newly freed immigrants in order to sell them back into bondage.

However, despite the difficult beginnings, these colonies slowly became spiritual and socioeconomic models for others to follow. Their inhabitants benefited from religious training and showed a fiercely independent will, *vis-à-vis* Europeans as well as neighboring African princes. Some received high-level training in industry and agriculture. The CMS played a decisive role due to its schools and the teaching it provided in church settings. In 1840 it was observed:

> The church in the colony of Sierra Leone is so evolved that it can now be left to its own devices to supply its pastoral ministry . . . It is only as a cradle of indigenous missionaries and as a base for indigenous missionary operations in other countries that the colony can still be considered part of the mission field.

Beginning in 1850, Sierra Leone had a fully autonomous Anglican bishop. After a dozen years, he was able to recruit his clergy from the local population.

## THE EVANGELIZATION OF THE INDIGENOUS POPULATION OF LIBERIA

Despite its uncertain beginnings, the colony of Sierra Leone inspired American philanthropists to launch a similar project. At the beginning of the nineteenth century, the United States had a population of more than 2 million blacks, which included

280,000 freedmen. It was especially with the latter in mind that in 1816 some Americans began to envision a return of blacks to Africa. Yehudi Ashmun, a black minister, took up the direction of this enterprise. The principal colony, founded in 1824, was given the name Monrovia in honor of the then-current American President, James Monroe. The country was christened Liberia in 1827. The American government soon lost interest, and beginning in 1841, the governor of Liberia was always black.

Most of the American freedmen were Christians, but as members of competing Protestant denominations, they were sometimes antagonistic to one another. They also lacked the missionary vision to reach out to the local population. A notable exception to this was Ashmun, who published an appeal in 1825 to mission organizations to come to Liberia to undertake missionary work.

The Society of the Evangelical Missions of Basel (the Basel Mission), founded in 1815, was looking for a field of activity at that time, and Ashmun's appeal seemed to be a response to their need. The mission sent five missionaries there between 1827 and 1829. Unfortunately, Ashmun died a little after their arrival, and they encountered more hostility than support from Monrovia's churches. The other missionaries did their best to fill the gap, but being only two, Sessing and Kiessling, they were not able to maintain the work. They established a school for indigenous children in Monrovia but, deprived of resources, fell back to Sierra Leone.

The Methodist Episcopal Mission (US) took up the task next. The pioneer of this work was Melville Cox, who arrived in 1833. Near death after several months in Africa, he asked that the following epitaph be engraved on his tomb: "May a thousand missionaries perish in Africa before anyone dreams of abandoning it!" Henceforth, the mission made it a priority to send black missionaries. The best known among them is the West Indian John Seys. When he arrived at the age of thirty-six, he found a church of only two hundred members. Under his influence and that of the African minister Brown, there were many conversions, including that of several tribal chiefs. Under pressure from the governor, who was frightened by his extraordinary influence that was spreading throughout the colony of Liberia, Seys was expelled seven years later. At that time the church had more than a thousand members.

Sophronia Farrington has been called the first "Missionary Lady" in West Africa. Sent by the Methodist Episcopal Mission, she arrived in Monrovia in 1836, the first of an immense and dedicated cohort whose labor would bear abundant fruit for more than a century and a half. Farrington resided for twenty years in Liberia and was sometimes the only foreign missionary in the colony.

## THE MISSION ON THE GOLD COAST

The work of Jacob Protten and other Moravian Brethren left a mark in Christiansburg in the course of the eighteenth century. A Danish governor in 1826 made known the desire of the indigenous population for the services of Christian ministers. The Basel Mission responded two years later, but over the course of the next dozen years it lost eight missionaries. Only one of them remained long enough to complete the preparatory work necessary for a Bible translation in the Tshi language.

Phillippe Kwaku, mentioned above, opened a school in Cape Coast, on the Gold Coast, that continued after his death in 1826. Beginning in 1820, this institution was provisioned with Bibles year after year by the British and Foreign Bible Society. A Bible study group that met regularly and had been organized by the governor asked for a missionary. Beginning in 1834, the Methodist Mission (WMMS) responded by sending a series of missionaries, but each in turn was unable to endure the climate. Finally, in 1838, the WMMS sent Thomas Birch Freeman, a biracial missionary who would have a considerable impact on vast regions of West Africa. He will be considered in the following chapter.

# CHAPTER 15

# *A Self-supporting Church*

## HENRY VENN: AN AVANT-GARDE MISSIOLOGIST

The developments presented in the previous chapter in some ways anticipate the vision of the most remarkable Protestant missiologist of the nineteenth century, Henry Venn, director of the Church Missionary Society (CMS) from 1841 to 1872.[228] In 1854 he announced and began to practice his theory of the "three self" church, which holds that the goal of mission is that a church become self-governing, self-supporting, and self-propagating. In effect, the church will administrate itself, assume its own financial burdens, and evangelize its own people as well as the unreached in neighboring regions. If this principle of "three selves" is respected, then the mission will eventually "die." Hence, Venn spoke of the euthanasia of the mission, of the need of mission organizations to accept that they must cease to exist when a church has been born. Only in this way can new churches grow and develop as they should, taking the gospel where it has not yet been preached.

It would be more than a century before this principle was widely accepted and ready for application—and this altered everything. The emergence of an autonomous church does not imply a rupture in its relations with the mission but, rather, a modification of the relationship. Henceforth the two would cooperate as partner churches, the missionary-sending church and the one receiving missionaries.

Venn's vision highlighted the dynamic character of the mission, which is always called to advance into new territories without becoming fixed there, and to build up newly founded churches so that they can continue the work the mission started. Venn summarized his thoughts in the last "instructions" that he gave to missionaries, which in hindsight seem prophetic:

1. Study the character of the people to whom you are sent and show great respect for their national particularities.
2. These racial particularities will probably grow as the mission progresses.

---

228 See M. Spindler, "Naître et grandir en église: La pensée d'Henry Venn," in René Luneau, ed., *Naître et grandir en église: Le role des autochtones dans la première inculturaton du christianisme hors d'Europe* (Lyon, France: Université Jean Moulin, 1987), 103–14.

3. Work to organize an indigenous church, one truly integrated into the nation.
4. This indigenous church will eventually reject denominational distinctions introduced by the various foreign missionary societies. In effect, our denominations—Methodist, Baptist, Anglican, etc.—come from the history of the European church and do not concern Africa.
5. The role of the missionary is outside the indigenous church. He must be willing to work within clear boundaries, never imposing his ideas and Western lifestyle.[229]

Venn hoped for a church that would remain within the Anglican communion but whose indigenous elements would predominate. Hence, it would have indigenous bishops, clergy, synods, disciplines, and liturgies.

This would not be an easy theory to implement. In 1861 the church in Sierra Leone was declared independent and the responsibility for the ministry was put into the hands of Africans. The local church also took over the institute of Fourah Bay, which became an exemplary mission school whose importance has already been underscored. It was Venn who pleaded that Samuel Ajayi Crowther receive episcopal ordination, and, hence, in 1864 he became the first African to be an Anglican bishop.

*Samuel Ajayi Crowther (1809–1892), the great African missionary of the nineteenth century, pioneer of the Niger basin.*

---

229 Jeanne Decorvet, *Samuel Ajayi Crowther: Un père de l'église en Afrique noire,* (Lavigny: Les Groupes Missionnaires, 1992), 160–61.

## SAMUEL AJAYI CROWTHER

The pioneers remembered in the history of missions are usually Westerners. Yet, rare were the European pioneers who enjoyed a long career in West Africa. Most soon died or, due to poor health, had to be repatriated before being able to accomplish much. The next several pages will be devoted to the lives of two African missionaries, for mission has never been exclusively Western. Moreover, it is important that the African church know that among its "Founding Fathers" are to be found indigenous leaders as remarkable as Samuel Crowther and Thomas Freeman.

Samuel Ajayi Crowther[230] (ca. 1809–1892) was born on the Gold Coast in the city of Ochogun, which lay in the forest and several days march from the coast. It had a population of twelve thousand inhabitants made up of the Yoruba people. In 1822 when Crowther was about twelve years old, he was captured in a raid, handed over to Portuguese slave traders, and put on a ship bound for America. The British Royal Navy, then patrolling the waters off the African coast to enforce the abolition of the slave trade, intercepted the Portuguese ship. The freed slaves were returned to the coast, while the several small children and adolescents found on board were taken to Freetown and given to British missionaries to look after. Crowther was placed with the Davey family, and he was educated and taught the gospel. In a letter written in 1841 he described his conversion:

> About three years after being freed from the slavery of men, I discovered that another and more terrible type of slavery exists, the slavery of sin and Satan. I cried to the Lord to open my heart . . . and, as was my desire, I was received into the visible church of Christ in this land to fight valiantly under his banner against spiritual enemies: the world, the flesh and the Devil.[231]

At the time of his baptism, Crowther received the Christian name of Samuel and the family name of one of the members of the committee of the London Missionary Society, Crowther. He became a teacher and was later sent to study theology in Britain. When he returned to Freetown many years later, he continued his education at the Institute of Fourah Bay, which had just been opened. The high mortality rate of European missionaries led to the decision to open the college, which would train Africans in an African environment and for the African church. Crowther was a member of the first class of students. One of his teachers said of him: "This is a boy well suited to study, much more than the others I have so far encountered, and he has real piety. He has good character, is hungry for knowledge, and possesses much energy for work."

At the conclusion of his studies Crowther became a professor at Fourah Bay. In 1829 or 1830 he married Susan Aseno, who was also a freed Yoruba slave. She supported her husband well during the fifty years of their common ministry, and their six children would in their turn also come to serve the gospel.

---

230 Most of the information about Samuel Ajayi Crowther is taken from the biography written by Jeanne Decorvet. See the preceding note.

231 J. Decorvet, op. cit., 37–38.

In 1841 Crowther was asked to participate in an exploratory expedition of the Niger basin. The purpose was twofold: to replace the slave trade with normal commercial trade on the river, and to open a way into the interior in order to share the gospel.[232] To these ends, the party surveyed the navigable branches of the river and sought to find places to introduce model farms along the riverbank as a way of promoting economic and agricultural development. They also sought ideal locations to place missionary bases, where the church might be planted and education provided for the population.

This first expedition was transported by three boats imported from Britain and manned by European crews. The party consisted of the missionaries Crowther and James Frederick Schön, as well as doctors, naturalists, geographers, sailors, farmers, volunteers, and a dozen freedmen who could speak the language of the local people to be encountered. The adventure continued for nearly four months and cost the lives of forty-one people, a third of the group. The mission directors responded expediently:

> Following the devastating results of the Niger expedition, the committee desires to emphasize the training of African refugees in Sierra Leone so that they can teach their own people and reduce to writing the numerous dialects of the people who border the river with a view to creating the translations indispensable to missionary work.

Despite the terrible losses of the expedition, it performed the useful service of showing that the Niger River was navigable up to several hundred kilometers into the interior, and that the local populations were friendly and desired to be instructed. There were a large number of people from this region living in Freetown, which suggests that sending native pastors and teachers into the region seemed a good response to the situation. With this plan in mind, in 1843 the mission directors sent Crowther to Britain so that he could be ordained there. During the following decade, about twenty more Africans were ordained, forming an African missionary team.

In 1846 Crowther, Henry Townsend, and Charles Andrew Gollmer traveled to the Yoruba country to begin their missionary work. This was Crowther's native land, which was closer to Freetown than the Niger basin. He worked for a dozen years in the city of Abeokuta, since it was from here that freed Yoruba Christians from Freetown had appealed to the CMS and the Methodist Mission for help. In 1842 the Methodists had sent the biracial minister Thomas Birch Freeman (see p. 514). The CMS came later, but its missionaries would stay longer—working with Crowther and Townsend.

At Abeokut, Crowther had the emotional experience of finding his mother, from whom he had been separated and without news since being captured as a child twenty-five years earlier. She had been carried away in slavery at the same time as

---

232 A dozen years later, these same objectives were also David Livingstone's as he explored South and Central Africa.

he, but her daughters had been able to redeem her. Crowther later recounted this poignant moment:

> This is today's text: You are to care for the orphan! Never have I felt the power of this text like today, when I must report that my mother, from whom I had been brutally separated for twenty-five years, came to find me with my brother. When she saw me, she began to tremble. She could not believe her eyes, and we embraced and looked at one another in silence, so great was our surprise: large tears were running down her emaciated cheeks . . . She was trembling while holding my hand and was calling me those famil-iar names that were formerly used for me by my grandmother, dead in slavery. I remember it well! We could not say anything significant but remained silent while sitting. From time to time, we threw each other looks full of affection, which oppression and violence had so long forbidden![233]

When it became clear to his mother that he had dedicated his life to the service of the one true God, she revealed an astonishing fact to him. At the moment of his birth, the soothsayer in their village had explicitly declared that he was not destined to serve any of the inferior gods, but the very high God, the Creator himself. Now Crowther's mother would be a part of his first group of catechumens and be baptized by him in 1848. For this occasion, Crowther translated the Anglican liturgy for the baptismal rite into Yoruba.

The city of Abeokuta was divided in various sections in which members of the different Yoruba tribes lived. They had been organized in this way by the founder of the city, chief Shodeke, to protect against slave raids. Chapels and schools were constructed in the different sections. Susan Crowther even took the initiative of forming a school for girls—something entirely new in this period. After three years, the churches claimed eighty communicants and two hundred catechumens. An even larger number had ceased to frequent the pagan worship services but did not yet dare to declare themselves openly to be Christians. The opposition of the priests and sorcerers of the local divinities was virulent. Some Christians were tortured, being whipped for days, but refused to deny their faith.

In 1851 Crowther was invited to come to Britain to plead the cause of the Niger mission, a costly enterprise that was encountering growing political opposition. He held meetings in numerous churches and at Cambridge University, where he ad-dressed a moving missionary appeal to the students. He was even able to present his case to Queen Victoria herself.

Chapels and schools were not the only accomplishments of this young church. The conditions of life improved for the inhabitants due to the introduction of medical care, the extraction of palm oil, and the cultivation of cotton. The missionaries also intervened in intertribal conflicts. Crowther and Townsend, for example, managed to stop a bloody confrontation between the Yoruba and the Adu by setting up their tent

---

233 J. Decorvet, op. cit., 85–86.

between opposing troops. In 1851 the Abeokuta combatants routed the formidable army of the Dahomeens—ten thousand male and six thousand female warriors. The entire population recognized the intervention of God. Following this deliverance, the missionaries brought all their moral authority to bear to prevent the massacre of the numerous Dahomeen prisoners.

Crowther tirelessly devoted himself to the translation of the Bible in Yoruba: the Gospel of Luke, the Acts of the Apostles, the Epistle to the Romans, a catechism, and the Prayer Book were printed in Britain. The complete New Testament appeared in 1865, and the entire Bible was completed in 1880.

In 1853 Crowther was asked to direct expeditions of reconnaissance and evangelization on the Niger River, a project that had been abandoned since the tragic events of 1841. Soon churches were built along this river way. In 1857 Crowther organized the Mission of the Niger. Leaving Abeokuta, he established his base on the coast at Lagos. The reach of his mission included the Niger basin and Benoue, and even encroached on some entirely Islamic regions. As an African, Crowther enjoyed easy access to tribal dignitaries, who showed him much respect. Even Muslim chiefs were favorable to him, impressed by his knowledge of Arabic and the Qu'ran. He spoke at length not only to great crowds of listeners assembled in marketplaces but also under the verandas of chiefs, some of whom took up the cause of the gospel. Many chapels and schools were erected due to his ministry.

Since the Niger basin is two thousand kilometers from Sierra Leone, the development of a church there required the establishment of a new diocese. Henry Venn, the director of the CMS, did not hesitate for an instant. He recognized that the diocese would need an African bishop and that his friend the Reverend Crowther was entirely fit for the position. Consequently, it was not in his own native country of Yoruba, but among the Lbo of the Niger basin, that this first African bishop exercised authority. On June 29, 1864, in Canterbury Cathedral, Crowther was consecrated a bishop in the Anglican Church. Perhaps the person in the audience most moved by the ceremony was the elderly Admiral Henry John Leeke. Forty-two years earlier, he had commanded the warship that had intercepted the Portuguese slave ship that was carrying the young Ajayi. At the same time, Crowther also received an honorary doctorate from Oxford University in recognition of his work of exploration and linguistics.

Crowther quickly returned to Africa and threw himself into his new work, crisscrossing his immense diocese, and establishing new mission stations. He also ordained evangelists and pastors, who were generally recruited at Fourah Bay, counseling and encouraging them during his regular visits. In 1865 he founded the Mission of the Niger Delta, and in 1870 he participated in the ordination ceremony of his youngest son, Dandelson, who would soon become the director of the mission.

During all these years, Bishop Crowther deepened his knowledge of local languages and customs, seeking to transform the old and rich African civilizations of Nigeria without destroying them. His directions to African ministers have a timeless quality:

Speak to the people with simplicity so that they can understand you. Avoid debates with Muslims or criticizing pagans; on the contrary, show sympathy and understanding to your listeners, whoever they be. We are not sent to censure, but to reveal the truth of the gospel in its fullness . . .

Respect the customs, laws, and traditions of your listeners. The old delight in spending the evening around the fire telling fables, stories, and proverbs. They love to pose riddles. All this is part of the people's education and develops their intelligence. Their proverbs are full of wisdom. Do not discourage songs, even if they are of pagan origin. Rather, correct, improve, and enrich them.

No one was better suited than Crowther to apply Venn's missiological principles since he had the discernment of a man who knew the culture from the inside.

Despite many years of outstanding service, Crowther's life did not end well. As the condescending colonial attitude of Europeans towards Africans became increasingly apparent, missionaries often became complicit in the prejudice of their era. Following the death of Henry Venn in 1873, things began to change. "New missionaries," imbued with a sense of their superiority and effectiveness, began to accuse an aging Bishop Crowther of laxness, reproaching him for too easily allowing the reintegration of repentant Christians, pastors among them, who had temporarily fallen back into pagan practices. Lacking confidence in his discernment, they attacked him for allowing the continuance of African customs that, in their judgment, were incompatible with the gospel.

*Bishop Crowther towards the end of his life, worn down from being the target of unjust criticism. (Photo: Oikoumene)*

In the 1890s a group of missionaries emerged, for the most part, from the Cambridge Revival. They established themselves in the region to the south of the Sudan, which was under the authority of Crowther. They were "young, capable, zealous, impetuous, but lacking in love." From their perspective, there was an urgent need to uproot iniquitous individuals and remove them from all influence in this society.

Crowther and his friends, for their part, thought that as the Christian community slowly became larger and increasingly mature, it would integrate itself harmoniously into the local setting. They sought to build bridges, to win the confidence of the population, to create a climate of reciprocal respect with the chiefs, whether they were pagan or Muslim. The two approaches were incompatible. L. Joubert writes:

At the time of his death, this good man, respected by all and anxious to live up to the confidence that had been placed in him, was faced with a plan of retribution and censure aimed at his African colaborers. But this plan was developed by the whites who, henceforth, were alone considered qualified to exercise authority in the young Church of the Niger.[234]

---

234 L. Joubert, *Journal des missions evangéliques* (Paris, 1976/1), 31.

Humble and peaceful, Crowther accepted a British missionary as a cobishop. Before censure and criticism, this bishop of more than eighty years declared: "If I am incompetent, I am ready to leave the mission to others and go as a pioneer to open new territories." Nevertheless, out of regard for his colleagues in the end he resigned, while young missionaries claimed the right to remove from office African pastors ordained by him and who had been active in the church for more than thirty years. At the news of his resignation, murmurs of revolt could be heard throughout the Niger basin. His colleagues felt that his resignation was simply a thinly veiled dismissal. His son Dandelson—at the head of the work in the Niger Delta where the church was flourishing—entreated him to resist the pressure of the Europeans. Schism seemed inevitable.

Among the Methodists and Baptists of the neighboring regions, the same problem appeared with equal intensity. The new generation of ministers put pressure on Crowther until he accepted the establishment of an independent and interdenominational African church. This was a matter of conscience for the old bishop who continued to be loyal to the mission that had entrusted him with the responsibility of the Niger basin. Finally, in faithfulness to the missiological principles defended by Henry Venn, he agreed to the birth of an independent church of the Delta. Broken by this trial, in the winter of 1891 Crowther fell victim to a cerebral stroke and became paralyzed. The Declaration of Independence was set for January 1, 1892 at Lagos, and despite the poor state of his health, Crowther was designated to announce it. He died on the eve of the inauguration of the new church.

The Cameroonian minister and theologian Kä Mana judged Crowther in this way:

> Crowther embraced the Christian faith in a crucial period in African history, at the moment when Europe decided to occupy the African continent and to administer it directly in the name of its economic interests. Welcomed into the bosom of the Anglican Church in which he was the first black student in theology, the first black pastor to be ordained, and the first African to be an Anglican bishop, Samuel Ajayi Crowther will be affirmed there as a founder of churches and a leader without equal in the Christian communities . . . Bishop Crowther laid the basis of a vision of African Christianity that can still inspire us today.[235]

Crowther is considered today as the father not only of the church, but also of the Federal Republic of Nigeria.

# THOMAS BIRCH FREEMAN (1809–1890)

We have already mentioned Thomas Birch Freeman, to whom the Methodist Mission (WMMS) had entrusted the work on the Gold Coast in 1838, a time when it had been disrupted by the death of several missionaries. Freeman was biracial and raised in Britain: his mother, Anna Birch, was an English servant, and his father was a freed slave from the Antilles. Freeman enjoyed a fruitful ministry. "Due to his astonishing

---

235 Kä Mana, *La nouvelle évangélisation en Afrique* (Paris: Karthala, 2000), 126–27.

work, churches were established in Ghana (Cape Coast, Kumasi), Nigeria (Abeokuta), and Dahomey (present-day Benin), which together formed an immense district of which he would remain the superintendent until 1857.[236]

Freeman was converted on the day that he was planning to disrupt a Methodist meeting. He was observing the proceedings in the hall through a keyhole in order to choose the most "opportune" moment to make a smashing entry, but what he heard of the message shook him to the point of bringing him to faith.

And so it was that in 1838 he took up the cause in Cape Coast among the Ashanti. His British wife died after a short while, and several years later he remarried an African who gave him four children. Freeman was quick to establish sound relationships with several local chiefs. In contact with various small groups of Christians that were dispersed throughout the region, he brought them together to construct chapels and insisted from the beginning on the necessity of forming an African pastorate.

After two and a half years in Cape Coast, he had erected seven chapels, baptized five hundred believers, and opened several schools. The field, it is true, had been prepared in the preceding century by Philippe Kwaku through regular Bible distribution and the efforts of the Basel Mission. Freeman attempted to establish the mission in Kumasi, the capital of the great Ashanti kingdom, but he experienced several reverses, including the massacre of Christians.

Many among the freed in Sierra Leone, who had come from Britain, had Yoruba relatives. When they heard talk of the new city of Abeokuta, they dreamed of returning to their native land. The Christians among them appealed to the CMS and the Methodist Mission, both of which became actively involved in the evangelization of Abeokuta. In

*Thomas Birch Freeman (1809–1890), an African pioneer missionary in Africa.*

1842 Freeman was moved by his mission to the Yoruba country where the needs were immense and urgent. First he established a base on the coast at Badagri, and from there he went to Abeokuta where Chief Shodeke received him favorably. Though open to the Christian faith, he was also especially anxious to obtain the support of the British in order to withstand the assaults of the neighboring peoples who were envious of the prosperity of his city.

At Christmas in 1842 when he returned to Badagri, Freeman was surprised to find three CMS missionaries there, including Crowther, who was *en route* to Abeokuta. There was collaboration rather than competition between the two missions. Since the WMMS lacked financial means, the CMS replaced it at Abeokuta. However, since wars often cut communications in this region, it was not until 1846 that the CMS was able to truly establish itself there.

---

236 André Roux, *Mission des églises, mission de l'église* (Paris: Le Cerf, 1984), 81.

Freeman did not settle in Abeokuta but prepared the field for the Methodist Mission in the neighboring region. He was particularly good at winning the sympathy of the chiefs. He went as far as Abomey, at Dahomey, where a warrior tribe was settled and was terrorizing the country. He knew how to negotiate with its chief, who showed him much respect. Though Freeman did not stop the invasions of the Dahomey tribe, he did at least succeed in slowing them down, and he was able to begin missionary work among them.

*Reception of missionaries by a Yoruba chief.*

Between 1838 and 1857, Freeman was active in three areas: the countries of Ashanti (Gold Coast), Yoruba, and Dahomey. He became the superintendent of a vast Methodist mission district that covered these three regions. A visionary and a pioneer par excellence, he was always ready for new initiatives. His ease in dealing with the African chiefs was a considerable asset. They appreciated his intelligence and courtesy as well as the respect that he showed for local customs. Sensible of the needs that he saw all around him, his principal weakness was that he did not know how to limit his work and often acted in a disorganized way. His mission did not have the means, either in men or money, to follow up on his exploratory efforts. This resulted in creating tension between him and his committee. Neither his value as a missionary nor his perfect probity was ever in question, but he was reproached for spending without counting the cost. He did, however, acknowledge his weaknesses: "I will have to be calmer, calculate better, and have less passion! It is unfortunate for me that at this point only one passion has absorbed my entire life: the extension of our work. I have envisioned too much, and I have neglected the financial question."

Then in 1857 Freeman left the ministry and offered himself to the city government of Accra. He continued, however, to counsel his successor in the superintendence of the mission, and in 1873 he took up a pastoral post in Accra. He died in 1890 at the age of eighty-one, greatly venerated by those who knew him.

Aside from his previously noted administrative deficiencies, he also had various other faults. Although he was biracial, he was always considered to be a European by the Africans because he never learned an African language. Moreover, he had a tendency to confuse mission and politics. Relying too heavily on the prestige of Britain, he encouraged many Africans to conflate Christianity and the West. For example, upon arriving in Abeokuta, he offered the king a Bible, saying: "It is thanks to this book that my country has become great." Lastly, his closeness to the chiefs was a double-edged sword: when one or another suffered a reverse, the mission was also bound to suffer. Freeman, nevertheless, was the most influential and enterprising among those of the Methodist Mission in West Africa during this period, and he gave considerable luster to the work, being one of the great figures in the West African missions of the nineteenth century.

# CHAPTER 16

# Coastal Regions of West Africa

## SENEGAL

The Portuguese in 1445 discovered the coast of Senegal, which was then called Senegambia because it was situated between the Senegal and Gambia rivers.[237] The Senegalese chief Behemoi was baptized in Lisbon in 1486, but the Christian presence in his country did not last long.

A Jansenist teacher named Epinat came in 1825 to settle in Saint Louis. He struggled to free many slaves, but soon despaired of success. Upon returning to France, he converted to Protestantism under the influence of the Reverend Henri Pyt.[238] He then returned to Senegal as an evangelist but was soon expelled. François Villégier, a missionary in Senegal in the latter part of the nineteenth century, commented: "As a pretext was needed to send him back to France, it was said that he was crazy. Perhaps, after all, it was believed that he was really affected by insanity. Could a reasonable man have been able to dream of regenerating these blacks who were then so supremely despised?"[239]

Between 1862 and 1863 the acting governor of this territory was the ship captain Jean-Bernard Jauréguiberry, future admiral and minister of the navy.[240] He was a childhood friend of the director of the Paris Mission, Eugène Casalis, and a "coreligionist and brother in Christ." He made an appeal to the Paris Mission, which in 1863 dispatched Louis Jaques, a Swiss of Vevey, to Saint Louis. For fear of calling too much attention to him, a public farewell was not held; and in order not to provoke a reac-

---

237 In 1626 the commercial company of Rouen established itself in Saint Louis, on the lower Senegal River. Later becoming a French colony, Senegambia was taken from France by the British during the eighteenth century. France retook possession in 1779, and the Catholic mission, which had been present there since 1659, returned the same year under the protection of the flag. The Catholic mission, however, had had little to do with the indigenous population, and it was only with the arrival of the Sisters of Cluny in 1819 that Catholic missions became more effective among the local population.

238 Pastor and evangelist, Henri Pyt (1796–1835) is one of the most representative figures of the evangelical revival of Geneva, which occurred at the beginning of the nineteenth century.

239 Jean Faure, op. cit., 293.

240 At that time the permanent governor was Louis Faidherbe. Jauréguiberry officially succeeded to the governorship in 1869 before being called to another position in France.

tion from the highly anti-Protestant clergy, Jauréguiberry named him the "personal chaplain of the governor." Anxious to avoid competition with the Catholic mission,[241] Jaques chose to reside in Casamance, which lay south of the Gambia River. Due to his efforts a missionary station with a school began to function in Sédhiou. Unfortunately, he had to abandon his post after two and a half years when the mission refused to accept his marriage to a divorcée. In the following years, three other missionaries took up the work, but two died after several months.

François Villégier worked in Senegal from 1870 to 1877, the only French missionary to stay so long. He translated the Gospel of Matthew into Wolof (the language of the Islamic population in the region of Saint Louis), opened a school, and evangelized the villages of the region. The first baptism took place in 1873.

The missionaries sent to Senegal were especially susceptible to the climate, and the work suffered from the brevity of their stays. Also, their regular travel between the capital and Casamance harmed the continuity of the work. In twenty years, eight missionaries were sent to Senegal, three accompanied by their wives. Three missionaries and one of their wives succumbed to fever; two had to be repatriated for reasons of health, and two for causes of dissension.

Amidst this bootless record, the name of Walter Taylor stands out. He was the only permanent member of the mission during a period of twenty years. The son of freed slaves and a Yoruba, Taylor chose to live in Sierra Leone. He was a cultivated man, having done his studies in the missionary college of Fourah Bay in Freetown. At the age of thirty, he moved to Senegal to begin work as an accountant in a commercial enterprise in Saint Louis, but he evangelized the Yoruba and established a church for them. Beginning in 1872, he worked with François Villégier, and then in 1878 he went to Paris to complete his studies at the House of Missions. At the conclusion of his stay in Paris, Taylor was ordained at the Oratoire du Louvre and, provided with a French passport to avoid expulsion, returned to Senegal. For a period of time he was the only French missionary in the country, but despite the circumstances, he persevered. In 1888 he visited some Protestant parishes in France, and his meetings resulted in several people being called to missionary service.

The most fruitful of Taylor's activities was in welcoming the non-Christian Bambara slaves who were fleeing from their Peuhls Muslim masters living in the interior of the country. He secured land at Pont-de-Khor, near to Saint Louis, where he organized the agricultural colony of Bethesda. Here the freed slaves could find the means to subsist. Taylor wrote in an 1880 report: "Since we began to give them asylum, we have been able to bring a number of them to the knowledge of Jesus Christ. Most of the communicant members of our church consist of these freedmen." In contrast, the evangelization of the indigenous Islamic population had little success, which for a long time threatened to undermine the survival of this Senegalese church. For, drawn from foreign fugitives, it lacked roots in the local population. He decided to retire there in 1891 after having experienced strained

---

241 This extreme prudence, which appeared from the beginning of Jauréguiberry's initiative, is due to this being the first time that the Paris Mission had undertaken work in a territory under French authority and where the Catholics had preceded it.

relations with the Paris Mission toward the end of his ministry. Taylor died in 1899 in his native country of Sierra Leone.

The French conquest of Bamako in 1883[242] presented the Paris Mission with a new field of opportunity. The Bambara population, having welcomed the French as liberators from the Muslim conqueror El Hadj Omar, now seemed open to the gospel. Louis Jaques, the pioneer missionary of Senegal, offered his services to the Paris Mission and in 1883 returned to Senegal with his second wife. Walter Taylor took them to the city of Kerbala, on the Senegal River, 160 kilometers from Saint Louis. There were numerous Bambara living there, many that he himself had previously freed. The population received them readily, but after the death of his wife and because of his difficulties in learning the local language, Jaques decided to return to France in 1887.

In 1902 the city of Dakar, which lay 150 kilometers south of Saint Louis, became the capital of French West Africa. The mission moved there in 1907, and a Protestant church was established in the city in 1913. A number of French ministers thrived in the city, but it could no longer be considered a truly missionary work. It was not until 1936 that another mission began to work in Senegal. This was the Worldwide Evangelization Crusade (WEC), an American organization. No other mission agency would work there until after the Second World War.

# GUINEA

Until the eighteenth century, the name Guinea denoted the Atlantic coast of West Africa, from Senegal to Gabon.[243] Fifteenth- and sixteenth-century European navigators discovered the coasts of the Gulf of Guinea but never penetrated into the interior of the continent. In the course of the nineteenth century, Europeans explored the upper course of the Niger River, reaching as far as Timbuktu (present-day Mali). This was the commercial center of ancient Africa, the link between North Africa and Black Africa, and for Westerners an almost mythical city.[244] The first French trading post was established on its coast in 1837. At that time Guinea was within the jurisdiction

*Walter Taylor and his wife, missionaries in Senegal for the Paris Mission, 1872 to 1891. (Service Protestant de Mission, Paris)*

---

242  Bamako is found in present-day Mali, but in the nineteenth century it was part of the sub-Saharan region then generally known as the Sudan.

243  This is why three states carry the name of Guinea: Guinea Bissau (formerly Portuguese), at the western end of the Gulf of Guinea; Equatorial Guinea (formerly Spanish), at the other extremity of the same gulf and to the south of Cameroon; and the best known of the three, the Republic of Guinea, with its capital in Conakry. A former French colony, the southern section of the Republic of Guinea is a small area of less than three hundred kilometers that adjoins the north of Guinea Bissau and the south of Sierra Leone. The more spacious continental part of Guinea, Conakry consists of the upper basin of the Niger and its tributaries, and it borders Mali and the Ivory Coast. It is this region that we are considering here.

244  In 1828 the French explorer René Caillié (1799–1838) became the first European to enter Timbuktu.

of Senegal, but in 1893 it became an autonomous colony. Later it was integrated into French West Africa.

The Fathers of the Holy Spirit settled in Boff in 1877 and in Conakry in 1890, and the White Fathers developed a work in the southeast in 1896. Islam offered strong resistance. It was introduced in the eighteenth century through a Holy War undertaken by the Fulani and became the majority religion, though parts of the population remained attached to their traditional tribal religions.

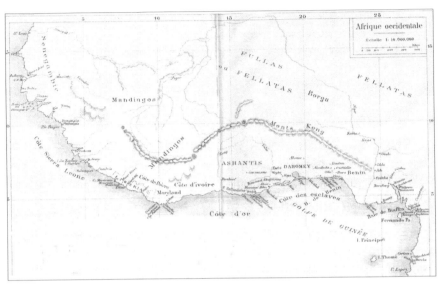

*West Africa about 1880—a few years before the Congress of Berlin*
*where colonial borders were defined.*

The first Protestant missionaries arrived in the region in 1797, eighty years before the Catholics. At that time the territory of Guinea was not yet clearly defined. Protestant missions in the area began when two Scottish Presbyterian missionaries, who had been working among the freedmen of Sierra Leone, advanced into the interior of lands that would later become Guinea. They had hoped to reach the indigenous tribes, but their efforts were short lived and ended in failure (see p. 500). In 1804 Anglican missionaries of the Church Missionary Society (CMS) attempted to reach the ethnic group called the Soussou. The population was hostile to them due to the slave traders, but they maintained a presence among them until 1818. They paid a heavy price for this because in less than ten years thirty of their number had died, and then the remaining missionaries gave up. Anglicans of the Society for the Propagation of the Gospel (SPG) sought to reach the Soussou in 1855. By 1866 they had established themselves on the Los Islands, near present-day Conakry. Later, the French colonial administration, wanting to develop the port of Conakry, sought workmen in Sierra Leone. Among the migrant workers were a good number of Protestants that the Anglicans succeeded in organizing. A church was constructed in 1900 and an Anglican bishop consecrated in 1901.

The Christian and Missionary Alliance (CMA) entered Sierra Leone in 1890 with the goal of extending its efforts far into the Sudan. Pioneer missionaries left Sierra Leone in 1900 and ventured as far as the border of Guinea, but it was not until 1918 that the governor authorized the establishment of the CMA in the colony. The missionaries, who evangelized as they went along, sought to pass through the Niger basin and enter the regions of the Sudan that began in Guinea. In 1923 they established their first mission station in Guinea, a place they named Baro, which lay at the confluence of the Niger and Niandan. Not long after this they established the station of Kankan, which became the center of the CMA mission in Guinea and where they set up a printing press. They succeeded in reaching a hundred villages along the Niger, some Muslim and others animist. The latter in general welcomed them with joy. In 1930 the field to be reached was enlarged through the establishment of the Macenta mission station. Its founder, Cova Zoumanigui, was a Guinean who left a highly profitable job in order to serve the Lord. Altogether, between 1923 and 1938 six new stations were established, and all enjoyed great success.

## GUINEA BISSAU

The first Catholics priests arrived in Guinea Bissau with the fifteenth-century explorers, and a diocese was established in the sixteenth century. But in the ensuing centuries the work stagnated. By 1900 Catholics were only 4 percent of the population, and in 1929 there was only one Catholic priest to serve the entire territory. The first and the only Protestant missionaries authorized to enter in the country were the representatives of the Worldwide Evangelization Crusade (WEC), who arrived in 1939.

## TOGO

The State of Togo is a narrow band of land that lies between Ghana and Benin. Its coast on the Gulf of Guinea extends a full fifty kilometers, but it recedes six hundred kilometers toward the north where it shares a border with Burkina Faso. Togo exists in its present form by virtue of the treaties signed between Germany, France, and Britain in 1885. The gospel was proclaimed for the first time in this region around 1842. The evangelists were Methodist and Anglican freedmen from Sierra Leone, who, like many others, were searching for their countries of origin along the Slave Coast. The Christians among their number formed small communities and attempted to reach the indigenous population with the message of the gospel.

The first Western missionaries in Togo were Germans of the Norddeutsche Missions-gesellslchaft—generally known as the Bremen Mission. In 1847 they settled in a region occupied by the Ewe, an ethnic group that largely bordered the territory of Tongo, toward the west. The missionary Bernhard Schlegel (d. 1859) fixed in written form one of the local dialects, which became the official Ewe language. He composed a grammar, readers, and a religious history, as well as translating the Gospels, several epistles, and Revelation. The first regions in which the Bremen Mission worked were in areas belonging to present-day Ghana. It established its first mission station in the territory of Togo proper in 1874.[245]

The work undertaken by the Bremen Mission was compromised by the ravages of the tribal wars between the Ewe and the Ashanti, and the high mortality rate among the missionaries. By the time the first Togolese minister was ordained in 1882, the mission had already sent 110 missionaries of which fifty-four had died and forty had had to be repatriated for reasons of health. These figures underscored the urgency of training an indigenous pastorate. About twenty young Ewe were duly sent to Germany to study at a school in Westheim that was sympathetic to their cause. They received good instruction and later became the leaders of their church.

Togo became a Germany colony in 1884, and the port of Lome served as its capital. Sanitary conditions soon improved, which increased life expectancy. Under these conditions, the work of the mission increased, extending beyond the region inhabited by the Ewe and encountering people speaking many different languages. In the early years of the twentieth century, the deaconesses of Hamburg helped out, creating boarding schools for the girls. By the First World War there were eight mission stations serving various ethnic groups, 164 annexes, and more than eleven thousand believers. The mission reached as far as Atakpame, 150 kilometers into the interior. By this time there were forty German missionaries. By 1911 a complete Bible had been translated in the Ewe language. Printed in Germany, the first copies arrived in Togo at the beginning of the First World War, just before Anglo-French troops expelled all the Germans from their colony, including the missionaries.

The Ewe church was henceforth left to its own devices and under the direction of indigenous ministers. In such circumstances, possessing the Bible in its own language and having a trained pastoral body were of vital importance. Unfortunately the territory was divided into two for political reasons. West Togo was placed under a British mandate and was later annexed to the Gold Coast (Ghana). Two-thirds of the members of the church established by the Bremen Mission lived in this territory. France made the eastern part of the country the colony of Togo.

The church in the colony of Togo had only a few indigenous ministers and was deprived of outside help for a long period. The educational work had to be abandoned, and the training of ministers in Germany was discontinued. In 1923 the Reverends Aku and Baëta from Lome appealed to the Paris Mission for help. Lacking means, the society was hard pressed to respond, though it clearly saw the need. In 1928 it sent Charles Maître, a missionary in Cameroon, to survey the field. He quickly confirmed that the need for missionaries was urgent. Charles Carrière, a schoolmaster, came as a volunteer in 1930, but it was not until 1934 that Jean Faure came to provide instruction for indigenous ministers, almost twenty years after the departure of the German missionaries. During all this time, the church had by default been placed in a situation of autonomy.

The missionaries sent by the Paris Mission where, from the beginning, working with a church that already had a significant history. The older Togolese ministers who

---

245 The first Catholic missionary appeared in 1861, being sent by the African Missions of Lyon.

had been trained by the Germans were well established and their status as colleagues with the new missionaries was clear. But the young ministers who succeeded them were poorly situated to maintain their status *vis-à-vis* the missionaries. They were supposed to direct the church, but the missionaries were their elders and had prepared them for the ministry. Moreover, in most of the neighboring countries it was the white missionaries who controlled the levers of power. Both sides regularly needed to redefine their respective roles.[246] For example, when a theological seminary was established, it was decided to place it under the responsibility of a Togolese minister.

## DAHOMEY (THE REPUBLIC OF BENIN)

The present State of Benin corresponds in part to the kingdom of Abomey, founded in the sixteenth century in the interior and occupied by formidable warriors. In the eighteenth century, it secured the port of Ouidah as an outlet to the sea to engage in commerce with the British and Portuguese. King Ghezo signed a treaty in 1850 with the French, whose influence was growing in the region. When King Behanzin, his successor, came into conflict with the French, the latter occupied the territory between 1890 and 1893 to protect its merchants and missionaries. Dahomey then became a part of the colony of French West Africa.

The Catholic presence in the area dates from the seventeenth century, but it was limited to the coast and essentially concerned only the Europeans who were engaged in trade there. Nevertheless, in 1800 there were about two thousand Catholic Dahomeans. The African Mission of Lyon began to work in the interior of the land in 1861. This was largely the work of Italian Father Borghero, who was highly influential and very much honored by the king of Abomey.

The Methodist Mission of London appeared in 1843 and for many years was the only Protestant mission in the country. Its first missionary was the biracial Thomas Birch Freeman. Departing from Yoruba country, he entered the kingdom of Abomey from the north and soon established good relations with the king. This mission reached out especially to two ethnic groups: the Gun, who lived on coast; and the Fon, who dwelled in the region of the royal capital of Abomey. Early in the twentieth century a college was opened in Puerto Novo to train catechists from Dahomey, south Togo, and the Ivory Coast.

The British Methodists, being conscious of the precariousness of an English-speaking mission in a French colony, asked the Paris Mission a little after 1920 to second some of its missionaries to their ranks. William J. Platt, the director of the British mission in Dahomey, welcomed Paul Wood-Lainé and Antonin Léthel, but they were soon reassigned to the Ivory Coast where the Methodists were also urgently asking for French Protestant missionaries (see p. 535). Later the French missionary André Roux lent support to the Methodists of Dahomey, serving there from 1934 to 1936.

---

246 This situation is examined by André Roux, who was a missionary to Togo from 1951 to 1953, in *Mission*, 111ff. The formal independence of the Evangelical Church of Togo was proclaimed in 1959, but forty years prior to this the church was already considered as autonomous and not under the tutelage of a mission.

# NIGERIA

We can only provide a brief glimpse of the first mission initiatives in the vast and densely populated country of Nigeria. Though the port of Lago had been occupied by the British since 1851, Nigeria did not become an integral part of the British Empire until 1900. The first messengers of the gospel came in 1842 from Sierra Leone, arriving in Abeokuta and Badagari in the southwest part of the country. They quickly organized a church amongst the numerous and dynamic ethnic groups of Yoruba.[247] But following ethnic wars, the missionaries were driven out of the Yoruba country for about fifteen years (1865–1880), and the church came entirely under the authority of African ministers.

Samuel Crowther founded the Niger Mission in 1865 and later conferred the direction of this work to his younger son, the Reverend Dandelson Crowther. The Niger Mission was subdivided in 1890 into two branches: the Niger Delta and Lower Niger Mission in the south, and the Sudan and Upper Niger Mission among the Islamic Haoussa peoples. The latter confronted great difficulties due to the local emirs.

The great city of Ibadan, which lay far into the interior of the country, was reached in 1853 by David Hinderer, an Anglican missionary. From 1846 to 1911 numerous American and British missions established themselves in Nigeria: first came Presbyterians and Jamaican Baptists from Cameroon, and then in 1850 Southern Baptists from the United States. In 1888 the church that issued from this mission declared its independence, creating the Native Baptist Church. The Anglican Church endured a schism in 1891 when Bishop Crowther was replaced by a British bishop. Other groups also separated themselves from their mission founders, giving birth to a number of new churches in the first years of the twentieth century. This is one reason why present-day Nigeria has so many African independent churches.

Among the missions that arrived at the end of the nineteenth and the first part of the twentieth centuries was the Qua Lboe Mission, an interdenominational organization of Northern Ireland. In 1893 in the east of the country, Primitive Methodists arrived, who had just been expelled from Fernando Po. In the same year, the Sudan Interior Mission (SIM) went farther north along the Niger River, eight hundred kilometers from the coast. After 1900 the work greatly expanded to include many of the various ethnic groups, and Nigeria became SIM's most extensive field.[248] The Sudan United Mission (SUM)[249] began in 1904 to work at Wase, a northern region that showed much resistance to the gospel. The SIM and the SUM began to establish collaborative bases in 1910 from which were formed a united church: the Council of the Mission of the North, the future Council of Evangelical Churches of Northern Nigeria. In 1911 the CMS, the Scottish Presbyterians, the Qua Iboe Mission, and the Methodists signed a convention of cooperation for purposes of evangelization and

---

247 This was previously reviewed when looking at the pioneer African ministries of Crowther and Freeman. (See pp. 509-17.)

248 In 1960, 650 SIM missionaries were working in Nigeria.

249 SUM was an evangelical, interdenominational, and international mission that began in 1904.

the training of evangelists, as well as to harmonize their practices in the area of church discipline.

The most famous missionary to Nigeria was Mary Slessor, nicknamed "the White Queen of Calabar." She was a British subject who enjoyed a remarkable ministry. From 1876 until her death in 1915, she successively evangelized several tribes with formidable reputations for bloodthirstiness. She was the first foreigner to live among them, and their customs were profoundly transformed by her witness. Most notably, she obtained the abolition of the systematic killing of twins and of the old who were incapable of providing for their own needs. Her prestige was such that the people spontaneously rallied to her decision, which led the British government to name her vice-consul for the entire region of Calabar. Her nickname of "Queen," how-

*Mary Slessor, despite her nickname "the White Queen of Calabar," lived in a state of destitution in order to carry the gospel into unknown and dangerous regions of Nigeria.*

ever, did not mean that she lived in luxury. Rather, she lived in the precarious manner of an African: often dwelling in a hut of dried mud, eating the local food, and being susceptible to endemic topical diseases. An independent woman, she sought regions remote from all European influence, and her prestige is explained by her capacity to identify with primitive people. She is probably the first single woman to have engaged in a pioneer ministry in the then-unknown regions of Africa.

The British government was tolerant towards Catholic Missions in Nigeria and in other places. The first Catholic priests disembarked in Lagos in 1862 and dedicated themselves especially to the Ibo people. Like the Protestants, they benefited from state grants for their educational work.

## GHANA (THE GOLD COAST)

The kingdom of Ghana was an important empire as early as the tenth century. It occupied one part of the Gulf Coast of Guinea and extended as far as the limits of the Sahara, where it encountered Islamic populations. Trading posts were established by the Portuguese in the fifteenth century, and the Danish and Dutch in the seventeenth and eighteenth centuries. The British began expelling other Europeans in 1850, and in 1874 the Gold Coast became a British Crown Colony.[250]

As noted in Book II, Chapter 16 this region was among the first in Africa to be reached by Protestant missions, an effort that began around 1740. The precursors of this effort were African ministers: Jacob Capitein, Jacob Protten, Philippe Kwaku. Among the most memorable of the Protestant missionaries was the biracial Thomas Birch Freeman, who began his work there in 1838. Following Methodist practice, Freeman emphasized lay witness and the evangelization of Africa by its own people.

---

250 The original name of Ghana was restored at the time of independence in 1960.

From early on, his approach bore fruit as the Methodist church grew quickly. (See the previous chapter for more on Freeman.)

In 1828 at the request of the Danish Trading Company, the Basel Mission established itself at Christiansburg and Akropong. The first four missionaries died in four years. It took great courage to replace them, but five new recruits took up the challenge, of whom two died in four months. The mission eventually sent ten missionaries, but after only a few years there was only one left alive. Many then called for the abandonment of a region so dangerous. Wilhelm Hoffmann, the new director of the House of Missions in Basel, conceived a new plan: he would send the only survivor, George Widmann, along with Andreas Riis, a Norwegian, to seek help from black Christians in Jamaica. The two missionaries returned to Christiansburg in 1843 with several Jamaican Moravians whom they had already trained. The work was then able to develop with more continuity and less loss of life. The first baptisms took place in 1846. Despite many obstacles, the Basel Mission pursued its task with new missionaries added in 1850. It placed special emphasis on the systematic study of the languages spoken in the region, and early on it opened a seminary for evangelists in Akropong. But at the same time it also moved in other directions. J.-F. Zorn writes, the Basel Mission "created a commercial and agricultural society with the aim of not only provisioning the mission but also training young Africans as craftsmen (carpenters, cartwrights, locksmiths, shoemakers, [book]binders, and farmers. The new products imported by the Jamaicans (coffee, tobacco, mangos, and cocoa) were also developed."[251]

At the end of the nineteenth century, there were thirteen stations where fifty missionaries were working, 150 annexes, and fifteen thousand Christians in the Gold Coast. At the beginning of the First World War, the missionaries of the Basel Mission, who were mostly Germans, were forced to leave. Though this resulted in the Presbyterian Church becoming autonomous, it benefited from the help of the United Free Church of Scotland and from the Dutch Reformed Church.

As was pointed out in regards to Togo, in 1847 the Bremen Mission undertook the work of evangelization among the Ewe ethnic group. At first the region in which it worked was attached to German Togo, but following the First World War a major part became integrated into the British Gold Coast. When the Bremen Mission was forced to leave, a Scottish mission, founded by the United Free Church of Scotland, took up the task. But this German mission was again authorized to work in the area in 1925.

The Gold Coast is one of the regions where the first Independent African Churches appeared. Under the influence of a black American church, the African Methodist Episcopal Zion Church was formed at the turn of the twentieth century. Following the three-month ministry of the black prophet William Wade Harris on the Gold Coast, his disciple, John Mackabah, founded the Church of the Twelve Apostles in 1914. (See the next chapter for more on Harris.) The Christian Council of Ghana (its current name) was formed in 1929 from a majority of the missions and Protestants churches of the country.

---

251 Zorn, "Missions protestantes," 1028. We note that the Basel Mission in the same period developed industrial and commercial projects similar to those of Calicut and on the southwest coast of India.

# CHAPTER 17

# *The Ivory Coast*

The Ivory Coast is a part of what in the nineteenth century was called the Slave Coast, which includes the region between the Gold Coast (present-day Ghana) and the Independent Republic of Liberia. In 1893 the French made it a colony, and it was later integrated into French West Africa.

The first Catholic mission in the region of the present-day Ivory Coast was established in 1637 by five Capuchin Fathers and a priest from Saint Malo. Three died, and the two survivors came to France in 1640 to seek additional help. They were blocked by the Dutch from returning to their post and deported to Recife, Brazil, where they pursued their missionary ministry. French Dominican missionaries sought to establish themselves on the same coast in 1687 and 1701, but the two attempts quickly ended in failure. It would not be until 1844 and 1850 that Catholic missionaries would disembark at Assinie and Grand-Bassam respectively. Lodged in the quarters of the French army and protected by it, they had scarcely any contact with the population and never learned the language. By 1852 all had died or left Africa.[252]

Finally in 1895, two years after the establishment of the French colony, the African Society of Missions of Lyon arrived in Grand-Bassam. This is considered to be the founding year of the Christian community in Ivory Coast. Although conditions were then more favorable and the missionaries achieved greater results than previously, their successes were limited until the First World War. Despite a cohort of twenty-three missionaries, at the beginning of the war there were little more than one thousand Christians and four hundred catechumens.

At the end of the nineteenth century, there were already several small groups of African Protestants in two or three coastal cities. Most of these were of the Fanai ethnic group from the neighboring British colony of the Ivory Coast. They generally worked as clerks, or "klarks" as they were known, in the commercial sector of the ports of the Ivory Coast. Gathering in several Methodist churches constructed for this purpose, they celebrated their worship services in English. A decree issued from Paris in 1922 that regulated "religious propaganda" declared that religious ceremonies

---

252 For this period, see Pierre Trichet, *Côte d'Ivoire: Les premières tentatives d'évangélisation, 1637–1852* (Abidjan: Éditions la Nouvelle, 1995).

could henceforth only be conducted in French, Latin, or a local language. This explains the actions of the French-speaking Methodist Mission of Dahomey, which will be examined below (see p. 534).

## THE ASTONISHING PROPHET WILLIAM WADE HARRIS

The Christian presence in the Ivory Coast was still quite limited in 1912. It was after this year that the evangelization of the population really began with the short but extraordinary ministry of an African preacher, the prophet William Wade Harris (circa 1860–1929). Originally from Liberia, he began to travel through the villages of the lower Ivory Coast in the course of the year 1913.

Harris was of the Grebo ethnic group, and his village was situated on the border of the French colony of Ivory Coast. His family practiced a traditional African religion, but he was converted due to the African minister in his village. Having attended a Methodist mission school, he was baptized and acquired a good knowledge of the Bible. He became a master of a boarding school, catechist, and preacher. At around fifty years of age, he spent time in prison on a charge of threatening subversive activity to liberate the Grebo from domination by the African Americans of Liberia.

He passed much of his time in prison by reading the Bible and praying. It was during this time that he received a vision: a "man stood behind him" and appealed to him "to evangelize his brothers on the Coast." The man, he believed, was the archangel Gabriel, clothed in the Spirit and great power, who opposed fetishes. Once he was released (probably in 1912), he began to evangelize his compatriots, but apparently without success. Then he crossed over into the neighboring French colony of the Ivory Coast where he exercised the prophetic gifts that he believed he had received.

From the beginning, he seems to have launched a veritable religious revolution in this vast territory. His sudden appearance as an evangelist of immense stature is all the more astonishing in that he was ignorant not only of French but also of the local languages of the Ivory Coast. In fact, he spoke pidgin English and needed a translator. Gaston Joseph, a French administrator, has written of him:

> The prophet appealed to the indigenous population to work in obedience to authority. He forbade the abuse of alcohol. He tolerated polygamy, but opposed adultery. He forbade theft. He asked that Sunday be considered a day of rest and contemplation. He proclaimed a marvelous afterlife for those who embraced [Christian] precepts and, through baptism, assured his proselytes that they had been made pure.[253]

Harris avoided all politics, and his personal disinterestedness was never in question. In effect, according to André Roux:

> All witnesses agreed on one point: he never sought to profit personally, whether in money or prestige. Accepting only the welcome that the African always offers his guests, room and board in

---

253 G. Joseph examines Harris in his book *La Côte d'Ivoire: Le pays, les habitants* (Paris: Larose, 1917), 160–61.

particular, he was a picture of simplicity and complete discretion. There was never about him the least trace of syncretism, nor of a racial complex.[254]

A Catholic priest who had personally known him wrote: "He asked for nothing and accepted nothing. He refused to associate with any sect or church, but he nonetheless urged his followers to affiliate with a church, providing only that it be Christian."[255]

In the manner of an Old Testament prophet, he preached monotheism, judgment, and repentance. Years later, many remembered his thundering voice commanding the people to throw away their fetishes and, like Elijah at Mount Carmel, threatening the recalcitrant with fire from heaven. Extraordinary results followed, which made the Catholic missionaries anxious: "His influence, founded on a remarkable hypnotic power and a system of imprudent intimidation, was immense . . . This hallucinating charlatan achieved in a few months what we, priests of Jesus Christ, have not even approached doing in twenty years. For the means that he employed were forbidden to us."[256]

The Catholic missionaries, however, kept their negative opinions to themselves as they saw their churches fill when Harris passed through. Sister Polyane, a Catholic religious of Jacqueville, recounts her experience in these words:

> Not more than three or four months ago, our indigenous population was still entirely plunged into the most profound paganism . . . All their lying devises were set aside due to the work of a single man, calling himself a prophet sent by God, and predicting all sorts of evil to those who would not heed his voice. All the fetishes have been burned or thrown in the sea . . . It is said everywhere that there has been a complete change of mind! Will it last? The future will tell, but at least it is possible.[257]

The ecclesiastical neutrality of the prophet did not continue. Soon he began to announce the coming of white preachers, warning that only the "whites of the Bible" (that is to say, the Protestants) should be heeded. Trained by the Methodist mission, Harris had received a biblical education centered on the good news of salvation in Christ. If he preached a single and formidable God to the idolaters, he also showed the love of this God who gave his Son to save humanity. He used a great walking stick in the form of a cross, which he insisted was only a symbol of the message of salvation in Jesus Christ. He explained that it had no power of its own, and at one point he even broke it to show that it was not a fetish. Harris affirmed that the Bible is the Book of God, the bearer of his good news. The Bible, he announced, called men

---

254 André Roux, *A l'ombre de la grande forêt* (Paris: Le Cerf, 1971), 31.

255 A response from African missions, February 1930, cited by Pierre Trichet, *Côte d'Ivoire: Les premières pas d'une église*. Vol. 2, *1914–1940* (Abidjan: Éditions la Nouvelle, 1995), 13.

256 Cited in part in J. Bianquis, *Le prophète Harris* (Paris: SMEP, 1924), 9; and in part in Trichet, op. cit., 20. Trichet said of Father Gorju that he was "filled with a visceral anti-Protestantism. Now, Harris was trained as a Protestant."

257 Trichet, op. cit., 9.

to turn from idols and put their confidence in God alone. Two recent historians have written:

> He was a born orator, who expressed himself in rough and abrasive language. He began by proclaiming: "God is all powerful, burn your fetishes and love one another. Bring me your idols and I will throw them into the fire, after which I will baptize you." It seems that with these few words he held a solution to the omnipresent problem raised by the sorcerers and the fetchers, one that swept the traditional spirits faraway.[258]

He would generally teach a group for a period of three days and then baptize those who responded to his call—sometimes these groups would number in the thousands. He always baptized in the name of the Father, Son, and Holy Spirit. Before taking his leave, he designated a dozen men to be the twelve "apostles" of their village, one among them being the spokesman. He did not seek to establish a "Harris" church; rather, he considered himself to be a messenger, a precursor in the manner of John the Baptist.

Kä Mana, in his history of the period, placed Harris among the other outstanding African preachers and prophets of the nineteenth century such as Simon Kimbangu, Simao Toko, and Samuel Ajayi Crowther.

> The history of African Christianity is also the history of great founding prophets who plowed the furrows of Christianity in the land, and who felt the urgent need to ponder, inspire, and construct the spiritual and material future of the African continent . . . Profoundly rooted in missionary Protestantism, and having a perfect mastery of its essentials, especially being grounded in the Scriptures . . . these men had a profound knowledge of African society in all its weaknesses, magical mentality, ethnic divisions, and confidence in the invisible forces that in this life do not always permit themselves to be deployed with all their force and splendor.[259]

Kä Mana further observes that if these prophets often gave vivid expression to "colonial Christianity," they were not complaisant in their own milieu of African culture, for they concentrated their missionary efforts on the defetishization of their societies.

Harris' ministry in the Ivory Coast continued scarcely more than a year. After spending four months on the Gold Coast, in September 1914 he returned to the Ivory Coast where he was welcomed by great crowds. While he continued to proclaim God's word along the coast, incessant appeals came to him from the interior. Unable to respond to these himself, he sent "minor prophets" in his place. Their preaching,

---

258  B. Sundkler and C. Steed, *A History of the Church in Africa*, eds. (Cambridge: Cambridge University Press, 2000), 199.

259  Kä Mana, op. cit., 122–23.

of course, had less force than that of Harris', and they did not possess his biblical knowledge or a comparable disinterestedness.

Early in the year 1915, not long after the start of the First World War, the French authorities expelled Harris. They were perturbed by his use of the English language, and they feared the trouble that the large crowds that followed him might create. On eight occasions he attempted to reenter the Ivory Coast, but each time he was turned back.

Despite the brevity of Harris' ministry and the limitations of his disciples, about 200,000 Ivorians burned their fetishes as a consequence of their work. Moreover, traces of his ministry remained, for innumerable villages erected large stone squares in anticipation of the "whites of the Bible" announced by the prophet.

When Harris was expelled from the Ivory Coast, he retired to his village in Liberia, near Cape Palmas. He was living there in anonymity and poverty when Pierre Benoit, a French Methodist missionary, found him in 1926. Marked by age, Harris was moved by this encounter with one of the "whites of the Bible" whose arrival he had predicted twelve years before. He dictated, no doubt at the urging of Benoit, a message for his followers in the Ivory Coast. Signed by his hand and dated September 25, 1926, the message is authenticated by a photograph of Harris and Benoit together.

> I, W. W. Harris, who have called you to the truth of the gospel and to baptism, have given this message to the Reverend P. Benoit so that he would bring it to you and so that you would obey it: All the men, women, and children who have been called and baptized by me must enter in the Wesleyan Methodist Church. I am myself a Methodist. No one should join a Roman Catholic Church if he desires to remain faithful to me . . . Read the Bible, it is the Word of God. Learn to read in order to able to know the Bible; it will be your guide. Be faithful in all things, and be firmly committed to the practice of the Ten Commandment and the Word of Jesus Christ, our only Savior. I send you my word and my message of joy. May the God of grace abundantly bless you.[260]

In the village where he passed his last years, William Wade Harris died in 1929 at the age of seventy.

Since the expulsion of the prophet in 1915, the churches born of his preaching were "sheep without a shepherd." According to the analysis of André Roux, over the course of the ensuing twenty years, three differing tendencies slowly became apparent among them:

> Some, while venerating the memory of Harris and claiming to be his followers, slowly abandoned all the religious practices and, without returning to the cult of fetishes, slipped into an indifference that favored ambient secularism, the "civilization of commerce" . . .

---

260 F. Deaville Walker, *Harris: Le prophète noir* (Privas, France: Pasteur S. Delattre, 1931), 174–75.

> In several regions a different line was followed. Among those who had heard Harris a series of "minor prophets" rose up who, with various motivations, became the leaders of groups that were often quite numerous . . . Most of them, unlike the master they claimed to follow, introduced elements of syncretism into their preaching . . .
>
> But between these two currents—one of forgetfulness and the other of syncretism—the great majority remained faithful to the spirit of the prophet and awaited, according to his word, those who would follow to continue his work.[261]

Roux estimated that sixty thousand remained within the orbit of Protestant missions,[262] while the rest drifted to the fringes. The requirement of monogamy, among others, contributed to many distancing themselves from the churches, Protestant as well as Catholic. Charles Daniel Maire remarks, moreover, that "some villages that had passed en masse to Methodism slowly built Harris churches. There were other more profound motives for creating Harris institutions: the more or less official refusal of the missionaries to pray for the sick and to give this ministry an important place constituted a deception . . . The reticence, indeed, the hostility, of the missionaries to accept traditional initiation ceremonies and seasonal holidays, which continued to be celebrated, did not contribute to retaining converts in the Methodist mission."[263] Roux writes that the return to an independent form of Harrisism appeared years afterwards in another way: "Later, when nationalism was awakened, it would produce a brusque explosion of neo-Harrisism, along lines similar to those of the 'Ethiopian' cults in which doctrine was less important than the expression of 'negritude' and the refusal of all European direction."[264] Among the numerous African independent churches that appeared in later years in the Ivory Coast and beyond, many would declare themselves to be the inheritors of Harris.[265] The ethnologist René Bureau describes them this way: "These churches claim to be of the Bible, but they accord much importance to the problems of sorcery. The worship service follows Protestant tradition, but polygamy is authorized. Yet the moral requirements are severe vis-à-vis alcohol, money, and sexuality.

## ARRIVAL OF THE WESLEYAN METHODIST MISSIONARY SOCIETY

The WMMS, located in London, had been active in Dahomey since 1854. When it learned that Christians in the Ivory Coast—the "klarks" mentioned above—claimed to be Methodists, they planned a reconnaissance trip to the region. This was undertaken in 1924 by William Platt, the director of the mission, and a colleague. To their

---

261 Roux, A l'ombre, 42–46.

262 Other historians, who see this number as exaggerated, estimate that twenty thousand people joined the Catholics and thirty-five thousand the Methodists.

263 Charles Daniel Maire, *Dynamique sociale des mutations religieuses. Expansion des protestantismes en Côte d'Ivoire* (Paris: EPHE, 1975), 138. Cited by Trichet, op. cit., 32–33.

264 Roux, A l'ombre, 50.

265 For the year 1960, Falk (op. cit., 287) gave the number of seventy thousand independent Harrisists.

great surprise, the phenomenon did not consist of a few groups of "klarks" but entire crowds that assembled to hear the word. The Harris converts enthusiastically held a celebration for the Methodist missionaries, who observed that the prophet's message was still very much alive. One of them reported: "I traveled several hundred kilometers and saw only three small fetishes . . . Some French officials and merchants assured us that before the arrival of Harris fetishism in this region was prodigious, and that it still prevails in the interior districts where his influence has not yet been felt."[266] The same author enthusiastically described his experience of a worship service in 1926, which was held for a Christian community of 1,300 that had probably never before received the visit of a missionary:

> It was an astonishing spectacle . . . I have never seen an audience crammed in like this . . . The heat was unendurable . . . What most surprised me was the order and perfect reverence that reigned, despite the crowd and heat . . . These blacks had been very noisy outside—almost violent in their exuberance—but at the threshold of the church all their agitation fell away. As soon as they entered the house of God, they became silent. Each man, each woman, knelt a moment, and then they calmly took their places, with neither noise nor chatting . . . They sang with all their hearts and souls, and moreover, they sang well. For the prayer, the entire assembly succeeded in kneeling, and I am not too sure how they did it. Then there was perfect silence, punctuated only by the light chorus of "Amen" that succeeded each specific request. It was evident that they had followed each word of the prayer. Then they softly repeated the Lord's Prayer.[267]

Paul Wood-Lainé, a French colleague of Platt's in Dahomey,[268] wrote of the journey:

> Some of the villages sent an escort as a way of welcoming the messenger of God. Everywhere the enthusiasm was marvelous. They listened avidly to the evangelical message. "Finally you have come," the people said. There were 350 churches in the process of being formed. One year later, we would inscribe the names of thirty thousand followers in our registers, all of them anxious for baptism. From village to village the cry was the same: "Send us teachers. We need men who can read the Book of God to us and speak to us of him."[269]

Platt asked his French colleagues in Dahomey, Antonin Léthel and Paul Wood-Lainé, to take this work in hand. After spending several months in the Ivory Coast

---

266 Walker, op. cit., 122.

267 Ibid., 88–89.

268 At the request of the Methodists, the interdenominational Paris Mission had sent several of its missionaries to Dahomey where their presence was needed, the country having been a French colony since the end of the nineteenth century (cf. p. 525).

269 Walker, op. cit., 70–71, as well as *L'oeuvre des missions protestantes*, conference of P. Wood-Lainé, cited by Trichet, *Côte d'Ivoire*, 30.

so that they could make a firsthand assessment, in August 1924 they addressed an appeal to the Protestants of France to take up the cause of these free churches that had been without leadership for ten years:

> The Protestant church of Ivory Coast . . . is a possibility so close to realization and so magnificent that we cannot dream of it without trembling. Who are we to undertake such a work? . . . The door so long sought is now here, for the Ivory Coast is the veritable door of the Sudan;[270] it is in the process of opening, and it is in this church, with its beautiful promise, that we will find a powerful army for the conquest of the interior.[271]

To compensate quickly for the absence of local teachers, Léthel summoned twenty-five young Africans from Dahomey. Though not well trained and "knowing little more of the gospel than the people to whom they were being sent to instruct," they were zealous.[272] Coming from another French colony, the catechists already spoke French, which avoided any infraction of the colonial rules. Under Léthel's supervision, some of these young people were responsible for as many as six to eight villages. Altogether, they acquitted themselves honorably in the performance of their tasks. The number of those sent by the Methodist Mission or contributed by the Paris Mission slowly increased. Nevertheless, this immense and urgent mission was always understaffed.

## BIRTH OF THE BIBLICAL MISSION IN THE IVORY COAST

### *The Surprising Role of the African Minister Mark Christian Hayford*

Two years after the arrival of the French Protestant missionaries, a call for more missionaries was heard in Paris, sounded this time by an African Baptist minister. Dr. Mark Christian Hayford (1864–1935) founded the Baptist Church and Mission in 1898 along the Gold Coast, his country of origin. During a journey through the Ivory Coast in 1919, he recognized the scope of the movement that the prophet Harris had begun several years earlier. Moreover, he saw the potential of the huge number of converts who, until then, lacked spiritual leaders able to teach them the word of God.[273] He succeeded in connecting fourteen of the Harris-inspired congregations to his Baptist Mission in the Gold Coast. The colonial administration, however, then required that religious services throughout the territory of the Ivory Coast be conducted in French, and at that time it was also preparing a law to forbid foreigners to evangelize.

---

270 The term Sudan then designated a territory much more vast than the modern Republic of Sudan. It included a sub-Saharan zone that extended the entire width of the continent, from the valley of the Nile in the east to the sources of the Niger and the Guinean jungle in West Africa.

271 The letter is published in full in Bianquis, op. cit., 36ff.

272 Walker, op. cit., 77.

273 Mark Hayford's brother Casely (1866–1930) was a lawyer with an interest in politics. In 1914 he encountered Harris and, enthused by the ministry of the prophet, published a brochure about him: Casely Hayford, *William Wade Harris: The West African Reformer; The Man and His Message* (London: C. M. Philips, 1915).

Consequently, Hayford could not live in the Ivory Coast, but he made a number of visits in the course of the following years.[274]

On the occasion of a journey to Britian in 1926, Hayford made a brief visit to France to present the needs of the Ivory Coast to Ruben Saillens, the director of the Institut Biblique de Nogent-sur-Marne. Hayford was then enjoying a growing popularity. He had met with the highest political personages in Britain and secured their approbation. In Paris he had an interview with Gaston Doumergue, the president of the Republic. In contrast, his contact with the Parish Mission did not turn out well. Since the preceding year, the Paris Mission had sided with the Methodist Mission, which expressed serious reservations with regard to Hayford.

*The Ghanan minister Mark Christian Hayford (1864–1935), who pleaded the cause of the Ivory Coast with French Baptists.*

Daniel Richard and his fiancée Laure Martzloff, students coming to the end of their studies at the Institut Biblique de Nogent, were struck by the urgency of the need expressed by Hayford. They were also members of the Baptist Church of the Tabernacle in Paris, whose pastor was Arthur Blocher. Convinced of a call from God and counting on the support promised by Dr. Hayford, they embarked in February 1927. Here was a new situation full of promise: French missionaries engaged by a mission directed by an African. At the last moment, Hayford decided not to accompany them. Instead, he left for the United States to attempt to secure more funding. He had, however, paid for the tickets of their voyage and agreed upon the monthly salary that they were to receive.

*Daniel and Laure Richard, pioneers of the Biblical Mission in the Ivory Coast.*

When they arrived in the Ivory Coast, they encountered a reality far different from the one that Hayford had described. During his journeys in the region in 1919 and 1920, Hayford had remained for too short a time to organize a church on the foundation established by the earlier work of the prophet Harris. The church was in the hands of Africans, and the person whom Hayford had said would be responsible for the Richards had long since left the country. The young couple, however, was warmly welcomed by a Methodist missionary, Willis Fletcher, who had been in Dabou for two years. He had registered the members of 234 Harrist churches as

---

274 "If Hayford had succeeded in establishing his Mission in the Ivory Coast, it would have been an extraordinary achievement, for an African church would have been founded by an African (the prophet Harris) and directed by an African (Dr. Hayford himself). In the period such a thing was virtually unthinkable. Yet Hayford thought it and even expressed it as early as 1903 in his book *West Africa and Christianity*. In this work he insisted not only that the gospel be brought to Africans by Africans but that the gospel be contextualized, to use the modern term" (Stefan Schmid, unpublished lecture).

Methodists. Dabou was at the heart of the region where the preaching of the prophet had had the greatest impact.

Daniel Richard soon discovered that the Baptist Churches he had come to help either no longer existed or had become Methodist, the Methodist mission having preceded him there. Moreover, he found himself without resources, for after paying the first month's salary, Dr. Hayford had ceased to communicate with him. Had Hayford been a smooth talker who had sought personal financial profit? The Paris Mission seemed to credit this version of the facts,[275] and inquiries made on the Gold Coast confirmed that a gap existed between Hayford's claims and the reality on the ground.[276]

After a period of questioning, the Richards wrote to their church that they had determined as an act of faith to live in the Ivory Coast despite the precariousness of their situation and the uncertain future of the mission. At the same time the church informed them that on Pentecost Sunday 1927 it had founded the Tabernacle Mission (later the Biblical Mission in the Ivory Coast) in order to assure them permanent support. Arthur Blocher traveled to London to negotiate with the Methodist Mission their respective fields of action. They agreed to assign the Tabernacle Mission responsibility for the southwest of the Ivory Coast as far as the border of Liberia.

The Richards established their base at Sassandra, the principal port of the west coast of the country. They sought to work with the Neyo tribe, fishermen whose villages dotted the coastal region. Yet, despite indications of Harris' earlier influence, the people seemed resistant to the gospel. Daniel Richard reported his observations to Paris:

> With what sadness I discovered in several villages the abandoned ruins of chapels that the Neyo had built [after Harris had passed through] . . . Hundreds of idols had been thrown into the sea, and adobe temples had been constructed. Alas! . . . abandoned without leaders, threatened with poison from the sorcerers, the Neyo who have not died have returned to fetishism . . . They are more pagan than other groups and do not concern themselves with our mission.[277]

Due to the absence of interest along the coast, Richard turned to the interior of the country, exploring the regions of Daloa, Man, and Danane. In this mountainous area, he encountered the Wobe and the Yakouba tribes, populous groups that were

---

275 The Protestant weekly *Le christianisme au XXe siècle* printed this warning in its January 21, 1926, issue: "A black of the Gold Coast, calling himself the Rev. Mark Hayford, is presenting himself to official persons in Paris (and in America)—and also among bankers and industrialists—to collect funds for the construction of a college in the Ivory Coast. We highly advise that any person who is solicited by him, even if he comes with letters of recommendation (perhaps authentic), give him nothing without first consulting with the director of the Paris Mission. Cited by S. Schmid, *Mark Christian Hayford, 1864–1935: Ein pionier aus Westafrika* (Bonn: Verlag für Kultur und Wissenschaft, 1999), 73.

276 See Schmid, op. cit., 82ff. Hayford took the Scottish Mission to court, charging it with defamation for the report it made in its inquiry into the real situation of the Baptist Church and Mission in the Gold Coast. He lost the case.

277 J. Decorvet, *Les matins de Dieu*, 2nd ed. (La Béude de Mazenc: La Croisade du Livre Chrétien, 1977), 51.

more open to the gospel than the inhabitants of the coast. Moreover, he came into contact with a tribe of the Ashantia ethnic group, which originated from the Gold Coast and had settled in the area about fifteen years before. The group lived at Buyo, in the country of Bete, about three hundred kilometers to the north of Sassandra. When Richard arrived in Buyo, writes Blocher, "he found a chapel already constructed and a handful of happy Africans to listen. These men and women turned to God, and after being instructed, were baptized. They were the first fruits of a vast field."[278]

After a year's vacation in France, the Richards returned to the Ivory Coast in 1930, now able to rely on support from a sister mission, the Christian and Missionary Alliance (CMA). The CMA first arrived in Africa in 1890 when it established itself in Sierra Leone; and it had been in Guinea since 1918. Conscious of the needs of the neighboring Ivory Coast, it established a base at Bouake in 1930 and took charge of some regions in the interior of the country, which lay to the east of the zone reserved for the Biblical Mission.

In 1934 the Worldwide Evangelization Crusade (WEC) also came to the Ivory Coast, establishing itself in the center and east. At the same time the Biblical Mission strengthened its work in the interior of the country while continuing to work in the coastal region of Sassandra and Tabou. The partition of the territory of the Ivory Coast between various missions avoided competition between denominations in the same area, but it also helped to create ethnic churches.

---

278 J. A. Blocher, in: R. Blanc, J. Blocher, E. Kruger, *Histoire des missions protestantes française,* (Flavion: Le Phare, 1970), 361.

# CHAPTER 18

# Protestant Mission and the Foundation of the Church in Cameroon

Cameroon was discovered by the Portuguese in 1472. Its name comes from the Portuguese word for prawns (*cameroes*), which are abundant in the waters of the Wouri River where it juts into the ocean at Douala (see map 11, p. 563). The Dutch supplanted the Portuguese in 1560, and in the eighteenth century they were in turn displaced by the British. In 1827 the British established the supply base of their antislavery navy on the island of Fernando Po, which lay in the Atlantic Ocean opposite to the estuary of the Wouri River. The Douala tribe, which lived in the estuary of Wouri, was gifted in commerce. Due to its trade with foreigners, it slowly assumed a dominant role throughout the coastal region.

## JAMAICAN PIONEERS

The evangelization of Cameroon began through the initiative of the freed Africans of the Antilles. The Baptist Missionary Society (BMS) had sent missionaries in 1813 to work among the slaves of Jamaica. In 1831 the missionaries showed solidarity with the slaves in rebellion against the colony, and when liberty was obtained in 1834, it was not only the occasion of great rejoicing, but also of revival. In their joy, the newly freed people decided to evangelize Africa, their native land. After some hesitation, the BMS agreed to help. In 1839 it sent two of its missionaries from Jamaica to reconnoiter Cameroon. These were the Reverend John Clarke and Dr. George Prince, the latter a former slaver trader.[279] Using Fernando Po as their base, they made several reconnaissance trips into the continent. They then returned to Jamaica where their report aroused much enthusiasm, and many freedmen offered to serve as missionaries in Africa. A number of Jamaicans and several British missionaries of the BMS embarked for Fernando Po in 1842.

---

279 The hesitation of the BMS was due to the failure of its efforts in Sierra Leone in 1795, three years after its founding. It had had to abandon the work there after only two years because of the insurmountable difficulties encountered by its missionaries. William Carey, the founder of the BMS, often said: "I hope that the Society will keep an eye fixed on Africa." He died several years before his wish was fulfilled through the work begun in Cameroon.

Among the Jamaicans was Joseph Merrick, a former printer turned pastor, and Alexander Fuller, a carpenter who would become responsible for the spiritual life of the Jamaican emigrants. The climate along the coast of Cameroon was much more dangerous for the Europeans than that of Fernando Po. Consequently, it was the Jamaicans who first settled on the continent at Bimbia at the end of 1843. These were Fuller, his two sons, and Merrick. Fuller died in 1847, but the work of his son Joseph Jackson Fuller, then only twenty years old, was crucial in the birth of the Cameroonian church, as we will see. Merrick succeeding in setting up a small printing press and then began translating and printing texts from the Bible as fast as he could. His printed material was highly popular among a population desirous of learning to read.

In 1845 the Spanish seized the island of Fernando Po and expelled most of the Protestant missionaries. Having little choice, the missionaries resettled themselves on the Cameroonian coast. Among the British missionaries, Alfred Saker was the only one to survive in the terrible coastal climate. He chose to reside at Douala and showed evidence of charisma as a pioneer missionary during thirty years of service in Cameroon. The printing press was moved by Merrick to Douala, and the Gospel of Matthew appeared in 1848. This occurred a little before the death of Merrick, whose brief ministry left a profound impression on the fledgling Church of Cameroon. Jaap Van Slageren writes:

> Without detracting from the remarkable work of the others, it is only just to note that it is Merrick who laid the foundations of Christianity in Cameroon. He was especially gifted in language, which allowed him to converse easily with the indigenous population in the Isubu language and to prepare Bible translations that later served as examples for Alfred Saker's work at Douala. Clarke, who praised Merrick so much that he was considered the absolute master Bible translator and linguistic researcher in West Africa, also testified to his peaceful and humanitarian influence in the society of the Isubu. His influence on King William of Bimbia was such that he convinced him to abolish the slave trade in his country, and his preaching of love and nonviolence so encouraged the people's efforts that many were moved to the point of transitioning toward a new and really Christian life.[280]

Although the Spanish expelled the missionaries from Fernando Po, they tolerated the indigenous Protestants there for many more years. Then in 1858 six Jesuits arrived with an order from the king of Spain forbidding all religions except Roman Catholicism. For several years, the Protestants held clandestine services, but when persecution became severe, most of the Protestants (ninety baptized) resolved to take refuge on the continent on the neighboring coast. Joseph J. Fuller founded a Victorian enclave for them.

---

280 Jaap van Slageren, *Les débuts du christianisme au Cameroun* (Leyden, The Netherlands: E. J. Brill, 1972), 22–23.

## ALFRED SAKER

Saker (1814–1880) was born in Kent of farming parents. Converted and baptized at the age of twenty, he later presented himself as a missionary candidate to the Baptist Mission, which appointed him to the Antilles. At the time he had been married for three years and was the father of two children.[281] The Sakers arrived in Africa in 1844, lending much help to the Jamaican pioneers at Fernando Po. The following year, before the measures of expulsion were taken by the Spanish, Saker moved to Douala and opened a school. He was accompanied by Thomas Johnson, a convert from Fernando Po.

Saker's primary objective being the translation of the Bible, he followed Merrick's work. He learned the rudiments of the biblical languages and asked that exegetical commentaries be sent to him from Europe. After seventeen years of effort, he completed the New Testament in 1862. Ten years later, he completed the entire Bible.[282] In translating the Scriptures, Saker's goal was to found an autonomous Cameroonian church as quickly as possible. In 1850, after five years in Cameroon, he gave the following testimony:

> Hence, I have lived a rather long time to witness what I have intensely desired for so long: the beginning of a good work in Cameroon and the foundation of a Christian church. May it be permitted to me to see thousands of souls joined to us. And I can hope it, for the Spirit of God accomplishes great work . . . There is still time for those men who, wanting what is in my life, to say to me: "What must I do to be saved?" The Christian community in all its smallness is recognized as a new force in this country.[283]

*Alfred Saker (1814–1880), pioneer missionary to Cameroon from 1845 to 1876.*

The first convert was baptized in 1849. Five more were baptized in 1851, including George Nkwe, a slave of Akwa, the great chief of the Douala and often hostile to the mission. In 1866 Nkwe became the first ordained Cameroonian minister. J. van Slageren explains, "Kkwe enjoyed a great role as counselor and peacemaker of the Douala, a people divided by internal quarrels that sometimes degenerated into civil wars. On the order of King Akwa, Nkwe was often present in the course of heated deliberations where his counsel restored a common outlook and avoided violent measures. This was all the more

---

281 His wife, Helen Jessup, had also received the conviction of a missionary call before being engaged to him.

282 When the Bible was published in 1872, the Old Testament had 854 pages and the New Testament 629. The written form of the language had been invented by Saker.

283 H. Nicod, *Conquérants du golfe de Guinée* (Paris: SMEP, 1947), 73.

remarkable in that Nkwe had kept the status of a slave and was supposed to pay a part of his salary to his owner."[284] At the time that Nikwe was baptized, a prince of Douala was also baptized under the name of Thomas Horton.

In 1850 during his first vacation in Britain, Saker recognized that the friends of the mission and even the committee of the BMS had doubts about the long-term prospects of Cameroon. He tried to restore their courage before taking his leave of them:

> I fear that some among you who desire the good of Africa are discouraged, but I believe that you must not be . . . In Cameroon there are now about a hundred people whom we can consider as converted to God. In the course of the past nine years, about forty have died while giving the encouraging witness that they were leaving for a better country. It is you and your agents who have been the instruments of their salvation. There are now eight indigenous catechists . . . The instruction given is an immense benefit . . . Churches have been founded, and, today, the desert is transformed into a garden of the Lord. If this is all that has been accomplished in the face of so much suffering and so many lives sacrificed, someone will ask if the result is worth the sacrifice? . . .
>
> Brothers, I think that you will agree with me that we must not allow ourselves to be discouraged . . . You are no doubt coming to the conclusion that I should return to Africa immediately. I can only say, I am ready.[285]

In 1855 Thomas Johnson, who came from Fernando Po, became the first African to be ordained a minister by Saker. For many years he had assumed the heavy burden of the church of Douala because of the death of several European missionaries and the absence of Saker during his various sojourns in Britian. Saker wrote of him: "I can only speak in rather elevated terms. His devotion and work are beyond all praise. Without him I would be nothing. He does not give me reasons for concern and disappoints none of my desires. The indigenous people have a profound affection for him."[286]

When the Christian community, whose ethical values were becoming far removed from that of the non-Christians, began to show considerable growth and to influence the spirit of the population, most of the traditional chiefs sought to eliminate it. Slageren writes:

> There followed a veritable and sometimes violent persecution in which the Christian women suffered most. The men, for their part, when they saw themselves mocked and calumniated and cheated of their goods and in their commercial transactions, began to move apart from the life of the tribe.[287]

284 Slageren, op. cit., 32.
285 Nicod, op. cit., 75–77.
286 Ibid., 81.
287 Slageren, op. cit., 36.

Saker sought to take a holistic view of human needs. He struggled energetically against slavery and ritual murders. He introduced fruit trees and truck farming into the country. With the Jamaican Fuller, a bricklayer by training who was ordained into the pastoral ministry in 1859,[288] he opened a vocational school where agriculture, brick making (until then entirely unknown), and construction were taught. It was necessary to establish this school as quickly as possible because of the persecution directed against Christians, for the young Christians who had been rejected by their society needed trades that would give them the means to survive.

Saker preached twice a day and trained others to preach. He quickly developed confidence in the converted Africans and often said, "I gave myself the rule of not doing any work myself that could be entrusted to another. What other method could have permitted me to accomplish all that has been done?"

*The brick church constructed by Alfred Saker in Douala.*

Saker was often the only European missionary in Cameroon. In order for the work to be extended into the interior of the land, others had to be enlisted. Consequently, between 1854 and 1864, the BMS accepted six missionaries, both British and Jamaican. The missionary team was soon convulsed by controversy. Some felt that Saker was so absorbed by the work of development that the task of evangelization suffered. He defended himself before the authorities of the BMS:

---

288 Fuller's wife died the year he was ordained. He remarried in 1861 to the daughter of a British missionary. It was the first mixed marriage celebrated religiously in Cameroon, and the British consul described it as a "scandalous event."

As for the material work that I do, it is not time lost since I find myself in a country where no industry exists, and among a population totally ignorant of all the elementary trades . . . Some claim that these material occupations have harmed our spiritual work and that I should have gone, Bible in hand, to seat myself here under a tree, or there under a shelter, to preach Jesus to the indigenous population. But this makes no sense as long as the people are not free of disease and hunger, as long as they do not have suitable roofs over their heads . . . For me apostolic work does not consist of preaching far off from men, but of going to each one in his hut, of sharing in his pains and cares, and of helping him to discover better ways of living and to realize them . . . When I have earned his attention, it is then possible to speak to him of the higher life that we have lost and that the God of love desires to give us, if we care to listen.[289]

E. B. Underhill, the secretary of the mission, came to Cameroon to inquire about Saker's work. He quickly saw the value in what he was accomplishing with his African and Jamaican colleagues. Slageren writes:

Saker is to be classed among the missionaries of the primitive period who venture into the dark places of Black Africa: men who are always of an independent and resolute character, which often makes life difficult for their entourage and even more so for their teammates . . .

But it is important to recognize that his merits were indispensable. Despite a weak constitution, Saker persisted for more than thirty years under extremely difficult conditions of life and work as the only white person ministering in Cameroon . . . He plead the cause of the Cameroonians while enlarging his work in every domain and striving for the people's spiritual as well as material welfare. He so touched the very soul of society that his example soon became a Douala proverb: "Do things like Saker."[290]

Saker, who saw four of his children die in Africa, retired to Britain in 1876 at the age of sixty-five. Sick and exhausted, he lived for only three years. David Livingstone declared of him: "He was the most remarkable missionary on the west side of Africa."

Together with Saker, others also laid the foundations of the Protestant church in Cameroon. These were Joseph Merrick and Joseph Jackson Fuller of Jamaica, Thomas Johnson of Fernando Po, and George Nkwe of Cammeroon. One secret of Saker's success is that he sought out freedmen and African elites for Christian service. But Cameroon is an extensive country, and this first generation could reach only a limited portion of its territory.

---

289 Nicod, op. cit., 118–20.
290 Slageren, op. cit., 30–31.

## THE GERMAN PERIOD

After the departure of Saker, Fuller became the leading missionary in Cameroon. He struggled courageously against the secret societies that were a veritable plague in the country. The Baptist Mission supported fourteen new missionaries in Cameroon between 1875 and 1884. At the end of this period, Germany became the master of the country. The British, being judged undesirable, were forced to leave. After signing an agreement that transferred the work of BMS to the Basel Mission, Fuller left the country in 1888.[291] The German colonial period lasted only about thirty years. Though a period of economic development for Cameroon, progress came at the price of brutal repression of independent-minded ethnic groups.

The first four missionaries of the Basel Mission began their work in 1886. Two succumbed in the first week. Several stations had been destroyed by war, and some of the congregations had been dispersed or declined due to the lack of pastoral care. When they reassembled, there were less than 250 baptized members.[292]

The transfer of responsibility was not without difficulty, for the Baptist churches refused to recognize the authority of the Basel Mission. More than infant baptism, the question of ecclesiastical discipline caused the greatest tensions. The Basel Mission was stricter than its predecessor, especially regarding adultery, polygamy, and the consumption of alcohol. Moreover the Baptists, having a congregational polity, allowed each local community a large measure of autonomy. The Basel Mission, in contrast, required a comprehensive submission of churches and pastors to its central authority. Some churches dissented and turned to the German Baptists for help. Beginning in 1891, the Baptist Mission of Berlin was able to support them.

In five years the Basel Mission lost ten out of the twenty missionaries that it sent out, and others had to be repatriated for reasons of health. Nevertheless, after troubled beginnings, it saw some encouraging results: its missionaries, more numerous than the British Baptists, benefited from the previous generation's sowing of the gospel seed. For example, they discovered villages along the Wouri River that had abandoned their fetishes and were worshiping the one true God. This was the fruit of the testimony of a Christian from the coast who, persecuted and reduced to slavery, was sold to a clan chief in the interior.

The gospel slowly spread beyond the estuary into the virgin forest. Beginning in 1896, a pause in the expansion of the work occurred as the mission wanted to strengthen its existing bases before extending into new fields. During this time the programs at all levels of education were rethought, teacher training was intensified, and a seminary for the preachers and catechists was inaugurated. Publications were emphasized, including a revision of Saker's translation of the New Testament (1901), a new edition of a hymn collection, and the production of a catechism and various other religious or educational books. Also, beginning in 1903, a monthly journal appeared.

---

291 Although Swiss, the majority of those sent by the Basel Mission were Germans.

292 In a Baptist mission, the number of baptized does not say everything. The influence of the gospel may touch a considerable number, but baptism is administered only after a sometimes lengthy time of testing.

As it had done previously in the Gold Coast and the Indies, the Basel Mission began a commercial society in 1898 in order to promote commerce at prices that made goods accessible to the population. The trade also served to provision stations and villages with useful merchandise. Above all, the project was intended to avoid the harmful effects of typical colonial commerce in which the sale of alcohol was the most lucrative part.

The colonial administration favored this project by freely conceding the field and by providing armed protection. Missionaries and representatives of the colonial power were of the same nationality and spoke the same language. Nevertheless, it would be an exaggeration to speak of an alliance between the colonists and missionaries. The latter often rose up against the strictly mercantile goals of colonization and against the contempt colonialists often bore for the population. Missionaries denounced numerous abuses in the German Protestant press, stirring debate in German society that reached even the Reichstag in Berlin.

Among the principal obstacles encountered were, in the north, the rapid progress of Islam, and in the South, by contrast, a lively competition with the Catholic mission. From the first years of the twentieth century, the Basel Mission sought to evangelize the plateau of Grassfields,[293] a region halfway between the virgin forest near the coast and the savanna land of northern Cameroon. In general, Christianity was well received there. One of the principal kings, desiring to learn to read, came to sit beside his son on the benches of a school that had just begun its courses. Eager for cultural and economic progress, the population was often less interested in the evangelical message. Also, resistance from the local religions was strong, even more so for Islam than Christianity.

On the eve of the First World War and after a little more than twenty-five years on the field, the Basel Mission was maintaining forty-six missionaries or missionary families at nineteen stations in Cameroon. There were four hundred annexes, fifteen thousand Christians, twenty-three thousand children in the schools, a hospital, a professional school, but only three Cameroonian ministers. These numbers underscore the importance of the Basel Mission's educational work in the vernacular language, but also its failure to produce indigenous leaders. The Baptists of the Berlin Mission, for their part, were responsible for six stations, twenty-five missionaries, a little over three thousand Christians, and 3,600 children in the schools. Some churches declared their independence from the mission and formed the Native Baptist Church, or the Independent Baptist Church, with about 2,500 members under the direction of the Reverend Joseph Dibundu.

In the course of the First World War, an army formed of Africans, British, and French troops seized strategic regions of the country.[294] In 1915 the German missionaries were imprisoned by the allies and the Swiss Germans expelled. Cameroon was then placed under a French and British mandate. The British obtained the region

---

293 The region was later known as Bamiléké.
294 It took seventeen months for the Allies to put an end to German resistance.

bordering on Nigeria, while the greater part of the country was entrusted to France, including the principal port, Douala.

## THE PARIS MISSION COMES TO THE RESCUE

The departure of the Germans left a void in leadership and many urgent needs unmet. Though short of personnel and means due to the war, the Paris Mission sent four missionaries to Cameroon in 1917. Each had experience in other countries: Elie Allégret in Gabon, André Oechsner de Coninck in Lesotho, Etienne Bergeret in New Caledonia, and Frédéric Christol in Zambia. These four took up the work that was formerly performed by over eighty missionaries from the Basel and Berlin missions. They were warmly received by all the churches: those of the Basel mission, the Baptists, and the Independents. By the third year of the war, the Cameroonian church was bereft of all exterior help, and almost everything was in need of reorganization. The only solution was to entrust as much of the work as possible to the Africans, while the responsibility of the missionaries would be limited to training the indigenous workers in their new responsibilities, providing counsel, and ensuring the coordination of efforts between different sectors. Elie Allégret adopted the motto: "The evangelization of Africa by Africans."

The missionaries and the Cameroonian church developed a progressive statement of understanding, and a synodal commission was named that included both Cameroonian ministers and missionaries. The opening of Bible schools and the reopening of primary schools was arranged, and it was decided that the salaries of the African ministers and evangelists would be assumed by the African church. The missionaries first sent by the Paris Mission understood that they were engaged not simply in the transfer of power from the Basel to the Paris Mission but, rather, in the transition of an African church toward autonomy. The mission saw itself as accompanying the Cameroonian church in this transitional period by aiding in its material and spiritual reconstruction following the destruction and disorganization of the war. Subsequent events showed how difficult it was to put these good intentions into practice.

Though church and mission sought to work together harmoniously, the relationship was vexed by the missionaries' desire to eliminate polygamy. The Cameroonian ministers were reluctant to do this, being convinced that the measure would be hotly resisted by the population. E. Allégret explained, "The firmness with which the missionaries imposed their decision corresponded to their desire to create a pure and holy church. In their view, 'the salvation of the black race depended on the constitution of Christian families of which polygamy is the negation.' They considered polygamy less as an element in African patrimonial culture than as an essential characteristic of paganism."[295] The stand taken by the missionaries against polygamy was also directly related to their concern for the dignity of women. In the social system of that time, the dowry paid for the second or third wife was the equivalent of buying a laborer—that is to say, it was a form of slavery.

---

295 Slageren, op. cit., 143.

At the end of the war, the committee of the Paris Mission wanted to retrive those missionaries that it had provisionally lent to others fields to fill the gap left by the removal of the Basel Mission. However, its continued support still seemed indispensable to the Church of Cameroon, which was rapidly expanding. In February 1919, a conference of churches in Cameroon occurred that included 310 delegates. It wrote to the committee of the Paris Mission to express its gratitude for the help given and to ask that the mission continue to work in collaboration with the church. In an act of faith, the committee decided at its June 2, 1919 meeting "to adopt North Cameroon as its eighth field of work."

The Bamiléké country (Grassfields) saw rapid progress in the period following the First World War, and the Basel Mission had already begun to reach this region when it was forced to abandon work during the war. In the aftermath of the conflict, the mission lost touch with the region. In 1920 Modi Din and other Cameroonian ministers sought to reestablish contact with this interior region. The work developed there in a remarkable and spontaneous fashion through the efforts of African evangelists. Numerous villages were stirred by a profound revival, which continued despite opposition and even persecution from tribal chiefs. If nothing else, the movement erected a human barrier to the advance of Islam. It was not until 1926 that the missionary Elie Robert came to settle in the Bamiléké country and establish the station of Mbo. The responsibility for the station soon passed to Frédéric Christol, who sought to adapt Christian life to the indigenous culture by avoiding useless disagreements. An agricultural school was established as was a training center for various types of trades: masonry, carpentry, gardening, tanning, chauffeuring, car repair, and much else. Medical work was also undertaken. At first there was a dispensary established at Mbo and then, in 1928, a hospital at Bafoussam, under the direction of Dr. Debarge. J. van Slageren writes:

> The penetration of the gospel into the Bamiléké region took place at a pace rarely seen in the history of the church . . . The movement was spontaneous and clothed in indigenous attire . . . Let us recall the context of the extraordinary work of the Reverend Modi Din. All of Grassfields, the British as well as the French parts [the Bamiléké country], was opened to the influence of this indefatigable traveler.[296]

However, Modi Din's[297] work was contested by missionaries who felt that it was too fast and superficial and that he admitted neophytes to baptism who were as yet uninstructed in the Christian faith. Paul Dieterlé, who succeeded Christol, was much stricter in his approach to local customs. He untiringly visited churches in order to keep them in the evangelical faith, but he often used his authority in a clumsy manner, which was not well received and produced unnecessary tensions.

---

296 Ibid., 185–86.

297 Modi Din was a man of a great firmness who was imprisoned for nearly three years for protesting against colonial policies during the time when Cameroon was under German authority. The missiologist Leenhardt, who encountered him in the course of a journey in Cameroon, is said to have been impressed by his personality, faith, and zeal.

The mission can be faulted for seeking to "Europeanize" this church in a misguided attempt to purify it from residual paganism. The result was the reverse of what was intended, producing a reaction against the mission and a desire for independence and Africanization. In addition to this, the large number of languages spoken in the region presented an unsolvable problem, for it was impossible to publish Bible translations or to have a seminary for catechists in each language. Conflict with authority and the fragmentation of the church due to tribalism put an end to the momentum of the revival.

The number of missionaries was slowly increasing. By 1927 after ten years on the field, the Paris Mission was supporting eighteen missionaries and six mission stations. Cameroonian leaders included 616 catechists and evangelists, and eleven pastors. One census reported that the church had 38,600 members, and 15,800 catechumens and students in schools. During the 1920s, there were twenty thousand New Testaments, nearly thirty thousand hymnals, and twenty thousand educational books published and distributed.

The success of the mission led logically to the organization of missionary conferences to discuss the general strategy of the work. These conferences were intended to supplement the synodal commissions held by the Cameroonian ministers; nevertheless, the ministers looked askance at these meetings about which they were informed after the fact. Hence, the period between the two World Wars saw mixed results. There was considerable growth due to the work of some remarkable Christian personalities, both African and European, but this was also a period marked by painful tensions and even some ruptures for which both sides share responsibility.

## COLLABORATION WITH OTHER MISSIONS

The Board of Foreign Missions of the Presbyterian Church (the northern Presbyterian Church in the U.S.), which had been present in Gabon since 1872, became engaged in 1885 in the southern part of nearby Cameroon. Its work was done with the agreement of the Basel Mission, and during the First World War, its missionaries originally came from a neutral nation. Throughout the war, even after the arrival of the French, the Presbyterians were able to pursue their work. Because the field to be occupied was much too vast, in 1920 the Paris Mission entrusted the American Presbyterians with the region south of the Sanaga River where there were about a hundred places of worship.[298]

In addition to the work it inherited from the Basel Mission, the Paris Mission also offered its aid to Baptist Churches. Only a few months after the coming of the French missionaries in 1917, a conference of the Baptist Churches of Cameroon was convoked. Most of the churches, including some of the Native Church, responded positively. Allégret and his colleagues encouraged them to unite with the denomination of the United Baptist Churches of Cameroon. In 1920 the Paris Mission contributed a French Baptist missionary, Charles Maître, who was entrusted with the direction of

---

298 The feelings of goodwill continued, for twenty-eight years later it is the Presbyterian Mission that gave the Paris Mission several stations in Gabon.

the entire work of the French Protestant Mission of Cameroon. Other Baptists joined the Paris Mission, notably the Reverends Maurice Farelly and Michel Rousseau.

After an absence of eight years, the colonial administration authorized the Basel Mission to return in 1922. The only condition was that its missionaries be Swiss or Alsatians. The mission stations of the Basel Mission that were located in territory under the British mandate were deprived of all exterior aid until 1925. At that time, the British finally allowed Swiss missionaries of the Basel Mission into their region. They found nine thousand Christians and 3,600 catechumens. In 1927 a German Baptist Mission was given the right to return to what was then British Cameroon. At the same time American Baptists were also allowed in.

In the course of the twentieth century, a variety of different denominational missions established themselves in Cameroon, including the Norwegian Lutheran Mission, which succeeded in founding a Lutheran Church in 1921.[299]

---

299 In 1948, the Sudan United Mission (SUM, or today VIA) entrusted its Swiss branch with the responsibility to witness among the Islamic population of Northern Cameroon. All of these missions avoided competition by working in different regions of the country. The Evangelical Church of Cameroon was established on 10 March 1957, forty years after the arrival of the Paris Mission. On the same date, the Union Baptist Church of Cameroon was also inaugurated. The two churches immediately began to work together, forming the Council of the Baptist and Evangelical Church of Cameroon. This institution coordinated the work undertaken by the two denominations. (This work is not elaborated here since it is beyond the chronological limits established for this book.)

# CHAPTER 19

# The Sudanese Regions

Today the name of Sudan denotes the nation located south of Egypt and west of Ethiopia, the former Anglo-Egyptian Sudan. But the term originally designated the vast region south of the Sahara, including Sudan, Chad, Niger, French Sudan (present-day Mali), Upper Volta (present-day Burkina Faso), and Mauritania. Islam penetrated these regions during the period from the eleventh through the eighteenth centuries. These countries are landlocked, except Mauritania on the Atlantic coast, and Sudan, which has access to the Red Sea.

Prior to the Islamization of these nations, traces have been found of a Christian presence that dates from the second half of the first millennium. This started with Nubian Christian merchants who, leaving the Valley of the Nile, ventured as far as Darfour (present-day west Sudan), Lake Chad, and even Mali. It is, however, difficult to evaluate the scope and the duration of this presence (see p. 131-32). Displaced by Islam, missionaries would not reintroduce Christianity into these countries until the twentieth century. In the more southern regions, missionaries encountered animistic populations that have been more open to Christianity than have the Muslims who dominate the north.

With the exception of the Anglo-Egyptian Sudan (the present-day Republic of Sudan), these countries were part of French West Africa[300] or, in the case of Chad, Equatorial French Africa.[301] The Catholic missions preceded the Protestant missions, which arrived around 1920. The churches in the region are, therefore, clearly more recent than those in Central Africa or South Africa or the coastal regions of West Africa. Moreover, their development has largely occurred in the last fifty years, which are not covered in this work. We will examine, rather, only the first twenty years of Protestant mission history in these countries.

---

300 French West Africa also included Senegal, Guinea, and Benin where Protestant missions had arrived earlier (see pp. 519ff), as well as the Ivory Coast (see chapter 7).
301 For the history of the Protestant mission in Chad, see p. 607f.

# MAURITANIA

This country is twice the size of France, and most of its territory lies in the Sahara.[302] The Maures, who form the majority of the population, were Islamicized by the Arabs in the fourteenth century. French trading posts were opened on the Atlantic coast in the seventeenth and eighteenth centuries, and French colonization began about 1855 through the efforts of Louis Faidherbe, the French governor of Senegal. The colony became a major undertaking for France at the beginning of the twentieth century, and achieved its independence in 1960, becoming the Islamic Republic of Mauritania.

Catholics, who for the most part were French, first entered the nation at the beginning of the twentieth century. Protestant missions were able to gain a foothold in several places but did not achieve long-term success. The Worldwide Evangelization Crusade withdrew its missionaries in 1965. In the capital, Nouakchott, there is a small community of expatriate Protestants who, for most part, have come from other African countries. In general, the population consists of Moroccan Arabs, who have a Bible in their own language.

# FRENCH SUDAN (THE REPUBLIC OF MALI)

In 1895 the White Fathers that formed the Catholic Mission set out from Senegal and reached Bamako, and the White Sisters followed a little latter. The first African priest was ordained in 1936. In 1919 the first Protestant mission entered the country, the Gospel Missionary Union. Until the end of the Second World War, its work was limited by a lack of missionary personnel. Nevertheless, the New Testament in Bambara left the press in 1937.[303] The Christian and Missionary Alliance (CMA) arrived in Freetown, Sierra Leone, in 1890. Its goal was to establish a base from which it could spread out into the interior of the continent as far as French Sudan and sub-Saharan West Africa. In 1896 A. B. Simpson, the founder of the mission, wrote:

> In Sudan another "advance" has sprung up. Our mission has been enriched with six new workers and a string of stations in the last year. The way from Freetown to Tibabadougo, near Niger, is totally open. And now, from this base, we envision a two-pronged movement into the interior, one in the northwest toward Timbuktu, and the other in the east toward Niger by Lake Chad.[304]

As noted above, the mission in Guinea began in 1919. In 1923 it began to work in Sikasso and in the southeast of French Sudan. The first years yielded little fruit, but in 1931 three missionaries lost their lives in a week, and the tragedy produced an unexpected reaction: twenty young people converted. This unleashed a movement of the Spirit in French Sudan and in neighboring countries where the CMA was working.

---

302 There were about 2 million inhabitants in the year 2000.

303 The complete Bible in this language was completed in 1958. During this period, the Gospel Missionary Union had extended its work to the center of the country, with eight missionary stations, a Bible school, and soon about forty places of worship.

304 Madeleine Vaillant, "Historique des missions protestantes in Haute-Volta with un état de la formation actuelle des autochtones" (bachelor's thesis, Faculté Libre de Théologie Évangélique, Vaux-sur-Seine, France, 1975), 20.

There were only four mission stations at the time, but seven were added in subsequent years. In 1936 the Institut Biblique de Ntorrosso opened, offering a four-year course of studies to train the future ministers of Sudan and its neighboring countries. A Bible school for young girls was also opened in Baramba.

Despite these efforts, the Christian churches remained very much minorities in Mali where Islam has been present since the eleventh century.

## UPPER VOLTA (BURKINA FASO)

Upper Volta, a region of French West Africa, became a French colony in 1902 but did not obtain its current borders until 1947.[305] It gained independence in 1960 and took the name Republic of Burkina Faso in 1984. Situated to the north of the Ivory Coast and Ghana, Burkina Faso does not have access to the sea and its northern section is located in the semidesert region of the Sahel. The population is composed of about fifty different ethnic groups, among which the Mossi form the largest. During the first half of the twentieth century, the country suffered from a large demographic hemorrhaging in which many people sought employment in the mines and plantations of the Ivory Coast and Ghana.

The feudal state of the emperor of the Mossi, who dominated the region before colonization, was rebellious against Islam. The first signs of a Muslim presence in this region were in the eleventh century, but effective Islamization began only in the eighteenth century and its growth was relatively slow in the course of the nineteenth century. By 1900 only 10 percent of the population was Muslim. During the twentieth century Islam expanded at the expense of the traditional religions, reaching 48 percent of the population by 1970.

The first Christian missionaries there were the White Fathers, who arrived in 1901. Choosing the region of Ouagadougou, they stimulated the development of the area, which later became the capital of the country. The first baptisms were celebrated in 1905, and the White Sisters reinforced the Catholic missionary presence in 1911. It was only in 1942, however, that the first indigenous priests were ordained.

The pioneers of Protestant missions were the Assemblies of God.[306] The American Pentecostals Wilbur Taylor and Harry Bright, who were working in Sierra Leone, heard of the Mossi and of their resistance to Islam. Taylor made a reconnaissance journey through the country in 1919, and the next year the colonial administration authorized the founding of a missionary station in the territory of this ethnic group. Taylor and Bright settled there in 1921 and after several years were joined by a dozen colleagues. There were rapid conversions, and several stations extended the field northward. In 1926 the missionary Arthur Wilson explained: "From the first months of work in Kaya, God gave us four men capable of being leaders, and permitted us to

---

305 The French colony of Upper Senegal and Niger, created in 1904, included French Sudan (Mali) and Upper Volta (Burkina Faso). Between 1919 and 1932, Upper Volta became a colonial territory and was then again partially integrated into Niger and partially into the Ivory Coast, and this continued until 1947. These modifications of status, name, and borders did not facilitate a comprehensive missionary effort into this region.

306 For the successive arrival of evangelical Protestant missions see Issaka F. Tapsoba, *Églises et mouvements évangéliques au Burkina Faso 1921–1989* (Ouagadougou, 1990).

transmit to them the vision of carrying the gospel to their people. He has truly used them to reach others who, in their turn, have received the same vision."[307] After fixing the language of the Mossi in writing, the first Bible texts were printed in their language at the end of 1929. During the 1930s, the missionaries of the Assemblies of God of France began to collaborate with the Americans. The first missionaries were Mr. and Mrs. Emile Chastagner, who founded the station of Tengodogo in 1931. A church quickly developed there due largely to the ministry of the evangelist Dentoumda Nizemba; and Pentecostalism remained the main current of Protestantism among the Burkinabé (people of Burkina Faso).

In 1923 the CMA began the evangelization of the southwest. The missionary Paul Freligh settled at Bobo-Kioulasso in order to work with the ethnic group called the Bobo. He was replaced in 1927 by the Johanson family. The CMA later enlarged its field of work to include the western part of the country, founding the Evangelical Christian Church.

Since the Sudan Interior Mission (SIM)[308] was already present in Niger, it entrusted the exploration of Upper Volta in 1930 to three Canadians directed by Dr. Roland Bingham. On the basis of their relationship, the SIM decided to take responsibility for the evangelization of the Gourmantche country in the eastern part of Upper Volta, close to Niger. Its first missionary team established itself at Fada N'Gourma in 1930. Their first tasks were evangelization, fixing the orthography for the Gourmantche language, and translating the Bible. The Gospel of Mark was completed in 1936. Among the pioneers, the Strong and Swanson couples were of particular importance.

In 1921 a man named Tidjite of the Lobi ethnic group, which lay in the southeast of the country, was on the eve of being initiated as a sorcerer. At that time he had a vision in which he heard a voice order him to destroy his idols and to await the coming of a white man who would announce the message of God to him. He obeyed and, after a time of persecution, part of the Lobi came to follow him. Then in 1931, Charles Benington, an Irishman from the Qua Iboe Mission, undertook an exploratory journey into French West Africa. Beginning from Nigeria where he exercised his ministry, Benington traveled to the village of Tidjite, of whose history he was completely ignorant. One of his colleagues, who arrived among the Lobi in 1934, recounts:

> One of the men who came before us to save us was the one of whom God had spoken eleven years before the arrival of the missionary, ordering him to destroy his fetishes because he was going to send him his Word. Though facing great opposition, he burned his fetishes in the marketplace, threw away his bow and arrows, made himself a sword, and procured for himself a red material of which he decorated his house. He was persecuted, bound hand and foot, left to die in a field, and finally carried to Ouagadougou to appear before the governor.[309]

---

307 *The Gospel among the Mossi People*, cited by Vaillant, op. cit., 22.

308 SIM continues to use its acronym but has changed its name to Serving in Mission.

309 Vaillant, op. cit., 25. The sword mentioned here was subsequently interpreted as "the sword of the Spirit," a symbol of the word of God, and the red scarf was interpreted as a symbol of the blood of Christ that purifies from all sin. Tidjite was evidently ignorant of the meaning of these symbols at the time when he chose them.

The work of the Qua Iboe Mission was restarted in 1937 by the Worldwide Evangelization Crusade (WEC), which was already present in the Ivory Coast. Jack Robertson was the first one sent by the WEC to Upper Volta. The evangelization of the region encountered much opposition from those who adhered to the local animistic religion, an opposition that was often occult in nature. Among the WEC missionaries was M. Davies, a Canadian who arrived in 1939. He founded the Evangelical Mission of the Pentecost in the years that followed the Second World War.

The training of indigenous pastors suffered from the dispersion and lack of consultation between the evangelical missions. The Assemblies of God opened a Bible School in Ouagadougou in 1933. Ten African pastors were trained in a year and left for the bush to evangelize the villages, but soon after this the school had to be closed due to the lack of missionaries available to teach. Arthur Wilson then took up the project, opening a Bible school in Kourbi. The first class consisted of about a hundred students, who financed their three-year course of studies by working as craftsmen.

In 1933 the CMA organized an evening Bible school in Bobo-Dioulasso, but again, due to lack of personnel, it could not continue. Instead, the CMA concentrated its efforts in Ntorrosso, Mali, where it provided Bible training to students in both these neighboring countries.[310]

# NIGER

The gospel had been preached in Niger as early as the seventh century, but the Berber Christians were driven from North Africa by Islam. Nubian Christian merchants may also have carried Christianity to the region before the tenth century, but nothing survived of these churches. Being isolated from the rest of Christendom, they were slowly eliminated by Islamization, which began in the eleventh century. As for the other countries of the Sahelian region, it was not until the twentieth century that a new evangelization effort was undertaken there.

The first French explorers discovered Niger in about the year 1890, and it became a French colony in 1922, attached to French West Africa. The Sudan Interior Mission (SIM) was the first missionary society in the colony, and it remained the largest since its arrival in Zinder in 1924. It worked especially among the Haoussa, in the South (Tsibiri, 1928). L'Institute Biblique de Niamey (the Bible Institute of Niamey) was one of SIM's chief accomplishments, which was intended to produce evangelists and ministers for Niger, Dahomey, and Upper Volta. Beginning in 1929, the Evangelical Baptist Mission also worked in Niger. Its work of evangelization was centered in the capital, Niamey. In the course of the twentieth century, Islam has made much progress in the region at the expense of traditional African religions. In contrast, the growth of Christian churches has been extremely slow.[311]

---

310 In 1970, Christians comprised 9.5% of the population of Burkina Faso. Catholics made up 7.7% of this, and Protestants only 1.8% (Barrett, *Encyclopedia*, 157).

311 According to Barrett, *Encyclopedia*, 547, the Muslims were 45.1% in 1900, and 90% in the middle of the 1990s. Protestants and Catholics were representing only .5% of the population in 1990 (7.7 million).

# ANGLO-EGYPTIAN SUDAN (THE REPUBLIC OF SUDAN)

The Republic of Sudan is the largest African nation, but its population density is small for its size. In 1823 Egypt seized the country, accelerating the process of Islamization but also making it a center of the slave trade. An Anglo-Egyptian Condominium was formed in 1899; and the independent Republic of Sudan was born in 1956. The population of the North is partially Arab and largely Islamic. In contrast, Islam has not taken hold in the South, whose Nilotic people are of the black race.

The northern part of Sudan close to Egypt was evangelized as early as the sixth century, and the three Nubian kingdoms in the valley of the Nile resisted Islam for centuries, eventually succumbing by the beginning of the sixteenth century (see 131-132). Despite many difficulties, three Coptic churches are currently present in Sudan, consisting mostly of Egyptians. They grew noticeably in the course of the twentieth century.[312]

The first missionaries of the modern era were Catholics who arrived in 1842 and four years later created a vicariate in Khartoum. In 1881 an independence movement led by the Mahdi and hostile to the West caused the church to almost entirely disappear. When "Holy War" was proclaimed, the Catholic missionaries were ready to flee but most were imprisoned and several died. The British reconquered Sudan in 1898, allowing Catholics, Anglicans, and Presbyterians to enter the field to evangelize the nation. The first baptisms were administered in 1911.

The British and Foreign Bible Society arrived in Khartoum in 1860, and in 1865 Christian Friedrich Spittler began to work there as a missionary. The Church Missionary Society (CMS) could not truly devote itself to evangelization until 1899, following the reconquest. It established itself in Omdurman, close to Khartoum. Its first missionaries were Frank Harpur and Llewellyn Gwynne, who were assisted by a colporteur from the Bible Society. They soon concentrated their efforts on the South to win the animist population, among whom they encountered a ready response. The Azande were the first to respond to the message of the gospel, soon followed by other ethnic groups. In 1914 the CMS began medical work and then intensified its efforts of evangelization through education. This was the origin of what is now the largest Protestant denomination in the country. In 1900 the United Presbyterian Church of North America also entered the field. From a previously established base in Egypt, the Presbyterians first came to Omdurman. They eventually established churches in both North and South Sudan. In 1935 when SIM was expelled from Ethiopia by the Italian colonial government, it too established itself in South Sudan. The Africa Inland Mission (AIM) did the same in 1937, with missionaries who had previously served in Kenya.

---

312 They were about thirty churches, organized in two dioceses, in 1970.

*Part Three*

# CENTRAL AFRICA
# AND MADAGASCAR

# The Belgian Congo:
## Exploration, Evangelization, and Foundation of a Church

David Livingstone passed the last years of his life in an area that might be considered the heart of Africa. It is a relatively confined place where the origins of three rivers are located. From here the Zambezi flows towards the Indian Ocean, the Congo towards the Atlantic Ocean, and the Nile towards the Mediterranean Sea. The explorer had sought to find the sources of the Nile, but he was consistently disappointed in his efforts. In his last attempt, he concluded that a river he had taken for a tributary of the Nile, the Lualaba, was in fact a tributary of the Congo that flowed toward the west. As for the immense basin of the Congo, it remained one of the last completely unexplored regions of the world. Its discovery was due to Henry Morton Stanley, whose vocation of explorer arose from his encounter with Livingstone (see p. 477).

## HENRY MORTON STANLEY

Born in America of British parents, Henry Morton Stanley (1841–1904) was abandoned by his family and placed in a hospice. Being mistreated, he fled and was taken in by a shopkeeper in New Orleans, but he remained an unsettled youth. He participated in the American Civil War, was imprisoned, changed sides, became a sailor, and then enrolled in the navy, which he soon deserted. Finally, he became an independent journalist, a profession in which his taste for travel, risk, and freedom found satisfaction. His encounter with Livingstone changed his life. It not only brought about his conversion, but through it he also discovered his vocation as an explorer.

After Livingstone's death, Stanley took up the torch and remained for some time in Uganda. Then in 1874, he set out from Mombassa (on the Indian Ocean, in present-day Kenya) on a great expedition that continued for 999 days. While Livingstone had for the most part traveled alone, Stanley went with a small private army. When he arrived at the sources of the Congo to begin his descent to its mouth in the Atlantic, his team included 260 persons, including women and children, and four Europeans. Upon the conclusion of the voyage there were no more than 108 left, which included thirteen women and six children. Stanley was the only surviving non-African. Diseases, drowning, and desertions had taken their toll on the contingent over the course of its two-and-a-half-year expedition, during which it had passed though lands made dangerous by climate, dense forests, river rapids, and the hostility of indigenous populations.

During his sojourn in Africa, Stanley was not directly involved in missionary activity, but his widely diffused letters and articles unambiguously served to promote the cause of mission. Here is an extract of a letter published in the popular press:

> May missionaries pious and full of good sense come here! . . . What a field and what a ripe harvest for the sickle of civilization . . . It is the Christian teachings in practice that can explain to the people how to become Christians, heal their diseases, construct houses . . . Do not be afraid to expend too much money for such a mission.

The descriptions that Stanley gave of Africans lacked the love that Livingstone had showed in his writings. In fact, he can be justly criticized for a lack of sensitivity to the humanitarian problems of the populations that he encountered. Jean Jacques Laufer concedes in his biography of Stanley that pleading his cause is difficult:

> Some have reproached him for his hardness, cruel repression, and the blood that he made run, the importance of which his jealous and often prejudiced subordinates—probably more culpable that he—exaggerated. Indeed, his was an iron will. He had a heavy hand and his anger towards those who set up obstacles to his grandiose achievements irritated him sometimes to the shedding of blood.
>
> He was often found to be egotistical and ambitious by those who did not understand the degree to which he mixed his deepest self and the legitimate aspirations of his personal life with the civilizing mission in which he invested himself. Egoist he was, indeed, as are most great achievers, those artists and men of action who sacrifice everything for their creative work.[313]

Stanley said: "I have not been sent into this world to be happy, nor to seek good fortune—I have had a mission to fulfill." And he added an ominous word for the sake of those who would travel his path: "I have removed from my vocabulary the words *impossible* and *failure*."

## OF EXPLORATION AND EXPLOITATION

The mouth of the Congo has been known since the fifteenth century, but explorers had never been able to go upstream very far. Stanley did not approach the mouth of the river from the sea but from having descended from the river's source. The information that he gained from his travel through this unknown country was of immense interest in missionary circles, as well as in the circles of politics and commerce.

---

313 Jean Jacques Laufer, *Stanley: Briseur d'obstacle* (Geneva: Labor & Fides, 1946), 220.

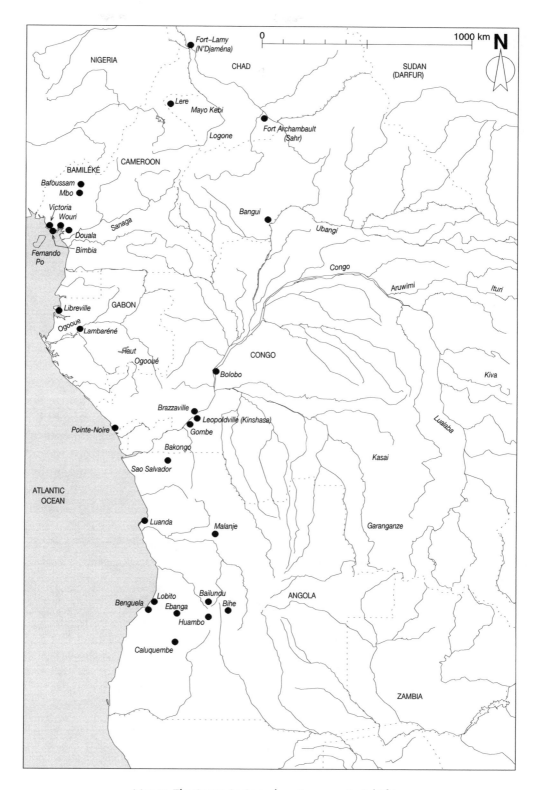

*Map 11: The Congo Basin and western equatorial Africa*

Leopold II, king of the Belgians, took note of the account that Stanley had rendered denouncing the treatment of Africans and the atrocities committed against them. In 1874 he convoked a conference, in which fourteen states participated, to lay the foundations of an international association with the following objectives: to abolish the slave trade, to establish honest international commerce in the Congo, to protect missions, and to end the rivalries between Protestants and Catholics in the region. When Stanley returned to Europe after his great expedition, King Leopold entrusted him with the task of continuing his explorations in the Congo basin, and he gave him funds to support his work for another five years. In 1885 the Congress of Berlin dissolved the international association and made the Congo an independent state in which Leopold II was recognized as the sovereign. Until his death in 1909, he considered this immense territory to be his personal property. Following his death, the Congo became a Belgian colony.

Though the reports of the explorers had initially produced a philanthropic reaction in the international community, this praiseworthy disposition quickly vanished before the enormous riches of the country. The production of rubber and the exploitation of resources buried in the earth, among others, stoked the fires of greed. Belgian companies, or companies based in Belgium, bought vast territories and sought to make quick profits from their investments with the complicity of the Belgian colonial administration. But in the spirit of "might makes right," this was done to the detriment of the exploited populations, which were reduced to slavery in their own land. The state decreed that the army would be maintained by the inhabitants, and one can easily imagine the state of a village in a poor region after the prolonged billeting of several thousand soldiers. A good example is the district of Monsambi where, from 1889 to 1902, the population declined from seven thousand to one thousand inhabitants, being reduced by diseases introduced by the white exploiters, the suppression of revolts, and the flight of voluntary exiles.

George Grenfell, a British Baptist missionary whose life will be examined later, arrived in the Congo in 1878. He observed horrors with his own eyes that exceeded even the cruelty of the Arab slave drivers, and he described raids on villages that attempted to force the population to deliver exorbitant quantities of ivory and rubber:

> Villages were burned and houses razed. Chiefs were attacked; the weak were shot without pity. The bodies were hanged upside down to serve as warnings for others, and their hands were cut off and carried to the commissioner—these were sometimes the hands of children. While their husbands were foraging in the forest, the women were at the mercy of the soldiers, and disease was sown throughout the country . . . The situation of the Israelites under the Medianites or the Assyrians was not more unfortunate than that of the Congolese under the Belgians.[314]

During this tragic period some have estimated the number of dead to have reached 5 million.

---

314 Félix Faure, *George Grennfell: Missionnaire au Congo, 1849–1906* (Paris: SMEP, 1928), 56–57.

# THE ARRIVAL OF THE FIRST PROTESTANT MISSIONARIES

In London in the year 1877 Henry Grattan Guinness founded the Livingstone Inland Mission (LIM). He had been profoundly interested in the explorations of Livingstone and was also influenced by the vision of Hudson Taylor, who had penetrated deeply into the interior of China to proclaim the gospel. The LIM's first missionary and the first Protestant missionary in the Congo was Henry Craven. Leaving Britain in January 1878, he was joined six months later by two colleagues, one of whom soon died. As for Craven, he had to take an early vacation in Britain for reasons of health. With the collaboration of his wife and the aid of several young Africans two had been brought to Europe for further training, he used this period of convalescence to translate extracts of the Bible into Kikongo. He returned to the Congo and died in 1885, after seven years of ministry.

*Henry Craven, first Protestant missionary in the Congo.*

The Livingstone Inland Mission was the first Protestant mission in the Congo, but due to a lack of strategy and too much haste the harvest did not measure up to initial expectations. Between 1878 and 1883, the LIM sent twenty-five missionaries and founded six stations in the province of Leopoldville, but not long after the death of Craven, deficient in both infrastructure and financial means, it ceased to exist. Its stations were given to other societies, the majority being taken up by the Baptist Missionary Society. The Baptists, applying a more ordered plan and taking careful account of the information supplied by the explorers, were more successful as in their turn they engaged in the Congo. It is true that, established about a century before in the time of William Carey, they also benefited from long experience.

## GEORGE GRENFELL

*George Grenfell (1849–1906), explorer and missionary in the immense basin of the Congo River.*

Born in 1849 in Cornouailles, George Grenfell (1849–1906) converted in the Sunday School of a Baptist church when he was about ten years old. As an adolescent, he read the stories of David Livingstone and had the conviction that God was calling him to Africa. He became an apprentice to a mechanic and for several years worked in a machine shop. Then in 1875 at the age of twenty-six, after a year in the Baptist College of Bristol, he embarked for Cameroon. At the time Cameroon was the only field of action in which the Baptist Missionary Society in Africa was engaged. Grenfell accompanied Alfred Saker, a missionary who had already worked in Cameroon for thirty years and was then returning after a vacation (see pp. 542ff). Stimulated by his admiration for Livingstone, Grenfell soon showed an interest in the exploration of the country's water courses, convinced that the mission should not be confined to the coastal regions.

After only a year, Grenfell traveled to Britain to marry and then returned to Cameroon. Sadly his young wife survived only a few months in the African climate. Several years later Grenfell married Rose Patience Edgerley, a Jamaican widow of a Cameroonian colleague. Due to her African origins, she could endure the climate of Central Africa better than a European, and she survived her husband. She was for him a precious assistant.

In 1878 about a year after the departure of Craven and his first LIM colleagues, the Baptist Mission asked Grenfell and his friend the Reverend Thomas Comber to take up the Congo as a new field of action. They left directly from Cameroon. The following year, Grenfell decided to make the capital of the kingdom of Bakongo, Sao Salvador (in present-day Angola), the base of the future Baptist Mission in the Congo. It was an eight-day march from the coast. Abandoned more than two centuries before, there was no trace left from the work of the Portuguese Catholic missionaries. King Don Pedro V welcomed the Protestants, assured them of his support and protection, and authorized them to settle in the area. Following the information provided by Stanley, an exploratory party soon left to travel up the river. Its efforts, however, were cut short after only four days. The king of Makuta welcomed them warmly but forbade them to go farther, fearing that he would lose control of the region's river trade over which he held a monopoly.

For a time missionaries circled around the blockade posed by King Makuta, establishing the first mission stations along the river in 1881. It is then that Grenfell returned to Britian to arrange for the construction of a steel riverboat, the *Peace*, which was twenty-three meters in length. It was taken apart and transported in eight hundred separate pieces, and then reassembled in Africa. Operational in 1884 and based in Stanley-Pool (which would become Leopoldville, and then Kinshasa), this boat rendered yeoman service over many years. Grenfell devoted himself to the work of reconnaissance along the Congo and some of its tributaries, like the Oubangui. His plan was to erect a dozen stations, about 150 kilometers distant from one another.

By 1886 Grenfell had undertaken five voyages of exploration and had traveled about twenty thousand kilometers. Due to his travels he could now draw up a map of large parts of the Congo's course. Many times his expeditions proved to be harrowing events, either because of the river's rapids and the surface rocks that ripped open the hull of the *Peace*, or because of attacks by the local population. Often the *Peace* would be threatened by aggressive local people in fast-approaching canoes and was able to escape only because of its speed. Grenfell recounted some of the challenges he faced upon returning from his second expedition:

> Thank God, we have returned safe and sound. It could have been
> otherwise, for we have encountered perils, and not small ones.

The winds were terrifying on several occasions,[315] and the rocks made three holes in the boat while we fled from the cannibals far into the night, and yet we have not been overcome. We have been attacked by the indigenous population about twenty times. Stones were thrown at us and arrows shot, and we were the target of more spears than we could count.[316]

But it was also common for the missionaries to be well received, as they were at Bolobo in 1887 in rather astonishing circumstances.

The *Peace* arrived at a time when the population was very excited, and it received a welcome that grew increasingly hostile with every passing moment. W. Holman Bentley, who was on board with his wife and small son, suddenly recalled that a young white woman had never before been seen in the country. He asked his wife to take the baby and come up on the bridge. Their appearance was greeted by an ovation on the shore. Spears and knives disappeared and the attention of the warriors was focused on them . . . Nothing could better satisfy this people covered with soot, oil, and red earth than to play the doting parents with a baby in their arms dressed in white. He was passed from one man to another and from one woman to another, eliciting admiration and joy in everyone. The mother was as anxious as she was grateful. Hostility gave place to good will. The station of Bolobo was soon established due to the unconscious influence of a baby.[317]

The missionaries had arrived just after the death of the king's wife, and the funeral ceremonies soon degenerated into orgies accompanied by human sacrifices. Yet the wives of the missionaries, young mothers, did not shrink from participating in such expeditions.

Grenfell also had occasion to assess the ravages caused by the Arab bands that came from the east coast as far as the center of Africa in order to hunt for slaves. In a single day, he saw the smoke of twenty-seven burning villages rise into the air where the inhabitants had been captured or killed by the troops of the terrifying Tippoo Tib. This Arab chief with a thousand soldiers was plundering an immense region of the Congo basin, but the armed intervention of the state succeeded in expelling the

*The riverboat* Peace, *a remarkable instrument for the exploration and evangelization of the Congo basin by George Grenfell.*

Arabs. Grenfell returned to this region about twenty years later. Though the population had diminished due to the trade in black slaves, the contrast with former times was extraordinary. F. Faure writes:

---

315  In certain straights the Congo was as wide as thirty kilometers, which made it like a lake agitated by rising waves.

316  Félix Faure, op. cit., 39.

317  Ibid., 43–44.

> Where before he had seen smoking villages and frightened fugitives, he now saw Christian homes and students studying . . . Deputations from the villagers bombarded Grenfell with demands for teachers, and in some places he saw that schools had already been constructed in the confidence that schoolmasters would soon arrive.[318]

While Grenfell was persevering in his river explorations, other missionaries were steadily increasing the number of mission stations as conditions allowed and reinforcements became available. Eight years after the arrival in the country of Grenfell and Thomas Comber a church was established at Sao Salvador. A missionary made this report:

> In 1886 Comber's domestic servant, responding to the teachings and influence of her master, declared herself a Christian. She was baptized in the presence of some principal men, several women, and fifty boys from the station's school. In special meetings that were held sometime after the church had been constructed with stones from the ruins of the ancient cathedral, not less than a hundred men and women were inscribed as members, and many publicly discarded their fetishes.

> Several of the king's wives became Christians and continued to attend the worship services despite the opposition of their master. They were determined to follow the new way. "It makes no difference to us even if they kill us," they said. "We do not fear dying for Jesus who died for us."[319]

Comber intervened with the king, who then ended his opposition and allowed several of his wives to join the church.

## UNION WITH THE MISSION OF EAST AFRICA

For a period of about twenty years, Grenfell supervised the entire field of the Baptist Mission. His explorations included crossing the cataracts of the Congo to find Lualaba, the river that Livingstone had discovered during his last peregrinations. Paddling up the Aruwimi, a tributary of the Congo that was not practicable for the *Peace*, he reached the outskirts of the Anglican mission field founded by Alexander Mackay in Uganda (see pp. 586ff). Hence he fulfilled the dream and prayer of Krapf, Livingstone, Coillard, and many others to unite the missionaries coming east from the Indian Ocean with those coming west up river from the Atlantic.

In the course of his travels, Grenfell often observed local customs of frightening cruelty as well as European acts of violence, arms trafficking, and the sale of alcohol. He recalled:

---

318 Ibid., 62.
319 Ibid., 40.

The bitterest experiences of this time have been imprinted as by fire on my spirit and memory. I saw the evil done by the trade of alcohol throughout the country, where bottles of wine and rum were used as currency while it was impossible to buy food in the market. I have seen slaves brought to the trading post of the white man and sold for wine or rum . . . I myself have faced the rifles of the soldiers of an Arab expedition. I have seen the cruel bonds that hold entire populations to their superstitious fears, which oblige them to condemn their own flesh and blood [their children] and to inflict horrible cruelties on them. I remained near to their open graves in order to prevent the interment of the living with the dead, and I have seen the blackest side of human nature. I declare that I know very well what is meant by the expression "indigenous custom."

Grenfell's family, which had elected to live on the *Peace*, was constantly on the move and so was sorely tried. There were four children living on the ship, including the eldest daughter. Still an adolescent, she had returned from Britain with the intention of assisting her father.

Though the conditions were difficult, Grenfell had no desire to abandon the country and asked for reinforcements from Britain. "If more men do not come soon," he wrote, "the mission in the Congo will collapse, and the work which has been so costly will be wasted." He had the special joy of discovering that the seeds of love, which he had sown with tears and in great personal danger, were bearing fruit. For example, the village of Bolobo, where the excited population had been calmed by seeing Mrs. Bentley's baby, was showing great interest in the gospel. In 1902 the Grenfell family stayed there for a long period and soon saw a revival among its people. "You will be happy to learn," wrote Grenfell, "that the people are disposed to hear and heed the message that they have so long despised. Many declare that they have given their hearts to the Lord Jesus, and the future appears very promising." It was now necessary to enlarge the chapel to provide for overflowing crowds, and the momentum spread to other villages. In another village Grenfell was welcomed with the singing of a hymn where, about twenty years earlier, he had been chased out at the point of a spear.

Back in Britain in 1891, Grenfell took possession of a new boat, the *Goodwill*. It was faster and more comfortable than the *Peace*, which was no longer adequate to assure communication and transportation between the numerous stations of the BMS. During his respite, Grenfell received the gold medal of the Royal Society of Geography.

In about twenty years, Grenfell had founded eight mission stations along the river, between Matadi and Stanleyville (present-day Kisangani). Jean Pirotte writes: "The BMS well illustrates the extensive method . . . judged to conform to that of the Apostle Paul. The missionary approached a new population, preached, strove to train a small group through Bible reading, and so created the nucleus of a local church.

Then he passed on to another region, leaving behind a trained group that was responsible for the growth of Christian life in that place."[320]

In May 1906, Grenfell found himself alone in the distant Eastern Province. His wife, who was in poor health, had remained behind in Bolobo. He was badly burned when his hut was deliberately set on fire while he was sleeping. Weakened by his wounds, he fell sick and his tired body soon succumbed to rheumatism and infection. He died on July 1, 1906, at the age of fifty-seven, until the end an explorer for the gospel.

## THE MULTIPLICATION OF PROTESTANT MISSIONS

At the time of Grenfell's death, the Baptist Missionary Society had twelve stations spread out along the length of the course of the great river. Its missionaries were in three provinces: Leopoldville, Equator, and the Eastern Province. The mission work continued to expand into these fields during the course of the twentieth century, but at a slower pace.

The American Baptist Missionary Union (ABMU),[321] established in 1814 to support the ministry of Adoniram Judson in Burma, arrived in 1884. It took over three of the LIM stations and founded four more in the following forty years.

The Svenska Missions Förabundet (Mission of the Free Church of Sweden) also arrived in 1884 in the province of Leopoldville. It took charge of a LIM station, established four others by 1900, and extended its work to Brazzaville Congo, which will be discussed below.

In 1886 Frederick Stanley Arnot arrived in Garanganze, the future province of Katanga, present-day Shaba. Originally of the same Scottish village as Livingstone, Arnot was associated with the Brethren Assemblies, but he left home without being supported by an organized missionary society. During his first two years, he was the only missionary in Garanganze, but then he was joined by two others. When for reasons of health he decided to take a vacation in Britain, the king of Garanganze would not allow him to leave without promising that he would return with a white wife for his harem. Arnot returned to Garanganze in 1889 with a team of twelve missionaries, which included five women whom he brought to the royal capital. The Garanganze Evangelical Mission (GEM) could then be established.

*Frederick Stanley Arnot, founder of the Garanganze Evangelical Mission.*

In 1891 the region was annexed to the Congo and was renamed the Province of Katanga. The Brethren Assemblies mission decided to keep the name Garanganze. Established five years before the annexation, it was also the only mission in the history of the Congo to precede the presence of the colonial administration and army. Among the GEM team was Dan Crawford, who

---

320 Jean Pirotte, cited by Zorn, "Missions protestantes," 1037.
321 It would later take the name American Baptist Foreign Mission Society (ABFMS).

arrived in 1889. He used modern techniques to communicate his message, employing a "magic lantern" to present biblical scenes while he spoke and a colleague sang hymns softly in the background. He also integrated himself into local life during the twenty-two years of his uninterrupted ministry. He adapted himself to the lifestyle of the population, as many other missionaries did in the nineteenth century. Moreover, he made a systematic effort to comprehend and penetrate the mental universe of the local people in order, as he said, "to think black"—an approach not often used. The population became attached to him and affectionately nicknamed him "the assembler of the people." By 1925 the GEM had about fifteen stations in Kantanga, and the work continued to prosper in the province during the coming years.

In 1884 the Methodist Episcopal Church of the United States ordained William Taylor as a "missionary bishop in Africa." Since 1870 he had worked in the Indies and Latin America, and so when he came to Africa he was already an accomplished missionary, fruitful and rich in experience. He arrived in the Congo in 1888 with about forty people, which included families with several children. Unaware that in the heart of Africa the difficulties confronting mission work were of an entirely different order than those encountered on other continents, he determined to undertake the gigantic enterprise of creating a chain of mission stations from the Atlantic Ocean to the Indian Ocean. Perhaps puffed up by prior successes in Asia, he appeared to be guilty of megalomania to the missionaries of other societies. In the event, the "Mission of Bishop Taylor" succeeded in constructing four stations in a dozen years. When Taylor returned to America in 1896, his mission quickly declined, lacking support from the mother church. Bishop Taylor will be encountered again when we examine the beginnings of Protestant missions in Angola.

Five other missionary societies arrived in the Congo before the end of the nineteenth century. The Christian and Missionary Alliance (CMA) established itself in the province of Leopoldville in 1888. The Congo Balolo Mission settled in the following year in the Province of Equator. (Founded under the impetus of H. Grattan Guinness, this mission was in some ways a resurrection of the LIM, which had ceased activities five years before.) The American Presbyterian Congo Mission established itself in Kasai in 1891. A few years later in 1897, the Westcott Mission (Plymouth Brethren in Britain) also settled in Kasai. The Disciples of Christ Congo Mission (from the American denomination of that name founded in 1823 by Thomas Campbell and his son Alexander Campbell) worked in the Province of Equator, beginning in 1899. (This mission developed an important medical and educational work, notably with women.) All five missions prospered and grew significantly in the course of the twentieth century.

At the end of the nineteenth century nine missionary societies were active in the Congo. Seven of them participated in a first general conference in Leopoldville in 1902. To obtain their objectives, J.-F. Zorn writes, the various societies coordinated their efforts, being "determined to face the hostility of the Catholic missions and the colonial religious politics vis-à-vis Protestantism."[322]

---

322 Zorn, "Missions protestantes," 1038.

# THE FIRST YEARS OF THE TWENTIETH CENTURY

Apolo Kivebulaya was a Ugandan who was sent in 1897 by the Church Missionary Society (CMS), an Anglican mission, to work in Ituri, east of the Congo. He undertook a remarkable work among the pygmies of the forest. Remaining single and living in extreme poverty, he showed much affection for these despised and feared peoples. He learned their dances, composed hymns for them, taught them some elementary rules of hygiene and self-discipline, and instructed them in artisan trades so that they would be assured of some income.[323] He also translated the Gospel of Mark into the language of the pygmies. J.-F. Zorn writes, "On the basis of this work, linguistic science was finally able to answer the question as to whether or not the pygmies had a structured language."[324] Kivebulaya, considered the apostle of the forests of Central Africa, was later named canon of the Anglican cathedral of Kampala, Uganda. He died in 1933.

After the departure of Kivelbulaya in 1925, there were no CMS missionaries to continue his work among the pygmies in the region of the Ituri, but missionaries of the Immanuel Mission, sent by the American Brethren Assemblies then entered the field. They first arrived in the great forest in 1926 and worked with the Africa Inland Mission (AIM), which arrived in 1912. Together they established the Nyankunde mission station. After the Second World War medical work was developed there, sustained by the Protestant missions and churches then in the region. One of the principal workers of the Immanuel Mission was Robert Deans (1880–1960), an American of Scottish origin who arrived in 1929. He established other mission stations, notably Lolwa in 1930, from which the work among the pygmies was greatly extended. William Deans, who participated with his father from the beginning of the mission, helped to develop various facets of the work. The mission eventually issued in the Immanuel Church, which is present today in northeast Congo.

In the course of the first quarter of the twentieth century, seventeen new Protestant societies arrived, the most important being the AIM, which came in 1912. This brought the total number of mission societies active in the region between 1878 and 1925 to twenty-eight. However, two of these lasted only a short time.[325]

---

323  Cf. Nguba Bahigwa, "Approche biblique pour une oeuvre missionaire en milieu pygmée: Cas des Mbuti de la forêt de l'Ituri" (master's thesis, Faculté de Théologie Evangélique de Bangui, 1992).

324  Neill, *History,* 326.

325  The book that furnished a large part of the information for this chapter was: E. M. Braekman, *Histoire du protestantisme au Congo* (Brussels: Librairie des Eclaireurs Unionistes, 1961). It gives statistics, which are rounded here, for the years 1907 and 1936 for the Protestant missions in the Congo:

    1907: 9 societies, 29 stations, 181 missionaries (of which there were 5 medical personnel and 27 hospitals and dispensaries), 25,000 adult members of churches, 25,000 catechumens, 600 catechists, no African pastor, a pastoral school of 20,500 students in the primary grades, and a population of 100,000 persons considered as Protestants.

    1936: 38 societies, 177 stations, 808 missionaries (of which there were 49 medical personnel and 72 hospitals and dispensaries), 240,000 adult members of churches, 180,000 catechumens, 14,400 catechists, 8 ordained African pastors and 200 non-ordained, 5 pastoral schools, 308,000 students in the primary grades (there were no secondary schools then), and a Protestant population of 638,000 persons.

The Belgian Congo Missionary Society had only a few programs in the Congo. Though very much a minority in Belgium, the Belgian Protestants nonetheless were conscious of their responsibilities in the Belgian Congo. The Union of the Belgian Evangelical Protestant Churches created the Belgian Congo Missionary Society in 1910. The Reverend Henri Anet, secretary general of the mission, wanted to move to Lower Kantanga in 1914 where he had obtained permission to work from the Belgian government; however, he was prevented from doing this by the outbreak of the First World War.

Later the mission society would concentrate its efforts in Rwanda when it was called to replace the German missionaries.[326] A citizen of both Belgium and Switzerland, Anet was known for his engagement in international missionary conferences. At the beginning of the Second World War, he retired, left Belgium, and moved to Switzerland where he died in 1952.

---

326 For more on the history of Protestant missions in Rwanda-Burundi, see pp. 584 and 590ff, as the pioneers in these countries came from Tanzania and Uganda.

# CHAPTER 21

# An African Prophet: Simon Kimbangu

The prophet William Wade Harris, who was presented in a preceding chapter, had an extraordinary impact in the Ivory Coast and was very important in the subsequent growth of the Ivorian church. However, his ministry continued for only about fifteen months, in 1913 and 1914 (see pp. 530ff). Simon Kimbangu (1889–1951) was another African prophet. He appeared in 1921 in the Belgian Congo, less than ten years after Harris and some thousands of kilometers from the Ivory Coast.

Kimbangu's ministry did not produce crowds as large as those of Harris', but he did help to give birth to a larger church than Harris', the Independent African Church. Kimbangu's ministry, however, was even briefer than Harris'. After only five months of ministry, he was condemned and incarcerated until his death, thirty years later. Despite some obvious differences that distinguished them, certain comparisons can be made between their brief careers. Both converted in the context of a Protestant mission in which they received succinct but accurate biblical training; both responded to a divine call that they received from outside of any missionary or ecclesiastical institution; and both were charged to proclaim a simple message that was devoid of Western theological elaboration or syncretism with African traditional religions.[327] Finally, both were also reduced to silence by colonial authorities who feared the emergence of a black power that was religious and independent.

Kimbangu was born in N'Kamba, in the Lower Congo. He was educated at the mission school at Ngombe-Lutete, married, was baptized with his wife in 1915, and became a teacher. The Baptist missionaries described him as "a man of superior intelligence who possessed a strong personality and knew his Bible well . . . A good and thoughtful man who read his Bible and conscientiously sought to fulfill his duty."[328]

In 1918, when the Spanish influenza was causing thousands of deaths in this region and throughout the world, Kimbangu heard a voice say: "I am Christ. My servants are unfaithful. I have selected you to witness to your brothers and to convert

---

327 We speak here of the messages of the prophets themselves, not how those messages were subsequently developed by their disciples, who may not have been entirely faithful to the original preaching. We refer to the remark of the African theologian Kä Mana (p. 532) that concerns the time of Kimbangu and Harris.

328 Marie Louise Martin, *Simon Kimbangu: Un prophète et son église* (Lausanne: Éditions du Soc, 1981), 61.

them." Despite the frequent repetition of this call, Kimbangu resisted it for three years, feeling himself incapable of such a task. On April 6, 1921, while he was going to a market, he passed through a village and found himself compelled by a force outside himself to enter a hut where a woman was in pain. He placed his hands on her and healed her in the name of Jesus Christ.

He considered this date to be the turning point of his life and birthday of the Kimbanguist church.[329] A little later he resurrected a child, and soon other miracles followed. Some took him to be a magician and feared him, but after this initial reaction had passed, many flocked to him with their sick. Some of the healing stories are almost identical to those found in the Gospels or the Acts of the Apostles. Those who recounted these stories no doubt wanted him appear to be an "African messiah." Though there are clearly legendary elements in the stories, the fact remains that there were a number of extraordinary events for which reliable testimony is abundant. Kimbangu's disciples were convinced that God was in the process of giving Africa its own Pentecost and that the Holy Spirit was working through Kimbangu.[330]

Kimbangu's message was similar to that of Harris'. "Throw away your fetishes," he told them, "and put your confidence in the one and all-powerful God. Repent and believe that God is offering you salvation through the sacrifice of Jesus Christ." He preached about the need for purity, warning against pagan dances, immorality, and polygamy. He taught his followers to love their enemies, submit to the authorities, and—more forcefully than Harris—practice monogamy. Despite later reports, he never attacked whites in his preaching. The fruit of this brief ministry was a spiritual revival throughout the lower Congo. The missions already present benefited from this movement, for he did not seek to create an independent church. Attendance at the services grew, and the people were buying Bibles and hymn collections even as they were throwing away their fetishes and amulets.

The reaction of the missionaries varied, but on the whole they were more reserved than enthusiastic. R. L. Jennings, head of the Baptist Mission in the region of N'Kamba, visited Kimbangu and wrote a report in which advised his colleagues, "Keep your people separate from N'Kamba!" Diangienda Kuntima, Kimbangu's son, spoke of this visit:

> He found some Zairian members following Jennings who immediately rejoiced. For them all the facts were clear, convincing, and edifying. Simon Kimbangu got his power from Jesus Christ. As for Reverend Jennings, he set off the campaign of defamation that later lead to the deportation and martyrdom of Simon Kimbangu.[331]

---

329 The formal founding of the Church of Jesus Christ by the prophet Simon Kimbangu took place thirty-five years later.

330 The conviction of the Kimbanguist church that their leader preached and healed by the power of the Holy Spirit was so strong that following the words "in the name of the Father, of the Son, and of the Holy Spirit" they frequently added, "who descended on Simon Kimbangu," or "who spoke by Simon Kimbangu." N'Kamba, the village of his birth and the origin of the movement, was often called the New Jerusalem—a new Jerusalem in the heart of Africa. However, the belief professed by some Kimbanguists that Kimgangu was an incarnation of the Holy Spirit appeared much later and contradicted the teaching of the founder.

331 Diangienda Kuntima, *L'histoire du Kimbanguisme* (Kinshasa: Kimbanguistes, 1984), 45.

Diangienda Kuntima suspected that Jennings, whose preaching was not as fruitful as Kimbangu's, was hostile due to jealousy.

Other missionaries were more positive. One missionary named Thomas said, "Kimbangu did not seek material gain; he healed in the name of Jesus. All our deacons have without question recognized the validity of his prophetic claims. They have asked us, 'You do not believe because he is black?'" Another missionary named Graham wrote:

> It seems to me that this is without question the most remarkable
> movement that the country has known. The prophets [Kimbangu
> and his aides] seem to have only a single goal: to spread the gospel . . .
> Many old members of our churches speak of a spiritual revival.[332]

This phenomenon, which swept up many people into the movement, caused the Catholic missionaries to call for the immediate intervention of the state, and the colonial administration to fear an insurrection. Léon Morel, the Belgian administrator of the district, seems to have seen things clearly. He recognized that Kimbangu knew the Bible well and that he had committed no crime for which he could be criticized. He came to the conclusion that Kimbangu wanted to found a religion inspired both by Protestantism and by religious practices based on fetishes. He wrote, not without perspicacity: "All the world can observe that European religions are constituted entirely of abstractions and do not correspond to the mentality of the Africans, who seek concrete facts and the assurance of protection. The teaching of Kimbangu convinces them, for he bases it on visible facts."

Kimbangu was surrounded by a dozen assistants whom he had ordained and authorized to practice a prophetic ministry. It was a means not only to extend the movement but also to keep it from growing in an uncontrolled fashion, which in fact happened soon after. In June 1921, hardly more than two months after Kimbangu first gained public notoriety, colonial authorities summoned Protestant and Catholic mission leaders and pressed them to condemn Kimbangu. The Protestants responded that they hoped he would disappear but ruled out the use of force against him. The Catholics, on the other hand, advocated brutal measures, and their opinion prevailed with the authorities.[333]

Several days later, armed forces attempted to arrest Kimbangu, but he was able to flee with his assistants and his seven-year-old eldest son, Charles Kisolokele. During the following five months, Kimbangu trained his disciples in secret. In September, he said that he had heard God order him to give himself up to the authorities. He then went openly to his village and exhorted his own to persevere, show courage, and practice nonviolence. He was arrested without offering resistance, shackled, and—while his disciples sang hymns—led away with his family. Less than a mother later, he was sentenced to 120 strokes of the lash and condemned to death. Here is the judgment of the court:

---

332  These reactions are cited by Martin, op. cit., 67–68.

333  In August of the same year, three British missionaries went to Brussels to ask the Belgian colonial minister to treat the prophet's movement with discernment and benevolence.

> Whereas Kibango [Kimbangu] sought, in explaining and in having his aides and followers explain the text of the Bible after his own fashion, to impose his will on the population, to affirm his prestige as he has already said in spreading and in having his aides spread false rumors of miracles, and to holding meetings to heal men as if he were sent by God to his village and elsewhere; that it is during these meetings that false ideas of religion have been inculcated in the indigenous population, and that they have been incited against the established powers.[334]

Convinced that the movement was solely religious and not revolutionary, the Protestants pleaded his cause, and the Belgian king commuted his punishment to a life sentence. He spent most of his thirty years of imprisonment in solitary confinement, with his Bible. In 1935 the director of the prison, noting his exemplary behavior, recommended his freedom. But the colonial authorities and Catholic archbishop opposed this, and he remained incarcerated until his death on October 12, 1951.

After Kimbangu's arrest, a conference of all the Protestant missionaries in the Lower Congo took place in November 1921. Having observed numerous ministers and evangelists join the Kimbanguists, the missionaries decided to curb the prophetic movement and block it from entering the churches. In response, the Kimbanguists said, in effect:

> Our God is the same as the one the Protestants worship; we have no more need of missionaries because we are great enough and intelligent enough to govern ourselves . . . We want to open Kimbanguist churches everywhere. We do not pray to Simon Kimbangu; we pray to God. Kimgangu is the one sent from God.[335]

Nevertheless, in 1922 the authorities forbade the Kimbanguists from meeting. Concentration camps were set up everywhere in the country, and massive numbers were deported to them. Persecution, which was often extreme, continued until 1957.[336] But, as it is often the case, it led to the expansion of the movement.

Some of those who continued to be followers of Kimbangu were called Ngunzists (the word Ngunza signifies prophet in Kikongo) and honored him even to the point of deification. The movement was characterized by syncretism, apocalypticism, and hostility to whites—all of which the prophet himself rejected. It promoted "possession" by the Holy Spirit, but the trances it produced generally resembled those typical of traditional religions. This was also true of its approach to healing and the breaking of spells. Persecution from the authorities had the unintentional consequence of uniting Kimbanguism and Ngunsism.

Kimbangu's youngest son, Joseph Diangienda, visited him several months before his death. Kimbangu said to him: "My son, if you kneel before me in order to ask me

---

334 Jules Chomé, *La passion de Kimbangu* (Brussels: Éditions Les Amis de la Presence Africaine, 1959), 66.

335 Martin, op, cit., 87.

336 Martin gives the number of thirty-seven thousand heads of families deported in thirty-six years, between 1921 and 1957.

to confer the Holy Spirit upon you, I will not do it. The Holy Spirit is the gift of God alone." Nevertheless, Kimbangu entrusted him with the direction of his disciples. Diangienda and his elder brother had been placed as children in a Catholic boarding school where the reading of the Bible was strictly forbidden. When Diangienda married in 1946, he felt constrained to accept the blessing of a Catholic priest.

Until the death of the prophet, Kimbanguism was a more or less informal religion in which the prophet's sons played important roles. Following his death, there was tension with the Protestants as an organizational structure slowly took shape. In the end, the Kimbanguists identified neither with the Protestants nor the Catholics. In 1956 they formally declared themselves to be "The Church of Jesus Christ on the Earth by the Prophet Simon Kimbangu." The Belgian government officially recognized the new religion at Christmas in 1959.

Soon after Kimbangu was arrested, his native village of N'Kamba was entirely destroyed in order to prevent a Kimbangu cult from emerging there. Nevertheless, his followers flocked to visit his wife who lived there in secret and in poverty. She bathed in the local water source, which then took on a sacred status.

Kimbangu's village, close to the border of Brazzaville Congo (today the Democratic Republic of Congo), soon became the center of the movement. While the prophet lived, the Congolese often crossed the river to hear him preach. Swedish missionaries sent the Reverend Samuel Matuba to make inquiries about this, and he made a favorable report about Kimbangu. At the outset, therefore, the Swedish mission had an open mind about the movement and hoped it might lead to a revival. It soon, however, developed reservations and then became hostile, expelling Matuba in 1922. This slowed down the momentum of the movement, but it succeeded in spreading to Brazzaville, and then to Libreville in Gabon. Matuba was imprisoned several times and even deported to Chad for five years. Recognition and freedom of worship were accorded to the Kimbanguists in French West Africa at the same time as in the Belgian Congo.

# CHAPTER 22

# The Pioneers in the Region of the Great Lakes

## KENYA: JOHANN LUDWIG KRAPF, LINGUIST AND STRATEGIST

Johann Ludwig Krapf (1810–1874) was born in Wurttemberg, Germany. After his studies in theology, he entered the pastorate but quickly abandoned it in order to prepare himself for ministry in mission. Like his compatriot Peter Heyling, the first Lutheran missionary in history who lived two centuries before (see p. 239-40), it was his passionate desire to bring new spiritual life to the old Coptic and Ethiopian churches, shut up in ancient liturgical traditions and the use of languages that had not been commonly understood for centuries. This project converged with that of the Church Missionary Society (CMS) to which he presented his candidature. Krapf arrived in Ethiopia in 1837 and began to work on the translation of the Bible. In 1842 he received an honorary doctorate from the University of Tübingen for his linguistic work and his collection of ancient Ethiopian manuscripts, but the Ethiopian king expelled him a little later (see p. 598). Krapf then traveled to Zanzibar where he worked among the freed slaves while he studied Swahili. It was not his intention to remain on the island of Zanzibar but to reach the interior of Africa in the hope of reentering Ethiopia from the south.

In 1844 he arrived in the port city of Mombassa and undertook the founding of a colony nearby for freed Christians from Zanzibar. In effect, he hoped to establish a bridgehead from which East Africa could be reached by African Christians. He was convinced that an evangelical black bishop would do more for the evangelization of this region of Africa than all the European missionaries put together. From then on, Krapf's priority was to place before the Christians of the country a Bible in their own language, a condition indispensable for establishing a church that could become truly national. In two years he produced a dictionary, grammar, and translation of the New Testament and Genesis. Unhappily, these works were of little use, being written in the Swahili of the Arabs, not the language of the Africans.

*Johann Ludwig Krapf (1810–1874).*

He was joined in 1846 by Johannes Rebmann, a compatriot from Wurttemberg who proved to be a valuable aide in the work of translation and exploration.

Krapf and Rebmann formulated an audacious and prophetic plan: they would establish a chain of mission stations from the Indian Ocean across the African continent to the Niger basin on the west coast, where their CMS colleague was then working, the future African bishop Samuel Ajayi Crowther. In Krapf's eyes this chain would form a dike to hold back the progress of Islam towards the south. Later, other missions would attempt to develop similar strategies to link the east and west coasts of the continent, but Krapf was the first one to have had this dream.

He was disappointed when the organization of the second station was bogged down in impassable difficulties: the lack of security (Krapf and Rebmann were robbed of all their baggage on several occasions), the obstruction of some of the kings, and the attacks launched by slave traders. There were simply too many obstacles to their progress toward the heart of Africa. They returned to the coast, walking in the night in order not to be noticed, without porters, money, or provisions.

Refusing to be discouraged, the two missionaries persevered in their explorations. They were the first Europeans to see Mount Kenya and Mount Kilimanjaro, the latter being the highest peak in Africa. Both public opinion and trained geographers concluded that the missionaries had been deceived by optical illusions when they claimed to have seen snow on the summits of mountains so close to the equator. Other CMS missionaries renewed the attempt to establish mission stations in the interior of the country, but they fell ill and returned home, sick and discouraged. Krapf had to return to Germany with his health gravely undermined. He traveled to Africa at the end of 1854, but once again he collapsed and had to return to Germany the following year. Until his death, he continued to revise the Bible translations he had undertaken in Africa. Ype Schaaf concludes an essay on this exceptional missionary with these words: "Johann Ludwig Krapf was one of the first linguists and strategists of the mission in Africa. He was also a pious Souabe of Wurttemberg, in health fragile and in endurance extraordinary."[337]

Nearly twenty years after the departure of Krapf, the missionary John Steer of Zanzibar found Rebmann in a small interior village. He was almost completely blind and had lost all contact with the mission, but he was comforted with the company of several Christians. He had passed twenty-nine years in Africa without ever returning home for a vacation.

Except for their excellent work of Bible translation, the efforts of these two pioneers did not leave much visible fruit in Kenya, but they prepared the way for their successors.[338] Due to the repeated appeals of Krapf, in 1862 missionaries of the United Methodist Mission began to work in Kenya. In 1886 the Bavarian Missionary Society also sought to follow in the tracks left by Krapf, but it was too imbued with the colonial spirit of the era. This mission was certainly animated by the gospel but also

---

337 Schaaf, op. cit., 81.

338 It is from Mombassa that Stanley began his 999-day journey across Africa. Despite being well prepared to travel to Lake Tanganyika, he would never have been able to find Livingstone if he had not benefited from the information left by Krapf and Rebmann many years earlier.

by the hope that the east coast of Africa, from Tanganyika to Somalia, would come entirely under the purview of Germany. It had scarcely any success.

In 1891 the Scottish Presbyterian Mission appeared on the field, and in 1895 it was the turn of the Africa Inland Mission. Sadly, almost all the early missionaries died due to the harshness of the climate. In 1902 American Quakers also arrived and eventually succeeded in establishing one of the strongest denominations in the country, and the evangelization of the highly populated region of Lake Victoria was begun in 1908 by the future Anglican bishop J. J. Willis, who journeyed from Uganda.

## TANGANYIKA (PRESENT-DAY TANZANIA)

### Beginnings and Developments in Evangelization

The Portuguese were the first Europeans to encounter the coastal inhabitants of southeast Africa. In the sixteenth century, Catholic missionaries attempted to establish a church on the coast close to the island of Zanzibar, but with little result. In the following century all their efforts disappeared with the decline of Portugal as a maritime nation. Setting out from the island of Reunion in 1860, three Catholic priests managed to settle in Zanzibar. They were followed in 1863 by priests of the Holy Spirit, who built the first mission station on the continent at Bagamoyo in 1868. It was intended to be a refuge for freed slaves and at the same time a bridgehead to Uganda, which the White Fathers successfully entered in 1878.

We have seen above that in 1846 Krapf and Rebmann left Zanzibar to journey through the vast regions of what is now Tanzania. Their reports aroused the interest of the British explorers John Speke and Richard Burton, who succeeded in discovering the region of the Great Lakes. In 1857 during his first visit to Britain after crossing Africa from west to east, David Livingstone made a moving appeal to the students of Oxford and Cambridge to evangelize this little-known part of Africa. This resulted in the Universities Mission to Central Africa sending the first missionaries to this region in 1860. Their original intent was to evangelize the Shire Highlands (present-day Malawi), but they quickly had to fall back to Zanzibar due to the difficulties they encountered. They founded a college there with the intention of preparing Africans to undertake the evangelization of the continent. In 1876 the mission once again launched into the interior of the land with the aid of the CMS.

Thanks to the efforts of Doctor John Kirk, the British consul to Zanzibar and former companion of Livingstone, the Sultan of Zanzibar signed a decree forbidding the slave trade in 1873.[339] The slave market of Zanzibar, one of the largest in Africa, was closed. This island, lying about fifty kilometers off the mainland, had throughout this period been the base of Protestant missions for East and Central Africa.

A high church Anglican mission, which had been in Zanzibar since 1864, moved to the continent in 1875. Three years later, evangelical Anglicans of the CMS—Britons, Australians, and New Zealanders—opened two mission stations there. The results, however, were minimal, and the stations were given to the Lutheran Mission of

---

339 This occured a month after the death of Livingstone.

Leipzig in 1898. The London Missionary Society (LMS) established a presence in the region of Ujiji and in areas south of Lake Tanganyika. Arthur Books, an LMS missionary, was killed in 1888 by rebellious Arab slave traders. The LMS decided in 1898 to hand over its mission activities in the area to a German Moravian mission.

These transfers are explained by the decisions made at the Congress of Berlin in 1885. From then until 1919, Tanganyika was a German colony and the principal mission field of the Protestant churches of Germany. The Berlin Mission arrived in Zanzibar in 1886 and moved to the continent the next year. Others followed, such as the Evangelische Missionsgesellschaft für Deutsch-Ostafrika (Evangelical Missionary Society for German East Africa) that emerged in 1886 out of the colonial enthusiasm of Bismarkian Germany. It evangelized Usambara, the coastal region north of Dar es Salaam. Ernest Johanssen was one of its pioneer missionaries who, in 1907, would launch the Protestant Mission in Rwanda. The Moravian Mission, already present on the Zambezi and the rivers of Lake Nyssa, in the last years of the nineteenth century founded about fifteen mission stations and took over, as noted above, those of the LMS. The Moravians emphasized Bible translation and undertook large medical and educational efforts.

After numerous protests by German Christians against the confusion of colonization and mission, some non-German missions were admitted into the region of Tanganyika. Among these was the Africa Inland Mission in 1908, a mission already active in the neighboring regions of Kenya.

Following the momentum of the international mission conference in Edinburgh in 1910, a missionary conference was held the following year in Dar es Salaam for German East Africa. The principal concern of the gathering was "the situation of the Christian missions and their task in the face of Islam."

The German period of colonization and missionary work in Africa ended with the defeat of the Second Reich in the First World War. German missionaries had to leave Tanganyika and were replaced by others, mostly Americans and Swedes. The United Free Church of Scotland took over the Moravian mission stations. Beginning in 1924, however, the Germans were authorized to return to their former stations. The Mission of Leipzig, after an absence of a dozen years, returned with the intention of guiding the African church into autonomy. It allowed the church to organize itself according to the typical Bantu social structure. Some American, Canadian, and Swedish Pentecostal missionaries entered the field in 1930. The Mennonites came in 1934 and worked in the region of the high plateau where they operated a Bible school and hospital in Shirati. To coordinate the work of the growing number of mission agencies and projects in the country, the Missionary Council of Tanganyika was formed in 1936. It was the precursor of the Christian Council of Tanzania, which today includes Lutherans, Moravians, Baptists, Mennonites, independent churches, Salvation Army, Quakers, and still others.

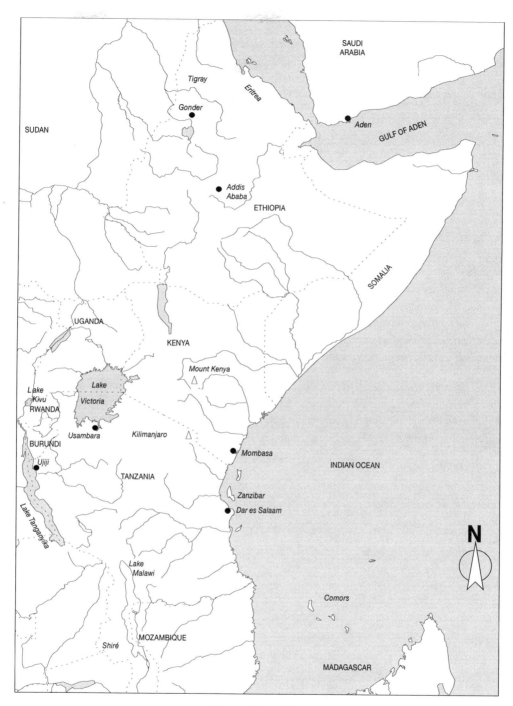

*Map 12: East Africa*

## THE MISSION IN UGANDA: ALEXANDER MACKAY

In the nineteenth century, the kingdom of Uganda (or Buganda) was one of the most powerful of Central Africa. It had a population of several million and a formidable army of 200,000 men. The army included ten thousand rowers of giant canoes, who sowed terror in the islands of Lake Victoria. The kingdom was the largest in Africa, extending to the north and west of the lake.[340] In 1858 John Speke became the first European to enter this land, and then Henry Morton Stanley sojourned there during his travels in 1874. Stanley wrote a description of the land and appealed to the Protestant public to send missionaries into this country where Islam was beginning to

*Alexander Mackay (1849–1890).*

infiltrate. In fact, the Arabs who had come with the intention of converting the population slowly abandoned this project in favor of the slave trade. They lost interest in Islamizing the inhabitants since their religion forbade them to make slaves of Muslims. Nonetheless, they never relaxed their opposition to Christian missions.

It was the Evangelical Anglicans of the Church Missionary Society (CMS) who responded to Stanley's appeal. In 1876 the CMS sent eight missionaries under the direction of Alexander Mackay (1849–1890). The son of a pastor in the Free Church of Scotland, Mackay converted at the time of his mother's death when he was sixteen years old. An engineer with a promising career before him, Mackay was also an assiduous reader of the Bible and a lay preacher much appreciated

by his listeners. Despite the attractive prospect of becoming the director of a large material factory for the railroads, he turned his back on his profession, convinced that God was calling him to serve in Africa. He was twenty-seven years old at the time of his departure.

When he arrived in Zanzibar, Mackay wrote in his journal: "In the name and in the power of God, I will set up my printing press on the shores of Lake Victoria, and I will not cease to labor until the story of the cross of Christ is printed in the language of Uganda and everyone has learned not only to read, but to believe it."[341]

Two years after his departure from Southampton, Mackay reached the south shore of Lake Victoria, one thousand kilometers from Zanzibar. He searched for two colleagues who had preceded him with all their equipment, but could not find them. His friends had been put to death by the king of the region for having helped a rebel seeking refuge among them. All their baggage, as well as the equipment brought to set up various machines, had been pillaged or dispersed. Two other members of the

---

340 The surface of the Lake Victoria is over twice the land area of Maryland, and it has numerous islands, some of which are densely populated. It is located on the equator at an elevation of one thousand meters.

341 August Glardon, *L'Ouganda et Alexandre Mackay* (Lausanne: Bridel, 1891), 80.

team had to be repatriated, and another two succumbed to malaria. Of the eight-man team that had left from Britain two years earlier, Mackay and his colleague the Reverend C. T. Wilson were the only ones to arrive. They appeared in the royal capital of Uganda (present-day Entebbe), which lies on the north shore of Lake Victoria, in September 1878. King Mtesa, the *kabaka* of Buganda, was favorably disposed to the missionaries because of his earlier encounter with Stanley. Though he had a formidable reputation, he showed himself amicable towards the missionaries and consented to welcome them to his palace.

Less than a month later, the White Fathers also presented themselves to the king. Cardinal Charles Lavigerie (1825–1892) had entrusted them with the task of opposing the advance of Islam in Central Africa. Unhappily, the first objective of these French priests was to persuade the king to oppose the Protestant missionaries, whom they described as bearers of a false religion, and their book, the Bible, as a "book of falsehoods." The king organized debates between the Protestants and Catholics, which much amused him. Following this, relations improved between the missionaries of the two confessions. This proved to be a temporary truce, however, for the Catholics and Protestants opposed each other in long and bitter confrontations at the end of the nineteenth century. This occurred in the context of a larger struggle for influence in the court between Christians and Muslims.

One of Mackay's methods of evangelization consisted of welcoming children into his home in order to give them a Christian education. Moreover, he never ceased to be surrounded by adults who desired to learn to read. Soon, several CMS missionaries arrived to reinforce his efforts.

Despite his promise to Stanley, the king did not become a Christian. Nevertheless, he appreciated Mackay's practical contributions. Architect, engineer, and blacksmith, Mackay was capable of constructing two-story houses and a variety of machines: water pumps, forges, weaving looms, and others. Mtesa entrusted the education of several of his sons to him. Though he was the greatest slave trader in East Africa, due to the influence of the missionaries he went as far as to provisionally forbid this human traffic. This resulted in increased opposition to the gospel from the powerful Arab merchants.

In 1882 four years after the arrival of Mackay, five baptisms were celebrated and several others soon followed. At the end of 1884, a church of more than one hundred members celebrated its first Holy Communion just as the trial of persecution first struck this young community.

An abrupt reversal of religious policy occurred when the king fell gravely ill. His entourage persuaded him that the cause of his sickness was the anger of Uganda's ancestral gods due to the presence of foreign religions in the realm. Islam, Catholicism, and Protestantism were all banned, while sorcery retook its traditional place. Villagers were captured each day on the roads, brought to the royal palace, and had their throats slit to appease the furor of the ancestors. This did not, however, prevent the death of the king in the autumn of 1884.

Mwanga, his son and successor, had been educated by the missionaries but was not a believer. He adopted a policy of neutrality regarding religion. Many of the converts to the Christian faith were people from the lowest social class, but when he saw some of the nobles and members of his entourage turn towards Jesus Christ, he grew fearful. Then a fierce persecution began, which Mackay experienced in his own family:

> Our first martyrs have won their crowns. On January 30, 1885, three young Christians were burned alive after being horribly mutilated. Their only crime was to be our disciples . . . Be that as it may, the work of God will survive. Some of our young Christians are very courageous, sometimes more courageous than prudent. While a certain number are hidden for fear of losing their lives, there are others whom we entreat in vain to hold themselves back, knowing the dangers to which they are exposed. Whether their retirement has been voluntary or not, I do not know of a single case of apostasy.[342]

In the face of widespread martyrdom, the growing number of believers seemed miraculous. The church passed from having one hundred to nearly two hundred members in the six months that followed the martyrdom of the three young people. There was even a stream of conversions among the officers of the court, though all were executed. Mackay testified:

> A violent persecution rose against the Christians; right and left, they were being slaughtered. Those in the court and the most visible among the Christians were the first seized. A dozen were cut in pieces the first day, and their limbs thrown here and there on the road. Then troops of armed men set out to complete this deadly work. More than thirty lost their lives. We were powerless, waiting to be arrested ourselves. We are in great danger . . . and we are experiencing an unspeakable sorrow.[343]

After ten years in Uganda, and for some of this time the only Protestant missionary, Mackay left the country in July 1887. Instead of returning to Britain as expected, he stopped in Ousambiro, south of Lake Victoria in present-day Tanzania. Here he organized a new mission station among the Ugandan refugees whom he discovered fleeing the bloody fury of King Mwanga. The excesses of the king finally produced an uprising in Uganda. The king fled and one of his non-Christian brothers seized the throne but proved incapable of reestablishing order. The kingdom passed for a time into anarchy.

In his miserable exile on an island in Lake Victoria, Mwanga appealed to Mackay for help and announced his conversion to him, confessing the evil of his conduct toward him and the Christians. The persecution he had begun had redounded on himself, but the depth of his repentance could not be doubted. After a year of observing the disorders that were ravaging Uganda, he reentered the country and was triumphantly reestablished on his throne. He then surrounded himself exclusively

---

342 Ibid., 137.
343 Ibid., 142.

with Christian counselors, Protestants and Catholics in equal number. The prime minister was one of Mackay's former students. The king's entourage paid close attention to his behavior, showed respect for the nation's laws, and even developed a constitution. Mackay seems to have believed in Mwanga's sincerity, but he did not live long enough to take the measure of the authenticity of his conversion and or see him persevere in the faith. For Mackay died the following year in Ousambiro, on February 8, 1890, due to an acute case of malaria. Only forty-one years old, he had lived for fourteen years in Africa.

The last letters Mackay wrote in his Ousambiro station were ardent pleas for the mission to be extended into the center of Africa. Here is an extract from one letter:

> How can I rest in peace knowing the imperative needs of Africa? The conversion of the pagans was supposed to be the work of the church and not a departure from its work. It is only when one sees the total ignorance and darkness in which so many millions of human beings are languishing that one truly recognizes that missionaries must be sent to do this work by the thousands, and by the tens of thousands. I am all the more struck by this when I reflect on the enormous waste of energy that occurs among Christians in Europe. Each little sect struggles to maintain its shibboleth with a handful of adherents in all the parishes instead of allowing their insignificant differences to fall by common accord and sacrificing and working together for the regeneration of the lost races.[344]

In the years following Mackay's death, the Ugandan church grew in striking fashion. A. Glardon writes:

> Nothing is more remarkable in the early history of the Ugandan Church than its evangelistic zeal . . . But almost the first thing that the Bagandan Christians realized was that the gospel that was good for them was also good for everyone else. Baganda teachers were pioneers in the kingdom of Unyoro, Toro, and Koki. Most famous of all these pioneers was Apolo Kivebulaya, who later became the canon of the cathedral in Kampala, and whose story of heroic witness and suffering is a modern epic.[345]

## THE INNOVATIVE VISION OF BISHOP ALFRED ROBERT TUCKER

The missionary work of the Ugandan Anglican Church grew during the peaceful period around the turn of the century. The Anglican Bishop Alfred Robert Tucker (1849–1914), who arrived in Uganda in the year of Mackay's death, worked fraternally with the African evangelists. For him, the church of Jesus Christ was a place where Ugandans and foreigners should have been able to serve together on a basis of perfect spiritual equality. Stephen Neill writes:

344 Ibid., 161.
345 Neill, *History*, 386. Concerning Apolo Kivebulaya, cf. also p. 572.

His plan for the Native Anglican Church, put forward in 1897, was to a large extent shattered on the inveterate opposition of the missionaries. As the number of missionaries increased they became entrenched, seeing themselves in positions of authority as rulers and directors and not being capable of the great imaginative effort required to see themselves as servants of the local church in real fellowship with Africans.[346]

Tucker's vision was only partially realized while he was the bishop in Uganda; he persevered, however, and sought to communicate his vision to others. In many respects, he was a pioneer of the relationship between church and mission that would be called "partnership," an approach that today is a fundamental element in all missiology.

At the beginning of Tucker's ministry in Uganda, the church, which had recently emerged from a period of persecution, scarcely included more than two hundred members. At his death, eighteen years later, the church was established in hundreds communities and included sixty-five thousand members. In 1927, forty years after the departure of Mackay and thirteen years after the death of Bishop Tucker, the mission and Anglican churches had fifty-four mission stations with ninety-five missionaries, 150,000 church members, sixty-six Ugandan pastors, three thousand evangelists, catechists, and teachers, and eighty-two thousand children in its schools. In 1918 the Africa Inland Mission (AIM) also began to establish itself in Uganda.

## RWANDA-BURUNDI

The two republics of Rwanda and Burundi (formerly Rwanda-Urundi) lie in hilly but fertile terrain and boast the densest populations on the African continent. During the period of colonization, they were generally associated with the Belgian Congo. These territories in the Great Lakes region, the very heart of Africa, were slow to come into contact with Europe. John Speke and Richard Burton were the first to explore them during their search for the sources of the Nile in 1858, and David Livingstone and Henry Morton Stanley also passed through in the 1870s. Rwanda and Burundi were then two small feudal kingdoms. At the Congress of Berlin in 1885 the two kingdoms were given to the Germans and integrated into German East Africa (Tanganyika). After the First World War, the allies transferred them to Belgium to supervise their development under the mandate system.[347] The mission was naturally affected by these political events.

The Catholics were the first on the scene. Two White Fathers under Cardinal Charles Lavigerie established a post in Urundi in 1879, but they were murdered after only two years. Their successors did not begin to arrive until 1889, and the Catholics

---

346 Ibid., 387.

347 Beginning in 1947, the supervision of the two nations was given to the United Nations. Consequently, Belgian subsidies for hospitals and schools, formerly reserved to Catholics, were then broadened to include Protestants. With this financing the state gained the right to supervise the management of the hospitals and schools, even the hiring of personnel. This was controversial, but the rule would remain in force until in 1962 when the two republics became independent.

only established their first permanent station in Rwanda in 1900. In 1912 Rwanda-Burundi was joined to the vicariate of Kivu. The first African Catholic priests were ordained in 1917 in Rwanda and in 1921 in Burundi. The Catholic mission benefited from the support of the Belgian administration in the areas of medical and educational work, in which it was largely subsidized by the state. Rwanda and Burundi soon became the most Catholic countries in Africa, with 50 to 60 percent of the population baptized in the Roman tradition.

*Ernst Johanssen (1864–1934)*
*with his family in Rwanda.*

In 1907 during the period of German colonization, the first Protestant missionary appeared in Rwanda. Ernst Johanssen (1864–1934), a Lutheran of the Bethel Mission, began his missionary career in Usambara, Tanganyika, in 1891. He was accompanied to Rwanda by an equally experienced colleague, Gerhard Ruccius, and by a group of African Christians, for the most part artisans who were animated by a real missionary spirit. This mission, the Berliner Evangelische Missionsgesellschaft für Ostafrika (Berlin East Africa Evangelical Mission Society), had in the past been compromised by Germany colonialism, but under the influence of Gustav von Bodelschwingh, it underwent a profound and happy transformation under a new name, Bethelmission (Bethel Mission). Johanssen explained the new pietistic and evangelical nature of the mission:

> For what purpose do we work? First of all we want to influence individuals with the message of the gospel, so that they become new men and women. Next we want to form a new community with them, one that allows itself to be permeated by the Spirit of Jesus Christ. In this way, they will be the instruments through which something new is introduced among the people. For their own gain, salvation, and liberation, they will come to taste an unknown joy and a new pleasure in life by experiencing Jesus, who came to give his own life for all of which man has need.[348]

When the missionary team from Usambara arrived in Rwanda, it made contact with the Catholic missionaries and was impressed by the quality of their work. When the king of the country asked the Protestant missionaries if the German colonial power was going to expel the French Catholic priests, Johanssen responded that there was enough room in the country for the two missions. Taking a broad view of missionary work, Johanssen explained:

> Even if there are many who pull us apart, all men who love Jesus Christ as Lord and Savior feel attracted towards those who know

---

348 E. Johanssen, *Klein anfänge: Grosse aufgaben* (1915). Cited by M. Twagirayesu and J. van Butselaar, *Ce don que nous avons reçu* (Kigali: Église Presbytérienne au Rwanda, 1982), 21.

> the same love. And we have no reason to suppose that this love
> does not exist among the representatives of another confession . . .
> The better one knows oneself on the human level, the better one
> will enjoy mutual understanding and respect.[349]

Uncommon words in a time of competition and often tense confrontations between confessions.

The principal concern of the Bethel missionaries was not the presence of the Catholics, but the appearance of Arab merchants, for Islam was until then unknown in these regions. For Johanssen, Islam was not simply a false religion that hindered evangelization; it was also a brake on the economic and moral development of the country, for it lowered the status of women and promoted polygamy. To avoid having the population come into contact with Muslim merchants, the missionaries opened small stores in the villages, and they set up a commercial missionary society to promote the introduction of Christian businessmen in Africa. They even imported a steamboat from Europe to transport merchandise on Lake Kivu, hence forestalling the intervention of the Arabs.

The Bethel Mission established three mission stations during its first years in the land, including one at Kirinda where Johanssen came to reside. Due to poor sanitary conditions among the population, the missionaries placed much emphasis on medical work. They also focused on agricultural development, which involved irrigation, animal husbandry, and the introduction of new seeds and plants from Germany. The work of evangelization was the chief responsibility of the African Christians of Usambara. The first baptisms took place after seven years. Progress was slow, but the evangelists were seeking depth of piety rather than quick but superficial growth.

This demanding approach proved prescient when the German missionaries had to leave Rwanda a dozen years later in 1916. At that time British and Belgian troops entered the country from the Congo. Belgium, which had obtained the political mandate for the country, did not authorize the return of the Bethel Mission after the war. Instead, the government solicited the Belgian Congo Missionary Society, founded in 1910, to take over the Bethel Mission stations. Due to limited resources, the society withdrew from its engagements in the Congo in order to concentrate on the work in Rwanda. It also sought other missions to participate in the work, a strategy that the colonial administration authorized on condition that they be French-speaking organizations. The first available missionary was Ernst von der Heyden who, ironically, had already served as a missionary in Rwanda from 1907 to 1914 for the Bethel Mission. Being Alsatian, he was German during the war but French afterwards. The Belgians in Rwanda had to turn a blind eye to the double standard of the colonial government that expelled German Protestant ministers while at the same time allowing German Catholic priests to remain. At the Kirinda mission station in 1921, five years after the departure of Johanssen, von der Henden wrote:

> We are like the dust in the universe before this immense task.
> On Sunday the hall is always full . . . It is miraculous to see how

---

349 Twagirayesu and van Butselaar, op. cit., 52.

> the living Word of God remains close to the hearts of the people here, and how it remains active despite many sins. One cannot be astonished enough that so many biblical truths continue to be known.[350]

Since 1919 a Belgian Seventh-day Adventist missionary, David Elie Delhove, had been working in Rwanda. It was observed that

> Delhove continues to teach the Bible as well as reading and writing at Kirinda. Since he is an Adventist, he has introduced some special practices . . . The Kirinda bell continues to ring, calling Christians to the worship of God. However, since 1919, it sounds Friday evening to announce the Sabbath.[351]

At the arrival of von der Heyden, Delhove sought to avoid tensions by opening a station in Gitwe, about twenty kilometers from there. In 1921 the Belgian Congo Missionary Society undertook the support of two Belgians, Arthur Lestrade and Josué Honoré, who took over two mission stations formerly established by the Bethel Mission. Renée Simul, a nurse who had pursued further training at the House of Missions in Paris, arrived in 1922 and soon married Lestrade. Finally, the society enlisted Edgard Durand, a Swiss who had studied in Belgium and then at the Faculté de Théologie de Genève. He traveled with his wife to Rwanda in 1924.

Though the missionary team was small and faced a massive task, it struck out on three fronts. First, it sought to translate the Bible into Kinyarwanda, the principal language of the country, limiting itself at first to certain books of the New Testament. Second, it sought to encourage Rwandan Christians to proclaim the gospel in their own country. Finally, it strove to preach a holistic gospel, one that touched all aspects of life. Lestrade wrote in 1930:

> Our principle is to train not only Christians but men, giving them the well-rounded education and technical training necessary for them to rise in society . . . Our mission attaches great importance to the education of young girls—the training of Christian wives and mothers for future generations.[352]

He often said, "The Bible in one hand, the saw in the other." The mission pursued medical work, opening children's hospitals in 1925 in Kirinda and Remera; it pursued education work, and in 1930, began to follow the official program of the Belgian government; and it pursued vocational training, concentrating in the construction trade. The work was undertaken with great enthusiasm and moved in several directions at once, but it was extremely limited in means, personnel, and finances. Still, despite these hindrances, the Presbyterian Church of Rwanda eventually issued from the work and ministry of the Belgian Protestant Mission, established by the Bethel Mission.

---

350 Ibid., 83.
351 Ibid., 73.
352 Ibid., 90.

The Anglicans were also involved in Rwanda. Though Belgian authorities feared British influence in Rwanda, they reluctantly allowed the Anglican Mission of Uganda to begin medical and evangelization programs in the country in 1925.[353] Two doctors, Len Sharp and Algie Stanley-Smith, pioneered this work.[354] They had been working in 1921 at Kabale in the southwest of Uganda, and even then had the goal of reaching the then "virgin" countries of Rwanda and Brundi. They undertook several reconnaissance trips with the intention of establishing a mission sometime in the future. In spite of the obstacles posed by the Belgian administration, they were able to establish themselves in Gahini, Rwanda, in 1925. Several years later, the mission experienced a revival that was also surging through many other Rwandan churches. This was the Balokole movement, which spilled over into the neighboring countries of Burundi and Uganda. The growth that the Anglican Church then enjoyed made it the second largest church in the country, after the Catholic Church. In 1925 the CMS called upon its missionary, the Reverend Harold Guillebaud, to translate the Bible in Kinyarwanda. Under the guidance of the British and Foreign Bible Society, Guillebaud worked with other Protestant missions, notably the Belgian Congo Missionary Society and the Seventh-day Adventists, to create a Bible translation for Rwandan Protestants. Benefiting from the work already completed by Belgian missionaries, the team of translators completed the New Testament, Psalms, and Pentateuch in 1936.

A number of other missions in the period between the two World Wars also entered the region. At the request of Delhove, the American Seventh-day Adventist mission began a very successful effort in 1921. Today, the Adventists constitute about a third of Rwandan Christians. During the period between the two World Wars, the American Free Methodists (1935), the Danish Baptists (1938), and the Swedish Pentecostalists (1940) undertook various missionary initiatives in Rwanda.

## URUNDI (THE REPUBLIC OF BURUNDI)

The Protestant missionary effort in Burundi paralleled that of Rwanda. The Neukirchener Mission, of Germany, began work there in 1911. In time these Lutheran pioneers founded five mission stations and saw extensive progress before having to leave in 1916. Their presence, however, had been too brief to found a church or to educate indigenous leaders. Unlike the situation in Rwanda, no other mission was able to take up the work again until 1928. The Belgian administration authorized the Danish Baptists to recultivate the field left fallow for a dozen years following the German expulsion. The Danes found a population prepared and impatient for the return of Protestant missionaries. Soon an indigenous church was established, and in 1934 it too was touched by the revival, during which the laity engaged in house-to-house evangelization.

Doctors Len Sharp and Algie Stanley-Smith, the founders of the Anglican Mission in Rwanda (see above), also worked in Buhiga and Matana, Burundi, in 1934.

---

353 The Anglicans were already at least indirectly present in 1897 in the person of the Ugandan missionary Apolo Kivebulaya, whose work among the pygmies was located in the border region between the Congo and Rwanda.
354 Born in China, Algernon (Algie) Stanley-Smith was the son of one of the "Cambridge Seven" who joined Hudson Taylor and the China Inland Mission (see p. 364).

According to a strategy worked out in advance in Uganda, they formed a "mixed and egalitarian" team of British and Ugandan Christians who undertook the task of evangelizing the country. The revival reinforced their determination and ability to engage in mission on an interracial basis, and thanks to the revival, the church experienced rapid growth. The medical work also developed quickly.

Sharp and Stanley-Smith came to believe that the CMS mission had lost its evangelical orientation. Wishing to benefit from an independent movement, they organized a medical mission that worked in Rwanda, Burundi, and Uganda. The church founded by this mission took the name Protestant Episcopal Church of Burundi.

The daughter of the missionary and translator Harold Guillebaud was the key worker in the translation of the Bible into the Kinyarwanda language of the country, which is related to the Kinyarwanda of Rwanda. The translation was completed in 1965. Until the Second Vatican Council, the Catholic clergy continued in its opposition to making the Bible available in the indigenous languages of the people.

The Seventh-day Adventists arrived in 1921, the Society of Friends (Kansas Yearly Meeting of Friends) in 1932, and the Free Methodists (American) in 1935. They took up the work that the Danish Baptists were not able to further due to their limited resources. The Swedish Pentecostals also appeared in 1935, and the World Gospel Union and the Brethren Assembly in 1938. From the churches that issued from these mission organizations (with the exception of the Pentecostals and Brethren Assembly) the Alliance of Protestant Churches of Burundi was formed. Energized by the spirit of the revival, Burundi Protestantism experienced much growth during this time.

# CHAPTER 23

# The Horn of Africa

## SOMALIA

To the east of Kenya and southeast of Ethiopia lies Somalia, a land politically troubled in the last decades of the nineteenth century due to European colonization. France occupied the northern coast on the Gulf of Aden in 1883; Britain established itself in a small section of the northern part of the country in 1887; and, finally, Italy declared a protectorate over most of the territory in 1889. The Catholics appeared in the country in 1881, sending several missionaries from Aden. In 1892 the Capuchins entered the section of the country under the Italian protectorate, but the church consisted almost solely of Italians who later left, following decolonization. The Catholic priests spent much of their time in social and educational work.

Protestants also took an interest. The Swedish Lutherans of the Evangelical National Missionary Society appeared in 1875 and undertook work in the areas of evangelism, medicine, education, and agriculture. The Italians often blocked their efforts. In 1935 after more than half a century in the country, the church had only 350 baptized members. Most were former Bantu slaves, but there also were a small number of Somalis. At this time, the Italian dictator Benito Mussolini expelled the Protestant missionaries and transferred their enterprises to the Catholic mission. The region under British authority had never had a missionary presence. The authorities had forbidden it, fearing the opposition of local Muslim chiefs.[355]

## ETHIOPIA

The former kingdom of Ethiopia looms large in the history of the African church. Christianity was introduced there in the first half of the fourth century and maintained itself over the course of the centuries despite almost constant pressure from Islam, especially between the eighth and sixteenth centuries[356] (see maps 12, p. 585,

---

355 It was not until after the Second World War that the Mennonites undertook educational, medical, and publishing work in Ethiopia. But they had to abandon these efforts in 1976. The Sudan Interior Mission arrived in 1954 and began the translation of the New and then the Old Testament.

356 See pp. 49-50, 132, and 175-76.

and 14, p. 648). In the sixteenth century the Ethiopian church[357] was almost entirely cut off from the rest of Christendom.[358] At the beginning of the nineteenth century, Abu Rumi translated the entire Bible into the Amharic language, producing a manuscript of 9,539 pages. This translation was purchased by William Jowett, a missionary of the British and Foreign Bible Society, and the four Gospels were printed in 1823 in Malta. The rest of the Bible was printed in London in 1840.

Protestant missionary societies hastened to begin work in Ethiopia in the nineteenth century. Though they knew that Christianity had a long history in this African country, they feared that it was soon to expire. The first Protestant missionaries to work there were Christian Kugler and Samuel Gobat. Sent in January 1826 by the Church Missionary Society (CMS), they patiently waited for four years in Egypt before they were able to enter Ethiopia, which was then divided into several hostile kingdoms. In 1830 they were able to engage the Tigre, the largest kingdom in the country, which lies in the north. Their caravan of twenty-two camels bore thousands of Amharic Gospels that had been printed in Malta. They were received with much interest, and the missionaries enjoyed full liberty to proclaim the gospel to this highly receptive population. But Kugler died at the end of the year 1830, and Gobat had to return to Europe for reasons of health in 1836.

As we observed above, Ludwig Krapf entered Ethiopia in 1837 (see p. 581). In Adoua, in the province of Tigre, he found Charles Isenberg and C. H. Blumhardt, two CMS colleagues who shortly before had preceded him into the country. Once he was able, Krapf dedicated himself to working with them to revise the Amharic translation of the Bible. But after only one year, they were expelled by the king of Tigre. Italian Catholics of the Lazarist order came into the region a little later, directed by Justin de Jacobis. They experienced persecution: an Ethiopian Lazarist was put to death and Jacobis was imprisoned.

The CMS missionaries left the region and settled in another kingdom toward the center of Ethiopia. Here they translated the Gospels into Oromo, the language of one of the ethnic groups of the Galla people. The Gospels began to appear in print 1841, and the entire New Testament was completed by 1875. Krapf introduced Ethiopian youth to Hebrew and to lives founded on the word of God. In 1842 King Sahela Selassie, who had invited him into his kingdom, now required the priest to leave under pressure from the Orthodox clergy. Capuchins missionaries arrived in 1846 but were expelled in 1855.

---

357 This is often called the "Coptic" church because of its link to the Egyptian Church, or "Orthodox" because of its liturgical and ecclesiologic traditions that are related to those of the Eastern Church.

358 According to the emperor Menelik, who reigned in Addis Ababa from 1889 to 1909, "Ethiopia is an island of Christians in a sea of Muslims."

*Johann Martin Flad*
*(1831–1915).*

# JOHANN MARTIN FLAD: APOSTLE OF THE FALASHAS

The missionary to enjoy the most remarkable ministry in Ethiopia during the second half of the nineteenth century is Johann Martin Flad (1831–1915) of Germany. While he was studying in 1852 at the Institute of Chrischona,[359] in Basel, Bishop Gobat came to expound the needs of Ethiopia, and Flad responded to his appeal. At the age of twenty-four, he accompanied Krapf on one of his many journeys to East Africa. He found the Ethiopian King Theodoros II not only well disposed to Protestantism and zealous in the reading of the Bible but one who aspired to become the religious reformer of his people. The king, called the Negus, permitted Flad to open schools, evangelize, and distribute the Scriptures. But not long after the king's wife died, he remarried; and under the influence of his new spouse, the king's behavior changed dramatically. He married multiple wives, became an alcoholic, and ruled his kingdom tyrannically, causing Flad and his colleagues much suffering. Nevertheless, the work continued. For example, missionaries who were residing in a Coptic monastery were able to worship regularly and convince many monks to read the Bible regularly, and a secretary of the king converted and became a zealous evangelist among his compatriots.

The Negus finally allowed Flad to take up his ministry again but on condition that he dedicate himself solely to the evangelization of the Falashas, Ethiopians of the Jewish religion. He baptized thirty-one of them in 1862. Flad sent his reports to Bishop Gobat, who sent them on to Britain where they excited the interest of the London Mission Society (LMS). The society sent two missionaries who had to promise that converted Falashas would be baptized in the Coptic Church. But the hostility of the king towards the Europeans, including the missionaries, was again aroused. They were cruelly treated, some were imprisoned for nearly five years, and the persecution spared neither their wives nor their children. They were finally freed in the Easter of 1868 when British troops reestablished the rights of incarcerated British officials. Defeated, King Theodoros II committed suicide.

Missionaries were evacuated with British nationals due to the anarchy then reigning in Ethiopia. The missionaries were able to return only sporadically with the camel convoys that transported Bibles. In effect, the Ethiopian Coptic Church looked askance at the activities of the missionaries, Catholics as well as Protestants, who were threatening its ancient religious traditions and were suspected of taking its converts from among the faithful of the established church. The missionaries who attempted to reform the church from the inside had scarcely any success. Considered as the apostle of the Falashas, Flad could not resettle in Ethiopia. Still, indefatigable and undaunted, he made numerous trips through Europe to plead the cause of the evangelization of the Falasha Jews of Ethiopia. He had also encountered and taught

---

359 The Pilgermission St. Chrischona center of studies, located in the region of Basel, was founded in 1840 by Father C. F. Spittler. One of his objectives was to reach Islamic populations by sending artisans to work among them. He believed that they would be able to witness more effectively through manual labor than preaching or education. Among the first ones sent from Chrischona were C. Schick and C. Palmer, who left for Abyssinia in 1846 in response to the appeal of Bishop Gobat.

Christian Falashas, some of whom were dedicated evangelists. One of these was Michael Argawi, who in 1910 made this observation:

> According to our calculations, since the beginning of the work in 1860, we have baptized seventeen thousand to eighteen thousand Falashas, including children. It is true that not all of them were deeply committed Christians, but many among those who died in the faith and many still living love the Lord with all their hearts.[360]

*Michael Argawi, a native evangelist of the Falashas, in front of his tukul. (Photo by Herman Norden)*

When Menelik II became the king of all Ethiopia in 1889, he moved the kingdom's capital to Addis Ababa and adopted a religious policy more subtle than that of his predecessors. By early in the twentieth century missions were able to begin to regain their footing in the country. The CMS returned to Addis Ababa in 1904 and extended its work throughout the land. In 1913 the British and Foreign Bible Society was authorized to open a Bible warehouse in the capital. The United Presbyterian Mission began to evangelize west Ethiopia in 1920. In 1927 the Sudan Interior Mission (SIM) also entered the country where it experienced much difficulty. It had fourteen mission stations when, in 1935, Mussolini's Italy seized Ethiopia and expelled all the Protestant missionaries. They were not able to return until 1942 when the British achieved victory over Italy. In the meantime, Ethiopian Protestants were persecuted but also experienced a great revival and engaged in the evangelization of their people. When the SIM missionaries returned after a seven-year absence, they were surprised to discover a church of eighteen thousand members, having had about sixty at the time of their departure.

The Evangeliska Fostrelands Stiftelsen (Evangelical Mission of Sweden) established itself in 1866 at Massawa, which lies in the southern part of the country, then in Egyptian territory but now part of Eritrea. The Swedes had previously attempted to work in Tigre, but in three years four of its eleven missionaries had died of fevers and two had been killed. The mission worked mostly among the Coptics rather than the Muslims or animists, operating a school, several mission stations, and a theological seminary. For nearly sixty years it was the only Protestant work in Eritrea. Tajeleng, the first evangelist trained at the seminary, was sent to the University of Berlin to teach in its eastern seminary. After a period of relative liberty, in 1885 Eritrea became an Italian colony and the Swedes suffered numerous restrictions. They nevertheless maintained their posts on the Red Sea where they welcomed large numbers of slaves who had been freed by the Italian navy. During the Italian period, the Catholics had much more freedom to operate.

---

360 J. Gauguin, *L'Ethiopie et l'evangile* (Neuchâtel: Delachaux & Niestlé, 1935), 62.

# CHAPTER 24

# *French Equatorial Africa*

## GABON

The pioneers in Gabon came from across the Atlantic. In 1842 the American Board sent Benjamin Griswold and John Leighton Wilson. Wilson had served in Liberia since 1834. Both settled on the right bank of the Gabon River in a place called Baraka, the location of the future capital, Libreville. They were readily accepted by the Mpongwe people, who soon brought them their children for education. However, after fifteen years the Church of Baraka did not have more than twelve members. The trade at the port permitted the making of easy money, and alcohol took its toll. Attempts to enter into the interior of the country were generally frustrated, and several stations erected in the dense forest were soon abandoned due to the death of the missionaries working there.

In 1863, after about twenty years, the New Testament was printed in Mpongwe, and later the Gospels were translated into the other languages spoken by the inhabitants of the interior regions. Then in the last quarter of the nineteenth century, the mission began to gain traction in the society. In 1870 the Board of Foreign Missions of the Presbyterian Church of the U.S.A. succeeded the American Board, for it was already established in neighboring Spanish Guinea. It would attempt to reach the Fang people, who lived in Guinea and in the interior of Gabon. In 1874 Doctor Robert Nassau settled on the shores of the Ogooue River, in Balambila, about two hundred kilometers from the coast. In 1877 Nassau established the first mission station of Lambarene, which lies about twenty-five kilometers from Balambila; and the first church in Ogooue was established in 1879. Three years later Nassau penetrated one hundred kilometers farther into the interior to erect the Talagouga mission station. The Fang proved to be quite receptive to the gospel.[361]

---

361 Robert Nassau recounts his first encounter with a Fang, which produced a surprising reaction: "A man was watching me fixedly, although calmly and discreetly. He eventually found the courage to address me in order to ask, "Are you not my brother. My brother died in such and such a period and went to the country of the white men?" His question suggests a belief system based on an ancient mythology that appears not only in Gabon but also in Cameroon. (Cited by Sundkler and Steed, op. cit., 273.)

*Robert Hamill Nassau, theologian, missionary, and doctor in Gabon.*

The scion of a noble Dutch family that included William of Orange, Robert Hamill Nassau emigrated to the United States and studied theology at Princeton Theological Seminary and medicine at the College of Medicine in Philadelphia. His subsequent career of forty-five years was nothing less than remarkable. He quickly learned three African languages, which were a great help to his ministry. His first wife and son, then less than two years old, died while he was working in the coastal regions. His second wife was taken from him in Ogooue, after having given birth to a baby they named Mary. Nassau hired an African governess to care for his child. The woman already had a child, but the father was a polygamist whom she did not want to marry. Nassau, an older man by this time, considered her as the mother of his daughter. His missionary colleagues and the American Committee viewed their relationship as the equivalent of a marriage and spoke against it, remonstrances that he chose to ignore. He remained in Africa until 1906, but from 1900 was generally estranged from his colleagues. In contrast, he had good relations with Elie Allégret and Urbain Teisserès, French missionaries who arrived following his rupture with his other colleagues (see below).

Professor P. R. Dekar, who studied the work of the Presbyterian American Mission in Cameroon and in Gabon, drew harsh conclusions about its missionaries: "In principle, they accepted African Christians as equals, friends, and protégés. But tragically, in practice, only Robert Hamill Nassau had personal relations with the African Christians."[362] Nassau wrote in his journal of his colleagues: "They know how to pray much better than me, but why don't they have black friends?" On his return to America, Nassau wrote a book that quickly became an important reference work in ethnology and the history of religions: *Fetishism in West Africa*. Despite the fruitfulness of his ministry, Nassau's work was largely forgotten or concealed because of the controversy surrounding his personal life. Albert Schweitzer, who arrived in Ogooue twenty-two years later, was fond of repeating, "I have always felt myself in some ways Dr. Nassau's successor."

France was present on the coasts of the Congo and Gabon for many years, and its colonial administration sought to extend its reach into the interior of the country where logging promised to be lucrative. Gabon was acquired as a colony by France in 1845. Savorgnan de Brazza (1852–1905), who began his African career as an explorer in the Congo and Gabon, later became the Commissary General of the French Congo (the middle areas of the Congo) on which Gabon depended. He was a great admirer of David Livingstone and, in an anxious time, was inspired by him to place his confidence in Africans and refrain from all use of force. He also had great respect for Protestant American missionaries. When he was alone and unknown at a time early in his experience in the Congo, he had received a cordial welcome and effective help from the missionaries, which he never forgot.

---

362 Ray Teeuwissen, "Le précurseur oublié: Avant Schweitzer; Il y avait Nassau," in *Le christianisme au XXe siècle*, no. 276 (October 13, 1990).

In 1883 the government degreed that only French was to be taught and used in the schools. Charged with executing this decree, Brazza saw its logic but did not want to implement it quickly or provoke the departure of the American missionaries. Nevertheless, the Paris Mission was asked to send missionaries as the Americans were not capable of learning French, and Alfred Boegner proposed that the American Mission be supplied with French teachers. In 1888 the Paris Mission dispatched three teachers to work in the schools in Libertine (formerly named Libreville) and Lambaréné, along with a Swiss artisan. Their mandate was not to replace the Americans but to work under their direction. Finally the Americans themselves officially asked the Paris Mission to take over the mission, but the French were reluctant to do this. Rather than replacing all the foreign missions in French colonies, they preferred to encourage English-speaking missionaries to persevere where they were. They also asked the French government to permit this even as the British allowed them to pursue their work in the colonies of Lesotho and Zambia.[363]

However, things quickly degenerated. Based on the experience of the Americans wanting to leave their stations in the Ogooue basin, the French envisioned the sending of instructors as a way to establish a foothold in Gabon. The following year, the missionaries Elie Allégret and Urbain Teisserès were asked to make an evaluation. Based on their report, the Paris Mission decided to become more formally engaged. The populations of Upper-Ogooue showed themselves more receptive to the gospel than the Mpongwe. The living conditions of the missionaries, however, were particularly trying: the stations along the river in the great forest were isolated, and the climate was humid and unhealthy. Fever and malaria ravaged the first dozen missionaries, ten of whom died during their first or second term of service. Despite the hardships, the work progressed: forty missionaries arrived in the course of the first ten years, and several new stations were established along the river. By 1897 Lambarene had a school for catechists, and the educational work greatly expanded.

*Savorgnan de Brazza (1852–1905), explorer and Commissary General of the French Congo and Gabon, who showed great respect for English-speaking Protestant missions.*

The distance of the stations from the interior required much local infrastructure to traverse: boats, peddlers, warehouses, and shops. In Lambarene by 1894 there were already twenty-two buildings erected to give shelter to the nearly one hundred people active in the mission station. The Paris Mission questioned this material growth, fearing that evangelization would suffer from it. The director Alfred Boegner asked especially about the causes of the rapid expansion of the mission. Aside from a thirst for the gospel and the zeal of the missionaries, was there not also on the part of the population a superficial attraction to the consumer goods and lifestyle of the Westerners? Taking the approach that it did, was the mission not risking the creation of a protected and privileged clientele?

---

363 For the position of the Paris Mission with regard to colonization, see p. 695ff

In 1908 the agronomist Felix Faure wrote a report based on his observations in Gabon wherein he argued for the necessity of integrating the gospel and work. He noted that the converts risked marginalization. No longer able to participate fully in the social and economic life of traditional African society, they were finding themselves cut off from a part of their means of existence, becoming, according to Faure, "*déclassé*" (lowered in class) and "*malheureux*" (unhappy). It was necessary, therefore, for the mission to offer them not only spiritual life and a new ethic but also the means to assure their subsistence in the new situation in which they found themselves. "While preaching of the gospel of repentance, forgiveness, and salvation that renews them, it is also necessary to preach the gospel of work that will free them," he concluded.[364] If this is not done, he argued, they will very quickly fall again into paganism or, perhaps worse, will be contaminated and demoralized by contact with the colonists who employ them.

In response to these diverse needs, the administrator of the Paris Mission, Onésime Beigbeder, proposed the founding of a society to take up the social and material aspects of the mission work, one that would specialize in training apt Africans to meet the challenges of the new society. In 1910 the mission established the Société Agricole et Industrielle de l'Ogooué (SAIO, Agricultural and Industrial Society of Ogowe). The society introduced wage labor and engaged personnel for the agricultural work. It also employed new methods of agriculture and new seeds, hoping that they would be spontaneously adopted in the villages when they had proved their value. A brickyard and sawmill also gave employment to workers and ameliorated the housing conditions of the local population. Caught in the tension between the need for commercial profitability and its philanthropic objectives, SAIO knew a precarious existence.

In 1924 the Paris Mission sent Jean and Jeanne Keller of Marseille to Lambarene. Lacking training, Jean did not take over the direction of SAIO until 1928. Not long after, he also became the president of the Gabon Mission. In 1930 he presided over the consecration of the first three Gabonese ministers who were entrusted with the responsibility for an entire district.

A Pentecostal-style revival profoundly affected the Church of Gabon in 1936. According to Keller, despite the inevitable excesses "this was a marvelous experience. It renewed a great number of the Christians who have known as never before the love and power of God, the reality of the deliverance and joy that are in Jesus Christ, and his call to a life more completely consecrated to his service."[365]

In 1931 a federation of all the Protestant missions working in French Equatorial Africa (AEF, its French acronym) and in Cameroon was founded through the work of Jean Keller and Henri Russillon of the Paris Mission, and M. Sodergren of the Swedish Evangelical Mission in the Middle-Congo region. A means of cooperation among missions, the Federation provided them with representation before government authorities, but its chief goal was "the full evangelization of the AEF and Cameroon, and

---

364 Zorn, "Missions protestantes," 104.
365 Jean Keller spoke these words at a ceremony celebrating the independence of the Evangelical Church of Gabon, Port-Gentil, June 30, 1961.

the division of these immense territories between the societies capable of performing the work."

Keller returned to France shortly before the Second World War to pursue the goal of cooperation and communication between the missionary societies. During the war, the governor general of the AEF decided to resist the "collaborationism" of Vichy, which led to a break in communications between Paris and the AEF colonies, and between the mission headquarters in Paris and the missionaries on the field. The International Mission Council was asked to assure support for those missionaries who had become "orphans." In contrast, the governor of French West Africa opted for Vichy, which resulted in negative repercussions for about 130 missionaries, the majority being British. There were some expulsions and some incarcerations, and a Methodist missionary in Benin named Taylor died in prison in Dakar. Keller obtained authorization to visit the colonies of French West Africa and to meet the representatives of ten missionary societies. They designated him as the general delegate to represent them and to defend their legitimate rights before the colonial administration.

## ALBERT SCHWEITZER (1875–1965)

The Mission in Gabon can hardly be described without discussing Doctor Albert Schweitzer, the best known French missionary of the twentieth century—though a part

*Doctor Albert Schweitzer (1875–1965), winner of the 1952 Nobel Peace Prize.*

of his life was lived outside the period covered by this work. Schweitzer was many things: a Doctor of philosophy, teacher of theology, director of a theological seminary in Strasbourg, preacher, lecturer, organist, and art critic. In 1905 he offered his services to the Paris Mission, declaring himself ready to set aside his career in Europe in order to help meet the extensive needs of Africa. He even decided to undertake the study of medicine to make himself more useful.

In 1911 Schweitzer completed his degree in medicine and announced, to the great astonishment of those close to him, his departure for Gabon. He wrote at the time: "Most will recognize that the entry of Christ in a life can change its course. Reading this in the New Testament, it seems quite natural: the unnaturalness begins when one puts it in practice. I am supposedly harming myself for not rebelling against this logic. Yet, how can so many brave people arrogate to themselves the right to bar a route that God wants to open?"[366]

The committee of the Paris Mission faced a difficult problem: while the mission work Schweitzer would undertake was clearly orthodox, he was known as a

---

366 Ernest Christen, *Schweitzer l'africain*, 6th ed. (Geneva: Labor & Fides, 1954), 73.

notorious liberal. He was himself conscious of the difficulty but believed that the obstacle could be surmounted. He wrote to the mission in 1905:

> Having heard your missionaries speak, having inhaled the air of this chapel, I know that our theological views accord admirably. And if you say that French missions have emerged from revival, I too know what revival is, for I sense that it is Jesus who has revived me. When I was immersed in my science, he said to me: "Go where I have need of you." And I want to follow him.[367]

Alfred Boegner, although in the opposite theological camp, pleaded his cause: "It is impossible," he said, "not to be struck by the intensity of his faith and of his vocation. He speaks of Jesus as the Master to whom he owes everything, to whom he looks for and awaits for orders, and to whom belongs his entire life."

Other members of the committee were clearly more reserved and, remembering the theological controversies that were then agitating French Protestantism, feared that accepting him as a candidate would discourage the more faithful supporters of the mission. Pastor Franz Anton Knittel, Schweitzer's curate, wrote that the doctor was not arguing from a high pulpit against orthodox doctrines but, rather, was advocating that "before becoming a missionary, it was necessary for him to feel saved and regenerated by the divine founder of the gospel, our Lord and Savior Jesus Christ." When the mission concluded that it was necessary to meet in order to ask him to explain some of his theological opinions, Schweitzer clearly refused: "When Jesus called his disciples, he did not say to them, 'Explain yourselves!' but 'Follow me!' This is the only condition to enter in his inner circle." It was also objected that Schweitzer was an Alsatian of German nationality, an inopportune status at that time for one who would work in a French colony.

Despite these difficulties, Schweitzer left for Gabon with his wife Helene in 1913. Due to the objections cited above, he was not fully accepted as a missionary of the Paris Mission but, as he put it, was recognized as a "temporary guest of the mission." The sale of his books (especially his study of Johann Sebastian Bach, which was a popular success) gave him the means to live without a salary from the Paris Mission.

He began medical work in Lambarene, and the hospital that he started aroused considerable interest in Europe due to the uncommon stature of its founder. He was more than an African missionary, having performed in the theological, philosophical, and musicological arenas. In theology, he held what was for his time a liberal interpretation of the teachings of Jesus, and he pleaded for a theology more mystical than dogmatic. He saw in the ethic of Christ a "respect for life" that influenced his medical beliefs and practices. In music, he dedicated himself to the study of Bach, emphasizing the pietistic sensibility of the great composer. Schweitzer received the Nobel Peace Prize in 1952,[368] an honor that gave him an almost mythic dimension that he had not sought.

---

367 This citation, as well as the two following, are taken from Zorn, "Missions protestantes," 593.
368 After forty years of intense labor in the hospital of Lambarene, Albert Schweitzer died in 1965.

His relations with those sent by the Paris Mission were generally harmonious. In his gracious fashion, he observed:

> I was always struck by the fact that the missionaries often showed themselves more liberal than the governing committees of their societies. They understood, by experience, that in distant countries and especially among primitives there exist no presuppositions that place a choice before Christians between dogmatic orthodoxy and liberal doctrine; here, it is only a matter of preaching the essentials of the gospel of the Sermon on the Mount and of bringing these men into the empire of the spirit of Jesus.[369]

# CHAD

Chad is a vast country[370] of which the northern part is largely desert and is occupied by populations that are generally nomadic and Muslim. The south, more fertile and populated, is inhabited by animistic tribal groups among whom Christian missions have encountered greater openness to the gospel.

Islam was carried by the Arab tribes into the north during the eleventh century. Other waves of Islamic penetration occurred in the sixteenth and seventeenth centuries, and in the course of the nineteenth century, the population endured the raids of Egyptian slave traders. In the second half of the nineteenth century British and German explorers entered the land. At the end of the nineteenth century, various Chadian kings allied themselves with the French in their struggle against Rabah, an Arab slave trader from Sudan who was finally defeated in 1900. Over the course of the next thirteen years France succeeded in occupying the entire country, and it became a protectorate linked to French Equatorial Africa. The French administration made Fort-Lamy (present-day N'Djamena) the capital of Chad, and the country obtained colonial status in 1922 (see map 11, p. 563).

Due to its geographical position, Chad was the last country of central Africa to be evangelized by Christian missionaries. An initial attempt had been made by the Capuchins in 1663 but without success. In the twentieth century, the first Catholic missionaries were the Fathers of the Holy Spirit, who came from Bangui in 1929. They settled in Kou, in the Logone, and ten years later in Fort-Archambault (present-day Sarh). Before the beginning of the Second World War, Capuchins, Jesuits, and Dominicans were all present in the country.

Protestants preceded the Catholics by a little more than ten years. The Fraternal Lutheran Mission sent J. I. Kaardal, an American of Norwegian origin, into Chad in 1920. Kaardal settled in Lere, in Mayo-Kebbi, in the southern part of the country. A short time before this, his mission was present in the region of North Cameroon, close to the Chadian border. In 1923 the colonial administration gave Kaardal full

---

369 A. Schweitzer, *Ma vie et ma pensée* (Paris: Albin Michel, 1960), 107–8. Cited by Zorn, "Missions protestantes," 598. It is evident that his colleagues would not all be in agreement with this analysis.

370 Chad has an area a little more than twice that of France, and its population was a little less than 4 million inhabitants at the time of its independence in 1960.

latitude to engage in religious work. A church in Lere and others among the villages of the Moundang tribe, who spoke the same language, were the fruit of his efforts. Later, Kaardal composed an alphabet for the people, opened schools, and began to teach literacy. He also translated the New Testament and some texts from the Old Testament.[371]

In 1925 the Baptist Mid-Missions, already active in the Lubangui-Chari neighborhood, founded a station in the south of the country at Fort-Archambault. The work was undertaken by the American missionary Paul Metzler. His wife, who was French, took responsibility for the first missionary school in Chad. The early years of the mission were difficult for Metzler, who had to endure the opposition of a pagan chief hostile to the gospel. He and those who became followers were threatened with death, and in its beginnings, the church was constrained to meet for worship services secretly at night. Despite this, the church grew, and eventually even the pagan chief himself converted.

In 1926 John Ramses Olley, a New Zealand member of the Brethren Assembly arrived in Fort-Lamy under the auspices of the Christian Missions to Many Lands. He had previously lived in North Africa and then Sudan and was animated by a desire to evangelize Muslims. He began his ministry in southern Chad, helped by Chadian Christians who had returned to their country after having accepted the gospel while living in Nigeria. After several years, Olley sought to evangelize regions farther to the north. The government prohibited this, but he nevertheless succeeded in establishing a Christian community in Abeche in 1930. For nearly thirty years, Olley traveled across the country during the dry season; during the rainy season, he lived in Fort-Lamy where he translated the New Testament in Mbai and Kim, the two local languages. The Evangelical Mission that he founded eventually issued in the Christian Assembly of Chad.

It was also in 1926 that the North American branch of the Sudan United Mission (SUM) asked the Canadian missionary Victor Veary and his wife Florence to go to Chad. They worked in Logone, in the south of the country. Several stations were established, including in 1939 one at Bebalem where a large hospital was soon organized. This mission eventually launched the Evangelical Church of Chad.

All these missions came to Chad without previously consulting with one another. Some even began work without knowing that other evangelists were already active there. They managed nevertheless to divide the country into several regions, concentrating particularly in the south where the population was animistic. They generally refrained from settling among the desert nomads in the north, who were largely Muslims.[372]

---

371 J. I. Kaardal remained in Chad for forty years, retiring in Cameroon in 1960.

372 The number of evangelical missions active in Chad visibly increased following the Second World War, notably in the Guera. But this period is beyond the chronological limits of this work.

# THE OUBANGUI-CHARI (CENTRAL AFRICAN REPUBLIC)

The biggest part of the territory of present-day Central Africa was still completely unknown to the rest of the world in about 1885 ... Recalling the remote lands reached by the explorers in Central Africa before 1885 [the date of the Congress of Berlin] gives one a sense of the daunting task that, in the fifteen years followings, would become hotly disputed by the four principal powers of the period.[373]

In 1903 France created the territory of Oubangui-Chari. Following the policy of King Leopold II in the Belgian Congo, it entrusted a great part of the territory to concessionary companies. These commercial companies had no other purpose than the exploitation of the resources of the territory for their own enrichment. Consequently, as P. Biames writes, "For nearly a half century the former colony of Oubangui-Chari was the most neglected and brutally exploited of all the French colonies of black Africa."[374] The population rose up in rebellion several times, but the most widespread peasant insurrection against the concessionary companies took place from 1929 to 1931.

The Catholic missionaries present were the priests of the Holy Spirit, who began their work in 1890 under the Vicar Apostolic Monsignor Augouard, in Bangui. The colonial governor, based in Brazzaville (Middle Congo), seems to have favored and even financially supported this missionary effort. Until 1925 it was limited to the region of Bangui, and then its work was extended throughout the territory with the aid of the Capucins and Jesuits.

Protestant missions entered the lists in 1920. William Clarence Haas of the Baptist Mid-Missions, an American organization, first arrived in 1912 but had to leave for reasons of health before having established a presence. Eight years later he returned with five colleagues with whom he established evangelism posts in Bangui and several other localities. The Brethren Church of California supported the Evangelical Mission of Oubangui-Chari, which arrived in Brazzaville in 1918. The intention of the mission was to reach all of Oubangui-Chari, but it was three years before it obtained permission for only four missionaries. In its first dozen years, the missionaries established three centers of activity among the Karre and fanned out in several directions to reach other language groups. They gave priority to Bible teaching, and the best students in the local schools were sent for further study to the Institute Biblique Central (Central Bible Institute).

The Sudan United Mission, which was already active in several countries of French Equatorial Africa, came to Oubangui-Chari in 1923. A year later the Swedes of the Orebro Mission also appeared, having previously established themselves in the French Congo. They opted to settle in the southwest of the country. In the same

---

373 P. Kalk, *Histoire de la République Centrafricaine* (Paris: Berger-Levrault, 1974), 11. Cited by N'Gouka Honor-Sylvestre, "La problématique des rapports mission-église en République Centrafricaine" (master's thesis, Faculté de Théologie Evangélique de Bangui, 1983), 9.

374 P. Biarnes, *L'Afrique aux africains* (Paris: Armand Colin, 1980). Cited by N'Gouka, op. cit., 10.

years, John Buyse of the Africa Inland Mission crossed the Oubanqui River from the Belgian Congo in order to evangelize the Zande tribe in the southeast. Others soon joined him, establishing several mission stations. In 1927 the Elim Mission, a Swiss Pentecostal effort, also came to engage in the work.

In their early days, all of these missions encountered obstacles to their work erected by the colonial administration. The country was already unsettled, and the government feared that missionaries would further trouble the society because they were foreign and because they were promoting the emergence of a trained African leadership. The government also treated French Catholic missions and Protestant missions differently. Roger Mehl writes of this striking contrast: "French colonial expansion was almost always accompanied by Catholic missionaries. Though this was the most secular period in French history, beyond the seas it appeared as a Catholic country and its domination as a Catholic domination."[375]

Protestant missions, anxious to establish the best relations possible with the colonial administration and not be suspected of anti-French leanings, tended not to be critical of the government. This drew much censure as it appeared that they were attempting to gain personal security in exchange for sacrificing the prophetic dimension of their ministries, and this in a country that was the victim of a particularly oppressive colonial regime. The mission continued to strive for the improvement of conditions in the population through engagement in education, medicine, and agriculture, with the principal emphases being on evangelization, church planting, Bible translation, and the training of Africans to work in Christian communities.

## THE MIDDLE CONGO (DEMOCRATIC REPUBLIC OF CONGO)

Christianity first entered the country[376] through Catholic missionaries, who arrived at the end of the fifteenth century when Diego Cao and his Portuguese sailors discovered the mouth of the Congo River. At that time the right bank of the river was part of the kingdom of the Mani-Kongo. But the Catholic Church planted at that time entirely disappeared, and there was little or no Christian presence there in the seventeenth and the eighteenth centuries. It was only at the end of the nineteenth century that Christian missions reappeared in this region.

Following the travels of Savorgnan de Brazza, the region to the northwest of the river (the right bank) came under French influence in 1880 rather than being part of the Belgian Congo. The French founded the cities of Pointe-Noire and Brazzaville. Catholic missions were introduced in 1883 by the Fathers of the Holy Spirit and the Vicariate of the French Congo was established in 1886. The first Congolese priests were ordained in 1895. Bishop Phillippe-Prosper Augouard (died in 1921) had the cathedral of Brazzaville constructed with wood imported from France. Though the Congolese

---

375 Roger Mehl, *Traité de sociologie du protestantism* (Neuchâtel: Delachaux & Niestlé, 1965), 151. It has been said that French secularity was not an "exportable commodity in the colonies."

376 The Popular Republic of the Congo, often referred to as Congo-Brazzaville to distinguish it from its neighbor the Democratic Republic of the Congo (previously Zaire), was formerly called the Moyen-Congo or French Congo.

forest was filled with wood suitable for building, he opted for imported wood for reasons of prestige.

Pietistic Swedes introduced the first Protestant mission, the Svenska Missions Förbundet (the Mission Covenant of Sweden), entering the lower basin of the Belgian Congo in 1884. It established its first mission station in 1909 on the north bank of the river in the French Congo, and achieved much in the areas of education, social transformation, and medicine. The Evangelical Church of the Congo that came from this ministry is now one of the largest in the country. This church experienced a revival in 1921 while it struggled against sorcery and superstition. In the same period, the preaching of Simon Kimbangu had a far-reaching effect in the region, and the Kimbanguist church enjoyed significant growth in both the French and Belgian Congos.

The Swedish mission, supported by the Free Church in Sweden, wanted to accord the same freedom it enjoyed at home to the African church that emerged from its work. Swedish missionaries led by Dr. Karl Laman wrote a constitution in 1929 about which many African church leaders were far from enthusiastic. One wrote:

> Having learned that our friends in Europe and our own white missionaries wished that the direction of the churches and of all the work of God be entrusted to us, the people of this country, we did not want to place ourselves in opposition to this . . . We dread this responsibility. But knowing that such is the will of God, and in the hope that we will not be left to ourselves, we will give ourselves to this work, in the name of the Lord.[377]

In the event, the constitution was not fully implemented, and the Evangelical Church of the Congo only achieved the status of an independent church when the country ceased being a colony. At that time, the African leader Jaspar Kimpolo proffered to the Mission Committee "his generous salutations and the expression of his gratitude for having offered autonomy to the church long before it had asked for it."

In 1935 the Salvation Army turned its attention to Brazzaville. Having already worked in the Belgian Congo, it was ready to apply its usual social approach to the establishment of a group of communities in the south of the country. In the early 1940s, a curious movement spread among the people from which the Salvation Army unintentionally benefited. This was the belief that the flag of the Salvation Army had a protective virtue against sorcery, disease, and even death, and that the letter "S" in its officers' uniforms signified Simon Kimbangu.

Finally, the northeast of the country was reached in 1921 by the Swedes of the Orebro Mission and by Pentecostal Baptists.

---

377 Sundkler and Steed, op. cit., 761–62.

# CHAPTER 25

# *Angola*

I n 1491 in the border region between the Congo and Angola, the Catholic Church inaugurated its first diocese in sub-Saharan Africa. However, in the subsequent five centuries, Catholicism scarcely left a trace there, not even during the era of slavery and Portuguese colonialism. All its efforts to establish itself in the society ended in failure. When Livingstone arrived in Angola, having crossed the breadth of Africa from east to west, he found scarcely anything of Christianity there except churches in ruins and several superstitious practices influenced by the faith. It is estimated that in 1870 the Catholic population consisted of barely fifteen thousand people out of a total of 3 million inhabitants. The Fathers of the Holy Spirit had to begin practically from scratch when they arrived in 1873. The Portuguese government encouraged conversions, but little progress was made in the struggle against illiteracy. After about fifty years, there may have been about a quarter of a million Catholics, but for the most part their Christian faith was sorely lacking in depth.[378]

## HELI CHATELAIN

Livingstone's account of his expedition across the African continent to the Atlantic port of Luanda, capital of present-day Angola, had a great impact in the West. Among his more impressionable readers was the fifteen-year-old Swiss boy Heli Chatelain (1859–1908). At the time he was bedridden for long months due to a disease of the hip. Struck by the image of Africa presented by Livingstone, he fervently asked God for healing so that he could dedicate his life to this continent.

Chatelain recovered, though he was handicapped for life. Still he kept his promise. In 1883, at the age of twenty-four, he decided to move to the United States and study medicine and theology. During this time, he encountered the Methodist Bishop William Taylor, founder of a mission to the Congo (see p. 621), who was then recruiting a youthful team for missionary service in Angola. Moved by Taylor's appeal, Chatelain presented himself as a candidate. At the end of 1884, Chatelain traveled to Britain where he intended to prepare himself for his adventure in Africa. He was accompanied by William Summers (1855–1888), a minister and medical doctor who was

---

also in the employ of Bishop Taylor. The two friends had the occasion to make the acquaintance of Henry Morton Stanley, with whom they discussed their plans.

At the beginning of 1885, Chatelain embarked from London for Luanda. These lines addressed to his family express his rigorous spirituality:

> Can the Christian speak of sacrifice? No, and this for two reasons: first of all, a single glance at the cross of Jesus Christ must cause us to understand that, before the Savior, there is no renouncement worthy of the name. Next, let us recall that if Jesus asks anything of us, it is with joy that we must say immediately: "He is the Lord." Our life, our money, our friends, all our joys are gifts from Him, and to renounce them on the order of the Master is to encounter a grace that is higher than these gifts, which comes from the one who expressed himself in these words: It is more blessed to give than to receive.[379]

When Chatelain and Sumer arrived in Angola, they were not the first Protestant missionaries there. To the north, in Sao Salvador near the Congolese border, the Baptist Mission from Britain had been present since 1879. Farther to the south and in the interior of the land in the region of Bihe and Bailundu, missionaries sent by the American Board had been busy since 1880 (see map 11, p. 563). Chatelain and Summers were the advance force of a missionary team then being assembled in the United States by William Taylor. The sixty-four-year-old Taylor disembarked several months later with twenty-three missionaries, which included six women. The missionaries also had a number of children with them.

Doctor Summers traveled into the interior of the country to find sites for the new arrivals, but due to illness Chatelain was not able to go with him. While managing the house in Luanda where new missionaries were welcomed and doing the initial work to establish a mission station, Chatelain taught French and English to the Portuguese colonists. In this way he supported himself, for it was one of Taylor's principles that every missionary must be self-supporting.

From the first year the American missionaries occupied several mission stations, often living in difficult physical conditions. It was not until the beginning of 1887 that Chatelain was prepared to make his first journey into the interior of the country. His purpose was to visit the mission stations, in particular their schools, to evaluate the ongoing work and determine the possibilities for new initiatives. The most immediate obstacle was financial: the missionary teachers had no exterior support and were reliant on student tuitions that Africans were ill-equipped to pay. Based on his experience in Luanda, Chatelain suggested that they offer classes to the Portuguese, who were numerous in the region and often desirous of learning English or French in order to conduct their commercial activities with greater ease. This would also create an opportunity to present the gospel to them, and their tuitions would finance the teaching of the African students. This model was a success and was imitated in many places.

---

379 A. Chatelain, *Héli Chatelain: L'ami de l'Angola* (Lausanne: Mission Philafricaine, 1918), 49.

Chatelain lived for some time in Malange, five hundred kilometers to the east of Luanda. While teaching there, he studied the local language, Kimbundu, which he tried to fix in writing. He translated a number of Bible texts—parables, stories from Genesis, the Gospel of John—and composed hymns. He evangelized using pictures of the life of Christ and speaking as much as he could in Kimbundu, his efforts being augmented by an interpreter using Portuguese.

In November 1887 Chatelain returned to Switzerland where he printed a primer (spelling book) to teach children, and a grammar in Kimbundu that was intended for missionaries so that they could learn to communicate as quickly as possible in the local language. He also sought the financial support that was indispensable for maintaining mission work. Most important, he decided at this time to leave the Taylor Mission, which he believed to be operating under erroneous principles:

> It seems to me that the time has come for me to prepare to cut the official lines that tie me to the Taylor Mission . . .
>
> As for the bishop . . . we perhaps resemble each other too much in independence of character and views to be able to work together in our respective positions, given the abyss that separates our educations and our personal tastes. I firmly believe that I cannot, without great sacrifice, be an active member of any denomination, and that my influence must be put to use in nonconfessional evangelization.[380]

Before returning to Angola, Chatelain spent six months in the United States. Curiously, he left for Africa as the guide of a scientific expedition composed of astronomers and naturalists who wanted to observe a solar eclipse and collect information about the flora and fauna of the country. According to Chatelain's terms of employment, in lieu of a salary he was to have freedom to pursue his missionary activities. He did not lack for work. The station in Luanda had greatly declined, and his linguistic work, especially the Kimbundu grammar, attracted the interest of the Portuguese authorities in Angola, who offered him their help so that he could continue his work. The time he spent in Africa on this occasion was not long.

Between 1890 and 1895, he visited the United States several times and was often consulted for his knowledge of linguistics and ethnology. His book *Folk-tales of Angola* included extensive information about the geography, climate, and population of the country. He described numerous customs and recorded a series of local short stories, which earned for him much notoriety among American intellectuals. During one year, Chatelain was even the American consul in Luanda. Beyond the immediate applause he received, his activities opened many doors for his missionary work.

---

380 Ibid., 122.

# THE PHILAFRICAN LEAGUE

In the course of his fifth trip to America, Chatelain started a project that he had been considering since he had left the Taylor Mission: a society, or league, whose purpose would be at once philanthropic, economic, cultural, and thoroughly spiritual in that he envisioned the evangelization of the continent and the foundation of an African church. The means to attain these ambitious objectives were the creation of a chain of mission stations that would begin at Benguela on the Atlantic coast and proceed across the interior of the continent as far as the Zambezi River, where François Coillard had been working since 1884.[381] The mission stations that formed the links in this chain would function as "cities of refuge" for freed slaves. They were also to be centers in the struggle against the slave trade in that they would be agricultural, artisan, and commercial colonies, organized according to Christian principles. Hence they would give training and employment to an indigenous workforce. The profits realized would provide salaries for the missionaries, permitting them to concentrate their efforts on evangelization, the pacification of the region, and the struggle against slavery. In each center, material printed in the local language would also provide a cultural dimension to the work.

The project aroused much interest and enthusiasm among Christians, especially in American universities. On May 27, 1896, the Philafrican Liberator's League was launched with the support of a number of well-known American personalities.

Chatelain and five Americans—two couples and a gentleman—found themselves in Benguela in September 1897. They faced a number of obstacles: no porter wanted to accompany them into uncertain regions, the authorities refused to recognize the freed slaves, and Chatelain fell gravely ill. Finally, the missionary team was accepted by a caravan of Boers, who furnished them with a wagon pulled by about twenty oxen. Chatelain's written analysis of the colonists shows his gift for keen observation:

> They are so much alike that it is hard to tell them apart from our Bernois peasants. They have a great respect for the Bible, but seem to read only the Psalms; sadly, they do not apply its precepts to the treatment of the indigenous people. They have need of a great revival and the best among them do not deny it . . . What missionaries the Boers would make, if the Spirit of God would work within them to melt their glacial orthodoxy! The women among them, with their chubby, rosy cheeks, are mothers of twelve to fifteen children! Many of the Boers are Huguenots by origin, and there are even Vaudois of the Piemont . . . What a strange mixture there is of good and evil among these survivors of the austere founders of the Reformation! On the one hand, it is

---

381 In the same period, George Grenfell also sought a "linking" that would extend from the Congo to Uganda, where Alexander Mackay's Anglican Mission was then at work. He succeeded a little before 1890 (see p. 566). About forty years earlier, Ludwig Krapf had envisioned a similar project that would join Kenya with the Anglican Mission in Nigeria. Stretching from east to west, the mission stations would have formed a dike to keep back the Islamic flood coming from the north. The project, however, encountered too many obstacles to be implemented (see p. 582).

sad to observe their hardness toward the indigenous population, and on the other hand, it is astonishing to see that so much good has been preserved in them, deprived of shepherds as they have been for so long a time.[382]

After five weeks, the caravan entered the Caluquembes country, which sits on a plateau more than 1,600 meters in elevation and two hundred kilometers to the southeast of Benguela. The Boers abandoned them there in a deep forest, refusing to go any farther into an unknown territory. The high altitude rendered the climate healthy, and Chatelain, therefore, chose to settle the first volunteers of the Philafrican League on this spot. In one of his first letters, he wrote:

> I have decided to establish our first station in the country of the Caluquembes, a day from here. The native people are perfectly ignorant and relatively free from the degrading influences of alcohol . . . The slave trade and slavery are worse than I believed them to be. God alone in time will provide a remedy. May these instruments be docile and patient. Pray that the Holy Spirit fills all our hearts and shines in the darkness that surrounds us!

They attacked the clearing, planting fruit trees and vegetables, and constructing log cabins. The station bore the name Lincoln,[383] the American President whose assassination had so disturbed Chatelain, who was six years old at the time. He then recommitted himself to the struggle against the misery of slavery, as Abraham Lincoln had done. Often alone in the task, Chatelain traveled through the region looking for villages. He had the gift of producing trust in the villagers, many of whom came to work in Lincoln in order to gain training.

*Heli Chatelain (1859–1908), founder of the Philafrican Mission in Angola.*

Soon, the interest of the people in the gospel became apparent. The inhabitants, who loved music, sang with pleasure to the accompaniment of a violin played by one of Chatelain's American colleagues. Once he had learned several phrases in Umbundu, Chatelain put them to music, sometimes to popular Swiss tunes that the people could easily learn and sing while walking. A neighboring king entrusted him with the education of his daughters and nieces.

But pillaging and plundering due to raids related to the slave trade were reducing the region to a state of chaos. Chatelain energetically sought the intervention of the authorities, which earned for him the hatred of numerous colonists who had an interest in these disorders. If the Caluquembes recognized him as a friend and called

---

382 Ibid., 208.
383 Later, it would be called Caluquembe, the name of the local people.

him *kahenda*, "the compassionate," others threatened him and sought his life. He wrote at the time:

> It is something, despite all my personal faults, to be the only one in this country who does not want to have slaves, who refuses to make use of brandy, either as a drink or a form of currency, who neither lies nor cheats, who observes the Sabbath, and who treats the blacks with the same equity as the whites. It is something to be able to speak of Jesus to these peoples, who have never heard his name pronounced. If, as in other places, the foundation of our cause must be sealed in the blood of martyrs, is it not a great good be able to give one's life for Christ who redeemed us by his blood?[384]

The missionary team at Lincoln was soon completed in 1898 with the arrival of two American doctors and a Swiss mechanic. In Switzerland interest grew for this missionary effort led by a Swiss citizen, and an auxiliary branch of the Philafrican League (which was increasingly called the Philafrican Mission) was formed in 1898. It came under the direction of Alida Chatelain, the sister and future biographer of Heli. In contrast, people grew impatient in the United States due to not seeing the chain of mission stations and the refuge centers for the freed slaves that had been planned. Chatelain defended himself, seizing the occasion to explain his vision of the work for which he was giving body and soul. His balanced and realistic understanding of how the gospel acts on the spiritual and social levels still merits our attention today. Here is his essential response:

> The purpose of the Philafrician League is not solely to provide a solution for the evils of African slavery but to apply the principles of Christ to all the social questions of the black continent. This program is so vast that there will always be—lest it be lost sight of—something to do for a society of this type. Alcoholism alone, which is one of the plagues we are attempting to suppress, will itself take a long time to workout. Moreover, we begin with the principle that to reconstruct the social life of Africa and put it in harmony with the laws of Christianity it will be necessary for the Spirit of God to regenerate as many individual Africans as possible. Hence, our work also embraces all the elements of a purely religious mission.
>
> Our work is an industrial and agricultural mission, interdenominational and largely lay. It is especially active where the need is most felt, the areas of slavery, polygamy, alcoholism, and witchcraft, those secular wounds of Africa . . .
>
> It is the place of governments, not ours, to liberate the slaves. Though it is true we could "redeem" them, this would be an indirect encouragement to the trade. Therefore, I do not approve of

---

384  H. Monnier, *Mission Philafricaine en Angola, 1897–1947* (Lausanne, 1947), 12.

this means except in certain exceptional cases, for example the sad case of one who already has a rope around his neck or who is about to be drowned for having committed an imaginary crime. What we can do, and what we are doing here, is to teach by word and example that the slave trade and slavery are sins, crimes in the eyes of God for which all are guilty who engage in it; . . . to prove that it is possible to live in this environment without slaves and without alcohol; to offer a refuge and an asylum to all the un-happy ones who desire to escape an illegal oppression.[385]

## NEW SWISS MISSIONARIES

The years 1900 and 1901 were a time of excruciating crisis. Chatelain's teammates found it increasingly difficult to bend to his authority. They had not come to lead the frugal lives of nonstop activity that the director imposed upon them; nor had they bargained for so much illness, which seemed to sap their wills. Those who did not return to America asked him to step down from directing the work and turn it over to a committee that they were forming. When he refused, they abandoned him, the last one leaving in January 1901. With the benefit of hindsight, Chatelain would observe that the departure of the missionaries produced a happy consequence, the rapid Africanization of the work.

In all his letters home Chatelain regularly asked for more Swiss workers. In 1903, three Swiss artisans joined him, occupying themselves with livestock, farming, and operating a much-used mill. The Lincoln mission station was steadily growing. Fugitive slaves sought refuge there, and entire villages elected to live nearby in order to benefit from the services being offered and to be protected from slave raids. Chatelain pleaded with the authorities to establish a garrison to pacify the region, an idea that was eventually accepted.

Despite the immensity of the task, Chatelain's two coworkers returned to Switzerland in 1907, each having served six and a quarter years. The atmosphere was probably not as serene as Alida Chatelain presented it in her letters, which were always positive and full of confidence in her brother. Rodolphe Bréchet writes, "Collaboration with Heli Chatelain was not easy, given his fire, demanding nature, force of character, and energy for work. On the other hand, his missionary experience, the vivacity of his exceptional intelligence, and his erudition were so far above that of the average devoted young artisans, who arrived from Switzerland with insufficient qualifications, that true consultation in the work was not easy."[386]

After ten years of uninterrupted service, in September 1907 Chatelain left Angola, weakened but anxious to personally present his mission's needs to the Swiss churches in order to recruit quality workers. When he arrived in the country, he was practically incapable of walking due to the weakness of his hip. Six months later, while he was planning to return as soon as possible, he had to confront the sad truth:

---

385 Chatelain, op. cit., 250.
386 Rodolphe Bréchet, *J'ai ouvert une port devant toi* (Lausanne: Alliance Missionaire Evangélique, 1972), 16.

his sickness was irreversible and was going to worsen. At the end of several weeks of acute suffering, which further undermined his health, he died on July 22, 1908. In the end he was greatly weakened, but peaceful. He was only forty-nine years old.

A little before his death, Chatelain expressed the wish that the Philafrican Mission become a Swiss Mission, attached to the National Protestant church of the French-speaking cantons. The leaders of the national Vaudoise church, after seeming to commit themselves to adopt "his" mission, changed their minds on the basis of a pessimistic report in 1912 that had been submitted by two of his missionaries. The Philafrican Mission lived on as an independent mission supported by believers from various denominations.

## THE MISSION AFTER CHATELAIN

After Chatelain's departure, various circumstances in Lincoln led to a difficult test of faith for the missionaries. Among other trials, a fire ravaged the station and the livestock were decimated by disease. In 1908 with only a single missionary on the site, the Swiss committee decided to cut short the training of Eugène Kaegi, a Vaudois blacksmith, in order to send him as quickly as possible. Together with his wife, Kaegi threw himself into the work of the mission, serving for thirty-one years. A man of winsome personality and deep spirituality, Doctor Bréchet said that he was "a mechanic with the temperament of an apostle."

In 1915 the Kaegis found themselves alone in the gap. War was then raging in Europe, which prevented the arrival of fresh replacements for those who had died or who had had to return home. Also, a terrible two-year drought caused an unprecedented famine, resulting in many deaths.

These accumulating problems retarded the growth of the work. Rodolphe Bréchet gave this diagnosis: "From the human perspective, fifteen years after the arrival of the pioneers, all was still in an embryonic state: a small nucleus of faithful Caluquembe, the baptism of the first five African Christians, the first Sunday school, the first youth group, the first boarding school for girls, the first annex with an African catechist, and finally twelve other baptisms."[387] The missionaries had not striven for rapid and superficial development. According to Chatelain's vision, the mission was not so much about implanting a few new religious beliefs and practices but of inculcating a new lifestyle and even a new socioeconomic organization that was modeled after the teachings of the Scriptures. They laid their foundation with care, only baptizing people who were well trained and zealous witnesses. Hence, the future appeared promising.

After being understaffed during the First World War, several new Swiss missionaries subsequently served for long periods at the station. A Belgian couple, Mr. and Mrs. Visser, settled close to Lincoln in 1926. Their presence enhanced relations between the mission and the Protestant churches of Belgium.

Marco Lucindo, a former student of the mission, was chosen to be the king of the Caluquembes in 1930. At first he refused this responsibility, believing it to be

---

387 Ibid., 19.

incompatible with his faith, but in the end, at the insistence of the Portuguese authorities, he accepted it for the good of his people. Kaegi reported the facts in these words:

> [Lucindo] felt the need intensely of the Holy Spirit's help to confront the frightening powers of paganism, which he knew better than anyone. He resolved not to install himself at the capital where his predecessors had lived. Here the relics of a paganism several hundred years old were preserved, the bones of ancient kings that it was sometimes necessary to consult with the sprinkling of blood. The atmosphere of this residence, impregnated as it was with the miasmas of the blackest superstitions, was not the place for a young king ambitious to lead his subjects to Christ the Savior. Instead, he resided on a small hill close to Lincoln. Marco asked the Swiss Christians to pray for him so that, in his delicate position, he would be able to glorify his Savior in all circumstances.
>
> Since he was the chief of his tribe, he was able to stand in for the missionaries in the morning service, which gave him occasion to witness to his faith before hundreds of his people.[388]

Lucindo reigned nearly five years before being deposed by the former king.

By 1933 the church in the region of Caluquembe had twenty-three annexes, commonly established at a walking distance of about four or five hours from each other. In Caluquembe there were about six hundred people attending the regular worship services; and at Ebanga, four hundred to five hundred people. In thirty neighboring villages there were fifteen catechists giving instruction to 760 neophytes.

At the beginning of 1942, during the war, Dr. Rodolphe Bréchet arrived with his wife, Amy. In September 1945, just after the war, they were followed by five compatriots; Edmée Cottier (a nurse), Alfred Hauenstein, Willy Maeder, and their wives. Cottier and Hauenstein gave priority to the evangelization of the villages while Bréchet established the hospital of Caluquembe and enjoyed a remarkable influence over a vast region.

## OTHER PROTESTANT MISSIONS

In general Protestant missions confronted numerous obstacles set up by the Portuguese government, which tended to favor Catholic missions. Emphasizing education, Protestant missions were one of the causes for the emergence of a new generation of Angolans who aspired to national independence.

Following the death of Chatelain, the Methodist mission under William Taylor persevered in its ministry among the Kimbundu, to the east of Luanda. Joseph Hartzell succeeded Taylor in 1896. The fruit of their efforts was the Evangelical Methodist Church. The Methodist Conference began in 1920, with two districts, Luanda and Malange. The mission contributed much to the education and development of the region.

---

388 Monnier, op. cit., 39.

The Église Evangélique du Centre de l'Angloa (Evangelical Church of the Center of Angola) gathered members from those converted by the American Board, mentioned at the beginning of this chapter, and the Mission of the United Church of Canada, which arrived after 1886 and enjoyed much success. In 1938 the new church had 100,000 members and 1,568 ministers.

Frederick Stanley Arnot was a leading missionary in the Congo among the Brethren Assembly (see p. 570). Witnessing to his faith in Katanga, close to the border, he encouraged his colleagues to establish a chain of mission stations from Bihe to Zambia. In the early years of the twentieth century, the Brethren were the most numerous of the Protestant missionaries in Angola. They translated the Bible into the local language and converted many to the service of God.

The Angola Evangelical Mission and the North Angola Mission, both American organizations, established themselves in the regions close to the Congolese border, in 1897 and 1925 respectively. Coming from neighboring Congo, the Kimbangu movement also spread rapidly here, from its origins in northern Angola.

Beginning in 1914, the south of Angola was evangelized by the African Evangelical Fellowship, a faith mission that was originally called the South Africa General Mission. Consequently, this part of the country has a majority Protestant population today. Finally, there was the small Portuguese Baptist Mission, which in 1936 established itself in Nova Lisboa (the present-day city of Huambo).

# CHAPTER 26

# *Madagascar*

Doctor Johannes Vanderkemp is remembered for the enthusiasm he had for this great island that had not yet heard the message of the gospel (see pp. 462ff). Death prevented him from beginning a mission there, though it was a task close to his heart. Fortunately the London Missionary Society (LMS), his mission, undertook this task a few years after his death through two Welsh missionaries, David Jones and Thomas Bevan. Because Vanderkemp's letters had raised considerable interest in Britain for the evangelization of Madagascar, about five thousand people gathered for the consecration ceremony that sent off the two missionaries and their families in December 1817. Sir Robert Farquhar, British governor of the Island of Mauritius, also lent his support. He hoped that the mission would contribute to ending the slave trade and to strengthening relations between Madagascar and Britain.

After several weeks on the Island of Mauritius, Jones and Bevan decided to explore Madagascar before bringing their families there. *En route*, they stopped at the Island of Bourbon (present day Reunion), where the French governor exclaimed to them: "To evangelize the Negroes, to change their hearts? You might as well seek to change the habits of my dog by preaching." This racist attitude did not shake the conviction of these pioneer missionaries, but they were well aware that the field they sought to sow was far from prepared to receive the gospel. The Malagasy historian Rabary remarked:

> Nothing seemed to prepare the inhabitants of Tananarive to receive Christian teaching. Everything appeared to present an obstacle, especially the inveterate practices of astrology, divination, the ordeal, idolatry, corruption . . . Polygamy was the rule and immorality was practiced openly and without a shadow of remorse. There was not the least fear of public opinion; rather, it was encouraged . . . The Malagasy believed in God but in an entirely miserable fashion: among them, God was less important than ancestors, fetishes, amulets, and ordeals. There was no true fear of divine law, no knowledge of sin, no sense of conscience. It

was impossible to build a spiritual edifice on such beliefs, or present serious evangelical teaching.[389]

## THE FIRST MISSIONARIES: COURAGE AND SACRIFICE

David Jones was the first missionary to establish himself with his family in Madagascar. They settled on the coast in Tamatave (Toamasina), where the climate was particularly unhealthy. Jones immediately took in charge ten young people from the ages of nine to fourteen. To economize, he first taught them the alphabet by writing on the sand of the seashore. He applied the Lancaster method, which called on the more advanced students to teach the others. This method was later systemically applied by the Protestant mission in Madagascar and contributed to the extraordinary success that education had there.

In December 1818, after less than two months, Jones' baby daughter and wife became ill and died in the space of two weeks. His daughter died on December 13, but two weeks later his wife seemed to improve. Jones, who was also sick at the time, wrote:

> On the December 26, we possessed sufficient strength to walk hand in hand in our bedroom. I said to her, "Allow me to take your arm for support, for you are stronger than I," and she was stronger. But alas! Alas! The following day I saw a great change in her for she was both deaf and mute. The next day, her aspect grew graver, for the signs of death could be seen in her countenance . . . On the 29th, at two-thirty in the morning, she left me.[390]

The graves had just been covered when the Bevan family arrived on January 6, 1819. Ignorant of the drama that had just transpired, they found Jones at death's door.

But, prophetically, Bevan said to him: "We are going to die and you will survive us." And less than a month later, Thomas Bevan, his wife, and their small child were all dead. Hardly more than three months after his arrival, Jones found himself alone in Madagascar with five tombs. Still gravely ill, he learned that some of the local people thought the families had died due to witchcraft while others, without the least evidence, believed the deaths were due not to fevers, but to poisoning. Jones then withdrew to the Island of Mauritius and remained there for a year to regain his health.

*David Jones.*

With a courage that compels admiration, he returned to Madagascar in 1820, but this time he went to the high plateau region where the climate was better. Governor Farquhar intervened to obtain authorization for him from Radama I, the young king of Imerina, whose kingdom included Tananarive (Antananarivo) and the high plateau

389 Augustin "Rabary" Rabarijama, *Les martyrs malgaches: Histoire des persecutions contre chrétiens à Madagascar, de 1835 à 1861* (Tananarive, Madagascar, 1910). Cited by Gustave Mondain, *Un siècle de mission protestante à Madagascar* (Paris: SMEP, 1920), 37–38.

390 Vincent Huyghues-Belrose, *Les premiers missionnaires protestants de Madagascar, 1795–1827* (Paris: Karthala, 2001), 253.

at the northern center of the island. En route toward the capital, Jones happened upon several processions of slaves who were being led to the coast for embarkation abroad. These sights inspired him to write lines full of sadness and indignation:

> I was revolted and anguished at the sight of all these poor people of all ages, chained to one another, who were being uprooted from their country to be sold like livestock. Some were just young people; there were some who were scarcely more than six or eight years old, poor children never before separated from their mothers. Ah! If one passed the same procession in the streets of London, what heart would not be moved and suddenly burn with the desire to launch a holy crusade against the ignoble trade.[391]

At its apogee, the slave trade captured three thousand to four thousand slaves per year. The slaves were first sent to the Mauritius and Bourbon islands, and from there transported to the Antilles, the United States, or Arabia.

In May 1821 David Griffith of the LMS arrived to lend his support to Jones. He was soon followed by the Reverend John Jeffreys, his wife, and four tradesmen, one of whom died after only a few weeks. Among the tradesmen was James Cameron, a remarkably cultured carpenter who would become a renowned missionary in Madagascar. Radama I was anxious for the welfare of his subjects and saw in the presence of these missionaries a chance of progress for his kingdom. In November 1820 he addressed a letter to the LMS. Here is a brief extract:

> At the time when the governor, Sir Farquhar, and I concluded an accord putting an end to the sale of slaves in the provenance of Madagascar, the missionary Mr. David Jones arrived in Antananarivo, the capital of my kingdom. He was accompanied by others sent from the British state, who visited me in order to ask permission to settle in my kingdom.
>
> I am satisfied with the declaration of Mr. Jones, your missionary, affirming that those sent from your society do not seek anything other than to enlighten minds by persuasion, by an initiation into the understanding of truth, and by the search for happiness. I ask you therefore, Sirs, to send us as many missionaries as your capacity permits you . . . I promise you that your missionaries will receive from my people protection, respect, and peace. The missionaries that we especially wish at this time are those who will teach the Christian religion, as well as various tradesmen to teach such things as weaving, carpentry, spinning.[392]

The king also desired education for his people. G. Mondain cites a letter from Jones, written in May 1821:

---

391 Mondain, op. cit., 40.
392 Vincent Huyghues-Belrose, in B. Hubsch, ed., *Madagascar et le christianisme* (Paris: Karthala, 1993), 202.

> I employ most of my time in teaching sixteen children or young people whom the king has entrusted to me. Three among them live with me. These are the children of Radama's sister, and one of them is the presumptive heir. The others are the children of dignitaries, all remarkably intelligent . . . They usually begin to read the English Bible within six months of learning the alphabet. Each Sunday, I teach the catechism and hymn singing. The king is enthusiastic about the progress [of the children] and often comes to hear them. These children have learned that they have immortal souls, and they know how to respond with seriousness to a crowd of questions about God, Jesus Christ, death, heaven, and evil, etc.[393]

A third of the children were girls, a ratio that would be maintained and, at times, increased to the benefit of the girls. Vincent Huyghues-Belrose notes, "This situation is exceptional even when compared to literacy later in Europe, a fact that merits underscoring."

Once the missionaries mastered the language, their efforts at teaching and evangelism were a success. Soon a school was inaugurated in the compound of the royal palace. Intended for the officers and their wives who were desirous of learning, it quickly attracted three hundred adult students. Griffith described the growing interest of the people in a letter:

> Since the month of April, we have opened twenty-two schools, with a total of two thousand students enrolled. The king himself has proved to be our true protector. We have been able to send some of the oldest students to direct the schools in the country, and the results have been more satisfying that we dared to hope . . . Our auditors are very numerous, and our city churches are jam-packed. Many people are obliged to remain standing and others must try to listen from outside by the windows. The services in the city are often attended by three or four thousand, indeed by five thousand; in the country, it is not rare to see meetings with two or three thousand.[394]

The organization of trade schools made up a large part of the work of the mission. The schools taught locksmithing, shoemaking, tanning, carpentry, soap making, and other trades. Courses were also offered in chemistry, architecture, agriculture, and even lithography. The missionaries emphasized hymn singing, which was a great success among this musical population. However, whatever the scope of success that the LMS missionaries enjoyed, it would have been premature to speak of a steady rate of conversions. The interest of the people was real, but their attachment to ancestral traditions, superstitions, and pagan practices had not slackened. The missionaries knew this, which is why they redoubled their efforts to translate the Scriptures in Malagasy, believing that the word of God would have a profoundly transformative

---

393 Mondain, op. cit., 41–42, note.
394 Ibid., 45–46.

effect on the society. In part they increased their labor with the aid of their most gifted students.

A printing press that had been sent from England in 1826 was utilized in Antananarivo (French Tananarive). Soon educational books and extracts from the Bible were available. The Gospel of Luke appeared in 1828, and already by 1830 the New Testament was completed along with several books of the Old Testament. This publication was a sensation, producing a veritable infatuation with Christianity among the people, especially the local elite.

## THE TIME OF PERSECUTIONS

In 1828 the king died abruptly and prematurely; he was only thirty-six years old. Rabary had this comment: "Radama had never enjoyed vigorous health, and his numerous travels and warlike expeditions often left him feverish and undermined his physical constitution. His lack of self control also contributed. For this prince, who exercised so remarkable a power over his subjects, never learned to control his own passions, which often led to unreserved drinking and debauchery."[395] It had been the king's ambition to conquer the entire island of Madagascar, and he believed that the technical prowess of the Europeans made available to him through the missionaries would serve his designs. F. H. Krüger wrote in 1886 that Radama I "sought civilization rather than Christianity, though he allowed the missionaries to do their work." He wanted his people to copy Europe in its material accomplishments, and to this end he would keep the missionaries under his control so that they would serve his ambitions. At the end of his reign when he sensed a growing reaction against Christianity and in favor of ancestral traditions, he forbade baptism and Holy Communion to his subjects.

Upon the king's death one of his wives acceded to the throne under the name of Ranavolona I. At first she showed herself more tolerant than her husband had been. She allowed about twenty baptisms, which included those close to power as well as slaves, women, and youth. Though converts were not yet numerous, thousands of people frequented the Christian meetings. There were many public discussions in which the missionaries encouraged new believers while denouncing certain practices and superstitions of the country's traditional religion. J.-F. Zorn writes that there was certainly "a movement toward Christianity, notably among the keepers of the sampy (objects of traditional worship) and the administrators of the regime, who saw in Christian doctrine the means to modernize and democratize the country."[396]

But these Christian advances produced a reaction during the second year of Ranavolona's reign. A part of the leadership class felt that its privileges were threatened by the evolutionary turn the society was taking. Those who were profiting from the slave trade were particularly concerned and mobilized themselves against the new religion. The queen took the lead in this reaction, ordering the assassination of

---

395  Ibid., 54–55.
396  Zorn, "Missions protestantes," 1046.

Rakotobe, the seventeen-year-old nephew of the king whom Radama had designated to succeed her. Educated by missionaries, he was a Christian.

The queen soon broke relations with Britain and hindered the work of the British missionaries. Nevertheless, there was a great thirst among the population to learn to read, and the work of education continued apace with more than four thousand students in school in 1835. In the same year, a royal decree forbade conversion to Christianity, and those who were already Christians were weighed down with heavy fines. The queen wrote a letter of warning on February 26, 1835, addressed to all the Europeans on the island

> I give you thanks for the good that you have done in my country and in my kingdom. The initiation of wisdom and knowledge . . . Do not be anxious, I will not change the habits and customs of our ancestors . . . On the contrary, if you see anyone among my subjects who wants to change the least of the rules established by the dozen great kings, my ancestors, I would not know how to consent . . . It is permissible to teach my people science and wisdom, but as for touching the customs of the ancestors, it will not be allowed, and I will entirely oppose it . . . However, as for teaching trades and wise practices that will benefit the inhabitants, continuing in these things will be fine. Such are my instructions, which I wanted you to know. Ranavalomanjaka.[397]

In a speech addressed to her subjects the following month, her tone clearly became more menacing:

> I will not allow the denigration of fetishes, the ridicule of divination . . . And as for baptism in the churches and prayers outside the home, as for the teaching of respect for the Sabbath . . . ah this! Who are the masters that reign in this country? Am I not the only sovereign here? Therefore, for you who are baptized, members of churches, organizers of prayer meetings, I give you one month to accuse yourselves. If you do not do it and wait to be discovered, I will exterminate you, me, Ranavalomanjaka, Queen, whom no one can deceive.

Between June 1835 and July 1836, all the missionaries were forced to leave the island and the schools were closed. Seven hundred Malagasy teachers and upper class students were sent to the army. The last missionaries to leave were David John[398] and Edward Baker, who strove to complete the printing of the first Bibles in Malagasy, which was accomplished on June 21, 1835. Working flat out, they managed to print thousands of Gospels, hymnals, tracts, and educational books. When they finally withdrew to the Island of Mauritius, they left behind a very young and small church, one that had been stripped of ministers and structures, one without formal places

---

397 Hubsch, op. cit., 226.
398 David John was originally David Jones but changed his name to avoid being confused with the first missionary to arrive on the island with Thomas Bevan in 1818.

of worship but whose members continued to meet in private houses. There were then only two hundred baptized Christians. But they had the word of God in their language, a few hundred New Testaments, and about one hundred complete Bibles. Christian houses were searched, but Bibles were concealed in holes dug in huts, rice pits, and caves far from the towns.

It is obvious that the missionaries would not have been able to plant this church without the active engagement of a large number of capable, zealous, and sacrificial Malagasy believers. Still, the spiritual discernment and remarkable work accomplished by a small group of missionaries in about fifteen years must be acknowledged. Afflicted by disease and death, they managed to fix a language in writing, educate thousands of children, and translate the entire Bible into a language that they had had to learn by ear. Seeing the Malagasies' interest in Christianity, they could easily have settled for producing a large number of superficial conversions. Instead, they gave priority to the translation of the Bible and, at the time of their enforced departure, left behind only a small cadre of believers. And this church, far from disappearing due to persecution, endured and even grew during an entire generation of isolation.

Amidst this small church courageously enduring tribulation, the attitude of several women was particularly exemplary. One of the first Christians to be persecuted for her faith was Rafaravavy. She belonged to a rich and influential family that was devoted to pagan practices, and her father was a high royal official. One day she went with her husband to the house of an idol maker to take delivery of a statuette. The craftsman was still in the process of sculpting the wooden figure, and after completing the final touches, he threw some of the wood chips from the idol into the fire in order to prepare a drink for his clients. A little later, Rafaravery recalled this scene as she heard a Malagasy evangelist read a passage from the prophet Isaiah (Isa 44:9–20) that showed the vanity of idols in terms that corresponded exactly with what she had seen in the house of the idol maker. She concluded that this was much more than a coincidence: God was speaking of current events to her through this biblical text. She immediately converted and became one of the first baptized Christians of Madagascar, taking the name Mary and devoting herself to a life of prayer and witness.[399]

Hardly had the last missionaries been expelled when she was denounced by three of her slaves and thrown in prison. Her father tried to persuade her to renounce her faith, but she was adamant. Finally, the queen spared her for the sake of the many services rendered to the state by her family. Persevering in her Christian faith, she was again arrested and this time condemned to death. As she lay in chains on the night before her execution and calmly prepared for martyrdom, a fire broke out that destroyed a quarter of the city and part of the royal palace. The normal activities of government were suspended for an indeterminate time, which caused her execution to be deferred. After a time of further detention, she was sold as a slave to a high ranking officer of the royal army and once again enjoyed the opportunity to meet with other Christians. Warned that she was going to be arrested again, she decided

---

399 Skeptical historians have concluded that this anecdote is mythic. Nonetheless, the conversion and the faithful witness of Rafaravavy are historical facts.

to flee with a small group of Christians. They wandered for months in the country, and in nearly every town through which they passed refuge was found among small communities of Christians ready to help them.

A little later, another Christian by the name of Rasalama was imprisoned and condemned to death. Going to the place of execution singing hymns in August 1837, she asked for a delay in order to gather her thoughts. While she was kneeling in prayer, her body was pierced through with lances. She was the first of many martyrs in the Malagasy church.

In 1840 Griffith and later Jones were able to return to Tananarive on the pretext of engaging in business affairs. They aided and encouraged the persecuted Christians, but both were soon expelled. Jones, who had been the first missionary in Madagascar in 1818, took up residence on the Island of Mauritius where he died the following year on May 1, 1841.

*Rasalama kneeling in prayer at the moment of her martyrdom, August 14, 1837.*

In 1849 two or three thousand Christians were incarcerated for having attended worship services, but rare were those who denied their faith. The majority of them were released after paying stiff fines. Twenty-six Christians, however, were either burned alive, decapitated, or stoned to death. Fourteen were thrown off the cliff of

Ampamarinana, which overhangs the royal palace of Tananarive, and their wives and children were sold as slaves.

William Ellis, previously a missionary in Oceania and then secretary of the LMS, entered Madagascar secretly in 1854 with 1,500 New Testaments, which the persecuted church needed urgently to nourish its faith.

The year 1857 was particularly dramatic. A conspiracy to depose the queen was exposed. It had been fomented by Frenchmen and several local Christians who had joined in. Feeling threatened and sensing that Christians were an increasingly numerous and powerful opposition force in her kingdom, the queen ordered her troops to begin a campaign of extermination. Among those who were arrested, about fifteen were stoned and then decapitated, and their heads were exposed on a pole as a spectacle to dissuade others from embracing the Christian faith. Dozens of believers were condemned to drink poison, and at least eight did not survive the ordeal. Many others were condemned to forced labor in the insalubrious marshes, bound with collars and heavy chains. The dying were decapitated and cut loose so that the survivors could continue their work.

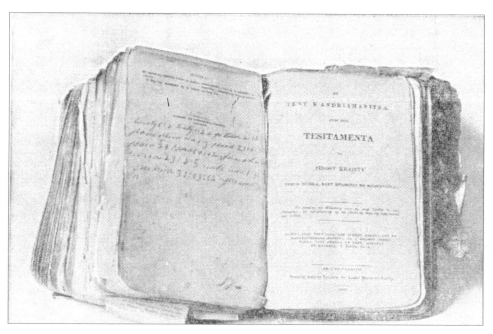

*One of the approximately one hundred Bibles in the Malagasy language printed just before the forced departure of the missionaries. They fed the faith of the Malagasy Christians during the long years of persecution.*

The persecution continued for thirty years, during which time the government made every effort to eradicate Christianity in the country. In the absence of pastoral leadership, the young converts resisted with impressive firmness, strengthened by a Bible that they were able to read in their own language. This provided the essential nourishment needed for the survival of these small, oppressed groups. Stephen Neill writes, "There could hardly be a more striking confirmation of the view held by almost all Protestant missionaries that the first duty of the missionary, after he has once learned the language, is to provide the people with the word of God, 'without note or comment,' in their own language."[400] In all New Testament simplicity, they joined in worship services, Holy Communion, and baptism. It is difficult to estimate the number of martyrs and secret conversions.

This time of tribulation ended with the death of the queen on August 16, 1861. She was succeeded by her son Radama II. Though not a Christian, one of his first acts upon acceding to the throne was to reestablish religious liberty. Henceforth all were free to practice the religion of their choice, to preach and teach the faith that they professed.

> [When this new era arrived,] men and women emerged from their hiding places in the forests where, rejected, they had been wandering for many years. They reappeared as the dead come from their tombs. Some still bore the traces of their chains and the strokes they had received. Others, reduced to the state of living skeletons due to undernourishment and illness, moved painfully along the routes that led to the capital . . . On arriving in their dear old city, they sang the hymn of pilgrims: "When the Lord returned again the captives of Zion, we were like them that dream." (Ps 126:1)[401]

## GROWTH IN A TIME OF FREEDOM

*James Cameron.*

Among the eight missionaries to return in 1862 were William Ellis and James Cameron. Cameron had been one of the first missionaries to work in Madagascar, serving there between 1826 and 1836. He left an enduring mark, but when persecution set in, he withdrew to serve in South Africa. On his return he sought out the Malagasy church. The Malagasy Christians received him with great joy and surrounded him with respect until his death in 1875 at the age of seventy-six. Ellis, for his part, took up the task of giving structure to the Malagasy church. He helped to organize the election of spiritual leaders (*mpitandrina*), selected from among those who had encouraged and taught the people during the persecution. He also inspired collections in Britain for the construction of new worship places.

After thirty years of pitiless persecution, what remained of this young and fragile church that was now freed to follow its own leadings? Remarkably not only had the believers survived, but their numbers had increased. Nevertheless, the huge task of restoration loomed before it, and an urgent appeal was made to mission agencies to help. In 1863 two Anglican missions responded simultaneously: the SPG, a largely High

---

400 Neill, *History*, 319.
401 *The Story of the LMS*, 353–54, cited by Neill, ibid.

Church organization; and the CMS, which was generally evangelical. The CMS continued in the work for only ten years. In 1866 two other organizations also committed themselves: the Norwegian Missions Society of the Free Lutheran Church, and the American Lutherans. In the following year the Quakers also joined in. The schools quickly increased their efforts, and before the end of the century nearly the entire population of the capital and the surrounding areas was literate. Printing was a priority. Ecclesiastic activities were also emphasized, especially the training of preachers and catechists, and the construction of chapels. In the meanwhile, King Radama II skillfully played off the rivalry between the French and British, largely favoring the French as well as the Catholic missions.

*King Radama II, who granted liberty to Christians, with his wife Ranavalona II. Succeeding her husband in 1868, Ranavalona declared herself a Protestant and sought to establish a Christian kingdom.*

In 1868 Radama II was assassinated, and Ranavalona II, his second wife, took his place. During the persecution, she had had clandestine contact with Christians, and upon her accession to the throne she immediately declared herself a Christian and a Protestant and had all the royal idols destroyed. She married her first minister, and the royal couple was baptized by a Malagasy minister in 1869. Under the new regime, the French and Catholic influence diminished. A Protestant chapel was constructed within the palace, and the government attempted to rule the country with principles and laws inspired by the Bible. The fascination for European civilization, however, was also important and enjoyed an influence at least as prominent as that of the gospel. The LMS missionaries sent from England were rather reserved in regard to the slide towards the development of a Protestant state.

By 1870 in Tananarive and its environs there were close to 150 places of worship and about forty thousand people attending every Sunday. Great stone churches were constructed, some able to hold as many as 1,200 people. In 1880 the LMS had more than a thousand chapels and 250,000 members, and other Protestant missions were also active and doing well.[402] There were also about eighty thousand Catholics. This rapid growth in church members overwhelmed the missionaries, who had always been insufficient in number.

Concern about the rapid expansion of the church was expressed in a letter from a missionary written in 1871 and published in the journal of the Malagasy Protestant church:

> While we all rejoice . . . there are also some things that must sadden us . . . Of the 231,759 persons [sic] who frequent the house of God, some, perhaps many, have come due to fear of the queen; consequently their Christianity consists only in abstaining from work on Sunday and making an appearance in the worship service. Now, when it is fear that leads people to prayer, the necessary result is going to be hypocrisy.[403]

The hazards of European politics would complicate the problem still more.

## FRANCE SUPPLANTS BRITAIN

In the field of European politics, Madagascar was a bone of contention between Britain and France. Although the Imerina monarchy maneuvered to maintain Madagascar's independence from the two powers, France ultimately succeeded in capturing the prize. The French parliament refused to annex Madagascar in 1885, but instead, made it a protectorate. Though this status was not supposed to affect the internal politics of the country, this was not how it turned out. The Jesuit missionaries, who were already present in small numbers on the island, coined the adage: "He who speaks French, speaks Catholic; he who speaks Protestant, speaks English." From then on, the British missionaries were thwarted in their efforts, notably in education. Five hundred Protestant churches were seized and transformed into Catholic churches. Following a new military campaign in 1895, France obtained the surrender of the queen. This humiliation resulted in a violent nationalist movement in the kingdom, and within a year, 150 Catholic chapels and six hundred Protestant churches were destroyed.

---

402 The rise in numbers cited from Barrett, *Encyclopedia*, 468 for Malagasy Protestants speaks for itself. There were 13,000 church members in 1867; 230,000 in 1870 (600 local communities); and 455,000 in 1895.

403 J.-F. Zorn, *Le grand siècle d'une mission protestante: La mission de Paris de 1822 à 1914* (Paris: Karthala/ Les Bergers et Les Mages, 1993), 166.

The French Undersecretary of State for the Navy, Félix Faure, convinced the French Protestants in 1884 to replace the British missionaries in the Malagasy Protestant Church. Alfred Boegner, director of the Paris Mission, responded that the mission could not imagine doing this unless it was invited to do so by the Malagasy Protestant Church. Also, a large number of evangelical French Christians did not favor supporting a missionary effort that so clearly smacked of colonial maneuvering. This branch of French Protestantism, which was strongly represented in the Paris Mission, was accused of being unpatriotic by the political press. However, after a dozen years the LMS itself appealed to the Paris Mission to take over the work. Its position had become difficult due to the anti-British politics of France. The Paris Mission continued to proclaim that it was above nationalistic chauvinism, that "its flag . . . [was] that of Jesus Christ and that it was in solidarity first and foremost with evangelical Christians in the world." But, also being in solidarity with the Malagasy Protestant Church, it finally submitted to pressure from the Jesuits to strip its British friends of their mission. The representatives of the Paris Mission successfully pleaded with French authorities to allow the LMS and the Norwegian Mission to remain in Madagascar.

Hence, in February 1896 the Paris Mission sent a group of missionaries to do reconnaissance. This included the Reverend Henri Lauga, Professor Frédéric Hermann Krüger, and Benjamin Escande, who until then had been in Senegal. At the end of the year, Lauga encouraged the committee of the Paris Mission to take over the direction of primary education in the Kingdom of Imerina from the LMS. At that time there were eight hundred schools and close to thirty thousand students. Henceforth, French Protestant expertise was brought to bear on the schools. In 1897 the Paris Mission sent fourteen men, thirteen women, and fifteen children to Madagascar. But several were quickly repatriated for reasons of health, and two missionaries, Paul Minault and Benjamin Escande, were killed in May 1897, probably by nationalists who had been involved in the previous year's uprisings. By 1902 Protestant missions had sixty thousand students in their schools, of which 26,800 were under the care of the Paris Mission.

In 1906 the new French governor, Dr. Victor Augagneur, took extreme antireligious measures, forbidding Christians from taking up collections outside of church buildings, prohibiting the public from singing and praying in cemeteries, and suppressing sorcery as a crime. Most important, he decided to close all the religious schools, Protestant as well as Catholic, under the pretext that classrooms were in church buildings. But the state was incapable of assuming responsibility for this work, and so 160,000 students were deprived of an education. The result of this unenlightened policy was that literacy rates in Madagascar in 1930 were lower than they had been in 1870.

Moreover, a noticeable decline in missionary effort was apparent in the years following 1905. There were cumulative reasons for this: decline of church callings in France, financial difficulties due to the separation of church and state, doctrinal tensions, and others. The decline in the number of schools (there were no more than 7,400 students in 1908) could be entirely attributed to Augagneur. The numbers attending worship services also took a downward turn. "Paganism was declining and Catholicism rising," the Protestant missionaries observed.

While Protestantism under the monarchy was still the official religion, it was in fact just one confession among others and even less prestigious than Catholicism. Faced with this situation, the mission in 1903 began to accelerate the process that was leading to autonomy for the Malagasy Protestant Church. It was hoped that this would stimulate indigenous leaders to take responsibility, and that the church would be perceived and in reality be a Malagasy institution—one owned and directed by the Malagasy. The churches related to the Paris Mission held an annual assembly, which created a synod of Reformed churches, the first step towards autonomy. In 1911 a Presbyterian-style constitution was adopted. Raymond Poincaré, the president of the Republic, signed a decree in 1913 that established the separation of church and state in Madagascar. Protestants perceived the secularity of the state as a guarantee of neutrality.

An intermissionary conference was also held in the same year that gave impetus to missionary work. It brought together delegates from European societies was well as Protestant missionaries working in Madagascar. They agreed to establish zones of activity in which each would work. The coastal regions were given to the French Protestant mission, which together with Malagasy ministers had begun to evangelize there in 1907. On the eve of the First World War the churches associated with the Paris Mission had about 140,000 members, about 30 percent of Malagasy Protestantism.[404]

In addition to the work of the foreign mission societies, Christianity in Madagascar received a fresh impetus in 1894 from a large, indigenous revival (*Fifohazana*) movement that swept through the province of Betsileo. The movement was initiated by a former soothsayer of the local religion, a man named Rainisoalambo, who had converted in 1884 and become a Lutheran minister. Following a profound spiritual experience, he received the gift of healing and began to preach the total abandonment of all practices linked to the traditional religion and worship of ancestors. The movement extended beyond the province of Betsileo in 1899 when Rainisoalambo established an order of lay preachers, the Disciples of the Lord. They went from place to place, two by two, to proclaim the gospel. Remaining in communion with the previously established Protestant churches, the Disciples of the Lord attempted to revive their waning faith. They also extended their movement farther along the coast, reaching coastal regions not yet evangelized. When the missionaries later discovered these regions, they were surprised to encounter many small, isolated groups of Christians in the bush, the fruit of the remarkable work of the Disciples of the Lord. The movement experienced several seasons of revival in the twentieth century, and centers of prayer and training were opened for the many Christians who desired to be affiliated with the movement.

404 According to Zorn, "Missions protestantes," 1050.

*Part Four*

# NORTH AFRICA AND THE NEAR EAST

# Evangelistic Presence in the Maghreb and Egypt

During the first centuries of the church, the entire south coast of the Mediterranean had a dense Christian population. Before the year 200, Christian communities existed from Egypt to Morocco. Alexandria, Carthage, and Hippo produced some of the greatest theologians in all of Christian history—Clement, Origin, Athanasius, Tertullian, Cyprian, Augustine, and others. Also, it should not be forgotten that monasticism, so influential for the development and growth of the church, was born in Upper Egypt.[405] However, except for the Copts of Egypt, the church there almost entirely disappeared due to the Islamization that followed the Arab conquest of the seventh century. Since the beginning of modern missions, northern Africa has been one of the most resistant regions of the world to the gospel, and one of the most neglected by Christians. The pages that follow tell this story.

## THE MAGHREB

Algeria and Tunisia were under Turkish domination from the sixteenth to the nineteenth century. During much of the Middle Ages and for a long time after, the southern coast of the Mediterranean was plagued by pirates, and numerous Europeans were captured there and enslaved. Those among them who converted to Islam were freed. In 1535 Charles V of Spain captured Tunis and freed thousands of slaves. Historian J. M. Sédès explains, "Every year the European fleets paid a heavy tribute in merchandise and men to the Muslim pirates. It is estimated that at the beginning of the seventeenth century, three thousand French slaves were held in Algeria and as many at Marrakech."[406] In 1645 St. Vincent de Paul obtained permission for several Lazarists to minister among the captive Christians in Tunisia and Algeria. They maintained themselves there in one way or another but were finally forced to leave in 1801. The slave trade in Europeans was theoretically abolished in Morocco in 1767. In 1819 the reunited allies determined at Aix-la-Chapell to put an end to these acts of piracy, but this was scarcely implemented. When France seized Algiers in 1830, it freed 122 captives.

---

405 For this period, see Book I, chapters 1 and 2.
406 J. M. Sédès, "Histoire des missions françaises," in *Que sais-je?* no. 405 (Paris: PUF, 1950), 26.

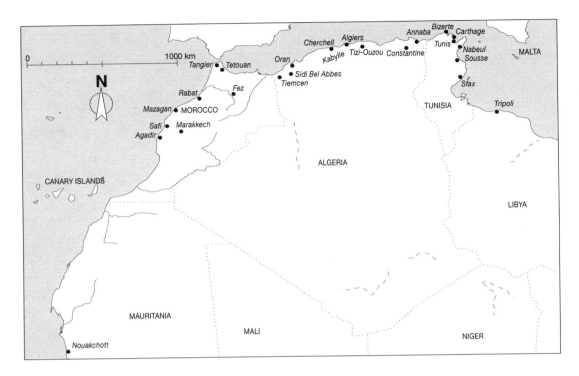

*Map 13: Northwest Africa*

# ALGERIA

The Turkish domination of Algeria, which began in 1516, came to an end in 1830 when France seized the country. Numerous French colonists settled in Algeria, and since the majority were Catholic, the church created a bishopric there in 1839. Bishop Antoine-Louis-Adolphe Dupuch was transferred out of the country in 1845, the French government having accused him of seeking to evangelize Muslims.

Charles Lavigerie (1825–1892), bishop of Nancy, was asked in 1866 by Governor General Marshal MacMahon of Algeria to head the Catholic Church of North Africa. He was named bishop of Algiers. Founder of the order of the White Fathers in 1868, his first recruits were farmers and village carpenters. They formed Christian peasant communities consisting of lay brothers and even entire families. Following a cholera epidemic, many of the resulting 1,800 orphaned children were adopted by these families and given a Christian education. The White Fathers acted prudently, procuring the services of hospitals, dispensaries, and colleges. Instruction in the colleges included sacred history, but there was no overt proselytism. Any Muslim who asked for baptism was referred to Lavigerie, a rarely used procedure.

Lavigerie had no less a dream than the reconquest of Islamic Africa in the name of the gospel. He made the White Fathers and White Sisters elite missionary orders. Priests were sent across the desert in 1875 and 1881 to Timbuktu, but each one was murdered by the Touareg.[407] In his desire to block the spread of Islam, Lavigerie sent missionaries as far as the kingdom of Buganda (Uganda), which Arabs were then beginning to enter. He also sent them to Tanganyika with hopes of checking the slave trade. He militated for the elimination of the traffic in slaves and was one of the promoters of the 1889 Brussels Conference that sought the abolition of the trade. A man of great determination who had the stature of a chief of state, he obtained freedom of worship for Algeria in spite of the opposition of MacMahon and the French government.

In 1830 the Paris Mission intended to send two missionaries to Algeria, Eugène Casalies and Thomas Arbousset, who were then concluding their studies at the House of Missions. When the French government objected,[408] it was with regret that they made plans for South Africa instead. Despite this setback, two other Protestant missions attempted to work in Algeria, the MacCall Mission and the Basel Mission. Both entered the country in 1830, but neither was able to remain long.

The Englishman George Pearse, one of the founders of the North Africa Mission (NAM) (see also p. 292), arrived in Algeria in 1876 with the intention of evangelizing French soldiers. On encountering the Kabyle people, he observed that they were more receptive to the gospel than the Arabs. At the age of sixty-five, Pearse built a small house for himself and his wife in the Kabyle village of Dejemaa Saharidj, which means "the gathering of springs." He was soon joined by Eugene Cuendet, a Swiss citizen who lived for fifty-two years in Algeria. This was the first station of the NAM. Pearse moved to Algiers in 1883 and continued primarily to evangelize the Kabyles emigrants. In 1884 the mission opened a center at Tlemcen, and then in 1886 two more at Constantine and Oran.

On at least three occasions, in 1886, 1901, and 1904, French deputies intervened in church matters to ask for the expulsion of the British missionaries in Algeria. Though this was at the instigation of the Catholic mission, the Protestants were suspected of espionage, if not traffic in arms. Some of their mission posts were temporarily abandoned until the synod of the Reformed Church of Algeria intervened in Paris to assert the truth of the matter.

In 1920 and 1925, the NAM missionaries engaged in work in Grande Kabylie. In Algeria, as in other countries of North Africa, NAM launched a literacy program and promoted traditional crafts and industrial work. These activities procured revenue for the population and placed both male and female workers under the influence of the gospel. The most important project was the carpet school that was opened in 1903 by Helena Day and located at Cherchell, a coastal city about one hundred kilometers west of Algiers. It employed eight weavers and several dozen young girls and women, who produced various sorts of carpets for export to Britain. Each day began

---

407 Following this, Lavigerie advocated the formation of "militias of Christ," an army to establish a Christian kingdom in the Sahara. From here evangelists would be able to spread out into all of Africa. But European governments opposed this project as too reminiscent of the crusades of sad memory.

408 The act of surrender signed by the dey Hussein of Algiers guaranteed the continuance of local customs and the Muslim religion, which ruled out the possibility of a Christian Mission. These strict arrangements were relaxed about twenty years later, in which time Lavigerie was able to secure religious liberty.

with a time of Bible study. The most difficult problem was that the young girls would become Christians but then marry a Muslim without their consent. And naturally the Muslims forbade their wives all contact with the mission.

Today wood sculpture is considered one of the original products of the Kabyle culture, but it was actually introduced in 1918 at the Djemaa Saharidj workshop by the missionary Thomas Warren.

In 1896 Emile Rolland, following an encounter with the evangelist Ruben Saillens,

*Emile Rolland, founder of the Rolland Mission in Tizi-Ouxou. (Photo: Rolland Mission)*

became convinced that he had a calling to be a missionary in Algeria. At the time he was working at the Peugeot workshops in the country of Montbéliard and was a member of the Baptist Church. The British of the North Africa Mission suffered from the interference of the French colonial administration, but Saillens helped them to understand the need for a French presence to make their work possible. The Rolland family left for Algiers at the end of the year 1896. They did not have the support of a mission, and the NAM could not assure backing for a French-speaking colleague. Rolland settled in Kabylie, at Djemaa Saharidj. He was especially active as a Bible colporteur and was helped by two NAM female missionaries. After seven years he moved to Algiers, where he worked with Lilias Trotter (see below).

In 1908 he moved to Kabylie, in Tizi-Ouzou, where he and his wife, Emma, created the Rolland Mission. It was sustained by a variety of French-speaking evangelical communities in Switzerland and France, particularly the Mennonite Assembly of Montbéliard. The mission purchased and restored several houses. One of the first ones to be completed was a home for students, in which there were soon conversions. During school vacations, teams of young Kabyles zealously evangelized neighboring villages.

Emma began a crafts center for women in Tizi-Ouzou. Her daughter and son-in-law write:

> Little by little Emma Rolland . . . understood that the Kabyle women, ignorant, superstitious, passionate, and subject to the power of men, were creations of God, intelligent, brave, and capable. Consequently, she needed to help them to develop themselves. She believed that their fathers would be less pressed 'to sell their daughters,' as one says, if they were earning an income. It was in this spirit that the Sewing Circle was conceived. At first they sewed lace . . . [but] quickly added raffia baskets.[409]

---

409 Guita Rolland and Alfred Rolland, *Un combat de la foi: 70 ans de vie missionnaire à Tizi-Ouzou* (Crempigny, France: Mission Rolland, 1997), 66.

A large number of Tizi-Ouzou girls came to learn a trade in the Sewing Circle. Later others came to work in carpet-weaving shops at the NAM center in Cherchell. In 1926 the mission established a girls' school, an entirely new initiative in the country. Later the mission set up a dispensary, which was directed by Marguerite Bancel, a French nurse. It also established a refuge for women who, due to Kabyle custom, would otherwise have been rejected. Finally, the mission founded a home for young people, to which the authorities on several occasions sent young delinquents. Modestly funded and operated with discretion on behalf of the weak and marginalized, the birth of this small Christian community, always miraculous in an Islamic land, was a witness to the love of God.

Emile Rolland died in 1934. His two sons were killed in the First World War, but his daughter Marguerite (Guita) married Emile's nephew, Alfred Rolland, and the couple served as missionaries in Algeria. They broadened the work and pursued it in the same spirit as the founder, persevering through the Second World War despite great difficulties and privations. Over the years, a large number of missionaries came to lend a hand to the Rolland family. Some came only for short periods, such as the youth who were sent by the Protestant Scouts, others for much longer. The Rolland Mission remained independent but was known to be tied to French-speaking Protestantism.[410]

*Lilias Trotter at age thirty-five.*

Another person who left an indelible mark on the mission history of Algeria is Lilias Trotter, (1853–1928). Born in London to a wealthy family, she was a highly talented artist with the promise of a brilliant career in painting. During an evangelistic campaign led by the American Dwight Moody, she felt God's call to be a missionary. She presented her candidature to the North Africa Mission, which declined to accept her because she suffered from a weak heart—a weakness that did not prevent her from serving as a missionary in North Africa for forty years. Undeterred, she set out with three friends for Algeria in 1888 as an independent missionary. The four went without a committee to support them or any mission training, and without either a strategy or a definite objective. Nor did they know anyone in Algiers or how to speak a single word of Arabic.

Without hesitation these young women took up residence in the Casbah of Algiers, which was completely new for Europeans. In order to learn the language they sought contacts with the population, and went from house to house to offer tracts and Bible texts. At first they suffered stiff opposition, not so much from Muslims as from Jews and even some Jesuit priests. Thanks to her ease in making contacts with the local population and her quick acquisition of Algerian Arabic, Trotter was able to reach out effectively to women. She received them in her home or visited them in their homes where they often lived isolated lives and suffered contempt for the place

---

410 The Rolland Mission continued to welcome the most destitute, especially children. It provided training for young girls and women, offering them food and presenting the gospel to them. Restrictions on their work became more stringent following Algerian independence in 1962. The last buildings were requisitioned by the Algerian government in 1977, and the Rolland Mission had to leave the country.

they held in the culture. She organized them into groups for prayer and Bible study. Soon other missionaries, both men and women, augmented the small team, which in 1907 was transformed into the Algiers Mission Band.

Lilias Trotter witnessed to her faith in cities and villages as far as the south of Algeria where the desert landscape appealed to her artistic sensitivity. She completed an adaptation of the Arabic Bible into modern Algerian Arabic. Mission historian P. Decorvet writes:

> The translation completed, she wanted the volume to be as close as possible to indigenous expectations. In this she neglected no detail: the paper was cream colored, rough, and had wide margins like Arab books. The text was printed lithographically and the characters traced by an elegant hand. In this way the Bible would be considered by the readers as one of their own, not a European book. Miss Trotter always insisted on the eastern origin of the Christian religion.[411]

She also composed numerous tracts, presented in an aesthetically pleasing format and in a narrative style designed to appeal to local readers. In this form they encountered a well-framed evangelical theology that demonstrated a profound knowledge of Islam. The material also emphasized important points of Christian theology: the holiness of God, the reality of sin and judgment, the grace offered through the crucified Christ, and the fatherly love of God. In particular, she studied Arab mysticism, in which she discerned an opening to the message of the gospel, and sought to dialogue with the Sufis of southern Algeria. She wrote a small book for them, which was adapted to their spirituality, *The Seven Secrets of the Way of God*. In this she explained the seven "I am" declarations of Jesus in the Gospel of John (I am the bread of life; the light of the world; the door; the good shepherd; the resurrection and the life; the way, the truth and the life; and the true vine).

By her understanding of Islam, her indefatigable zeal, and her sympathy, Trotter wrote a remarkable page in the history of missions in Muslim countries. Even if her ministry did not produce many visible results, she was a source of inspiration for other missionaries, especially for her beautiful literary productions.[412]

At the end of the nineteenth and beginning of the twentieth centuries several Protestant missions arrived in Algeria from Britain, America, Scandinavia, and France. Thomas Hocart of the Methodist Churches in France was in Kabylie as early as 1886, and Emile Brès joined him in 1906. The Board of Foreign Missions of the Methodist Episcopal Church sent workers in 1909. Medical and education programs were put in place, and soon there were several dozen new Christians and a few Christian communities established. The work, however, was difficult and never flourished.

---

411 P. Decorvet, *Victoire sur l'impossible* (Vevey, Switzerland: Les Groupes Missionnaires, 1963), 69.

412 In 1965 the Algiers Mission Band united with the North Africa Mission and the Southern Morocco Mission. These organizations had always collaborated together and shared the same vision of Christian mission in the Muslim world.

The Echoes of Service mission of the Brethren Assembly in Britain established several evangelism posts beginning in 1910. These slowly gathered a number of convert groups, mostly in Kabylie. Other missions also came to Algeria: the British and Foreign Bible Society, the Church Mission to the Jews (an Anglican organization), the Salvation Army, and the Evangelical Baptists. In the cities of Algiers, Oran, and Sidi-Bel-Abbè, a number of Christian communities developed as a result of the evangelization efforts of these European missions. The Reformed Church (linked to the French Reformed Churches) established as many as twenty parishes, but these generally had only occasional contact with the Protestant missions. In 1940 these missions established the Council of Evangelical Missions, which later became the Association of Protestant Churches and Institutions in Algeria.

# MOROCCO

As early as the second century there were already Christians in the regions of present-day Tangier and Rabat, as well as Volubilis (the region of Fez). They suffered from imperial persecution, then from schisms due to heresies, and finally invasion by Germanic barbarians. The church disappeared completely by the year 700, following the Arab conquest.

At the beginning of the thirteenth century, five Franciscans friars were martyred for attempting to proclaim the gospel in Moroccan cities. Despite later attempts at evangelism, there was practically no Christian presence in the country before the middle of the nineteenth century. The Catholic Church attempted to gain a foothold in Rabat, establishing a prefecture in 1859, and an episcopal vicariate in 1908. The Catholic population of Morocco was then made up almost entirely of people of Spanish and French origin. Morocco was a French protectorate between 1912 and 1956, and then regained its national sovereignty.

The first Protestant mission in the region was the London Jews' Society, which came in 1875—in 1900 there were more than 150,000 Jews in Morocco, or about 3 percent of the population. Other missions followed: the North Africa Mission in 1884, the Southern Morocco Mission in 1888, and the Gospel Missionary Union in 1894. In the next generation the Emmanuel Mission for the Sahara, an American group, came in 1926; and then the Anglicans of the Bible Churchmen's Missionary Society opened several evangelism posts in 1929, which were attached to the Anglican diocese of Sierra Leone.

The North African Mission was more active in Morocco than any other organization. It established several medical centers, the largest being Tulloch Memorial Hospital, in Tangier, named for a young missionary who died of typhoid fever shortly after his arrival in 1886. The hospital, founded by Doctor T. G. Churcher, was renowned throughout the region for the quality of the care it provided. A nursing school was annexed to it. As it was impossible in the Moroccan cultural context to open a hospital for both men and women, a second hospital for women was added, using a renovated house in the center of Tangier. While visiting the villages in the northern part of the country to perform follow-up care for the patients that had been treated in Tangier, the medical teams observed immense sanitary needs in the rural regions of Morocco. Due, however, to the lack of personnel, they could only open a few dispensaries.

The NAM purchased a farmhouse on a hill close to Tangier in 1897 for use in arboriculture and winegrowing, and the farm provided practical training for numerous young people. Later, an independent Canadian missionary converted the house into the Raymond Lulle Orphanage. Many of the orphans in their adult lives became active members of the small Christian community of Tangier. Another pilot farm project was also established in Tetouan.

The Southern Morocco Mission (SMM), the fruit of an evangelism campaign that brought revival to the lowlands of Scotland shortly before 1860, was another important society that sought to evangelize Morocco. The Presbyterian John Anderson was converted on the occasion of the Scottish revival and later became engaged in an intense effort to evangelize his country. When he fell sick, he was urged by physicians to move to a warmer land. He opted for southern Morocco where he was struck by the masses of Muslims he saw who were totally ignorant of the grace of God. When he returned to Scotland, he pleaded their cause. His first missionary recruit was the young farmer Cuthbert Nairn, who in 1888 went to Tangier with his sister Jessie and then to southern Morocco. Nairn lived for fifty-two years in Morocco, principally in Marrakech where he built a dispensary. He was killed there in 1944 by a demented patient. During these years, Anderson was instrumental in the establishment of the Bible Training Institute of Glasgow, which began in 1892. Here many servants of God were taught, some of whom later participated in his mission.

Six months after Cuthbert and Jessie Nairn had left Scotland a dozen more candidates were in Anderson's office to offer their services. In the absence of a well-structured organization, only three among them could be accepted. Nevertheless, five years after it began, the SMM had four principal centers in the cities of Mogador, Mazagan (El Jadida), Marrakech, and Safi. Several other centers were subsequently added, notably one in Agadir. The SMM sought to situate itself in strategic places in order to pursue medical work—the needs were immense—and evangelism through colportage and the distribution of brochures. The translation of the Gospels was achieved in several Berber dialects.

The SMM never became a large mission, but it had as many as twenty missionaries in 1900 at the apogee of its growth. Most of these were Scottish. It had less than ten missionaries during the Second World War, but in 1959 when it merged with NAM, it had a dozen.

# TUNISIA

Despite the Arab conquest in 697, a bishop still existed in Carthage as late as 1076. Then Christianity seems to have disappeared entirely except for the occasional missionary: Raymond Lulle in the late thirteenth and early fourteenth centuries, several Franciscans and Dominicans in the thirteenth and fourteenth centuries, and a Lazarus chaplain with some captives in the seventeenth century. Beginning in 1830 France exercised some control over Algeria. In 1881 before intervening in upper Kabylie to subdue an uprising, it took the opportunity to seize Tunisia when the economy collapsed and disorders seemed certain. The French installed a protectorate regime in 1883 that continued until 1956. Missions enjoyed more liberty in Tunisia—and in Morocco—than they did in Algeria.

The archbishop of Carthage was reestablished with the appointment of Cardinal Lavigerie in 1884 at the beginning of the French protectorate. As a practical matter, however, the Catholic Church was concerned only with European colonists. At the request of a military chaplain, a Reformed parish was established in 1889 for the Protestant colonists. The first Protestant mission that sought to evangelize North Africa was the London Jews' Society, an Anglican mission. It was present intermittently in Tunis beginning in 1829, but it became permanent in 1860. The mission established a Bible depot, a worship place, and a school.[413]

The NAM sought to establish itself there not long after it was formed in 1882, but as noted above, Tunisia became a French protectorate in an unstable period in its history. Consequently, it was not until 1900 that the mission succeeded in founding centers successively in several cities: Sfax, Sousse, Kairouan, Tunis, Bizerte, and Nabeul. Due to a lack of workers, these centers were not long maintained. Because the sanitary conditions of the country were disastrous, missionaries played an important role in introducing modern medicine and hygiene, which allowed them to be accepted by the population. Doctors established dispensaries at Tunis, Sousse, and Sfax, but the NAM did not have the means to found a hospital in Tunisia as it had done in Morocco.

In 1908 an American Methodist Mission sought to form a small Christian community and focused primarily on children. Pentecostals and Adventists arrived a little later. But despite these efforts and those mentioned above Tunisia was largely neglected by Christian missions.

# EGYPT

A biblical land and site of ancient Christianity, Egypt fell into the hands of the Arabs in 642, only ten years after the death of Mohammed. Unlike North Africa (Maghreb), the church largely resisted Islamization, thanks especially to the existence of the Bible in the Coptic language spoken by the people.

Hemmed in on all sides by Islam and partially cut off from the rest of Christendom, the Egyptian church held firm, but its centuries-old liturgical tradition became ossified. Due to commercial and cultural lines of communication in the eastern basin of the Mediterranean, there were also other Orthodox churches in Syria, Greece, and Armenia. The Roman Catholic Church, which had nearly disappeared in this part of the world by the end of the Middle Ages, grew in the second half of the nineteenth century through the efforts of various missionary orders.

---

413 Among the population of 1.6 million people in 1900, there were 80,000 Jews, about 5 percent of the total (Barrett, *Encycolpedia*, 750).

As with Ethiopia, from the time Protestant missions first entered the country they sought both to revive and reform the Coptic Church, but without much success. The first to arrive were the Moravians, who remained from 1752 to 1783. The Anglicans' CMS envisioned Egypt as a base from which they would reach out to Ethiopia and from there to other regions of the African continent. William Jowett (1787–1855), when canvassing Egypt in 1819, was welcomed by the patriarch of Alexandria. Together with the British and Foreign Bible Society, he set up a printing press in Malta in 1818 that would eventually produce Bibles for the entire Near East (see below, p. 652). Their objective was to reach Muslims and Jews with the help of the Coptic Church. But this collaboration effort did not work out, and the CMS withdrew in 1862. It returned, however, in 1882 when the British acquired political supremacy in Egypt and established an Anglican Church there. It consisted of several mission stations and a hospital in Old Cairo. The hospital became a center for evangelism at the same time that it was providing medical care. At first attached to the diocese of Jerusalem, a separate Anglican diocese for Egypt was created in 1920.

In 1855 Christian Friedrich Spittler, who had initiated mission work in Chrischona, envisioned with Samuel Gobat the creation of an "apostolic route" from Jerusalem to Gondar (Abyssinia). Three mission stations were established in Egypt along the valley of the Nile, which were to be the initial steps along the route. But these were soon abandoned when it was decided that the project was unrealistic.

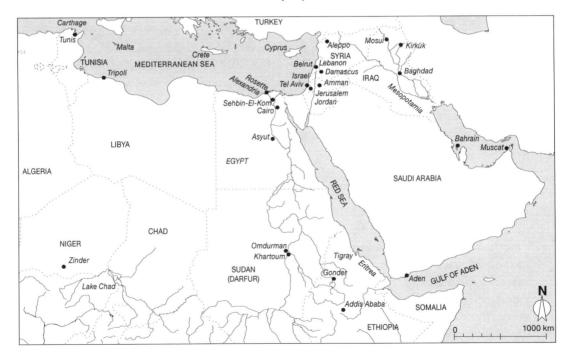

*Map 14: Northeast Africa and the Near East*

In 1854 three missionaries of the United Presbyterian Church of North America undertook the task of evangelizing the people of the ancient Coptic Church living in

Alexandria and Assiout, respectively in Lower and Upper Egypt. They hoped to breathe a spirit of reform into the church but had little more success than the Anglicans. Eventually they formed the Evangelical Coptic Church, which in 1875 had six hundred members of which 10 percent were originally Muslim. At this time a splinter group made up of Darbyites formed the Brethren Assembly, which from the outset was under Egyptian leadership. By 1914 there were forty-seven missionaries, about forty local communities, twenty pastors with diplomas from the Presbyterian Seminary of Assiout, and a little more than five thousand members. The church gave priority to education, forming several secondary colleges. In 1921 the former Presbyterian missionary Charles Watson founded the University of Cairo, which was independent of the mission. Samuel Zwemer, an American Presbyterian missionary and specialist in Islam (see pp. 657ff), established a printing press and launched the journal *The World of Islam*. In 1926 the Evangelical Coptic Church became autonomous. With twenty-five thousand members, it was the largest Protestant church in the country.

Several Christian university movements in Great Britain, which emerged as a result of a revival, participated in the evangelization of Egypt in the period following the British capture of this land in 1882. One of these was the Student Volunteer Missionary Union, which first sent Douglas Thornton in 1899. He came to Cairo where he died due to exhaustion from overwork in 1907. His successor, W. H. Temple Gairdner, became a renowned Arabist whose Arabic-language poems were widely regarded. Stephen Neill writes that Thornton and Gairdner "worked on the principle of a frank, friendly, and courteous approach to Muslims, one of the main instruments of their service being the bilingual periodical *Orient and Occident*, which was used for the calm and temperate exposition of Christian truth in its relationship to Islam"[414] At the Edinburgh World Missionary Conference in 1910, Gairdner was one of the key workers on the commission responsible for studying relations between Christian missions and other religions. One participant said of him: "Some have shown us how to refute Islam. He has shown us how to love Muslims." Others, however, reproached him for an excessive openness to other religions. In his Edinburgh report, Gairdner wrote:

> Christianity, "religion of the Light of the world," cannot ignore any light, even "broken;" it must take them all into consideration and absorb them all into its ample home. Moreover, the Church of Christ is itself in part enveloped in mists of incredulity and imperfections. This . . . "broken light" still has aspects of its own truth to discover, half or in fact entirely forgotten . . . Hence, "in going into the whole world," the Church of Christ can recover all the light that is in Christ and become, like its Chief—and as he wants it to become in its turn—"the light of the world."[415]

---

414 Neill, *History*, 369.

415 W. H. T. Gairdner, *Edinburgh 1910: An Account and Interpretation of the World Missionary Conference* (London: Oliphant, Anderson & Ferrier, 1910), 135–36. Cited by J. Blandenier, "Mission et religions du point de vue protestant et oecuménique (période 1910–1928)," in F. Jacquin and J.-F. Zorn, eds., *L'altérité religieuse: Un défi pour la mission chrétienne* (Paris: Karthala, 2001), 289–90.

The North Africa Mission established its first station in Alexandria in 1892, and later two others also in Lower Egypt—Rosette in 1897 and Sehbin el-Kom in 1899. Unlike the work mentioned above, which focused on the Coptic minority, the objective of these new stations was to evangelize Muslims, a task that it engaged in more ardently and also more perilously than any other had before.

Other missions also worked in Egypt. A Free Methodist Church was founded there in 1895, and in 1908 the Assemblies of God sought to establish itself in Alexandria, Assiout, and Cairo. By 1929 the Assemblies possessed a dozen stations whose ministers were all Egyptians. It also had a large membership, consisting mostly of the Coptic minority.[416]

# LIBYA

A country that in the ancient past was Christian, Libya had fallen to the Arabs in 644 when Tripoli was taken. Later, the Turks dominated the country until 1911, at which time it became an Italian colony. With the defeat of Italy in 1943 during the Second World War, The British administered the country for the next eight years. The Kingdom of Libya was established in 1951 and the republic in 1969.

Between 1850 and 1890 Franciscans worked in Tripoli and, despite the obstacles set up by the Turkish Administration and the local religious authorities, saw the Catholic community grow from two thousand to 5,500 members. In 1914 during the Italian period, a Vicar Apostolic was created that was concerned largely with the colonists. At this time there were also a number of Coptic and Orthodox immigrants.

In 1889 when the country was still under the Turks, the North African Mission was established but encountered many difficulties. Rather than engage in direct evangelism it concentrated on medical work and children's education. Theirs was a Christian witness based in acts of compassion that persevered for many years, chiefly through the dispensary opened by M. Reid and continued by Dr. James Liley.[417] No church, however, emerged during the period covered by this book.[418]

---

416 In the year 2000, a little more than 10 million of the 68.5 million inhabitants were Christians, or about 15.1 percent. There were also more than 68 denominations represented (Barrett, *Encyclopedia*).

417 After serving the Libyan people for eighty years, the dispensary had to be closed in 1969 when Colonel Khadafi came to power.

418 Barrett, *Encyclopedia*, 455–457, estimates that in 1968 there were forty thousand Catholics and 2,650 Protestants, almost all non-Libyans. Moreover, a Baptist church has existed in Tripoli since 1965, an Evangelical Coptic church since 1968, and a Korean Presbyterian church since 1970.

# CHAPTER 28

# The Gospel in the Near East

Though the Near East is part of Asia, it is included in this section devoted to Africa because it is historically more Mediterranean than Asiatic in culture and politics. Moreover, Protestant missions have tended to see Egypt and the Near East as a single block. The geographical region treated here covers approximately the present-day states of Israel, Lebanon, Jordan, Syria, and Turkey. It also peripherally covers the Middle Eastern lands of Armenia, Iraq, and Arabia.[419]

It is difficult to present the missionary work in the latter nations because of their vexed political and military history over the last two centuries. The interventions of the Ottoman Empire and then the Western nations altered their borders many times. In the nineteenth and early twentieth centuries none of the countries listed above existed as such within their present borders. Since it is difficult to analyze the missionary activity in the region country by country, the experience of specific mission societies, whose work generally transcended present-day national boundaries, will be highlighted.

An observation of the preceding chapter about North Africa is also valid here: the regions that formed the center of the Islamic world have generally been neglected by Christian missions, which have tended to prefer less refractory fields.

Finally, Judaism, Christianity, and Islam emerged from this part of the world, the crossroads of the monotheistic religions, and nearly all Christian denominations have shown an interest in the Holy Land, the heart of the Near East. In attempting to understand the nature of the Christian presence in this region, it is not always easy to distinguish between a truly missionary motivation and those that are more concerned with religious politics. It should also be added that Protestants have been less than unanimous in their attitudes toward the ancient churches of the region: Syrian, Greek Coptic, Maronite, and others.

For these various reasons, an exhaustive picture of missions in the Near East cannot be given here for the century and a half period covered by this work.

---

419 The beginning of the Protestant mission in Iran is covered on p. 338.

## APPROACH TO ISLAM

The Middles Ages were not only the time of the Crusades but also a period in which serious attempts were made to understand Islam in order better to refute it. For example, some intellectuals, principally in the twelfth and thirteenth centuries, dedicated themselves to a careful study of Arabic and Quranic literature (see pp. 104ff), and the Reformers of the sixteenth century also expressed some vague desires for the further study of Islam.[420] In general, however, ignorance and a lack of interest prevailed in the West until the nineteenth century. At the beginning of the era of modern missions, one of the first people to show an interest in this field was not a university intellectual but a man of the earth, Karl Gottlieb Pfander. He was employed by the Basel Mission and worked in the region that sits astride the border between Persia and northern India, present-day Pakistan. He published *Mizan-al-Haqq* (*The Way of the Truth*) in 1829, more a polemical work than a study of Islam. He also wrote a number of tracts of the same type, which were translated into various languages of the East—Arabic, Persian, Turkic, Urdu, and others.[421] Later Sir William Muir (1821–1905), a layman working for the British government in the Punjab, wrote the well-documented *Life of Muhammad*. He also discovered and published *The Apology of Al-Kindi*, a defense of the Christian faith against its Muslim critiques by a nineteenth-century intellectual in Baghdad.

From these slim beginnings it would be necessary to await the appearance of Samuel Zwemer, Temple Gairdner, and the great world missionary conferences of the first part of the twentieth century before a fuller knowledge of Islam could be acquired.

## MALTA: CENTER OF CHRISTIAN LITERATURE WRITTEN IN ARABIC

We will begin this study with the Mediterranean island of Malta, which is not actually in the East but in the first half of the nineteenth century enjoyed a far from negligible role as an "aircraft carrier" for Protestant missions to the Near East, as Jean-Michel Hornus has expressed it.[422] In 1800 the British captured the island from Napoleon, who had seized it two years earlier. Britain then annexed it in 1811. Several missions established printing presses there to produce, under the protection of British law that they would not have benefited from in the East, Arabic publications intended for the Near East, Egypt, and Ethiopia. There were also publications in modern Greek.

The LMS was the first mission organization there, arriving in 1808. It was followed by the CMS in 1815, under the leadership of William Jowett (see below, p. 598).

---

420 Ibid., 255, 265–68.

421 Pfander engaged in several public debates with Muslim intellectuals in India. In 1854, Imad-ud-din, a well-regarded professor who had pleaded for a purified Islam, gave a reply to Pfander. Following this confrontation, he entered a period of personal inquiry and introspection. In 1866 he decided to convert to Christianity, and his autobiography became a great stimulus for Christian missions among the Muslims. In 1884, he became the first Indian honored with a doctorate in theology, which was awarded by the Archbishop of Canterbury in recognition of his contributions to Christian literature in India.

422 Jean-Michel Hornus, "Cent cinquante ans de présence évangélique au Proch-Orient (1808–1958)," *Foi et Vie* 78 (1979).

From Malta, Jowett had frequent contact with ecclesiastical dignitaries in various countries of the Near East. He had been asked by his mission to collaborate with the Orthodox churches in order stimulate them to proclaim the gospel to the Muslims, a task which would have been undertaken principally through the publication of the Bible. Jowett worked in Bible distribution on Malta until 1830. CMS's printing press on Malta was shut down in 1842, its essential activities having been transferred to Beirut in 1834.

## THE LONDON JEWS' SOCIETY

The London Society for Promoting Christianity Amongst the Jews, more commonly known as the London Jews' Society (LJS), was an Anglican organization.[423] After several unsuccessful attempts to establish missionaries in the Middle East, notably in Iraq in 1820, the LJS finally succeeded with William Lewis in 1823. Lewis served in Lebanon where he sought to create a center for the various Protestants groups then working in the Near East. This proved to be unsuccessful due to the distrust of the Maronite clergy. The efforts of Protestant missions, nevertheless, were concerted to the extent of dividing the territory into discrete units, with the LJS concentrating on Palestine. Lewis exercised an itinerant ministry during the twelve years until his death. A permanent station was founded in Jerusalem in 1833 with several missionaries, and the work extended as far as Jaffa (Tel Aviv), Hebron, and Lod. The Anglo-Jewish community that was in place in Jerusalem in 1838 generally flourished over the next hundred years. During this period, the LJS missionary Joseph Wolff, himself a converted Jew, traveled through the Near East, especially Iraq and the whole of Mesopotamia, in an attempt to establish contact with the Jewish Diaspora in those countries.

## THE ANGLO-PRUSSIAN BISHOPRIC OF JERUSALEM

The LJS and Christian Bunsen, a counselor of the King of Prussia, conceived the rather surprising idea of creating an Anglo-Prussian bishopric in Jerusalem—one that would be both Anglican and Lutheran. This would show in a concrete way the essential unity of Protestantism in Jerusalem. The project was justified on the eschatological theory that the conversion of the Jews would occur shortly before the return of Christ to Jerusalem. The first bishop to be consecrated for the position was the Anglican Michael Solomon Alexander, who arrived in Jerusalem in 1843. He was succeeded three years later by Samuel Gobat (1799–1879) of Switzerland, who remained in this ministry for thirty years. Originally of Cremines, in the canton of Bern, Gobat had been a CMS missionary in Abyssinia.

*Samuel Gobat (1799–1879), Anglican Bishop of Jerusalem from 1846 to 1876.*

Although the mission among the Jews had been the raison d'être for this project, Gobot did not emphasize the evangelization of the Jews. Rather, he sought to bring

---

423 The current name is the Church's Ministry Among Jewish People (CMJ).

Eastern Christians to the evangelical faith. He appealed to the CMS and to German and Swiss Pietists (he had close relations with Christian Spittler and the work of the St. Chrischona Pilgrim Mission) to develop schools and welcome the children orphaned by the massacres in Lebanon. He succeeded in opening churches in Jerusalem in which the worship services were celebrated in English and German, but more often in Hebrew and Arabic. His missionary zeal for Africa did not slacken, and he became one of the promoters of the project to establish an "apostolic route" from Jerusalem to Abyssinia (mentioned above), an idea that was later abandoned. His efforts also resulted in the establishment of Anglican parishes in Syria, Lebanon, and Jordan.[424] Despite these successes, the bishopric was somewhat artificial in that its many purposes were poorly defined and the unity it was supposed to manifest was somewhat fragile. Moreover, Gobal was more an apostle than an ecclesiastical diplomat. He was strongly opposed by some Anglicans who believed that his proselytism was undermining relations between the Orthodox and Anglican churches. In 1882 there was much tension between Prussians and Anglicans on the occasion of the nomination of a new bishop, and beginning in 1887 the office of bishop would no longer be limited exclusively to Anglicans.

The Anglicans succeeded in establishing a church in Jordan in 1860, and the Lutherans were also soon present there, maintaining five parishes and an orphanage. There were no other Christian churches present in the Transjordan region until the 1920s when the Christian and Missionary Alliance[425] began to send missionaries in the region, and in 1929 when the Assemblies of God set out to evangelize Amman.

## THE AMERICAN BOARD

The American Board of Commissioners for Foreign Missions began in 1810, and its first missionary, Adoniram Judson, sailed for the Indies two years later. The American Board supported two young ministers in the Near East beginning in 1819. These were Levi Parsons, who died three and a half years later in Alexandria, and Pling Fisk, who began work in Beirut in 1823. The first Arab convert was martyred, and afterwards most of the members of the church were of Christian background. These included two Armenian priests of high rank and, in the south of Lebanon, a large group of Greek Orthodox members who came en masse into Protestantism. In 1834 the printing press that had previously been established in Malta was transfered to Beirut where it produced numerous Bible texts translated into modern Arabic.

The American Board and the American Mission of the Presbyterian Church joined together in 1931 to establish a theological seminary in Beirut. This was a partial failure in that most of the ministers who studied there eventually emigrated to the United States. More successful were the small Bible schools that more closely reflected the

---

424 Gobat wrote a journal of his sojourn in Abyssinia, *Sejour en Abyssinie*, published by the Society of the Mission of Geneva in 1834 and translated into English as *Journal of Three Years' Residence in Abyssinia* (1853). It was republished by Negro Universities Press in 1969. On the basis of his letters and circulars, his life was made the object of a book that was prepared by his family: *Samuel Gobat, Bishop of Jerusalem, his life and work: a biographical sketch* (London: J. Nisbet, 1884).

425 The CMA worked in Syria where it founded churches in Damascus and Homs.

local culture. They attracted ministers from small communities who returned home upon graduation. On the other hand, the Syrian Protestant College quickly acquired an excellent reputation and attracted students from countries throughout region. In 1920 it became the famous American University of Beirut.

Churches were planted in Alep and Tripoli in 1841, and later also in Lebanon and Syria. In 1879 the mission, which had been Congregationalist, was placed under the authority of the American Presbyterian mission.

William Goodell (1792–1867), under the American Board, established a mission station in 1831 among the Armenians of Constantinople. The Armenian Apostolic Church at first welcomed the missionaries, but Matthew II Tchouadjian, the patriarch named in 1841, was hostile to these evangelicals and in 1846 condemned them in two successive declarations. A Protestant Armenian church then emerged and experienced rapid growth. Due to the continuing conflict between the missionaries and Armenian leaders, the Union of Evangelical Armenian Churches in the Near East was established shortly before the genocide perpetrated against Armenian people in the decades prior to the First World War. In 1925 a synod was formed for the dispersed Armenians in Syria and Lebanon, but it did not benefit from the support of the American Board. The Armenian evangelicals also had churches in Europe (especially France) and the United States where many had emigrated.

The American Board also established a mission station in Mosal, Iraq, a little after 1850. As a result of its work, evangelical Arab churches were established there as early as 1855. Later there were also parishes in Kirkuk, Baghdad, and Basra, which were generally led by Egyptian ministers.

## PRESBYTERIAN MISSIONS

The American Presbyterian churches sent the brothers Henry and Samuel Jessup to work in Lebanon in 1856 and 1863 respectively. Later about twenty other missionaries also arrived, which included a few doctors. They made slow progress, but soon several small Christian communities were formed, made up largely of former Orthodox Christians. The principal centers of activity were Beirut, Sayda, Tripoli, Aley, and Zahle. A secondary school was opened in 1840 in Aley, about twenty kilometers south of Beirut. The synod of Syria was established in which missionaries, ministers, and parish delegates first met in 1881. A cultural center was opened in Nabatye in 1922, a large hospital in Dayr el-Zor in 1924, and a rural center in Jibrael (nearby to Tripoli) in 1944.

The Presbyterian Church of Scotland created a committee for mission among the Jews in 1838. In order not to encroach on the activities of the London Jews' Society, it worked largely in Galilee and, in 1842, in Constantinople as well. Its initiatives were halted due to a division in the church in Scotland, which produced the Church of Scotland and the Free Church of Scotland—both Presbyterian churches. The Free Church established churches in Damascus in 1843, Beirut in 1864, and Smyrna in 1882. (Its Beaconsfield Memorial Hospital was destroyed by a tragic fire in the city in 1922.) In 1885 the mission of the Free Church built the Sea of Tiberias Hospital. Its projects were often carried out in collaboration with the Presbyterians of North Ireland and Canada. The work focused as much on Muslims as Jews, but the majority of converts were nonetheless from the Eastern churches.

The Arab Mission of the American Reformed Church entered Iraq in 1889, and in 1920 was joined in its efforts by two other American missions, the Evangelical Reformed Church and Presbyterian Church in the U.S.A.

The work of the Presbyterians in the Arabian Peninsula will be considered below (see pp. 657ff).

## CHRISTIAN ACTION IN THE ORIENT

This work came into being in 1922 at the initiative of the Alsatian minister Paul Berron. He originally came to Turkey in 1914 with a German mission (Alsace was then German) in order to bring help to Armenian victims of Turkish persecution.[426] When the First World War broke out, he was named chaplain of the German "Soldiers Home" in Turkey, then in Amman in Jordan, and finally in Alep in Syria. He did all this while continuing to make the Armenian refugees his priority.

After the war Berron became French and worked in Syria under the French mandate. However, no longer able to serve through a German mission, he went to Strasbourg to instigate a new mission, Action Chretiénne en Orient (ACO, Christian Action in the Orient).[427] Its objectives were threefold: material aid to Armenians, spiritual work among the Eastern Christians, and mission among the Muslims.[428]

The first ACO missionaries were Alice Humbert-Droz from Switzerland and Hedwige Bull from Estonia, who left for Aleppo, Syria, in 1922 and engaged the Evangelical Armenian Church as fellow workers in both their medical and evangelistic work. In 1925 ACO opened a hospital in Beirut, and later it also opened an orphanage, which was generally intended to serve Armenian children.

In 1932 ACO also developed an evangelistic outreach in Arabic to Muslims, which encountered numerous difficulties. The evangelists who had the best access to the population were Armenians, who were indigenous to the region. In 1938 Anne-Marie Beck, an Alsatian teacher, arrived and was soon able to proclaim the gospel in three Eastern languages. She married Elias Tartar, a Syrian tailor who was an Orthodox convert to Protestantism. He dedicated himself entirely to the evangelization of Jews and Muslims.

The mission also sought to establish some contacts in Upper Mesopotamia with Turkish and Iraqi Christians of various denominations—Catholic Syrians, Greek Orthodox, Armenians, and Nestorians—who immigrated into these largely Muslim regions following the First World War and subsequent political upheavals. But ACO did not attempt to found new churches. Some Aramaic-speaking Muslim villages were reached by Armenian evangelists, but without much result.

---

426 This mission was the Deutscher Hilfsbund für christliches Liebeswerk im Orient.

427 Later it would become a Swiss auxiliary committee with a secretary in Lausanne. Until 1948 its most energetic leader was the Reverend Henri Nussié.

428 Cf. P. Berron, *Une oeuvre missionnaire en Orient et en Occident: Origine et développement de l'action chrétienne en Orient* (Strasburg, France: Oberlin, [1962?]), 22–23.

## SAMUEL ZWEMER AND THE ARABIAN MISSION

We have already mentioned the presence of Presbyterians in Arabia, but there were other mission efforts in the last part of the nineteenth century that were ventured in the Arabian Peninsula, the heart of historical Islam.

Thomas Valpy French (1825–1890), a CMS missionary in the Indies since 1850, was consecrated the Anglican bishop of Lahore in 1877. At the age of sixty-six, he decided to attempt a difficult adventure in Arabia. He disembarked at Mascat, Oman, in 1880 and was joined by two young American Presbyterians, James Cantine and Samuel Zwemer. French died three months later, but his companions persevered in the task. They succeeded in launching the Arabian Mission, establishing their base in Basra, Iraq, and opening posts in Mascate, Aden, and Bahrain. They made Bible distribution their priority. Several small churches were formed in Arabia, but their members consisted almost entirely of Westerners employed in the country. In 1938 at the time of the world missionary conference of Tambaram, one of the veterans of the Arabia Mission, Paul Harrison, recounted how in fifty years they had registered five conversions of Arab Muslims. The participants were moved upon hearing him conclude his address with these words: "The church of Arabia greets you."

Samuel Marinus Zwemer (1867–1952) was born in the state of Michigan, the thirteenth of fifteen children whose father was a minister. Conscious at an early age of God's call to mission, he studied theology and medicine. The Reformed Board refused to accept him as a missionary to Arab countries, which was considered a futile exercise. Therefore, he formed with his friend James Cantine the Arabian Mission in 1889. Briefly joined by French, they persevered in the task on the Arabian coast in the Persian Gulf, encountering much opposition and few results. Cantine died after a few years, and Zwemer's only companion was then a young Syrian who had recently converted. He married Amy Wilkes, a nurse of a British Anglican mission, and the couple settled on the island of Bahrain, evangelizing the area through the use of tracts and Bible texts. During eight days in 1904, they suffered the lost of their two daughters, ages seven and four.

Other missionaries joined them, and as we have seen, the Arabian Mission opened several stations in the Arabian Peninsula. Through his writing and conference addresses, Zwemer slowly acquired a reputation as an eminent Islamicist. In 1910 he participated in the World Missionary Conference at Edinburgh where his contributions on Islam were highly valued. The Presbyterian Church of Cairo offered him a position in 1912. With the agreement of the CMS, he accepted, believing that Cairo would become the nerve center for an itinerant ministry to Muslims around the world. From Cairo, he helped to initiate missionary enterprises among Muslims in the Indies, Indochina, China, and South Africa. He was a professor, writer,[429] evangelist, apologist, and much-appreciated counselor to missions engaged in Islamic countries. He was also a noted preacher in the churches of the West and among

---

429 As noted above (p. 649), he established a journal, *The World of Islam*, which recorded the mission work occurring in Muslim lands.

American Christian students. To his young listeners he pleaded the cause of missions in Islamic lands.

Zwemer was innovative in his approach to Muslims. He combined, writes Ruth Tucker, "traditional evangelism and the more contemporary concept of 'sharing' that was characteristic of the student volunteers.[430] He dealt with Muslims on a plane of equality—sharing his own faith (a very conservative theology) as he sought to learn more about theirs, always showing them the utmost respect."[431]

In 1929 he began the last phase of his career when he accepted the often repeated offer from Princeton Theological Seminary to be the chairman of its department of History of Religion and Christian Missions. In this new post he continued to pursue his study of Islam with the aim of finding openings to make the good news of Jesus Christ more accessible to the followers of Muhammad.[432]

Zwemer was a much beloved-personality for the joy he communicated and even, according to his friends, his roguish spirit.[433] He remained ebullient throughout the difficulties he suffered as a missionary in sometimes dangerous regions. He was often cheerful even through the difficult periods of mourning when he lost his children on the mission field, his first wife in 1937, and, two years before his death, his second wife in 1950. Zwemer did not have occasion to see many Muslims convert as a direct result of his ministry, but he contributed amply to the understanding of Islam by Western Christians and helped them to see the need to redouble their efforts to evangelize Islamic peoples.

It is necessary to acknowledge, as Jean-Michel Hornus does, that "practically all Protestants of the Near East were [in the period described here] attached to the Eastern churches, and that missions were dedicated to other purposes, largely to aid."[434]

> The conversion to Protestantism by Muslims and Jews in the Near East has been extremely rare, due to the rigor of the community structures. On the other hand, the schools and dispensaries, initially conceived as a means to reach those to whom one hoped to proclaim the gospel, were generally transformed into entirely secular or Islamic universities and modern hospitals.[435]

It remains true, however, that medical work has often provided an opening for Christians to witness to their faith, as the wife of a medical missionary in Beirut explained:

---

430 The Student Volunteer Movement was headed by John Mott, who helped to nourish Zwemer's faith in his youth.

431 Tucker, op. cit., 279.

432 In the course of his long life, Zwemer wrote about fifty books on the mission of the church, mostly regarding Islamic missions.

433 On one occasion he was so boisterous that the maitre d' in the restaurant where he was dining with his friends had to ask him to be quiet so as not to trouble the other diners. The anecdote is unimportant in itself, except that is unexpected of an eminent missionary.

434 Hornus, op. cit., 34.

435 Ibid., 11.

The Muslim of Arabia is violently opposed to our Christian message and does not desire it a bit. But he certainly desires medical care and has a terrible need for it. He desires it so much that he will open his home and heart to a Christian doctor. Consequently, the doctor or nurse who has a true passion for the souls of these people can accomplish marvelous works of evangelization and personal witness.[436]

436 Mrs. Tucker Callaway (wife of a medical missionary in Beirut in the 1930s), cited in ibid., 71.

# SECTION V

## PROTESTANT MISSION
## IN LATIN AMERICA

# From Protestant Immigration to Evangelization

W e will begin with a brief sketch of Protestantism in Latin America in the period prior to modern missions. In the first volume of this work, Christianity in this region was almost entirely a history of Catholic missions. During the period from the initial discovery to the early nineteenth century, Protestants were present largely due to immigration.

The first Catholic missionaries generally belonged to one of three religious orders: Augustinians, Franciscans, and Dominicans. Some bore with them a humanist and reformist vision of the church. Influenced by Desiderius Erasmus, they hoped to establish a revived form of Christianity in the New World, one unaffected by the divisions then rocking the church in Europe. But as the Counter-Reformation raged in Latin America, the Inquisition generally snuffed out any reformist inclinations. Moreover, it opposed all forms of "Indianization" of the church and even strove to prevent the translation of the Bible into vernacular languages. The first tribunal of the Inquisition in Lima was held in 1570, and another was held in Mexico in 1571. The trials led to the burning of "Lutheran" books and the expulsion of suspects. The works of Erasmus or those in the reformist spirit of Erasmus underwent the same fate. Jean Pierre Bastian writes, "Due to the effectiveness of the repression brought to bear by the Inquisition, Protestant ideas were absent from the colonies during the seventeenth century."[437] In the end all political subversion and any progressive ideas were condemned as "Lutheran."

Despite this intense hostility, Protestantism appeared briefly in the Antilles in the seventeenth century when Oliver Cromwell's fleet seized Jamaica in 1655, and Danish and Dutch colonists settled on several islands of the Lesser Antilles between 1660 and 1690. Protestants during this period were hardly the moral superiors of Catholics, for they too inflicted terrible suffering on black slaves, and even ministers possessed slaves. The 1696 "slave code" in Jamaica specified: "All property owners must see that their slaves are instructed in the principles of the Christian religion and facilitate their conversion by making a maximum effort to prepare them for baptism." But for

---

437 Jean-Pierre Bastian, *Le protestantisme en Amérique latine: Une approche socio-historique* (Geneva: Labor & Fides, 1994), 57.

most this part of the code remained a dead letter, and the colonial chaplains did not generally feel called to evangelize slaves.

It was not until the Moravians arrived in 1732 that Africans of the Antilles encountered missionaries, and naturally their efforts were hindered by frequent opposition from the colonists (see pp. 265ff). In the second half of the eighteenth century, the Methodists dedicated themselves to the evangelization of the slaves, and unlike the Moravians, they were also engaged in the antislavery struggle.

In the course of the eighteenth century, the ideas of the Enlightenment seeped into Spain. The enlightened policies of the Bourbons of Spain favored the economic development that came with the emigration into South America of foreign merchants, whatever their nationality or religion. Finally, like the capture of St. Sabastian (1808),[438] it was not the ideas of the French or American revolutions that rung down the curtain on Spanish colonialism in Latin America; rather, it was the fall of the Spanish dynasty brought about by the Napoleonic conquest. The resulting political vacuum triggered a movement that resulted in independence in a dozen Latin American nations.

## PROTESTANT IMMIGRATION

Religious tolerance first began to emerge in Latin America when its newly independent governments signed commercial treaties with the United States and the Protestant nations of Europe. Wanting to end its economic dependence on Spain and form new relationships with others, the Latin American nations were constrained to concede religious liberty in exchange for trading partners. Authorization was given to erect Protestant chapels for the use of those employed by American and European trading companies. This occurred in Rio de Janeiro in 1816, Buenos Aires in 1824, Caracas in 1834, and Lima in 1849—and others followed.

Brazil first granted non-Catholics toleration in 1824. By 1871 it is estimated that about 300,000 Germans had settled in the south of the country, and more than half of these were Protestants. But it was not until 1891 with the advent of the new republic that religious liberty was inscribed in the constitution. In Argentina this did not occur until 1853 when a new liberal constitution granted religious liberty, opening the door to Protestant immigration. Uruguay granted religious toleration to Protestants in 1856, which prompted Italians of the Vaudoise Church (*Chiesa Valdese*) to settle there. This organized their social and religious life much as it had been for centuries in Piemont, each village having its own chapel, school, and teacher—and, if possible, its own pastor.

The Protestant churches that emerged due to immigration in nineteenth-century Latin America were not large. Moreover, these groups strove to preserve their national and confessional identity and, therefore, did not tend to mingle with the rest of the population. They were not evangelists. Traditional Protestantism slowly became a fixture in the large cities, and its members were generally middle class and, sometimes, of the leading class. Jean André Meyer writes, "Relatively modest in numbers,

---

438 Ibid., 67.

these churches had a remarkable influence due to the social quality and ascension of their members. They had the highest percentage of schools and universities in all of Protestantism."[439] It is certain that Protestantism enjoyed an influence far greater than one would suppose from the small numbers that made up its churches and religious societies.[440]

Protestant organizations at the local and regional levels appeared to be quite innovative when compared to the traditional hierarchy of the Catholic Church and the civil structures that it inspired. Protestant assemblies, conventions, and synods,[441] which tended to follow modern and democratic processes, influenced liberal politicians who wanted to establish parliamentary forms of government for their countries, and Protestant polity inspired many in the Latin American political elite. During the second half of the nineteenth century, this explains why some politicians, as we will see later, hoped for the growth of Protestant influence and appealed to Protestant mission organizations to send missionaries.

## THE INFLUENCE OF BIBLE SOCIETIES: JAMES THOMPSON

In the newly independent states, conservatives and liberals were often in conflict. Over the course of the nineteenth century it was the liberals who slowly gained sway. They had the will to build modern and prosperous states, which was implied in their literacy and educational efforts that until then were nonexistent in these nations. In this context, the first agents of the Protestant Bible societies were welcomed with great interest; and at the same time that they were making Bibles available, they were also militating for popular education.

The best known and most active of the Bible colporteurs was the Scottish Baptist minister James Thompson (1781–1854).[442] He was originally employed by the British and Foreign School Society, which sent him to Buenos Aires in 1819. At this time he was also an agent of British and Foreign School Society, which was founded in 1808 and originally named the Royal Lancastrian Society. During the first half of the nineteenth century, Thompson was at the forefront of the movement to introduce a system of mutual teaching. His pedagogy consisted of quickly training monitors among the best students and then directing those students to teach reading and writing to the others. In this way, the effectiveness of the teaching was multiplied. This project won over the Argentine President Bernardino Rivadavia, who was anxious at the time to reform Catholicism and reorganize public education. He looked favorably on Thompson who, while he worked in Buenos Aires, was the head of about a hundred schools.

In 1821 Thompson was enlisted by the president of Chile to open several schools. In the following year General José de San Martin named him the director of public education in Peru where he launched programs to translate the New Testament in

---

439 Jean André Meyer, *Histoire du christianisme*, vol. 12, ed. J. M. Mayeur et al. (Paris: Desclée, 1995), 998–99.
440 For Mexico, Bastian (op. cit.) states that in 1910 there were 100,000 Protestants out of 14 million inhabitants. Altogether in Latin America, including the Caribbean, Neill, *History*, 391, estimates them at 500,000 in 1914.
441 An example would be the Lutheran Synod of Rio Grande do Sul created in 1886.
442 Some, such as Bastian (op. cit.), spelled his name as Thomson.

Quechua and Aymara. Thompson contributed to the foundation of "philanthropic societies" in Equator and Colombia in 1824 and 1825. Despite the support of the liberal clergy in Colombia,[443] the hostility of the traditionalist hierarchy forced him to depart before he was able to consolidate the work he had undertaken. In 1827 he went to Mexico where José Maria Mora, a Catholic priest as well as a liberal engaged in the economic development of his country, became an agent of the Bible Society and served for about twenty years. In the course of his work Thompson also traveled to the Antilles.

A large number of those sent by the British and American Bible societies followed in Thompson's tracks, but their goal was not to found Protestant churches; rather, they aimed at reforming Latin American Catholicism through Bible distribution and literacy programs—the latter included cultural, educational, social, and sometimes medical themes. The majority of the Catholic clergy were conservative and hostile to these initiatives, and they confiscated and destroyed Bibles in great numbers. The Bible societies were not highly successful in terms of statistics, but their efforts tended to foment transformation. In the second half of the nineteenth century, liberals who attempted to reform these same countries tended to follow the Protestant and Bible society model to achieve their aims.

## THE BEGINNING OF PROTESTANT MISSIONS: ALLEN GARDINER

With the exception of the Bible societies, the Protestant missionary societies did not tend to be highly active in South America during the first half of the nineteenth century. In general, European missionary societies made the evangelization of pagan populations or the adepts of Eastern religions their clear priority, not Christianized populations even if their faith was only superficial. They were more interested in Africans than Amazonian Indians, of whom there was little talk. Moreover, the rare attempts to evangelize the biracial or European population of the cities and ports—Buenos Aires, Montevideo, Rio de Janeiro—were considered by the Catholic clergy as proselytism. Hence their work was systematically obstructed, making the efforts of evangelical pioneers largely untenable.

One of the factors that stimulated the interest of American Protestants in the evangelization of the Amerindian populations was the tragedy of a pioneer missionary, Allen Gardiner (1794–1851), among the native people at the southern extremity of the continent. An officer of the British navy, Gardiner heard the gospel in his youth but did not make a clear decision about it at the time. His naval life, however, was full of danger, which led him to ponder the question of death and the life beyond. Following a naval battle in which he believed he might have lost his life, he bought a Bible and began to read it secretly. Later when he attended a religious ceremony in a pagan temple in China he perceived how much the biblical message, in contrast, carried certitude and hope. These reflections as well as the death of a family member

---

443 In this context the term "liberal" does not indicate a theological tendency in conflict with orthodoxy, nor an economic school, but a democratic and nonauthoritarian administration of political as well as ecclesiastical institutions.

led him to conversion, an experience that took away his timidity and made him a zealous witness among the officers and marines of the Royal Navy. He was then twenty-seven years old.

His ship landed a little later at Tahiti, which was now largely a Christian island due to the efforts of the London Missionary Society (LMS). He was struck by how much this island differed from other places he had visited while sailing the world's seas—places characterized by violence, the lure of gain, and the depredation of morals. Now convinced of the importance and urgency of mission, he also perceived the vanity of his own ambition to rise up through the ranks of the military hierarchy.

Having visited numerous ports of call, he was particularly struck by the moral and spiritual misery that reigned in the ports of South America. He also learned of the oppression of the Amerindian populations which lived in inhospitable regions at the southernmost end of the continent. Spanish colonization had made them implacable rebels. On returning to Britain, he joined the LMS and proposed to become a missionary in South America. At the time, however, the society did not envision taking up a new field of activity in the Atlantic region. This refusal profoundly shook him. Gardiner then sought to become a vicar in an Anglican parish, but again his candidacy was declined. Finally, he returned to the British navy and soon obtained the rank of captain. He married Julia Susanna, who died in 1834 after having given him five children.

His experience led him to devote himself once again entirely to the service of God. At forty years of age, he left the navy to become a missionary among the Zulus in South Africa. He successfully established the first missionary station in Port Natal, called Berea, but his efforts to extend evangelization farther into the region were dashed by the Boer War, and he was constrained to return to Britain.

After a second marriage, Gardiner left for South America with his family and arrived in Rio de Janeiro in 1838. He began to crisscross the vast regions Argentina on horse or mule, distributing Portuguese and Spanish Bibles. His objective was to settle in the heart of a nonevangelized Indian tribe in order to learn the language. Though he was warmly welcomed for stays of short duration, no village chief wanted a European family to settle permanently in his territory.

He made other unfruitful attempts among the Araucaria Indians of southern Chile and then moved on to Patagonia. There he benefited from a black American deserter who had been in the area for three years and had learned the local language. Using this man as a translator, Gardiner made promising contacts with a tribe. He then returned to Britain to urge the great mission societies—CMS, LMS, and Wesleyan—to extend their efforts into South America. When they demurred, he founded the Patagonia Missionary Society, which he largely financed himself.

In 1844 Gardiner returned to Argentina with a young colleague, Robert Hunt. The two missionaries had much difficulty finding the tribe with which Gardiner had previously established contact. When they finally located the Patagonians, their reception was not what was expected. The Patagonians, who were completely destitute, seized their baggage, stole their clothes, and then used up their provisions, which had been intended to supply their needs for several months. After a few days when their goods were completely exhausted, the tribal people became aggressive. The two missionaries, without any remaining provisions, left the territory and returned to Britain. Against the advice of his mission committee, Gardner remained adamant in his conviction of the need to establish a mission among the Indians of the South American continent.

Gardiner left with a young Spanish colleague, Manuel Gonzales, for Bolivia in 1845. They benefited from the support of government authorities but were opposed by the Catholic clergy. Despite opposition, they undertook the evangelization of an Indian tribe in the Gran Chaco plain, which was then still partially attached to Bolivia. And soon another young Spaniard joined them. Gardiner returned to Britain to demonstrate to his committee the necessity of establishing a permanent base in Bolivia, and he pleaded the cause of the evangelization of the Amerindian tribes about whom European Christians showed little interest. To raise their consciousness, he wrote *A Voice of South America*. The book was well received and allowed Gardiner to send additional missionaries to work in the Patagonia Mission.

Gardiner's next objective was to evangelize the Fuegians, inhabitants of the Tierra de Fuego, an archipelago at the southern tip of the South American continent separated from Patagonia by a narrow channel. Here he did not have to face obstacles thrown up by Catholic missions since even the Jesuits had never gone so far south in their two centuries of relentless work on the continent.

The scientist Charles Darwin had occasion to see the Fuegians at the time of his voyages along the South American coast. He described them as the most miserable and primitive savages that he had ever encountered. Upon seeing their faces, which he described as flat and simian, he believed he had found a confirmation of his theory of evolution. He also noted that their homes resembled molehills more than houses. "I have always thought," he wrote, "that even the best missionaries would not manage to make men of these savages."

Gardiner was convinced, however, that they would accept the gospel if it were preached in their own language. An earlier attempt had been made to evangelize this people, in 1826 by another officer of the Royal Navy, Robert Fitzroy, who had been accompanied by a young missionary named Richard Matthews. Their encounter with the Fuegians had occurred at precisely the same time as Darwin's scientific expedition. But the missionaries were soon forced to flee, having been accosted and robbed of all their possessions. They came away with three orphans, whom they brought to Britain. One of them later desired to return to his country. Having learned English, he would render important service at the time of another missionary attempt, as we shall soon see.

Gardiner embarked once again for Tierra de Fuego in 1850. He was fifty-six years old and accompanied by six men: a surgeon, an employee of a hotel trained as a catechist, a carpenter, and three fishermen from Cornouaille. They came prepared with supplies for six months and anticipated a ship to resupply them before the end of this period. Gardiner wrote this message to his friends: "When we saw this abandoned people but knew that they were called to eternal life like us, we dedicated ourselves to proclaim the gospel to them in their own language. My word of farewell is, Pray for us!" This was the first and last letter that they received from him.

The attempts of the missionary team to establish contact with the seminomadic Fuegians were without success. A storm so damaged their boat that the cabin could barely serve as a dormitory, and some of their provisions were lost. After six months, they became anxious about the ship that was supposed to resupply them. They survived by stretching their provisions to make them last and by trying to fish, though without much success. The Fuegians in the neighborhood gave them no help, being suspicious and undernourished themselves. Then began their desperate struggle against the cold and snowstorms of the Antarctic in winter. They divided themselves into two groups that lived on beaches several kilometers from each other. This was intended to increase their chances of finding help or being found by the resupply ship. As winter advanced, it became increasingly less plausible to them that a ship would risk the raging sea, which bristled with reefs and icebergs. They suffered from scurvy and other diseases linked to cold and malnutrition. On June 11 the first death occurred among them. Then at the end of August one after another died while the survivors found it increasingly difficult to summon the strength to inter the bodies of their fallen companions. On September 4 the last of Gardiner's teammates made a final entry in his journal:

> My faithful work companion has arrived at the end of his suffering here below. He is now with the assembly of the blessed, in the presence of the Lord whom he has served until the end . . . I had no water, and in the fear of being tormented by thirst, I prayed to the Lord to help me find a little. He granted my prayer. Yesterday, while I was rising, I was able to collect a sufficient quantity of water from a rock from which it was flowing. What good I have received from my heavenly Father! Blessed be his name.[444]

Gardiner wrote the following on September 5, the eve of his death:

> Great and marvelous is the goodness of the Lord towards me. Until now he has sustained me: I have been four days without food and have experienced neither hunger nor thirst . . . I am sustained in perfect peace by his abundant grace, refreshed in feeling the love of my Savior, and assured that all is prepared with wisdom and mercy. And I pray to be capable of receiving the full blessing that is reserved for me. I simply wait for his good time and pleasure in which he will dispose of me according to his will. I want to be in him, whether I live or die. I commend my body and my soul to his care and his protection, and I pray intensely that, in his goodness, he will keep my dear wife and children in the shadow of his wings. May he comfort them, strengthen them, guide them and fully sanctify them, and may we be able together, in a luminous and eternal world, to praise and adore his goodness and grace.

---

444 Burckhardt and Grundemann, op. cit., 325–26.

> We are plucked as brands from the fire by his precious blood in order to benefit from filial adoption and to become inheritors of his heavenly kingdom. Amen.[445]

Before succumbing, he still had the strength to copy in a trembling hand this verse of a psalm: "My soul waits for the Lord—for my repose is in him." Gardiner's death—and that of his six companions—occurred just one year after his departure from Britain.

The circumstances of this terrible experience are well known to us through Gardiner's journal, which was found close to his body by the members of the expedition that set out to find the missing party four months later. The journal was published and had a huge impact. The author expressed neither regrets nor doubts but only the peace and even joy experienced by him and his companions. He pleaded that these supposedly inaccessible people not be abandoned, for they had the same need of the good news as all other human beings. He even took care to develop a detailed new strategy so that a renewed Patagonia mission would avoid the errors that they had made in attempting to reach the Fuegians. He recognized that in his zeal he had been too much in haste. In the future there should first be a well-equipped mission station on the Falkland Islands, which lay several hundred kilometers from the continent. From there, brief incursions could be made to Tierra de Fuego, which would accustom the people to seeing missionaries and teach them that they had nothing to fear from them. Then the difficult step of taking several young Fuegiens to live among the missionaries could be taken. Finally, the missionaries would have to learn their language and settle among them. This approach would take years, Gardiner observed.

Despite his conversion in 1821 and his missionary call, Gardiner encountered little more than trials, refusals, and failures in his many attempts to advance the cause of God's mission. His disappointments make his unshakeable faith and perseverance to the end all the more striking. His story produced a rise in missionary consciousness among Christian people, especially in Britain. The secular press dedicated numerous headlines and articles to the dramatic last scene of his life. Some stories were full of admiration for the abnegation of the missionary team while others were critical of the expedition's poor organization. Indeed, many were scandalized that so much human life was expended by men trying to take their religion to a savage people.

Here is a portion of a prayer written by Gardiner on his birthday, June 21, 1851, which came ten days after the death of the first member of his team:

> I pray to you, my heavenly Father, so that, if it is in accord with your just will, you would lower your compassionate gaze upon my companions and me who are overwhelmed by the lack of food, and for whom you would want to supply what is necessary . . . I desire to learn an entire submission of my will to yours and to abase all the pride in my heart.

---

445 Phyllis Thompson, *An Unquenchable Flame: Biography of Allen Gardiner; Founder of the South American Missionary Society* (London: Hodder & Stoughton, 1983), 182.

Lord, I pray that you would be honored in my person, either by my life, or by my death, and that I may never be separated from you. Sustain me by your grace and deliver me from the anxiety of worry, murmurs, and incredulity . . .

I am bold still to present a request before your throne of grace, O merciful Lord: I pray to you that you would prepare the day when your servants will finally enter among the poor pagans of these regions. Permit, O God, that we would be instruments to begin this great and blessed work. But if you find it good to put an end to our pilgrimage and to allow us to wither away and die here, I entreat you to arouse others and to send workers to this harvest. Show Lord, for the manifestation of your glory and grace, that nothing is too difficult for you.[446]

The call that resounded in the last lines of his journal would be heard, and others would imitate Gardiner's example, supported by the Patagonia Missionary Society founded by him.[447] In 1854 a British ship landed a small group of missionaries and colonists on one of the Falkland Islands where they established a station. Then, following Gardiner's counsel, they cautiously made many brief and discreet visits to the beaches of Tierra de Fuego in order to build confidence in the population. They eventually succeeded in persuading a few young people to come and live among them and to learn their language. The young Fuegian that Robert Fitzroy had brought to Britain about thirty years earlier would now play a decisive role. This occurred in 1858 when they had been in the Falklands for four years. In the following year, the visits to Tierra de Fuego increased. The inhabitants appeared to be friendly, and the numbers coming to welcome and barter with them on the beach increased until they reached about 300. One Sunday the small missionary team felt emboldened to celebrate a worship service in their presence. During the service, a group from a neighboring tribe interrupted and a British sailor was killed with the stroke of a mace. The others ran towards the dinghy with the intention of rowing to the ship anchored off the coast, but the oars had been taken away. All were massacred. Even the young Fuegians with whom they had been in close contact joined in the bloodbath. One of them, however, ran to and fro while crying and wringing his hands, begging in vain for his brothers to spare the missionaries.

At this time a ship was crossing the Atlantic with a British minister and two students from the Bible Institute of Chrischona on board. They were coming to join the outreach to the Fuegian, entirely ignorant of these tragic events. When they arrived, they did not give up but courageously took over the work. They knew that it would take a great deal of patience and prudence to successfully communicate the gospel message to this hostile people. In 1874, twenty-one years after the death of Gardiner and his companions, thirty-six converts were baptized. And soon, along this dangerous shore where merchant ships regularly sank while attempting to round Cape

---

446 Thompson, op. cit., 174.
447 It later changed its name to South American Missionary Society.

Horn, shipwrecked sailors were surprised to receive help rather than being despoiled and massacred. In 1862 other Chrischona missionaries began to settle in Patagonia, and the population slowly became less aggressive, but it took long and arduous work before a Christian community could be formed. Darwin was wrong about the Fuegians, but it had taken close to fifty years of perseverance since Fitzroy's first attempt before a church was finally born in this desolate land.

*Map 15: Latin America*

# CHAPTER 30

# Development of Protestant Mission in Latin America

As we have seen, the creation of Bible societies and the missionary example of the Protestant churches aroused much interest and sympathy in the liberal and progressive environment that emerged in Latin America in the nineteenth century. Protestant missionaries, despite the attitude of the Catholic clergy who accused them of proselytism, were often given great latitude in their work, as we have seen in the case of James Thompson and others of the British and Foreign Bible Society. Protestant missionaries began to arrive just as the region's political leaders started to yearn for the social benefits that missions could provide. When missionaries arrived in Mexico in 1870, President Benito Juarez expressed the wish that Protestantism would expand "so that the Indians would learn to read instead of passing their time lighting candles."

This was also true in other countries. The president of Colombia requested an increase in the number of missionaries so that they could establish schools and churches. He even went so far as to offer them property owned by the Catholic Church that he had requisitioned. It was in this favorable context that in 1856 the American Presbyterians started a large educational program in order to continue the work that Thompson had begun about thirty years before. Justo Rufino Barrios, president of Guatemala from 1873 to 1885, asked for a United Presbyterian Church of North America missionary to come in order to support his liberal and anti-Catholic policies. Of course, though Protestantism seemed to respond to their religious and political needs, even the most liberal were not disposed to accept North American control over their countries.

Historic North American Protestantism, despite its diversity of denominations and differing views on slavery, had generally consistent goals: a wide distribution of the Bible, education for the people, and teaching of the evangelical faith. The call to personal conversion remained at the center of the mission societies' theology, but they also actively founded social works as well as numerous primary, secondary, and professional schools. Liberal governments were then striving to organize public education but were unable to reach either the backward regions or the marginalized. For those who were neglected by the state, indigenous Protestant societies and their supporting missions performed an indispensable task. Education buildings were generally constructed alongside churches, and ministers often took up the task of being schoolmasters. The content of their programs did not differ from that of the public schools, but their pedagogical methods were more advanced, emphasizing individual responsibility and democratic values. The liberals were naturally sympathetic to this approach.

European mission societies were hesitant to consider Latin America as "virgin" territory, the population having been Christianized from the time of the Iberian colonization. Consequently, European Anglican, Lutheran, and Reformed missions generally limited their activities to their coreligionists who had emigrated to the continent.[448] In contrast, the North American Protestant churches and missions were not reticent to act, and indeed they intensified their efforts at the end of the nineteenth century. This was especially so of those who were in the revival tradition: Methodists, Baptists, and many others who were evangelical or Pentecostal. They believed that South American Catholicism was largely a religious veneer and, for the aboriginal populations, one mixed with residues of their traditional faiths. At the time of the Protestant Pan-American Congresses (Panama in 1916, Montevideo in 1925, Havana in 1929), Latin America was unhesitantly affirmed to be a mission field, not a Christian land.

Foreign influences became increasingly prevalent in Latin America during the course of the twentieth century, especially methods of evangelization borrowed from the techniques of mass communication. But there was less financial dependence on North American churches and missions in this region than in other mission fields.

The missions also engaged in the evangelization of the animistic Amerindian tribes of the forests and in the translation of Bible texts into several of their unwritten languages. It was not, however, until the middle of the twentieth century—the period outside of the chronological limits of our study—that the evangelization of these tribes and the translation of the Bible into their languages were taken up in earnest.

We must be content with a brief country-by-country review of the early progress of Protestant missions.[449] It is sometimes difficult with the fragmentary evidence that we have at our disposal to distinguish between the envoys sent to instruct their coreligionists and those sent as evangelists to the non-Protestant population. We will not mention the preliminary work undertaken by James Thompson, itinerant agent of the British and Foreign Biblical Society, since he has already been considered above. In fact, as a missionary between 1819 and 1827, he preceded by several decades some of the first Protestant missionaries in the region, and all of those in the nations of South America with the exception of Uruguay and Paraguay. Despite the brief duration of his stay in many countries, he was able to open schools in almost every country in which he worked and to lay the foundations for Bible distribution centers.

---

448 At the end of the nineteenth century, baptized Catholics comprised from 80 to 90 percent of the South American population. Under the influence of European delegates, the 1910 Edinburgh mission conference declared Latin America to be a Christian land and not, therefore, an object of missionary concern.

449 Much of the material here is derived from Barrett, *Encyclopedia*.

# SOUTH AMERICA

## Argentina

Because the climate of Argentina is similar to that of much of Europe, many Europeans who wanted to immigrate to South America made this country their destination, and until the end of the nineteenth century, the growth of Argentine Protestantism was due largely to immigration. The American Methodists, who arrived in 1836, limited their efforts for several dozen years to work among the European immigrants. The first Reformed Europeans arrived in 1843, followed by the Vaudois of Piedmont; and several Reformed churches united in 1859. German and Scandinavian Lutherans appeared at the end of the nineteenth and the beginning of the twentieth centuries, and Russian Baptists of German origin first disembarked in 1878.

One of the first truly missionary enterprises was undertaken by the Church and Missionary Alliance (CMA) in 1897. Consistent with its general policy, the CMA prioritized those regions lacking evangelical missions, but it also worked in Buenos Aires and Cordoba. The Southern Baptists of the U.S. sent missionaries in 1903, as did the Brethren Assemby in the first years of the twentieth century. Surprisingly, despite several efforts in 1909, the Pentecostals remained relatively few in number until the Second World War. This was in contrast to their much greater engagement in other countries of South America, such as Brazil and Chile.

## Brazil

The largest country of Latin America is also the one that has the greatest mixed-race population. It is a "melting pot" for nearly all the races on the continent: Indians, Portuguese, Africans, Chinese, Japanese, Germans, and others. It was the American Methodists who first attempted missionary work in Brazil in 1830, but obstruction from the authorities did not allow this. In 1855 Doctor Robert Kelley and his wife launched an independent work in Rio de Janeiro. Their mission, Help for Brazil, eventually produced a Congregational church. Opposed by the Catholic clergy, Kelley called on the government to enforce the new constitution, which guaranteed religious liberty. This gave him room to maneuver for the next twenty years.

The Presbyterians arrived in 1859 and by 1888 had established the Igreja Presbiteriana do Brasil (Presbyterian Church of Brazil). They also funded the Makenzie Institute in San Paulo, the only Protestant institution in South America to obtain university status in those years. An independent Presbyterian Church separated from it in 1903 for doctrinal reasons.

Other missions followed. Under the impetus of the minister and future missionary bishop William Taylor, American Methodists began a spiritual and charitable work among the disfavored social classes in the north of Brazil in 1876. This population had had no previous contact with Protestantism, and the work developed slowly. The Protestant Episcopal Church of the United States began to work in the southernmost part of Brazil in 1889. And the Lutheran Evangelical Church of Brazil (part of the Missouri Synod) was established in 1890 when it split off from the Lutheran Evangelical

Church. The new church consisted largely of Germans living in southern Brazil who had first arrived in the middle of the century.

A little after the birth of Pentecostalism in Chile a similar movement appeared among the Italian immigrants of Sao Paulo. Two Swedish Pentecostal ministers, who had come from Chicago in 1910, contributed to the creation of the first Brazilian Pentecostal churches. From this start the movement expanded rapidly but also gave rise over time to a number of dissident movements.

## Paraguay

It was not until 1856 that the first Protestants had access to Paraguay, and as in other South American countries, the first efforts were made by Bible societies. Thirty years later in 1886 a Methodist missionary began to evangelize the land. The New Testament Missionary Union began several communities in 1902, which from the beginning were financed indigenously and without elaborate ecclesial structures. In 1889 Wilfried B. Grubb, an American layman, penetrated the region of Chaco where the Lengua Indians lived, a tribe with so fierce a reputation that even government agents did not dare to approach. Grubb and his several companions learned their language and soon won their friendship, and he developed such influence with them that the Paraguay government gave him the official title *Pacificator de los Indios*. It took Grubb eleven years to master the language, and it was another six before he celebrated the first baptism. In 1910, after twenty-one years among the Lengua, he observed:

> Where formerly it was dangerous for the white man to go without an armed party, anyone can now wander alone and unarmed, so far as any risk from the Indians may be apprehended, over a district larger than Ireland. From out of a chaotic mass of savage heathenism we have now, by the aid of Divine power, the satisfaction of having admitted into the Church of Christ 149 Lenguas, and of this number there are no fewer than thirty-five communicants.[450]

The first Mennonites in Paraguay were refugees who fled Russia after the Bolshevik Revolution of 1917. Sensitive to the needs of the Indians, they appealed to their North American coreligionists to undertake spiritual and medical work among them. The Mennonites became the largest church in the country after the Roman Catholic. The Russian Baptists came in 1920, and German-Russian Mennonites in 1930.

## Uruguay

North American Methodists were, in 1838, the first Protestant missionaries in Uruguay. Their work was interrupted by political troubles that led to a long civil war, but they took up the work again in 1878. Although its numbers remained modest, the Methodist Church produced several of the most remarkable leaders of the country, which was also the case in other countries of Latin America. Other churches also

---

450 Neill, *History*, 391–92.

came. The Iglesia Evangelica Valdese del Rio de la Plata (Vaudoise Church) was established by the first Italian immigrants, who arrived in 1856. For a long time several of their congregations were led by laymen, their first pastor not being ordained until 1877. And U.S. Southern Baptists came from Argentina to Montevideo in 1911. Their progress was slow due to a lack of laborers.

## Bolivia

Bolivia is one of the last South American nations to welcome the permanent presence of Protestant missionaries. The first arrived in 1895 and belonged to the Brethren Assembly. Having strict admission policies, its congregations did not grow quickly. A little later in 1898 Canadian Baptists started an agricultural development project and opened schools, but their projects were neither successful nor were they able to grow the church. In 1901 the Methodist Mission arrived, which devoted itself to education, medical work, and animal husbandry. The Evangelical Mission of the Andes established itself in Bolivia in 1907 and produced the Evangelical Christian Union. It was dedicated above all to the evangelization of the Quechua Indians. Its missionaries were the first to translate the New Testament into the Quechua language, and they prepared ministers in several Bible institutes.

## Chile

Chile and Argentina have the largest proportion of European immigrants among the countries of Latin America. The first Protestant missionary to reside in Chile was David Trumbull, a former chaplain in the American navy who came to Valparaiso in 1845. By 1873 he managed to unite Christians from various ecclesiastical traditions to form the nucleus of the Presbyterian Church. The development of the church, however, was slowed by the difficulty of finding indigenous leaders. The Lutherans, who arrived in 1846, grew faster but almost exclusively among those of German origin.

It was in Chile in 1877 that the Methodist William Taylor[451] introduced the principle of self-supporting missions. He opened schools paid for by the parents of the students and hired laymen who received a poor salary and were expected to find ways to provide for their own needs. This principle, which Taylor later found to be inapplicable in Africa, led to the rapid growth of Methodism in Chile, especially between 1893 and 1907. In 1910, however, the church experienced a division due to differing positions taken on the emergence of Pentecostalism.

Various Baptist churches were founded at the turn of the twentieth century, notably one of German origin in 1892, and other by Southern Baptists in 1917. They also experienced several divisions that, paradoxically, resulted in the Baptist movement being more widespread in the country though reduced in numbers. Some were Pentecostal, and Chile became highly important in the extension of Pentecostalism in South America. (See below.)

---

451 A minister in the Methodist Episcopal Church of the United States, William Taylor enjoyed a fruitful ministry in Latin America and in 1884 was consecrated a "missionary bishop in Africa" (see the sections on Brazil and Peru). He later led a large number of missionaries into the Congo and Angola (cf. pp. 571, 613).

The missionaries Henry Weiss and Albert Dawson applied to the Christian and Missionary Alliance (CMA) in 1896, hoping to contribute to the evangelization of Chile. The CMA, which was just then beginning and had not yet become involved in Latin America, did not accept their offer. Consequently Weiss and Dawson set out as independent missionaries. Due to their success, however, the CMA's mission committee was pleased to integrate them into their work in 1898.

In the nineteenth century the Anglican missionary society in South America chose to work among the Araucanian Indians. At the time of the Spanish conquest of Chile, these tribes had fled to the extreme south of the country and resolutely rejected Catholicism. The Anglicans, however, succeeded in proclaiming the gospel among them, and there were some conversions. The long and demanding work that the Anglicans had undertaken received public approbation from the government on several occasions.

## Peru

Bolivia, Paraguay, Equator, and Peru are the South American nations in which Indian character has been best preserved. The first Methodist missionaries arrived in Peru in 1877, sent by Bishop William Taylor. After an arid period, their work suddenly experienced surprising success in 1891 through the efforts of an agent of the American Bible Society, Francisco Penzotti. He had come in 1888 after having been incarcerated several times.

Missionaries of the Brethren Assembly chose to work in Lima in 1896 and to collaborate with the Regions Beyond Missionary Union, which arrived a little later. By 1907 John Ritchie, an Assembly missionary, enjoyed great success in the expansion of the evangelical movement in Peru throughout the first half of the twentieth century. His principal work was in the distribution of Bibles and Christian books, as well as work in the countryside. The evangelization of the Indians of the eastern coastal regions was undertaken by the South American Indian Mission in 1921, and then in 1946 by the Wycliffe Association, which had access to numerous tribes. In 1925 the CMA established itself in Huanuco in a mountainous region that no Protestant mission had yet visited, and in 1930 the CMA added the capital, Lima, to its field of work.

## Ecuador

Three missionaries of the Gospel Missionary Union (GMU) arrived in Ecuador in 1896 and were the first Protestants to establish a permanent missionary presence. Eloy Alfaro, the new strong man of the country, was a liberal who promulgated a new constitution. This led to the breaking of the concordat with the Holy Sea, which until then had been the principal obstacle to the work of the American Bible Society[452] and the entry into the country of Protestant missionaries. The Methodists had been unsuccessful in establishing themselves there in 1877. The GMU attempted to minister among a diverse number of Indians, especially the Jivaros of Amazonia and the Quechua of the Andes, among whom numerous conversions took place. In 1897 the CMA

---

452 Penzotti, of the American Bible Society, forbade the unloading of a cargo of Bibles in Guayaquil in 1888. He wrote to the government: "The Bible will not enter Ecuador as long as this regime is in place."

also began to work among Indian groups in the eastern coastal regions and in the Sierra Mountains in the northeast of the country. This was the CMA's first mission field in Latin America.

Clarence W. Jones sought authorization to establish a missionary radio station in several countries of Latin America. Finally in 1930 he received permission from the Congress of Equator to broadcast from Quito. On Christmas day 1931 The Voice of the Andes (HCJB) broadcast its first message from a station close to the capital that had a 250-watt transmitter. On Easter day 1940, President Andres Cordova of Equator inaugurated a new transmitter that had ten thousand watts. Due to the mountains surrounding Quito, a 3,200-meter antenna was set up. Soon letters were addressed to the station from all over South America and from as far away as Russia, Japan, India, and New Zealand. This correspondence witnessed to the fine reception that the message enjoyed on practically the entire surface of the planet.

## Colombia

Colombia is the South American nation most marked by Spanish influence, and it was here that the Protestant missionaries suffered much from the Catholic clergy. The Presbyterian Church from the United States sent missionaries to Bogotá as early as 1856, and its missionaries were the only ones working in the country until the end of the century. Through their accomplishments in the areas of sanitation and education, they won the respect of the government and the general population. The Presbyterian Church enjoyed only modest growth, but it was engaged in numerous activities and succeeded in training a number of local leaders.

Missions that were already active in neighboring countries entered Colombia during the first years of the twentieth century: The Evangelical Alliance Mission (TEAM) in 1906, the Gospel Missionary Union (GMU) in 1908, and the Christian and Missionary Alliance (CMA) in 1923. The latter devoted itself primarily to the distribution of the gospel in print.

## Venezuela

The first Protestant congregation was established in Venezuela in 1883 by the members of the Brethren Assembly. It began to grow quickly in 1910, becoming one of the principal Protestant denominations of the country. The Pentecostals of the Asambleas de Dios in Venezuela, however, appeared in 1916 and quickly became the largest Protestant church in the country. In contrast the Iglesia Presbiteriana formed by the American Presbyterian missionaries in 1897 experienced slow growth. The Evangelical Free Church Association began in 1898 but then was restarted in 1920 by an independent couple. The church collaborated with The Evangelical Alliance Mission (TEAM), which had been in the country since 1906. TEAM set up a printing press in 1907 and founded a journal, *La Estella de la Manana* (The Morning Star), which was distributed throughout Latin America.

## British Guiana (Present-day Guyana)

Until the beginning of the nineteenth century Guiana was under Dutch domination together with its neighbor Surinam. Protestant missions developed there sooner than in the Spanish colonies. As early as 1743 Lutherans from the Netherlands were present, and in 1766 the Scottish Presbyterians also appeared. Both denominations were established in the country but without direct missionary participation. Two other mission societies deserve mention. The London Missionary Society began work there in 1807. Its missionaries were Anglicans, and the church that they founded at Georgetown in 1810 later embraced the emerging Anglo-Catholic tradition and maintained close contact with the Roman Catholic Church. Also, Canadian Presbyterians founded the Guiana Presbyterian Church in 1885.

## Dutch Guiana (Present-day Suriname)

In 1875 Dutch Guiana became one of the first mission fields undertaken by the Moravian Brethren (see p. 270). The Reformed and the Dutch Lutherans also established churches there in 1750 and 1751 respectively. The Lutherans included among their members a good number of Creoles, while the Reformed Church attracted mostly European colonists. The Wesleyans engaged in evangelism in the country in 1920 and the Salvation Army in 1926.

## French Guiana

France was active in the eastern section of the Guianas at the beginning of the seventeenth century, but it was only in 1677 that it obtained confirmation of its rights, which were previously contested by the Dutch and British. In 1852 the French made Guiana into a penal colony that became commonly know as Devil's Island. During the Second Empire, eighteen thousand convicts were sent there. The first Protestant missionary in Guyana was a French minister over sixty years old. Responding to a call for ministers made by Ruben Saillens in an evangelical journal, he disembarked at Cayenne and worked for several years among the convicts and "relegated," freed prisoners who were nonetheless required to live in Guiana for the remainder of their lives.

Charles Péan (1901–1991), an officer of the Salvation Army, later made numerous visits to Guiana beginning in 1928. In his book *Terre de Bagne* (Prison *Land*), written in 1930, he succeeded in stirring popular opinion against the use of the island as a prison, which resulted in its being closed down in 1945. The Salvation Army then played a large role in reintroducing the former convicts into society.

In 1928 M. Large, a missionary of the British Brethren Assembly, undertook a ministry among the convicts of Saint-Laurent du Maroni. He settled near Cayenne and began to gather a small group of sympathizers in the shop of M. Parris, a shoemaker. He was expelled after several years, accused of helping several convicts to escape.[453] In 1932 Anna-Magdalena Lanicca, a language professor from Switzerland, joined the Large family as an instructor. After the departure of the Larges, she at-

---

453 Though Large was able to produce evidence of his innocence he was not allowed to return to Guyana.

tended meetings of the Evangelical Assembly and, with the help of other Christians, created the House of Emmanuel for abandoned children. In 1947 her work was taken up by Willy and Elisabeth Moret, a young couple from Aubonne sent by Assemblées évangéliques de la Suisse Romande (Assemblies of French-speaking Switzerland). At that time French Guiana became one of the church's principal fields of work.

# CENTRAL AMERICA

## Mexico

The American Bible Society dispatched an agent in 1824 to distribute Bibles in Mexico, but all proselytism was forbidden by law. According to President Guadalupe Victoria (1786–1843), "the demands of religious tolerance were not concordant with the Mexican constitution . . . and would not be accepted by the Mexican people." When the Indian Benito Juarez took power by force of arms in 1856 and promulgated a liberal constitution, the Catholic Church opposed it so vehemently that the government adopted an anticlerical policy in 1860. The government returned to these policies with renewed vigor in 1910, an approach that also limited the activities of the Protestant missions and churches. Between 1926 and 1935, nearly three hundred Catholic priests were martyred.[454]

As noted above, Juarez encouraged the contribution of Protestant missionaries. Between 1862 and 1870, two American Baptist missions founded several mission stations, and the American Board established itself at Monterrey and Guadalajara. The American Presbyterians entered Mexico in 1872, forming the Presbyterian Synod of Mexico in 1901. The Methodists appeared in 1873, and an autonomous Methodist Church of Mexico emerged in 1930. In 1880 Mexico became the first Latin American country to receive Southern Baptists.

The multiplication of Protestant missions was thwarted for a period of about twenty years by the antireligious laws of 1910. This brake on missionary action did not prevent certain evangelical and Protestant churches from experiencing strong growth—notably the Pentecostals.

## Guatemala

The Presbyterian Church in the U.S.A. arrived in Guatemala in 1882 at the request of President Justo Rufino Barrios. It was his hope that Protestantism would become a positive factor in the economic development and social progress of the country. The mission of the Primitive Methodist Church collaborated with the Presbyterians in 1921, launching the Quiché Bible Institute in San Cristobal. Their intention was to increase the work of evangelization among the Quiché Indians.

Congregational minister C.I. Scofield[455] founded the Central American Mission in 1890 as a faith mission. He arrived in Guatemala in 1899, and by 1927 the mission

---

454 Graham Green, *The Power and the Glory*, (London: Heinemann, 1940).

455 Scofield is best known for the reference Bible that bears his name, but his work in the evangelization of Central America is often overlooked. The first missionary of the Central American Mission was William McDonnell, who came to Costa Rica in 1891.

succeeded in establishing the Iglesia Evangelica Centroamericana as an autonomous institution.

The Pentecostal movement appeared in 1916, eventually producing the Full Gospel Tabernacle Church; and the Assemblies of God entered the country in 1937. As in most other Latin American countries, Pentecostalism rapidly became the dominant Protestant movement in the nation.

## Honduras

The most important missionary work in Honduras was that of the Central American Mission, which first arrived in the country in 1896. Methodist missionaries, however, were there as early as 1860. The other missions, notably that of the Quakers, began to arrive in the first years of the twentieth century. An Evangelical Church was established in 1920, and the Moravian Church in 1930. It was only in 1937 that the first missionaries of the Assemblies of God entered in the country, arriving from El Salvador.

## El Salvador

As with Honduras, the Central American Mission arrived in El Salvador in 1896 and became one of the principal Protestant missions. The Church of God, headquartered in Cleveland, soon followed, and then came the American Baptists and Seventh-day Adventists. The Assemblies of God appeared in 1922 and enjoyed rapid growth, becoming the largest Protestant denomination in the country though still smaller than the Roman Catholic Church.

## Nicaragua

In 1849 the German Moravian Mission undertook the work of evangelizing the Mosquito Indians along the eastern coast of Nicaragua. It established several schools and a Bible institute. The Central American Mission, present in the neighboring countries, sent missionaries to Nicaragua in 1900 but experienced slow growth. Assemblies of God missionaries came in 1936 and built on the foundations laid by the Independent Pentecostals who had come in 1912. The American Baptist Mission picked up the work in 1923 that had been initiated some years earlier by an independent Baptist missionary. The mission engaged in educational and medical work, establishing, for example, a school for nurses. The work of the various Baptist missions as well as other churches eventually produced the National Baptist Convention, whose work enjoyed a remarkable scope over the years.

## Costa Rica

A small country that at the end of the nineteenth century had a population of only about 300,000, Costa Rica was pleased to welcome a large number of black immigrants from the Antilles. Various Antillean churches and missions sent missionaries to work among this immigrant population. Among the sending organizations were the Baptist Missionary Society of Jamaica, which arrived in 1887, and the Baptist Convention of the Caribbean, which received help from the British Baptist Mission to undertake the work of evangelism. The first North American missionaries to arrive were sent by the Central American Mission in 1891. Others soon followed: the Methodists in 1917, Pentecostal missionaries who organized the Assemblies of God in 1932, and other Pentecostal groups still later.

## Panama

Methodist immigrants from the Caribbean came to Panama as early as 1815. Between 1855 and 1900, thirty thousand freedmen from several Antillean islands settled as farmers in the interior of the land. In 1882 the Methodist Synod of Jamaica decided to send ministers to care for their coreligionists. Baptists and Anglicans of the SPG also sent ministers several years later.

With the aid of the United States, Panama broke off from Colombia in 1903 and became an independent nation. A number of American missionary societies then seized the opportunity to send missionaries to Panama: the Salvation Army in 1904; the Methodists, the Church of God, and the Seventh-day Adventists in 1905; and carrying forward the work of the SPG, the Episcopal Church of the United States in 1906. Following the First World War, a number of Pentecostal missions arrived, the first being the International Church of the Foursquare Gospel in 1927.

# THE ANTILLES

## Cuba

In 1512, just twenty years after Christopher Columbus discovered the New World, Dominican priests arrived in Cuba. The Anglicans were the first to celebrate Protestant religious services on the island in 1741, but it was not until 1871 that a minister of the Episcopal Church of the United States was able to settle in Cuba. This church, however, included only British and North American immigrants. Its efforts to reach out to the general population were thwarted by the American Civil War and then by the Spanish-American War, which saw the defeat and expulsion of the Spanish in 1898.

During this troubled time, Cuban refugees in Florida were evangelized by the Methodists, and two among them returned to Havana as missionaries in 1873. The Baptist Convention sent Cuban exiles back into their country in 1883 as Bible colporteurs. With the end of the conflict in Cuba in 1898, the Methodists built some of the best schools on the island as well as several dispensaries in rural regions. The American Presbyterians arrived in 1898 and continued the work begun in 1884 by a Cuban who had formed several Presbyterian congregations. Congregationalist and Disciples of Christ missionaries arrived in Cuba respectively in 1909 and 1918. Their churches were eventually merged into the Presbyterian Synod.

## Jamaica

Jamaica is not part of Latin America as its official language is English. Apart from several small islands colonized by the Danish, Dutch, and British, Jamaica is also the only state of Central America with a Protestant majority. Discovered by Columbus, Catholic missionaries worked there during the first half of the sixteenth century. The

British supplanted the Spanish in 1655, and an Anglican church was then established, intended for British nationals. The Quakers were the pioneer Protestant evangelists, arriving in 1671. The Moravians came in 1754, and the Methodists in 1789.

The first Baptist missionary was the Virginia freedman George Lisle, who came to Kingston in 1783. He formed a church comprised mostly of slaves but also of a minority of indigenous Indians. The Baptist Missionary Society (founded by William Carey in 1792) was called in to help in 1813. The fruit of their efforts was the Jamaica Baptist Union, which became autonomous in 1842. Remarkably, the Baptist Missionary Society of Jamaica was established in the same year that the church became independent. It immediately sent freedmen as missionaries into Fernando Po and Cameroon, where their efforts were crucial in founding churches in these places (see p. 546). As noted above, this society also sent missionaries to Costa Rica in 1887. Later it also sent missionaries to Panama.

The Salvation Army began to work there in 1887, and other missions also came before the end of the century. In 1900, out of a population of about 720,000, 39 percent were Anglicans, and 35 percent belonged to various other Protestant communities.

The Church of God, located in Cleveland, sent the first Pentecostal missionaries to the island in 1917. They began a church that in the course of the twentieth century became the largest Protestant denomination on the island.

## Haiti

The island of Hispaniola, discovered by Columbus in 1492, became a Spanish colony. After various politico-military events, the French seized it but were later themselves expelled due to the revolution led by Jean-Jacques Dessalines, a descendant of African slaves. He proclaimed a republic in 1803, but soon the Spanish and French reoccupied the island, holding the east and west sides respectively. The reunification that followed independence in 1822 was only provisional. In 1844 the western part became the republic of Haiti with French as the official language. (The eastern part became the Dominican Republic. See below.) The majority of the population, however, was African or biracial people who spoke Creole.

The British Methodists sent the first two Protestant missionaries in 1807, and they evangelized the numerous English-speaking blacks who had come to Haiti as escaped slaves. After eleven years they were expelled but not before one of them managed to reduce the Creole language into written form. The literature that he furnished the Haitians allowed thousands among them to learn to read and write. The church they established became the oldest Protestant church in Haiti and made up a large part of the intellectual and social elite of the country. Unfortunately, many of its members emigrated to the United States or Europe. While these events were unfolding, the Episcopal Church of Haiti was founded by a black American in 1861.

Various Baptists missions began to arrive in 1823, but the results of their efforts were meager except for the establishment of the Baptist Convention of Haiti. A century later, during the American occupation from 1915 to 1934, the American Baptist mission evangelized the island with much greater success and provided training for indigenous ministers that was generally superior to that of other Protestant denominations. During the 1930s, a variety of Pentecostal missions also founded churches.

## Dominican Republic

A British Methodist minister arrived in 1834 to work among the English-speaking blacks, but his efforts were not followed up until early in the twentieth century. This made the Dominican Republic one of the last countries of Latin America to welcome Protestant missionaries. In 1907 the Free Methodist Church (from the U.S.) continued the ministry begun by an independent missionary about fifteen years earlier. The Protestant churches of Puerto Rico joined the meager effort to evangelize the country in 1911. Faced with a dearth of missionaries, the Methodists and Presbyterians founded the Committee of Christian Action in 1920, which later included the Moravians. The church born from this interdenominational effort was the Iglesia Evangelica Dominicana, which became independent in 1953. A Puerto Rican Pentecostal evangelist settled in the capital, Saint Domingue, in 1933, and responsibility for the work he had begun was undertaken by the Assemblies of God in 1941.

## Puerto Rico

The Spanish, who landed on the island in 1493, were expelled from it as a result of the Spanish-American War in 1898. This opened the island to Protestant missions, and six principal denominations responded to the challenge between 1899 and 1900. The Methodists undertook the work of expanding and developing education, while the Seventh-day Adventists, who arrived in 1909, focused largely on medical work. The Presbyterians, who were the first to arrive, benefited from the work accomplished by a businessman of the Reformed confession who, in 1860, had settled in the eastern part of the island. They constructed a well-equipped hospital in 1904 and began to develop a nondenominational theological college that was inaugurated in 1919. Some of the churches that were the fruit of these missionary efforts decided in 1931 to form the United Evangelical Church of Puerto Rico. Pentecostalism came to Puerto Rico in 1916, brought by a Puerto Rican who had been converted in Hawaii where he had gone to find work. A number of Pentecostal organizations were able to grow quickly on the island.

Thanks especially to the quality of the educational institutions that it was adept at creating, Protestantism trained an elite in the country, which allowed it to be represented at all levels of Puerto Rican society and government.

## Guadeloupe and Martinique

These two islands of the Antilles were originally Spanish but in 1946 became French. Columbus discovered Guadeloupe in 1493 and Martinique in 1503. Due to the resistance of the Caribbean Indians, the Spanish decided not to attempt to colonize these territories. On Guadeloupe, the first Catholic missionaries were killed by the native population in 1523. In the seventeenth century Dominican, Capuchin, Jesuit, Carmelite, and other missionaries returned to Guadeloupe and Martinique. On both islands

Catholicism remained strongly mixed with ancestral African beliefs. French commercial companies established themselves in Martinique in 1635.

In the seventeenth-century Guadeloupe (and perhaps also Martinique) had a Reformed community composed of colonists, but this later disappeared. In the end, the aboriginal population entirely disappeared and was replaced by slaves brought from Africa. In the following century, the Moravians attempted to evangelize Guadeloupe while working in various islands of the Antilles. They succeeded in producing a short-lived Christian community. The Protestant churches currently present on these islands are of recent origin. The Seventh-day Adventists sent missionaries in 1924 to Martinique, but the work of establishing Evangelical and Pentecostal churches did not begin until after the Second World War. The latter groups experienced rapid growth.

## THE RISE OF PENTECOSTALISM

In surveying the history of Protestant missions in the nations of South and Central America during the first third of the twentieth century, the contribution of Pentecostal missionaries has been mentioned in almost every instance. The Pentecostals were able to establish churches quickly and often, and generally their congregations were the largest within the wider Protestant community. It is appropriate, therefore, to examine further the birth of this Latin American "Pentecostal phenomenon," which has a missional dimension.

Pentecostalism appeared at the beginning of the twentieth century and was a new element in the heart of Latin American Protestantism. It was a religious movement at variance with historic Protestantism and had a strong appeal to underprivileged classes. It appeared for the first time on the continent at Valparaiso, Chile, between 1902 and 1910. While it manifested strong Latin American cultural traits, it also had affinities to the revival movements that had appeared a short time before in California and Wales. There were supernatural signs, trances, visions, exorcisms, and miraculous healings. The same phenomena appeared several years later at the other end of Latin America, among the rural migrant workers of north Mexico. They also appeared at this time in Sao Paulo, Brazil, among the Italian immigrants newly arrived from the United States. The historic churches dismissed Pentecostal behavior as irrational, contrary to the Scriptures, and attributable to excitement and fanaticism. The relationship between these two types of Protestantism was conflicted from the beginning.

Jean Pierre Bastian describes these two expressions of South American Protestantism in these words:

> The first, forged in the societies of thought from radical liberalism, considered Protestantism as an individual and social instrument of regeneration through education. Hence, it created a religious and political avant-garde that was supposed to contribute, in the long run, to the transformation of the peoples . . . according to the norms of the earlier Protestant Reformation . . .

In contrast, the schismatic religious movement that arose in Chile and would soon spread throughout the continent was not interested in propagating a democratic culture and educating the masses. It showed itself, rather, to be a religion of the oppressed . . . It was a denunciation and judgment of the elites for their inability to communicate and appeal to the people . . . Though a popular religion of Protestant inspiration, it was rooted in an oral tradition that would supplant [traditional] Protestantism and change the power relationships at the heart of Latin American religion.[456]

From the start, Pentecostalism experienced spectacular growth throughout Latin America.[457] Traditional Protestantism on the continent, which was rooted in immigrant communities and attributable to the work of American missions, tended to be highly structured and was associated with interdenominational and federative organizations. Pentecostalism, in contrast, enjoyed an unguided and protean proliferation. Among Pentecostals, only the Assemblies of God organized itself in networks. The others tended to remain limited to a single region, and their growth was often due to several inspired preachers whose influence in the area sometimes seemed beyond all control.

The Pentecostal movement quickly encountered much success among the destitute who seemed to gather on the edges of the great cities. They were often migrant Indians or biracial in origin, whom poverty had driven from the countryside. Theologically they were Protestants in that they emphasized the inspiration of the Bible, interpreted it literally, objected to Roman Catholic traditions and rites, and practiced an ecclesiology centered on the local community. At the same time, the movement was rooted in the indigenous religious culture. It was attractive to many because of its miraculous signs and wonders and because of its similarities to traditional Latin American religions. Pentecostalism permitted an emotional expressiveness that was typically Latin American and had a popular appeal that historic Protestantism, which seemed to be more suited to the declining elite, was incapable of matching.

---

456 Bastian, op. cit., 135–37.

457 For example, the Assemblies of God in Brazil had 14,000 members in 1930; 120,000 in 1950; and 950,000 in 1965. In Chile, where the movement began, the Pentecostals were a third of the 62,000 Protestants in 1929. By 1961 they counted more than 500,000 members, four times more than all the other Protestants combined.

# SECTION VI
## CONCLUDING POINTS

# CHAPTER 31

# *Protestant Mission and Colonization*

It is frequently said that Christian missions in the nineteenth and twentieth centuries benefited from colonization. According to some, not only did they do nothing to combat colonialism, but they opened the way for it, either willingly or otherwise. The history of missions can not avoid this question. But all simplistic responses are partial and undoubtedly biased. Colonization took different forms according to the periods, places, and policies of the colonizer. The missionaries themselves did not have the same sensibilities as they faced this problem. Their responses depended in part on their theological views about the relationship between church and state. They were also influenced by their nationalities: for example, they might be hostile to colonization if the colonizer were of a different nationality, did not trust them, and treated them as foreigners. Finally, attitudes changed over time as the effects of colonization became more apparent. We will limit ourselves to general remarks and the highlighting of key facts that will shed light on a subject already touched on in several places in the text.

## COLONIALISM AND THE MISSIONAL CHURCH

The modern colonial era took shape in the course of the nineteenth century and continued a little beyond the middle of the twentieth century. Its initial form consisted of the establishment of temporary commercial trading posts on the coasts of Africa and Asia. As these became more profitable, they became permanent and the colonizers began to insert themselves far into the interior of the lands, sometimes engaging in police efforts against slavery or to secure exclusive rights to minerals or other local products. Once begun, colonization was not easily confined.

The Congress of Berlin, which began at the end of 1884 and continued into 1885, might be compared to the Yalta talks of the Big Three after the Second World War. It made a modern form of colonization official in Africa. The European powers agreed to renounce territorial disputes and operate only within their own zones of influence; hence, the influence of a colonizer was to stop at the borders of the neighboring colonies. Moreover, no part of Africa was to be under the sovereignty of traditional African powers, and frontiers were to be clearly demarcated, sometimes without regard for the languages and ethnic groupings of the people directly concerned. Europe behaved as though it owned Africa and had every right to confer upon it "the benefits of civilization," to use the chant of the period.

As realpolitik rarely mixes well with philanthropy, it was inevitable that the ambitions of the colonizers would often be at odds with the interests of the colonized. At times even the progress of local populations was feared as this could increase the people's self-confidence and decrease their docility. A fundamental difference in attitudes was given expression by Victor Augagneur, the French governor of Madagascar in the first years of the twentieth century. In a reply to a Protestant missionary protesting against the methods employed by the colonial administration, Augagneur said, "What we want is to make the indigenous people into manual laborers, and you missionaries want to make them into men!"[458]

The mixed motives of the colonizers did not prevent some positive achievements, especially in the areas of medicine and education. Colonization also worked to pacify regions long embroiled in ethnic conflicts. And of course there were many colonial administrators, civil servants, and military personnel who acted admirably and in the interests of the local people.

It is no longer politic today to praise the era of colonization, which makes it all the more imperative to be mindful that at the time for Westerners of goodwill this was not a scandalous or shameful period of history. Our role here is not to tabulate the balance sheet for colonization, justifying or condemning it. Rather, we will try to understand how missional Christians envisioned it then.

The era of colonization and the height of the great age of missions coincided in time, and few would say that this was a mere chronological coincidence. Would Christian missions have been as far-reaching as they were without colonization? This seems difficult to imagine. Nonetheless, the tremendous momentum of religious revivalism that opened the period of the modern mission movement closely preceded the century of colonization in Africa. Also missionary pioneers envisioned the relationship between Europe and the countries of the Global South (to employ a modern term) in a way often very different from that of the politicians and business leaders of the time. Knowing their own history, they were aware that during the first three centuries of the Christian era, the gospel would not have spread as quickly as it did without the *Pax Romana*. That the peace imposed by Rome is generally recognized by Christians as a part of the *praeparatio evangelica* and a disposition of Providence does not justify the crimes committed by the Roman Empire in the name of conquest, as Saint Augustine argued in his magisterial *City of God*. Moreover, it is undeniable that the Christianization of Europe was accelerated by the political support it received from Emperor Constantine in the fourth century and by the brutal conquests of Charlemagne in Northern Europe five centuries later. This past has bequeathed to Christian European an ambiguous legacy that has tainted the subsequent history of

---

458 Maurice Leenhardt, "Les missions protestantes françaises," in *Protestantisme français*, ed. Marc Boegner (Paris: Plon, 1945), 391.

the church. Hence the relationship between colonization and mission is not without analog within the history of the West.

The motivation of missionaries in the colonial period was both religious and spiritual. Yet to the extent that they incarnated the gospel as flesh and blood human beings, they were not able to disassociate themselves or the message from their material, social, and cultural circumstances. They cared for the sick through modern medical science; they improved farming through modern irrigation techniques; they constructed clean and sturdy houses by the standards of the West; and they taught literacy while helping whole cultures to make the transition from the oral to the written stage of development. In effect, they intervened in the lives of whole populations to make profound changes. The results were eminently positive, but they were also tremendously disruptive to the cultural identity of peoples and their long-term effects cannot be measured. Were the missionaries the shock troops of cultural imperialism or incarnate witnesses to the gospel?

Two contradictory accusations are often made against mission. Sometimes it is reproached for being interested only in the destiny of souls and preaching about the life beyond, while neglecting the material and social life and the realities of the here and now. On the other hand, it is often also accused of introducing foreign values into local cultures by intervening in various "worldly" areas: teaching, medical care, agricultural techniques, and others. These interventions, it is said, are far from being culturally neutral for the historical developments that allowed their emergence in the West were based on very different values from those of traditional non-Western cultures.

The proclamation of the gospel is inevitably challenging to traditional worldviews. The biblical worldview, for example, leads cultures to approach reality in ways totally different from those associated with animism. The desacralization of nature and the rejection of a magical understanding of cause and effect in nature are not so much a product of Western thought as they are the implications of a biblical understanding of the world and history. Some analogous remarks could also be made in comparing the Christian worldview with those held in Hindu, Buddhist, and Islamic societies. Western civilization, of course, is not a pure product of Christianity, but it is an amalgam in which centuries of Christendom have had an effect. None of this should be understood to excuse insensitivity on the part of Christian missionaries to the value of the ancestral traditions of the people they evangelized, nor does it excuse disrespect for the "savages" and the lack of interest shown in understanding the reasons for their behavior.

Colonization developed in a particular historical context.[459] On one hand, Europe benefited from long centuries of progress in multiple areas due to a rich Greco-Roman and Judeo-Christian heritage. Following more than a millennium of Christian civilization, the Renaissance, Enlightenment, and Industrial Revolution produced an increase in knowledge and riches that was self-sustaining and continuously ex-

---

459 We are concerned here with the colonization of Africa. In the confrontation with Asian civilizations, the problem cannot be posed in the same terms.

panding. On the other hand, Africa was long deprived of a Christian worldview and suffered from difficulties in communications due to low population levels. It was also beset with high mortality rates due to the harsh climate and endemic diseases, and it was weakened by the hemorrhaging of the population due to the slave trade. The ineluctable collision of these two civilizations inevitably threatened the more vulnerable one. Even Westerners of goodwill and generous spirit often saw themselves as the representatives of a superior civilization, an attitude that was generally manifested as a benevolent paternalism. Moreover, the writing of some of the most dedicated and humble pioneer missionaries can sometimes appear shocking today.

Nonetheless, in every period of history God has raised up prophets and protesters against the majority view. Though contested and judged subversive, these prophetic voices were well informed about what was happening in the field, and their message was common among the missionaries of the colonial period. David Bosch writes:

> It is simply inadequate to contend that mission was nothing other than the spiritual side of imperialism and always the faithful servant of the latter. Reality was more ambivalent . . . Throughout the history of mission, there has always been a persistent minority which, admittedly within limits, withstood the political imposition of the West on the rest of the world.[460]

However, the missionaries of the colonial period were not all heroes, prophets, or *avant-garde* ethnologists. They were confronted with disease, poverty, depression, isolation, tribal conflicts, and xenophobic populations. In this context they sometimes sought to make their work less difficult and more effective by using the colonial structures that were readily available to them. Who among us, then, will cast the first stone? Moreover, as European Christians of the colonial period were not impervious to the thoughts and prejudices of their time neither were the missionaries.[461] People in all ages—even our own—are products of their time. Therefore we should not judge our predecessors by modern standards, especially as those standards are greatly indebted to the mistakes of the past from which we benefit by hindsight. Finally, we should remember that one day we too will be judged by our successors, a consideration that should give us pause before making hasty judgments.

Before considering the attitude of the principal colonizing countries towards mission, it should be remembered that Christian missions preceded the colonial era and even the Iberian conquests of the fifteenth and sixteenth centuries. Christianity, in fact, has been missionary from its first days. The first Christians themselves lived

---

460 Bosch, *Transforming Mission*, 310.

461 The Dutch missiologist H. Kraemer wrote in his famous work *The Christian Message in a Non-Christian World*: "Most Western Christians, like most human beings, are incapable of escaping the cultural, mental, and social framework to which they are accustomed and in which they usually have to express their religious life. Hence they consider their own theological methods or the forms of their ecclesial and cultural life to be as fitting for the Christians of Africa and Asia as for themselves. This is a grave mistake. But, while denouncing it, one should remember that it is very rare to encounter human beings capable of forgetting themselves and effectively transposing the best of their lives into any other cultural and social forms other than their own. The difficulty is congenital and semi-biological." Translated into French in *La lumière des nations* (Neuchâtel: Delachaux & Niestlé, 1944), 74.

under the tyranny of a colonial power, and they reached out to evangelize that power. In its faithfulness to Christ, the church has always been missionary, even in the times when, far from being supported by governments, it was persecuted.

In antiquity and in the Middle Ages, mission was not the sole prerogative of the European churches. African Christianity during antiquity—before Islamization—reached into the interior of the continent with missionaries, particularly along the valley of the Nile. Syro-Persian Christianity was also missionary in the first millennium, reaching out to the Indies and as far as China and Mongolia, and establishing churches that continued to spread and grow over the centuries. It is the Eurocentrism of much of church history that has hidden the existence of non-Western and non-Roman Christian missions from popular view. Book I of this volume gives much evidence for this point of view.

Lesslie Newbigin's historical analysis sheds light on the reasons for the false identification of Christianity with Western civilization, a misunderstanding that ill served Western missionaries as they came into contact with other cultures:

> The rise of Islam and the consolidation of its power right across North Africa and the Middle East had the effect of isolating Western Christendom from any real contact with the ancient cultures of India and the Far East, and from the peoples of Sub-Saharan Africa. The Eastern Churches, except for that of Russia, found themselves in the position of tolerated minorities that could exist only by refraining from challenging the faith of Islam. Christianity was the folk religion of a diminishing minority of the world's peoples, squeezed into a smaller and smaller part of the western peninsula and islands of the Eurasian continent . . . To put it in one sentence, the Church had become the religious department of European society rather than the task force selected and appointed for a world mission . . . During the last few centuries, the vision of a world missionary task has been recovered, and in the nineteenth and twentieth centuries the Church has become for the first time a worldwide community.[462]

## THE PARIS MISSION AND COLONIZATION

> The colonial enterprise and the crimes that it legitimates will in a brief time produce the moral decline of some of the people who were until now walking at the forefront of civilization. The human conscience will eventually so cauterize itself that finally all excesses will become possible.[463]

The words are those of the Reverend Tommy Fallot (1844–1904), an ardent supporter of the Paris Mission and a great figure in the social reform movements of the nineteenth century. Fallot also denounced the horrors of war, and spoken ten years

---

462 Lesslie Newbigin, *Honest Religion for Secular Man* (Philadelphia: Westminster, 1966), 102–3.
463 Roux, *Mission*, 167–68.

before the beginning of the First World War, his words were prophetic. They were a rare protest in a time when colonization was a source of pride for those who considered themselves to be the benefactors of the "uncivilized."

Jean Bianquis, the Secretary General of the Paris Mission, was another discordant and moving voice of the time. He wrote in 1906:

> The fact of colonial conquest places before the conscience a singularly sensitive question. On the European continent, we readily protest against the right of conquest, but the day will surely come when our consciences, grown more sensitive, will raise up this same protest on behalf of countries overseas . . .[464] We will have accomplished all the duties we owe to the indigenous populations of our colonies only on that faraway day when we will have made them our equals in liberty.[465]

In 1822, during the period when the Paris Mission was established, there was a revival movement sweeping through much of the Western world. The international character of the movement was reflected in the composition of the directing committee of the Paris Mission, in the variety of students in the House of Missions, and in the makeup of the missionary bodies in Lesotho and Zambezi where Swiss and Italians from the Piemont were in the majority.

French Protestantism, long persecuted by a royal totalitarianism, was ready to put liberty and respect for the human person at the head of its moral and political values. The historian André Roux has written: "It is well understood that in France the climate was marked by a Protestant sensibility . . . And that Protestant opinion willingly took a position against the colonial power in order to defend indigenous societies whose situation reminded them of their own past."[466] After ten years of reticence, the Paris Mission finally decided to assume responsibility for Madagascar from the British but refused to introduce into the island "the wagons of the colonizer." The same hesitation can be detected with regard to Gabon.

It was French Protestantism's evangelical element, later joined by the liberals, on the committee of the Paris Mission that opposed the mixing of mission and colonization. Léon Pilatte, the editor of the periodical *L'Église Libre*, defended this position in the August 1886 issue of his review. In summarizing the article, J.-F. Zorn observed that Pilatte "questioned the new fashion of pleading the cause of mission in the church by appealing to patriotism. He believed that the Macedonian call was abused when it was used by the French government to support colonialism with self-interested appeals: "'Come over to help us in Tunisia, Gabon, Madagascar, the Congo;

---

464 A seventeenth-century Dutch merchant made a similar remark concerning the Indonesians: "We must recognize that they fight for the liberty of their country even as we ourselves have for so long fought with all our strength for ours." Cited by C. L. Van Doorn, in *Les églises chrétiennes et la décolonisation*, ed. Marcel Merle (Paris: Armand Colin, 1967), 335.

465 Roux, op. cit., 168.

466 André Roux, "Les protestants français," in Merle, op. cit., 219.

and,moreover, help us to complete and consolidate our conquests!' . . . A door opened by the government is not necessarily a door opened by God."[467]

In its earliest years the Paris Mission was engaged in Lesotho, a region that was not subject to European sovereignty or under its protection. Later, French missionaries counseled the Lesotho king to seek a British protectorate in order to avoid having the kingdom fall under Boer domination.[468] This was 1843 when the goal of colonization was to free Africans not proceed to the occupation of their lands, as it would be at the end of the century.

Apart from some coastal trading posts, at this time France's presence in Africa was limited to Algeria where it forbade all proselytism. Following the Congress of Berlin, France occupied vast regions in western and equatorial Africa. A number of French Protestant organizations believed that it was now their responsibility to evangelize these lands. When Zambia came under British control, French Protestants declined to go there and even proposed leaving Lesotho to British missionaries. In effect, the limited resources of French Protestantism were to be concentrated in French colonies. But the committee of the Paris Mission set aside these considerations, refusing to abandon mission fields that it had entered and churches that it had established.

Roger Holland, pastor of the Free Churches and a member of the committee in 1900, affirmed: "My response will be simple: We cannot abandon our noncolonial missions [those outside the French colonial system], for then we would be unfaithful to the spirit of the society. The church of Jesus Christ is not a national society."[469] The committee's missions that lay outside the French system, he added, show everyone that the object of the Paris Mission is subject to no man or national flag but to our Lord Jesus Christ. The mission work of the well-known Baptist minister and evangelist Ruben Saillens was undertaken with the same commitment to God, not country.[470]

The relations between French Protestant missions and French colonialism were not above acrimony and conflict, which explains at least in part why the movement to abandon colonialism in France was led by Protestants. André Roux concluded in 1963: "Altogether, French Protestantism found itself impelled by its spirituality and history to promote the movement to accelerate the process of decolonization and emancipation of the subject peoples that began in 1945."[471]

## THE ATTITUDE OF PROTESTANT MISSIONS TOWARD OTHER COUNTRIES

Due to their history and the places where their missionaries were engaged, did French Protestants have a more critical attitude about colonization than their coreligionists of other Western nations? To respond, we must examine the activities of several

---

467 Zorn, *Missions protestantes*, 90. The italics indicate Pilatte's words.

468 This may be one of the causes of the French government's hesitation to allow British Protestant missions in their colonies. Moreover, in 1900 the French allied themselves with the Boers in their conflict with Britain.

469 R. Hollard, *Missions colonials et missions noncolonials* (Paris: Report to the Conference to the Auxiliary Committees, 1900).

470 See Zorn, *Le grand siècle*, 182.

471 Merle, op. cit., 248.

other colonial powers. The Swiss will not be mentioned here because they had no colonies. This is also true of the Scandinavian countries with the exception of Denmark, which in the nineteenth century still possessed several trading posts on the coasts of Africa, the Indies, and the Antilles. The Swiss and the Scandinavians, however, were very much engaged in missions in the nineteenth and twentieth centuries.

### British Missions

British Christians were at the forefront of the mission movement at the beginning of the nineteenth century, and throughout the period Britain was the leading commercial and military power of the world.[472] It was to British colonies that British missionaries first ventured. However, the commercial companies acting in the name of the British government did not lend them their support. André Raux notes that

> William Carey and his colleagues, the Serampore trio, did not settle in the British territories of India but in a small Danish trading post. And they were a source of conflict for the British East India Company, as missionary pioneer Robert Morrison would be in China in 1807.[473]

Anxious above all to maintain order to expand its lucrative activities, the company was concerned that Christian evangelism would produce hostile reactions among the local religious leaders. In 1833, however, the British government ordered the British East India Company to guarantee freedom of action to the missionaries.

The Anglican Church, whose supreme head is the British monarch, often found itself in an ambiguous position. But non-Anglican missionaries were also engaged in mission work in British colonies, such as the Baptist Carey and the Presbyterian Livingstone. There were also non-British missionaries, such as Coillard of France. All of these appealed to the British Parliament and Crown for protection. The principal motivations of the missionaries were to eliminate cruel pagan ritual practices such as infanticide and the cremation of widows in India, and to end the slave trade, the trade in arms and alcohol, and territorial aggression.

In India an independence movement gained much popular support during the years from 1918 to 1920. It was commonly recognized that the education system begun by the missionaries contributed much to this nationalist movement. The missionaries clearly opposed the injustices perpetrated against the nationalists in the effort to suppress the movement, but they refrained from direct political involvement to end colonization. Some Indian churches reproached the missionaries' "timidity" and neutrality, which they felt was cowardice and complicity with imperialism. The British missionaries in Africa received the same harsh reproach.

British Protestant missions were not alone among missions that favored the decolonization of the churches in Africa and Asia,[474] though it must also be admitted

---

472 In 1815, 90 percent of the merchant navies plowing the oceans were built to fly the British flag.

473 André Roux, "Problématique de la mission," in *Église et théologie*, no. 77 (1962).

474 Though the first Anglican dioceses were created in India in 1813, it was not until 1912 that the first Indian bishop, V. Z. Azariah, was consecrated.

that indigenous peoples often had to apply pressure to obtain their autonomy. Curiously, it was the pioneer missionaries a century earlier who sometimes pleaded for the rapid emancipation of churches however recently established. Henry Venn, the director of the evangelical Anglican organization CMS, had as early as 1854 called for the triple autonomy of the African churches (financial, administrative, and missionary), but his plans seemed to have been forgotten.

## German Missions

Emperor Wilhelm I (1798–1888), with the help of Chancellor Otto von Bismarck, sought to make his empire a great European and colonial power. The Prussian colonial empire, however, was less extensive and more ephemeral than that of the British, and the Germans lost it following the First World War after only about thirty years. One of the advocates of German colonization in Africa was Friedrich Fabri, the director of the Rhineland Missionary Society. He believed that Germany would be able to resolve its economic and social problems through colonization. Once Germany possessed overseas territories, the government called on mission societies to participate. In the eyes of the nation's political leaders, missionaries were necessary "to reinforce the German character of these regions." A slogan of the time was, "Only German missionaries for German colonies." A missionary publication in 1885 explained:

> If the colonies, about whose conquest we rejoice and whose extension we desire, are really to offer us and our people new blessings, new and lasting sources of prosperity, our well being requires that we not only introduce rifles and munitions, not only clothes and tools, but also and above all the Word of God.[475]

The majority of over fifteen Germany mission societies worked in German colonies, but many of their missionaries also served in countries that never became German colonies. For the most part, however, the dozen mission societies formed in Germany during the thirty years of the colonial period dedicated themselves solely to German colonial territories. This was the case in particular with the Evangelische Missionsgesellschaft für Ostafrika (Evangelical Missionary Society for East Africa), which was founded in 1886 by a group of ministers at the instigation of politicians and officers in the colonial army.

The confusion between Christian and national interest caused numerous, lively debates. The Reverend Franz Michael Zahn, inspector of the German missionary Society of the North, warned of the danger that one day they would "see mission, which belonged to the kingdom of God, appropriated and 'nationalized' by the German people." Zahn even saw danger in missions established by the same nation that had colonized a county. In such a case, he admitted that he would have difficulty "conserving the neutrality that a missionary must rigorously keep in the political realm."

Zahn's was not an isolated voice. The director of the Hermansburg Mission, Ludwig Harms, took up the defense of Africans and protested vigorously and passionately against the manner in which the white colonists of the Transvaal were treating

---

475 *Allgemeine mission zeitschrift* 12, cited by Merle, op. cit., 284–85.

the indigenous population. The best economists reproached the German missionary societies for not lining up on the side of the government and sometimes even for opposing its representatives as was the case in Cameroon.

The great German missiologist Gustav Warnek made it known that he had serious reservations about the confusion between the competing missionary and nationalist visions of the Berliner Evangelische Missiongesellschaft für Ostafrika (Berlin East Africa Evangelical Missionary Society). This mission, however, reversed itself when the Reverend Friedrich von Bodelschwingh (1831–1910) joined its governing body. Inspired by Pietism and possessing great spiritual breath, Bodelschwingh convinced the mission "to replace the emphasis on nationalism with an emphasis on the salvation of man. Henceforth, the training given by the mission was determined more by the need to liberate Africans than to increase their output under colonial tutelage."[476] Of symbolic and practical importance, the seat of the mission was moved from Berlin to Bethel where Bodelschwingh's work was established. Following the First World War a defeated Germany was relieved of its colonial possessions. When German missionaries were free to return to their former mission fields ten or twenty years later, they found that conditions had entirely changed.

## Dutch Missions

In the middle of the seventeenth century when the Dutch supplanted the Portuguese in Ceylon, the Protestant missionaries had the Portuguese priests expelled, and there were some forced conversions to Protestantism. This unfortunate and unfruitful episode (see p. 341) preceded the modern era of mission by a century and a half.

In 1795 the Dutch Evangelical Missions Society became the first Protestant mission organization to appear on the European continent, but it did not have a mission field under its direct responsibility in the first period of its history. In the 1850s the Dutch Reformed Church moved into a time of renewal of its missionary commitment, and a number of missionary societies were established. It undertook the evangelization of Indonesia, convinced that God had entrusted this vast country to Holland so that it would be brought to Christ.

Abraham Kuyper (1837–1920), orthodox Calvinist theologian and prime minister of the Netherlands from 1901 to 1905,[477] was concerned with the question of colonialism in general, and with the Dutch East Indies in particular. He pleaded for the rights of colonized peoples and advocated that they be accorded gradual independence. To prepare the people for the postcolonial period, he worked to ensure that schools were preparing leaders for an independent future and that nationals served on the local and regional councils whose responsibility and autonomy would increase over time.

---

476 Twagirayesu and Butselaar, op. cit., 19–20.
477 He was one of the founders of the Free University of Amsterdam and the *Gereformeerde Kerk*. Cf. Pierre Courthial, "Le mouvement réformé de reconstruction chrétienne," in *Hokhmma*, no. 14 (1980), 57.

# AMERICAN CHRISTIANS AND COLONIZATION

When the momentum of modern missions swept up the American churches at the beginning of the nineteenth century, America had shaken off British colonial rule only a few short years before. This was no doubt one of the reasons for the anticolonialist tradition of American Christians, which they maintained through the nineteenth century.[478] This was still the case at the beginning of the twentieth century, despite America's recent conquest of the Philippines, Puerto Rico, and Cuba, and the establishment of colonies in all but name. The missionary Charles Forman wrote of the Philippines at the time:

> After America had imposed its hegemony on the territory, the missionaries spent more time protesting against the enactments of the American government than in praising its high achievements; they enjoined it to respect the noble goals that it had announced at the beginning of its intervention.[479]

At the same time, Americans felt an increasing moral responsibility for the peoples of the world due to their optimism and confidence in their national destiny. In the confluence of democracy and Christianity that occurred in the first half of the twentieth century, American missionaries were often ranked on the side of American nationalism. John Mott (1865–1955), Chairman of the Executive Committee of the Student Volunteer Movement for Foreign Missions, wrote soon after the World Missionary Conference of Edinburgh (1910) in support of nationalism:

> The development and spread of the spirit of national and racial patriotism is, however, the most significant fact of all. It is not an evil thing. It cannot and should not be checked. Christ never by teaching or example resisted or withstood the spirit of true nationalism. Wherever His principles, including those pertaining to the supreme claims of His Kingdom on earth, have had the right of way, they have served to strengthen national spirit and not to weaken it. But it is a matter of profound concern to the Western world. Who can measure what it will mean for mankind when not only Japan but also China with her unlimited resources and India with her 300 million people take their place among the great civilized powers? The influence which they will exert upon the life and thought of the world must be enormous, whatever its nature; whether it will be Christian or not depends largely on the direction given to it today. It is the duty of the Church to bring pure Christianity to bear at once in order to help to educate, purify, unify, guide, and strengthen the national spirit. The possibilities are great if the Christian Church will identify itself freely and largely with all these noble national aspirations. If Christianity will show that it has a message not merely for individuals but for society and for the nation

---

478 At the time they were rejecting colonialism and gaining their independence, white Americans scarcely changed their relations with the black and Indian populations.

479 *The International Bulletin of Missionary Research* (1982), cited by Bosch, op. cit., 421.

as a whole, that it can adapt itself to the people whom it seeks to save, and that it does not deem it essential, even desirable, that the ordered life of the Christian community in Asia and Africa should follow in every respect the lines of European and American Christianity, it may attract instead of repel these rising nations. Their newly found life when ruled by Christ will be a source of strength to their own nations and to the Christian faith.[480]

Mott's optimism suggests, at least in retrospect, a certain naiveté, but in many respects his diagnosis later proved to be correct. Still, it was Marxist ideology, not Christianity, that became the most effective instrument used by colonized people to shake off Western imperialism. Naturally, Americans found themselves in the opposite camp, being carried there by the large number of its Christians missions.

# EVALUATION

We have considered the question of colonialism from the perspective of Protestant missions. Was there a noticeable difference of attitude about colonization between Catholic and Protestant missions?

Marcel Merle, who directed the collective work *Les églises chrétiennes et la décolonisation* (*Christians Churches and Decolonization*) that we have cited here several times, wrote about Protestantism in his conclusion:

> In certain cases churches such as the Reformed Church of France found themselves less compromised than others due to their minority status within the colonial enterprise. But other Protestant churches, such as those in the Low Countries and Great Britain, gave the impression of being allied with power. It is the minority or majority situation of the church, not its confessional tradition, that seems to have determined its reaction to decolonization.[481]

While self evident, this conclusion is only partly true. For a mission's theology also influenced its choices and the way it understood the relationship between church and mission, and church and state. Catholic missions were the inheritors of the system of the Patronat.[482] Though this system was no longer officially viable in the nineteenth century, the concept of Christendom that underlay it continued to be influential, suggesting that church and state had reciprocal roles in colonial territories under Catholic sway.

In Protestantism, the development of missiological thought was marginal during the period of the Reformation when Europe was still operating in a climate favorable

---

480 John R. Mott, *The Decisive Hour of Christian Missions* (New York: Student Volunteer Movement for Foreign Missions, 1911), 35–36.

481 Merle, op. cit., 504.

482 Patronat begins from the medieval principle that the Pope exercises supreme authority on behalf of Christ. As such, the Pope is the vicar of the entire earth, including the non-Christian world. He delegates this power to Catholic kings on condition that they take responsibility for both the religious and political spheres of life. David Bosch writes, "Colonialism and Mission, as a matter of course, were interdependent; the right to have colonies carried with it the duty to Christianize the colonized" (Bosch, 227).

to Christendom. That the Reformers did not develop a clear missiology in this period was in this respect a blessing, for they did not saddle the churches with a tradition of state-sponsored mission. Instead, Protestant missions issued from the Pietist and Methodist revivals, which emphasized individual conversion and in general advocated the separation of church and state. They encountered indifference from the official ecclesiastical authorities and distrust from the civil authorities. R. Mehl writes, "Missionary activity was in general the work of churches that did not feel themselves tied to a well-organized Christendom or a specific type of civilization."[483] Hence, even in countries where Protestants were a majority, the history of the sending churches prevented their missions from being allies of the state.

As these reflections suggest, understanding the attitude of Protestant missions toward colonialism requires a knowledge of how Protestant missional thought evolved during the colonial era, especially in the case of Britain. Colonization by Protestant nations in the seventeenth century was largely concerned with lay commercial interests, and colonial chaplains focused their attention on the spiritual life of the colonists. Those who sought to evangelize the local populations were rare.

The missionary pioneers of the eighteenth century and of the first half of the nineteenth century were influenced by Pietism. They were first and foremost citizens of the kingdom of God and only secondarily citizens of earthly nations. They sought above all else the salvation of non-Christians, not the prestige or enrichment of their nations. In this period many commercial companies judged the presence of these pioneer missionaries to be undesirable, and as noted above, there were conflicts between the missionaries and the colonizers. Despite this attitude, the pioneers still no doubt felt that their civilization was more apt than any other to promote the well being of the world's populations. They were, however, little inclined to adopt a racist approach to those they were going to encounter. Though full of consternation over the harmful effects of paganism, they were nonetheless convinced by the teachings of Scripture of the unity of the human species and the universal character of the gospel. It is evident that they were genuinely curious about the people among whom they came to live and sought without prejudice to understand their habits, language, customs, and beliefs. Moreover, most went abroad without any prospect of returning to their own countries. It is no accident that among their number were many forerunners in the sciences of anthropology and linguistics.

The notion that Christians had a responsibility to send and support missionaries steadily gained sway in the nineteenth century. The newsletters of William Carey and other eminent pioneers made their mark on the time. Reports of the missionaries' remarkable achievements in the areas of education, medicine, and linguistics eventually overcame much of the misunderstanding that attended the early missionary enterprise. The life of a Livingstone, one of the great national heroes of Britain, lent the cause of missions a luster difficult to imagine today. The popular press seized on it, and eventually the growing prestige of missions came to influence the era's politicians. This was especially the case with the British parliament. Mission supporters

---

483 R. Mehl, *Décolonisation et missions protestantes* (SMEP, 1964), 34.

first sought liberty from Parliament for the missionaries to work,[484] then protection for them once they were in place, and finally support to accomplish their work. The convictions of the missionaries led them not only to seek the progress of the gospel in the world but also to improve the quality of life among the populations among whom they lived. Hence mission came to be seen by the colonizing states as a worthy and useful endeavor.

Analyzing the period that began around 1880, David Bosch went so far as to use the term "complicity" to describe the relationship between missionaries and colonizers. This is too severe though there are flagrant cases where it is applicable.[485] Two trends help explain the age. First, with the Congress of Berlin in 1885 one enters the golden age of colonization. The West did not doubt its superiority and saw no conflict between its interests and the well being of the colonized peoples. Missionaries in this period rarely contested the legitimacy of colonization but did denounce specific abuses in which colonized people were the victims. Yet colonial attitudes often appeared among missionaries as the last years of Bishop Samuel Ajayi Crowther sadly illustrate. (See p. 513-14).

Due to the success of missions and the growing interest of the general Western public in countries overseas, missions were no longer the prerogative of nonconformist and sometimes marginal adventurers. Having become popular, missions began to seem "tame" and even institutional. The following numbers are significant: the CMS, an evangelical Anglican mission established in 1799, sent out 991 missionaries during its first ninety years of existence, or about an average of eleven per year; but in the twenty-five years following 1889, it sent out 1,478 missionaries, or about an average of sixty per year.

Colonization is a page of human history marked like all others by numerous ambiguities. Noble intentions were mixed and often in conflict with sordid interest. All through human history great empires have been engines of civilization, but there is not one among them that has not produced its share of victims sacrificed on the altar of political self-interest. Since leaving the Garden of Eden, the glory of the few has been built on the humiliation of the many. The history of the West in the last few centuries has not escaped this rule. As for the church, though it belongs to the kingdom of God, it has its feet on the earth and, more often than necessary, is bogged down in the marshes. This is the price it pays for being incarnate in the world. It does its important work while trying to avoid being conformed to the world; but being made up of human beings rather than angels, the people of God often fail to be the signs of God's kingdom of justice and peace for which the church is to hope and prepare.

It belongs to each generation of Christians to exercise vigilance in the face of the pressing issues of its time. The era of political colonization largely came to an end by the beginning of the 1960s, but it has continued on in the form of an economic domination through which the West profits while millions of people elsewhere in

---

484 As we have seen, the British East India Company was directed in 1833 by the British government to guarantee the missionaries the liberty needed to develop their activities.

485 See Bosch, op. cit., 310 (as well as the second part of Chapter 9: "The Missionary Motifs in the Enlightenment Era").

the world live in poverty. While we look askance at our ancestors for their colonial delusions, what will our successors say of the neocolonialism of our day, and of the indifference that often allows it to continue?

# CHAPTER 32

# *The World Missionary Conferences*

Protestantism in general has been characterized by personal piety and strong individualism, and this tendency was greatly reinforced by eighteenth- and nineteenth-century revivalism. Such an approach to Christianity has both strengths and weaknesses. It brings forth personal initiative and responsibility as individuals hear and respond to God's call on their lives. The dynamism that results from this does not easily allow itself to be paralyzed or diverted by the bureaucratic inertia of ecclesiastical institutions. But individualism also runs the danger of isolation, subjectivism, vain competition, and absence of consultation and strategic coherence.

These advantages and dangers have been apparent since the dawn of modern evangelical missions. Wise mission leaders have been quick to see the need to avoid the danger of rampant individualism on the mission field. Being animated by the same spiritual sensibility, from the outset mission societies have generally cooperated with one another, opening their schools to the nationals of other societies, and helping one another when missionaries found themselves in difficulty. They were conscious that, despite differing denominations and nationalities, they were all serving the same cause and seeking to obey the same Lord.

But with the growth and development of missions in the second half of the nineteenth century, the complexity and variety of the work increased the danger that missionaries would begin to work competitively or at cross purposes. It was to ward off this danger that within the mission-sending countries there began to be intermissionary regional conferences for the purpose of sharing information about needs and projects, developing and coordinating coherent strategies, and affirming fraternal communion.

As early as 1810 William Carey dreamed of organizing a world missionary conference in South Africa. Johannes Vanderkemp was well disposed to the idea but the practical obstacles proved to be too great and the dream was never realized. Fifty years later the idea reappeared. The first mission conference took place in Liverpool in 1860, the second at Midway in 1878, and the third in London in 1888. The New York mission conference in 1900 brought together two thousand delegates and seven hundred missionaries, but without French-speaking representation. To prepare for this conference, the work of 249 mission societies in the Protestant world were surveyed to promote a greater understanding of the work. The sites of these conferences, however, reflected the Anglo-Saxon predominance in the Protestant missionary world.

The first quarter of the twentieth century was a time of transition for Protestant missions. Profiting from the huge momentum that missions had gained in the nineteenth century, the movement continued to experience growth and development into the new century. Yet, simultaneously, there was growing uncertainty about the role of Western churches in the evangelization of the world. Equally important, the theological fissures already apparent in the nineteenth century would continue to deepen and widen in the years to come until they threatened to disrupt the movement. The three world missionary conferences at Edinburgh in 1910, Jerusalem in 1928, and Tambaram in 1938 were not only landmarks in the history of mission but also the new ecumenical movement that would attempt to redress the growing division.

## THE WORLD MISSIONARY CONFERENCE AT EDINBURGH, 1910

The conference that was held in June 1910 in Scotland, a land that has furnished many eminent pioneers in mission work, included 1,200 participants from about 150 mission societies. A little over a thousand of the delegates were British or American, and only 170 represented societies from continental Europe—and only a few of these were French speakers. Eighteen delegates represented the non-Western "young churches," and the only black person was a Liberian of American origin. Several Asians, however, played a significant role on the platform.

Edinburgh 1910 was more significant than preceding conferences in part because it devoted more time to missiological reflection and because it decided to create the International Missionary Council.[486] The participants were lifted by a rising tide of optimism that one might find difficult to imagine today. The extraordinary changes that had occurred in the course of a century of Protestant missions filled their imaginations with thrilling expectations for the future.[487] This spirit, moreover, was not limited to missionary circles. The West, confident in the worth of its civilization, seemed to believe in the limitless progress of material comfort and the increase of wealth. It also felt a burden of responsibility for civilizing the entire planet, for ought not what had succeeded so well in Europe and North America become a factor in the development of other places in the world? One could describe the years from 1880 to 1920 as the "golden age of colonization." It was in this context of unbridled optimism that the Edinburgh conference was held, where the voices raised to warn of the dark

---

486 The International Missionary Council (IMC) is considered to be the precursor of the World Council of Churches founded in 1948. It was in New Delhi in 1961 that the IMC would merge into the WCC as one of its principal departments.

487 This was only a center after the career of William Carey. If the conference had taken place in 1810 the assembly would have included a handful of Europeans—mostly Moravians—and no North American missionaries at all.

side of colonialism were all too rare. This would not be the case eighteen years later at the time of the Jerusalem conference.

The Edinburgh conference, writes David Bosch, marked "the apogee of an optimistic and pragmatic conception of mission," but it would be unjust to perceive it only as a reflection of the period. On reading the records of the conference and the comments of the participants, it is impossible not to be struck by their spirituality, their insistence on prayer, their meditation on the Scriptures. Edinburgh was a witness to the clear and firm theological conviction of the salvation universally available in Christ, the urgent duty of Christians to take this message to all peoples of the earth, and the need to rely more on the power of the Holy Spirit than on human expertise and financial power.

One of the great motivations of the conference was expressed in the slogan coined in 1886 by the American evangelical leader A. T. Pierson: "the evangelization of the world in this generation," which was immediately taken up by the Student Volunteer Movement. John Mott (1865–1955), one of its earliest leaders, made it the title of a book in 1900.

Mott, a Methodist layman from the United States, was the president and leading figure of the Edinburgh conference. A little after the conference, he published *The Decisive Hour of Christian Missions*, a summary of the data obtained by the conference that exercised a considerable influence on Protestantism in general. This work is remarkable for its well-documented account of the then-current state of missions in the world, its enthusiasm, and the spirituality that animated it. The book witnesses to the missionary dynamism and evangelical zeal not only of the conference but of the age.

*The plenary hall of the World Missionary Conference
held at Edinburgh in 1910 (partial view). (Ecumenical photo)*

Jean de Visme, a delegate at Edinburgh from the Paris Mission, expressed the general impression he had after attending the conference:

> The hour to which we have arrived in the history of the kingdom of God on the earth and in consequence in the destiny of the church is a solemn one and perhaps of unique importance; it is an hour in which we must learn to profit . . . The entire earth is open before us today . . . In a great rush of faith, prayer, and love, the Christian Church must take the eternal gospel in hand and with it take possession of the entire earth in the name of Jesus Christ.

Elie Allégret, missionary of the SMEP in Gabon between 1899 and 1903, concurred: "Edinburgh has above all been a council of war for the conquering church . . . that at last must carry out the orders of its chief to take the gospel to every people on earth."

The picture, however, should be examined in greater detail, for Edinburgh brought together participants from a variety of different perspectives. The enthusiasm, optimism, and sense of urgency for mission were not shared by all. "The evangelization of the world in this generation" was a slogan that, according to Stephen Neill, "excited enthusiasm in many, but also numerous critics." David Bosch notes that "the World Missionary Conference of Edinburgh in 1910 . . . gathered an interesting range . . . of Social Gospel Christians and 'saviors of souls,' as well as missionary organizations that represented both the established church and moderate evangelicals."[488] For some, the return of Christ was imminent, and, therefore, it was urgent to save as many souls as possible before the Day of Judgment. For others, the need for urgency was suggested by the historical context in which they lived. Due to colonization and technological progress in the areas of communication and travel, the Christian West was in a highly favorable position to spread the gospel message. Moreover, not occupying a field was to leave it to others: nationalism, materialist ideologies, or the other great religions of the world.[489]

Still others at Edinburgh contested the validity of haste. For them, mission was a long and demanding enterprise that required not only enthusiasm but also perseverance and thorough preparation. In their eyes, priority should be given to education and leadership development so that the young churches would have a solid foundation upon which to build. This was the position of the Pietist Gustav Warneck, the founder of Germany missiology. He believed that he discerned at Edinburgh an approach that would lead to superficial evangelism and the founding of churches before they were ready. Finally, there were those whom Bosch calls the "social Christians," who urged that Christian missions should embrace responsibility for the whole of society. They advocated a program that included Christianization, education, new economic systems, and new political structures. They would risk a clean sweep of all that had existed before in order to replace it with a new form of civilization based on

---

488 Bosch, op. cit., 439.
489 For John Mott's exposition of this approach, see p. 701.

the European or North American model and an expression of the Christian faith that was clearly Western.

In his *A History of Christian Missions*, Stephen Neill contests the pertinence of the criticisms made of the slogan of the Student Volunteer Movement:

> The slogan was based on an unexceptionable theological principle—that each generation of Christians bears responsibility for the contemporary generation of non-Christians in the world, and that it is the business of each such generation of Christians to see to it, as far as lies within its power, that the gospel is clearly preached to every single non-Christian in the same generation. This is of universal and permanent obligation; it applies to Christian witness both within what is commonly called Christendom and beyond it. If the principle is to be rejected, the New Testament must first be rewritten.[490]

Beyond the divergences indicated above, what were the themes generally accepted at Edinburgh in 1910? Two at least can be observed. First, the martial rhetoric of conquest that characterized many of the addresses given at Edinburgh did not lead to a new form of fanaticism or a narrow, bellicose spirit. On the contrary, the attention given to the members of other religions and to those religions themselves was full of respect and sympathy, suggesting a real effort to understand.[491] Conversely, this openness to the serious religious reality that exists outside of the Christian revelation did not lead to a desire for demobilization or an intention to weaken the imperative to evangelize the world. Second, the range of positions expressed at Edinburgh was quite wide, but there were commonly shared fundamental principles: an affirmation of the finality and authoritative character of the Christian revelation, of the universality of the gospel message, and the confession of Christ as the only Savior of humanity.

As noted above, the International Missionary Council (IMC) was the permanent organization to issue from the Edinburgh conference. The uncertain path that ran from the first world missionary conference of Liverpool in 1860 to that of Edinburgh in 1910 strongly suggested the need for regular conferences. However, due to the interruption of the First World War, it was not until 1921 that the IMC was formally constituted, presided over by John Mott. His presence assured that there would be continuity of thought and action following Edinburgh. The IMC became the vehicle through which the subsequent world missionary conferences were held: Jerusalem in 1928, and Tambaram in 1938.

The ambitious program laid out at Edinburgh has not been accomplished, far from it. The participants in the conference were not utopians, but they were visionaries. Their conference reinvigorated the missionary vision of Christian people and led to profound changes in the "spiritual geography" of the world over the course of the

---

490 Neill, *History*, 394.

491 For a fuller study of the positions expressed at the Edinburgh conference regarding other religions, see Blandenier, "Mission," 283–307.

twentieth century. Though Kenneth Scott Latourette believed that the "Great Century of Mission" had come to an end in 1914, Stephen Neill believed that the Edinburgh conference, though marking the end of an age, also helped to extend the reach of the nineteenth-century missionary movement well into the next century.[492]

# JOHN MOTT

As the principal planner and founder of the International Missionary Council, John Mott merits more than a passing mention in this work. He was neither a missionary nor the secretary of a mission society, but he was nonetheless one of the great figures of Protestant missions at the end of the nineteenth and first part of the twentieth centuries. Whatever their theological leanings and missiological particularities, the mission societies of the time all benefited from his work and from his more than common capacities. Friend and counselor to several heads of state, winner of the Nobel Peace Prize in 1946, Mott was one of the most influential Protestant leaders of the era.

Mott was born and raised in Iowa and was a member of the Methodist Episcopal Church. While a college student, he became active in the Young Men's Christian Association (YMCA) and remained active in this movement for the next forty years, sixteen of which he served as Secretary General. The evangelists J. Kynaston Studd (the brother of C. T. Studd) and Dwight Moody played a decisive role in his conversion and subsequent career path. While many at the time predicted that he would enter a legal or political career, perhaps becoming a head of state, all he wanted was to remain a layman while dedicating his life to the cause of world evangelization. He was one of the original "Mount Hermon One Hundred" that launched the Student Volunteer Movement for Foreign Missions (SVM), and he soon headed the organization. Later he played a key role in founding the World Federation of Christian Students (WFCS), which would eventually include nearly three thousand universities on five continents.

*John Mott (1865–1955), first president of the International Missionary Council.*

He dedicated his life to fulfilling the watchword of the SVM, "The Evangelization of the World in this Generation." Given his long years of service, it was entirely appropriate that he would be the chairman of the Edinburgh conference in 1910.

As a speaker, conference-goer, and organizer of young Christians, Mott traveled untiringly throughout the world. For example, at the time of his first trip to China 3,500 literati pressed into a hall in Canton to hear his message, which led to 150 of them asking for baptism.

Mott was neither a theologian nor particularly interested in the theological aspects of the Christian faith. He nevertheless found himself embroiled in the controversies that agitated the American Protestant mission world in the early years of

492 Neill, *History*, 395–96.

the twentieth century, dividing evangelicals and progressives. The Fundamentalists on the right and the Liberals on the left reproached him for not joining their ranks. He wrote at the time:

> There are not two sets of good news, one concerning social problems and the other individual concerns. There is only one Christ, who lived, died, and was resurrected . . . He is the Savior of the individual and at the same time the only power capable of transforming the environment in which men live, and the quality of their relations.

Mott affirmed and maintained throughout his life that the conversion of non-Christians to Jesus Christ is the essential task of mission.

Animated by this principal concern, Mott saw the division of the Christian world as an obstacle to mission. Consequently, in his later career he lent much of his strength and prestige to the creation of the World Council of Churches. When he was over eighty years old, he wrote:

> If Protestant missions continue to work as organizations that are ignorant of one another, pursuing diverse goals with different methods, what hope will we have? It would be criminal not to plan together . . . We will only arrive there by abandoning our party spirit, our national spirit, by breaking down barriers and racial lines . . . May men of action who are conscious of the necessity of the hour assume a prophetic attitude . . . In the midst of so much change, the world of missions must not be static. Why should it alone preserve the forms of the past? Indeed, the past must be respected, but with a clear vision for what will be tomorrow and the assurance that God desires that new things be achieved . . . May the errors of the past instruct us. Denominationalism has too often been sectarian. Some have considered it to be a raison d'être and have forgotten the kingdom of God . . . God desires that that we rise above ourselves and our petty ecclesiastical concerns until we are united even as Christ prayed. This unity must not be affirmed only at the end of the world but immediately, so that all will recognize the power of the gospel.[493]

## THE JERUSALEM MISSIONARY CONFERENCE OF 1928

Unlike Edinburgh, the Jerusalem conference made no attempt to be a great congress. It was, rather, an enlarged session of the International Missionary Council (IMC). There were only two hundred participants and a third of them represented "young churches." The smallness of the gathering lent itself to theological debate, which revealed the difficulties and divisions of Protestantism in this period.

In certain respects, the Jerusalem conference sought to pursue the course set out at Edinburgh, which was certainly what Mott and many other members of the IMC

---

493  B. Valloton, *Un homme: John R. Mott* (Paris: UCJG, 1951), 168–72.

had hoped would occur. But the times had changed. The atrocities of the First World War, the Bolshevik Revolution and the emergence of the anti-Christian Soviet empire, the social troubles experienced by the industrialized countries, and the inkling of difficulties to come in the next decade left their mark on the troubled conscience of the age. To these must be added the first stirrings of nationalism and the rising liberation movement among colonized peoples—especially in India in the 1920s under the leadership of Mahatma Gandhi. The shining optimism that lit up the mission movement of the preceding era seems to have dimmed. World opinion about Western civilization became more critical; a belief in its universal supremacy was shaken; and it was now easier to dissociate Christianity from the West.

*The participants at the Jerusalem Missionary Conference. (Photo: Oikoumene)*

At several places the official documents of the conference gave expression to concerns that would often be at the forefront of subsequent conferences. There was a shift in emphasis from individual spirituality towards the problems of society. In his critical analysis given in the final address in the conference, the former China missionary and well-known Anglican missiologist Roland Allen took exception to the desire to make Christianity the means of remodeling civil society. He discerned the obvious inconsistency of a conference that advocated a Western-style reform while at the same time wanting to dissociate Christianity from its Western forms.[494]

Nonetheless, many speakers addressed in clear and militant terms the tension that existed between blacks and whites in North America and South Africa due to racism. Others focused on the problems specific to urban populations in the large Asian nations, the poverty of rural populations, the wrongful aspects of colonialism, the ravages of war, and the struggle to build permanent peace between peoples.

---

494 Roland Allen, *Jerusalem: A Critical Review of "The World Mission of Christianity"* (London: World Dominion, 1928).

The title of the final message delivered at the Jerusalem conference suggested an unbridled triumphalism: "For the conquest of the World." Yet, beneath appearances attitudes had clearly changed. The preamble of the address is a better refection of this altered reality:

> The world suffers today from a state of profound instability and insecurity. Scientific development and commercial expansion have modified the course of human thought, provoking a crisis among ancient religions [including Christianity]. Some venerable institutions have been discredited or put into question. This includes the moral order that until recently seemed well established but is now contested. Many today question if there is an absolute Truth and perfect Good.[495]

Though uttered three-quarters of a century ago, these words closely reflect the view of reality commonly held today, unlike those of Edinburgh that come from an entirely different time. No doubt Mott and the other Christian leaders who took part in the editing of the final declaration retained their fundamental convictions, but they were also clearly aware that the West too had grave insufficiencies, and that the Western version of Christianity was not the only legitimate expression of the faith. "We condemn all the more," they declared, "the desire to immobilize our gospel in ecclesiastical forms whose meaning proceeds from the experiences of the Western churches."[496]

The approach of Edinburgh did not entirely disappear, but now mission and church leaders also took into account other trends. Hence, Stephen Neill wrote in his *A History of Christian Missions* of the influence of theological liberalism on missiology in the period following the First World War. In a paragraph entitled, "Missionary Uncertainties," he wrote:

> But in these years of rapid missionary expansion, a very different gospel had been growing up and taking hold of the minds of a great many Christians, especially in America. The liberal was not by any means so sure that Jesus Christ was the last Word of God to man. He was repelled by the exclusive claim to salvation through Christ alone. He tended to take a much more favorable view of the other religions than his more conservative colleagues, and to look forward to some kind of synthesis of religions rather than to the disappearance of any of them. The real enemy is secularism. Adherents of all the great religions should stand together in defense of the spiritual reality of man's life. There should be no hostility between them, the spirit of proselytism being replaced by the willingness to learn from one another.

This point of view was strongly represented at the second of the great World Missionary Conferences that was held at Jerusalem in 1928. It is strange to contrast the

495 *Pour la conquête du monde: Message de la Conférence Missionnaire de Jérusalem* (Paris: SMEP, 1928), 1–2.
496 Ibid., 6.

confident tone of the Edinburgh pronouncements with the almost hesitant accents of what was said at Jerusalem. Clearly a comprehensive change was taking place in the theological climate, in attitudes to other religions, and in the understanding of the missionary task.[497]

The leaders of some of the evangelical missionary societies of the "second wave" (see Book II, Chapter 2) were conscious of this new direction and chose not to participate in the Jerusalem conference, although there was an evangelical wing present. Francis Steele, secretary of the American branch of the North Africa Mission in the 1950s, wrote of the new trend:

> Since the Edinburgh Conference of 1910, a process of theological dilution slowly undermined the foundations of evangelical missions. The second world conference that took place in Jerusalem in 1928 clearly departed from the doctrine of scriptural authority. The influence of theological liberalism shifted the emphasis to a concern for social issues instead of personal salvation.[498]

Several preparatory studies drafted by specialists in world religions caused apprehension among some of the European delegates. Being influenced by the theology of Karl Barth, they admired his struggle against a liberalism that he believed to be anthropocentric. The final message attempted to reconcile these divergent positions, which resulted in a text that was inconsistent in places. Hence the text contained some passages that were consistent with the essentials affirmed at Edinburgh and others that diverged from them:

> The nature of the gospel forbids us to think that it would be good for some but not for others. Either it is true for all, or it is not the truth. But so many questions have been raised and are stilling being raised concerning the raison d'être of missions and the right to do missionary work . . . that we must state our own attitude for the sake of the future of the work and for our own sake's . . . The obligatory character of the missionary work proceeds from the nature of God to whom we have given our hearts.[499]

The following, however, reveals a different perspective:

> We observe and confess that Christianity has not sufficiently sought out and recognized the sound and noble elements that are contained in non-Christian religious systems. This would have permitted it to experience a more profound personal communion with the members of these systems and in consequence to be better able to attract them to the living Christ. We know that even without a conscious knowledge of the Savior some men are able to follow the light that they possess and thereby triumph over some of the evils that afflict humanity. This must inspire us all the

---

497  Neill, *History*, 455.
498  Steele, op. cit., 42.
499  *Pour la conquête*, 5–6.

more to aid these men to discover that light in all its fullness and power in Christ.[500]

The Edinburgh Conference, wrote Stephen Neill, marked the end of an age. The new age, however, did not begin at Jerusalem. That would not occur until the period of decolonization that followed the Second World War. The Jerusalem conference came at the beginning of a long period of transition during which the gap between the evangelical and ecumenical wings of the Protestant missionary movement widened and deepened. This would become increasingly apparent on the mission field during the 1930s.

## THE TAMBARAM CONFERENCE 1938

This conference, held in December 1938, comes at the end of our period of study. Its most distinguishing feature was that a majority of its participants were representatives of non-Western churches. Of the 480 participants, more than half came from what today would be called the Global South, and a large majority of these were Asians. The conference was supposed to be held in Hangchow, China, but due to the Sino-Japanese War, it was held instead in Tambaram, near Madras, India, where it was welcomed by the churches of South India. While the war was then raging in China, the beat of marching boots could already be heard in Europe where the Second World War would explode some months later. This dramatic moment gave the meetings a markedly somber quality. Moreover, some of the participants came from Asia and Eastern Europe where Christians were being persecuted. For them the time had passed for merely holding forth on how the sociopolitical engagement of Christians could improve societal conditions. Rather, it was now time to prepare the church to hold fast amidst adversity and render testimony that the kingdom of God was at hand.

The Tambaram conference was concerned with practical problems and avoided theological debates that then seemed out of place. Marc Spindler has written that it "was concerned much of the time with the progress of the young churches towards autonomy, and what the economic and political conditions of this autonomy would be. To oversimplify, it could be said that the theme of the Three-Self church—as classically stated since the time of Henry Venn—dominated the debates of the Tambaram conference. This was a missiological debate in the strictest sense. The IMC did not want to direct this transition, but it did want an organizational process that would allow for coordination and consultation between the national churches and the mission societies."[501]

The representatives of the Asian and African churches insistently appealed to the "older" churches to set aside their traditions and confessional distinctions in order to gather around the cross of Christ and thereby strengthen the Christian witness

---

500 Ibid., 9.

501 Marc Spindler, "Hendrick Kraemer et la question du syncretism: Le malentendu de Tambaram," in Jacquin and Zorn, op. cit., 311–12.

"so that the world would believe."[502] This appeal, heard throughout the church in the years immediately following the war, played its part in the establishment of the World Council of Churches in 1948.

Jacques Matthey underscored the importance placed on the theme of the church at the time of the conference: "The majority of the participants at Tambaram (Madras) represented the 'young churches' whose importance was recognized. They insisted on the central role of the Church as messenger of the gospel in a world marked by the recrudescence of militant paganism. They particularly valued the witness of the local church. For years to come Tambaram also expressed the Protestant position on the exclusive claims of Christianity among the religions of the world, which removed the sensitive question of syncretism."[503]

Much credit for the "exclusivist" position that Matthey defined was owed to Dutch missiologist Hendrick Kraemer, who played a decisive role at Tambaram. Phillippe Chanson explained:

> Kraemer . . . defended a clear discontinuity between the Christian faith and the non-Christian religions of the naturalist type . . . Though he acknowledged a cultural syncretism in the outward forms of Christianity, he pled for a biblical realism that recognized the fundamental reality that God could not be incorporated into the ranks of the divinities of non-Christian religions . . . which led to passionate debates, especially with lay Indian theologians.[504]

Amidst the well-known differences among the representatives of the divergent traditions, traditional theology emerged to dominate the conference. Hence for example, in his analysis of the documents produced by the sixteen work groups of the conference, the Singhalese minister and theologian D. T. Niles summarized the first document, *The Faith by which the Church Lives*, in classical language:

> The term sin is written in blood in the Bible, but men often have the tendency to write it in gray. The conference sought to see and write this word once again in blood. If sin was only an error, man would simply need illumination . . . but if sin signifies the essential fallenness of man and his rebellion against God, then man needs an objective redemption. God must do for man what man cannot do for himself.[505]

Whatever concerns the participants of the Tambaram conference had for the undoing of the traditional Western version of Christianity, the central character of the message of redemption was clearly affirmed. The report of the commission responsible for reflecting on non-Christian religions underscores this point:

---

502 The welcoming churches at the Tambaram conference were well placed to plead for this unity because already in 1908 four Reformed and Congregationalist churches united to form the United Church of South India; and in 1947 the Methodists and Anglicans also joined this new church.

503 Jacques Matthey, "Conférences missionaires mondiales," in I. Bria et al., eds., *Dictionnaire oecuménique de missiologie: Cent mots pour la mission* (Paris: Cerf, 2001), 60.

504 Phillippe Chanson, "Syncrétisme," in Bria, op. cit., 330–31.

505 N. T. Niles, *The Tambaram Conference and After* (n.p., n.d.), 2.

Our message is that God was in Christ, reconciling the world to himself. We believe that God revealed himself to Israel, preparing the way for his full revelation in Jesus Christ our Lord. We believe that Christ is the Way, the Truth and the Life for all, and that he alone is adequate to the needs of the world. This is why we want to witness to him throughout the world.[506]

The keynote address delivered by the Reverend Toyohiko Kagawa, an evangelist from Japan, set the tone. Its title was "The Message of the Cross," and he began in no uncertain terms:

On Calvary, I see the blood of Jesus, which flows from his body on the cross! I hear the sound of his agony as the Lamb of God, dying for the sins of humanity! This occurred for me, and for my nation, and for my race, and for the entire world! I have sinned, and Jesus died for me. My race has sinned, and He died for my race. And all humanity has sinned, and He died for us all. Forgive us, Lord, in his name and because of the blood of Jesus Christ, our Redeemer and Savior![507]

## EVALUATING THE CONFERENCES

It is no easy task to understand the work of mission, the progress of world evangelization, and the evolution of missiological thought as these things have developed on all the mission fields of the earth. In this effort the role of the great mission conferences should not be underestimated, if only because the participants were not, for the most part, armchair missologists but men and women engaged on the field.

Did these conferences influence missiological thought, or did they merely reflect the thoughts of the time? It is difficult to say. What is certain is that they acted as catalysts to thought and they serve today as helpful landmarks in the development of Protestant missiology and practice. But the documents produced by these conferences are not always clear. There was no preliminary sorting of the participants according to their theological positions, and as we have seen, there were inconsistencies that found their way into the printed records of the conferences. Still, the contradictions in the record reflect the reality of the conferences themselves. It was this imprecision that led some evangelicals not to attend the conferences in order not to lend them credibility. Nevertheless, the records made at Edinburgh, Tambaram, and even to some extent at Jerusalem show that evangelicals were well represented. If they were not in the majority, it is at least clear that the statements emerging from the conferences were well rooted in evangelical soil where Protestant missions have always had deep roots.

However the three conferences are interpreted, it is clear that the theory and practice of mission were not in these years engraved in stone. Less than thirty years

---

506 Spindler, "Hendrick Kraemer," 313.

507 E. De Billy in *L'église universelle au pays des parias* (Paris: SMEP, 1938), 6. Billy was a French Methodist missionary in the Ivory Coast and one of the few French-speaking delegates at Tambaram.

separate the first and third conferences, but these were years of tremendous up-heaval in the West.

The atmosphere at Edinburgh 1910 was full of certitude. The participants were the conscious inheritors of the "heroic" period of mission. They knew that nine-teenth-century missions had been costly in human lives and that men and women of conviction had willingly made those sacrifices. Now that the conditions had become easier, it was vital to continue down the trail that they had blazed. This work could now be taken up with optimism, if not euphoria, and done with a sense of urgency. They knew that they should press on with the evangelization of the world "in this generation," for the favorable time of missions in which they lived might well be limited.

Though the Western world was shaken to its core between 1910 and 1928, not everyone at the Jerusalem conference drew the same conclusions from this experi-ence. For some, the crisis of the West made the claims of the European and North American churches to be the bearers of the unique message of universal salvation untenable. Others retained the firm conviction that the gospel was more than ever the only message offering hope for the regeneration of a lost humanity, as much in the West as in the rest of the world.

That the "young churches" were in the majority at Tambaram witnesses to the reality that the mission work of the previous century had borne abundant fruit that was now ripening into maturity. At the same time the influence of the European churches were clearly in decline. The West had lost its moral authority and was no longer a model to be followed by others. For the first time since antiquity the world could not be neatly divided into two compact blocks, Christendom on one side and the non-Christian world on the other. Christianity was now a minority everywhere in the world. The churches continued to be called to witness to the unique message of the gospel of Christ, but now the message was incarnated in varied cultures, no longer only that of the West. Seen from this perspective, the Tambaram conference lifted the curtain on a new act in mission history—one, however, that was delayed for a decade due to the interruption of the Second World War.

Book II opens in 1792 with the establishment of the Baptist Missionary Society in London, which began the modern era of Protestant missions. This beginning point was easy to determine. In contrast, it was more difficult to settle on an ending point for the narrative. We opted for the end of the Second World War, which set the stage for the postcolonial period. Over the following two decades independence would come to most of Europe's colonies. This, of course, would strongly affect the relations between the Western churches and the younger churches born of their mission programs.

However, this is too neat a picture. It should not be thought that by 1945 the pioneer work of missions had been completed and the only remaining task was to establish new relations between the old churches of the West and the new churches of what would now be called the Majority World. There were in fact still many ethnic groups that had neither heard the gospel of Jesus Christ proclaimed, nor possessed the Bible in their own language. There were still immense masses that for political or religious reasons remained inaccessible to traditional missionary work. Moreover, although the number of Christians on the earth quadrupled between 1900 and 2000, increasing from 500 million to two billion, they still remain only about a third of the globe's total population. This is due to the demographic explosion that has especially affected the least evangelized countries.

Hence, this book is interrupted rather than concluded. This is not ignominious, since it is in this way that the Acts of the Apostles—the first history of mission—also ends. The words "the end of mission" will be written by the one who is Lord of the church as well as of history, not us. He will do so when the good news of the kingdom will have been preached in the entire world to serve as witness to all the nations (Matthew 24:14).

It would be audacious to give a global evaluation of the events narrated in this work. Moreover, such an evaluation does not ultimately belong to us. The apostle Paul, remarking on the value of the work that he and other missionaries had accomplished, noted: "If any man builds on this foundation [Jesus Christ] using gold, silver, costly stones, wood, hay or straw, his work will be shown for what it is, because the Day [of the Lord] will bring it to light" (1 Cor 3:12,13).

Two aspects of mission, however, ought to be set forth. First, the reading of a book such as this might give one the false impression that mission is now outdated. The work of our predecessors is certainly worthy of our attention, but it is not for us to idealize them or to duplicate their work in our time. To approach an understanding of the history of mission is to glimpse God at work in the past through the fragility and ambiguities of human enterprises, and it is to draw lessons from past experience that might help us to accomplish the tasks before us today. Since the time of the pioneer missionaries, great changes in religion, culture, politics, and economics have altered relations between the West and other parts of the world; and many of these changes are due in no small measure to the missionaries themselves. Some churches have been born, come to maturity, and are now sending out missionaries of their own. Churches that are centuries old and others that have existed only for decades are now working together to proclaim throughout the world the name of Christ—the earth's only hope, whether it knows it or not, whether it wants him or not. To imagine that at this point missions should repeat the past or that missionaries should imitate their predecessors would be to misunderstand our place in the history of God's mission.

This takes us to a second point: when Carey and his contemporaries traveled overseas, Europe was then the center of the world and the center of Christendom (the United States at that time had only a small population of about 8 million inhabitants). Beyond the European continent and the nominal Catholicism of Latin America, Christians were tiny minorities in different places around the globe. Two centuries later, the majority of Christians are now living outside the West and are demonstrating a spiritual dynamism that sharply contrasts with the tired "old churches" in much of Europe. This extraordinary reversal could well lead to the resowing of our countries by those who are the fruit of our ancestors' obedience. But this is a distant vision that lies well outside the purview of this study.

It is sufficient for us to understand, as our predecessors did, that the mandate of mission is addressed to the entire church and concerns the entire world. The gospel is not a Western product; rather, it is the gift of God to all humanity. It comes to us through his Son, who was born of a woman, who lived among a small Near Eastern people at the crossroads of the continents, and whom God set apart for the salvation of the world. No one has exclusive rights to the message; none can claim that it is indispensable for some people but dispensable for others; and none are more in need of the gift than others or, conversely, less worthy to receive it. This conviction of the universal nature of the gospel has been shared by the missionaries whose stories have been told here and who often paid a high price for their beliefs, even on occasion laying down their lives. Whatever the limitations and deficiencies of their work, they had full authority to pass on the gospel message to all the peoples of the world; and that authority resides with us as well, even to the end of the age.

# Bibliography

Abbreviations: SMEP: Société des Missions Évangéliques de Paris; G.M.: Éditions des Groupes Missionaires; L&F: Labor & Fides.

## GENERAL WORKS

Barrett, D. B. *World Christian Encyclopedia*. 2 vols. New York: Oxford University Press, 2001.

Blandenier, J. "Mission et religions du point de vue protestant et oecuménique (période 1910–1928)." In F. Jacquin and J. F. Zorn, eds. *L'altérité religieuse: Un défi pour la mission chrétienne*. Paris: Karthala, 2001.

Blocher, J. A., and J. Blandenier. *L'évangélisation du monde: Précis d'histoire des missions*. Vol. 1, *Des origines au XVIIIe siècle*. Lavigny: G.M., 1998.

Burckhardt, G., and R. Grundemann. *Les missions évangéliques*. 4 vols. French translation. Lausanne: Bridel, 1884–1887.

Comby, J. "Deux mille ans d'évangélisation." *Bibliothèque d'histoire du christianisme* 29 (1992): 172–73.

Delacroix, S., ed. *Histoire universelle des missions catholiques*. 4 vols. Paris: 1957–1959.

Flachsmeier, H. R. *Geschichte der evangelischen Weltmission*. Giessen, Germany: Brunnen-Verlag, 1963.

Foster, J. *A partir de Jérusalem*. Neuchâtel: Delachaux & Niestlé, 1961.

Gairdner, W. H. T. *Edinburgh 1910: An Account and Interpretation of the World Missionary Conference*. London: Oliphant, Anderson & Ferrier, 1910.

Latourette, K. S. *A History of the Expansion of Christianity*. 7 vols. New York: Harper & Brothers, 1937–1945.

———. *A History of Christian Missions in China*. London: SPCK, 1929.

Mayeur, J. M., C. Pietri, A. Vaucher, and M. Venard, eds. *Histoire du christianisme*. Paris: Desclée, 1995.

Merle, M., ed. *Les églises chrétiennes et la decolonisation*. Paris: Armand Colin, 1967.

Nagel, L. *Les Missions évangéliques au XIXe siècle*. Neuchâtel: The Basel Mission.

Neill, S. *A History of Christian Missions*. Grand Rapids: Eerdmans, 1964.

Newbigin, L. *Honest Religion for Secular Man*. Philadelphia: Westminster, 1966.

Société des missions évangéliques. *Petite histoire des missions chrétiennes par un laïque.* 2nd ed. Paris: SMEP, 1929.

Sédès, J. M. "Histoire des missions françaises." *Que sais-je?* 405. Paris: PUF, 1950.

Spindler, M. "Naître et grandir en église: La pensée d'Henry Venn." In *Naître et grandir en église: Le role des autochtones dans la première inculturaton du christianisme hors d'Europe*, René Luneau, ed. Lyon, France: Université Jean Moulin, 1987.

Tucker, R. A. *Aux extrémités de la terre: Histoire biographique des missions chrétiennes.* French translation. Miami: Vida, 1989.

## GENERAL WORKS: AFRICA, MADAGASCAR, AND POLYNESIA

De Benoist, J. R. *Église et pouvoir au Soudan français, 1885–1945.* Paris: Karthala, 1987.

Falk, P. *La croissance de l'église en Afrique.* Kinshasa: Institut Supérieur Théologique de Kinshasa, 1985.

Hubsch, B., ed. *Madagascar et le christianisme.* Paris: Karthala, 1993.

Laux, C. *Les théocraties missionaries en Polynésie au XIXe siècle.* Paris: L'Harmattan, 2000.

Linden, J. *Christianisme et pouvoir au Rwanda, 1900–1990.* Paris: Karthala, 1999.

Raison-Jourde, F. *Bible et pouvoir à Madagascar au XIXe siècle: Invention d'une identité chrétienne et construction de'un etat.* Paris: Karthala, 1991.

Schaaf, Y. *L'histoire et le role de la Bible en Afrique.* Lavigny: G.M., 1994; 2nd ed. 2000.

Sundkler, B., and C. Steed, eds. *A History of the Church in Africa.* Cambridge: Cambridge University Press, 2000.

Trichet, P. *Côte d'Ivoire: Les premières pas d'une église.* Vol. 2, *1914–1940.* Abidjan: Éditions la Nouvelle, 1995.

———. *Côte d'Ivoire: Les premières tentatives d'évangélisation, 1637–1852.* Abidjan: Éditions la Nouvelle, 1995.

## PROTESTANT MISSIONS

Blanc, R., J. Blocher, and E. Kruger. *Histoire des missions protestantes françaises.* Flavion, Belgium: Le Phare, 1970.

Blanquis, J. *Les origines de la Société des Missions Évangéliques de Paris, 1822–1830.* 3 vols. Paris: SMEP, 1930–1935.

Eppler, P. *Geschichte der Basler Mission 1815–1899.* Basel, Switzerland: Verlag der Missionsbuchhandlung, 1900.

Grandjean, A. *La mission romande.* Lausanne: Bridel, 1917.

Hollard, R. *Missions colonials et missions noncolonials.* Paris: Report to the Conference to the Auxiliary Committees, 1900.

Joseph, G. *La Côte d'Ivoire: Le pays, les habitants.* Paris: Larose, 1917.

Mehl, R. *Décolonisation et missions protestantes.* Paris: SMEP, 1964.

Roux, A. "Problématique de la mission." In *Église et théologie*, no. 77, 1962.

Snead, A. C. *Missionary Atlas: A Manual of the Foreign Work of the Christian and Missionary Alliance.* Harrisburg, PA: Christian Publications, 1936.

Vallotton, B. *Un home: John R. Mott.* Paris: U.C.J.G., 1951.

Wallis, E. and Bennet, M. *De toute tribu et de toute langue.* Lavigny: G.M., 1972.

Zorn, J.-F. *Le grand siècle d'une mission protestante: La mission de Paris de 1822 à 1914.* Paris: Karthala/ Les Bergers et Les Mages, 1993.

———. "Missions protestantes en Afrique austral." In *Histoire du christianisme,* vol. 11, Paris: Desclée, 1995.

# AFRICA AND MADAGASCAR

Anderson, D. *We Felt Like Grasshoppers: The Story of Africa Inland Mission.* Nottingham, England: Crossway Books, 1994.

Asch, S. *L'église du prophète Kimbangu.* Paris: Kaarthala, 1983.

Berthoud, R. *Du Transvaal à Lourenço Marques.* Lausanne: Bridel, 1904.

Biber, C. *Cent ans au Mazambique.* Lausanne: Éditions du Soc, 1988.

Blaser, K. ed. "Mission et photographie," *Le fait missionaire,* no. 10. Lausanne, 2001.

Braekman, E. M. *Histoire du protestantisme au Congo.* Brussels: Librairie des Eclaireurs Unionistes, 1961.

Bréchet, R. *J'ai ouvert une port devant toi.* Lausanne: Alliance Missionaire Evangélique, 1972.

De Billy, E. *En Côte d'Ivoire: Mission protestante d'A.O.F.* Paris: SMEP, ca. 1930.

Decorvet, J. *Les matins de Dieu* [History of the Biblical Mission in the Ivory Coast]. 2nd ed. Nogent-sur-Marne, France: Mission Biblique en Côte d'Ivoire, 1977.

Dieterlen, H. "François Coillard." In *Récits missionnaires illustré,* no. 13. Paris: SMEP, 1926.

Dinnen, S. *Faith on Fire: Norman Grubb and the Building of WEC.* Fearn, Scotland: Christina Foucs, 1997.

Ellengerger, V. *Sur les Hauts-Plateaux du Lessoute.* Paris: SMEP, 1930.

Faure, J. *Histoire des missions et églises protestantes en Afrique occidentale des origines à 1884.* Yaoundé: CLE, 1978.

———. *Togo: Champ de mission.* Paris: SMEP, ca. 1942.

Huyghues-Belrose, V. *Les premiers missionnaires protestants de Madagascar, 1795–1827.* Paris: Karthala, 2001.

Joubert, L. "Mission et colonization en Afrique noire." In *Les missions protestantes et l'histoire* Montpellier: Actes du IIe Colloque, 1971.

Kuntima, D. *L'histoire du Kimbanguisme.* Kinshasa: Kimbanguistes, 1984.

Leenhardt, M. *Le mouvement éthiopien au sud de l'Afrique de 1896 à 1899.* Cahors, France: Couesiant, 1902.

Livingstone, D., and H. M. Stanley. *Du Zambèze au Tanganyika.* Paris: Gheerbrant, 1969.

Maire, C. D. *Dynamique sociale des mutations religieuses. Expansion des protestantismes en Côte d'Ivoire.* Paris: EPHE, 1975.

Mehl, R. *Traité de sociologie du protestantism.* Neuchâtel: Delachaux & Niestlé, 1965.

Mondain, G. *Un siècle de mission protestante à Madagascar.* Paris: SMEP, 1920.

Monnier, H. *Mission Philafricaine en Angola, 1897–1947.* Lausanne, 1947.

Nicod, H. *Conquérants du golfe de Guinée.* Paris: SMEP, 1947.

Northcott, C. *Livingstone en Afrique.* Neuchâtel: Delachaux & Niestlé, 1960.

Page, M. E. "The Arabs and the Slave Trade" In *Livingstone: Man of Africa: Memorial Essays 1873–1973*, Briglal Pachai, ed. London/New York: Longmans, 1973.

Rolland, G., and A. Rolland. *Un combat de la foi: 70 ans de vie missionnaire à Tizi-Ouzou.* Crempigny, France: Mission Rolland, 1997.

Roux, A. *L'evangile dans la forêt: Naissance d'une église en Afrique noire.* Paris: Cerf, 1971.

——. *A l'ombre de la grande forêt.* Paris: Le Cerf, 1971.

Rusillon, H. *Une énigme missionaire: Les destinées de l'église chrétienne dans l'Afrique du Nord.* Paris: SMEP, 1931.

Saint-John, P. *Souffle de vie: La mission au Ruanda.* Lavigny: G.M., 1973.

Schmid, S. *Mark Christian Hayford, 1864–1935: Ein pionier aus Westafrika.* Bonn: Verlag für Kultur und Wissenschaft, 1999.

Slageren, J. *Les débuts du christianisme au Cameroun.* Leyden, The Netherlands: E. J. Brill, 1972.

Smith, F. G. *Velona! Le triomphe des martyrs malgaches.* Chalon-sur-Saône, France: Europresse, 1988.

Steele, F. *Not in Vain: The Story of North Africa Mission.* Pasadena, CA: William Carey Library, 1981.

Tapsoba, I. F. *Églises et mouvements évangéliques au Burkina Faso 1921–1989.* Ouagadougou, 1990.

Teeuwissen, R. "Le précurseur oublié: Avant Schweitzer; Il y avait Nassau." In *Le christianisme au XXe siècle*, no. 276, 1990.

Twagirayesu, M., and J. van Butselaar. *Ce don que nous avons reçu: Histoire de l'église presbytérienne au Rwanda.* Kigali: Église Presbytérienne au Rwanda, 1982.

Walker, F. D. *Harris: Le prophète noir.* Privas, France, Pasteur S. Delattre, 1931.

## ASIA

Berron, P. *Une oeuvre missionnaire en Orient et en Occident: Origine et développement de l'action chrétienne en Orient.* Strasbourg, France: Oberlin, [1962?].

Broomhall, M. *The Jubilee Story of the China Inland Mission.* London: China Inland Mission, 1915.

Decorvet, J., and G. Rochat. *L'appel du Laos.* Yverdon, Switzerland: Imprimerie H. Cornaz, 1946.

Dupertuis, S. "L'evangile au pays du million d'éléphants: Laos 02; Cent ans de mission." *Dossier vivre* 20. Geneva: Je Sème, 2002.

Hornus, J.-M. "Cent cinquante ans de présence évangélique au Proche-Orient, 1808–1958." *Foi et Vie* 78 (March 1979): 2–108.

Lyall, L. T. *Passion pour l'extraordinaire: Mission à l'intérieur de la Chine, 1865–1965.* Thun, Switzerland: Union Missionnaire d'Outre-mer, 1965.

Murao, M. S., and W. H. Murray Walton. *Japan and Christ.* London: Church Missionary Society, 1928.

Richter, J. *Mission und evangelisation im Orient.* Gütersloh, Germany: Bertelsmann Verlag, 1930.

# PACIFIC AND LATIN AMERICA

Bastian, J.-P. *Le protestantisme en Amérique latine: Une approche socio-historique*. Geneva: L&F, 1993.

De Melo Chaves, M. *Pionniers de la foi* [Establishment of Protestantism among the people of Brazil]. Translated by E. G. Léonard. Carrières-sous-Poissy, France: La Cause, n.d.

Leenhardt, M. *De la mort à la vie: Centenaire de la Nouvelle Calédonie*. Paris: SMEP, 1953.

——. *La grande terre: Mission de Nouvelle Calédonie*. Paris: SMEP, 1922.

Vernier, C. *Tahitiens d'autrefois; Tahitiens d'aujourd'hui*. Paris: SMEP, 1934.

Vernier, H. *Au vent des cyclones: Puai noa mai te vero*. Paris: Les Bergers et Les Mages, 1986.

# MISSIONARY BIOGRAPHIES

## Africa

Bianquis, J. *Le prophète Harris*. Paris: SMEP, 1924.

Blandenier, M. *A toute creature* [Abridged biographies of F. Coillard, C. Studd, H. Taylor, W. Booth]. 3rd ed. Lavigny: G.M., 1981.

Chatelain, A. *Héli Chatelain: L'ami de l'Angola; Foundateur de la Mission Philafricaine, 1859–1908*. Lausanne: Mission Philafricaine, 1918.

Chomé, J. *La passion de Kimbangu*. Brussels: Éditions Les Amis de la Presence Africaine, 1959.

Christen, E. *Schweitzer l'africain*. 6th ed. Geneva: L&F, 1954.

Clavier, H. *Thomas Arbousset pionnier*. Paris: SMEP, 1963.

Decorvet, J. "Samuel Ajayi Crowther: Un père de l'église en Afrique noire." *Foi Vivante* 309 (1992).

Decorvet, P. *Victoire sur l'impossible: Miss Trotter à la rencontre de l'islam*. Vevey, Switzerland: G.M., 1963.

Dieterlen, H. *Adolphe Mabille: Missionnaire*. Paris: SMEP, 1898.

——. *Eugène Casalis, 1812–1891*. Paris: SMEP, 1930.

Faure, F. *George Grenfell: Missionnaire au Congo, 1849–1906*. Paris: SMEP, 1928.

Favre, E. *François Coillard: Enfance et jeunesse; Coillard: Missionaire au Lessouto; Coillard: Missionaire au Zambèze*. 3 vols. Paris: SMEP, 1908–1913.

——. *La vie d'un missionaire français: François Coillard*. Paris: SMEP, 1922.

——. *Les vingt-cinq ans de Coillard au Lessouto*. Paris, SMEP, 1933.

Hayford, C. *William Wade Harris: The West African Reformer; The Man and His Message* London: C. M. Philips, 1915.

Huffman, R. M. *A Passion for the Impossible: The Life of Lilias Trotter*. Wheaton: Harold Shaw, 1999.

Junod, H. A. *Ernest Creux et Paul Berthoud: Foundateurs de la Mission Suisse en Afrique du Sud*. Lausanne: Mission Suisse dans l'Afrique du Sud, 1933.

Junod, H. P. *Henri-Alexandre Junod: Missionnaire et savant, 1863–1934*. Lausanne: Mission Suisse dans l'Afrique du Sud, 1934.

Laufer, J. J. *Stanley: Briseur d'obstacle*. Geneva: Labor & Fides, 1946.

M'Bokolo, E. *David Livingstone: Exploration dans l'Afrique australe et le basin du Zambèze, 1840–1864*. Paris: Karthala, 1981.

Mackenzie, R. *David Livingstone: The Truth behind the Legend*. Eastbourne, England: Kingsway, 1993.

Martin, M. L. *Simon Kimbangu: Un prophète et son église*. Lausanne: Éditions du Soc, 1981.

Northcott, C. *David Livingstone: His Triumph, Decline and Fall*. London: Lutterworth, 1973.

———. *Robert Moffat: Pioneer in Africa*. New York: Harper & Brothers, 1961.

Pachai, B., ed. *Livingstone: Man of Africa*. London: Longman Group, 1973.

Pigott, B. *L'appel du désert: Vie de Lilias Trotter; Messagère de Dieu chez les musulmans*. Dieulefit, France: Nouvelle Société d'Éditions de Toulouse, 1937.

Siordet, J. E. *Adèle Mabille, née Casalis, 1840–1923*. Paris: SMEP, 1933.

Spartalis, P. J. *Karl Dumm: Last of the Livingstones*. Bonn: Verlag für Kultur und Wissenschaft, 1994.

## Asia

Barnaud, J. *William Carey: Le pionnier des missions moderns*. Paris: SMEP, 1935.

Beck, J. R. *Dorothy Carey: The Tragic and Untold Story of Mrs. William Carey*. Grand Rapids: Baker Book House, 1992.

Blocher, J. A. *Robert Morrison: L'apôtre de la Chine, 1782–1834*. Paris: Les Bons Semeurs, 1938.

Bosshardt, A. *Conduit par sa main*. Lavigny: Les Groupes Missionnaires, 1983.

Crossman, E. *Fleuve de lumière* [Biography of James O. Fraser]. Lavigny: G.M., 1985.

Dewanji, M. *William Carey and the Indian Renaissance*. Delhi: William Carey Study and Research Centre, 1996.

Drewery, M. *William Carey: A Biography*. Grand Rapids: Zondervan, 1978.

Farelly, R. *William Carey*. Paris: Société de Publications Baptistes, 1984.

Grubb, N. *Charles Studd: Champion de Dieu*. 5th ed. La Bégude-de-Mazenc, France: Croisade du Livre Chrétien, 1977.

Hayes, E. H. *Robert Morrison: China's Pioneer*. Westminster: Livingstone, 1925.

Morrow, H. W. *Splendeur de Dieu* [Biography of Adoniram Judson, pioneer in Burma]. Neuchâtel: Delachaux & Niestlé, 1955.

Nommensen, L. I. *Cinquante-six ans parmi les cannibals*, (trans. M. L. Pilloud). Lausanne: La Concorde, 1960.

Pollock, J. *The Cambridge Seven*. London: InterVarsity, 1969).

Steer, R. *Hudson Taylor: L'evangile au coeur de la Chine*. Lavigny: G.M., 1996.

Taylor, H. *L'aventure de la foi* [The abridged biography]. Lavigny: Les Groupes Missionaires, 1986.

Taylor, H. *Vie de Hudson Taylor*. Lavigny: G.M., 1979.

Walker, F. D. *William Carey: Missionary Pioneer and Statesman*. Chicago: Moody, 1925.

*Pacific and Latin America*

Brunel, G. *John Williams: Apôtre des mers du Sud.* 2 vols. Cahors, France: Coueslant, 1931.

Paton, J. G. *John G. Paton: Le grand apôtre des cannibals.* Translated and abridged by C. Galland. Geneva: 1898.

———. *Missionary to the New Hebrides: An Autobiography.* London: Hodder & Stoughton, 1891.

Thompson, P. *An Unquenchable Flame: Biography of Allen Gardiner; Founder of the South American Missionary Society.* London: Hodder & Stoughton, 1983.

## SELECTED MISSIOLOGICAL WORKS

Allen, R. *Jerusalem: A Critical Review of "The World Mission of Christianity."* London: World Dominion, 1928.

———. *Missionary Methods: St. Paul's or Ours?* 2nd ed. London: World Dominion, 1930.

Blandenier, J., M. Blandenier, A. Heiniger, and W. Schulthess. *Mission renouvelée.* Lavigny: G.M., 1975.

Blaser, K. *Repères pour la mission chrétienne.* Geneva: L&F, 2000.

Bosch, D. *Transforming Mission: Paradigm Shifts in Theology of Mission.* New York: Orbis Books, 1991.

———. *Dynamique de la mission chrétienne: Histoire et avenir des modèles missionnaires.* Paris: Karthala, 1995.

Collective. *Dictionnaire oecuménique de missiologie: Cent mots pour la mission.* Paris: Cerf, 2001.

Collective. *La culture au risque de l'evangile: Rapport de Willowbank.* Lausanne: Presses Bibliques Universitaires, 1979.

Collective. *Pour la conquête du monde: Message de la Conférence Missionaire de Jérusalem.* Paris: Conseil International des Missions, 1928.

Friesen, S. *Missionary Responses to Tribal Religions at Edinburgh, 1910: Studies in Church History.* Vol. 1. New York: Peter Lang Publishing, 1996.

Gairdner, W. H. T. *Edinburgh 1910: An Account and Interpretation of the World Missionary Conference.* London: Oliphant, Anderson & Ferrier, 1910.

Griffiths, M. *Envoyer, c'est partir un peu.* Lavigny: G.M., 1997.

Hiebert, P. G. *Mission et culture.* Saint-Légier, Switzerland: Emmaüs, 2002.

Johnstone, P. *Flashes sur le monde.* Fontenay-sous-Bois, France: Éditions Farel, 1979.

Kä Mana. *Foi chrétienne: Crise africaine et reconstruction de l'Afrique.* Lomé: CETA, 1992.

———. *La nouvelle évangélisation en Afrique.* Paris: Karthala, 2000.

Karamago, A. *Dieu au pays des mille collines.* Lausanne: Éditions du Soc, 1988.

———. "L'evangile en Afrique: Ruptures et continuité." Thesis. Yens sur Morges, Switzerland: Cabedita, 1990.

Kraemer, H. *La lumière des nations.* Neuchâtel: Delachaux & Niestlé, 1944.

Matthey, J. *Et pourtant, la mission* [Approach to mission found in the book of Acts]. Aubonne: Éditions du Moulin, 1984.

Mott, J. *L'heure decisive des missions chrétiennes.* French translation. Saint-Blaise, Switzerland: Foyer Solidariste, 1912.

Newbigin, L. *En mission sur le chemin du Christ.* Aubonne: Éditions du Moulin, 1989.

——. *The Relevance of Trinitarian Doctrine for Today's Mission.* Edinburgh: House Press, 1963.

——. *Une religion pour le monde séculier.* Tournai, Belgium: Casterman, 1967.

Nida, E. *Coutumes et cultures.* Lavigny: G.M., 1984.

Richardson, D. *L'éternité dans leur coeur.* French translation. Lausanne: Jeunesse en Mission, 1982.

Ries, J. *Les chrétiens parmi les religions: Des Actes des Apôtres à Vatican II.* Paris: Desclèe, 1987.

Roux, A. *Mission des églises, mission de l'église.* Paris: Cerf, 1984.

Scott, J. *Mission chrétienne dans le monde monderne.* Lavigny: G.M., 1977.

Spindler, M. *La mission: Combat pour le salut du monde.* Neuchâtel: Delachaux & Niestlé, 1967.

Van Lin, J., and M. Spindler. *La théologie protestante des religions non-chrétiennes de 1910 à 1938.* Paris: Centre Protestant d'Études et de Documentation, 1979.

## MISSIOLOGICAL JOURNALS

*Perspectives missionaires.*

*Revue de missiologie protestante.*

*Secrétariat de rédation*: Jean-François Hérouard, 12 rue Perdonnet, FR-75010 Paris, France; jfherouard@opcareg.org.

# Index of People, Institutions, and Ethnic Groups

## A

Abgar, 20–21
Addai, 20
Aedesius, 49–50
Affonso I, 171–72
Africa Inland Mission (AIM), 296, 558, 572, 583–84, 590, 610
Afrikaner, Jonker, 464
Aglipay, Gregory, 385
Alamans, 53–55, 68
Alcuin, 82, 90, 100
Alexander VI (pope), 140, 148
Alexander VII, 186
Algiers Mission Band, 213, 276, 644
Algonquin, 145, 168, 228, 288
Allan, George, 295
Allégret, Elie, 549, 551, 602–03, 710
Allen, Roland, 714
Alopen, 121
Amand, 75, 89–90, 100
American Baptist Missionary Union (ABMU, or American Baptist Foreign Mission Society, ABMB), 290, 372, 570
American Board of Commissioners for Foreign Missions, 289, 371, 654
Anderson, John, 646
Anet, Henri, 573
Angles, 53, 70, 72
Anjiro, 180–83

Anskar, 83–85, 87, 90, 100, 241
Antislavery Society, 499
Arabs, 51, 77–78, 90–91, 110, 130–32, 138, 175, 554, 558, 564, 567, 569, 581, 584, 586–87, 592, 607, 639, 641, 644–47, 650, 654–57
Araucanian (ethnic group), 678
Arawaks, 215, 270
Arbousset, Thomas, 411, 418, 641
Archives, 21, 123, 153, 238
Arnot, Frederick Stanley, 570, 622
Ashanti (ethnic group), 515–16, 524, 539
Ashmun, Yehudi, 505
Asser, 486
Atger, François, 418
Athanasius, 50, 639
Audétat Fritz, 393–94
Augustine of Canterbury, 70–73
Augustine of Hippo, 28, 54, 130, 145, 240, 639, 692
Avars, 87
Azande (ethnic group), 558
Azariah, Vedanayagam Samuel, 336

## B

Bacon, Roger, 104
Bailey, Wellesley, 301
Baker, S. W., 425
Bambara (ethnic group), 520–21, 554
Bamiléké (ethnic group), 550
Bancel Marguerite, 643

Baptist Mid-Mission, 608

Baptist Missionary Society (BMS), 279, 289, 308, 310–11, 327–28, 341, 372, 474, 541, 544–45, 547, 565, 569–70, 682, 684

Bar Sawma, 125–26

Bardesanes, 22

Barnabas, 6, 12

Barotse (ethnic group), 486, 488, 493

Barrett, David (Encyclopedia), 458

Bartholomew, 10, 26, 138, 218, 222

Basel Mission, 290, 349, 401, 499, 502, 505, 515, 528, 547–52, 599, 641, 652

Bastian, Jean Pierre, 219, 663, 686

Batak (ethnic group), 401–03

Beatrice, Donna, 172

Beck, Anne-Marie, 656

Beck, Jean, 261

Bede the Venerable, 71

Beigbeder, Onésime, 604

Belgian Congo Missionary Society, 573, 592–94

Bell, Schall von, 189–91

Benedict of Nursia, 69–70, 75, 115

Benington, Charles, 556

Bennet, Cephas, 378

Benoit, Pierre, 533

Bentley, W. Holman, 567

Bergeret, Etienne, 549

Berlin Mission, 547–49, 584

Berron, Paul, 656

Berthoud, Paul and Mabille, 486

Betchouana, or Tswana (ethnic group), 464

Bete, 539

Bethel Mission (Evangelische Mission-sgesellschall für Ostafrika), 247, 591–94

Bevan, Thomas, 623–34

Beza, Theodore, 211

Bianquis, Jean, 696

Bibliander, Theodore, 201, 207–09

Biblical Mission in the Ivory Coast (Mission Biblique en Côte d'Ivoire), 536–38

Bingham, Roland, 294, 298, 556

Blandina, 30

Blocher, Arthur, 537–39

Blue Cross, 420, 452

Blumhardt, Christian H., 502, 598

Boardman, George, 376–77

Boardman, Richard, 248

Boardman, Sarah, 378

Bobo (ethnic group), 556–57

Bodelschwingh, Fredrich von, 700

Bodelschwingh, Gustav von, 591

Boegner, Alfred, 420, 603, 606, 635

Boers, 461, 482, 486, 488, 616–17

Boleslaus II, or Boleslaus the Pious, 95, 97

Boniface, 74–76, 90, 100

Boniface IV, 67

Boniface VIII (pope), 112

Bosch, David, 35, 63, 694, 704, 709–10

Bosshardt, Alfred, 370

Bouchet, Juste, 491

Bougainville, Louis-Antoine, 166, 411, 415

Boyle, Robert, 225

Brainerd, David, 246–48

Braun, Peter, 269

Bréchet Rodolphe, 619–21

Bremen Mission (see also Norddeutsche Missions-gesellslchaft), 523–24, 528

Brent, Charles Henry, 386

Brès, Emile, 644

Bright, Harry, 555

Brigitte, 61

British and Foreign Bible Society, 288, 321, 355, 391, 396, 506, 558, 594, 598, 600, 645, 648, 673

Bruce, Robert, 339–40

Brügger, Willy, 393–94

Brunel, Gaston, 420

Bucer, Martin, 199, 202, 207

Bullom (ethnic group), 499, 501

Bulu, Joeli, 426

Burdon, J. S., 355

Burgunds, 53–56
Burton, Richard, 467, 500, 583, 590
Buyse, John, 610

**C**

Cakchiquel (ethnic group), 302
Caluquembes (ethnic group), 617, 620–21
Calvin, John, 197, 199, 201–02, 209, 211,
    213–15, 219, 221, 226
Cameron, James, 363, 369, 625, 632
Campanius, Johann, 227, 232
Campbell, Thomas and Alexander, 571
Capitein, Jacob, 497–98, 527
Capuchins, 143–44, 168, 529, 597–98,
    607, 685
Carey, Dorothy, 311, 314–15, 319
Carey, Felix, 311, 324, 329, 373
Carey, William, 241, 275, 279, 289,
    307–31, 333, 337–38, 341, 345, 347,
    371, 373–74, 410–11, 565, 684, 698,
    703, 707
Casalis, Eugene, 481, 519
Cassels, W. W., 364
Cavelier de la Salle, 168
Celsus, 27, 33–34
Central American Mission, 681–83
Charlemagne, 81–82, 90, 99–100, 103, 692
Charles I, 225
Charles II, 225, 232
Charles V, 144, 152, 155–56, 639
Chastagner, Émile, 556
Chatelain, Alida, 618–19
Chatelain, Heli, 613–21
Chiang Kai-Shek, 370
Chin (ethnic group), 372, 379
China Inland Mission (CIM), 290, 292,
    353, 358, 360–70, 380
Chinese Evangelization Society (CES), 354
Chrischona (Pilgermission St-Chrischo-
    na), 599, 648, 654, 671–72
Christian Action in the Orient (Action
    Chretiénne en Orient, ACO), 656

Christian and Missionary Alliance
    (CMA), 295–96, 382, 386–88, 390,
    395–97, 523, 539, 554, 556–57, 571,
    654, 675, 678–79
Christian Missions to Many Lands, 608
Christian VI, 258, 264, 277
Christol, Frédéric, 487, 549–50
Church Missionary Society (CMS),
    289, 474, 500, 507, 522, 558, 572, 581,
    586, 598
Cita, evangelist Lao, 393, 395
Clement of Alexandria, 26, 29, 92, 112,
    127–28
Clotilda, 55–56, 71
Coillard, François, Christina, 474, 481–93,
    568, 698
Coligny, Gaspard de (admiral), 213–15,
    218–19, 222–23
Colomba, 64, 100, 341
Colomban, 62, 65–69, 74–75, 89, 100
Columbus, Christopher, 139, 143, 149,
    153, 307, 683–85
Comber, Thomas, 566, 568
Congo Balolo Mission, 571
Congress of Berlin, 458, 522, 564, 584,
    590, 609, 691, 697, 704
Coninck, André Oechsner de, 549
Constance, 42, 263
Constantine (emperor), 17, 22, 30, 32–33,
    38, 41–42, 49, 55, 81, 91–92, 94, 96,
    190, 641, 692
Constantius Cholrus, 32–33
Contesse, Charles, 391, 393
Contesse, Gabriel, Marguerite, 390–93
Cook, James, 409–10, 415
Cornelius (bishop), 37
Cornelius (Roman captain), 5
Cox, Melville, 505
Craven, Henry, 565–66
Crawford, Dan, 570
Creux, Ernest, 486
Croats, 90
Cromwell, Oliver, 225, 287, 663

Crowther, Samuel Ajayi, 502, 508–15, 526, 532, 582, 704

Cru, Louis, 449

Cuendet, Eugene, 641

Cupidon, John Cyprian (bishop of Carthage), 502

Cyprian (bishop of Aquitaine), 28–29, 56, 639

Cyril (*see also* Constantine), 91–94, 100

## D

Daniel, Ebenezer, 341

Daniel of Winchester, 76

Danish-Hallo Mission, 288, 312

Dardier, Henri, 487

Darwin, Charles, 668, 672

Daumas, François, 481

David, Christian, 258, 263

David of Basra, 24

Davidson, Benjamin, 294

Dawson, Albert, 678

Dayak (ethnic group), 401

Deans, Robert, 572

Deans, Williams, 572

Debarge, 550

Decorvet, Philippe, 644

Delhove, David Elie, 593–94

Delord, Philadelphe, 450–51

Deutsche, Blindenmission (German Mission to the Blind; later, Christoffel Blindemission), 340

Diangienda, Joseph, 576–79

Dibundu, Joseph, 548

Diderot, 166

Dieterlé, Paul, 550

Dieterlen, Hermann, 484, 486

Diocletian, 32–33, 41, 79

Diognetus (epistle to), 37, 39

Dionysius (Denys) (bishop of Paris), 31

Dionysius (Denys) of Corinth, 36

Dober, Leonard, 265–67, 277

Dominic Guzman, 116

Dominicans, 106–08, 115–16, 125, 141, 143, 145–49, 151–52, 155–56, 175, 191, 198, 386–97, 529, 646, 663, 685

Douala (ethnic group), 541–46, 549

Duff, Alexander, 332–33

Dufour, Marie, 394

Dupetit-Thouars, 416

Durand, Edgard, 593

Dusun (ethnic group), 398

Dyak (ethnic group), 398

Dyer, Maria (Taylor), 356, 360

## E

Echoes of Service, 645

Edwards, Jonathan, 245, 248

Egede, Hans, 255–62, 335

Egede, Paul, 258, 262

Elim Mission, 610

Eliot, John, 227–32, 246–47, 273, 287

Ellis, William, 631–32

Ephraim, 22

Erasmus, Desiderius, 205–07

Erasmus of Rotterdam, 205, 663

Erik IX, 87

Erik the Red, 86–87

Escande, Benjamin, 635

Eskimo, 276

Ethelbert, 71–72

Eusebius of Caesarea, 9, 25–26, 30, 34, 37, 39

Eusebius of Nicomedia, 47–48

Evangelical Mission against Leprosy, 301

Evangelical Mission in Laos, 388, 395

Evangelische Missionsgesellschaft für Ostafrika (Evangelical Mission Society for East Africa, *see also* Bethel Mission), 584, 591, 699–700

Evangeliska Fostrelands Stiffelsen (Evangelical Mission of Sweden), 600

Ewe (ethnic group), 523–24, 528

Ezena, 50

## F

Falashas (people), 599–600

Falk, Peter, 465

Fallot, Tommy, 695
Fang (ethnic group), 601
Farelly, Maurice, 552
Farquhar, Robert, 623–25
Farrington, Sophronia, 505
Faulding, Jennie (Taylor), 362
Faure, Felix, 567, 604, 635
Faure, Jean, 503, 524
Favre, Edouard, 491
Félix, Bernard, 394
Flad, Johann Martin, 599
Fletcher, Willis, 537
Foster, John, 321
Fountain, John, 317
Fourah Bay (College), 502, 508–09, 512, 520
Francis of Assisi, 114, 116–17
Francis Xavier, 166, 177, 179, 184–85, 187–89, 340, 382, 397, 399
Franciscan, 104, 110, 114–18, 125–26, 128–29, 141, 143–44, 146–48, 172, 188, 191, 198, 343, 384, 386, 399, 645–46, 650, 663
Francke, Auguste, 249–50
Franks, 53–56, 65, 71, 83, 91, 185
Fraser, James O., 369, 380
Frederic IV, 250, 252, 256–58
Freeman, Thomas Birch, 499, 506, 509–10, 514–17, 525–28
French, Thomas Valpy, 657
Fridolin, 74
Frumentius, 49–50
Fulani (ethnic group), 522
Fuller, Alexander, 542
Fuller, Andrew, 308, 311, 327
Fuller, Joseph Jackson, 542, 545–47
Funé, Jean, 396

## G

Gairdner, W. H. Temple, 649, 652
Gall, 66–68, 96
Galla (ethnic group), 598
Gandhi, Mahatma, 337, 714
Garanganze Evangelical Mission, 570

Gardiner, Allen, 666–71
Gautbert, 83
Geddie, John, 438–39, 442
Geza, Duke, 96
Glenny, Edward, 292–93, 297
Gobat, Samuel, 598–99, 648, 653
Gollmer, Charles Andrew, 510
Gospel Missionary Union (GMU), 554, 645, 678–79
Goths, 19, 46–47, 49, 53, 56
Gourmantche (ethnic group), 556
Grant, Asahel, 339
Grassfields (see also the Bamiléké ethnic group), 548, 550
Grebo (ethnic group), 530
Gregory I, or Gregory the Great (pope), 70–73
Gregory II (pope), 74
Gregory III (pope), 75
Gregory IV (pope), 83, 90
Gregory X (pope), 125
Gregory XV (pope), 186
Gregory of Tours, 31, 55–57
Gregory Thaumaturgus, 19, 35
Gregory the Illuminator, 25, 119
Grenfell, George, 564–70, 616
Griffith, David, 625–26, 630
Griswold, Benjamin, 601
Grotius, Hugo, 236–37, 239
Grubb, Norman, 300–01
Grubb, Wilfried B., 676
Guarani, 156–65, 168
Guillebaud, Harold, 594–95
Guinness, Henry Grattan, 292–93, 297, 565, 571
Gun (ethnic group), 525
Gundaphore, 10, 23–24
Gustav I Vasa, 224
Gützlaff, Karl, 343, 349–50, 387

## H

Haas, William Clarence, 609
Haensel, Charles, 502
Haoussa (ethnic group), 557

Harris, William Wade, 528, 530–38, 575–76

Hartzell, Joseph, 621

Hasseltine, Anna (Judson), 371

Hawels, Thomas, 410

Hayford, Mark Christian, 536–38

Henrique, Don, 171

Henry of Uppsala, 87

Henry the Navigator, 137–38

Heurnius, Justus, 234–35, 287, 399

Heyden, Ernst von der, 592–93

Heyling, Peter, 237, 239–40, 287, 581

Hinderer, David, 526

Hocart, Thomas, 644

Hoffmann, Wilhelm, 528

Honoré, Josué, 416, 593

Horne, Melville, 500

Hosius, 33

Hoste, D. E., 364, 366

Hottentots, 273–75, 461–64

Hough, George, 374

Howe, William, 417

Hsi (Pastor), 365

Hubmaier, Balthasar, 203

Hughes, Grace, 328

Humbert of Romans, 107

Huns, 53–54, 121

Hurons, 145, 168

Huss, John, 263

Hutchinson, J., 422, 424

Hutter, Jacob, 203–04

Hutterite, 204

**I**

Ibo (ethnic group), 527

Ignatius of Antioch, 36

Ignatius of Loyola, 111, 141, 175, 177

Igorot (ethnic group), 386

Inuit (see also Eskimo), 86, 255, 257–62, 264

Irenaeus of Lyons, 30, 35

Iroquois, 145, 168, 271–72

Isabella of Castile, 139, 148

**J**

Jacobites, 23, 50, 109

Jalla, Adolphe, 488, 493

Jalla, Louis, 487

Jansenist, 191, 519

Jaques, Louis, 519–21

Jauréguiberry, Jean-Bernard, 449, 519–20

Jeanmairet, Dorwald, 487

Jefferson, John Clark, 412

Jennings, R. L., 576–77

Jerome, 39, 149

Jesuits, 111, 121, 141–42, 144–49, 156–57, 159–69, 172–73, 175–77, 179, 181, 183, 185, 187–93, 198, 229, 240, 280, 333, 337, 340–41, 343, 348, 382, 384, 386, 395, 397, 416, 542, 607, 609, 634–35, 643, 668, 685

Jessup, Henry and Samuel, 655

Jivaros (ethnic group), 678

Johanson, 556

Johanssen, Ernst, 584, 591–93

John (apostle), 6, 9, 17–18, 30, 184, 267, 415

John I, 103, 137

John III, 177

John VIII (pope), 90, 92–93

John XIX (pope), 85

John XXII, 128

John Chrysostrom, 23

John Damascus, 105–06

John of Brienne, 116

John of Montecorvino, 126, 128

John of Persia, 24

Johnson, James, 502

Johnson, Thomas, 543–44, 546

Jones, Clarence W., 679

Jones, David, 623–25, 630

Jones, John (Loyalty Islands), 356, 448–49

Jones, John Taylor, 387

Joubert, Louis, 466, 479, 513

Jowett, William, 598, 648, 652–53

Juàrez, Benito, 673, 681

Judson, Adoniram, 313, 371–76, 378–79, 387, 570, 654

Julian the Apostate, 38, 42, 131
Justin Martyr, 7, 35–36, 39
Justinian (emperor), 18, 29, 32, 78, 131, 240, 242

**K**

Kä, Mana, 514, 532
Kaardal, J. I., 607–08
Kachin, (ethnic group), 372, 379–80
Kaegi, Eugène, 620–21
Kajarnak, 261–62
Kam, Joseph, 270, 399
Kanak, 447, 449–53
K'ang-His, 191–92
Kanzo, Uchimura, 383
Kapéa, 450
Karen (ethnic group), 372, 375–76, 378–80
Karre (ethnic group), 609
Keller, Jean, 604–05
Kelley, Robert, 675
Keraits, 124
Kilian, 74
Kimbundu (ethnic group), 615, 621
Kimbangu, Simon, 532, 575–79, 611, 622
Kirk, John, 474, 478, 583
Kisolokele, Charles, 577
Kivebulaya, Apolo, 572, 589
Knight, Charles, 502
Ko Tha Byn, 375
Krapf, Johann Ludwig, 568, 581–83, 598–99
Krishna Pal, 319, 325
Krüger Frédéric-Hermann, 635
Kublai Khan, 125–26
Kugler, Christian, 598
Kumm, Karl and Lucy, 297–99
Kuntima, Diangienda, 576–77
Kuyper, Abraham, 700
Kwaku, (Quaque) Philippe, 497–99, 506, 515, 527

**L**

Laman, Karl, 611
Langereau, Edmond, 449
Langereau, François, 451

Lanicca, Anna-Magdalena, 680
Lapp, 224
Las Casas, Bartholoméw de, 143, 148–56, 219, 238
Latourette, Kenneth Scott, 34, 712
Lauga, Henri, 635
Lavigerie, Charles (cardinal), 587, 591, 640–41, 647
Lawry, Walter, 422
Leenhardt, Maurice, 447, 451–52, 492
Lengua (ethnic group), 676
Leopold II, 564, 609
Leprosy Mission, The, 301–02
Léry, Jean de, 213, 215–16, 218
Lesotho (ethnic group – see also Bassouto), 474, 481–82, 484–87, 489, 491, 494, 549, 603, 696–97
Lestrade, Arthur, 593
Léthel, Antonin, 525, 535
Lewanika, 487–88
Liele, George, 249
Liley, James, 650
Lisu (ethnic group), 369, 380
Livingstone, David, 65, 173, 289, 296–97, 465–68, 470–79, 486, 491, 493, 546, 561–62, 565–66, 568, 570, 583, 590, 602, 613, 703
Livingstone Inland Mission (LIM), 565
Lobi (ethnic group), 556
London Jews Society, 645, 647, 653, 655
London Missionary Society (LMS), 289, 319, 331, 333, 335, 343, 345, 349, 351, 355, 367, 371, 387, 398, 410–12, 414–17, 419, 421–22, 426–27, 430, 435–37, 447–49, 462–63, 466, 468, 474, 500, 584, 599, 623, 625–26, 631, 634–35, 652, 667, 680
Lucindo, Marco, 620–21
Luke (evangelist), 6–9, 18, 49
Lulle, Raymond, 646
Luther, Martin, 108, 132, 197–201, 203, 205, 207, 209, 239–40, 249, 251, 263
Lyall, Leslie T., 355

# M

Mabille, Adolphe, 486
MacGilvary, David, 390–91
Mackabah, John, 528
Mackay, Alexander, 568, 586–90
Magyars, 87, 90, 96
Maire, Charles-Daniel, 534
Maître, Charles, 524, 551
Makenzie, Institute, 675
Malpan, Abraham, 334
Mandela, Nelson, 462
Mandingue (ethnic group), 502–03
Marcus Aurelius, 17, 30–31
Mark (evangelist), 6, 10–11, 25
Marks, J. E., 379
Marshman, Joshua, 318–19, 321–22, 324,
    326–28, 345–46
Martel, Charles, 74, 79
Martin, Frederic, 267
Martin of Tours, 43–45, 56, 72, 100, 115
Martyn, Henry, 338–39
Massachusetts, 145, 225–26, 228–29,
    231, 371
Mathaia, 450
Mathieson, J. W. and Mary, 439, 441
Matthew (evangelist), 10, 26, 50
Matuba, Samuel, 579
Maurice, John, of Nassau-Siegen, 238
Mayhew, Thomas, 227
McDougall, Francis Thomas, 398
Mehl, Roger, 610, 703
Meiji, (emperor), 383
Melanchthon, Philipp, 207
Menelik II, 600
Merrick, Joseph, 542–43, 546
Mesrop Machdotz, 25, 119–20
Methodius, 90–95, 100
Metzler, Paul, 608
Milne, William, 346–47, 351, 398
Minault, Paul, 635
Mirian, 48–49
Modi Din, 550
Moffat, Robert and Mary, 289, 463–66, 468

Mohammed, 647
Mohican, 272
Mojos, 158–59, 163–64
Mokalapa, Willie, 492–93
Molapo, 482–84
Montecorvino, John of, 126–28
Montesinos, Antonio de, 143, 149–51
Montoya, Antonio Ruiz de, 157, 160–61
Moody, Dwight L., 299, 364–65, 643, 712
Moravian, 91–93, 245, 248, 258–61, 263–
    65, 267–73, 275–80, 288, 308, 319,
    338, 341, 461–63, 498–99, 505, 528,
    584, 648, 664, 682, 684, 686
Moret, Willy and Elizabeth, 681
Morrison, Robert, 289, 318–19, 343–49,
    351, 356, 364, 398, 698
Moshesh, 482
Mossi (ethnic group), 555–56
Mott, John R., 701–02, 709, 711–13, 715
Moulton, J. E., 308, 425
Moundang (ethnic group), 608
Mpongwe (ethnic group), 601, 603
Mtesa, 587
Mwanga, 588–89

# N

Nairn, Cuthbert, 646
Namaqua (ethnic group), 464
Nassau, Robert Hamill, 601–02
Neesima, Shimeba, 382
Neill, Stephen, 319, 336, 350, 358, 364,
    367, 369, 375, 388, 401, 430, 445, 467,
    590, 631, 649, 710–12, 715, 717
Nero, 9, 17, 29
Nestorian, 23, 77, 109, 120–27, 129–30,
    185, 337, 339–40, 343, 372, 399, 656
Nevius, John L., 381
Newbigin, Lesslie, 283, 695
Neyo (ethnic group), 538
Niles, D. T., 718
Nina, 48–49, 120
Nisbet, Henry, 436, 438–39
Nkwe, George, 543–44, 546
Nobili, Robert de, 185–86

Nommensen, Ludwig, 401–03
Norddeutsche Missions-gesellschaft (Bremen Mission), 523
North Africa Mission (NAM), 292–93, 298, 641–43, 645, 650, 716
Norwegian Mission Society of the Free Luther Church, 633
Nott, Henry, 415

## O

Olga, 97–98
Olley, John Ramses, 608
Onguts, 124–25, 127
Origen, 9, 12, 19, 27, 33, 35–36, 39
Orosius, 54
Ostrogoths, 47, 53–54

## P

Paez, Pedro, 176
Palladius, 59
Pantaenus, 26, 39
Papeiha, 431
Paravar (ethnic group), 340
Paris Mission (Société des Missions évangéliques de Paris), 290, 417–21, 449–51, 466, 481, 486, 488, 491, 519–21, 524–25, 537–38, 549–52, 603–07, 635–36, 641, 695–97, 710
Parker, William, 355–56
Parthia, 8–10, 25
Pascal, Blaise, 192
Paton, John, 408, 427, 437–45
Patrick, 57–64, 100
Patterson, John Coleridge, 448
Paul (apostle, see also Saul of Tarsus), 5–12, 14, 16, 18–19, 33, 38, 49, 67, 93–94, 185, 205, 220, 269, 329, 344, 435, 569
Paul III, 154
Paul V (pope), 190–91
Peán, Charles, 680
Pearse, George, 292–93, 641
Pellissier, Jean Pierre, 482
Penn, William, 227, 232
Penzotti, Francisco, 678

Peregrinus de Castello, 69, 128
Peuhl (ethnic group), 500, 502, 520
Pfander, Karl Gottlieb, 652
Philafrican Mission or League, 616–18, 620
Philafrican League (Philafrican Mission in Angola – see also Philafrican), 616, 618
Philafrican Mission in Angola (see also Philafrican), 617
Philip (evangelist), 6, 8, 49
Philip, John, 466
Picts, 64
Pierce, Jonathan, 376
Pike, Kenneth L., 303
Pilatte, Léon, 696
Pitman, Charles and Elizabeth, 431, 434
Peter (apostle), 5–6, 8–9, 18–19, 45, 67, 75
Peter Alphonse, 105
Peter of Ghent, 144–45
Peter the Hermit, 104
Peter the Venerable, 105–06, 201, 207
Pirmin, 74
Plackett, Dorthy (Carey), 308, 315
Plancius, Peter, 233–34
Platt, William J., 525, 534–35
Pliny, 15, 18–19
Plütschau, Heinrich, 250, 252
Pocahontas, 227
Polo, Marco, 125
Polycarp, 30, 38
Pomare I, 410, 412
Pomare II, 412–16, 427
Pomare Vahine, 414, 416–17
Praying Indians, 229, 247
Prester John, 124, 175
Protten, Jacob, 498–99, 505, 527
Pyt, Henri, 519

## Q

Qua Iboe Mission, 526, 556–57
Quakers, 232, 242, 248, 583–84, 633, 682, 684
Quechua (ethnic group), 295, 666, 677

Quiché (ethnic group), 681

**R**

Radama I, 624–28
Radama II, 632–33
Rafaravavy, 629
Rainisoalambo, 636
Ram Mohan Roy, 326, 333
Ranavalona II, 633
Rasalama, 630
Rauch, Christian Heinrichm 272
Raymond of Pennafort, 106
Rebmann, Johannes, 582–83
Reeves, Charles, 294
Rhenius, Karl, 334–35
Rhodes, Alexandre de, 187, 395
Rhodes, Cecil, 188
Ricci, Matthew (or Matteo), 181, 189–92
Richard, Daniel and Laure (née Martzloff),
    537–39
Riis, Andreas, 528
Ringeltaube, Walter Tobie, 355
Robert, Elie, 550
Robertson, Jack, 557
Roffe, Geoffroy Edward, 395
Rolland Emile and Emma, 642–43
Rolland, Guita and Alfred, 643
Roux, André, 525, 530, 533–34, 696–97
Ruccius, Gerhard, 591
Rufinus of Aquileia, 48, 50
Rumohr, Charlotte (Carey), 328
Rupert, 74
Ryland, John, 309

**S**

Sahela, Selassie, 598
Saillens, Ruben, 537, 642, 680, 697
Saker, Alfred, 542–47, 565
Salah, Pierre, 502
Salvation Army, 337, 380, 399, 584, 611,
    645, 680, 683–84
Saly, 393, 395
Saravia, Adrian, 198, 210–11, 236
Saul of Tarsus (see also Paul), 6, 12, 18
Savonarola, Jerome, 149–50, 207

Savorgnan de Brazza, 602–03, 610
Saxons, 53, 70–71, 73, 81–82, 96, 100, 708
Schaaf, Ype, 173, 465, 582
Schlegel, Bernhard, 523
Schmidt, George, 270, 273–75, 461–62
Schön, J. T., 502, 510
Schumann, Solomon, 270
Schwartz, Christian Frederich, 252–55,
    288, 312, 334–35, 341
Schweitzer, Albert, 602, 605–06
Scots, 58, 63–64, 69
Scott, Peter, 296
Seys, John, 505
Sharp, Len, 594–95
Simons, Menno, 205
Simpson, Albert, 295–96, 554
Slavs, 54, 81, 83, 87, 89–90
Slessor, Mary, 527
Slovenes, 89–90
Smith, Mary, 463
Society for the Propagation of the Gos-
    pel (SPG), 225, 246, 255, 287, 379, 497,
    499, 522, 632, 683
Soter (bishop), 30
Southern Baptists, 337, 526, 675, 677, 681
Southern Morocco Mission (SMM),
    645–46
Spangenberg, August Gottlieb, 267, 269, 279
Speke, John, 467, 583, 586, 590
Spener, Philip Jacob, 240, 242, 249–51
Spittler, Christian, 558, 648, 654
Stack, Matthew, 259, 261
Stam, John and Betty, 370
Stanley, Henry Morton, 468, 470–71,
    477–78, 561–62, 564, 566, 586–87,
    590, 614
Stanley-Smith Algie, 594–95
Steer, John, 582
Steer, Roger, 358
Stephen (one of the seven, Acts 6–7),
    5–6, 96
Stephen II (pope), 75
Stephen V (pope), 94
Stevenson, Robert Louis, 445

Studd, Charles T., 229–301, 364, 712
Sudan Interior Mission (SIM), 293–94, 556–57, 600
Sudan United Mission (SUM), 297–98, 526, 608–09
Suisse Romande Mission, 681
Summer Institute of Linguistics (SIL), 302
Summers, William, 613–14
Sun Yat-sen, 368–70
Sung, John, 369
Svenska Mission Förbundet, 570, 611
Swanson, 556

**T**

Tacitus, 15, 29
Tagore, Rabindranath, 324
Tamerlane, 129–30
Tamils, 181, 294, 335, 342
Tanielo (Samoan evangelist), 447
Tartar, 126–27, 209, 242
Tartar, Elias, 656
Tataio (Samoan evangelist), 447
Taylor, Hudson, 290, 292–93, 299, 301, 350–51, 353, 357, 360, 362–63, 365, 367–68, 391, 565
Taylor, Hugh, 391
Taylor, Walter, 520–21
Taylor, Wilbur, 555
Taylor, William (Methodist bishiop), 571, 613–14, 621, 675, 677–78
Taylor Mission, 615–16
Teisserès, Urbain, 602–03
Temne (ethnic group), 499
Tertullian, 28, 33, 35, 37, 639
The Evangelical Alliance Mission (TEAM), 679
Theodosius (emperor), 22, 42
Thomas (apostle), 9–10, 23–24, 126, 157, 266, 277, 279, 333, 340
Thomas, John, 311–12, 317, 319, 323
Thomas, John (Polynesia), 422, 424–25
Thomas Aquinas, 107
Thomas Cana, 22, 121
Thomas of Tolentino, 129

Thompson, James, 665–66, 673–74
Thompson, Thomas, 497
Thornton, Douglas, 649
Tidjite, 556
Tippoo Tib, 567
Tonga (Polynesian ethnic group), 408, 410, 422–26, 434
Top, Albert, 257–60
Topinambous, 158, 215–17, 220–21
Touareg (people), 132, 641
Townsend Cameron, 302–03, 510–11
Trajan, 18, 95
Trigault, Nicolas, 190–91
Trotter, Lilias, 642–44
Trumbull, David, 677
Tuahine (Polynesian evangelist), 431
Tucker, Alfred Robert, 590
Tucker, Ruth, 658
Turner, George, 438–39

**U**

Ulfilas, 46–47, 53
Ultra-Ganges Mission, 346–48, 398
Underhill, E. B., 546
Underwood, Horace, 380
Unemura, Masakisa, 384

**V**

Valerian, 22
Valignano, Alessandro, 188
Van Slageren, Jaap, 542–44, 546, 550
Vandals, 47, 53–54, 78
Vanderkemp, Johannes, 462–63, 466, 623, 707
Veary, Victor, 608
Vedamanikkam, 335
Venn, Henry, 507–08, 512–14, 699, 717
Verbiest, Ferdinand, 190–91
Vernier, Frédéric, 419–20
Vernier, Paul-Louis, 420–21
Victoria (queen), 415, 442, 511
Viénot, Charles, 418–20
Vikings, 84–86, 255
Villegagnon, Nicolas Durant de, 213–15, 219, 221–22

Villégier, François, 519–20
Vincent de Paul, 639
Visigoth, 47, 53–54, 56, 74
Visser, Mr. and Mrs., 620
Vladimir, (king of Russia), 97–98
Voetius, Gisbertus, 235–36, 287

W
Ward, William, 317, 319, 321–22, 328, 372, 411
Warnek, Gustav, 700
Watchman Nee, 369
Weiss, Henry, 678
Wellesley, Lord, 301, 322, 325
Weltz, Justinian von, 240–43, 250, 255, 287
Wenceslaus (Vaclav), king of Bohemia, 94–95
Wesley, John, 248, 269, 288
Wesleyan Methodist Missionary Society (WMMS), 289, 336, 502, 506, 514–15, 534
Whitecross, Margaret, 442
Whitefield, George, 245, 248
Wilberforce, William, 248, 269, 288
Wilfrid, 69, 73
William of Tripoli, 107–08
Williams, John, 289, 408, 412, 424, 427–38, 445
Williams, Roger, 277, 231
Willibrord, 69, 73–75
Willis, J. J., 583
Willy, Maurice, 390, 91, 393
Wilson, Arthur, 555, 557
Wilson, John Leighton, 601
Winfrid (see also Boniface), 74
Wobe (ethnic group), 538

Wolfall, Robert, 225, 256
Wolfe, John, 380
Wolff, Joseph, 653
Wolof (ethnic group), 502, 520
Wood-Lainé, Paul, 525, 535
Worldwide Evangelization Crusade (WEC), 299–301, 364, 521, 523, 539, 557
Wycliffe, John, 115, 207, 263
Wycliffe Association, 678
Wycliffe Bible Translators, 302
Wycliffe University, 303

X
Ximenez de Cisneros, 148–49

Y
Yahbh-Alllaha II, 126, 129
Yakouba (ethnic group), 538
Yoruba (ethnic group), 502, 509–12, 515–16, 520, 525–26

Z
Zambezian (groups), 175, 491, 493
Zande (ethnic group), 610
Zeisberger, David, 272–73
Ziegenbalg, Bartholomäus, 250–53, 288
Zinzendorf, Nicolas von, 258, 261, 263–67, 269, 271–74, 277–79, 498
Zorn, Jean-François, 336, 380, 407, 464, 487, 528, 571–72, 627, 696
Zoumanigui, Cova, 523
Zulus (people), 484, 667
Zwemer, Samuel, 649, 652, 657–58
Zwingli, Ulrich, 199–201, 207–08

# Index of Places

## A

Abeche, 608
Abeokuta, 510–12, 515–17, 526
Abomey, 516, 525
Abyssinia, 175, 240, 287, 648, 653–54
Acadia, 167–68
Accra, 498, 517
Addis Ababa, 600
Aden, 49–50, 138, 597, 657
Adiabene, 20, 23
Africa
  East, 297–98, 568, 581, 584–85, 587, 599
  North, 27–30, 35, 53, 78, 112, 130, 132,
    224, 521, 557, 608, 640–41, 643, 647,
    651, 695
  South, 273, 275–76, 290, 299, 335, 461–
    63, 465–66, 482, 493, 503, 553, 632,
    641, 657, 667, 707, 714
  West, 139, 296, 298, 461, 497–98, 502–
    03, 505–06, 509, 517, 519, 521–22,
    525, 529, 542, 553–57, 579, 605
Agadir, 646
Akropong, 528
Alep, 655–56
Alexandria, 6–7, 10–11, 15, 24, 26–27, 29,
    39, 50, 54, 77, 79, 123, 639, 648–50, 654
Aley, 655
Algeria, 112, 130, 292–93, 639–45, 647, 697
Algiers, 213, 276, 639–45
Alodia, 131

Amarapura, 313, 373
Amazon, 149, 159
Ambon, 399
America, 63, 139–40, 151, 171, 214, 222–23,
    226–27, 230–32, 245–46, 248–49,
    271–72, 279, 297, 344, 378–79, 461,
    471, 499, 503, 509, 561, 571, 602, 616,
    619, 644
  Central, 146, 681, 686, 701, 715
  North, 145–46, 167, 169, 223–26, 229,
    246–48, 269, 271–72, 276, 287, 289,
    558, 648, 708, 714
  South, 139–40, 148–49, 156, 158, 242, 270,
    388, 664, 666–67, 675, 678–79, 686
Amiens, 43, 83
Amman, 654, 656
Amsterdam, 226, 233–34, 242, 266, 497
Andes, 149, 156, 295, 677–79
Aneityum, 438–39
Angola, 171, 173, 469, 566, 571, 613–15,
    617, 621–22
Aniwa, 442–44
Annam, 187, 193, 388, 395–96
Antananarivo (see also Tananarive),
    624–25
Antigua, 269
Antilles, 143, 258, 261, 265–66, 268–69,
    277, 514, 541, 543, 625, 663–64, 666,
    682–83, 685–86, 698
Antioch (Pisidian), 6, 11

Antioch of Syria, 6, 15
Arabia, 8, 10, 13, 26, 50, 77, 108, 121, 123,
    338, 625, 651, 657, 659
Argentina, 158, 664, 667, 675, 677
Armenia, 10, 19, 23–25, 46, 49, 119–20,
    124, 126, 647, 651
Aruwimi, 568
Asia, 6, 9, 17, 21, 23, 53, 78, 90, 118–19,
    121, 123–26, 128–30, 132–33, 139, 175,
    177, 179, 187, 198–99, 206, 250, 283,
    318, 321, 342, 346–47, 390, 398, 457,
    571, 651, 691, 698, 702, 717
Asia Minor, 6, 8, 17–19, 27, 30, 35, 46, 48,
    77, 103, 124, 205, 338
Assinie, 529
Assiout, 649
Aswan, 297–98
Atakpame, 524
Athens, 6, 11–12, 14, 24, 29, 54, 220
Atlantic, 130, 132–33, 156, 214, 469–70,
    521, 541, 553–54, 561, 568, 571, 601,
    613, 616, 667, 671
Australia, 299, 301, 365, 412, 438
Australian Islands, 419–20
Austria, 53, 90, 203, 240, 264
Ava, 376
Axum, 49–50
Ayuthia, 386–87
Azerbaijan, 339

## B

Badagri, 515
Bafoussam, 550
Baghdad, 79, 109, 120, 123, 125, 129, 652, 655
Bahrain, 657
Bailundu, 614
Bakongo (kingdom), 566
Balambila, 601
Bali, 399
Balkans, 10, 47, 95, 132
Bamako, 521, 554
Banana Island, 500
Bangkok, 313, 349, 387
Bangladesh, 289, 313, 320, 331, 336–37

Bangor, 65, 69
Baraka, 601
Baramba, 555
Barotse, 486, 488, 493
Basel, 31–32, 66, 69, 349, 549, 599
Batavia, 237, 399
Battambang, 387, 397
Bavaria, 74, 90
Belgium, 32, 73, 301, 340, 487, 564, 573,
    590, 592–93, 620
Bengal, 311–13, 317, 320–21, 323–26, 331,
    342, 372
Benguela, 616–17
Benoue, 512
Berlin, 500, 548–49, 564, 591, 700
Betchuanaland (Botswana), 468
Bethel, 247, 591–94, 700
Bethelsdorf, 463
Bethesda (agricultural colony, Senegal), 520
Bethlehem, 271, 482
Bethulie, 482
Betsileo, 636
Bhamo, 313, 363
Bihe, 614, 622
Bimbia, 542
Birka, 83–84, 88
Bizerte, 647
Bobbio, 67–69
Bobo-Kioulasso, 556
Boff, 522
Bogotá, 679
Bolivia, 158–59, 163, 295, 668, 677–78
Bolobo, 567, 569–70
Bolovens, 394
Bombay, 129, 294
Bordeaux, 31, 45, 54, 56, 126
Borneo, 129, 397–99, 401, 403
Botswana (see also Betchuanaland), 464
Bouake, 539
Bougainville, 166, 409, 411, 415
Bourbon (Reunion Island), 623, 625, 664
Bourges, 31, 89
Brazil, 140, 148, 158–59, 173, 213–15, 219,
    221, 238, 529, 664, 675–76, 686

Brazzaville, 570, 579, 609–11
Bregenz, 66–67, 69
Bremen, 83–84, 86–88, 523–24, 528
Buenos Aires, 158, 160, 664–66, 675
Bulawayo, 491
Bulgaria, 94–95
Burkina Faso (see also Upper Volta), 523, 553, 555–56
Burma (Myanmar), 301, 313, 320, 329, 363, 371–75, 377–80, 387, 570
Burundi (see also Urundi), 590–91, 594–95
Buyo, 539
Byzantium, 24, 54, 89–91, 119

C

Cairo, 648–50, 657
Calabar, 527
Calcutta, 138, 312–14, 317–18, 322, 327, 331–33, 342, 371, 376, 398, 411
California, 146–47, 299, 609, 686
Caluquembe (Lincoln missionary station), 617, 620–21
Cambodia, 387–88, 390, 397
Cambridge, 225, 228, 338, 364–65, 583
Cameroon, 298, 514, 524, 526, 541–52, 565–66, 602, 604, 607, 684, 700
Canterbury, 69–70, 72, 210, 512
Canton, 184, 343–48, 350, 364, 370, 712
Cape Coast, 497, 506, 515
Cape Palmas, 533
Cape Town, 273–74
Cappadocia, 8–9, 19, 25, 46, 119
Caraibes, 216
Carmel, 531
Carmelite missionaries, 147, 337
Carthage, 24, 28–29, 37, 54, 78, 158, 639, 646–47
Casamance, 520
Caucasus, 24, 48–49, 120
Cayenne, 680
Celebes, 399, 401
Central African Republic (see also Oubangui-Chari), 609

Ceylon (Sri Lanka), 121, 237, 253, 273, 276, 294, 340–42, 398, 700
Chaco, 158, 668, 676
Chad, 298, 553, 579, 607–08
    Lake, 130–31, 553–54
Chalcedon, 119, 130
Chang'An, (Xian), 49, 121–23
Chefoo, 363, 381
Cherchell, 641, 643
Chiapas, 156
Chicago, 365, 376
Chieng Mai, 387
Chile, 158, 665, 667, 675–78, 686–87
China, 121, 123–30, 138, 183–84, 186–87, 189–93, 276, 293, 295, 299, 301, 313, 318–19, 343–51, 353–70, 380–82, 387–88, 395, 397–98, 465, 565, 657, 666, 695, 698, 701, 712, 714, 717
Clapham, 288
Cochinchina, 186–88, 388
Cologne, 24, 31–32, 55, 99, 126
Colombia, 158, 301, 666, 673, 679, 683
Colombo, 253, 341
Conakry, 522
Congo, 139, 171, 173–74, 295, 297, 299–300, 364, 469, 472, 474, 561–73, 575–76, 578–79, 590, 592–93, 602–04, 609–11, 613, 622, 696
River, 565, 610
Constantine, 17, 22, 30, 32–33, 38, 41–42, 49, 55, 81, 91–92, 94, 96, 190, 641, 692
Constantinople, 41, 46–47, 79, 89–92, 94–95, 97–98, 104, 120, 126, 130, 132, 137, 655
Cook (Islands), 431–32
Copenhagen, 250, 253, 255–57, 260–61, 266, 498
Cordoba, 103, 143, 158, 675
Corinth, 6–7, 15, 24, 36
Costa Rica, 682, 684
Crete, 8
Cuba, 139, 146, 148, 150, 683, 701
Cyprus, 6, 16, 112, 129

## D

Da Nang (see also Tourane), 395
Dabou, 537–38
Dacia, 95
Dahomey (Benin), 515–16, 525, 530, 534–
    36, 557
Dakar, 521, 605
Dalat, 396
Dalmatia, 7, 10
Daloa, 538
Damascus, 18, 24, 49, 79, 103, 105–06, 655
Danane, 538
Danube, 13, 46–47, 89, 96
Dar es Salaam, 584
Darfur, 131
Dayr el-Zor, 655
Debhatta, 312–13
Denmark, 74, 83–85, 87, 224, 250, 255–59,
    264, 269, 277, 322
Dhaka, 313, 337
Djemaa Saharidj, 642
Dominican Republic, 139, 143, 265,
    684–85
Douala, 541–46, 549
Driesdenburg, 499
Dura Europus, 22, 24, 49

## E

Ebanga, 621
Ecuador, 678
Edessa, 10, 20–22, 104
Edinburgh, 299, 462, 500, 584, 649, 708–
    11, 713, 715–16, 719–20
Egypt, 8, 11, 19, 25, 27, 31–32, 39, 50,
    77–78, 116, 120, 130–31, 207, 240,
    276, 287, 293, 297, 553, 558, 598, 639,
    647–52
El Jadida (see also Mazagan), 646
El-Mina, 497
El Salvador, 682
Elim (missionary station), 610
Elvira, 33

England (see also Great Britain, the Unit-
    ed Kingdom), 11, 33, 40, 53, 58–59,
    63, 65, 72–74, 85, 126, 210, 224–29,
    233, 245, 248, 252, 288, 296, 298,
    307–08, 312, 315, 317, 319, 338, 348,
    354, 357, 360, 362–63, 365, 371, 465,
    627, 634
Entebbe, 587
Ephesus, 6, 8–9, 15–16, 19, 24, 36, 120
Equatorial Guinea (Spanish), 301
Eritrea, 600
Erromanga, 435–37
Ethiopia, 10, 13, 23, 49–50, 78, 123–24,
    132, 175, 240, 294, 553, 558, 581, 597–
    600, 648, 652
Europe, 6, 13, 31, 44, 53–54, 60, 64, 69–
    70, 73, 78–79, 81, 83–84, 87, 89–91,
    97, 99–100, 105, 108, 111, 115, 119,
    125, 129, 132–33, 137, 142, 149, 156,
    160–63, 166, 177, 188, 191, 198–99,
    203, 205, 221, 226, 236, 239, 248–49,
    251–52, 257–58, 263–64, 266–68, 274,
    276, 284, 287, 292, 324, 335, 339, 347,
    349–50, 356, 363–64, 415, 433, 458,
    466, 471–72, 479, 486–87, 490, 493,
    499–500, 503–04, 514, 543, 564, 589–
    90, 592, 598, 605–06, 611, 620, 626–27,
    655, 663–64, 675, 684, 692–93, 702,
    708, 717

## F

Fada N'Gourma, 556
Faiffo, 396
Falkland Islands, 670
Far East, 138, 183, 232, 238, 301, 371, 380,
    394, 399, 695
Fernando Po, 137, 526, 541–44, 546, 684
Fez, 24, 29, 79, 645
Fiji (Viti, Islands), 408, 422, 426
Fitzroy, Robert, 668, 671–72
Flanders, 32
Florida, 146–48, 223, 683
Formosa (Taiwan), 237, 349
Fort-Archambault (Sarh), 607–08

Fort-Lamy (N'Djamena), 607–08

France, 45, 62–63, 103–04, 111, 132, 138, 141, 159, 167, 169, 186, 213–15, 218, 221–23, 236, 263, 301, 388, 390, 416–20, 449, 451–53, 482, 486–87, 490–91, 507, 519–21, 523–24, 529, 536–37, 539, 549, 554, 556, 597, 602, 605, 607, 609–10, 634–35, 639–40, 642, 644, 646, 655, 680, 696–98, 702

Freetown, 499–500, 502, 504, 509–10, 520, 554

French Equatorial Africa, 553, 601, 604, 607

French West Africa, 521–22, 525, 529, 553, 555–57, 579, 605

Friendly Islands, 422, 425–26

Fulda, 69, 75, 88

## G

Gabon, 521, 549, 551, 579, 601–06, 696, 710

Galatia, 6, 9, 38

Galilee, 18, 655

Gambia (country, river), 243, 502–03, 519–20

Ganges, 319–20, 325

Garanganze (Katanga, present-day Shaba), 570

Gaul (see also France), 30–33, 43–44, 53, 55–56, 58–59, 65, 72–73, 75, 83

Geneva, 32, 211, 215–16, 218–19, 221–22, 225, 231, 481, 491

Georgetown, 680

Georgia (Caucasus), 23–24, 48–49, 120

Germany, 31–32, 53, 66, 69–70, 73–75, 95–97, 99, 203, 233, 239–40, 245, 249, 252–53, 258, 264, 276, 297, 349, 365, 401–02, 498, 523–24, 547, 581–84, 591–92, 594, 599, 699–700, 710

Ghana, 497, 515, 523–24, 527–29, 537, 555

Gitwe, 593

Glasgow, 347, 438, 468, 500, 646

Gnadental, 275, 462

Goa, 138, 177–81, 183, 185

Godthaab, 256, 258–59

Gold Coast (Ghana, see also Ivory Coast), 243, 497–98, 505–06, 509, 514, 516, 524, 527–29, 532, 536, 538–39, 548

Gondar (Abyssinia), 648

Great Britain (see also England and the United Kingdom), 12, 33, 57, 59, 70, 72, 224, 232, 250, 314, 317–18, 320, 327–28, 337, 346–47, 350, 357, 379, 387, 398, 410, 415, 435–36, 462, 467, 469, 497, 502, 511–12, 515, 517, 523, 569–70, 583, 587–88, 613–14, 623, 628, 632, 634, 641, 649, 652, 667, 671, 702–03

Greece, 6–7, 10, 29–30, 125, 205, 647

Greenland, 63, 86, 225, 255–62, 264–65, 276–77, 335

Guadalajara, 145, 681

Guadeloupe, 143, 685–86

Guatemala, 154, 156, 302, 673, 681

Guiana (Dutch, see also Suriname), 242, 270, 287, 680

Guiana (French), 680–81

Guinea (Conakry, country), 266, 268, 276, 301, 399, 498, 500, 521–23, 527, 539, 554, 601

Guinea (gulf), 138, 521, 523, 527

Guinea Bissau, 523

Guyana (British), 158, 680

## H

Haiphong, 396

Haiti, 139, 143, 145, 149, 684

Halle, 249–53, 255, 264, 290, 312

Halmahera, 401

Hangchow, 360–61, 717

Hanoi, 393, 396

Hapai Island, 424–25

Havana, 674, 683

Hawai, 421, 685

Hedeby, 83–84, 88

Helvetia, 32

Herrnhut, 258–61, 264–66, 268, 270–75, 278, 338, 498

Holland (*see also* Low Countries), 89, 226, 233, 236, 240–42, 266, 270, 340–42, 398, 403, 461, 697, 700
Honan, 364
Honduras, 682
Hong Kong, 349–50, 355, 368
Hooghly (river), 313, 317, 319
Huambo (Novo Lisboa), 622
Huanuco, 678
Hué, 396
Hungary, 96

I

Ibadan, 526
Iceland, 86, 88
Illyricum, 7, 9
India (Indies), 10, 22–24, 26, 49, 78, 116, 121, 123, 126, 129–30, 138–40, 177–81, 184–85, 193, 250, 252–53, 255, 264, 276, 289, 294, 299, 301, 312, 317, 321, 323–24, 326, 328–29, 331–38, 340, 364, 371–74, 379, 388, 398, 410, 652, 679, 695, 698, 701, 714, 717
Indies (*see also* India, Pakistan, and Bangladesh), 23–24, 26, 46, 138–39, 142, 151, 171, 192, 233–34, 237, 250, 252, 275, 280, 289, 311–12, 314–16, 320–22, 327, 335, 338, 373, 399, 548, 571, 654, 657, 695, 698
Indochina, 187–88, 344, 386, 388–90, 395–96, 657
Indonesia, 125, 178, 180, 188, 237–38, 276, 397, 399–400, 700
Iona, 64–65
Iran (*see also* Persia), 24, 331, 338
Iraq, 651, 653, 655–57
Ireland, 57–67, 69, 292, 298, 301, 526, 656, 676
Ispahan, 188, 339–40
Israel, 5, 7, 13, 227, 229, 651, 719
Italy, 29–30, 32, 37, 53, 56, 58, 67, 90, 104, 116, 132, 177, 186, 189, 203, 263, 487, 597, 600, 650

Ituri, 572
Ivory Coast, 139, 301, 525, 529–30, 532–39, 555, 557, 575

J

Jaffa, 653
Jaffna, 341–42
Jamaica, 249, 269, 276, 528, 541, 546, 663, 682–84
Japan, 123, 180–84, 187–89, 301, 370, 382, 383–84, 679, 701, 719
Java, 129, 234, 237, 287, 344, 349, 399–401
Jerusalem, 5–9, 11, 16–18, 23–24, 37, 49, 54, 77, 79, 104, 133, 203, 424, 648, 653–64, 711, 716–17, 719
   Conference of 1928, 711, 713–16, 720
Jibrael, 655
Jordan, 651, 654, 656
Judea, 5–6, 13, 16, 205

K

Kabylie, 293, 641–42, 644–45, 647
Kairouan, 79, 647
Kampot, 397
Kankan, 523
Karachi, 337
Kasai, 571
Katanga (present-day Shaba, *see also* Garanganze), 570, 622
Kaya, 555
Kenya, 138, 296, 558, 561, 581–82, 584, 597
Kerala, 23, 426
Kerbala, 521
Khanbalik, 125–26, 128–29
Khartoum, 298–99, 558
Kiev, 63, 88, 97–98
Kingston, 684
Kinshasa (*see also* Leopoldville), 566
Kirinda, 592–94
Kirkuk, 655
Kisangani (*see also* Stanleyville), 569
Kivu (province and lake), 591–92
Kompong Chhang, 397
Korea, 125, 301, 349, 380–82

Kottayam, 334
Kou, 607
Kourbi, 557
Kuala Lumpur, 398
Kumasi, 515
Kurdistan, 130, 339
Kuruman, 464, 468

L

Labrador, 276
Lagos, 293, 502, 512, 514, 527
Lahore, 337, 657
Lambarene, 601, 603–04, 606
Laos, 388, 390–95
Lapland, 224
Latin America, 148, 169, 197, 280, 283–84,
    384, 457, 571, 663–66, 672–79, 681–83,
    685–87
Lausanne, 290
Lealuyi, 488, 492
Leeward Islands, 414, 417, 419–20, 428
Leopoldville (Stanley Pool, present-day
    Kinshasa), 565–66, 570–71
Lere, 607–08
Leribe, 482–87
Lesotho (or Lesouto), 474, 481–82, 484–
    87, 489, 491, 494, 549, 603, 696–97
Liberia, 504–05, 529–30, 538, 601
Libya, 27, 31, 130, 293, 650
Lifou, 447–50
Lincoln (see also Caluquembe), 617–21
Lithuania, 99
Logone, 607–08
Lolwa, 572
Lome, 524
London, 24, 33, 210, 225, 253, 288–89,
    293, 327–29, 345, 366, 390, 410, 414,
    421, 465, 469, 475, 525, 534, 538, 565,
    598, 614, 625, 643, 707
Louang-Phrabang, 390–91, 395
Loyalty Islands, 408, 431, 447–51
Lualaba, 471, 561, 568
Luanda, 173, 469, 613–15, 621
Lucon, 386

Luxeuil, 66–67, 69, 74
Lyon, 15, 24, 30–32, 35, 54, 125, 222, 525, 529
Lystra, 6, 11, 220

M

Macao, 187, 193, 343–49
Macedonia, 6, 91, 696
Macenta, 523
Madagascar, 176, 463, 623–25, 627, 630–32,
    634–36, 692, 696
Madoura, 336
Madras, 10, 23, 250, 252, 255, 334–36,
    426, 717–18
Maghreb, 27, 29, 78, 639, 647
Majorca, 110, 112–13
Makuria, 131
Malabar, 22, 49, 121, 129, 178, 186, 251, 334
Malacca, 138, 180, 187, 237, 345–47,
    397–98
Malange, 615, 621
Malawi, 583
Malaysia, 180, 340, 346, 397–98, 400
Mali (see also French Sudan), 130–31, 521,
    553–55, 557
Malta, 213, 240, 598, 648, 652–54
Manchuria, 129, 349, 363, 380–81
Mandalay, 313, 379
Manila, 385–86
Mare, 447–51
Marmoutier, 44
Marquises Islands, 411, 420
Marrakech, 639, 646
Marseille, 11, 30, 70, 393, 604
Martinique, 265, 685–86
Mascate (Oman), 657
Massachusetts (colony), 145, 225–26,
    228–29, 231, 371
Massawa, 600
Matadi, 569
Maurice (Island), 32
Mauritania, 553–54
Mayence, 31, 54, 69
Mayo-Kebbi, 607
Mazagan (El Jadida), 646

Mbo, 550

Mecca, 77, 79

Mediterranean, 11, 13, 27, 30–31, 50, 79, 99, 132, 561, 639, 647, 651–52

Mekong, 390

Merv, 49, 123–24

Mesopotamia, 8, 10, 13, 18, 21–22, 77, 653, 656

Mexico, 144–47, 154, 156, 302, 663, 666, 673, 681, 686

Milan, 24, 30, 42, 54, 67, 69

Mindanao, 386

Mogador, 646

Moluccas (Spice Islands), 180, 237, 399

Mombassa, 138, 561, 581

Mongolia, 123–24, 129, 276, 357, 363, 695

Monobaze, 23

Monrovia, 505

Monterrey, 681

Montevideo, 666, 674, 677

Montmartre, 31, 141, 177

Moorea, 412, 414–15, 427–28

Morija, 482

Morocco, 13, 117, 137, 293, 639, 645–46, 647

Moulmein, 313, 377

Moulton, 308, 425

Mozambique, 138, 175

Mudnabatti, 313–14, 316, 322

Myanmar (see also Burma), 372

Mymensingh, 313, 337

**N**

Nakhon-Phanom, 387

Namaqualand, 463

Nanking, 349–50, 355

Narbonne, 31, 79

Natal, 484, 667

N'Djamena (see also Fort-Lamy), 607

Negros (Island), 385

Nha Trang, 396

Niamey, 557

Niandan, 523

Nicaragua, 682

Nicodemia, 42

Niger (country), 513, 553–54, 556–57

Niger River, 294, 298–99, 504, 508, 510–12, 514, 521, 523, 526, 582

Nigeria, 131, 293–94, 298–99, 512, 514–15, 526–27, 549, 556, 608

Nile, 27, 78, 117, 131–32, 297–99, 469–72, 553, 558, 561, 590, 648, 695, 718

Ningpo, 349, 356–57

Nobatia, 131

Nong Boua, 393

Nouakchott, 554

Noumèa, 450

New Caledonia, 408, 447, 449–51, 549

New England, 225–29, 232, 246, 287, 371, 497

New Guinea, 399, 431

New Hebrides, 419, 427, 435–39, 442, 444

New Zealand, 299, 337, 608, 679

N'Kamba, 575–76, 579

Norway, 84–86, 98, 224, 257, 259

Nousiainen, 87–88

Nova Lisboa (present-day Huambo), 622

Ntorrosso, 555, 557

Nubia, 78, 123, 131–32, 297, 553, 557–58

Nyankunde, 572

Nyasa (Lake), 469, 473–74

**O**

Oceania, 177, 193, 631

Ochogun, 509

Ogooue, 601–04

Oman (see also Mascat), 657

Omdurman, 558

Oran, 641, 645

Orange (River), 463

Orange (State), 482, 484

Orient, 126, 133, 199, 237, 347, 656

Osrhoene, 20–21, 24

Ouagadougou, 555–57

Oubangui-Chari (Central Africa), 566, 609–10

Ouidah, 525

Ousambiro, 588–89

## P

Pacific, 140, 147, 156, 193, 283, 289, 407–10, 412–13, 416, 420–21, 427, 433, 439, 452
Pakistan, 289, 331, 336–39, 652
Paksé, 394–95
Palestine, 9, 11, 13, 18, 69, 77, 653
Panama, 143, 158, 674, 683–84
Panay, 385
Pannonia, 43, 93, 96
Papeete, 410, 412, 414, 416, 418–19
Paraguay, 145, 149, 156–58, 160–61, 163–64, 166–68, 229, 674, 676, 678
Paramaribo, 158, 270
Paris, 31, 54, 56, 69, 71, 110, 112–13, 126, 141, 177, 184, 191, 213, 215, 218, 239, 264, 390, 418, 449, 466, 481–82, 486–87, 490–91, 520, 529, 536–38, 593, 605, 641
  Low Countries (see also Holland), 210, 487, 497, 702
Patagonia, 149, 667–68, 670–72
Pathan, 337
Peking, 190, 366, 370
Pennsylvania, 145, 232
Pernambouc, 158, 238
Persia (Iran), 331, 338–40, 652
Peru, 148, 154, 156, 164, 665, 678
Petchiburi, 387
Philae, 131
Philippines, 140, 188, 193, 294, 302, 384–85, 400, 701
Phnom Penh, 397
Pointe-Noire, 601
Poland, 96–97
Polynesia, 410, 420, 427, 435, 447
Pont, 35, 215
Pont-de-Khor, 520
Poona, 294
Portugal, 131–32, 137, 139–41, 171–73, 175, 177, 232, 236–37, 239, 372, 583
Pretoria, 486
Puerto Novo, 525
Puerto Rico, 265, 685, 701

Punjab, 78, 301, 337, 339, 652

## Q

Quebec, 145, 167–68, 272
Quilimane, 469
Quito, 158, 679

## R

Rabat, 29, 645
Raiatea, 412, 417, 420, 427–28, 430–32, 434
Rangoon, 313, 372–75, 378–79
Rarotonga, 413, 427, 429, 431–34, 447
Recife, 158, 529
Regents (colony, town), 501
Remera, 594
Rhineland, 89, 401, 699
Rhode Island, 231, 321
Rhodesia, 474
Northern Rhodesia (Zambia, see also Zambezi), 494
Rio de Janeiro, 158, 214, 221, 412, 664, 666–67, 675
Romania (see also Dacia), 10, 95–96
Rome, 7–9, 12–17, 21–22, 24, 27, 30, 35–37, 41–42, 53–54, 56, 60–61, 67, 69–71, 74–75, 79, 85, 89–93, 95–97, 104, 110, 112, 120, 125–26, 128, 141, 149, 173, 186, 188, 191–92, 235, 692
Rosette, 650
Rotterdam, 205, 233, 462
Rouen, 31, 69, 84
Roxbury, 228–29
Russia, 63, 94, 97–98, 132, 276, 369, 384, 676, 679, 695
Rwanda, 573, 584, 590–95

## S

Sabah (North Borneo), 397
Safi, 646
Sahara, 130, 132, 137, 293, 527, 553–54, 613, 645, 695
Sahel, 555
Saigon, 388, 390, 395–96
Saint Croix, 266–67, 269, 279
Saint Domingo, 143, 149, 151

Saint Louis (Senegal), 130, 519–21

Saint Maurice, 32

Samaria, 5–6, 227

Samoan Islands, 424, 427, 434–36, 450

San Cristobal, 681

San Ignacio-Mini, 158–59, 163

Sanaga River, 551

Santal (mission), 337

Sao Paulo, 158–59, 675–76, 686

Sao Salvador, 139, 171, 173, 566, 568, 614

Saporo, 383

Sarawak, 397–98

Sassandra, 538–39

Sayda, 655

Scandinavia, 32, 46, 81–84, 87, 90, 97, 143, 255, 365, 644

Scotland, 57–58, 63–64, 213, 296, 298, 331–32, 336, 360, 438–39, 463, 468, 474, 487, 528, 584, 586, 646, 655, 708

Sédhiou, 520

Sefula, 487–88

Seleucia-Ctesiphon, 22

Senegal, 130, 519–22, 554, 635

Serampore, 255, 313, 317–25, 327–28, 333, 338, 345, 347, 372, 374, 698

Sesheke, 487

Sfax, 647

Shaba (Katanga, see also Garanganze), 570

Shanghai, 355, 360, 364–65, 368, 370

Shansi, 364–66

Shirati, 584

Shire Highlands (Malawi), 583

Siam (Thailand), 184, 187, 313, 386–92, 395

Sicily, 29, 70, 103

Sidi-Bel-Abbè, 645

Siem Reap, 397

Sierra Leone, 137, 499–505, 508, 510, 512, 515, 520–23, 526, 539, 554–55, 645

Sikasso, 554

Singapore, 347–48, 398

Slave Coast, 498, 523, 529

Smyrna, 30, 38, 655

Society Islands, 409, 413–14, 421

Socotra, 49, 121, 123

Somalia, 583, 597

Sousse, 647

South Carolina, 249

Spain, 10–12, 31, 33, 53, 74, 103, 105–06, 113, 117, 132, 140–41, 148, 151, 155–57, 160, 162, 164, 181, 186, 223, 225, 232, 236, 384–85, 542, 639, 664

Sri Lanka (see also Ceylon), 121, 253, 289, 294, 331, 340

Stanley-Pool (Kinshasa, see also Leopold-ville), 566

Stanleyville (Kisangani), 569

Sudan (French Sudan), 27, 50, 131, 293–95, 297–99, 513, 523, 526, 536, 553–55, 607–08

Sudan, Republic of, formerly the Anglo-Egyptian Sudan, 298, 553, 558

Suisse Romande, 681

Sumatra, 129, 276, 397, 399, 401–03

Surinam (see also Dutch Guiana), 173, 242, 270, 276, 278, 287, 680

Sweden, 46–47, 83–85, 87, 224, 236, 570, 600, 611

Switzerland, 32, 53, 66–67, 203, 222, 366, 390, 392, 487, 491, 493, 573, 615, 618–19, 642, 653, 656, 680–81

Sylhet, 313, 337

Syria, 6, 15, 18, 50, 77, 103, 112, 121–22, 647, 651, 654–56

**T**

Tabou, 539

Tabriz, 123, 339

Tahiti, 289, 311, 408–22, 430–31, 449, 667

Talagouga, 601

Tamatave (Toamasina), 624

Tambaram, 657, 708, 711, 717–20

Tambaram (Conference of 1938), 657, 708, 711, 717

Tananarive (Antananarivo), 623–24, 627, 630–31, 634

Tanganyika (Tanzania), 297, 471, 583–84, 590–91, 641

Tanganyika, Lake, 471, 584